International Institutions in the New Global Economy

The International Library of Writings on the New Global Economy

Series Editor: Helen V. Milner
B.C. Forbes Professor of Politics and International Affairs
Princeton University, USA

1. Environment in the New Global Economy (Volumes I and II)
   Peter M. Haas

2. Foreign Aid in the New Global Economy
   Peter Burnell and Oliver Morrissey

3. International Monetary Relations in the New Global Economy (Volumes I and II)
   Benjamin J. Cohen

4. International Conflict and the Global Economy
   Edward D. Mansfield

5. The Political Economy of Financial Crises (Volumes I and II)
   Roy E. Allen

6. International Institutions in the New Global Economy
   Lisa L. Martin

Wherever possible, the articles in these volumes have been reproduced as originally published using facsimile reproduction, inclusive of footnotes and pagination to facilitate ease of reference.

For a list of all Edward Elgar published titles visit our site on the World Wide Web at
www.e-elgar.com

International Institutions in the New Global Economy

Edited by

Lisa L. Martin

Clarence Dillon Professor of International Affairs
Harvard University, USA

THE INTERNATIONAL LIBRARY OF WRITINGS ON THE NEW GLOBAL ECONOMY

An Elgar Reference Collection
Cheltenham, UK • Northampton, MA, USA

Published by
Edward Elgar Publishing Limited
Glensanda House
Montpellier Parade
Cheltenham
Glos GL50 1UA
UK

Edward Elgar Publishing, Inc.
136 West Street
Suite 202
Northampton
Massachusetts 01060
USA

A catalogue record for this book is available from the British Library

ISBN   1 84376 425 3

Printed and bound in Great Britain by MPG Books Ltd, Bodmin, Cornwall

Contents

Acknowledgements

The editor and publishers wish to thank the authors and the following publishers who have kindly given permission for the use of copyright material.

American Economic Association for article: Kyle Bagwell and Robert W. Staiger (1999), 'An Economic Theory of GATT', *American Economic Review*, **89** (1), March, 215–48.

Blackwell Publishing Ltd for articles: Paul R. Milgrom, Douglass C. North and Barry R. Weingast (1990), 'The Role of Institutions in the Revival of Trade: The Law Merchant, Private Judges, and the Champagne Fairs', *Economics and Politics*, **2** (1), March, 1–23; Liliana Botcheva and Lisa L. Martin (2001), 'Institutional Effects on State Behavior: Convergence and Divergence', *International Studies Quarterly*, **45** (1), March, 1–26; Alastair Iain Johnston (2001), 'Treating International Institutions as Social Environments', *International Studies Quarterly*, **45** (4), December, 487–515.

Cambridge University Press for article: Daniel L. Nielson and Michael J. Tierney (2003), 'Delegation to International Organizations: Agency Theory and World Bank Environmental Reform', *International Organization*, **57** (2), Spring, 241–76.

International Journal for article: Robert O. Keohane (1990), 'Multilateralism: An Agenda for Research', *International Journal*, **XLV** (4), Autumn, 731–64.

Johns Hopkins University Press for articles: Lisa L. Martin (1993), 'Credibility, Costs, and Institutions: Cooperation on Economic Sanctions', *World Politics*, **45** (3), April, 406–32; John R. Oneal and Bruce Russett (1999), 'The Kantian Peace: The Pacific Benefits of Democracy, Interdependence, and International Organizations, 1885–1992', *World Politics*, **52** (1), October, 1–37; Strom C. Thacker (1999), 'The High Politics of IMF Lending', *World Politics*, **52** (1), October, 38–75.

MIT Press Journals and the IO Foundation and the Massachusetts Institute of Technology for articles: James D. Fearon (1998), 'Bargaining, Enforcement, and International Cooperation', *International Organization*, **52** (2), Spring, 269–305; Michael N. Barnett and Martha Finnemore (1999), 'The Politics, Power, and Pathologies of International Organizations', *International Organization*, **53** (4), Autumn, 699–732; B. Peter Rosendorff and Helen V. Milner (2001), 'The Optimal Design of International Trade Institutions: Uncertainty and Escape', *International Organization*, **55** (4), Autumn, 829–57, references; Thomas H. Oatley (2001), 'Multilateralizing Trade and Payments in Postwar Europe', *International Organization*, **55** (4), Autumn, 949–69, references.

MIT Press Journals and the World Peace Foundation and the Massachusetts Institute of Technology for articles: Robert O. Keohane (1982), 'The Demand for International Regimes', *International Organization*, **36** (2), Spring, 325–55; John Gerard Ruggie (1992), 'Multilateralism: The Anatomy of an Institution', *International Organization*, **46** (3), Summer, 561–98; Robert Powell (1994), 'Anarchy in International Relations Theory: The Neorealist–Neoliberal Debate', *International Organization*, **48** (2), Spring, 313–44; James D. Morrow (1994), 'Modeling the Forms of International Cooperation: Distribution versus Information', *International Organization*, **48** (3), Summer, 387–423.

Oxford University Press for article: Monika Bütler and Heinz Hauser (2000), 'The WTO Dispute Settlement System: A First Assessment from an Economic Perspective', *Journal of Law, Economics, and Organization*, **16** (2), October, 503–33.

Sage Publications, Inc. for article: Kenneth W. Abbott and Duncan Snidal (1998), 'Why States Act through Formal International Organizations', *Journal of Conflict Resolution*, **42** (1), February, 3–32.

Every effort has been made to trace all the copyright holders but if any have been inadvertently overlooked the publishers will be pleased to make the necessary arrangement at the first opportunity.

In addition the publishers wish to thank the Marshall Library of Economics, Cambridge University, and the Library of Indiana University at Bloomington, USA for their assistance in obtaining these articles.

Book title!

Introduction

Lisa L. Martin

FS3

F02   F13

Institutionalization is a hallmark of the new global economy. International institutions, which are integrated structures of norms, and formal international organizations (IOs) both led to the formation of the global economy and have resulted from its development. International economic interactions are largely institutionalized. That is, they occur within a framework of norms, rules, and organizations. Many of these rules have been made explicit and formally agreed by states; others remain more informal. It is difficult to understand the functioning of the global economy without an understanding of its institutionalization. The growth of this institutional framework has attracted extensive attention from political scientists, who ask why states have created these institutions and what their consequences are for patterns of economic interaction.

This collection surveys the best articles that have been published since 1981 on the role of institutions in the global economy. In this Introduction, I provide a brief intellectual history of the field and describe the analytical frameworks that characterize it. International institutions have become a vibrant field of study in political science and are gaining increasing attention from economists. This collection focuses on positive, explanatory studies of international institutions and IOs. While many of these positive studies have normative implications, I do not focus here on the voluminous work that takes a primarily normative approach, for example, papers that criticize the World Bank or International Monetary Fund (IMF) and propose changes in their design. I also leave aside the European Union (EU), which encompasses the most heavily institutionalized set of economic relationships in the global economy, as adequate treatment of the EU would require a volume of its own.

Modern study of international institutions and IOs began in the early 1980s. Prior to this time, the study of IOs was quite policy orientated and descriptive, lacking an overarching analytical framework.[1] This lack of a theoretical foundation meant that, although individual studies generated strong insights, they did not cumulate to create a coherent picture of or debate about the role of IOs in the world economy. This situation changed with the publication of an edited volume by Stephen Krasner, *International Regimes*[2] and of Robert Keohane's book *After Hegemony*.[3] Papers in *International Regimes* of most relevance to economic issues are reprinted in this volume. These articles cast international institutions in a new light and suggested a new explanatory framework for studying them. The puzzle that motivated this new research began with two observations: that international economic cooperation in the 1970s was stable in spite of substantial shifts in the distribution of international economic power, and that organizations such as the Bretton Woods institutions and the General Agreement on Tariffs and Trade (GATT) were prominent features of the economic landscape. Keohane and others argued that these two observations were connected to each other, and that the existence of institutions and IOs explained the persistence of economic cooperation.

The fundamental logic of this line of work is summarized in Keohane's 1982 article, 'The Demand for International Regimes' (Chapter 1).[4] In order for states to cooperate, they must overcome a range of collective-action problems. No external enforcement exists in the international economy, so any agreements must be self-enforcing. This means that states must find ways to avoid temptations to cheat, such as reneging on agreements to encourage trade by erecting protectionist barriers. Avoiding such temptations requires high-quality information about the actions and preferences of other states, and about the likely consequences of cheating on agreements. In addition, states must coordinate their actions, for example, agreeing on common technological and public health standards. IOs provide forums in which states could mitigate collective-action problems that threaten stable patterns of cooperation. IOs can perform monitoring functions, providing assurance that others are living up to the terms of their commitments. They are forums for negotiating to resolve coordination problems, and to learn about the preferences and constraints facing other governments. They create structures for enforcement and dispute resolution, although actual enforcement powers typically remain in the hands of member states.

Through these functions, IOs become a valuable foundation for cooperation and for the global economy. Thus patterns of cooperation can be more resilient in the face of underlying shifts in economic power and interests. The initial work applying this 'contractual' view of institutions concentrated on international regimes, defined as sets of principles, norms, rules, and decision-making procedures.[5] One advantage of examining regimes, as compared to the earlier focus on individual IOs, is that it allowed researchers to consider informal institutions as well as formalized bodies. While in more recent years much attention has shifted back to formal IOs, the understanding that informal bodies of norms sustain cooperation in the global economy underlies even work on individual organizations today.

While research on international regimes represented a major step forward in the analysis of international institutions, it was subject to criticism from a number of perspectives. Friedrich Kratochwil and John Ruggie recognized the contributions of regime analysis, but worried that it was moving too far from the analysis of specific IOs, thus missing some important internal organizational dynamics.[6] Stephan Haggard and Beth Simmons surveyed a number of weaknesses of regimes analysis from the perspective of those undertaking positive empirical research on regimes.[7] Because the concept of regimes was broadly defined, much effort went into determining whether or not regimes actually existed in various issue areas, and whether changes in patterns of behavior reflected changes *within* regimes or *of* regimes. It is not clear that these descriptive debates added a great deal to our understanding of the causes and consequences of institutions in the international environment.

Other major weaknesses of the literature included its state-centric focus and neglect of domestic politics. Giulio Gallarotti argued that IOs systematically failed in their attempts to manage difficult problems in international relations;[8] the inability of IOs to resolve serious conflict, in his analysis, reflected not just random mistakes, but a systematic pattern of failure. IOs could even have perverse effects, exacerbating conflict rather than mitigating it. For these reasons, Gallarotti argued against relying too heavily on formal IOs to manage international relations. Oran Young criticized the regimes literature for neglecting the role of political leadership.[9] Many of these criticisms have been echoed in recent years as the theoretical and empirical analysis of institutions and IOs has progressed.

One of the most telling critiques of the regimes literature came, perhaps paradoxically, from the editor of the *International Regimes* volume, Stephen Krasner.[10] Krasner charged that the work on regimes was too focused on market failures: instances where all could potentially benefit from mutual cooperation, but where collective-action problems, such as high transaction costs, prohibited states from reaching the 'Pareto frontier'. In his survey of efforts to cooperate in the field of communication, he found that states had little trouble reaching the Pareto frontier. It was relatively easy for them to identify the set of bargains from which it would be impossible to make all better off. Instead, they found themselves trapped by distributional conflict, having to choose among bargains that benefited some while harming others. Thus the most significant problem plaguing efforts at international cooperation was not providing a good contractual environment to overcome transaction-cost problems, such as informational limitations, but a coordination problem in which states disagreed over which of multiple Pareto-efficient equilibria they preferred. Krasner's insight has led to a revision of early work on regimes, which claimed that coordination problems would be relatively easy to solve.[11] A new focus on how institutions might aid in resolving coordination problems has added depth to our understanding of IOs' functions.[12]

In the 1990s the theory of international institutions became deeper and richer. Ruggie and Keohane brought the concept of multilateralism back into the study of institutions. Keohane (1990, Chapter 3) defined multilateralism simply as cooperation among three or more states, while Ruggie (1992, Chapter 4) conceptualized multilateralism as a set of norms that prescribed certain patterns of behavior such as non-discrimination.[13] Both served to redirect attention to variation among types of institutions, a highly productive move for the field. Another debate arose regarding the problem of compliance with the rules of IOs, and with international agreements more generally. A managerial school, representing the views of legal scholars, argued that states generally wanted to comply with international rules, and that variation in compliance was therefore not a compelling puzzle.[14] Political scientists responded by noting that the managerial argument was plagued by selection bias: if states almost always complied with the rules, it was likely because they would only accept rules that demanded minimal changes in their patterns of behavior. The appropriate question, therefore, was not so much compliance as how different structures of rules would promote far-reaching changes in behavior that left states open to exploitation, or 'deep cooperation'.[15] Interestingly, both the managerial and contractual schools agreed on the conclusion that variation in patterns of compliance was not a terribly important question, although they came to this conclusion by very different paths. Nevertheless, empirical research on variation in compliance has continued, leading to some intriguing findings.[16]

Other theoretical developments focus on the form and design of IOs. One body of work asks why IOs are becoming more 'legalized': they more often incorporate legalistic features such as third-party dispute settlement.[17] Researchers have begun to explore the advantages and possible disadvantages of legalization for promoting international cooperation. Another body of work focuses on design principles for IOs. Starting from the assumption that IOs are designed to resolve collective-action problems, analysts have derived a number of hypotheses about the form of IOs.[18] For example, if states design an IO to reduce the transaction costs of monitoring members' behavior, we would expect the organization to have relatively centralized monitoring capacities. Using logic like this, dimensions of IOs such as their centralization and autonomy from member states can be explained. David Lake broadens our theoretical perspective on institutions by noting that the typical IO constitutes only one point on a wide spectrum of forms of international organization, ranging from complete anarchy to hierarchical organization, as in empires.[19] Kenneth Abbott and Duncan Snidal (1998, Chapter 8) returned to one of the initial questions posed by the regimes literature, about why sometimes states cooperate informally, while at other times they choose to create formal IOs.[20] Coming from a contractual perspective, Abbott and Snidal argue that transaction costs and tradeoffs between autonomy and the benefits of commitment explain patterns of formalization.

Much recent work on international institutions and IOs has turned to rigorous empirical analysis, applying the kinds of models and analytical frameworks described above. Much international trade is now regulated by structures of rules and formal organizations, most notably the GATT/World Trade Organization (WTO) on the international level. This phenomenon has drawn the attention of economists. Kyle Bagwell and Robert Staiger (1999, Chapter 12) offer a general economic theory of the structure of the GATT/WTO.[21] They begin from the observation that the only feasible and self-enforcing bargains on international trade are those that preserve the existing terms of trade; if deals change the terms of trade, at least one of the parties to the bargain will refuse to live up to its terms. The structure of GATT/WTO is thus designed to promote liberalization – reduction in barriers to exchange – while maintaining existing terms of trade. This principle explains why norms such as non-discrimination and reciprocity are so important in trade institutions, and why they go hand-in-hand. Other economists have focused on the WTO's dispute resolution mechanism, asking whether it is optimal from the perspective of promoting trade and examining its effectiveness.[22]

Beyond the WTO, another notable development in the institutionalization of trade has been the proliferation and strengthening of regional trade organizations. Dispute settlement is a prominent feature of regional trade organizations, as it is of the WTO. James McCall Smith asks about variation in the legalization of dispute resolution mechanisms, and finds that it is largely explained by asymmetry in the powers of states that belong to the organizations.[23] Small states prefer legalized mechanisms that bind large states, while large states prefer to avoid legal constraints, so that they can exercise their bargaining power. Frederick Abbott also examines a regional organization, the North American Free Trade Agreement (NAFTA), from the perspective of legalization.[24] While Abbott finds legalization an important strategy in the Americas, in Asia it has gained little foothold for a variety of reasons surveyed by Miles Kahler.[25] A number of hypotheses exist for explaining variation in legalization and formalization across regions and issue areas, but systematic empirical exploration of these hypotheses is one of the significant remaining challenges for scholars of IOs. The impact of domestic economic interests on regional trading arrangements, and the relationship between the WTO and such arrangements, have also received rigorous empirical scrutiny.[26] Other authors ask about the role of escape clauses and other mechanisms of flexibility in IOs, especially trade organizations.[27]

The other type of economic IO that has drawn extensive attention from political scientists is the international financial institution (IFI). IFIs, such as the IMF and the World Bank, play a major role in the world of international finance and money, and we are just beginning to understand how the interaction of politics and economics works in these institutions. Some analysts, such as Strom Thacker (1999, Chapter 11), demonstrate that the IMF's patterns of lending respond to the geopolitical interests of the United States, its dominant member.[28] Others focus on the delegation of authority to the IFIs, asking why states would choose to allow them what appears to be a substantial degree of autonomy. Some analysts find that delegation has not undermined the interests of the most powerful member states, as delegation is itself a strategy for promoting these interests.[29] For example, Daniel Nielson and Michael Tierney (2003, Chapter 19) demonstrate that the World Bank's environmental policies correlate highly with measures of the environmental interests of the United States.[30] On the other hand, Erica Gould is more skeptical about the ability of member states to maintain control over IFI actions once they delegate authority. She argues that the IMF, in its use of conditionality, often responds to private financial actors rather than state interests.[31]

Through these theoretical developments and high-quality empirical analyses, our understanding of the purposes and functioning of international institutions and IOs has increased tremendously in recent years. However, a strong criticism of this style of analysis has also arisen. In the United States, the contractual approach to IOs that traces its roots to the early analysis of regimes continues to dominate the field. A number of authors working from a more sociological perspective have presented a powerful challenge to contractualism. They argue that IOs do far more than assist states in crafting and living up to self-enforcing agreements. They do not merely change the contractual environment, they reach more deeply into states to change fundamental interests and promote norms. IOs can socialize states under certain conditions (Alastair Johnson, 2001, Chapter 18).[32]

Other authors find that IOs continue to suffer from systematic pathologies – pathologies that contractual theorists often miss because they do not appreciate the bureaucratic dynamics of institutions as organizations (Michael Barnett and Martha Finnemore, 1999, Chapter 13).[33] Further criticism of the accepted wisdom about IOs comes from within the rationalist-contractual school. This school has argued, based on game theory's folk theorems, that IOs can facilitate cooperation by enhancing the shadow of the future for states. However, as James Fearon (1998, Chapter 9) shows, if the underlying collective-action problem involves distributional conflict as well as enforcement problems, states that care more intensely about the future may actually find it more difficult to cooperate.[34] If any bargain that they strike today will hold far into the future, as it will in an institutionalized environment, states will bargain hard and hold out for better deals.

The new global economy is highly institutionalized. Understanding this phenomenon has led to the development of a vibrant field of political science centered on the study of international institutions and IOs. This field continues to hold, in spite of telling challenges, to a primarily contractual view that sees institutions as solutions to collective-action problems. In recent years the study of IOs has moved beyond this powerful insight to develop more nuanced theories of IOs' form, function, and effects, and to begin to subject these theories to systematic empirical scrutiny. As the papers reproduced in this volume attest, the study of international institutions is a productive one, but one in which many questions remain open to further rigorous research.

Notes and References

1. See Lisa L. Martin and Beth Simmons (1998), 'Theories and Empirical Studies of International Institutions', *International Organization*, **52** (4), Autumn, 729–57.
2. Stephen D. Krasner (1983), *International Regimes*. Ithaca, NY: Cornell University Press.
3. Robert O. Keohane (1984), *After Hegemony: Cooperation and Discord in the World Political Economy*. Princeton, NJ: Princeton University Press.
4. Robert O. Keohane (1982), 'The Demand for International Regimes', *International Organization*, **36** (2), Spring 1982, 325–55.
5. Stephen D. Krasner (1982), 'Structural Causes and Regime Consequences: Regimes as Intervening Variables', *International Organization*, **36** (2), Spring, 185–205.

27. B. Peter Rosendorff and Helen V. Milner (2001), 'The Optimal Design of International Trade Institutions: Uncertainty and Escape', *International Organization*, **55** (4), Autumn, 829–57; Barbara Koremenos (2001), 'Loosening the Ties that Bind: A Learning Model of Agreement Flexibility', *International Organization*, **55** (2), Spring, 289–325; George Downs and David M. Rocke (1995), *Optimal Imperfection? Domestic Uncertainty and Institutions in International Relations*. Princeton, NJ: Princeton University Press.

28. Strom C. Thacker (1999), 'The High Politics of IMF Lending', *World Politics*, **52** (1), October, 38–75.

29. Lisa L. Martin (2002), 'Agency and Delegation in IMF Conditionality', May, manuscript.

30. Daniel L. Nielson and Michael J. Tierney (2003), 'Delegation to International Organizations: Agency Theory and World Bank Environmental Reform', *International Organization*, **57** (2), Spring, 241–76.

31. Erica Gould (2003), 'Money Talks: Supplementary Financiers and International Monetary Fund Conditionality', *International Organization*, **57** (3), Summer, 551–86.

32. Alastair Iain Johnston (2001), 'Treating International Institutions as Social Environments', *International Studies Quarterly*, **45** (4), December, 487–515.

33. Michael N. Barnett and Martha Finnemore (1999), 'The Politics, Power, and Pathologies of International Organizations', *International Organization*, **53** (4), Autumn, 699–732.

34. James Fearon (1998), 'Bargaining, Enforcement, and International Cooperation', *International Organization*, **52** (2), Spring, 269–305.

[1]

The demand for
international regimes

Robert O. Keohane

We study international regimes because we are interested in under-standing order in world politics. Conflict may be the rule; if so, in-stitutionalized patterns of cooperation are particularly in need of explana-tion. The theoretical analysis of international regimes begins with what is at least an apparent anomaly from the standpoint of Realist theory: the exis-tence of many "sets of implicit or explicit principles, norms, rules, and decision-making procedures around which actor expectations converge," in a variety of areas of international relations.

This article constitutes an attempt to improve our understanding of in-ternational order, and international cooperation, through an interpretation of international regime-formation that relies heavily on rational-choice analysis in the utilitarian social contract tradition. I explore why self-interested ac-tors in world politics should seek, under certain circu͏—ablish international regimes through mutu͏ —͏ ount

The original idea for this paper germinated sponsored conference on International Poli͏ neapolis, Minnesota, in June 1978.

I am indebted to Robert Holt and Anne Kr͏ that meeting. Several knowledgeable friends, McKeown, James N. Rosse, and Laura Tyson, ͏ me think about the issues discussed here. For article I am especially grateful to Robert Bates, J Field, Albert Fishlow, Alexander George, Ernst son, Robert Jervis, Stephen D. Krasner, Helen Mi͏ John Ruggie, Ken Shepsle, Arthur Stein, Susan St͏—ge, Harrison Wagner, and David Yoffie. I also benefited from discussions of earlier drafts at meetings held at Los Angeles in October 1980 and at Palm Springs in February 1981, and from colloquia in Berkeley, California, and Cam-bridge, Massachusetts.

International Organization 36, 2, Spring 1982
0020-8183/82/020325-31 $1.50

for fluctuations over time in the number, extent, and strength of international regimes, on the basis of rational calculation under varying circumstances.

Previous work on this subject in the rational-choice tradition has emphasized the "theory of hegemonic stability": that is, the view that concentration of power in one dominant state facilitates the development of strong regimes, and that fragmentation of power is associated with regime collapse.[1] This theory, however, fails to explain lags between changes in power structures and changes in international regimes; does not account well for the differential durability of different institutions within a given issue-area; and avoids addressing the question of why international regimes seem so much more extensive now in world politics than during earlier periods (such as the late 19th century) of supposed hegemonic leadership.[2]

The argument of this article seeks to correct some of these faults of the hegemonic stability theory by incorporating it within a supply-demand approach that borrows extensively from microeconomic theory. The theory of hegemonic stability can be viewed as focusing only on the supply of international regimes: according to the theory, the more concentrated power is in an international system, the greater the supply of international regimes at any level of demand.[3] But fluctuations in demand for international regimes are not taken into account by the theory; thus it is necessarily incomplete. This article focuses principally on the demand for international regimes in order to provide the basis for a more comprehensive and balanced interpretation.

Emphasizing the demand for international regimes focuses our attention on why we should want them in the first place, rather than taking their desirability as a given. I do not assume that "demand" and "supply" can be specified independently and operationalized as in microeconomics. The same actors are likely to be the "demanders" and the "suppliers." Furthermore, factors affecting the demand for international regimes are likely simultaneously to affect their supply as well. Yet supply and demand language allows us to make a distinction that is useful in distinguishing phenomena that, in the first instance, affect the desire for regimes, on the one hand, or the ease of supplying them, on the other. "Supply and de-

[1] See especially Robert O. Keohane, "The Theory of Hegemonic Stability and Changes in International Economic Regimes, 1967–1977," in Ole R. Holsti, Randolph Siverson, and Alexander George, eds., *Changes in the International System* (Boulder: Westview, 1980); and Linda Cahn, "National Power and International Regimes: The United States and International Commodity Markets," Ph.D. diss., Stanford University, 1980.

[2] Current research on the nineteenth century is beginning to question the assumption that Britain was hegemonic in a meaningful sense. See Timothy J. McKeown, "Hegemony Theory and Trade in the Nineteenth Century," paper presented to the International Studies Association convention, Philadelphia, 18–21 March 1981; and Arthur A. Stein, "The Hegemon's Dilemma: Great Britain, the United States, and the International Economic Order," paper presented to the American Political Science Association annual meeting, New York, 3–6 September 1981.

[3] The essential reason for this (discussed below) is that actors that are large relative to the whole set of actors have greater incentives both to provide collective goods themselves and to organize their provision, than do actors that are small relative to the whole set. The classic discussion of this phenomenon appears in Mancur Olson Jr., *The Logic of Collective Action: Political Goods and the Theory of Groups* (Cambridge: Harvard University Press, 1965).

mand'' should be seen in this analysis as a metaphor, rather than an attempt artificially to separate, or to reify, different aspects of an interrelated process.[4]

Before proceeding to the argument, two caveats are in order. First, the focus of this article is principally on the *strength* and *extent* of international regimes, rather than on their *content* or *effects*. I hope to contribute to understanding why international regimes wax and wane, leaving to others (in this volume and elsewhere) the analysis of what ideologies they encompass or how much they affect ultimate, value-laden outcomes. The only significant exception to this avoidance of questions of content comes in Section 5, which distinguishes between control-oriented and insurance-oriented regimes. Second, no claim is made here that rational-choice analysis is the only valid way to understand international regimes, or even that it is preferable to others. On the contrary, I view rational-choice analysis as one way to generate an insightful interpretation of international regimes that complements interpretations derived from analyses of conventions and of learning (illustrated in the articles in this volume by Young and Haas). My analysis is designed to be neither comprehensive nor exclusive: I suggest hypotheses and try to make what we know more intelligible, rather than seeking to put forward a definitive theory of international regimes.

The major arguments of this article are grouped in five sections. First, I outline the analytical approach by discussing the virtues and limitations of "systemic constraint-choice analysis." Section 2 lays the basis for the development of a constraint-choice theory of international regimes by specifying the context within which international regimes operate and the functions they perform. In Section 3 elements of a theory of the demand for international regimes are presented, emphasizing the role of regimes in reducing transactions costs and coping with uncertainty. In Section 4, I use insights from theories of information and uncertainty to discuss issues of closure and communication. Section 5 suggests that control-oriented regimes are likely to be increasingly supplemented in the 1980s by insurance regimes as the dominance of the advanced industrial countries in the world political economy declines.

1. Systemic constraint-choice analysis: virtues and limitations

The argument developed here is deliberately limited to the *systemic* level of analysis. In a systemic theory, the actors' characteristics are given by assumption, rather than treated as variables; changes in outcomes are explained not on the basis of variations in these actor characteristics, but on the basis of changes in the attributes of the system itself. Microeconomic theory, for instance, posits the existence of business firms, with given utility

[4] I am indebted to Albert Fishlow for clarifying this point for me.

functions, and attempts to explain their behavior on the basis of environmental factors such as the competitiveness of markets. It is therefore a systemic theory, unlike the so-called "behavioral theory of the firm," which examines the actors for internal variations that could account for behavior not predicted by microeconomic theory.

A systemic focus permits a limitation of the number of variables that need to be considered. In the initial steps of theory-building, this is a great advantage: attempting to take into account at the outset factors at the foreign policy as well as the systemic level would lead quickly to descriptive complexity and theoretical anarchy. Beginning the analysis at the systemic level establishes a baseline for future work. By seeing how well a simple model accounts for behavior, we understand better the value of introducing more variables and greater complexity into the analysis. Without the systemic microeconomic theory of the firm, for instance, it would not have been clear what puzzles needed to be solved by an actor-oriented behavioral theory.

A systems-level examination of changes in the strength and extent of international regimes over time could proceed through historical description. We could examine a large number of cases, attempting to extract generalizations about patterns from the data. Our analysis could be explicitly comparative, analyzing different regimes within a common analytical framework, employing a methodology such as George's "focused comparison."[5] Such a systematic comparative description could be quite useful, but it would not provide a theoretical framework for posing questions of why, and under what conditions, regimes should be expected to develop or become stronger. Posing such fundamental issues is greatly facilitated by *a priori* reasoning that makes specific predictions to be compared with empirical findings. Such reasoning helps us to reinterpret previously observed patterns of behavior as well as suggesting new questions about behavior or distinctions that have been ignored: it has the potential of "discovering new facts."[6] This can be useful even in a subject such as international politics, where the variety of relevant variables is likely to confound any comprehensive effort to build deductive theory. Deductive analysis can thus be used in interpretation as well as in a traditional strategy of theory-building and hypothesis-testing.

This analysis follows the tradition of microeconomic theory by focusing on constraints and incentives that affect the choices made by actors.[7] We

---

[5] Alexander L. George, "Case Studies and Theory Development: The Method of Structured, Focused Comparison," in Paul Lauren, ed., *Diplomacy: New Approaches in History, Theory, and Policy* (New York: Free Press, 1979).

[6] Imre Lakatos, "Falsification and the Methodology of Scientific Research Programmes," in Lakatos and Alan Musgrave, eds., *Criticism and the Growth of Scientific Knowledge* (Cambridge: Cambridge University Press, 1970).

[7] Stimulating discussions of microeconomic theory can be found in Martin Shubik, "A Curmudgeon's Guide to Microeconomics," *Journal of Economic Literature* 8 (1970): 405–434; and Spiro J. Latsis, "A Research Programme in Economics," in Latsis, ed., *Method and Appraisal in Economics* (Cambridge: Cambridge University Press, 1976).

assume that, in general, actors in world politics tend to respond rationally to constraints and incentives. Changes in the characteristics of the international system will alter the opportunity costs to actors of various courses of action, and will therefore lead to changes in behavior. In particular, decisions about creating or joining international regimes will be affected by system-level changes in this way; in this model the demand for international regimes is a function of system characteristics.

This article therefore employs a form of rational-choice analysis, which I prefer to term "constraint-choice" analysis to indicate that I do not make some of the extreme assumptions often found in the relevant literature. I assume a prior context of power, expectations, values, and conventions; I do not argue that rational-choice analysis can derive international regimes from a "state of nature" through logic alone.[8] This paper also eschews deterministic claims, or the *hubris* of believing that a complete explanation can be developed through resort to deductive models. To believe this would commit one to a narrowly rationalistic form of analysis in which expectations of gain provide both necessary and sufficient explanations of behavior.[9] Such beliefs in the power of Benthamite calculation have been undermined by the insufficiency of microeconomic theories of the firm—despite their great value as initial approximations—as shown by the work of organization theorists such as Simon, Cyert, and March.[10]

Rational-choice theory is not advanced here as a magic key to unlock the secrets of international regime change, much less as a comprehensive way of interpreting reality. Nor do I employ it as a means of explaining particular actions of specific actors. Rather, I use rational-choice theory to develop models that help to explain trends or tendencies toward which patterns of behavior tend to converge. That is, I seek to account for typical, or modal, behavior. This analysis will not accurately predict the decisions of all actors, or what will happen to all regimes; but it should help to account for overall trends in the formation, growth, decay, and dissolution of regimes. The deductive logic of this approach makes it possible to generate hypotheses about international regime change on an *a priori* basis. In this article several such hypotheses will be suggested, although their testing will have to await further specification. We shall therefore be drawing on microeconomic theories and rational-choice approaches heuristically, to help us con-

---

[8] I am indebted to Alexander J. Field for making the importance of this point clear to me. See his paper, "The Problem with Neoclassical Institutional Economics: A Critique with Special Reference to the North/Thomas Model of Pre–1500 Europe," *Explorations in Economic History* 18 (April 1981).

[9] Lance E. Davis and Douglass C. North adopt this strong form of rationalistic explanation when they argue that "an institutional arrangement will be innovated if the expected net gains exceed the expected costs." See their volume, *Institutional Change and American Economic Growth* (Cambridge: Cambridge University Press, 1971).

[10] Two of the classic works are James March and Herbert Simon, *Organizations* (New York: Wiley, 1958); and Richard Cyert and James March, *The Behavioral Theory of the Firm* (Englewood Cliffs, N.J.: Prentice-Hall, 1963).

struct nontrivial hypotheses about international regime change that can guide future research.

The use of rational-choice theory implies that we must view decisions involving international regimes as in some meaningful sense voluntary. Yet we know that world politics is a realm in which power is exercised regularly and in which inequalities are great. How, then, can we analyze international regimes with a voluntaristic mode of analysis?

My answer is to distinguish two aspects of the process by which international regimes come into being: the imposition of constraints, and decision making. Constraints are dictated not only by environmental factors but also by powerful actors. Thus when we speak of an "imposed regime," we are speaking (in my terminology) of a regime agreed upon within constraints that are mandated by powerful actors.[11] Any agreement that results from bargaining will be affected by the opportunity costs of alternatives faced by the various actors: that is, by which party has the greater need for agreement with the other.[12] Relationships of power and dependence in world politics will therefore be important determinants of the characteristics of international regimes. Actor choices will be constrained in such a way that the preferences of more powerful actors will be accorded greater weight. Thus in applying rational-choice theory to the formation and maintenance of international regimes, we have to be continually sensitive to the structural context within which agreements are made. Voluntary choice does not imply equality of situation or outcome.

We do not necessarily sacrifice realism when we analyze international regimes as the products of voluntary agreements among independent actors within the context of prior constraints. Constraint-choice analysis effectively captures the nonhierarchical nature of world politics without ignoring the role played by power and inequality. Within this analytical framework, a systemic analysis that emphasizes constraints on choice and effects of system characteristics on collective outcomes provides an appropriate way to address the question of regime formation.

Constraint-choice analysis emphasizes that international regimes should not be seen as quasi-governments—imperfect attempts to institutionalize centralized authority relationships in world politics. Regimes are more like contracts, when these involve actors with long-term objectives who seek to structure their relationships in stable and mutually beneficial ways.[13] In

[11] For a discussion of "spontaneous," "negotiated," and "imposed" regimes, see Oran Young's contribution to this volume.

[12] For a lucid and original discussion based on this obvious but important point, see John Harsanyi, "Measurement of Social Power, Opportunity Costs and the Theory of Two-Person Bargaining Games," *Behavioral Science* 7, 1 (1962): 67–80. See also Albert O. Hirschman, *National Power and the Structure of Foreign Trade* (1945; Berkeley: University of California Press, 1980), especially pp. 45–48.

[13] S. Todd Lowry, "Bargain and Contract Theory in Law and Economics," in Warren J. Samuels, ed., *The Economy as a System of Power* (New Brunswick, N.J.: Transaction Books, 1979), p. 276.

The demand for international regimes

some respects, regimes resemble the "quasi-agreements" that Fellner discusses when analyzing the behavior of oligopolistic firms.[14] In both contracts and quasi-agreements, there may be specific rules having to do with prices, quantities, delivery dates, and the like; for contracts, some of these rules may be legally enforceable. The most important functions of these arrangements, however, are not to preclude further negotiations, but to establish stable mutual expectations about others' patterns of behavior and to develop working relationships that will allow the parties to adapt their practices to new situations. Rules of international regimes are frequently changed, bent, or broken to meet the exigencies of the moment. They are rarely enforced automatically, and they are not self-executing. Indeed, they are often matters for negotiation and renegotiation; as Puchala has argued, "attempts to enforce EEC regulations open political cleavages up and down the supranational-to-local continuum and spark intense politicking along the cleavage lines."[15]

This lack of binding authority associated with international regimes has important implications for our selection of analytical approaches within a constraint-choice framework: it leads us to rely more heavily on microeconomic, market-oriented theory than on theories of public choice. Most public-choice theory is not applicable to international regime change because it focuses on the processes by which authoritative, binding decisions are made within states.[16] Yet in international politics, binding decisions, arrived at through highly institutionalized, rule-oriented processes, are relatively rare and unimportant, and such decisions do not constitute the essence of international regimes. Traditional microeconomic supply and demand analysis, by contrast, assumes a situation in which choices are made continuously over a period of time by actors for whom "exit"—refusal to purchase goods or services that are offered—is an ever-present option. This conforms more closely to the situation faced by states contemplating whether to create, join, remain members of, or leave international regimes. Since no binding decisions can be made, it is possible to imagine a market for international regimes as one thinks of an economic market: on the basis of an analysis of relative prices and cost-benefit calculations, actors decide which regimes to "buy." In general, we expect states to join those regimes in which they expect the benefits of membership to outweigh the costs. In such an analysis, observed changes in the extent and strength of international

[14] William Fellner, *Competition among the Few* (New York: Knopf, 1949).

[15] Donald J. Puchala, "Domestic Politics and Regional Harmonization in the European Communities," *World Politics* 27,4 (July 1975), p. 509.

[16] There are exceptions to this generalization, such as Tiebout's "voting with the feet" models of population movements among communities. Yet only one chapter of fourteen in a recent survey of the public-choice literature is devoted to such models, which do not focus on authoritative decision-making processes. See Dennis C. Mueller, *Public Choice* (Cambridge: Cambridge University Press, 1980). For a brilliantly innovative work on "exit" versus "voice" processes, see Albert O. Hirschman, *Exit, Voice, and Loyalty* (Cambridge: Harvard University Press, 1970).

regimes may be explained by reference to changes either in the characteristics of the international system (the context within which actors make choices) or of the international regimes themselves (about which the choices are made).

This constraint-choice approach draws attention to the question of why disadvantaged actors join international regimes even when they receive fewer benefits than other members—an issue ignored by arguments that regard certain regimes as simply imposed. Weak actors as well as more powerful actors make choices, even if they make them within more severe constraints. (Whether such choices, made under severe constraint, imply obligations for the future is another question, one not addressed here.)[17]

2. The context and functions of international regimes

Analysis of international regime-formation within a constraint-choice framework requires that one specify the nature of the context within which actors make choices and the functions of the institutions whose patterns of growth and decay are being explained. Two features of the international context are particularly important: world politics lacks authoritative governmental institutions, and is characterized by pervasive uncertainty. Within this setting, a major function of international regimes is to facilitate the making of mutually beneficial agreements among governments, so that the structural condition of anarchy does not lead to a complete "war of all against all."

The actors in our model operate within what Waltz has called a "self-help system," in which they cannot call on higher authority to resolve difficulties or provide protection.[18] Negative externalities are common: states are forever impinging on one another's interests.[19] In the absence of authoritative global institutions, these conflicts of interest produce uncertainty and risk: possible future evils are often even more terrifying than present ones. All too obvious with respect to matters of war and peace, this is also characteristic of the international economic environment.

Actors in world politics may seek to reduce conflicts of interest and risk

---

[17] Anyone who has thought about Hobbes's tendentious discussion of "voluntary" agreements in *Leviathan* realizes the dangers of casuistry entailed in applying voluntaristic analysis to politics, especially when obligations are inferred from choices. This article follows Hobbes's distinction between the structure of constraints in a situation, on the one hand, and actor choices, on the other; but it does not adopt his view that even severely constrained choices ("your freedom or your life") create moral or political obligations.

[18] Kenneth N. Waltz, *Theory of International Politics* (Reading, Mass.: Addison-Wesley, 1979).

[19] Externalities exist whenever an acting unit does not bear all of the costs, or fails to reap all of the benefits, that result from its behavior. See Davis and North, *Institutional Change and American Economic Growth*, p. 16.

by coordinating their behavior. Yet coordination has many of the characteristics of a public good, which leads us to expect that its production will be too low.[20] That is, increased production of these goods, which would yield net benefits, is not undertaken. This insight is the basis of the major "supply-side" argument about international regimes, epitomized by the theory of hegemonic stability. According to this line of argument, hegemonic international systems should be characterized by levels of public goods production higher than in fragmented systems; and, if international regimes provide public goods, by stronger and more extensive international regimes.[21]

This argument, important though it is, ignores what I have called the "demand" side of the problem of international regimes: why should governments desire to institute international regimes in the first place, and how much will they be willing to contribute to maintain them? Addressing these issues will help to correct some of the deficiencies of the theory of hegemonic stability, which derive from its one-sidedness, and will contribute to a more comprehensive interpretation of international regime change. The familiar context of world politics—its competitiveness, uncertainty, and conflicts of interest—not only sets limits on the supply of international regimes, but provides a basis for understanding why they are demanded.

Before we can understand why regimes are demanded, however, it is necessary to establish what the functions of international regimes, from the perspective of states, might be.[22]

At the most specific level, students of international cooperation are interested in myriads of particular agreements made by governments: to

---

[20] Olson, *The Logic of Collection Action;* Bruce M. Russett and John D. Sullivan, "Collective Goods and International Organization," with a comment by Mancur Olson Jr., *International Organization* 25,4 (Autumn 1971); John Gerard Ruggie, "Collective Goods and Future International Collaboration," *American Political Science Review* 66,3 (September 1972); Duncan Snidal, "Public Goods, Property Rights, and Political Organization," *International Studies Quarterly* 23,4 (December 1979), p. 544.

[21] Keohane, "The Theory of Hegemonic Stability"; Charles P. Kindleberger, *The World in Depression, 1929–1939* (Berkeley: University of California Press, 1974); Mancur Olson and Richard Zeckhauser, "An Economic Theory of Alliances," *Review of Economics and Statistics* 48,3 (August 1966), reprinted in Bruce M. Russett, ed., *Economic Theories of International Politics* (Chicago: Markham, 1968). For a critical appraisal of work placing emphasis on public goods as a rationale for forming international organizations, see John A. C. Conybeare, "International Organizations and the Theory of Property Rights," *International Organization* 34,3 (Summer 1980), especially pp. 329–32.

[22] My use of the word "functions" here is meant to designate consequences of a certain pattern of activity, particularly in terms of the utility of the activity; it is not to be interpreted as an explanation of the behavior in question, since there is no teleological premise, or assumption that necessity is involved. Understanding the function of international regimes helps, however, to explain why actors have an incentive to create them, and may therefore help to make behavior intelligible within a rational-choice mode of analysis that emphasizes the role of incentives and constraints. For useful distinctions on functionalism, see Ernest Nagel, *The Structure of Scientific Explanation* (New York: Harcourt, Brace, 1961), especially "Functionalism and Social Science," pp. 520–35. I am grateful to Robert Packenham for this reference and discussions of this point.

maintain their exchange rates within certain limits, to refrain from trade discrimination, to reduce their imports of petroleum, or progressively to reduce tariffs. These agreements are made despite the fact that, compared to domestic political institutions, the institutions of world politics are extremely weak: an authoritative legal framework is lacking and regularized institutions for conducting transactions (such as markets backed by state authority or binding procedures for making and enforcing contracts) are often poorly developed.

Investigation of the sources of specific agreements reveals that they are not, in general, made on an *ad hoc* basis, nor do they follow a random pattern. Instead, they are "nested" within more comprehensive agreements, covering more issues. An agreement among the United States, Japan, and the European Community in the Multilateral Trade Negotiations to reduce a particular tariff is affected by the rules, norms, principles, and procedures of the General Agreement on Tariffs and Trade (GATT)—that is, by the trade regime. The trade regime, in turn, is nested within a set of other arrangements—including those for monetary relations, energy, foreign investment, aid to developing countries, and other issues—that together constitute a complex and interlinked pattern of relations among the advanced market-economy countries. These, in turn, are related to military-security relations among the major states.[23]

Within this multilayered system, a major function of international regimes is to facilitate the making of specific agreements on matters of substantive significance within the issue-area covered by the regime. International regimes help to make governments' expectations consistent with one another. Regimes are developed in part because actors in world politics believe that with such arrangements they will be able to make mutually beneficial agreements that would otherwise be difficult or impossible to attain. In other words, regimes are valuable to governments where, in their absence, certain mutually beneficial agreements would be impossible to consummate. In such situations, *ad hoc* joint action would be inferior to results of negotiation within a regime context.

Yet this characterization of regimes immediately suggests an explanatory puzzle. Why should it be worthwhile to construct regimes (themselves requiring agreement) in order to make specific agreements within the regime frameworks? Why is it not more efficient simply to avoid the regime stage and make the agreements on an *ad hoc* basis? In short, why is there any demand for international regimes apart from a demand for international agreements on particular questions?

An answer to this question is suggested by theories of "market failure" in economics. Market failure refers to situations in which the outcomes of

---

[23] Vinod Aggarwal has developed the concept of "nesting" in his work on international regimes in textiles since World War II. I am indebted to him for this idea, which has been elaborated in his "Hanging by a Thread: International Regime Change in the Textile/Apparel System, 1950–1979," Ph.D. diss., Stanford University, 1981.

market-mediated interaction are suboptimal (given the utility functions of actors and the resources at their disposal). Agreements that would be beneficial to all parties are not made. In situations of market failure, economic activities uncoordinated by hierarchical authority lead to *in*efficient results, rather than to the efficient outcomes expected under conditions of perfect competition. In the theory of market failure, the problems are attributed not to inadequacies of the actors themselves (who are presumed to be rational utility-maximizers) but rather to the structure of the system and the institutions, or lack thereof, that characterize it.[24] Specific attributes of the system impose transactions costs (including information costs) that create barriers to effective cooperation among the actors. Thus institutional defects are responsible for failures of coordination. To correct these defects, conscious institutional innovation may be necessary, although a good economist will always compare the costs of institutional innovation with the costs of market failure before recommending tampering with the market.

Like imperfect markets, world politics is characterized by institutional deficiencies that inhibit mutually advantageous coordination. Some of the deficiencies revolve around problems of transactions costs and uncertainty that have been cogently analyzed by students of market failure. Theories of market failure specify types of institutional imperfections that may inhibit agreement; international regimes may be interpreted as helping to correct similar institutional defects in world politics. Insofar as regimes are established through voluntary agreement among a number of states, we can interpret them, at least in part, as devices to overcome the barriers to more efficient coordination identified by theories of market failure.[25]

The analysis that follows is based on two theoretical assumptions. First, the actors whose behavior we analyze act, in general, as rational utility-maximizers in that they display consistent tendencies to adjust to external changes in ways that are calculated to increase the expected value of outcomes to them. Second, the international regimes with which we are concerned are devices to facilitate the making of agreements among these actors. From these assumptions it follows that the demand for international regimes

[24] Of particular value for understanding market failure is Kenneth J. Arrow, *Essays in the Theory of Risk-Bearing* (New York: North Holland/American Elsevier, 1974).

[25] Helen Milner suggested to me that international regimes were in this respect like credit markets, and that the history of the development of credit markets could be informative for students of international regimes. The analogy seems to hold. Richard Ehrenberg reports that the development of credit arrangements in medieval European Bourses reduced transaction costs (since money did not need to be transported in the form of specie) and provided high-quality information in the form of merchants' newsletters and exchanges of information at fairs: "during the Middle Ages the best information as to the course of events in the world was regularly to be obtained in the fairs and the Bourses" (p. 317). The Bourses also provided credit ratings, which provided information but also served as a crude substitute for effective systems of legal liability. Although the descriptions of credit market development in works such as that by Ehrenberg are fascinating, I have not been able to find a historically-grounded theory of these events. See Richard Ehrenberg, *Capital and Finance in the Age of the Renaissance: A Study of the Fuggers and Their Connections*, translated from the German by H. M. Lucas (New York: Harcourt, Brace, no date), especially chap. 3 (pp. 307–333).

at any given price will vary directly with the desirability of agreements to states and with the ability of international regimes actually to facilitate the making of such agreements. The condition for the theory's operation (that is, for regimes to be formed) is that sufficient complementary or common interests exist so that agreements benefiting all essential regime members can be made.

The value of theories of market failure for this analysis rests on the fact that they allow us to identify more precisely barriers to agreements. They therefore suggest insights into how international regimes help to reduce those barriers, and they provide richer interpretations of previously observed, but unexplained, phenomena associated with international regimes and international policy coordination. In addition, concepts of market failure help to explain the strength and extent of international regimes by identifying characteristics of international systems, or of international regimes themselves, that affect the demand for such regimes and therefore, given a supply schedule, their quantity. Insights from the market-failure literature therefore take us beyond the trivial cost-benefit or supply-demand propositions with which we began, to hypotheses about relationships that are less familiar.

The emphasis on efficiency in the market-failure literature is consistent with our constraint-choice analysis of the decision-making processes leading to the formation and maintenance of international regimes. Each actor must be as well or better off with the regime than without it—given the prior structure of constraints. This does not imply, of course, that the whole process leading to the formation of a new international regime will yield overall welfare benefits. Outsiders may suffer; indeed, some international regimes (such as alliances or cartel-type regimes) are specifically designed to impose costs on them. These costs to outsiders may well outweigh the benefits to members. In addition, powerful actors may manipulate constraints prior to the formation of a new regime. In that case, although the regime *per se* may achieve overall welfare improvements compared to the immediately preceding situation, the results of the joint process may be inferior to those that existed before the constraints were imposed.

3. Elements of a theory of the demand for international regimes

We are now in a position to address our central puzzle—why is there any demand for international regimes?—and to outline a theory to explain why this demand exists. First, it is necessary to use our distinction between "agreements" and "regimes" to pose the issue precisely: given a certain level of demand for international agreements, what will affect the demand for international regimes? The Coase theorem, from the market-failure literature, will then be used to develop a list of conditions under which international regimes are of potential value for facilitating agreements in world politics. This typological analysis turns our attention toward two central problems, *transactions cost* and *informational imperfections*. Questions of information, involving uncertainty and risk, will receive particular attention, since their exploration has rich implications for interpretation and future research.

The demand for agreements and the demand for regimes

It is crucial to distinguish clearly between international regimes, on the one hand, and mere *ad hoc* substantive agreements, on the other. Regimes, as argued above, facilitate the making of substantive agreements by providing a framework of rules, norms, principles, and procedures for negotiation. A theory of international regimes must explain why these intermediate arrangements are necessary.

In our analysis, the demand for agreements will be regarded as exogenous. It may be influenced by many factors, particularly by the perceptions that leaders of governments have about their interests in agreement or nonagreement. These perceptions will, in turn, be influenced by domestic politics, ideology, and other factors not encompassed by a systemic, constraint-choice approach. In the United States, "internationalists" have been attracted to international agreements and international organizations as useful devices for implementing American foreign policy; "isolationists" and "nationalists" have not. Clearly, such differences cannot be accounted for by our theory. We therefore assume a given desire for agreements and ask: under these conditions, what will be the demand for international regimes?

Under certain circumstances defining the demand and supply of agreements, there will be no need for regimes and we should expect none to form. This will be the situation in two extreme cases, where demand for agreements is nil and where the supply of agreements is infinitely elastic and free (so that all conceivable agreements can be made costlessly). But where the demand for agreements is positive at some level of feasible cost, and the supply of agreements is not infinitely elastic and free, there may be a demand for international regimes *if* they actually make possible agreements yielding net benefits that would not be possible on an *ad hoc* basis. In such a situation regimes can be regarded as "efficient." We can now ask: under what specific conditions will international regimes be efficient?

One way to address this question is to pose its converse. To ask about the conditions under which international regimes will be *worthless* enables us to draw on work in social choice, particularly by Ronald Coase. Coase was able to show that the presence of externalities alone does not necessarily prevent Pareto-optimal coordination among independent actors: under certain conditions, bargaining among these actors could lead to Pareto-optimal solutions. The key conditions isolated by Coase were (a) a legal framework establishing liability for actions, presumably supported by governmental authority; (b) perfect information; and (c) zero transactions costs (including organization costs and costs of making side-payments).[26] If all these conditions were met in world politics, *ad hoc* agreements would be costless and regimes unnecessary. *At least one of them must not be fulfilled if international regimes are to be of value, as facilitators of agreement, to independent utility-maximizing actors in world politics*. Inverting the Coase theorem provides us, therefore, with a list of conditions, at least one of which must apply if regimes are to be of value in facilitating agreements among governments:[27]

    (a) lack of a clear legal framework establishing liability for actions;
    (b) information imperfections (information is costly);
    (c) positive transactions costs.[28]

In world politics, of course, *all* of these conditions are met all of the time: world government does not exist; information is extremely costly and often impossible to obtain; transactions costs, including costs of organization and side-payments, are often very high. Yet the Coase theorem is useful not merely as a way of categorizing these familiar problems, but because it suggests how international regimes can improve actors' abilities to make mutually beneficial agreements. Regimes can make agreement easier if they provide frameworks for establishing legal liability (even if these are not perfect); improve the quantity and quality of information available to actors; or reduce other transactions costs, such as costs of organization or of making side-payments. This typology allows us to specify regime functions—as devices to make agreements possible—more precisely, and therefore to understand demand for international regimes. Insofar as international regimes can correct institutional defects in world politics along any of these three dimensions (liability, information, transactions costs), they may become efficient devices for the achievement of state purposes.

Regimes do not establish binding and enforceable legal liabilities in any strict or ultimately reliable sense, although the lack of a hierarchical struc-

[26] Ronald Coase, "The Problem of Social Cost," *Journal of Law and Economics* 3 (October 1960). For a discussion, see James Buchanan and Gordon Tullock, *The Calculus of Consent: Logical Foundations of Constitutional Democracy* (Ann Arbor: University of Michigan Press, 1962), p. 186.

[27] If we were to drop the assumption that actors are strictly self-interested utility-maximizers, regimes could be important in another way: they would help to develop norms that are internalized by actors as part of their own utility functions. This is important in real-world political-economic systems, as works by Schumpeter, Polanyi, and Hirsch on the moral underpinnings of a market system indicate. It is likely to be important in many international systems as well. But it is outside the scope of the analytical approach taken in this article—which is designed to illuminate some issues, but not to provide a comprehensive account of international regime change. See Joseph Schumpeter, *Capitalism, Socialism, and Democracy* (New York: Harper & Row, 1942), especially Part II, "Can Capitalism Survive?"; Karl Polanyi, *The Great Transformation: The Political and Economic Origins of Our Time* (1944; Boston: Beacon Press, 1957); and Fred Hirsch, *Social Limits to Growth* (Cambridge: Harvard University Press, 1976).

[28] Information costs could be considered under the category of transaction costs, but they are so important that I categorize them separately in order to give them special attention.

ture does not prevent the development of bits and pieces of law.[29] Regimes are much more important in providing established negotiating frameworks (reducing transactions costs) and in helping to coordinate actor expectations (improving the quality and quantity of information available to states). An explanation of these two functions of international regimes, with the help of microeconomic analysis, will lead to hypotheses about how the demand for international regimes should be expected to vary with changes in the nature of the international system (in the case of transactions costs) and about effects of characteristics of the international regime itself (in the case of information).

International regimes and transactions costs

Neither international agreements nor international regimes are created spontaneously. Political entrepreneurs must exist who see a potential profit in organizing collaboration. For entrepreneurship to develop, not only must there be a potential social gain to be derived from the formation of an international arrangement, but the entrepreneur (usually, in world politics, a government) must expect to be able to gain more itself from the regime than it invests in organizing the activity. Thus organizational costs to the entrepreneur must be lower than the net discounted value of the benefits that the entrepreneur expects to capture for itself.[30] As a result, international cooperation that would have a positive social payoff may not be initiated unless a potential entrepreneur would profit sufficiently. This leads us back into questions of supply and the theory of hegemonic stability, since such a situation is most likely to exist where no potential entrepreneur is large relative to the whole set of potential beneficiaries, and where "free riders" cannot be prevented from benefiting from cooperation without paying proportionately.

Our attention here, however, is on the demand side: we focus on the efficiency of constructing international regimes, as opposed simply to making *ad hoc* agreements. We only expect regimes to develop where the costs of making *ad hoc* agreements on particular substantive matters are higher than the sum of the costs of making such agreements within a regime framework and the costs of establishing that framework.

With respect to transactions costs, where do we expect these conditions to be met? To answer this question, it is useful to introduce the concept of *issue density* to refer to the number and importance of issues arising within a given policy space. The denser the policy space, the more highly interdependent are the different issues, and therefore the agreements made about

[29] For a discussion of "the varieties of international law," see Louis Henkin, *How Nations Behave: Law and Foreign Policy*, 2d ed. (New York: Columbia University Press for the Council on Foreign Relations, 1979), pp. 13–22.

[30] Davis and North, *Institutional Change and American Economic Growth*, especially pp. 51–57.

them. Where issue density is low, *ad hoc* agreements are quite likely to be adequate: different agreements will not impinge on one another significantly, and there will be few economies of scale associated with establishing international regimes (each of which would encompass only one or a few agreements). Where issue density is high, on the other hand, one substantive objective may well impinge on another and regimes will achieve economies of scale, for instance in establishing negotiating procedures that are applicable to a variety of potential agreements within similar substantive areas of activity.[31]

Furthermore, in dense policy spaces, complex linkages will develop among substantive issues. Reducing industrial tariffs without damaging one's own economy may depend on agricultural tariff reductions from others; obtaining passage through straits for one's own warships may depend on wider decisions taken about territorial waters; the sale of food to one country may be more or less advantageous depending on other food-supply contracts being made at the same time. As linkages such as these develop, the organizational costs involved in reconciling distinct objectives will rise and demands for overall frameworks of rules, norms, principles, and procedures to cover certain clusters of issues—that is, for international regimes—will increase.

International regimes therefore seem often to facilitate side-payments among actors within issue-areas covered by comprehensive regimes, since they bring together negotiators to consider a whole complex of issues. Side-payments in general are difficult in world politics and raise serious issues of transaction costs: in the absence of a price system for the exchange of favors, these institutional imperfections will hinder cooperation.[32] International regimes may provide a partial corrective.[33] The well-known literature on "spillover" in bargaining, relating to the European Community and other integration schemes, can also be interpreted as being concerned with side-

[31] The concept of issue density bears some relationship to Herbert Simon's notion of "decomposability," in *The Sciences of the Artificial* (Cambridge: MIT Press, 1969). In both cases, problems that can be conceived of as separate are closely linked to one another functionally, so that it is difficult to affect one without also affecting others. Issue density is difficult to operationalize, since the universe (the "issue-area" or "policy space") whose area forms the denominator of the term cannot easily be specified precisely. But given a certain definition of the issue-area, it is possible to trace the increasing density of issues within it over time. See, for example, Robert O. Keohane and Joseph S. Nye, *Power and Interdependence: World Politics in Transition* (Boston: Little, Brown, 1977), chap. 4.

[32] On questions of linkage, see Arthur A. Stein, "The Politics of Linkage," *World Politics* 33,1 (October 1980): 62–81; Kenneth Oye, "The Domain of Choice," in Oye et al., *Eagle Entangled: U.S. Foreign Policy in a Complex World* (New York: Longmans, 1979), pp. 3–33; and Robert D. Tollison and Thomas D. Willett, "An Economic Theory of Mutually Advantageous Issue Linkage in International Negotiations," *International Organization* 33,4 (Autumn 1979).

[33] GATT negotiations and deliberations on the international monetary system have been characterized by extensive bargaining over side-payments and complex politics of issue-linkage. For a discussion see Nicholas Hutton, "The Salience of Linkage in International Economic Negotiations," *Journal of Common Market Studies* 13, 1–2 (1975): 136–60.

payments. In this literature, expectations that an integration arrangement can be expanded to new issue-areas permit the broadening of potential side-payments, thus facilitating agreement.[34]

It should be noted, however, that regimes may make it more difficult to link issues that are clustered separately. Governments tend to organize themselves consistently with how issues are treated internationally, as well as vice versa; issues considered by different regimes are often dealt with by different bureaucracies at home. Linkages and side-payments become difficult under these conditions, since they always involve losses as well as gains. Organizational subunits that would lose, on issues that matter to them, from a proposed side-payment are unlikely to support it on the basis of another agency's claim that it is in the national interest. Insofar as the dividing lines between international regimes place related issues in different jurisdictions, they may well make side-payments and linkages between these issues less feasible.

The crucial point about regimes to be derived from this discussion of transactions costs can be stated succinctly: the optimal size of a regime will increase if there are increasing rather than diminishing returns to regime-scale (reflecting the high costs of making separate agreements in a dense policy space), or if the marginal costs of organization decline as regime size grows. The point about increasing returns suggests an analogy with the theory of imperfect competition among firms. As Samuelson notes, "increasing returns is the prime case of deviations from perfect competition."[35] In world politics, increasing returns to scale lead to more extensive international regimes.

The research hypothesis to be derived from this analysis is that increased issue density will lead to greater demand for international regimes and to more extensive regimes. Since greater issue density is likely to be a feature of situations of high interdependence, this forges a link between interdependence and international regimes: increases in the former can be expected to lead to increases in demand for the latter.[36]

The demand for principles and norms

The definition of international regimes provided in the introduction to this volume stipulates that regimes must embody principles ("beliefs of fact, causation, and rectitude") and norms ("standards of behavior defined in

[34] Ernst B. Haas, *The Uniting of Europe* (Stanford: Stanford University Press, 1958).

[35] Paul A. Samuelson, "The Monopolistic Competition Revolution," in R. E. Kuenne, ed., *Monopolistic Competition Theory* (New York: Wiley, 1967), p. 117.

[36] Increases in issue density could make it more difficult to supply regimes; the costs of providing regimes could grow, for instance, as a result of multiple linkages across issues. The 1970s Law of the Sea negotiations illustrate this problem. As a result, it will not necessarily be the case that increases in interdependence will lead to increases in the number, extensiveness, and strength of international regimes.

terms of rights and obligations'') as well as rules and decision-making procedures.[37] Otherwise, international regimes would be difficult to distinguish
from any regular patterns of action in world politics that create common
expectations about behavior: even hostile patterns of interactions could be
seen as embodying regimes if the observer could infer implied rules and
decision-making procedures from behavior.

Arguments about definitions are often tedious. What is important is not
whether this definition is "correct," but that principles and norms are integral parts of many, if not all, of the arrangements that we regard as international regimes. This raises the question of why, in interactions (such as those
of world politics) characterized by conflict arising from self-interest, norms
and principles should play any role at all.

The constraint-choice framework used in this article is not the best approach for describing how principles and norms of state behavior evolve
over time. The legal and sociological approaches discussed in this volume by
Young are better adapted to the task of historical interpretation of norm-
development. Nevertheless, a brief analysis of the function of principles and
norms in an uncertain environment will suggest why they are important for
fulfilling the overall function of international regimes: to facilitate mutually
advantageous international agreements.

An important principle that is shared by most, if not all, international
regimes is what Jervis calls "reciprocation": the belief that if one helps
others or fails to hurt them, even at some opportunity cost to oneself, they
will reciprocate when the tables are turned. In the Concert of Europe, this
became a norm specific to the regime, a standard of behavior providing that
statesmen should avoid maximizing their interests in the short term for the
sake of expected long-run gains.[38]

This norm requires action that does not reflect specific calculations of
self-interest: the actor making a short-run sacrifice does not know that future
benefits will flow from comparable restraint by others, and can hardly be
regarded as making precise calculations of expected utility. What Jervis calls
the norm of reciprocation—or (to avoid confusion with the concept of reciprocity in international law) what I shall call a norm of generalized
commitment—precisely forbids specific interest calculations. It rests on the
premise that a veil of ignorance stands between us and the future, but that
we should nevertheless assume that regime-supporting behavior will be
beneficial to us even though we have no convincing evidence to that effect.

At first glance, it may seem puzzling that governments ever subscribe
either to the principle of generalized commitment (that regime-supporting
behavior will yield better results than self-help in the long run) or to the
corresponding norm in a given regime (that they should act in a regime-
supporting fashion). But if we think about international regimes as devices to

---

[37] Stephen D. Krasner, article in this volume, p. 186.
[38] Robert Jervis, article in this volume, p. 364.

facilitate mutually beneficial agreements the puzzle can be readily resolved. Without such a norm, each agreement would have to provide net gains for every essential actor, or side-payments would have to be arranged so that the net gains of the package were positive for all. Yet as we have seen, side-payments are difficult to organize. Thus, packages of agreements will usually be difficult if not impossible to construct, particularly when time is short, as in a balance of payments crisis or a sudden military threat. The principle of generalized commitment, however, removes the necessity for specific clusters of agreements, each of which is mutually beneficial. Within the context of a regime, help can be extended by those in a position to do so, on the assumption that such regime-supporting behavior will be reciprocated in the future. States may demand that others follow the norm of generalized commitment even if they are thereby required to supply it themselves, because the result will facilitate agreements that in the long run can be expected to be beneficial for all concerned.

The demand for specific information

The problems of organization costs discussed earlier arise even in situations where actors have entirely consistent interests (pure coordination games with stable equilibria). In such situations, however, severe information problems are not embedded in the structure of relationships, since actors have incentives to reveal information and their own preferences fully to one another. In these games the problem is to reach some agreement point; but it may not matter much which of several is chosen.[39] Conventions are important and ingenuity may be required, but serious systemic impediments to the acquisition and exchange of information are lacking.[40]

The norm of generalized commitment can be seen as a device for coping with the conflictual implications of uncertainty by imposing favorable assumptions about others' future behavior. The norm of generalized commitment requires that one accept the veil of ignorance but act *as if* one will benefit from others' behavior in the future if one behaves now in a regime-supporting way. Thus it creates a coordination game by ruling out potentially antagonistic calculations.

Yet in many situations in world politics, specific and calculable conflicts of interest exist among the actors. In such situations, they all have an interest in agreement (the situation is not zero-sum), but they prefer different types of agreement or different patterns of behavior (e.g., one may prefer to

---

[39] The classic discussion is in Thomas C. Schelling, *The Strategy of Conflict* (1960; Cambridge: Harvard University Press, 1980), chap. 4, "Toward a Theory of Interdependent Decision." See also Schelling, *Micromotives and Macrobehavior* (New York: Norton, 1978).

[40] For an interesting discussion of regimes in these terms, see the paper in this volume by Oran R. Young. On conventions, see David K. Lewis, *Convention: A Philosophical Study* (Cambridge: Cambridge University Press, 1969).

cheat without the other being allowed to do so). As Stein points out in this volume, these situations are characterized typically by unstable equilibria. Without enforcement, actors have incentives to deviate from the agreement point:

> [Each] actor requires assurances that the other will also eschew its rational choice [and will not cheat, and] such collaboration requires a degree of formalization. The regime must specify what constitutes cooperation and what constitutes cheating.[41]

In such situations of strategic interaction, as in oligopolistic competition and world politics, systemic constraint-choice theory yields no determinate results or stable equilibria. Indeed, discussions of "blackmailing" or games such as "prisoners' dilemma" indicate that, under certain conditions, suboptimal equilibria are quite likely to appear. Game theory, as Simon has commented, only illustrates the severity of the problem; it does not solve it.[42]

Under these circumstances, power factors are important. They are particularly relevant to the supply of international regimes: regimes involving enforcement can only be supplied if there is authority backed by coercive resources. As we have seen, regimes themselves do not possess such resources. For the means necessary to uphold sanctions, one has to look to the states belonging to the regime.

Yet even under conditions of strategic interaction and unstable equilibria, regimes may be of value to actors by providing information. Since high-quality information reduces uncertainty, we can expect that there will be a demand for international regimes that provide such information.

Firms that consider relying on the behavior of other firms within a context of strategic interaction—for instance, in oligopolistic competition—face similar information problems. They also do not understand reality fully. Students of market failure have pointed out that risk-averse firms will make fewer and less far-reaching agreements than they would under conditions of perfect information. Indeed, they will eschew agreements that would produce mutual benefits. Three specific problems facing firms in such a context are also serious for governments in world politics and give rise to demands for international regimes to ameliorate them.

(1) Asymmetric information. Some actors may have more information about a situation than others. Expecting that the resulting bargains would be unfair, "outsiders" may therefore be reluctant to make agreements with "insiders."[43] One aspect of this in the microeconomic literature is "quality uncertainty," in which a buyer is uncertain about the real value of goods

[41]Arthur A. Stein, article in this volume, p. 312.

[42] Herbert Simon, "From Substantive to Procedural Rationality," in Latsis, ed., *Method and Appraisal in Economics;* Spiro J. Latsis, "A Research Programme in Economics," in ibid.; and on blackmailing, Oye, "The Domain of Choice."

[43] Oliver E. Williamson, *Markets and Hierarchies: Analysis and Anti-Trust Implications* (New York: Free Press, 1975).

being offered. In such a situation (typified by the market for used cars when sellers are seen as unscrupulous), no exchange may take place despite the fact that with perfect information, there would be extensive trading.[44]

(2) Moral hazard. Agreements may alter incentives in such a way as to encourage less cooperative behavior. Insurance companies face this problem of "moral hazard." Property insurance, for instance, may make people less careful with their property and therefore increase the risk of loss.[45]

(3) Deception and irresponsibility. Some actors may be dishonest, and enter into agreements that they have no intention of fulfilling. Others may be "irresponsible," and make commitments that they are unlikely to be able to carry out. Governments or firms may enter into agreements that they intend to keep, assuming that the environment will continue to be benign; if adversity sets in, they may be unable to keep their commitments. Banks regularly face this problem, leading them to devise standards of "creditworthiness." Large governments trying to gain adherents to international agreements may face similar difficulties: countries that are enthusiastic about cooperation are likely to be those that expect to gain more, proportionately, than they contribute. This is analogous to problems of self-selection in the market-failure literature. For instance, if rates are not properly adjusted, people with high risks of heart attack will seek life insurance more avidly than those with longer life expectancies; people who purchased "lemons" will tend to sell them earlier on the used-car market than people with "creampuffs."[46] In international politics, self-selection means that for certain types of activities—for example, sharing research and development information—weak states (with much to gain but little to give) may have greater incentives to participate than strong ones. But without the strong states, the enterprise as a whole will fail. From the perspective of the outside observer, irresponsibility is an aspect of the problem of public goods and free-riding;[47] but from the standpoint of the actor trying to determine whether to rely on a potentially irresponsible partner, it is a problem of uncertainty and risk. Either way, information costs may prevent mutually beneficial agreement, and the presence of these costs will provide incentives to states to demand international regimes (either new regimes or the maintenance of existing ones) that will ameliorate problems of uncertainty and risk.

4. Information, openness, and communication in international regimes

International regimes, and the institutions and procedures that develop in conjunction with them, perform the function of reducing uncertainty and

[44] George A. Ackerlof, "The Market for 'Lemons': Qualitative Uncertainty and the Market Mechanism," *Quarterly Journal of Economics* 84,3 (August 1970).

[45] Arrow, *Essays in the Theory of Risk-Bearing.*

[46] Ackerlof, "The Market for 'Lemons' "; Arrow, *Essays in the Theory of Risk-Bearing.*

[47] For an analysis along these lines, see Davis B. Bobrow and Robert T. Kudrle, "Energy R&D: In Tepid Pursuit of Collective Goods," *International Organization* 33,2 (Spring 1979): 149–76.

risk by linking discrete issues to one another and by improving the quantity and quality of information available to participants. Linking issues is important as a way to deal with potential deception. Deception is less profitable in a continuing "game," involving many issues, in which the cheater's behavior is closely monitored by others and in which those actors retaliate for deception with actions in other areas, than in a "single-shot" game. The larger the number of issues in a regime, or linked to it, and the less important each issue is in proportion to the whole, the less serious is the problem of deception likely to be.

Another means of reducing problems of uncertainty is to increase the quantity and quality of communication, thus alleviating the information problems that create risk and uncertainty in the first place. Williamson argues on the basis of the organization theory literature that communication tends to increase adherence to group goals: "Although the precise statement of the relation varies slightly, the general proposition that intragroup communication promotes shared goals appears to be a well-established empirical finding."[48] Yet not all communication is of equal value: after all, communication may lead to asymmetrical or unfair bargaining outcomes, deception, or agreements entered into irresponsibly. And in world politics, governmental officials and diplomats are carefully trained to communicate precisely what they wish to convey rather than fully to reveal their preferences and evaluations. Effective communication is not measured well by the amount of talking that used-car salespersons do to customers or that governmental officials do to one another in negotiating international regimes. Strange has commented, perhaps with some exaggeration:

> One of the paradoxes of international economic relations in the 1970s has been that the soft words exchanged in trade organizations have coexisted with hard deeds perpetuated by national governments. The reversion to economic nationalism has been accompanied by constant reiterations of continued commitment to international cooperation and consultation. The international bureaucracies of Geneva, New York, Paris and Brussels have been kept busier than ever exchanging papers and proposals and patiently concocting endless draft documents to which, it is hoped, even deeply divided states might subscribe. But the reality has increasingly been one of unilateral action, even where policy is supposedly subject to multilateral agreement.[49]

The information that is required in entering into an international regime is not merely information about other governments' resources and formal negotiating positions, but rather knowledge of their internal evaluations of the situation, their intentions, the intensity of their preferences, and their

---

[48] Oliver E. Williamson, "A Dynamic Theory of Interfirm Behavior," *Quarterly Journal of Economics* 79 (1965), p. 584.

[49] Susan Strange, "The Management of Surplus Capacity: or How Does Theory Stand Up to Protectionism 1970s Style?", *International Organization* 33,3 (Summer 1979): 303–334.

willingness to adhere to an agreement even in adverse future circumstances. As Hirsch points out with respect to the "Bagehot Problem" in banking, lenders need to know the moral as well as the financial character of borrowers.[50] Likewise, governments contemplating international cooperation need to *know* their partners, not merely know *about* them.

This line of argument suggests that governments that successfully maintain "closure," protecting the autonomy of their decision-making processes from outside penetration, will have more difficulty participating in international regimes than more open, apparently disorganized governments. "Closed" governments will be viewed with more skepticism by potential partners, who will anticipate more serious problems of bounded rationality in relations with these closed governments than toward their more open counterparts. Similarly, among given governments, politicization of issues and increases in the power of political appointees are likely to reduce the quality of information and will therefore tend to reduce cooperation. Thus as an issue gains salience in domestic politics, other governments will begin to anticipate more problems of bounded rationality and will therefore perceive greater risks in cooperation. International cooperation may therefore decline quite apart from the real intentions or objectives of the policy makers involved.

This conclusion is important: international policy coordination and the development of international regimes depend not merely on interests and power, or on the negotiating skills of diplomats, but also on expectations and information, which themselves are in part functions of the political structures of governments and their openness to one another. Intergovernmental relationships that are characterized by ongoing communication among working-level officials, "unauthorized" as well as authorized, are inherently more conducive to information-exchange and agreements than are traditional relationships between internally coherent bureaucracies that effectively control their communications with the external world.[51]

Focusing on information and risk can help us to understand the performance of international regimes over time, and therefore to comprehend better the sources of demands for such regimes. Again, reference to theories of oligopoly, as in Williamson's work, is helpful. Williamson assumes that cooperation—which he refers to as "adherence to group goals"—will be a function both of communication and of the past performance of the oligopoly; reciprocally, communication levels will be a function of cooperation. In addition, performance will be affected by the condition of the environment. Using these assumptions, Williamson derives a model that has two points of equilibrium, one at high levels and one at low levels of cooperation.

[50] Fred Hirsch, "The Bagehot Problem," *The Manchester School* 45,3 (1977): 241–57.

[51] Notice that here, through a functional logic, a systemic analysis has implications for the performance of different governmental structures at the level of the actor. The value of high-quality information in making agreements does not force governments to become more open, but it gives advantages to those that do.

His oligopolies are characterized by substantial inertia. Once a given equilibrium has been reached, substantial environmental changes are necessary to alter it:

> If the system is operating at a low level of adherence and communication (i.e., the competitive solution), a substantial improvement in the environment will be necessary before the system will shift to a high level of adherence and communication. *Indeed, the condition of the environment required to drive the system to the collusive solution is much higher than the level required to maintain it once it has achieved this position. Similarly, a much more unfavorable condition of the environment is required to move the system from a high to a low level equilibrium than is required to maintain it there.* [52]

It seems reasonable to suppose that Williamson's assumptions about relationships among communication, cooperation or adherence, and performance have considerable validity for international regimes as well as for cartels. If so, his emphasis on the role of information, for explaining persistent behavior (competitive or oligopolistic) by groups of firms, helps us to understand the lags between structural change and regime change that are so puzzling to students of international regimes. In our earlier work, Nye and I observed discrepancies between the predictions of structural models (such as what I later called the "theory of hegemonic stability") and actual patterns of change; in particular, changes in international regimes tend to lag behind changes in structure. [53] But our explanation for this phenomenon was essentially *ad hoc:* we simply posited the existence of inertia, assuming that "a set of networks, norms, and institutions, once established, will be difficult either to eradicate or drastically to rearrange." [54] Understanding the role of communication and information in the formation and maintenance of international regimes helps locate this observation in a theoretical context. The institutions and procedures that develop around international regimes acquire value as arrangements permitting communication, and therefore facilitating the exchange of information. As they prove themselves in this way, demand for them increases. Thus, even if the structure of a system becomes more fragmented—presumably increasing the costs of providing regime-related collective goods (as suggested by public goods theory)—increased demand for a particular, well-established, information-providing international regime may, at least for a time, outweigh the effects of increasing costs on supply.

These arguments about information suggest two novel interpretations of puzzling contemporary phenomena in world politics, as well as providing the

---

[52] Williamson, "A Dynamic Theory of Interfirm Behavior," p. 592, original italics.

[53] *Power and Interdependence*, especially pp. 54–58 and 146–53. Linda Cahn also found lags, particularly in the wheat regime; see "National Power and International Regimes."

[54] *Power and Interdependence*, p. 55.

basis for hypotheses that could guide research on fluctuations in the strength and extent of international regimes.

Understanding the value of governmental openness for making mutually beneficial agreements helps to account for the often-observed fact that effective international regimes—such as the GATT in its heyday, or the Bretton Woods international monetary regime[55]—are often associated with a great deal of informal contact and communication among officials. Governments no longer act within such regimes as unitary, self-contained actors. "Transgovernmental" networks of acquaintance and friendship develop, with the consequences that supposedly confidential internal documents of one government may be seen by officials of another; informal coalitions of like-minded officials develop to achieve common purposes; and critical discussions by professionals probe the assumptions and assertions of state policies.[56] These transgovernmental relationships increase opportunities for cooperation in world politics by providing policy makers with high-quality information about what their counterparts are likely to do. Insofar as they are valued by policy makers, they help to generate demand for international regimes.

The information-producing "technology" that becomes embedded in a particular international regime also helps us to understand why the erosion of American hegemony during the 1970s has not been accompanied by an immediate collapse of international regimes, as a theory based entirely on supply-side public goods analysis would have predicted. Since the level of institutionalization of postwar regimes was exceptionally high, with intricate and extensive networks of communication among working-level officials, we should expect the lag between the decline of American hegemony and the disruption of international regimes to be quite long and the "inertia" of the existing regimes relatively great.

The major hypothesis to be derived from this discussion of information is that demand for international regimes should be in part a function of the effectiveness of the regimes themselves in providing high-quality information to policy makers. The success of the institutions associated with a regime in providing such information will itself be a source of regime persistence.

Three inferences can be made from this hypothesis. First, regimes accompanied by highly regularized procedures and rules will provide more information to participants than less regularized regimes and will therefore, on

[55] On the GATT, see Gardner Patterson, *Discrimination in International Trade: The Policy Issues* (Princeton: Princeton University Press, 1966); on the international monetary regime, see Robert W. Russell, "Transgovernmental Interaction in the International Monetary System, 1960–1972," *International Organization* 27,4 (Autumn 1973) and Fred Hirsch, *Money International*, rev. ed. (Harmondsworth, England: Pelican Books, 1969), especially chap. 11, "Central Bankers International."

[56] Robert O. Keohane and Joseph S. Nye, "Transgovernmental Relations and International Organizations," *World Politics* 27,1 (October 1974): 39–62.

information grounds, be in greater demand. Thus, considerations of high-quality information will help to counteract the normal tendencies of states to create vague rules and poorly specified procedures as a way of preventing conflict or maintaining freedom of action where interests differ.

Second, regimes that develop norms internalized by participants—in particular, norms of honesty and straightforwardness—will be in greater demand and will be valued more than regimes that fail to develop such norms.

Third, regimes that are accompanied by open governmental arrangements and are characterized by extensive transgovernmental relations will be in greater demand and will be valued more than regimes whose relationships are limited to traditional state-to-state ties.[57]

Perhaps other nontrivial inferences can also be drawn from the basic hypothesis linking a regime's information-provision with actors' demands for it. In any event, this emphasis on information turns our attention back toward the regime, and the process of institutionalization that accompanies regime formation, and away from an exclusive concern with the power structure of world politics. The extent to which institutionalized cooperation has been developed will be an important determinant, along with power-structural conditions and issue density, of the extent and strength of international regimes.

From a future-oriented or policy perspective, this argument introduces the question of whether governments (particularly those of the advanced industrial countries) could compensate for the increasing fragmentation of power among them by building communication-facilitating institutions that are rich in information. The answer depends in part on whether hegemony is really a necessary condition for effective international cooperation or only a facilitative one. Kindleberger claims the former, but the evidence is inconclusive.[58] Analysis of the demand for international regimes, focusing on questions of information and transactions costs, suggests the possibility that international institutions could help to compensate for eroding hegemony. International regimes could not only reduce the organization costs and other transactions costs associated with international negotiations; they could also provide information that would make bargains easier to strike.

How effectively international regimes could compensate for the erosion of hegemony is unknown. Neither the development of a theory of international regimes nor the testing of hypotheses derived from such a theory is likely to resolve the question in definitive terms. But from a contemporary policy standpoint, both theory development and theory testing would at least

---

[57] These first three inferences focus only on the *demand* side. To understand the degree to which norms, for example, will develop, one needs also to look at supply considerations. Problems of organization, such as those discussed in the public goods literature and the theory of hegemonic stability, may prevent even strongly desired regimes from materializing.

[58] Kindleberger has asserted that "for the world economy to be stabilized, there has to be a stabilizer, one stabilizer." *The World in Depression,* p. 305.

help to define the dimensions of the problem and provide some guidance for thinking about the future consequences of present actions.

5. Coping with uncertainties: insurance regimes

Creating international regimes hardly disposes of risks or uncertainty. Indeed, participating in schemes for international cooperation entails risk for the cooperating state. If others fail to carry out their commitments, it may suffer. If (as part of an international growth scheme) it reflates its economy and others do not, it may run a larger-than-desired current-account deficit; if it liberalizes trade in particular sectors and its partners fail to reciprocate, import-competing industries may become less competitive without compensation being received elsewhere; if it curbs bribery by its multinational corporations without comparable action by others, its firms may lose markets abroad. In world politics, therefore, governments frequently find themselves comparing the risks they would run from lack of regulation of particular issue-areas (i.e., the absence of international regimes) with the risks of entering into such regimes. International regimes are designed to mitigate the effects on individual states of uncertainty deriving from rapid and often unpredictable changes in world politics. Yet they create another kind of uncertainty, uncertainty about whether other governments will keep their commitments.

In one sense, this is simply the old question of dependence: dependence on an international regime may expose one to risks, just as dependence on any given state may. Governments always need to compare the risks they run by being outside a regime with the risks they run by being within one. If the price of achieving short-term stability by constructing a regime is increasing one's dependence on the future decisions of others, that price may be too high.

Yet the question of coping with risk also suggests the possibility of different types of international regimes. Most international regimes are *control-oriented*. Through a set of more or less institutionalized arrangements, members maintain some degree of control over each other's behavior, thus decreasing harmful externalities arising from independent action as well as reducing uncertainty stemming from uncoordinated activity. A necessary condition for this type of regime is that the benefits of the regularity achieved thereby must exceed the organizational and autonomy costs of submitting to the rules, both for the membership as a whole and for each necessary member.

Control-oriented regimes typically seek to ensure two kinds of regularity, internal and environmental. Internal regularity refers to orderly patterns of behavior among members of the regime. The Bretton Woods international monetary regime and the GATT trade regime have focused, first of all, on members' obligations, assuming that, if members behaved according to the rules, the international monetary and trade systems would be orderly. Where all significant actors within an issue-area are members of the regime, this assumption is warranted and mutual-control regimes tend to be effective.

Yet there are probably few, if any, pure cases of mutual-control regimes. Typically, an international regime is established to regularize behavior not only among the members but also between them and outsiders. This is a side-benefit of stable international monetary regimes involving convertible currencies.[59] It was an explicit purpose of the nonproliferation regime of the 1970s, in particular the "suppliers' club," designed to keep nuclear material and knowledge from diffusing rapidly to potential nuclear powers. Military alliances can be viewed as an extreme case of attempts at environmental control, in which the crucial benefits of collaboration stem not from the direct results of cooperation but from their effects on the behavior of outsiders. Alliances seek to induce particular states of minds in nonmembers, to deter or to intimidate.

Observers of world politics have often assumed implicitly that all significant international regimes are control-oriented. The economic literature, however, suggests another approach to the problem of risk. Instead of expanding to control the market, firms or individuals may diversify to reduce risk or may attempt to purchase insurance against unlikely but costly contingencies. Portfolio diversification and insurance thus compensate for deficiencies in markets that lack these institutions. Insurance and diversification are appropriate strategies where actors cannot exercise control over their environment at reasonable cost, but where, in the absence of such strategies, economic activity would be suboptimal.[60]

In world politics, such strategies are appropriate under similar conditions. The group of states forming the insurance or diversification "pool" is only likely to resort to this course of action if it cannot control its environment effectively. Second, for insurance regimes to make sense, the risks insured against must be specific to individual members of the group. If the catastrophic events against which one wishes to insure are likely (should they occur at all) to affect all members simultaneously and with equal severity, risk sharing will make little sense.[61]

---

[59] Charles P. Kindleberger, "Systems of International Economic Organization," in David P. Calleo, ed., *Money and the Coming World Order* (New York: New York University Press for the Lehrman Institute, 1978); Ronald McKinnon, *Money in International Exchange: The Convertible Currency System* (New York: Oxford University Press, 1979).

[60] Arrow, *Essays in the Theory of Risk-Bearing*, pp. 134–43.

[61] In personal correspondence, Robert Jervis has suggested an interesting qualification to this argument. He writes: "If we look at relations that involve at least the potential for high conflict, then schemes that tie the fates of all the actors together may have utility even if the actors are concerned about catastrophic events which will affect them all. They can worry that if some states are not affected, the latter will be much stronger than the ones who have been injured. So it would make sense for them to work out a scheme which would insure that a disaster would not affect their relative positions, even though this would not mean that they would all not be worse off in absolute terms." The point is certainly well taken, although one may wonder whether such an agreement would in fact be implemented by the states that would make large relative gains in the absence of insurance payments.

The demand for international regimes 353

International regimes designed to share risks are less common than those designed to control events, but three examples from the 1970s can be cited that contain elements of this sort of regime:

(1) The STABEX scheme of the Lomé Convention, concluded between the European Community and forty-six African, Caribbean, and Pacific states in 1975. "Under the STABEX scheme, any of the 46 ACP countries dependent for more than 7.5 percent (2.5 percent for the poorest members of the ACP) of their export earnings on one of a list of commodities, such as tea, cocoa, coffee, bananas, cotton, and iron ore, will be eligible for financial help if these earnings fall below a certain level."[62] STABEX, of course, is not a genuine mutual-insurance regime because the guarantee is made by one set of actors to another set.

(2) The emergency sharing arrangements of the International Energy Agency, which provide for the mandatory sharing of oil supplies in emergencies, under allocation rules devised and administered by the IEA.[63]

(3) The Financial Support Fund of the OECD, agreed on in April 1975 but never put into effect, which would have provided a "lender of last resort" at the international level, so that risks on loans to particular countries in difficulty would have been "shared among all members, in proportion to their quotas and subject to the limits of their quotas, however the loans are financed."[64]

Control-oriented and insurance strategies for coping with risk and uncertainty have different advantages and liabilities. Control-oriented approaches are more ambitious; when effective, they may eliminate adversity rather than simply spread risks around. After all, it is more satisfactory to prevent floods than merely to insure against them; likewise, it would be preferable for consumers to be able to forestall commodity embargoes rather than simply to share their meager supplies fairly if such an embargo should take place.

Yet the conditions for an effective control-oriented regime are more stringent than those for insurance arrangements. An effective control-oriented regime must be supported by a coalition that has effective power in the issue-area being regulated, and whose members have sufficient incentives to exercise such power.[65] Where these conditions are not met, insurance regimes may be "second-best" strategies, but they are better than no strategies at all. Under conditions of eroding hegemony, one can expect the increasing emergence of insurance regimes, in some cases as a result of the

---

[62] Isebill V. Gruhn, "The Lomé Convention: Inching toward Interdependence," *International Organization* 30,2 (Spring 1976), pp. 255–56.

[63] Robert O. Keohane, "The International Energy Agency: State Influence and Transgovernmental Politics," *International Organization* 32,4 (Autumn 1978): 929–52.

[64] OECD *Observer*, no. 74 (March–April 1975), pp. 9–13.

[65] The optimal condition under which such a coalition may emerge could be called the "paper tiger condition": a potential external threat to the coalition exists but is too weak to frighten or persuade coalition members to defect or to desist from effective action. OPEC has been viewed by western policy makers since 1973 as a real rather than paper tiger, although some observers keep insisting that there is less to the organization than meets the eye.

unwillingness of powerful states to adopt control-oriented strategies (as in the case of STABEX), in other cases as replacements for control-oriented regimes that have collapsed (as in the cases of the IEA emergency sharing arrangements and the OECD Financial Support Fund or "safety net"). Economic theories of risk and uncertainty suggest that as power conditions shift, so will strategies to manage risk, and therefore the nature of international regimes.

6. Conclusions

The argument of this paper can be summarized under six headings. First, international regimes can be interpreted, in part, as devices to facilitate the making of substantive agreements in world politics, particularly among states. Regimes facilitate agreements by providing rules, norms, principles, and procedures that help actors to overcome barriers to agreement identified by economic theories of market failure. That is, regimes make it easier for actors to realize their interests collectively.

Second, public goods problems affect the supply of international regimes, as the "theory of hegemonic stability" suggests. But they also give rise to demand for international regimes, which can ameliorate problems of transactions costs and information imperfections that hinder effective decentralized responses to problems of providing public goods.

Third, two major research hypotheses are suggested by the demand-side analysis of this article.

(a) Increased issue density will lead to increased demand for international regimes.
(b) The demand for international regimes will be in part a function of the effectiveness of the regimes themselves in developing norms of generalized commitment and in providing high-quality information to policymakers.

Fourth, our analysis helps us to interpret certain otherwise puzzling phenomena, since our constraint-choice approach allows us to see how demands for such behavior would be generated. We can better understand transgovernmental relations, as well as the lags observed between structural change and regime change in general, and between the decline of the United States' hegemony and regime disruption in particular.

Fifth, in the light of our analysis, several assertions of structural theories appear problematic. In particular, it is less clear that hegemony is a necessary condition for stable international regimes under all circumstances. Past patterns of institutionalized cooperation may be able to compensate, to some extent, for increasing fragmentation of power.

Sixth, distinguishing between conventional control-oriented international regimes, on the one hand, and insurance regimes, on the other, may

The demand for international regimes 355

help us to understand emerging adaptations of advanced industrialized countries to a global situation in which their capacity for control over events is much less than it was during the postwar quarter-century.

None of these observations implies an underlying harmony of interests in world politics. Regimes can be used to pursue particularistic and parochial interests, as well as more widely shared objectives. They do not necessarily increase overall levels of welfare. Even when they do, conflicts among units will continue. States will attempt to force the burdens of adapting to change onto one another. Nevertheless, as long as the situations involved are not constant-sum, actors will have incentives to coordinate their behavior, implicitly or explicitly, in order to achieve greater collective benefits without reducing the utility of any unit. When such incentives exist, and when sufficient interdependence exists that *ad hoc* agreements are insufficient, opportunities will arise for the development of international regimes. If international regimes did not exist, they would surely have to be invented.

[2]

ECONOMICS AND POLITICS   0954-1985
Volume 2   March 1990   No. 1

THE ROLE OF INSTITUTIONS IN THE REVIVAL OF TRADE: THE LAW MERCHANT, PRIVATE JUDGES, AND THE CHAMPAGNE FAIRS

PAUL R. MILGROM, DOUGLASS C. NORTH AND
BARRY R. WEINGAST*

A good reputation can be an effective bond for honest behavior in a community of traders if members of the community know how others have behaved in the past — even if any particular pair of traders meets only infrequently. In a large community, it would be impossibly costly for traders to be perfectly informed about each other's behavior, but there exist institutions that can restore the effectiveness of a reputation system using much less extensive information. The system of judges used to enforce commercial law before the rise of the state was such an institution, and it successfully encouraged merchants (1) to behave honestly, (2) to impose sanctions on violators, (3) to become adequately informed about how others had behaved, (4) to provide evidence against violators of the code, and (5) to pay any judgments assessed against them, even though each of these behaviors might be personally costly.

How can people promote the trust necessary for efficient exchange when individuals have short run temptations to cheat? The same question arises wh[...] traders are legislators swapping votes, mediev[...] or modern businesspeople trading promises ab[...] these situations, one of the important ways in [...] another's honest behavior is by establishing a [...] language of economics, if the relationship itself [...] could lose by dishonest behavior, then the relatio[...] would be unwilling to surrender this bond unless t[...] was large.

Variants on this basic idea are found througho[ut] (Klein and Leffler, 1981; Shapiro, 1983; Shapiro and Stiglitz, 1984), politics (Axelrod, 1984, 1986; Calvert, 1986) and game theory (Abreu, 1988; Aumann, 1985; and Fudenberg and Maskin, 1986). Even in a community in which any particular pair of people meet rarely, it is still possible (as we show) for an individual's reputation in the group as a whole to serve as a bond for his good and honest behavior toward each individual member. This illustrates the important fact that a reputation system may sometimes work only when it encompasses

*Department of Economics, Stanford University; Department of Economics, Washington University; Hoover Institution, Stanford University. The authors thank Robert Aumann, Gary Becker, Peter DeMarzo, Avner Greif, Michihiro Kandori, Bart Lipson, Uwe Schimack and the participants at numerous workshops for helpful conversations. Mr Milgrom and Mr Weingast thank the National Science Foundation for partial support.

2   MILGROM, NORTH AND WEINGAST

sufficiently many traders and trades, that is, there are economies of scale and scope in reputation systems.

These conclusions about the potential effectiveness of a reputation system, however, leave us with a puzzle: If informal arrangements based on reputations can effectively bond good behavior, then what is the role of formal institutions in helping to support honest exchange? The legal apparatus for enforcing business contracts in many ages and many parts of the world, the suppliers' organizations that negotiate contracting patterns among modern Japanese firms, the complex institutional structure that facilitates agreements among US Congressmen,[1] the notaries that recorded agreements in the Italian city-states in the middle ages, and the organization of international trade via the Champagne fairs are all examples of institutionalized arrangements to support trade and contracting. All involve the creation of specialized roles which would not be necessary if reputations alone could be an adequate bond for trade. But, why can't a simple system of reputations motivate honest trade in these various settings? And, what role do formal institutions play when simple reputational mechanisms fail?

We embed our study of these questions in the time of the revival of trade in Europe during the early middle ages. At that time, without the benefit of state enforcement of contracts or an established body of commercial law, merchants evolved their own private code of laws (the *Law Merchant*) with disputes adjudicated by a judge who might be a local official or a private merchant. While hearings were held to resolve disputes under the code, the judges had only limited powers to enforce judgments against merchants from distant places. For example, if a dispute arose after the conclusion of the Champagne Fair about the quality of the goods delivered or if agreements made at the Fair for future delivery or for acceptance of future delivery were not honored, no physical sanction or seizure of goods could then be applied.

The evolution and survival for a considerable period of a system of private adjudication raises both particular versions of our general questions and new questions about the details of the mechanism. What was the purpose of the private adjudication system? Was it a substitute for the reputation mechanism that had worked effectively in earlier periods (Greif, 1989)? Also, if there was no state to enforce judgments, how did they have any effect? How could a system of adjudication function without substantial police powers?

The practice and evolution of the Law Merchant in medieval Europe was so rich and varied that no single model can hope to capture all the relevant variations and details. Our simple model is intended to represent certain universal incentive problems that any successful system would have to solve. It abstracts from many of the interesting variations that are found across time and space as well as from other general problems, such as the spatial diversion of traders and trading centers and the interactions among competing trading systems.

---

[1]Either by facilitating coordination (Banks and Calvert, 1989) or by preventing reneging on agreements (Weingast and Marshall, 1988).

We begin in section 1 with a discussion of the medieval Law Merchant and related institutions. We set the theoretical context for our analysis in section 2. It is well known, as we have explained above, that in long-term, frequent bilateral exchange, the value of the relationship itself may serve as an adequate bond to ensure honest behavior and promote trust between the parties. We argue in section 2 that even if no pair of traders come together frequently, if each individual trades frequently enough within the community of traders, then transferable reputations for honesty can serve as an adequate bond for honest behavior *if members of the trading community can be kept informed about each other's past behavior*. Well informed traders could boycott those who have violated community norms of honesty, if only they knew who the violators were. It is the costliness of generating and communicating information − rather than the infrequency of trade in any particular bilateral relationship − that, we argue, is the problem that the system of private enforcement was designed to overcome.

In section 3, we introduce our basic model of a system of private enforcement and develop our core thesis that the role of the judges in the system, far from being substitutes for the reputation mechanism, is to make the reputation system more effective as a means of promoting honest trade. The formal system is more complex than the simple informal system of reputations that preceded it, but that was a natural outcome of the growing extent of trade. In a large community, we argue, it would be too costly to keep everyone informed about what transpires in all trading relationships, as a simple reputation system might require. So the system of private judges is designed to promote private resolution of disputes and otherwise to transmit *just enough* information to the right people in the right circumstances to enable the reputation mechanism to function effectively for enforcement. In order to succeed, such a system must solve a number of inter-connected incentive problems: Individual members of the community must be induced to behave honestly, to boycott those who have behaved dishonestly, to keep informed about who has been dishonest, to provide evidence against those who have cheated, and to honor the decisions of the judges. All of these problems can be resolved by the system if certain institutional constraints are satisfied, as we show in section 3. Briefly, the costs of making queries, providing evidence, adjudicating disputes, and making transfer payments must not be too high relative to the frequency and profitability of trade if the system is to function successfully.

Intuitively, the system of private judges accomplishes its objectives by *bundling* the services which are valuable to the individual trader with services that are valuable to the community, so that a trader pursuing his individual interest serves the community's interest as well. Unless a trader makes appropriate queries, he cannot use the system to resolve disputes. The requirement that the traders make queries provides an opportunity for the judge to collect payments for his services even if no actual disputes arise. As applied to the Champagne Fairs, the local lord or his agents could appoint honest judges, register transactions, and tax them.

In section 4, we make a brief digression to assess how *efficiently* the system of private judges accomplishes its task. We argue that no system can restore the

4   MILGROM, NORTH AND WEINGAST

effectiveness of the community reputation mechanism without incurring costs that are qualitatively similar to those incurred by the system of private judges, and moreover that the latter system seems to have been designed in a way that kept these transaction costs low.

Our analysis in section 3 gives the judge a passive role only. In section 5, we study the possibility that the judge may threaten to sully the reputations of honest traders unless they pay bribes. We show how the system can survive some such threats, though we do not attempt a comprehensive evaluation of all the kinds of bribes and extortion that might be tried in such a system.

Concluding remarks, relating our model to a broader institutional perspective, are given in section 6.

1. THE MEDIEVAL LAW MERCHANT

The history of long-distance trade in medieval and early modern Europe is the story of sequentially more complex organization that eventually led to the "Rise of the Western World." In order to capture the gains associated with geographic specialization, a system had to be established that lowered information costs and provided for the enforcement of agreements across space and time. Prior to the revival of trade in the early middle ages, few institutions underpinned commercial activity; there was no state to enforce contracts, let alone to protect merchants from pirates and brigands. In contrast, modern Western economies possess highly specialized systems of enforcing contracts and protecting merchants, resulting in widespread geographic specialization and impersonal exchange. The story of this evolution has been told elsewhere (e.g., Lopez, 1976; North and Thomas, 1973). Our purpose in this section is to suggest the outlines of an important step in this evolution, namely the early development of commercial law prior to the rise of large-scale third-party enforcement of legal codes by the nation-state.

A large number of problems had to be resolved in order to support the expansion of trade. First, as trading communities grew larger, it became harder within each community for merchants to monitor one another's behavior. New institutions were required to mitigate the types of cheating afforded by the new situation. Second, as trade grew among different regions, institutions were needed to prevent reneging by merchants who might cheat in one location, never to be seen again.

In response to these problems, a host of institutions arose and evolved over time. Towns with their own governments became homes for merchants who developed their own law separate from the traditional feudal order (Pirenne, 1925; Rorig, 1967). Merchant gilds arose to provide protection to foreign merchants away from their homes, but also protection to local merchants against fly-by-night foreign merchants who might never be seen again (DeRoover, 1963; Thrupp, 1948). Key to understanding the ability of merchants from widely varying regions to enforce contracts was the evolution of the *Lex Mercatoria* or Law Merchant — the legal codes governing commercial transactions and administered by private judges drawn from the commercial ranks. While practice varied across time and

INSTITUTIONS IN THE REVIVAL OF TRADE   5

space, by the end of the 11th century, the Law Merchant came to govern most commercial transactions in Europe, providing a uniform set of standards across large numbers of locations (Benson, 1989). It thereby provided a means for reducing the uncertainty associated with variations in local practices and limited the ability of localities to discriminate against alien merchants (Berman, 1983; Trakman, 1983). Thus, "commercial law can be conceived of as coordinating the self-interested actions of merchants, but perhaps an equally valuable insight is gained by *viewing it as coordinating the actions of people with limited knowledge and trust*" (Benson, 1989, p. 648, emphasis added).

While the governments of towns supported the development of markets and were intimately involved in developing merchant law (Pirenne, 1925; Rorig, 1967), they often could not provide merchants protection outside their immediate area.[2] Nor could they enforce judgments against foreign merchants who had left town prior to a case being heard. Thus, merchant law developed prior to the rise of a geographically extensive nation-state. But this raises a key problem in the theory of enforcement, for what made these judgments credible if they were not backed up by the state? Ostracism played an important role here, for merchants that failed to abide by the decisions of the judges would not be merchants for long (Benson, 1989; DeRoover, 1963; Trakman, 1983).

The Law Merchant and related legal codes evolved considerably over time. In addition to providing a court of law especially suited for merchants, it fostered significant legal developments that reduced the transaction costs of exchange (North, 1989, ch. 13). As agency relationships became common — whether between partners in different locations or between a sedentary merchant who financed a traveling one — a new set of rules governing these agreements was required. The same also held for the new practices of credit agreements and insurance. Here, we note the development of law covering agency relations (DeRoover, 1963; Greif, 1989), bills of exchange, and insurance (North, 1989, ch. 13).

The benefits of all these developments, however, could only be enjoyed as long as merchants obeyed the Law Merchant. Moreover, since disputes arise even among honest merchants, there needed to be a system for hearing and settling these disputes. To see how these feats of coordination might have been accomplished, we develop a game theoretic model of the judicial enforcement system — a model inspired by the Law Merchant and by the Champagne Fairs. The latter played a central role in trade in the 12th and 13th centuries (DeRoover, 1963; North and Thomas, 1973; Verlinden, 1963), and included a legal system in which merchants could bring grievances against their trading partners. However, it is not clear why such a system would be effective. What prevents a merchant from cheating by supplying lower quality goods than promised, and then leaving the

---

[2]Of course, considerable variation existed across locations, especially between northern and southern Europe. In the latter area, city-states arose, providing law and protection beyond the immediate area of the city. Further, over time, as the nature of governments changed, so too did their involvement in the legal and enforcement process.

6   MILGROM, NORTH AND WEINGAST

Fairs before being detected? In these circumstances the cheated merchant might be able to get a judgment against his supplier, but what good would it do if the supplier never returned to the Fairs? Perhaps ostracism by the other merchants might be an effective way to enforce the payment of judgments. However, if that is so, why was a legal system needed at all?

Another part of the inspiration for our formal model is the system of notaries that was widely used to register the existence of certain types of contracts and obligations. Typically, notaries were used for long-term contracts such as those for apprenticeships, sales of land, and partnerships (Lopez and Raymond, 1955). The extensive use of notaries in certain areas to register agreements suggests that reputation via word of mouth alone was insufficient to support honest behavior and that a third party without any binding authority to enforce obligations was nonetheless quite valuable for promoting honest exchange.

2. COMMUNITY ENFORCEMENT WITHOUT INSTITUTIONS

With the exception of barter transactions, in which physical commodities are exchanged on the spot, virtually all economic transactions leave open the possibility of cheating. In the Champagne Fairs, where merchants brought samples of their goods to trade, the quantities they brought were not always sufficient to supply all the potential demand. Then, the merchants sometimes exchanged promises – to deliver goods of like quality at a particular time and place, or to make payment in a certain form. Promises, however, can be broken.

To represent the idea that cheating may be profitable in a simple exchange, we use the Prisoners' Dilemma (PD) game as our model of a single exchange transaction. Although this PD model is too simple to portray the richness of even simple contracts, it has the advantage that it is very well known and its characteristics in the absence of institutions have been thoroughly studied, so that the incremental contribution made by the Law Merchant system will be quite clear. Moreover, the PD game represents in an uncluttered way the basic facts that traders have opportunities and temptations to cheat and that there are gains possible if the traders can suppress these temptations and find a way to cooperate.

The Prisoners' Dilemma game that we employ is shown below, where $\alpha > 1$ and $\alpha - \beta < 2$.

	Honest	Cheat
Honest	1, 1	$-\beta, \alpha$
Cheat	$\alpha, -\beta$	0, 0

Each player can choose to play one of two strategies: Honest or Cheat. As is well known, Honest behavior maximizes the total profits of the two parties. However, a trader profits by cheating an honest partner ($\alpha > 1$) even though cheating imposes a still larger loss on his honest partner $(1 - (-\beta) > \alpha - 1)$.

It is clear that if this game is played only once, it is in each player's separate interest to play Cheat, since that play maximizes the player's individual utility regardless of the play chosen by the competitor. Consequently, the only *Nash equilibrium* of the game is for both to play Cheat. Then both are worse off than if they could somehow agree to play Honest.

Now suppose that the players trade repeatedly. Let a_{it} represent the action taken by player i in period t; let $\pi_i(a_{1t}, a_{2t})$ represent the resulting payoff earned by player i in period t; and let δ be the discount factor applied to compute the present value of a stream of payoffs. If trade is frequent, then δ is close to one; if trade occurs only once (or is quite infrequent), then δ is (close to) zero. A player's time weighted average payoff over the whole sequence of trades is given by:

$$\bar{\pi}_i = (1 - \delta) \sum_{t=0}^{\infty} \delta^t \pi_i(a_{1t}, a_{2t}) \qquad (1)$$

In this repeated trading relationship, if the players can condition their actions in each period on what has transpired in the past, then they have an instrument to reward past honest behavior and to punish cheating. For the PD game, Axelrod (1984) has shown that for δ close enough to 1 there is a Nash equilibrium in which each player adopts the Tit-for-Tat (TFT) strategy — according to which the player chooses honest play at $t = 0$ and for any later t plays whatever his partner played in the immediately preceding period (that is, at $t - 1$).

The central idea that frequent trading with the same partner, or "clientization," makes it possible to find an equilibrium with efficient trading applies even for more refined solution concepts, such as subgame perfect equilibrium. It has been shown to hold for virtually all repeated games, regardless of the number of players, the number of strategies available to each, or the magnitudes of the payoffs (Fudenberg and Maskin, 1986). What is less fully appreciated is that the same conclusion holds in a community of traders in which players change partners often and cheaters may never again have to face the cheated partner — provided that information about the behavior of the traders is widely shared in the community.

To see this, suppose that there are N traders and that there is some rule M that matches them at each stage. Let h_t be the history of trade through date t and let $M(h_t, i)$ be the identity of the trader who is matched with trader i at date $t + 1$ at history h_t. Consider the Adjusted Tit-for-Tat (ATFT) strategy according to which player i plays Honest at date 0 and then plays Cheat at date $t + 1$ if two conditions hold: (1) i made the play at date t that was specified by his equilibrium strategy and (2) $M(h_t, i)$ did not make the play at date t that was specified by his equilibrium strategy. If either condition fails, then the ATFT strategy calls for i to play Honest. The ATFT strategy formalizes the idea that a trader who cheats will be punished by the next merchant he meets if that merchant is honest, even if that merchant is not the one who was cheated.

One might wonder what reason the merchant who was not cheated has to carry out the punishment. Within the PD model, the answer is twofold: First, punishing the cheater is directly profitable, because the punishment is delivered by playing Cheat. Second — and this is the reason that applies even in more general models — a merchant who fails to deliver a punishment, say by participating in a boycott, when he is supposed to do so is himself subject to punishment by the community of merchants. The community, in its turn, will carry out the punishment, for the very same reasons. Theorem 1 below verifies that this system is in fact sometimes an equilibrium, that is, no merchant could gain at any time by deviating from its rules provided he expects other merchants to adhere to the rules in all future play.

Theorem 1. For δ near enough to one — specifically if

$$\delta \geq \text{Max}[\beta/(1 + \beta), (\alpha - 1)/(1 + \beta)] \tag{2}$$

— the Adjusted Tit-for-Tat strategies are a subgame perfect equilibrium in the community trading game for *any* matching rule M.

Proof. By the Optimality Principle of dynamic programming, it suffices to show that there is no point at which player i can make a one-time play different from the equilibrium play that raises his total payoff. By inspection of the strategies, it is clear that the player may face one of four decision situations according to whether condition (1) only is satisfied, condition (2) only is satisfied, or both or neither of (1) and (2) are satisfied. If just condition (1) or condition (2) (not both) is satisfied, then a current period deviation by player i is unprofitable if:

$$(1 - \delta)[\alpha - \delta\beta] + \delta^2 \cdot 1 \leq (1 - \delta) \cdot 1 + \delta \cdot 1 \tag{3}$$

which holds if and only if $\delta \geq (\alpha - 1)/(1 + \beta)$. If (1) and (2) are both satisfied, deviation is unprofitable if:

$$(1 - \delta)[0 - \delta\beta] + \delta^2 \cdot 1 \leq (1 - \delta) \cdot \alpha + \delta \cdot 1 \tag{4}$$

and this is satisfied for all $\delta \geq 0$. If neither (1) nor (2) is satisfied, then deviation is unprofitable if:

$$(1 - \delta)[0 - \delta\beta] + \delta^2 \cdot 1 \leq -(1 - \delta) \cdot \beta + \delta \cdot 1 \tag{5}$$

which holds if and only if $\delta \geq \beta/(1 + \beta)$. ∎

Our formal analysis verifies that it is not necessary for any pair of traders to interact frequently — that is, for traders to establish client relationships — in order for the boycott mechanism to be effective. However, that simple conclusion relies on the condition that the members of the community are well enough informed to know whom to boycott. This condition is probably satisfied in some communities, but it is more problematical in others. For example, merchants engaged in long-distance trade could not be expected to know, of their own knowledge, whether another pair of merchants had honored their mutual obligations. Unless social and economic institutions developed to fill in the knowledge gap or unless other means of enforcement were established, honest behavior in

INSTITUTIONS IN THE REVIVAL OF TRADE   9

a community of self-interested traders could not be maintained. Our model in the next section shows how a particular institution could have resolved this problem.

3. THE LAW MERCHANT ENFORCEMENT SYSTEM

We now consider in more detail a model of trade in which outsiders cannot readily observe what has transpired in a given bilateral trade. While "disputes" may arise in which one party accuses the other of cheating, none of the other players have a method of freely verifying the parties' claims. Even if the dispute itself can be observed by others, they cannot costlessly determine whether cheating by one has actually occurred or whether the other is opportunistically claiming that it did.

In our model, we suppose that choices in each bilateral exchange are known only to the trading pair, so that each individual possesses direct information *solely about his own past trading experiences.*[3] To capture the idea that traders know little of their partners' past trading behavior, we use an extreme model of matching due to Townsend (1981). In Townsend's matching model, there is an infinity of traders indexed by ij where $i = 1$ or 2 and j is an integer which may be positive or negative. At period t, trader $1j$ is matched with trader $2, j + t$.[4] In particular, no two traders ever meet twice and no trader's behavior can directly or indirectly influence the behavior of his future trading partners. In the absence of institutions, players possess *no information* about their current partner's past behavior.

Under these conditions, the opportunities available to a player in any period cannot depend in any way on his past behavior. Strategies such as TFT and ATFT become ineffective. So, in our Prisoners' Dilemma game, it can never be in the players' interest to be honest. We have established the following:

Theorem 2. In the incomplete information Prisoners' Dilemma with the Townsend matching rule, the outcome at any Nash equilibrium is that each trader plays Cheat at every opportunity.[5]

With limited information about the past behavior of trading partners and no institution to compensate, there are no incentives for honest behavior. It is evident that incentives could be restored by introducing an institution that provides full information to each trader about how each other has behaved. Such an institution, however, would be costly to operate. Moreover, efficient trade does not require that every trader know the full history of the behavior of each other trader. For

---

[3]This is also the premise of the game-theoretic analysis of Kandori (1989).

[4]This matching rule is often called the "Townsend Turnpike," for Townsend suggested that one way to think of it is as two infinitely long sets of traders moving in opposite directions.

[5]Kandori (1989) has shown that there exist other matching rules for which, despite the absence of sufficient bilateral trade and each player's ignorance about what has happened in trades among other players, there may nevertheless be a code of behavior that supports efficient exchange. However, as Kandori argues, the resulting system is "brittle" and leads to a breakdown of honest trade when there are even minor disturbances to the system. Both Kandori (1989) and Okuno and Postlewaite (1989) consider other institutional solutions to this problem.

example, in the ATFT strategy considered in the preceding section, a trader need only know his own history of behavior and whether his partner has defected in the immediately preceding period to determine his own current behavior. One part of the problem is to arrange that the traders are *adequately* well informed so that they can sanction a Cheater when that is required.

However, there is a second problem that the institutions must overcome: Traders may not find it in their individual interests to participate in punishing those who cheat. As one simple example, if trade is expected to be profitable, a trader will be reluctant to engage in a trade boycott. The institutions must be designed both to keep the traders adequately informed of their responsibilities and to motivate them to do their duties.

In the model we develop below, this second problem has multiple aspects. First, traders must be motivated to execute sanctions against Cheaters when that is a personally costly activity. Second, traders must be motivated to keep well enough informed to know when sanctions are required, even though information gathering activities may be personally costly and difficult to monitor. In effect, one who keeps informed about who should be punished for past transgressions is supplying a public good; he deters the traders from cheating against *others*. Moreover, in our model, no other trader except his current partner will ever know if a trader does not check his partner's past history, so the trader could avoid supplying the public good without facing any sanction from future traders. Third, traders who are cheated must be motivated to document the episode, even though providing documentation may be personally costly. After all, from the cheated trader's perspective, what's lost is lost, and there may be little point in "throwing good money after bad." But if players who are cheated are unwilling to invest in informing their neighbors, then, just as surely as if the neighbors are unwilling to invest in being informed, the Cheater will profit from his action and Honest trade will suffer. These are the problems that the trading institution in our model must solve.

The institution that we model as the resolution of these problems is based on the presence of a specialized actor — a "judge" or "law merchant" (LM) who serves both as a repository of information and as an adjudicator of disputes. The core version of our model is based on the following assumptions. After any exchange, each party can accuse the other of cheating and appeal to the LM. Any dispute appealed to the LM is perfectly and honestly adjudicated at cost C to the plaintiff. (We consider the case of a dishonest LM later.) The LM's pronouncements include the ability to award damages if the defendant is found to have cheated the plaintiff. However, payment of the damage award is *voluntary* in the sense that there is no state to enforce payment. Finally, we assume that any party can visit the LM prior to finalizing a contract. At that time, for a cost of Q, the party can *query* the LM for the records of previous judgments about any other player. Without querying the LM, players have *no* information about their current partners' trading history.

By structuring this sequence of events around the basic trade transaction, we

INSTITUTIONS IN THE REVIVAL OF TRADE 11

create an "extended" stage game called the *LM system stage game* with the following sequence of play:

(a) Players may query the LM about their current partner at utility cost $Q > 0$. In response to a query, the LM reports to the traders whether a party has any "unpaid judgments." Whatever transpires at this stage becomes common knowledge among the LM and the two partners.

(b) The two traders play the (Prisoners' Dilemma) game and learn the outcome.

(c) Either may appeal to the LM at personal cost $C > 0$, but only if he has queried the LM.

(d) If either party makes an appeal, then the LM awards a judgment, J, to the plaintiff if he has been Honest and his trading partner has Cheated (we call this a *valid appeal*); otherwise, no award is made.

(e) If a judgment J is awarded, the defendant may pay it, at personal cost $f(J)$, or he may refuse to pay, at cost zero.

(f) Any unpaid judgments are recorded by the LM and become part of the LM's permanent record.

The players' utilities for the extended stage game are determined as the sum of the payments received less those made. For example, a player who queries, plays Honest, is Cheated, and appeals, receives $-Q - \beta + -CJ$ if the other party pays the judgment and $-Q - \beta - C$ if he does not.

The function $f: \mathfrak{R}^+ \to \mathfrak{R}^+$ represents the utility cost of paying a given judgment. We naturally assume that f is increasing and continuous. Thus, the greater the size of the judgment, the greater the cost to the defendant. We also assume that $f(x) \geq x$: The cost of paying a judgment is never less than the judgment itself. This excludes the possibility that the payment of judgments adds to the total utility of the players.

The desired behavior of the parties in various contingencies under the Law Merchant system is fully described by the *Law Merchant System Strategy* (LMSS) as follows.

At substage (a), a trader queries the Law Merchant if he has no unpaid judgments on record, but not otherwise.

At substage (b), if either player has failed to query the Law Merchant or if the query establishes that at least one player has an outstanding judgment, then both traders play Cheat (which we may interpret as a refusal by the honest trader to trade); otherwise, both play Honest.

At substage (c), if both parties queried at substage (a) and exactly one of the two players Cheated at substage (b), then the victim appeals to the LM; otherwise, no appeal is filed.

At substage (d), if a valid appeal was filed, the LM awards damages of J to the aggrieved party.

At substage (e), the defendant pays the judgment J if and only if he has no other outstanding judgments.

Theorem 3. The Law Merchant System Strategy is a symmetric sequential equilibrium strategy of the LM system game if and only if the following inequality holds.

$$(1 - Q)\delta/(1 - \delta) \geq f(J) \geq \max[(\alpha - 1), f(C)] \qquad (6)$$

If this condition is satisfied, then the average payoff per period for each player (at the equilibrium) is $1 - Q$.

Remark. The condition in Theorem 3 can be satisfied only if $1 - Q$ is positive (because the right-hand-side is at least $\alpha - 1 > 0$).

Proof. To establish that the LMSS is a symmetric sequential equilibrium strategy, we again appeal to the Optimality Principle of Dynamic Programming. If we show that there is no point at which a single change in the trader's current action only (followed by later adherence to the LMSS) can raise the trader's expected payoff at that point, then there is no point at which some more complicated deviation can be profitable, either.

In evaluating his expected payoffs, the player must make certain conjectures about what other players have done in the past in order to forecast what they will do in the future. To verify the equilibrium, we may assume that the trader believes that all other traders have played according to the LMSS in all past plays except those where the trader has actually observed a deviation. We may also assume that the trader believes that all others will adhere to the LMSS in all future plays. To derive the conditions under which the LMSS is an equilibrium strategy, we work backward through a typical extended stage game.

First, we check when it "pays to pay judgments," that is, under what conditions a player will find it more profitable to pay any judgment rendered against him than to refuse to pay. (We ignore the sunk portion of the payoff which is unaffected by later behavior.) Paying the judgment J yields an additional payoff of $-f(J)$ in the current period. In future periods, the player will spend Q to query the LM and earn a trading payoff of 1, for a total of $1 - Q$. In terms of lifetime average payoff, paying the judgment leads to $-(1 - \delta)f(J) + \delta(1 - Q)$. If the trader refuses to pay the judgment, then his current period payoff is zero ànd, given the system, his payoff is also zero in every subsequent period. Therefore, it "pays to pay judgments" if and only if $-(1 - \delta)f(J) + \delta(1 - Q) \geq 0$, or equivalently,

$$f(J) \leq (1 - Q)\delta/(1 - \delta). \qquad (7)$$

Second, does it pay the victim to appeal at substage (c), incurring personal cost C? Given the strategies, the trader expects the judgment to be paid. So he will appeal if and only if $J \geq C$. It is convenient to write this condition as:

$$f(J) \geq f(C). \qquad (8)$$

If there are no unpaid judgments and the LM has been queried, does it pay the trader to play Honest? If he does, then his current period payoff will be $1 - Q$. If he Cheats and later adheres to the strategy (which entails paying the

INSTITUTIONS IN THE REVIVAL OF TRADE   13

judgment), then his payoff will be $-Q + \alpha - f(J)$. Equilibrium requires that the former is larger, that is:

$$f(J) \geq \alpha - 1. \tag{9}$$

Does it pay the trader otherwise to play Cheat? With the given strategy, his future opportunities do not depend on his play in this case, and Cheat always maximizes the payoffs for the current period, so the answer is that it does pay, regardless of parameter values.

Does it pay the players to query the LM if neither has an outstanding judgment? If a player does so, his current period payoff is expected to be $1 - Q$. If not, it will be zero. In both cases, his payoffs per period for subsequent periods are expected to be $1 - Q$. So, it pays if and only if

$$Q \leq 1. \tag{10}$$

However, condition (10) is redundant in view of conditions (7) and (9).

Does it pay a party with an outstanding judgment to query? No, because the party's expected payoff is $-Q$ if he queries and 0 if he does not.

Thus, regardless of the circumstances wrought by past play, there is no situation in which a one-time deviation from the Law Merchant System Strategy that is profitable for a trader provided that conditions (7)–(9) hold. These are the conditions summarized in formula (6).   ∎

Corollary.   There is a judgment amount J which makes the LMSS a symmetric sequential equilibrium strategy (that is, satisfying formula (6)) if and only if

$$(1 - Q)\delta/(1 - \delta) \geq \max[(\alpha - 1), f(C)]. \tag{11}$$

Conditions (7)–(10) show the relationship among the various parameters for the LM system to support the efficient cooperation. Each corresponds to one of the problems we described in introducing the model. Condition (7) requires that Cheating and then paying a judgment not be profitable; put simply, the judgment must be large enough to deter Cheating. Condition (8) requires that judgments exceed the cost of an appeal, that is, the judgment must also be large enough to encourage the injured party to appeal. Otherwise, information about Cheating will never reach the LM and Cheating will go unpunished. The two previous conditions require that the judgment be large enough, but condition (9) requires that it not be so large that the Cheater would refuse to pay, for then the injured party would not expect to collect, and so would find it unprofitable to appeal. Notice that the feasibility of satisfying all these conditions simultaneously depends on the technology of wealth transfer summarized by f. If the traders live at great distances from one another and if their principal asset holdings are illiquid (such as land and fixed capital, or reputation and family connections), then wealth transfers may be quite costly ($f(J)/J$ may be large) and the fines required by the LM system then will not work.

Finally, condition (10) requires that it be worthwhile for the traders to query the LM. In our model, this condition is implied by the others, but that need not be true for extensions of the model. If traders do not query the LM, then they will have insufficient information to administer punishments, so once again Cheating will go unpunished. The LM institution encourages queries by making them a condition for appealing to the LM, and, as we have seen, querying deters Cheating. At equilibrium, traders who fail to query are constantly Cheated by their trading partners.

If condition (6) fails, then the LMSS is not an equilibrium strategy. However, the condition is satisfied for a wide range of plausible parameter values. Table 1 below gives some acceptable values for the parameters. In it, we assume that $f(x) = x/(1 - p)$ where p is the percentage of value that is lost when assets are transferred. The LMSS is an equilibrium strategy for some J with the given combinations of parameters and for any other combination with lower transaction costs (lower p, Q, and C), less temptation to cheat (lower α), and more frequent trade (higher δ). In the table, $J = C/(1 - p) = \alpha - 1$ is the judgment which is just sufficient to provide the incentives for not cheating and for complaining about being cheated.

For example, in the last line of Table 1, Cheating is seven times more profitable than playing Honest at each current round, the cost of querying the LM consumes one-third of the profits of Honest venturers, the cost of complaining is three times the profits of the venture, and half of any assets transferred in settlement of a judgment are lost. The judgment itself is six times what the Cheater could expect to earn from Honest trade with his next partner (nine times net of transaction costs). Nevertheless, if the inter-trade discount factor is at least 0.9, the LM system is in equilibrium and supports honest behavior, filing of valid complaints, and payment of judgments.

4. MINIMIZING TRANSACTION COSTS

Theorem 3 shows that the LM system restores cooperation even when the players know little about their partners' histories. There are transaction costs necessary to maintain this system, however: That the average payoff per period is $1 - Q$ reflects the transaction cost of Q per period incurred by each trader to support the Law Merchant system.

TABLE 1   SAMPLE PARAMETERS FOR WHICH THE LAW MERCHANT STRATEGY IS A SEQUENTIAL EQUILIBRIUM STRATEGY

Transaction Costs Parameters			Temptation to Cheat	Discount Factor	Penalty or Judgment
Q	C	p	α	δ	J
0.50	0.5	50%	2.0	0.67	1.0
0.50	1.0	50%	3.0	0.80	2.0
0.33	3.0	50%	7.0	0.90	6.0

Notice that the cost, C, of making and investigating a claim and the cost $f(J) - J$ of making the transfer do not appear in the expression for the average payoff. These costs do appear in condition (6): The Law Merchant system is not viable if the cost of making and investigating a claim or the cost of paying a judgment is too high, for then the traders cannot reasonably expect that the others will make claims and pay judgments when they should. However, once these costs are low enough that the threat to file claims with the Law Merchant is credible, they act only as a deterrent: These costs are never actually incurred at equilibrium in our model of the Law Merchant system.

Is the Law Merchant system the least expensive way to induce Honest behavior from rational traders at every stage? Theoretically, any institution that restores incentives for Honest trading by restoring the effectiveness of decentralized enforcement must inform a player when his partner has cheated in the past. If the temptation to Cheat is small and the value of continued trading is high, then this information need not be perfect, as in our model. So it may be possible to induce honest behavior using a less costly information system — one that costs only $q < Q$ to inform a trader adequately well — and correspondingly to increase the traders' average payoffs from $1 - Q$ to $1 - q$.[6] However, using imperfect information to economize on information costs calls merely for a refinement of the Law Merchant system — not for something fundamentally different. It is not possible to provide correct incentives without incurring some information cost of this kind and, as we have seen, the LM system avoids the unnecessary costs of dispute resolution and loss on transfers.

In operation, the Law Merchant system would appear to be a low cost way to disseminate information, for two reasons. First, the LM system centralizes the information system so that, for information about any partner, a player need only go to one place. He need not incur costs trying (i) to establish who was his current partner's previous partner, and (ii) to find the partner to make the relevant inquiry. Second, for the Prisoners' Dilemma, it is not sufficient to know only one period's history, but several.[7] The LM system not only centralizes this information but provides it in a very simple form: all that needs to be communicated is whether there are any outstanding judgments. For large communities, locating each of one's partner's previous partners and asking them for information is likely to be more expensive than the centralized record-keeping system of the Law Merchant.

Given the lack of quantitative evidence about the full costs of running different kinds of institutions, it is not possible to write down a convincing formal model to establish that the LM system minimizes costs in the class of feasible institutions.

---

[6]And, given that our model has a fixed starting date, there is really nothing to be learned from the initial query, so that could be eliminated with some small cost savings. However, this is just an artifact of our desire for modeling simplicity and not an inherent extra cost of the system.

[7]Kandori (1989) shows that in the repeated Prisoners' Dilemma, players must know at least two periods of history for each partner to sustain an equilibrium with Honest behavior.

What we can say confidently is that the *kind* of costs incurred by the LM system are inevitable if Honest trade is to be sustained in the face of self-interested behavior and that the system seems well designed to keep those costs as low as possible.

5. DISHONEST LAW MERCHANTS

Our analysis in section 2 proceeded on the assumption that the Law Merchant has no independent interest in the outcome of his decision. In addition, he is diligent, honest, and fair.

One need not look far in history (or, for that matter, in the modern world) to see that judges are not always so perfect. Within our model, there are many small amendments that could be made to insert opportunities for bribery and extortion. Although we do not provide a systematic treatment of these, we shall give a brief development of one of them to emphasize the simple idea that the Law Merchant business is itself valuable and that LMs may wish to maintain their reputation for honesty and diligence in order to keep the business active.

The most obvious problem with this reputation based account is that it seems to presume that a trader who is extorted by the Law Merchant can somehow make his injury widely known to the community of traders. It might be that the Law Merchant is a more sedentary merchant than the long-distance traders whom he serves, so that idea is perhaps not so far-fetched. Nevertheless, we shall argue that even if, in the spirit of our earlier analysis, there is no way for the trader to inform others about his injury, it may still be an equilibrium for the LM to behave honestly, due to the "client" incentives in the long-term relationship between the LM and each individual trader. More precisely, we will show that there is an equilibrium of the system in which every trader expects that if he pays a bribe he will be subjected to repeated attempts at extortion in the future; this dissuades the trader from paying any bribe. Then, a Law Merchant who commits to his threat to damage the reputation of a trader succeeds only in losing business, so he does not profit from making the threat.

To set the context for the formal extension, we modify the Law Merchant system stage game to regard the Law Merchant as a player. In the original version, the LM was allowed no choices, but let us nevertheless suppose that the LM earned a payoff of $2\epsilon > 0$ per contract, which is paid for as part of the $2Q$ that the parties spend to query the LM.

Next, we create a Modified Law Merchant System game in which our basic model is altered to allow the LM to solicit bribes. Initially, we consider only one kind of bribe — that extorted from a trader with no unpaid judgments by an LM who threatens to report falsely that there *are* unpaid judgments. Thus, we assume that before the traders make their queries, the LM may demand that one of the traders who has no unpaid judgment pay a bribe, $B \geq 0$. The amount B demanded is chosen by the LM. If the bribe is not paid and a query is made, the LM is committed to report falsely that the trader has an unpaid judgment.[8] The trader next decides whether to pay the bribe. The stage game then continues as previously described. When a bribe of B is paid, the LM's payoff is increased by B and the victim's payoff is reduced by an equal amount.[9]

Now consider the following variation of the Law Merchant System Strategy for the traders. If a player has no unpaid judgments and no bribe is solicited from him at the current stage, then he plays the LMSS as previously described. If the player has never before paid a bribe and a bribe is solicited, then he refuses to pay the bribe and does not query the LM in the current period. If the player has ever before paid a bribe, then he pays any bribe up to $\alpha - Q$ that is demanded of him. A player who has paid a bribe at the current round plays Cheat at that round and refuses to pay any judgment made against him. We call this specification the Extended Law Merchant System Strategy (ELMSS).

The Law Merchant's expected behavior is specified by the LM's Bribe Solicitation Strategy (BSS). If one of the present traders has no unpaid judgment but has previously paid a bribe, then the LM demands a payment of $\alpha - Q$. Otherwise, the LM does not demand any payment.

Theorem 4. If condition (6) holds and, in addition,

$$\alpha \leq 1 + (1 - Q)(2\delta - 1)/(1 - \delta), \tag{12}$$

then there is a sequential equilibrium of the Modified Law Merchant System game in which each trader adopts the strategy ELMSS and the Law Merchant adopts the strategy BSS.

Proof. Once again, we check that there is no contingency after which a one-time deviation by any player is profitable, when each player expects that the others have adhered to the strategy except where deviations have been explicitly observed, and each expects that all will adhere to it in the future. As before, we begin again from the last stage and work forward.

Consider a trader who has paid a bribe and cheated, and been assessed a judgment of $J > 0$. He expects a zero future payoff in each future period if he pays the judgment (because he will be extorted again and again). He expects the same zero payoff if he does not pay, since he will then have an unpaid judgment on his record. Since $-f(J) < 0$, he will find it most profitable to refuse to pay the judgment.

Having paid a bribe B, a trader expects to earn α this period and zero in the

---

[8]If the Law Merchant cannot commit to this action, then it is easy to show that there is an equilibrium in which the trader ignores the threat and the LM does not carry it out. It is no doubt true that some threats are disposed of in just this way — the victim simply calls the LM's bluff. We are interested in showing that the reputation mechanism can sometimes function even when the LM's threat must be taken at face value.

[9]If we assumed that transfers are costly here, as in the case of judgments, then the victim would become more reluctant to pay and bribery would be less likely to succeed.

future if he cheats today, or 1 this period and zero in the future if he does not. Since $\alpha > 1$, cheating is most profitable.

Given that a player has paid a bribe before, if a bribe B is demanded today, then the profits from paying the bribe, querying, and cheating are expected to be $\alpha - Q - B$; not paying leads to profits of zero. Hence, it is at least as profitable to pay the bribe whenever $B \le \alpha - Q$.

If a trader has paid a bribe before, the strategy specifies that he will pay any bribe up to $\alpha - Q$ in the current period. In this case, according to the strategies, no trader's play in future periods will depend on whether the LM demands a bribe or on the amount of the bribe, so his most profitable play is to demand $\alpha - Q$.

Suppose a trader has not paid a bribe before and a bribe, B, is demanded currently. If the trader pays the bribe then, according to the strategy, he will cheat and refuse to pay the judgment. The resulting payoff is $\alpha - B - Q$ in the current period and, as a trader with an unpaid judgment, zero in future periods. If he refuses to pay the bribe, then his expected payoff is zero in the current period and $1 - Q$ in subsequent periods. So, it is most profitable for him to refuse to pay if

$$(1 - \delta)(\alpha - B - Q) + \delta \cdot 0 \le (1 - \delta) \cdot 0 + \delta \cdot (1 - Q),$$

which is equivalent to condition (12).

Finally, when facing a trader who has never before paid a bribe, the LM expects that any demand for a bribe will be refused and that the trader will also not query in the current period, leading to a loss of revenues of ϵ, with no effect on play in future periods. Hence, it is most profitable for the LM not to demand any bribe in this case. ∎

Theorem 4 pertains to a model in which only one kind of dishonest behavior by the LM is possible. The problem of discouraging other kinds of dishonest behavior may require other strategies. From our preliminary analysis, it appears that the most difficult problem is to deter the LM from soliciting or accepting bribes from traders who have an unpaid judgment but wish to conceal that fact. By concealing the judgment, cheating, and refusing to pay the new judgment, the trader could "earn" $\alpha - Q$ and a portion of that might be offered as a bribe to the LM. As we add richness to the possibilities for cheating, it is natural to expect that the necessary institutions and strategies must respond in a correspondingly rich way.

6. CONCLUSION

We began our analysis by studying an environment in which private information about behavior in exchanges is a potential impediment to trade. Under complete information, even if meetings among particular pairs of traders are infrequent, informal norms of behavior are theoretically sufficient to police deviations. But when information is costly, the equilibrium may potentially break down and informal means may not be sufficient to police deviations.

The Law Merchant enforcement system that we have studied restores the equilibrium status of Honest behavior. It succeeds even though there is no state with police power and authority over a wide geographical realm to enforce contracts. Instead, the system works by making the reputation system of enforcement work better. The institutions we have studied provide people with the information they need to recognize those who have cheated, and it provides incentives for those who have been cheated to provide evidence of their injuries. Then, the reputation system itself provides the incentives for honest behavior and for payment by those who are found to have violated the code, and it encourages traders to boycott those who have flouted the system. Neither the reputation mechanism nor the institutions can be effective by themselves. They are complementary parts of a total system that works together to enforce honest behavior.

Our account of the Law Merchant system is, of course, incomplete. Once disputes came to be resolved in a centralized way, the merchants in Western Europe enhanced and refined their private legal code to serve the needs of the merchant trade — all prior to the rise of the nation-state. Without this code and the system for enforcement, trade among virtual strangers would have been much more cumbersome, or even impossible.[10] Remarkably, the Law Merchant institution appears to have been structured to support trade in a way that minimizes transaction costs, or at least incurs costs only in categories that are indispensable to any system that relies on boycotts as sanctions.

Our model is a stylization, not set in a particular locality at a particular date. Necessarily, then, it omits many important elements that some historians will argue are essential to understanding the institutions that are found there and then. However, our core contention that institutions sometimes arise to make reputation mechanisms more effective by communicating information seems almost beyond dispute. The Mishipora, described in the Hebrew Talmud, according to which those who failed to keep promises were punished by being publicly denounced; the use of the "hue and cry" to identify cheaters in medieval England; the famed "Scarlet Letter," described in Hawthorne's famous story; and the public stocks and pillories of 17th century New England, which were sometimes used to punish errant local merchants, are all examples of institutions and practices in which a principal aim is to convey information to the community about who has violated its norms.

It is our contention that an enduring pattern of trade over a wide geographical area cannot be sustained if it is profitable for merchants to renege on promises or repudiate agreements. In the larger trading towns and cities of northern Europe in the 10th through 13th centuries, it was not possible for every merchant to know

---

[10]Of course, merchants could and did communicate extensively, writing letters, engaging in trial relations, and checking the credentials of their trading partners. Where possible, they also relied on family members and client relationships to provide reliable services. But with geographic specialization in production, these devices alone could not allow merchants to escape the need to rely on the promises of individuals with whom they were not well acquainted.

the reputations of all others, so extensive trade required the development of some system like the Law Merchant system to fill in the gap.

Many of the key characteristics of our model correspond to practices found at the Champagne Fairs. While merchants at the Fairs were not required to query prior to any contract, the institutions of the Fair provided this information in another manner. As noted above, the Fairs closely controlled entry and exit. A merchant could not enter the Fair without being in good standing with those who controlled entry, and any merchant caught cheating at the Fair would be incarcerated and brought to justice under the rules of the Fair. So anyone a merchant met at the Fair could be presumed to have a "good reputation" in precisely the sense of our model. It did not indicate that all free merchants had never cheated in the past; but it did indicate that anyone who had been convicted of cheating had made good on the judgment against him. Moreover, because merchants might disappear rather than pay their judgments, judges at the Fairs had to balance the size of their judgment so that the value of being able to attend future Fairs exceeded the award.

According to Verlinden (1963, p. 132): "At the end of the 12th century and during the first half of the 13th, the Champagne Fairs were indeed the centre of international commercial activity of the western world." This is a long time for a single fair to maintain such dominance, but the Champagne Fair had two advantages over its potential competitors. First, it had an effective system for enforcing exchange contracts. Second, as we observed earlier, there are important economies of scope and scale in reputation mechanisms. Other, smaller fairs that tried to compete with the Champagne Fairs on an equal footing would have to contend with merchants who participated only long enough to make a profitable cheating transaction and then return to the Champagne Fairs where their participation rights were intact.

Despite this observation, it must be counted a weakness of the model that it does not fully account for trade outside of a single trading center. Even if the Law Merchant and related systems were effective underpinnings for local trade, how was information about a trader's dishonesty in one location transmitted to another? The model in this paper is too simple to handle this problem, but we hope to extend our approach to the institutions that developed during the middle ages to protect against the added problems raised by spatial separation. This includes the merchant gilds in northern Europe, the consulates of the Italian city states, and the organization of alien merchants into colonies (like the Steelyard in medieval London) with local privileges and duties. These institutions can also be understood from the perspective developed in this paper — they are designed to reinforce reputation mechanisms that alone are insufficient to support trade.

The Law Merchant system of judges and reputations was eventually replaced by a system of state enforcement, typically in the late middle ages or the early modern era in Western Europe. Enforcement of the private codes by the state added a new dimension to enforcement, especially in later periods when nation-states exercised extensive geographic control. Rather than depend for punishment upon the decentralized behavior of merchants, state enforcement could seize the property of individuals who resisted paying judgments, or put them into jail. If judgments could be enforced this way, then, in principle, the costs of keeping the merchants well informed about one another's past behavior could be saved. To the extent that the costs of running state adjudication and enforcement were roughly similar to the costs of running the private system and to the extent that taxes can be efficiently collected, a comprehensive state-run system would have the advantage that it eliminates the need for each individual to pay Q each period. As the volume of trade increased in the late middle ages, the cost saving from that source would have been substantial.[11] Thus our approach suggests that the importance of the role of the state enforcement of contracts was not that it provided a means of enforcing contracts where one previously did not exist. Rather, it was to reduce the transaction costs of policing exchange.[12]

In closing, we return to the broader implications of our work for the study of institutions. In complete information settings, institutions are frequently unnecessary because decentralized enforcement is sufficient to police deviations. However, this conclusion fails in environments where information is incomplete or costly. In the context of our model, the Adjusted Tit-for-Tat strategy requires that a trader know his current partner's previous history. When such information is difficult or costly to obtain, decentralized enforcement mechanisms break down. Institutions like those of the Law Merchant system resolve the fundamental problems of restoring the information that underpins an effective reputation system while both economizing on information and overcoming a whole array of incentive problems that obstruct the gathering and dissemination of that information.

PAUL R. MILGROM   DOUGLASS C. NORTH   BARRY R. WEINGAST
Department of Economics   *Department of Economics*   *Hoover Institution on War,*
Stanford University   *Washington University*   *Revolution and Peace*
Stanford   *St. Louis, MO 63130*   *Stanford University*
CA 94305   *Stanford*
                                                       CA 94305

REFERENCES

Abreu, Dilip, 1988, On the Theory of Infinitely Repeated Games with Discounting, *Econometrica* 39, 383–96.
Aumann, Robert, 1985, Repeated Games, in George Feiwel (ed.), *Issues in Contemporary Microeconomics and Welfare*, Macmillan Press, London, 209–42.
Axelrod, Robert, 1984, *The Evolution of Cooperation*, Basic Books, New York.

[11]Historically, the successful state enforcement came in a series of stages. As suggested above, state enforcement began with the adoption of the legal codes by a wide range of cities and towns. Some of these evolved over time into large city-states (e.g., Venice or Genoa) or, later, became part of a larger nation-state (e.g., London). For a discussion of the evolution of legal codes underpinning merchant trade, see North (1987).

[12]As we emphasized in section 4, however, a full evaluation of state enforcement must also assess the potential for corruption in the enforcement mechanisms of state enforcement.

Axelrod, Robert, 1986, An Evolutionary Approach to Social Norms, *American Political Science Review* 80, 1095–1111.

Banks, Jeffrey and Randall Calvert, 1989, Equilibria in Coordination Games. MS, University of Rochester.

Benson, Bruce, 1989, The Spontaneous Evolution of Commercial Law, *Southern Economic Journal*: 644–61.

Berman, Harold, 1983, *Law and Revolution: The Formation of Western Legal Tradition*, Harvard University Press.

Calvert, Randall, 1989. Reciprocity Among Self-interested Actors, in Peter C. Ordeshook, ed., *Models of Strategic Choice in Politics*, Michigan University Press.

Fudenberg, Drew and Eric Maskin, 1986, The Folk Theorem in Repeated Games with Discounting or with Incomplete Information, *Econometrica* 54, 533–554.

DeRoover, Raymond, 1963, The Organization of Trade, *Cambridge Economic History of Europe*, Vol. III.

Greif, Avner, 1989, Reputation and Coalitions in Medieval Trade: *Journal of Economic History*, 49, 857–82.

Jones, William Catron, 1961, *The Settlement of Merchants' Disputes by Merchants: An Approach to the Study of the History of Commercial Law*, PhD dissertation, University of Chicago.

Kandori, Michihiro, 1989, *Information and Coordination in Strategic Interaction Over Time*, PhD dissertation, Stanford University.

Klein, Benjamin and Keith Leffler, 1981, The Role of Market Forces in Assuring Contractual Performance, *Journal of Political Economy.* 89, 615–41.

Lopez, Robert S., 1976, *Commercial Revolution of the Middle Ages, 950–1350*, Cambridge University Press, Cambridge.

Lopez, Robert S. and Irving W. Raymond, 1955, *Medieval Trade in the Mediterranean World*, Columbia University Press, New York.

Mitchell, W., 1904, *Essay on the Early History of the Law Merchant*, Cambridge University Press, Cambridge.

North, Douglass, 1987, Institutions, Transactions Costs, and the Rise of Merchant Empires, in James Tracey (ed.), *The Economics of the Rise of Merchant Empires*, Vol. 2.

North, Douglass, 1989, *Institutions, Institutional Change, and Economic Performance*, Book MS, Washington University.

North, Douglass and Robert Thomas, 1973, *Rise of the Western World*, Cambridge University Press, Cambridge.

Okuno-Fujiwara, M. and Andrew Postlewaite, 1989, Social Norms in Random Matching Games, mimeo, University of Pennsylvania.

Pirenne, Henri, 1925, *Medieval Cities: Their Origins and the Revival of Trade*, Princeton University Press.

Rorig, Fritz, 1967, *The Medieval Town*, University of California Press, Berkeley.

Scutton, Thomas E., 1909, General Survey of the History of the Law Merchant, in *Select Essays in Anglo American Legal History*, compiled by the Association of American Law Schools.

Shapiro, Carl, 1983, Premiums for High Quality Products as Returns to Reputations, *Quarterly Journal of Economics* 98(4), 659–679.

Shapiro, Carl and Joseph Stiglitz, 1984, Equilibrium Unemployment as a Worker Discipline Device, *American Economic Review* 74(3), 433–444.

Thrupp, Silvia, 1948, *The Merchant Class of Medieval London*, University of Chicago Press, Chicago.

Townsend, Robert M., 1981, Models of Money with Spatially Separated Agents, in J.H. Kareken and Neil Wallace (eds.), *Models of Monetary Economies*, Federal Reserve Bank, Minneapolis.

Trakman, L., 1983, *The Law Merchant*, Littleton, Rothman and Co.

Verlinden, C., 1963, Markets and Fairs, *Cambridge Economic History of Europe*, Vol. III.

Weingast, Barry R. and William Marshall, 1988, 'The Industrial Organization of Congress; or Why Legislatures, like Firms, are not Organized as Markets, *Journal of Political Economy* 96, 132–163.

[3]

ROBERT O. KEOHANE

Multilateralism:
an agenda for research

FS3 fo2

Multilateralism can be defined as the practice of co-ordinating
national policies in groups of three or more states, through ad
hoc arrangements or by means of institutions. Since the end of
World War II, multilateralism has become increasingly important in world politics, as manifested in the proliferation of multinational conferences on a bewildering variety of themes and
an increase in the number of multilateral intergovernmental
organizations from fewer than 100 in 1945 to about 200 by 1960
and over 600 by 1980.[1] Bilateralism has been revived on some
issues in the 1980s, particularly with regard to trade, yet the
number and variety of multilateral arrangements continue to
increase.

   In the international relations literature, multilateralism has
served as a label for a variety of activities more than as a concept
defining a research programme. When a scholar refers to multilateralism, it is not immediately clear what phenomena are to be
described and explained. Before we can understand multilateralism, we need to think about how we should conceive of it and

Stanfield Professor of International Peace and Chair of the Department of Government, Harvard University, Cambridge, MA; author of *After Hegemony: Cooperation and Discord in the World Political Economy* (1984) and *International Institutions
and State Power: Essays in International Relations Theory* (1989).

I appreciate the comments of Jeffrey Frieden, Stanley Hoffmann, Nannerl O.
Keohane, Lisa Martin, Joseph S. Nye, John Gerard Ruggie, and Mark Zacher
on an earlier draft.

1 Harold K. Jacobson, *Networks of Interdependence: International Organizations and
the Global Political System* (2nd ed; New York: Knopf 1984), 37-50 and appendix A.

analysis. Neorealism emphasizes the weakness of international institutions and the fragility of co-operation, stressing that 'in a condition of anarchy ... relative gain is more important than absolute gain,' or at least that states consistently seek to minimize gaps in gains favouring their partners.[4]

If neorealism is defined in this way, rather than vaguely in terms of neopositivist methodology or reliance on self-interested state behaviour, it becomes possible to delineate a contrasting view that does not deny the importance of states or denigrate efforts to specify and test causal propositions.[5] What I have called neoliberal institutionalism shares neorealism's emphasis on the significance of self-interested state action[6] and the importance of structural analysis at the systemic level. However, it argues that state behaviour can only be understood in the context of international institutions, which both constrain states and make their actions intelligible to others, and it denies that states consistently search for relative gains.[7] Its most fundamental claims are that international relations would be unintelligible without some degree of institutionalization, because they would lack shared expectations and understandings, and that variation in the commonality, specificity, and autonomy of institutions will affect the constraints and incentives facing states and will therefore exert impacts on state behaviour in world politics.

4 The quotation is from Kenneth N. Waltz, *Man, the State and War* (New York: Columbia University Press 1959), 198. The most systematic expositor of the view that relative gains are of crucial importance in world politics is Joseph Grieco. See his *Cooperation among Nations: Europe. America and Non-Tariff Barriers to Trade* (Ithaca NY: Cornell University Press 1990).

5 Robert O. Keohane, *After Hegemony: Cooperation and Discord in the World Political Economy* (Princeton NJ: Princeton University Press 1984), and *International Institutions and State Power: Essays in International Relations Theory* (Boulder CO: Westview 1989), especially chaps 1 and 7.

6 Although we are more likely to stress other motivations as well: see Keohane, *After Hegemony*, chap 7.

7 Neoliberal institutionalists explicitly agree that *under some conditions* states seek relative gains, but they emphasize that behaviour seeking relative gains is 'conditional on the nature of prevailing rules and expectations' rather than an essential or defining characteristic of world politics. See Keohane, 'Neoliberal institutionalism: a perspective on world politics,' in Keohane, ed, *International Institutions and State Power*, 11; also *After Hegemony*, chap 7.

The most thorough neorealist treatment of co-operation, by Joseph Grieco, accepts the neoliberal view of the significance of international institutions: 'realist theory would agree – perhaps to the surprise of some neoliberals – that international institutions *do* matter for states as they attempt to cooperate.'[8] In this respect, Grieco returns to the classical realist tradition of E.H. Carr and Hans J. Morgenthau, both of whom devoted considerable attention to international law and organization, while emphasizing the utopianism of visions of universal harmony and the limitations of judicial or legislative processes in resolving serious international disputes. Carr emphasized 'the bargaining process,' in which power was crucial, but he did not seek to deny the significance of the institutional context within which bargaining took place. Morgenthau devoted much of *Politics among Nations* to the roles of international institutions, and he even wrote an article on a 'functional theory of international law.'[9] A number of realists therefore agree with institutionalists both that international institutions are significant and that they operate within a bargaining system in which power plays a paramount role.

To argue that international institutions are significant, however, is only to claim that it is worthwhile to study them, not to specify how strong they are or what it is about them that should be studied. In seeking to identify clearly what needs to be explained, neither the neorealist nor the neoliberal institutionalist formulation is very helpful. Waltz's formulation of neorealist theory, although commendably precise in a number of respects, is vague on its own dependent variable. Waltz's balance of power theory, which he regards as the 'distinctively political theory of international politics,'[10] only predicts that balances of power will

8 Grieco, *Cooperation among Nations*, 233-4.
9 E.H. Carr, *The Twenty Years' Crisis, 1919-1939* (2nd ed; London: St Martin's Press 1946); Hans J. Morgenthau, *Politics among Nations: The Struggle for Power and Peace* (New York: Knopf, various editions from 1948 onwards), and 'Positivism, functionalism, and international law,' *American Journal of International Law* 34(1940), 260-84.
10 Waltz, *Theory of International Politics*, 117.

periodically recur. Likewise, my own formulation of institution-alist theory has been stronger at offering general arguments about why international institutions exist than at specifying vari-ations in their forms or patterns of state behaviour within them. Both neorealism and neoliberal institutionalism have empha-sized contextual and causal arguments at the expense of careful identification of sources of variation in state behaviour which need to be explained.[11] In this essay I seek to redress the balance by identifying four key puzzles of multilateralism and only sug-gesting possible explanations. My puzzles are:

1 Under what conditions do institutions matter?
2 What accounts for the rise of multilateral institutions?
3 What explains variations in membership, strength, and scope?
4 What accounts for variations in property rights and rules?

Following closely from the discussion about the significance of international institutions, I will begin with the issue of impact. How much difference do international institutions make for state policy, and what explains variation in impact?

UNDER WHAT CONDITIONS DO INSTITUTIONS MATTER?
Oran Young has recently observed that much less attention has been paid to the impact of international institutions than to their origins or their patterns of development over time: 'The ultimate justification for devoting substantial time and energy to the study of regimes must be the proposition that we can account

---

11 David Laitin made this point to me long ago about my own work, although I have only recently taken it to heart. Stephan Haggard and Beth A. Simmons emphasize the importance of accounting for variation in 'Theories of interna-tional regimes,' *International Organization* 41(summer 1987), 491-517. Some recent books have sought to be clearer on such sources of variation than the previous literature. Stephen Walt, *The Origins of Alliances* (Ithaca NY: Cornell University Press 1987), tries to distinguish between balancing and bandwagoning and to test alternative explanations of such behaviour. In *Cooperation among Nations*, Grieco has sought to specify variation in co-operation in the Tokyo Round codes. Although I disagree with both his formulation of neoliberal theory and his selection of critical cases – and therefore with his theoretical conclusions – his attempt to specify variation to be explained is laudable.

for a good deal of the variance in collective outcomes at the international level in terms of the impact of institutional arrangements. For the most part, however, this proposition is relegated to the realm of assumptions rather than brought to the forefront as a focus for analytical and empirical investigation.'[12] Young's statement needs to be qualified, however. Scholars have shown that international régimes can affect both the *capabilities* and the *interests* of states. International régimes can affect capabilities by serving as a source of influence for states whose policies are consistent with régime rules or which are advantaged by the régime's decision-making procedures. In *Power and Independence*, Joseph S. Nye and I referred to these influence resources as 'organizationally dependent capabilities.'[13] Régimes may also alter the underlying power capabilities of states, whether by reinforcing the dominance of rich, powerful states (as dependency theory argues) or by dissipating the hegemon's resources (as claimed by some versions of hegemonic stability theory).[14]

International institutions may alter calculations of interest by assigning property rights, providing information, and altering patterns of transaction costs. Short-run self-interest is affected by constraints imposed on policy choices by agreed-upon rules; long-run conceptions of self-interest may be reshaped as a result, in part, of practices engaged in over a period of time. We are familiar with how international trade régimes have tended to reinforce the awareness, among the governments of the industrialized countries, of the benefits of non-discriminatory trade; but it is also increasingly clear, as Nye argued several years ago, that the rules and institutions of Soviet-American security régimes

---

12 Oran R. Young, *International Cooperation: Building Regimes for Natural Resources and the Environment* (Ithaca NY: Cornell University Press 1989), 206-7.

13 Robert O. Keohane and Joseph S. Nye, Jr, *Power and Interdependence: World Politics in Transition* (Boston: Little, Brown 1977), 56.

14 For a useful summary of the possible effects of régimes on interests and capabilities, see Stephen D. Krasner, 'Regimes and the limits of realism: regimes as autonomous variables,' in Krasner, ed, *International Regimes* (Ithaca NY: Cornell University Press 1983), esp 361-4.

have helped to reshape the conceptions of their interests held by the American and Soviet governments.[15]

Nevertheless, as Young points out, these hypothetical propositions about interests and capabilities have not been subjected to systematic empirical assessments. Consider the issue of capabilities. Arguments continue to rage about whether United States power has really declined significantly since the end of the 1960s.[16] It could be that United States power has declined and that such practices as liberal trade, promoted by general rules (which others may violate or evade more effectively), have accelerated that decline. But those who are sceptical about the 'declinist' thesis emphasize the ability of the United States to exercise influence in international institutions and the consistency of many of its practices with institutional norms as counterweights to erosions in its relative financial and technological capabilities. And even if the decline of the United States could be empirically established, further investigation might show that American influence in international institutions has retarded rather than accelerated the erosion of American power.

The fundamental difficulty in assessing the impact of international institutions is that causal inference is difficult where experimental or statistical research designs are infeasible. We do not have a hypothetical institution-free baseline from which to measure the impact of actual institutions on state capabilities. We might be tempted to attribute co-operation among states in

15 Joseph S. Nye, Jr, 'Nuclear learning and U.S.-Soviet security regimes,' *International Organization* 41(summer 1987), 371-402. On interests, see Robert O. Keohane, 'The demand for international regimes,' in *International Organization* 36(spring 1982), 325-55. For some recent evidence on East-West régimes, see Volker Rittberger, ed, *International Regimes in East-West Politics* (London: Pinter 1990).

16 The most comprehensive statements of the case for decline are made by Robert Gilpin, *War and Change in World Politics* (New York: Cambridge University Press 1981), and Paul Kennedy, *The Rise and Fall of the Great Powers* (New York: Random House 1987). Two sophisticated arguments against the 'declinist' view are Joseph S. Nye, *Bound to Lead: The Changing Nature of American Power* (New York: Basic Books 1990), and Henry Nau, *The Myth of America's Decline* (New York: Oxford University Press 1990).

accordance with international rules to constraints on short-range self-interest, or to changes in long-range self-interest, resulting from those rules. But both the co-operation and the institutions could in principle be reflections of some third set of forces, such as patterns of complementary interests and underlying distributions of power, without institutions having any effect at all. If it were possible to use an experimental design, we would control for other explanatory factors, such as distributions of power and interest, and vary institutional characteristics. Unfortunately, we cannot actually perform such an experiment.

Yet this inability to use strict experimental methods does not prevent us from investigating the impact of institutions. Some important work along these lines has already been done,[17] but more would be useful. To investigate the impact of institutions on interests, one possible approach is to identify situations in which institutional rules are 'inconvenient': that is, in which they conflict with governments' perceptions of what their self-interests would be if there were no such institutions. In these instances of inconvenient commitments, we should expect that if institutions were unimportant, the rules would be violated, but that insofar as the rules are obeyed, we can infer that institutions had an impact. In my own empirical research I am seeking a better understanding of the conditions for institutional impact by examining major cases of inconvenient commitments in the history of American foreign policy since 1789. My purpose is to determine under which conditions institutional commitments are more or less likely to be kept. At the current stage in my work, only a few points seem clear: there is substantial variation in the extent to which commitments seem to matter, both across issues and over time; enforcement of commitments against the United States has been quite rare; and unenforceable commit-

17 See Oran R. Young, *Compliance and Public Authority* (Baltimore MD: Johns Hopkins University Press 1979); Peter M. Haas, 'Do regimes matter? Epistemic communities and Mediterranean pollution control,' *International Organization* 43(summer 1989), 377-405. Haas emphasizes the impact of transnational networks of scientists, or 'epistemic communities,' on patterns of compliance.

ments are nevertheless sometimes honoured, although no single motivation, whether based in reciprocity, concern about reputation, or moral principle, seems reliably to ensure compliance.

WHAT ACCOUNTS FOR THE RISE
OF MULTILATERAL INSTITUTIONS?

The rise of multilateral institutions has not been linear: increased bilateralism appeared in the 1980s on issues such as trade in textiles under the Multi-Fibre Arrangement and trade in products such as automobiles and consumer electronics which are covered by voluntary export restraints. Despite these countervailing tendencies, for the postwar period as a whole states have relied increasingly on multilateral arrangements, and the most important of those arrangements have become institutionalized. How should we account for this trend?

Much work on multilateralism has focussed on co-operation as a variable: the extent to which governments' policies are effectively co-ordinated in such a way as to become consistent with one another. Unfortunately, co-operation is easier to define, or to specify in an experimental situation, than to operationalize. Because both conflicting interests and power are always involved in bargaining processes leading to co-operation, the extent of the role coercion played in the formation of institutions or in the co-ordination of policy becomes a matter of judgment. It may be difficult to distinguish what Young refers to as 'negotiated' and 'imposed' orders from one another: one state's co-operation is another's imposition.[18] Furthermore, states' policies are not, unlike game-theoretic choices, dichotomously co-operative or conflictual: multilateral co-operation is a systems-level *result* of policy choices by a number of states rather than an attribute of any given actor or its policies.[19]

18 Oran R. Young, 'Regime dynamics: the rise and fall of international regimes,' in Krasner, ed, *International Regimes*, esp 101-4.
19 In her dissertation, on monetary co-operation and discord in the interwar period, Beth A. Simmons has taken a significant step forward by operationalizing not co-operation – the joint product of action by at least two states – but the specific behaviour required of deficit and surplus states if monetary co-operation is to

Nevertheless, it is possible to trace the evolution of co-operation in an issue-area over time, or to compare the extent of cooperation in different issue-areas at a given moment in time.
There has been more co-operation on trade issues among the
advanced capitalist countries since World War II than in the
interwar period; there is more co-operation on trade in manufactured goods than there has been in agricultural trade; and
co-operation has been based on more liberal principles in trade
than in services. It may be easier to devise reliable operational
indicators of changes in institutional multilateralism than in
changes in co-operation per se. The number, budgets, memberships, and scope of activity of international organizations provide plausible measures of institutional multilateralism, to which
there is nothing directly comparable in the co-operation literature.

The institutionalist literature written in the 1980s took its
cue from micro-economics, seeking to explain institutionalized
co-operation by using the metaphor of supply and demand. In
this view, institutions are supplied by states acting as 'political
entrepreneurs who see a potential profit in organizing collaboration.'[20] Hegemonic states may have incentives to serve as entrepreneurs, but relatively small groups of states can also overcome
collective action problems to do so.[21] The key variable here is
concentration of capability, as in Waltz's theory. Because capabilities became somewhat less concentrated among the advanced
industrialized democracies after the 1950s, supply explanations
do not account for increasing multilateralism.[22]

At any rate, favourable conditions on the supply side – not
necessarily hegemony – could only be necessary conditions for

---

occur. The relevant standards of behaviour are different for deficit countries
than for surplus ones; but in each case they can be specified and the actions of
the countries evaluated against them.

20 Keohane, 'The demand for international regimes,' 339.

21 Duncan Snidal, 'The limits of hegemonic stability theory,' *International Organization* 39(autumn 1985), 579-614.

22 Game-theoretical formulations such as Snidal's, with their emphasis on strategic
interaction and the role of k-groups, did, however, help to explain why expectations of discord drawn from naive hegemonic stability theory were incorrect.

multilateralism. To obtain a fuller account, one must look at demand as well as supply. The most obvious source of changing demands lies in the changing interests, or preferences, of states. Preferences may be altered by changes in domestic political institutions or coalitions. For instance, Nazi Germany was less willing to enter into multilateral arrangements in the 1930s than was its Weimar predecessor; after World War II, the Federal Republic of the 1950s was positively anxious to be included in arrangements that would have been anathema to the Nazis. The post–New Deal, post–World War II United States was much more willing to engage in international co-operation than the protectionist, insulated United States of most of the interwar period. Preferences can also change in two different ways as a result of increasing levels of interdependence. First, even if states were unitary decision-makers, under conditions of interdependence their ability to attain their objectives would be increasingly affected by the actions of others. As interdependence rises. therefore, the opportunity costs of not co-ordinating policy increase, compared with the costs of sacrificing autonomy as a consequence of making binding agreements. The result can be expected to be increased demand for multilateral agreements. Second, increased interdependence is likely to affect domestic political institutions and coalitions, as Peter Katzenstein and Peter Gourevitch have shown.[23]

Recent work by Ronald Rogowski suggests a possible extension of the Gourevitch-Katzenstein line of argument to account for increasing co-operation among the advanced industrial democracies. Rogowski's theory builds on the Stolper-Samuel-

23 On the effects of interdependence on political institutions in small European states, see Peter J. Katzenstein, *Small States in World Markets* (Ithaca NY: Cornell University Press 1985). Peter Gourevitch's discussion of the effects of interdependence on political coalitions appears in his *Politics in Hard Times* (Ithaca NY: Cornell University Press 1985). On the relationship between selected international organizations and United States foreign policy, with explicit attention to the issue of the influence of intergovernmental organizations on United States domestic politics, see Margaret P. Karns and Karen A. Mingst, eds, *The United States and Multilateral Institutions: Patterns of Changing Instrumentality and Influence* (Boston: Unwin Hyman 1990), esp chap 11 by the editors.

son theorem from the economics of international trade, which predicts that locally abundant factors of production will benefit from trade liberalization and that only locally scarce factors can benefit by protection.[24]

Rogowski extends the Stolper-Samuelson theorem to politics, arguing that increasing exposure to trade will result in political conflict between owners of scarce and abundant factors of production, respectively. Furthermore, he infers that owners of abundant factors will be strengthened politically by openness. It follows that the liberalization of the postwar international political economy, led by the United States, should have strengthened owners of abundant factors of production, including capital, in all major industrial countries. These actors will favour further openness and will increasingly have the capabilities to obtain it. Thus the domestic political structures of other industrialized countries should, by this theory, have become more conducive to policies of economic openness during the postwar period, even as the United States became less dominant. On this interpretation, recent patterns of co-operation could reflect shifts in interests, in favour of openness, as a result of the interaction between economic interdependence and domestic politics.[25]

Another source of change in the demand for institutions, in addition to rising levels of interdependence and changes in

24 Ronald Rogowski, *Commerce and Coalitions: How Trade Affects Domestic Political Alignments* (Princeton NJ: Princeton University Press 1989), 3. The full statement of the theory by Rogowski includes producers who use scarce factors intensively as beneficiaries of protection, and producers who use locally abundant factors intensively as beneficiaries of economic openness.

25 *Ibid*, esp 170-1. A weakness in Rogowski's theory is the assumption that capital and labour can be treated as homogeneous, mobile factors of production: in modern economies, capital and labour may be quite specific to sectors. In industries such as textiles and autos, on the one hand, and aircraft and computers, on the other, foreign trade interests seem to follow sectoral lines more than those of capital versus labour. *In the short run*, Rogowski's assumption that economic sectors that are advantaged by changes in openness will become stronger politically is also questionable, because deprivation of traditional benefits may be a stronger mobilizing force than opportunities for new gains. Other interest-based theories may be more plausible; but the general point remains: changes in interests could account for increased reliance on multilateral institutions.

domestic politics, lies in what Jeffrey Frieden refers to as the 'contractual environment.'[26] In the absence of appropriate institutions, the abilities of states to make agreements may be thwarted by externalities, uncertainty, informational asymmetries, and fears that partners will behave opportunistically. Even strong converging interests arising from a combination of complementary domestic structures and international interdependence are not sufficient to explain the emergence of multilateral institutions, because if no contractual problems existed, no institutions would be needed, and if contractual problems were utterly severe, no institutions would be possible. For international institutions to be devised, contractual problems must be significant but not overwhelming.

To account for the rise of international institutions, advocates of a contractual approach make two principal arguments:

1 Institutions perform the functions of reducing uncertainty and the costs of carrying out transactions for their members; but institutions are themselves costly to create and maintain. As the number and importance of related issues within a given policy domain increase, the costs of creating new institutions will fall relative to the costs of inventing new rules and procedures for each issue that arises. In other words, increases in issue density will lead to a *demand for the creation of multilateral institutions*.

2 International institutions that succeed in establishing relatively clear rules, which provide standards for judgment of behaviour, and in stabilizing expectations, thus reducing uncertainty, will become valued and will therefore tend to create a *demand for the maintenance of multilateral institutions*.[27] According to this line of argument, we should expect that a

26 Jeffrey Frieden, personal communication.
27 These arguments are made in Keohane, 'The demand for international regimes,' and in *After Hegemony*, chaps 5-6. It is interesting to note that Morgenthau's argument for the conditions under which alliances will occur is similar: it is cast in functional terms and stresses the role of alliances in reducing uncertainty 'when the common interests [of potential allies] are inchoate in terms of policy and action' and therefore need to be made 'explicit and operative.' *Politics among Nations*, 4th ed, 177.

combination of increasing interdependence (leading to high levels of issue density) and the success of existing institutions will tend to lead both to an expansion of institutional tasks and an increase in the number of functioning international institutions. If collective action dilemmas are serious, increases in the number of players, and especially in the diffusion of capabilities among them, will raise the costs of co-operation. However, multilateral institutions may not suffer as a result; indeed, rules such as those in the General Agreement on Tariffs and Trade (GATT) limiting unconditional most-favoured-nation treatment to members can be interpreted as institutional responses to collective action problems.

Although under conditions of increasing interdependence and a record of institutional success we can expect the tasks assumed by international institutions to expand, this increase in activity will not be uniform across issue-areas, because specific features of the environment will be important. As explored later in this essay, different situations vary in the requirements for institutions to monitor rule compliance or even to help states enforce common standards: in some cases rules may be self-enforcing; in others they may be enforceable with appropriate institutions; in still others no conceivable international arrangements will ensure compliance with inconvenient rules.

The contractual line of argument has many ramifications for different aspects of multilateralism, as sketched in the sections below. However, it has only begun to be tested, and the results from case-studies are mixed. International régimes often seem to reduce uncertainty and transactions costs, in response to rising interdependence.[28] However, several case-studies of régime change find contractual arguments insufficient to ac-

---

28 See, particularly, Keohane, *After Hegemony*, chaps 8-10, and the chapters in Krasner, ed, *International Regimes*, and in Kenneth A. Oye, ed, *Cooperation under Anarchy* (Princeton NJ: Princeton University Press 1986). See also Mark W. Zacher, 'International commodity trade regimes,' *International Organization* 41(spring 1987), 173-202, and Ethan B. Kapstein, 'International coordination of banking regulations,' *International Organization* 43(spring 1989), 334. In their review of United States relations with multilateral institutions, Karns and Mingst conclude that rule-creation activities by multilateral institutions are important to the United States, but that information gathering and surveillance are less so. See *The United States and Multilateral Institutions*, esp 291-6.

count for observed behaviour, arguing that the effects of institutions to which they point were insignificant,[29] that ideological hegemony was important,[30] or that changes in states' conceptions of their preferences, as affected by transnational networks, were more important than contractual theories assume.[31] It is difficult at this point to generalize about the relative importance of these contractual factors, compared with the effects of shifts in the distribution of capabilities and changes in the interests or preferences of states, as shaped by changes in interdependence, interacting with domestic politics. There seems to be some merit in the contractual arguments, but effects predicted by these arguments are neither uniform nor overwhelmingly strong.

It is important to emphasize in this connection that sensible adherents of the contractual approach would propose it not as a *substitute* for the analysis of power, interests, or interdependence, but rather as a useful *supplement* to those traditional modes of political analysis. It is emphasized below not as a theoretical panacea but as a relatively novel way of throwing light on some puzzles of multilateralism. It is particularly important that my discussion of contractualism should not be interpreted as implying that international institutional arrangements are 'optimal' in any sense of that word. Any clear separation between functional and power arguments is misleading.[32]

An interpretation of institutional change that focusses on capabilities, interests, interdependence, domestic political struc-

29 Andrew M. Moravcsik, 'Disciplining trade finance: the OECD export credit arrangement,' *International Organization* 43(winter 1989), 173-205, esp 198.

30 Jack Donnelly, 'International human rights: a regime analysis,' *International Organization* 40(summer 1986), 637.

31 Roger K. Smith, 'Explaining the non-proliferation regime: anomalies for contemporary international relations theory,' *International Organization* 41(spring 1987), 253-82; Peter M. Haas, *Saving the Mediterranean: the Politics of International Environmental Cooperation* (New York: Columbia University Press 1990), esp 183-9. Haas (187) finds that 'all the factors that the cooperation under anarchy school identifies as contributing to cooperation were present to some extent in the Med Plan,' but that 'they do not account for the full extent of the Med Plan.'

32 The classic statement remains that of Ernst B. Haas, in *Beyond the Nation-State: Functionalism and International Organization* (Stanford CA: Stanford University Press 1964), chap 2, 'Functionalism refined,' 26-50.

ture, and the contractual environment emphasizes the role of constraints within which choices are made. Such an approach does not deny that the thought processes of and the actions taken by decision-makers in international organizations are often significant: particular initiatives and policies, which may benefit or harm millions of people, may depend upon the imagination, courage, and capacity for learning of leaders of international organizations. They may also depend on the accumulation of scientific knowledge, on the basis of which better decisions can be made.[33]

Nevertheless, the argument I am making sees organizational decision-making as dependent on politically compelling demands for multilateral institutions and on the political power and interests required to create and support such institutions. Scientific knowledge is certainly significant in modern politics: indeed, it may play a role in the process by which states determine their own preferences, and it certainly affects beliefs about international interdependence and the potential benefits of international institutions. Yet its impact on decision-makers in international organizations themselves can only materialize if prior conditions make possible the creation, maintenance, and expansion of multilateral institutions.

How, then, should we account for the rise of multilateralism in the postwar world? We need not only to judge the relative importance of power, interdependence, domestic politics, and the contractual environment but also to see how these forces interact. Understanding these interactions will require close study of political and economic processes within issue-areas as

33 For a thorough exploration of learning and adaptation in international organizations, and a defence of the importance of organizational decision-makers, see Ernst B. Haas, *When Knowledge is Power: Three Models of Change in International Organizations* (Berkeley CA: University of California Press 1990), particularly 7-15. Haas describes three patterns of organizational change – incremental growth, turbulent non-growth, and managed interdependence – and very cleverly distinguishes learning from adaptation. His account of variation in life histories among international organizations is persuasive, even if his work does not provide a convincing basis for abandoning what he calls a 'structuralist' account of the rise of multilateralism in general.

well as systematic comparative analysis of patterns across issue-areas. Both types of study will seek to connect those shifts with changes in distributions of capabilities, patterns of interdependence, domestic political coalitions, and multilateral institutional activity.

The contractual theorist should expect to find an incremental pattern of change, promoted by officials of international organizations as well as by those of central governments: we should observe responses of institutions to problems involving externalities, uncertainty, and high costs of transactions. Explanations stressing interdependence would expect central governmental officials, facing trade-offs between objectives, to take the lead. Theories relying on changes in domestic politics should expect to observe shifting political coalitions in major countries, with policy change instituted by new political leadership or prompted by pressure from below. Our ultimate objective should be to understand under which conditions each of these explanations, or their combination, coupled with structural power theories, accounts for the rise in multilateralism.

WHAT EXPLAINS VARIATIONS IN
INSTITUTIONAL MEMBERSHIP, STRENGTH, AND SCOPE?
Interest-based and contractual explanations of the rise of multilateralism since 1945 could also be employed to investigate variation in the incidence of multilateralism, as opposed to uncoordinated policy or bilateralism across issue-areas, and in the degree of institutionalization of multilateral arrangements. Much such variation needs to be explained. In the world political economy, issues of trade have been more institutionalized than those of money and much more so, at least on a global basis, than those involving oil; but some trade issues have been subject to bilateral arrangements whereas others are regulated in a genuinely multilateral way. Some commodities, such as coffee, have been subject to elaborate international régimes; others have not. With respect to the physical environment, international régimes governing tanker discharges, fisheries in many

areas of the open sea, and Antarctica have preceded comparable attempts to regulate deep-sea mining, transboundary flows of pollutants including nuclear fallout, or actions that adversely affect the atmospheric ozone layer. Even among those areas in which international regulation takes place, differences exist in patterns of representation, secretariat autonomy, the status of experts, revenue base, voting, budgeting, the monitoring of compliance, and a variety of other organizational character-istics.[34]

As in explanations for the rise of multilateralism, accounts of variation across issue-areas could focus on the distribution of power, on interdependence or domestic politics as determinants of states' preferences, or on the contractual environment. Even for the same states, domestic politics differs across issue-areas; and the states that are involved in different issue-areas are not the same. Thus, complementary interests in one area may con-trast with conflicting interests in another as a result of differences in domestic politics. The distribution of capabilities and the intensity of interdependence are also different across issue-areas. Contractual environments also vary: externalities, un-certainty, and transaction costs differ from one issue-area to another.

To explain variation across issue-areas, theories of organiza-tional learning also have to be taken into account, because varia-tions in learning may differentiate issue-areas from one another over time. In *When Knowledge is Power*, Ernst Haas shows that both concentration of power in states with similar preferences and agreement on objectives rooted in scientific knowledge were necessary conditions for successful organizational learning. Haas has explored issues of learning in such depth that I have nothing to add; in this essay, therefore, I will focus on other dimensions of institutional variations: patterns of institutional membership, the strength of multilateral regulation, and the scope of multilateral institutions. I will also avoid probing varia-

34 For a list of these and other factors, see *ibid*, 64, table 1.

tions in detailed organizational arrangements or patterns of influence.[35] Yet my general point – that students of multilateralism should be seeking to account for variation across institutions and issue-areas – applies to these organizational issues as well as to the questions addressed below.

Institutional membership

Different international institutions apply different criteria for membership. Two questions differentiate the major situations. (1) Is membership in principle open to all states within a certain geographical area that accept certain general principles and rules, or is it explicitly limited on the basis of domestic political arrangements or as a function of selection by present members? (2) If the former, how rigorously do members employ the criteria embedded in the rules?

Restricted institutions – for example, the North Atlantic Treaty Organization (NATO), the Organization of the Petroleum-Exporting Countries (OPEC), the Organization for Economic Co-operation and Development (OECD), the European Community – deliberately limit membership to a relatively small number of states that have some set of interests in common or that have specified domestic political arrangements. The rationale for these institutions, as currently constituted, would disappear were their memberships to become universal. *Conditionally open institutions* – for example, the International Monetary Fund (IMF), GATT, the GATT codes – are open in principle to states that are willing to accept a set of prescribed commitments, which not all states may be able (much less willing) to do. Conditionally open institutions adopt measures to exclude non-providers from benefits secured by co-operation. For instance, during the

35 Robert W. Cox and Harold K. Jacobson et al, *The Anatomy of Influence: Decision Making in International Organization* (New Haven CT: Yale University Press 1973), is a classic study of variations in patterns of influence in eight international organizations over twenty years. Its research design represents an exemplary use of the comparative method, although it lacks a larger theoretical framework within which its relatively narrow focus – determinants of influence in the organizations – could be located.

Tokyo Round of the 1970s, major GATT members perceived that they could benefit from agreements on a number of specific issues, such as government procurement and subsidies, but that many GATT members would not make commitments to provide benefits (for example, open markets for foreign suppliers and transparency and limitation of export-promoting subsidies) on these issues. They therefore agreed to codes open to all GATT members, but they sought to limit their benefits to those countries that adhered to the obligations of the codes. *Open institutions* such as the United Nations system can be joined by all sovereign states, with the exception perhaps of pariah states, with minimal further requirements for membership. Some institutions that were originally conceived as conditionally open, requiring commitments and a certain form of government, such as the United Nations (which initially excluded defeated enemies and certain states considered fascist such as Franco's Spain), have become open institutions; others that began as open ones, such as certain fisheries régimes, have become only conditionally open.[36]

Multilateral institutions of all three types are doubtless constructed to help powerful states achieve their interests. I would suggest, consistent with a contractual perspective, that the differences in form among them are closely connected with differences in function. Restricted institutions either seek to achieve gains vis-à-vis outsiders (a function for which there must be outsiders to exploit) or to build strong bonds of community (requiring similar political systems). They arise for the former reason when states perceive unexploited opportunities in their relationships with potential adversaries, whether in security or economic affairs. In 1948 the future NATO states discerned unexploited opportunities in their relationship with the Soviet Union. OPEC perceived comparable opportunities at its formation in 1960 and especially during the 1970s: greater cohesion, it was

---

36 For a distinction between open-to-entry common-property régimes and restricted common-property régimes, see Young, *International Cooperation*, 51.

752   INTERNATIONAL JOURNAL

thought, could produce higher oil prices or maintain the high prices already attained. The European Community uses its enhanced bargaining power to exploit opportunities with its trading partners and also seeks to build community among its own membership. Whatever else they do, restricted institutions engage in *cartelization*.

Conditionally open institutions are designed largely to cope with the dilemma of insufficient contributions, or 'free riding,' associated with problems of collective action. In a word, they are designed to foster *collaboration*.[37] If no price were imposed for membership in such institutions, co-operation would be highly sub-optimal, because the contributors would not receive reciprocal benefits from the free riders and would therefore reduce their own contributions. To achieve either specific reciprocity (tit for tat) or diffuse reciprocity in which a benefit does not depend on a specific quid pro quo, some conditions for membership are essential. The original conception of the United Nations, in which opposition to fascism was a condition for membership, reflects this conception of conditional openness. To understand the value of charging 'a price for admission,' consider what would happen to GATT if states were asked to abide by rules of non-discrimination without the assurance that their trading partners would do so!

Open institutions serve as forums for the exchange of opinions, but the benefits that members are willing to confer on each other are limited due to the difficulty of enforcing rules or ensuring reciprocity in concessions. Open institutions arise when none of the three principal reasons for limitation – the desire to exploit unexploited opportunities vis-à-vis adversaries, the search for community, and the need to control free-rider problems – is compelling. Open institutions may be useful in pure co-ordination games but are unlikely to be very effective

---

37 This is to say that 'supralateral' institutions – in which diffuse reciprocity prevails (see *supra* note 2) – must necessarily either have restricted membership or membership that is conditional on adherence to fairly demanding rules. I am indebted to John Ruggie for making this connection.

in situations requiring collaboration or suasion.[38] In general, open institutions are likely to be limited principally to symbolic issues and to operations involving relatively small quantities of resources. In this connection, the contrast is instructive between GATT, limited to states accepting its obligations, and the United Nations Conference on Trade and Development (UNCTAD), which is open to all United Nations members and serves chiefly as a forum for symbolic activity.[39] Insofar as significant resources are allocated by open institutions, informal means of controlling them will be used to circumvent the organization's nominal decision-making practices.[40] Open institutions controlled by the entire membership are normally limited to the function of *consultation*.[41]

38 In co-ordination games, players may prefer different outcomes but have no incentives to diverge from equilibria that have been reached: co-ordination games therefore do not require arrangements to ensure enforcement. Collaboration games, by contrast, contain strong incentives to defect from established equilibria. Finally, in suasion games, states have such asymmetrical interests that equilibrium outcomes leave at least one player dissatisfied. It typically seeks to link other issues to the issue in question, through promises or threats. For these distinctions, see Lisa L. Martin, 'Strategic interaction, multilateralism and institutions,' unpublished paper, April 1990. Martin builds on an article by Arthur A. Stein, 'Coordination and collaboration: regimes in an anarchic world,' in Krasner, ed, *International Regimes*, 115-40.

39 See Joseph S. Nye, Jr, 'UNCTAD: poor nations' pressure group,' in Cox and Jacobson, *Anatomy of Influence*, 334-70.

40 Cox and Jacobson, *Anatomy of Influence* (426), find that organizations controlled by their 'participant subsystems' – that is, by their members in accordance with formal rules – were 'those whose work has little salience for states, especially powerful states.' Organizations with high salience were controlled by powerful members, irrespective of nominal decision-making procedures. Cox and Jacobson do not explore whether their finding could be accounted for in part by the different susceptibility of the organizations they studied to collective action problems as well as to measures taken by powerful states to maintain their control. It should also be noted that although Cox and Jacobson imply that salience explains patterns of influence, it is quite conceivable that the relationship is reciprocal: control of an international organization by a majority composed of small states may lead powerful countries to withhold resources from it, thereby reducing its political salience. Likewise, with respect to the argument made in the text, it is plausible that the form of a multilateral institution will affect its functions as well as vice versa.

41 In distinguishing cartelization, collaboration, and consultation, I have adapted a very useful suggestion from Jeffrey Frieden.

754   INTERNATIONAL JOURNAL

The strength of multilateral regulation

In a pioneering paper, Brent Sutton and Mark Zacher ask a question that has not been given sufficient attention: 'What is regulated internationally and what is not regulated internationally in the world, and why?' They use theories of market failure, uncertainty, and transaction costs to account for variations in the degree of regulation of specific issues within the general domain of international shipping. Across areas such as international shipping services, financial transactions, market access, liability for damages, and crime, there is substantial variation in the extent to which regulation occurs.[42]

Vinod Aggarwal focusses on a similar variable, which he calls the 'strength' of an international régime, referring to 'the stringency with which rules regulate the behavior of countries.' Extreme 'weakness' of a régime denotes lack of regulation in the Sutton-Zacher sense. Aggarwal seeks to specify changes in the strength of international textile régimes between 1950 and the early 1980s and to account, chiefly on the basis of international and domestic structures, for variations in the strength of these régimes, particularly what he sees as the precipitous decline of the Multi-Fibre Arrangement after 1977.[43]

The most extensive and sophisticated efforts to explain what issues are regulated through multilateral institutions were undertaken by students of regional political integration in the 1960s and early 1970s. They developed a highly differentiated

---

42 Brent A. Sutton and Mark W. Zacher, 'Mutual advantage, imposition, and regime formation: evolution of international shipping regulations,' paper delivered to the 14th World Congress of the International Political Science Association, Washington, DC, 28 August-1 September 1988. Sutton and Zacher are currently working on a larger project comparing the evolution of régimes for shipping, air transport, telecommunications, and postal services, relying to a considerable degree on what I am referring to as a contractual analytical framework. For a published presentation of this theoretical argument, see Mark W. Zacher, 'Toward a theory of international regimes: explorations into the bases of mutual interests,' *Journal of International Affairs* 44(no 1, 1990), 1-19.

43 Vinod K. Aggarwal, *Liberal Protectionism: The International Politics of Organized Textile Trade* (Berkeley: University of California Press 1985), 20-1, 181-2. See also Haggard and Simmons, 'Theories of international regimes,' 496.

and sophisticated conception of integration, which is related to the 'strength' of régimes but which is explicitly multidimensional. These scholars not only sought to assess the descriptive argument that European politics was becoming more centralized and less subject to veto by individual states but also tried to account for inter-regional variation in the success of integrative efforts. Seeking to compare regional organizations, Nye began with a conception of integration as 'forming parts into a whole,' but he found it necessary to disaggregate political integration into a number of components, of which the most relevant for multilateral institutions in general are *institutional integration* and *policy integration*. Institutional integration is reflected in the bureaucratic growth and expansion of jurisdiction by the multilateral institutions themselves, acting either bureaucratically or with a system of less than unanimous voting by members. Policy integration is indexed by the scope of institutional action, the salience of fields in which multilateral institutions have authority, and the locus of decision – whether in the multilateral institution as a whole or in individual member-states.[44]

The choice of political integration as a dependent variable followed from the concerns of students of regional organizations

---

44 Joseph S. Nye, Jr, *Peace in Parts: Integration and Conflict in Regional Organization* (Boston: Little, Brown 1971; reprinted by University Press of America 1987), 26, 49. For a discussion of the 'locus' and 'scope' of decision-making in Europe between 1950 and 1970, see Leon N. Lindberg and Stuart A. Scheingold, *Europe's Would-Be Polity: Patterns of Change in the European Community* (Englewood Cliffs NJ: Prentice-Hall 1970). In a brilliant essay published in 1975, John Gerard Ruggie constructed a dimension, which he described as 'the instrumentalities of regimes,' which paralleled the concerns of integration theory. He distinguished among a common framework for national behaviour, a joint facility coordinating national behaviour, a common policy integrating national behaviour, and a common policy substituted for independent national behaviour. In that paper, Ruggie also argued that international behaviour is institutionalized; distinguished types of interdependence; introduced the concept of international régime into the international relations literature, defining it essentially as it is still commonly defined; and even inaugurated the concept of 'epistemic communities.' In other words, Ruggie in this short paper foreshadowed much of the conceptual work of the next decade. See John Gerard Ruggie, 'International responses to technology: concepts and trends,' *International Organization* 29(summer 1975), 557-84.

in the 1960s and early 1970s: they took co-operation through multilateral institutions as given, as least in Europe, and sought to understand whether it was leading to political community, federalism, or some new form of institutional, functionally driven collaboration. They also sought to explore how general this 'integration process' might become. However, the failure of regional integration outside Europe, and the stalling of the European integration process for almost twenty years after 1966, soon led scholars to shift their focus away from integration theory's emphasis on unification towards more decentralized modes of encouraging co-operation among states that remained legally and politically sovereign.

The reinvigoration of the European Community with the Single European Act and current discussions of a loosely defined 'political union' have begun to prompt renewed attention to processes of political integration. Much of this work has played down the European Community's institutions by focussing on intergovernmental bargains, which seem to constitute the most important dimension of European politics.[45] However, there has also been renewed interest in Ernst Haas's concept of 'supranationality,' referring not to an end-point of unity but to 'a cumulative pattern of accommodation in which the participants refrain from unconditionally vetoing proposals and instead seek to attain agreement by means of compromises upgrading common interests.'[46] The European Community is becoming an example of the 'pooling and sharing of sovereignty,' described well neither by the metaphor of 'cooperation under anarchy' – because the elaborate networks of rules, obligations, and organizations

45 For two good recent examples, see Wayne Sandholtz and John Zysman, '1992: recasting the European bargain,' *World Politics* 42(October 1989), 1-30, and Andrew Moravcsik, 'Negotiating the Single European Act: national interests and conventional statecraft in the European Community,' Working Paper 21, Center for European Studies, Harvard University, January 1990. Stanley Hoffmann and I also stress intergovernmental bargains in 'European Community politics and institutional change,' chapter 16 in William Wallace, ed, *Dynamics of European Integration* (London: Pinter forthcoming), 276-300.

46 Ernst B. Haas, 'Technocracy, pluralism and the New Europe,' in Stephen R. Graubard, ed, *A New Europe?* (Boston: Houghton Mifflin 1964), 66.

are far from anarchic – nor by the image of centralization implicit in the concept of political integration.[47] Yet as a multilateral institution it is *sui generis*, and studying it alone is unlikely to improve our systematic understanding of sources of variation in multilateralism.

The concepts of institutional and policy integration may, however, be helpful in studying such variation. The end of the Cold War in Europe is likely to unleash a series of changes in world politics which will surely have institutional ramifications. We can expect that the institutional innovations that result will vary considerably along the dimension of institutional integration. To account for this variation, scholars could profit not only by recalling the sophisticated discussions of the concept of integration in the regional integration literature but also by reflecting on that literature's imaginative consideration of relevant explanatory variables – which Nye referred to as 'process mechanisms,' 'structural conditions,' and 'perceptual conditions.'[48] Many of the hypotheses used to explain variations in regional integration could help to account for variations in the institutional strength or policy scope of contemporary multilateralism.

From the standpoint of research design, a major obstacle to empirical testing of regional integration theory is that there was only one case of substantial success – the European Community. A research programme with fourteen sets of variables and essentially two outcomes (success in Europe, failure elsewhere) is underspecified and therefore not testable. However, there is considerable variation in institutional integration among the scores of important multilateral institutions in existence today; and we are likely to observe more variation in the future. With sufficiently parsimonious paring of integration theory to essentials, and an assiduous search for sufficiently similar cases of

47 Keohane and Hoffmann, 'European Community politics and institutional change,' 279-82.
48 Nye, *Peace in Parts*, 64-87.

multilateralism, progress in explaining variations in institutional integration seems possible in the 1990s.

The scope of multilateral institutions
The political integration literature is also valuable insofar as it directs our attention to variation in the policy scope of multilateral institutions. We observe substantial variation in the scope of international régimes, ranging from narrowly regional to global. Such variation is apparent on such diverse issues as trade, currency areas, shipping, and regulation of the physical environment. Consider, for example, the natural resource régimes studied by Oran R. Young. Multilateral institutionalized régimes are often quite narrowly regional: Young mentions the North Pacific halibut régime, the Fraser River salmon régime, and the North Pacific fur seal régime. Yet global régimes have also been instituted, as in the case of whaling.

Young suggests from a normative standpoint that the optimal size of a regional authority for natural resources should reflect costs and benefits. Relatively small regional organizations avoid serious collective action problems and can tailor their rules to the specific conditions of the area; at some point in their expansion, transaction costs will tend to rise more rapidly than justified by the gains of increased size, such as economies of scale and the internalization of externalities within a régime.[49] Young is using what I have called a contractual approach to make a normative point, but the point is also relevant to explanation: if we assume calculating rationality by actors, we can expect that actual arrangements will *roughly* correspond to this cost-benefit logic.[50] One worthwhile way to evaluate the validity of contractual arguments would be to see whether they could explain variations in the scope of institutionalized multilateralism across issue-areas.

The scope of international régimes depends not simply on

49 Young, *International Cooperation*, 121-4.
50 Young's argument is of course similar to arguments for optimal currency areas in economics.

intra-institutional decisions but on patterns of *competition* among international institutions. In the United Nations system, for example, specialized agencies struggle fiercely for mandates and budgets, often to the detriment of co-ordinated action by the system as a whole.[51] One result of the postwar settlement of 1990 in Europe will be a struggle by European institutions – NATO, the Community, the Conference on Security and Co-operation in Europe, the Council of Europe – for mandates from states to play prominent roles in important policy areas.

WHAT ACCOUNTS FOR VARIATIONS IN PROPERTY RIGHTS AND RULES?

Ernst Haas has observed that 'all international organizations are deliberately designed by their founders to "solve problems" that require collaborative action for a solution.'[52] Problems are solved by multilateral institutions largely by creating rights and rules: as Young has argued, 'the core of every international regime is a cluster of rights and rules [whose] exact content is a matter of intense interest to these actors.'[53] People who construct institutions have purposes in doing so, and the rights and rules of institutions reflect visions of what sorts of behaviour should be encouraged or proscribed. Multilateral institutions vary in their purposes even within issue-areas, as the contrast between GATT's espousal of non-discriminatory trade and UNCTAD's emphasis on special privileges for developing countries illustrates. The content of the rights and rules of multilateral institutions changes over time. Even if we understood why certain areas of activity are regulated while others are not, and the strength and scope of multilateral institutions, we would not fully comprehend multilateralism unless we had some insights into the purposes that it is meant to serve.

The rights allocated by international régimes can be com-

---

51 The classic analysis is *A Study of the Capacity of the United Nations Development System*, a report by Sir Robert Jackson (New York: United Nations 1969).
52 Haas, *When Knowledge is Power*, 2.
53 Young, *International Cooperation*, 15.

mon-property rights, permitting free use of areas such as outer space or the deep seabed, or property rights vested in particular entities – private actors, states, or international organizations. On issues of environmental management, the option of common-property rights remains available, although areas treated as commons are progressively shrinking as technological advances facilitate access to them and as crowding effects – pollution, overexploitation of resources, and the like – become more evident. Property rights may also be contingent: multilateral insurance arrangements may be designed to provide benefits to countries hurt by lower commodity prices or by environmental catastrophes.[54]

On issues of international economic exchange, as well as many resource issues, the principal dividing line is between advocates of market arrangements and supporters of politically authoritative allocation. The debate about principles and purposes becomes a debate over markets and authority.

John Ruggie has argued that the postwar international economic order reflected a compromise that he has called 'embedded liberalism': 'Movement toward greater openness in the international economy would be coupled with safeguards that acknowledged and even facilitated the interventionist character of the modern capitalist state.'[55] Henry Nau has criticized Ruggie's view, holding that the first twenty years after World War II were characterized by market-oriented liberalism and successful economic growth, but that after the mid-1960s increasing state interventionism and attempts to meet popular demands for short-term benefits led to inflation and reduced growth rates, until markets were re-emphasized and supported by the Reagan

54 On insurance régimes, see Keohane, 'The demand for international regimes,' 167-70. However, Peter Haas finds an Interstate Guarantee Fund in the Med Plan to have been virtually a 'dead letter': *Saving the Mediterranean*, 186.

55 John Gerard Ruggie, 'Embedded liberalism revisited: progress in international economic relations,' in Beverly Crawford and Emmanuel Adler, eds, *Progress in International Relations* (New York: Columbia University Press 1990), 4. See also Ruggie, 'International regimes, transactions and change: embedded liberalism in the postwar economic order,' in Krasner, ed, *International Regimes*, 195-231.

administration.[56] Aggarwal has shown that international régimes in the textile trade have changed their nature – the objects promoted by the régime – over time, becoming more protectionist, particularly after 1977.[57] For all three authors, the fundamental conceptual point is the same: to emphasize the importance of social purposes and principles in shaping international institutions. Purposes matter, and they may change over time.[58]

The purposes of multilateral institutions not only have changed over time; they vary across issue-areas in the extent to which they are designed to support, supplement, or supplant a world market economy. Multilateral arrangements to maintain currency convertibility, the GATT régime limiting the rights of states to impose restrictions on trade, and international legal institutions providing for enforcement of contracts support the market. Lending by the World Bank or the IMF to developing countries, or arrangements such as the Multi-Fibre Arrangement in textiles, supplement, and may therefore distort, market arrangements. Proposals for a New International Economic Order or for an authoritative régime to control extraction of seabed minerals would have supplanted market mechanisms with authoritative allocation, involving either political allocation of resources or limitations on the rights of non-state actors.

Purposes matter, but so does power. The most straightforward way to account for these variations is to focus on both purposes and power together. In a major study of efforts by the Third World to transform international institutions during the 1970s, Stephen D. Krasner has sought to explain the variations in the success of Third World countries, across issue-areas, in changing market-oriented principles and norms into authorita-

56 Nau, *The Myth of America's Decline*.
57 Aggarwal, *Liberal Protectionism*, 24, figure 3.
58 Haas, *When Knowledge is Power*, emphasizes reshaping of purposes *internally*, through actions by the leaders of international organizations who learn from a combination of scientific knowledge and experience. Aggarwal, Nau, and Ruggie all stress the purposes of actors external to the international organizations, particularly leaders and high-level bureaucrats within states.

tive rules controlled by themselves. Krasner argues that 'Third World states have been able to change, to some degree, all regimes to which they had access, or in which their sovereignty could be used effectively.' But where access was denied, as in the Antarctic Treaty régime, or where the relevance of juridical sovereignty was low, as in the area of official capital transfers, the Third World has not been successful.[59] Even if otherwise weak states gain access to rule-making, their political adversaries may be able to deny legitimacy to the results: for example, the United Nations has not been able to establish itself as the principal regulator of direct foreign investment because the industrialized capitalist countries prefer to endorse voluntary codes of conduct drawn up by the OECD.

Another possible way to account for these variations would be to adopt what could be called an 'archaeological' approach to international institutions. Because institutions tend to persist over time, their rules may reflect, to some extent, the views of dominant states at the time of their founding. Understanding variation in rules across issue-areas may therefore be facilitated by examining the differences in the ideas and ideologies held by dominant groups not simply contemporaneously, but at the time when various multilateral arrangements were instituted.[60] Krasner's finding that institutional arrangements such as access rules affected the Third World's political success suggests that the characteristics of institutions themselves, derived from their origins, may affect their susceptibility to radical alteration.

59 Stephen D. Krasner, *Structural Conflict: The Third World against Global Liberalism* (Berkeley: University of California Press 1985). The quotation appears on 122-4. Krasner's book is exemplary in that it is one of the few studies of multilateralism that seeks seriously to explain variations in institutional patterns across issue-areas.

60 Judith Goldstein has pioneered this form of analysis in her examination of the institutions of protection in United States trade policy. See Goldstein, 'The political economy of trade: institutions of protection,' *American Political Science Review* 80(March 1986), 161-84.

CONCLUSIONS

The major argument of this essay is that multilateralism should be the subject of a systematic research programme. It meets the tests for a fruitful area in which to carry out research:

1 *Significance*. Multilateral institutions appear to be becoming more important in world politics and seem likely to remain significant in their effects on state policies, as well as on account of their own activities, during the foreseeable future.

2 *Unsolved puzzles*. We do not have very much solid scientific knowledge about the sources of change in multilateral institutions over time or the causes of variation across issue-areas. It is intriguing to ask why multilateralism has become so much more prevalent; precisely what the impact of multilateral institutions has been; why their institutional arrangements – including membership, strength, and scope – vary so much; and what accounts for variations in the rights and rules that they establish, and in the principles underlying those rights and rules.

3 *The availability of diverse explanatory perspectives*. A good deal of thinking has already been done about multilateral institutions, although we hardly have well-specified theories. Approaches that could be useful for explaining variations among issue-areas and multilateral institutions include: neo-realist arguments stressing relative state capabilities; arguments about interdependence and domestic politics, separately or together; contractual theories emphasizing responses to externalities, uncertainty, and transaction costs; and models of organizational adaptation and learning. None of these perspectives has established itself as superior, but all contain promising elements.

4 *Relative tractability*. Much work in international relations is bedevilled by the existence of very small numbers of instances of any reasonably homogeneous phenomenon. Many explanatory variables seem relevant, so the investigator is caught between the Scylla of indeterminacy (more

account for variations in its extent or form. My purpose in this essay is to specify some dimensions of multilateralism and to make some suggestions about possible lines of explanation of the variations thus identified. My method is to review some of the major clusters of research that have dealt with aspects of multilateralism, seeking to identify what scholars were endeavouring to explain in each research programme, and then to review the theories that they sought to devise to achieve such explanation.[2]

As noted in the definition, I limit multilateralism to arrangements involving *states*. Transnational relations are important, and issues involving transnational business alliances are fascinating; but the scope of multilateralism is so broad, even when limited to states, that I deliberately restrict the term to intergovernmental arrangements. My principal interest, furthermore, is in multilateral institutions. Institutions can be defined as persistent and connected sets of rules, formal and informal, that prescribe behavioural roles, constrain activity, and shape expectations. When we ask whether an observed pattern of behaviour constitutes or reflects an international institution, we ask whether we can identify persistent sets of rules that affect the behaviour of the actors, which in most important cases are, but need not necessarily be, states.

Multilateral institutions, then, are multilateral arrangements with persistent sets of rules; they can be distinguished from other

---

2 In working papers prepared for a research project on multilateralism, John Ruggie distinguishes what he calls 'the architectural notion of multilateralism' from multilateral institutions as conventionally defined. This architectural notion of multilateralism requires that units are indivisibly linked, that they interact on the basis of generalized principles of conduct, and that these interactions rely on expectations of diffuse rather than specific reciprocity. As Ruggie notes, this 'institution of multilateralism' is 'an extremely demanding organizational form,' requiring more self-abnegation than typically found in international régimes. I suggest that Ruggie's concept be labelled 'supralateralism,' to distinguish it more clearly from multilateralism as conventionally conceived. See 'Multilateralism: the anatomy of an institution,' a proposal by John Gerard Ruggie and collaborators, University of California Institute on Global Conflict and Cooperation, San Diego, July 1990.

forms of multilateralism, such as ad hoc meetings and short-term arrangements to solve particular problems. These institutions may take the form of international régimes – institutions with explicit rules, agreed upon by governments, that pertain to particular sets of issues in international relations – or bureaucratic organizations, which assign specific professional roles to their employees. In fact, however, régimes are usually accompanied by organizations: an international organization is established to monitor and manage a set of rules governing state behaviour in a particular issue-area. References in this essay to multilateralism will refer to multilateral institutions.

This review will suggest that multilateralism serves as a label for a cluster of fascinating issues for research. Furthermore, these issues may be connected in ways that have not been fully recognized in the literature.

THE SIGNIFICANCE OF INTERNATIONAL INSTITUTIONS

My focus on multilateral institutions presumes that institutions are significant in contemporary world politics. Yet the most influential book on international politics published during the past fifteen years essentially ignores international institutions, and its theoretical framework denies that they are fundamentally important. Kenneth Waltz's articulation of a systemic theory of international relations, self-consciously deductive and rigorous yet consistent with the core propositions of realism, challenged institutionalists by playing down the role of international institutions within 'self-help systems,' just as it annoyed students of foreign policy by stressing the primacy of international structure, without by any means denying the need for a theory of foreign policy.[3] Waltz's argument, which has come to be referred to as 'neorealism,' separates unit-level from structural elements in international politics and emphasizes the merits of structural

---

3 The *locus classicus* is Kenneth N. Waltz, *Theory of International Politics* (Reading MA: Addison-Wesley 1979). For a clear statement by Waltz on both controversies, see his 'A response to my critics,' in Robert O. Keohane, ed, *Neorealism and Its Critics* (New York: Columbia University Press 1986), 322-45.

explanatory variables than cases) and the Charybdis of truncated, invalid analysis.[61] The existence of a number of multilateral institutions, with comparable activities, memberships, and organizational arrangements, would make it possible to soften this dilemma through systematic comparative analysis. Indeed, such analysis could benefit from using sophisticated quantitative methods more often than it does now. Lisa Martin, for instance, has shown that such an analysis can tell us quite a bit about patterns of co-operation with respect to economic sanctions: for instance, the extent of co-operation on economic sanctions has been quite modest during the last several decades, but it increases with the costs of sanctions and the assistance given to the target; bandwagoning prevails over balancing; and co-operation takes place more frequently when institutions are available than when they are absent.[62] Systematic quantitative analysis should be seen not as an alternative to case-studies but as complementary to such well-established qualitative methods. Cases whose typicality or atypicality are known can more validly be used to suggest general conclusions than those picked arbitrarily; furthermore, quantitative analysis can suggest propositions that can be further evaluated through case-studies.

This issue of *International Journal* presumably reflects its editors' convictions that the time has come for systematic study of multilateral institutions. I share that view and hope that this essay and its successors will persuade you, our readers, not only to agree but to reflect on how you might participate in making this investigation a co-operative, and perhaps even more institutionalized, endeavour.

61 To methodologists, the latter problem is known as 'missing variable bias.' Stanley Hoffmann states the dilemma succinctly: 'single-cause analysis is invalid, multiple causation is valid but too complex for scientific treatment, since it is not possible to follow in all their meanderings the interrelations among a large number of factors.' Hoffmann, *Janus and Minerva* (Boulder CO: Westview 1987), 454.

62 Lisa L. Martin, 'Coercive Cooperation: Explaining Multilateral Economic Sanctions,' doctoral dissertation, Harvard University, 1990.

[4]

Multilateralism: the anatomy
of an institution John Gerard Ruggie

In 1989, peaceful change, which a leading realist theorist had declared a very low-probability event in international politics less than a decade before,[1] accommodated the most fundamental geopolitical shift of the postwar era and perhaps of the entire twentieth century: the collapse of the Soviet East European empire and the attendant end of the cold war. Many factors were responsible for that shift. But there seems little doubt that multilateral norms and institutions have helped stabilize their international consequences. Indeed, such norms and institutions appear to be playing a significant role in the management of a broad array of regional and global changes in the world system today.

In Europe, by one count at least fifteen multilateral groupings are involved in shaping the continent's collective destiny.[2] The European Community (EC) is the undisputed anchor of economic relations and increasingly of a common political vision in the West. And the former East European countries want nothing so much as to tie their economic fate to the EC, a goal that the EC

This article was prepared as the background discussion paper for the Ford Foundation West Coast Workshop on Multilateralism. Several other papers prepared for that workshop are being published in this and other issues of *International Organization,* and the entire set will be presented in John Gerard Ruggie, ed., *Multilateralism Matters: The Theory and Praxis of an Institutional Form* (New York: Columbia University Press, forthcoming). I thank the Ford Foundation for making the project possible and the University of California Institute on Global Conflict and Cooperation for orchestrating it. I am also very grateful to the other participants in the workshop for proving that multilateral cooperation under anarchy is not only feasible but can also be mutually profitable and fun; to Robert O. Keohane for his extensive and helpful critiques of an earlier draft of this article, which forced me to rethink and clarify several key issues; to Ernst B. Haas for his constructive comments; and to David Auerswald for research assistance.

1. See Robert Gilpin, *War and Change in World Politics* (New York: Cambridge University Press, 1981), p. 15: "Although ... peaceful adjustment of the systemic disequilibrium is possible, the principal mechanism of change throughout history has been war, or what we shall call hegemonic war (i.e., a war that determines which state or states will be dominant and will govern the system)."

2. See William M. Clarke, "The Midwives of the New Europe," *Central Banker* 1 (Summer 1990), pp. 49–51; and Bruce Stokes, "Continental Shift," *National Journal,* nos. 33 and 34, August 1990, pp. 1996–2001.

International Organization 46, 3, Summer 1992

members have facilitated through the creation of the European Bank for Reconstruction and Development and, in some cases, through the prospect of association agreements. Yet the author of another influential realist treatise published a decade ago gave the EC only a few fleeting references—and then only to argue that it would never amount to much in the international "structure" unless it took on the form of a unified state, which it shows no signs of doing even now.[3]

In the realm of European security relations, the central policy issue of the day concerns the adaptation of the North Atlantic Treaty Organization (NATO) to the new European geopolitical realities and the question of whether supplementary indigenous West European or all European multilateral security mechanisms should be fashioned.[4] The Soviet Union, contrary to most predictions, posed no obstacles to German reunification, betting that a united Germany firmly embedded in a broader Western institutional matrix would pose far less of a security threat than a neutral Germany tugged in different directions in the center of Europe.[5] But perhaps the most telling indicator of institutional bite in Europe today is the proverbial dog that has not barked: no one in any position of authority anywhere is advocating, or quietly preparing for, a return to a system of competitive bilateral alliances—which surely is the first time that this has happened at any comparable historical juncture since the Congress of Vienna in 1815.[6]

3. See Kenneth N. Waltz, *Theory of International Politics* (Reading, Mass.: Addison-Wesley, 1979), especially the references to a united Europe on p. 180 and the discussion on pp. 201–2.

4. Moreover, Hungary and Czechoslovakia have already joined the Council of Europe, and both have raised the issue of forging some type of affiliation with NATO. See "Prague Courts NATO," *Los Angeles Times,* 19 March 1991, p. M1.

5. Mearsheimer and others who discount the efficacy of institutions have drawn dire inferences from the end of the cold war for the future of European stability. In contrast, Snyder, Van Evera, and others who take institutions seriously have been much more prone to see an adaptive political order ahead. See John J. Mearsheimer, "Back to the Future: Instability in Europe After the Cold War," *International Security* 15 (Summer 1990), pp. 5–56; Jack Snyder, "Averting Anarchy in the New Europe," *International Security* 14 (Spring 1990), pp. 5–41; and Stephen Van Evera, "Primed for Peace: Europe After the Cold War," *International Security* 15 (Winter 1990–91), pp. 7–57.

6. In 1989, according to Weber, "some foreign policy thinkers in Paris reverted to old ideas, suggesting a new alliance with Poland, the emerging Eastern European states, and perhaps the Soviet Union as well in opposition to Germany. These flirtations with bilateral treaties and a new balance of power have been mostly left by the wayside." See Steve Weber, "Security After 1989: The Future with Nuclear Weapons," in Patrick Garrity, ed., *The Future of Nuclear Weapons* (New York: Plenum Press, forthcoming). By comparable historical junctures, I mean 1848, 1919, and 1945. After 1848, what was left of the Concert of Europe system rapidly degenerated into a system of competitive alliances; after World War I, France in particular sought the protection of bilateral alliances against Germany; and after World War II, several West European countries sought bilateral alliances with the United States and with one another. Among the useful sources for the two earlier periods are the following: Rene Albrecht-Carrie, *A Diplomatic History of Europe Since the Congress of Vienna* (New York: Harper & Row, 1958); E. H. Carr, *International Relations Between the Two World Wars* (New York: St. Martin's Press, 1961); Henry W. Degenhardt, *Treaties and Alliances of the World,* 3d ed. (Essex: Longmans, 1981); and A. J. P. Taylor, *The Struggle for Mastery of Europe,* 1848–1918 (New York: Oxford University Press, 1971).

Security relations in the Asia-Pacific region make the same points in the negative. In the immediate postwar period, it was not possible to construct multilateral institutional frameworks in this region. Today, the absence of such arrangements inhibits progressive adaptation to fundamental global shifts. The United States and Japan are loath to raise serious questions about their anachronistic bilateral defense treaty, for example, out of fear of unraveling a fragile stability and thereby triggering arms races throughout the region. In Asia-Pacific, there is no EC and no NATO to have transformed the multitude of regional security dilemmas, as has been done in Europe with Franco-German relations, for example. Indeed no Helsinki-like process through which to begin the minimal task of mutual confidence building exists in the region.[7] Thus, whereas today the potential to move beyond balance-of-power politics in its traditional form exists in Europe, a reasonably stable balance is the best that one can hope to achieve in the Asia-Pacific region.[8]

At the level of the global economy, despite sometimes near-hysterical predictions for twenty years now of imminent monetary breakup and trade wars that could become real wars, "just like in the 1930s,"[9] the rate of growth in world trade continues to exceed the rate of growth in world output; international capital flows dwarf both; and the eighth periodic round of trade negotiations, which had been prematurely pronounced dead, is moving toward completion—this time involving difficult domestic and new transnational issues that the originators of the regime never dreamed would become subject to international rules. And despite considerable tension between them, the United States and Japan continue, in Churchill's phrase, to "jaw-jaw" rather than "war-war" over their fundamental trade differences.[10]

Limited multilateral successes can be found even in the global security realm. One is in the area of nuclear nonproliferation. Many responsible officials and policy analysts in the 1960s predicted that by the 1980s there would

---

7. Some proposals along these lines are offered by Stuart Harris in " 'Architecture for a New Era' in Asia/Pacific," *Pacific Research* 3 (May 1990), pp. 8–9.

8. Latin America seems to fall somewhere in between. According to one recent assessment, "While the United States was ignoring and undermining multilateralism in the Western hemisphere, the Latin American nations themselves were moving towards greater co-operation, or *concertacion*, as they call it, to some degree as a response to United States policy." See Richard J. Bloomfield and Abraham F. Lowenthal, "Inter-American Institutions in a Time of Change," *International Journal* 45 (Autumn 1990), p. 868.

9. This refrain was begun by C. Fred Bergsten in "The New Economics and U. S. Foreign Policy," *Foreign Affairs* 50 (January 1972), pp. 199–222. For a recent rendition, see "Echoes of the 1930s," *The Economist*, 5 January 1991, pp. 15, 16, and 18.

10. On recent developments in the General Agreement on Tariffs and Trade (GATT), see Gilbert R. Winham, "GATT and the International Trade Regime," *International Journal* 45 (Autumn 1990), pp. 796–882. One real problem is that the variety of extant trade arrangements today is well beyond the scope of the traditional GATT terminology and that no new consensus exists about what types of unilateral, bilateral, and other measures are compatible or incompatible with the underlying multilateral character of GATT. This gives added relevance to the type of conceptual clarification I am proposing here.

exist some two dozen nuclear weapons states.[11] As it has turned out, however, the total set of actual *and potential* problem states today consists of only half that number. According to a former official of the U.S. Arms Control and Disarmament Agency and an analyst at the Lawrence Livermore National Laboratory, this is at least in part due to the nonproliferation treaty (NPT) regime: "Virtually every nonproliferation initiative has turned out to be much more effective than expected when it was proposed or designed, and nonproliferation success has been cheaper than expected. The fact that the nuclear proliferation problem has been 'bounded' by the NPT regime means that policy initiatives can be focused on a handful of states."[12]

Moreover, after years of being riveted by the cold war, the United Nations (UN) has been rediscovered to have utility in international conflict management: its figleaf role proved useful in Afghanistan, and its decolonization function aided Namibia. It serves as one means by which to try to disentangle regional morasses from Cambodia to the Western Sahara. And perhaps of greatest importance for the new, post–cold war era, the posture adopted by the UN Security Council to sanction Iraq for its invasion and annexation of Kuwait constituted the organization's most comprehensive, firm, and united response ever to an act of international aggression.[13]

Seen through the lenses of conventional theories of international relations, which attribute outcomes to the underlying distribution of political or economic power, the roles played by normative constraints and institutions in the current international transformation must seem paradoxical. Norms and institutions do not matter much in that literature to begin with; they are viewed as by-products of, if not epiphenomenal adjuncts to, the relations of force or the relations of production. What is more, insofar as the conventional literature has any explanation at all of extensive institutionalization in the international system, the so-called theory of hegemonic stability is it. But in addition to all the other historical and logical problems from which that theory suffers,[14]

11. Regarding these predictions, see Mitchell Reiss, *Without the Bomb: The Politics of Nuclear Nonproliferation* (New York: Columbia University Press, 1988), pp. 3–36.

12. See Thomas W. Graham and A. F. Mullins, "Arms Control, Military Strategy, and Nuclear Proliferation," paper presented at a conference entitled "Nuclear Deterrence and Global Security in Transition," Institute on Global Conflict and Cooperation, University of California, La Jolla, 21–23 February 1991, p. 3. As Graham and Mullins point out, states have left the "problem" list more rapidly than they have joined it in recent years. See also Joseph F. Pilat and Robert E. Pendley, eds., *Beyond 1995: The Future of the NPT Regime* (New York: Plenum Press, 1990).

13. As Heisbourg has suggested, it is also quite possible, though difficult to prove, that "without the decisions of the U. N. Security Council, there would have been no [international] coalition capable of weathering close to seven months of crisis and war [and] the U. S. Congress would not have approved offensive military operations in the absence of the Security Council's Resolution 678, which authorized the use of force." See Francois Heisbourg, "An Eagle Amid Less Powerful Fowl," *Los Angeles Times,* 10 March 1991, p. M5.

14. See Robert O. Keohane, "The Theory of Hegemonic Stability and Changes in International Economic Regimes, 1967–1977," in Ole R. Holsti, Randolph M. Siverson, and Alexander L. George, eds., *Change in the International System* (Boulder, Colo.: Westview Press, 1980), pp.

merely finding the hegemony to which the current array of regional and global institutional roles could be ascribed is a daunting, if not insurmountable, challenge.

The fact that norms and institutions matter comes as no surprise to the "new institutionalists" in international relations; after all, that has long been their message.[15] But, curiously, they have paid little explicit and detailed analytic attention to a core feature of current international institutional arrangements: their multilateral form. A literature search keyed on the concept of multilateralism turns up relatively few entries, and only a tiny number of these are of any interest to the international relations theorist. The focus of the new institutionalists has been on "cooperation" and "institutions" in a generic sense, with international regimes and formal organizations sometimes conceived as specific institutional subsets.[16] For example, no scholar has contributed more to the new institutionalism in international relations than Robert Keohane. Yet the concept of multilateralism is used sparingly in his work, even in a literature survey on that subject. And the definition of multilateralism that he employs is purely nominal: "the practice of co-ordinating national policies in groups of three or more states."[17]

The nominal definition of multilateralism may be useful for some purposes. But it poses the problem of subsuming institutional forms that traditionally have been viewed as being expressions of bilateralism, not multilateralism—instances of the Bismarckian alliance system, for example, such as the League

131–62; Arthur A. Stein, "The Hegemon's Dilemma: Great Britain, the United States, and the International Economic Order," *International Organization* 38 (Spring 1984), pp. 355–86; Duncan Snidal, "The Limits of Hegemonic Stability Theory," *International Organization* 39 (Autumn 1985), pp. 579–614; and John A. C. Conybeare, *Trade Wars: The Theory and Practice of International Commercial Rivalry* (New York: Columbia University Press, 1987).

15. I mean to include here both strands of theorizing identified by Keohane: the rationalist and the reflectivist. See Robert O. Keohane, "International Institutions: Two Approaches," *International Studies Quarterly* 32 (December 1988), pp. 379–96.

16. See Stephen D. Krasner, ed., *International Regimes* (Ithaca, N. Y.: Cornell University Press, 1983); Kenneth A. Oye, ed., *Cooperation Under Anarchy* (Princeton, N. J.: Princeton University Press, 1986); and Robert O. Keohane, *After Hegemony* (Princeton, N. J.: Princeton University Press, 1984).

17. See Robert O. Keohane, "Multilateralism: An Agenda for Research," *International Journal* 45 (Autumn 1990), p. 731. After introducing the concept of multilateralism and defining it in this manner, Keohane essentially goes on to discuss international institutions in the generic sense. See also Keohane, *After Hegemony,* in which there are but two fleeting references to multilateralism, both to specific agreements in trade; and Keohane, *International Institutions and State Power* (Boulder, Colo.: Westview Press, 1989), which contains no entry under multilateralism in its index. I must admit that these criticisms apply as well to my own writings on the subject of institutions. Keohane has kindly referred to a 1975 paper of mine as having "foreshadowed much of the conceptual work of the next decade." Alas, it also foreshadowed this blind spot, having been concerned primarily with differentiating the study of international organization from the study of formal international organizations—hence, the introduction of the concept of "regimes." See Keohane, "Multilateralism," p. 755, fn. 44, referring to Ruggie, "International Responses to Technology: Concepts and Trends," *International Organization* 29 (Summer 1975), pp. 557–83.

of the *Three* Emperors. In short, the nominal definition of multilateralism misses the *qualitative* dimension of the phenomenon that makes it distinct.[18]

In a superb discussion of this issue, attempting to sort out the enormous variety of trade relations in the world today, William Diebold insists for starters on the need to distinguish between "formal" and "substantive" multilateralism, by which he means roughly what I mean by nominal versus qualitative. "But that is far from the end of the matter. The bilateral agreements of Cordell Hull were basically different from those of Hjalmar Schacht."[19] That is to say, the issue is not the number of parties so much, Diebold suggests, as it is the kind of relations that are instituted among them. It is this substantive or qualitative characteristic of multilateralism that concerns me in the present essay, not only for trade but also for the institutional dimension of international relations in general.

Nor is the missing qualitative dimension captured entirely by the concepts of international regimes or intergovernmental organizations. There are instances of international regimes that were not multilateral in form, such as the Nazi trade and monetary regimes, to which we will return momentarily. As for multilateral formal organizations, although they entail no analytic mystery, all practitioners of the new institutionalism agree that these organizations constitute only one small part of a broader universe of international institutional forms that interest them.

The missing qualitative dimension of multilateralism immediately comes into focus, however, if we return to an older institutionalist discourse, one informed by the postwar aims of the United States to restructure the international order. When we speak here of multilateralism in international trade, we know immediately that it refers to trade organized on the basis of certain principles of state conduct—above all, nondiscrimination.[20] Similarly, when we speak here of multilateralism in security relations, we know that it refers to some expression or other of collective security or collective self-defense.[21] And when President George Bush today enunciates a "new world order" for the Middle

---

18. In the UN context, what Keohane defines as multilateral is called multi*national*—for example, the multinational (non-UN) observer team in the Sinai. In the UN, only that is considered multilateral which is duly authorized by a multilateral forum. But if Keohane's definition is analytically too loose, the UN conception is too limiting, as I discuss later in my article.

19. See William Diebold, Jr., "The History and the Issues," in William Diebold, Jr., ed., *Bilateralism, Multilateralism and Canada in U. S. Trade Policy* (Cambridge, Mass.: Ballinger, 1988), p. 1. Diebold seeks to formulate some principled basis for distinguishing what kind of recent trade measures—unilateral, bilateral, and what he calls plurilateral—are consistent with, and what kind undermine, the principles of multilateralism on which the GATT regime is based.

20. See ibid.; Richard N. Gardner, *Sterling-Dollar Diplomacy in Current Perspective*, rev. ed. (New York: Columbia University Press, 1980); Jacob Viner, "Conflicts of Principle in Drafting a Trade Charter," *Foreign Affairs* 25 (July 1947), pp. 612–28; Herbert Feis, "The Conflict over Trade Ideologies," *Foreign Affairs* 25 (January 1947), pp. 217–28; and Robert Pollard, *Economic Security and the Origins of the Cold War* (New York: Columbia University Press, 1985).

21. See Robert Dallek, *Franklin D. Roosevelt and American Foreign Policy* (New York: Oxford University Press, 1979); John Lewis Gaddis, *The Long Peace* (New York: Oxford University Press, 1987), pp. 3–47; and Pollard, *Economic Security and the Origins of the Cold War*.

East and elsewhere—universal aspirations, cooperative deterrence, and joint action against aggression[22]—whether it constitutes vision or rhetoric, the notion evokes and is entirely consistent with the American postwar multilateralist agenda, as I argue below. In sum, what is distinctive about multilateralism is not merely that it coordinates national policies in groups of three or more states, which is something that other organizational forms also do, but that it does so on the basis of certain principles of ordering relations among those states.

Thus, there exists a compound anomaly in the world of international relations theory today. An institutional phenomenon of which conventional theories barely take note is both widespread and significant; but at the same time, the particular features that make it so are glossed over by most students of international institutions themselves. This article is intended to help resolve both parts of the anomaly.

The premise of the present article is that we can better understand the role of multilateral norms and institutions in the current international transformation by recovering the principled meanings of multilateralism from actual historical practice; by showing how and why those principled meanings have come to be institutionalized throughout the history of the modern interstate system; and by exploring how and why they may perpetuate themselves today, even as the conditions that initially gave rise to them have changed.

This "grounded" analysis of the concept suggests a series of working hypotheses, which require more extensive testing before strong validity claims can be made for them. Nevertheless, I and my fellow contributors to this symposium on multilateralism believe that the hypotheses are sufficiently interesting and that the case we make for them is sufficiently plausible to warrant such further study, and we present them here in that spirit.[23] The argument, in brief, goes something like this: Multilateralism is a generic institutional form of modern international life, and as such it has been present from the start. The generic institutional form of multilateralism must not be confused with formal multilateral organizations, a relatively recent arrival and still of only relatively modest importance. Historically, the generic form of multilateralism can be found in institutional arrangements to define and stabilize the international property rights of states, to manage coordination problems, and to resolve collaboration problems. The last of these uses of the multilateral form is historically the least frequent. In the literature, this fact traditionally has been explained by the rise and fall of hegemonies and, more recently, by various functional considerations. Our analysis suggests that a

---

22. George Bush, cited in "President Bush's Address to Congress on End of the Gulf War," *The New York Times*, 7 March 1991, p. A8.

23. See the following articles in this issue of *IO*: James A. Caporaso, "International Relations Theory and Multilateralism: The Search for Foundations"; Miles Kahler, "Multilateralism with Small and Large Numbers"; and Steve Weber, "Shaping the Postwar Balance of Power: Multilateralism in NATO." See also the contributions to Ruggie, *Multilateralism Matters*.

permissive domestic environment in the leading powers of the day is at least as important and, in some cases, more important. When we look more closely at the post–World War II situation, for example, we find that it was less the fact of American *hegemony* that accounts for the explosion of multilateral arrangements than it was the fact of *American* hegemony. Finally, we suggest that institutional arrangements of the multilateral form have adaptive and even reproductive capacities which other institutional forms may lack and which, therefore, may help explain the roles that multilateral arrangements play in stabilizing the current international transformation.

The meanings of multilateralism

At its core, multilateralism refers to coordinating relations among three or more states in accordance with certain principles. But what, precisely, are those principles? And to what, precisely, do those principles pertain? To facilitate the construction of a more formal definition, let us begin by examining an historical instance of something that everyone agrees multilateralism is not: bilateralism.

Earlier in this century, Nazi Germany succeeded in finely honing a pure form of bilateralism into a systemic organizing principle. Now, as Diebold notes, the everyday term "bilateral" is entirely neutral with regard to the qualitative relationship that is instituted among countries.[24] So as to give expression to its qualitative nature, the Nazi system therefore typically has been referred to as bilateral*ist* in character or as embodying bilateral*ism* as its organizing principle. In any case, once the New Plan of the Nazi government took effect in 1934, Hjalmar Schacht devised a scheme of bilateralist trade agreements and clearing arrangements.[25] The essence of the German international trade regime was that the state negotiated "reciprocal" agreements with its foreign trading partners. These negotiations determined which goods and services were to be exchanged, their quantities, and their price. Often, Germany deliberately imported more from its partners than it exported to them. But it required that its trading partners liquidate their claims on Germany by reinvesting there or by purchasing deliberately overpriced German goods. Thus, its trading partners were doubly dependent on Germany.

This trade regime in turn was linked to bilateralist monetary clearing arrangements. Under these arrangements, a German importer would, for example, pay marks to the German Reichsbank for its imports rather than to the foreign source of the goods or services, while the foreign counterpart of the

24. Diebold, "The History and the Issues."
25. The classic and appropriately titled study of the Nazi system is Albert O. Hirschman's *National Power and the Structure of Foreign Trade* (1945; reprint, Berkeley: University of California Press, 1980). See also Leland B. Yeager, *International Monetary Relations: Theory, History, and Policy* (New York: Harper & Row, 1976), pp. 357–76.

transaction would receive payment in home country currency from its central bank—and vice versa for German exports. No foreign exchange changed hands; the foreign exchange markets were bypassed; and artificial exchange rates prevailed. The permissible total amounts to be cleared in this manner were negotiated by the two states.

German bilateralism typically but not exclusively focused on smaller and weaker states in East Central Europe, the Balkans, and Latin America, exchanging primary commodity imports for manufactured exports. But the scheme had no inherent limit; it could have been geographically universalized to cover the entire globe, with an enormous spiderweb of bilateralist agreements radiating out from Germany.[26]

The nominal definition of multilateralism would not exclude the Schachtian bilateralist device: it coordinated economic relations among more than three states. Nor is the fact decisive that negotiations took place bilaterally: after all, many tariff reductions in the General Agreement on Tariffs and Trade (GATT) are also negotiated bilaterally. The difference is, of course, that within GATT bilaterally negotiated tariff reductions are extended to all other parties on the basis of most-favored-nation (MFN) treatment, whereas the Schachtian scheme was inherently and fundamentally discriminatory, so that bilateral deals held only on a case-by-case and product-by-product basis, even if they covered the entire globe in doing so.

Let us examine next an institutional arrangement that is generally acknowledged to embody multilateralist principles: a collective security system. None has ever existed in pure form, but in principle the scheme is quite simple. It rests on the premise that peace is indivisible, so that a war against one state is, ipso facto, considered a war against all. The community of states therefore is obliged to respond to threatened or actual aggression, first by diplomatic means, then through economic sanctions, and finally by the collective use of force if necessary. Facing the prospect of such a community-wide response, any rational potential aggressor would be deterred and would desist. Thus, the incidence of war gradually would decline.

A collective security scheme certainly coordinates security relations among three or more states. But so, too, as noted above, did the League of the Three Emperors, which was nothing more than a set of traditional alliances.[27] What is distinct about a collective security scheme is that it comprises, as Sir Arthur Salter put it a half-century ago, a permanent potential alliance "against the *unknown* enemy"[28]—and, he should have added, in behalf of the *unknown* victim. The institutional difference between an alliance and a collective security

---

26. Several major states, including Great Britain and the United States, had limited agreements with Germany involving *Sondermarks*—marks which foreigners could earn through the sale of specified products to Germany but which Germany in turn restricted to particular purchases from Germany.

27. Taylor, *The Struggle for Mastery of Europe,* chap. 12.

28. Arthur Salter, *Security* (London: Macmillan, 1939), p. 155; emphasis in original.

scheme can be simply put: in both instances, state A is pledged to come to the aid of B if B is attacked by C. In a collective security scheme, however, A is also pledged to come to the aid of C if C is attacked by B. Consequently, as G. F. Hudson points out, "A cannot regard itself as the ally of B more than of C, because theoretically it is an open question whether, if an act of war should occur, B or C would be the aggressor. In the same way B has indeterminate obligations towards A and C, and C towards A and B, and so on with a vast number of variants as the system is extended to more and more states."[29] It was precisely this difference between a collective security system and an alliance that ultimately doomed the fate of the League of Nations in the U. S. Senate.[30]

The United States frequently invoked the collective security model in leading the anti-Iraq coalition in the Persian Gulf crisis and then in war, though what if any permanent institutional consequences will follow from that effort remains to be seen.[31] NATO reflects a truncated version of the model, in which a subset of states organized a collective self-defense scheme of indefinite duration, de jure against any potential aggressor though de facto against one. Nevertheless, internally the scheme was predicated on two multilateralist principles. The first was the indivisibility of threats to the collectivity—that is, it did not matter whether it was Germany, Great Britain, the Netherlands, or Norway that was attacked, nor in theory by whom—and the second was the requirement of an unconditional collective response.[32]

We are now in a position to be more precise about the core meaning of multilateralism. Keohane has defined institutions, generically, as "persistent and connected sets of rules, formal and informal, that prescribe behavioural roles, constrain activity, and shape expectations."[33] Very simply, the term "multilateral" is an adjective that modifies the noun "institution." Thus,

29. See G. F. Hudson, "Collective Security and Military Alliances," in Herbert Butterfield and Martin Wight, eds., *Diplomatic Investigations* (Cambridge, Mass.: Harvard University Press, 1968), pp. 176–77. See also Charles A. Kupchan and Clifford A. Kupchan, "Concerts, Collective Security, and the Future of Europe," *International Security* 16 (Summer 1991), pp. 114–61.

30. Contrary to folklore, Woodrow Wilson was not prepared to commit the United States to specific and automatic military obligations under the League of Nations; his collective security scheme would have relied on public opinion, arms limitations, and arbitration more than on enforcement mechanisms. Senator Henry Cabot Lodge's fundamental objection to the League of Nations was that its permanence and universalism would entail limitless entanglements for the United States. Lodge in turn favored stronger and more specific security guarantees to France and against Germany. See Lloyd E. Ambrosius, *Woodrow Wilson and the American Diplomatic Tradition* (New York: Cambridge University Press, 1987), pp. 51–106.

31. The key shortcoming of collective security UN style is, of course, that the UN has no means of its own to implement a military response to aggression, since no state has ever negotiated an Article 43 agreement making standby forces available. After the war in the Persian Gulf, the U. S. ambassador to the UN, Thomas Pickering, proposed the reconsideration of Article 43 provisions in speeches before the Veterans of Foreign Wars on 4 March 1991 and before the American Bar Association on 26 April 1991 in Washington, D. C.

32. French absence from the unified command and U. S. control over nuclear weapons complicate matters further.

33. Keohane, "Multilateralism," p. 732.

multilateralism depicts a *generic institutional form* in international relations. How does multilateral modify institution? Our illustrations suggest that multilateralism is an institutional form which coordinates relations among three or more states on the basis of "generalized" principles of conduct—that is, principles which specify appropriate conduct for a class of actions, without regard to the particularistic interests of the parties or the strategic exigencies that may exist in any specific occurrence. MFN treatment is a classic example in the economic realm: it forbids discrimination among countries producing the same product. Its counterpart in security relations is the requirement that states respond to aggression whenever and wherever it occurs—whether or not any specific instance suits their individual likes and dislikes. In contrast, the bilateralist form, such as the Schachtian device and traditional alliances, differentiates relations case-by-case based precisely on a priori particularistic grounds or situational exigencies.

Bilateralism and multilateralism do not exhaust the institutional repertoire of states. Imperialism can be considered a third generic institutional form. Imperialism also is an institution that coordinates relations among three or more states though, unlike bilateralism and multilateralism, it does so by denying the sovereignty of the subject states.[34]

Two corollaries follow from our definition of multilateralism. First, generalized organizing principles logically entail an indivisibility among the members of a collectivity with respect to the range of behavior in question. Depending on circumstances, that indivisibility can take markedly different forms, ranging from the physical ties of railway lines that the collectivity chooses to standardize across frontiers, all the way to the adoption by states of the premise that peace is indivisible. But note that indivisibility here is a *social construction,* not a technical condition: in a collective security scheme, states behave as if peace were indivisible and thereby make it so. Similarly, in the case of trade, it is the GATT members' adherence to the MFN norm which makes the system of trade an indivisible whole, not some inherent attribute of trade itself.[35] Bilateralism, in contrast, segments relations into multiples of dyads and compartmentalizes them. Second, as discussed in further detail below, successful cases of multilateralism in practice appear to generate among their members what Keohane has called expectations of "diffuse reciprocity."[36] That is to say, the arrangement is expected by its members to yield a rough equivalence of benefits in the aggregate and over time. Bilateralism, in contrast, is premised

34. See Michael Doyle, *Empires* (Ithaca, N. Y.: Cornell University Press, 1986), pp. 19–47. Some of the more predatory expressions of the Nazi arrangements came very close to if they did not actually constitute the imperial form.

35. Obviously, the existence of nuclear weapons, economic interdependence, externalities, or other technical factors can and probably does affect the social constructions that states choose. I am not imputing causality here, simply clarifying a concept.

36. Robert O. Keohane, "Reciprocity in International Relations," *International Organization* 40 (Winter 1986), pp. 1–27.

on specific reciprocity, the simultaneous balancing of specific quids-pro-quos by each party with every other at all times.[37]

It follows from this definition and its corollaries that multilateralism is a highly demanding institutional form. Its historical incidence, therefore, is likely to be less frequent than that of its alternatives; and if its relative incidence at any time were to be high, that fact would pose an interesting puzzle to be explained.

The obvious next issue to address is the fact that, as Keohane points out, the generic concept of international institution applies in practice to many different types of institutionalized relations among states.[38] So too, therefore, does the adjective multilateral: the generic attribute of multilateralism, that it coordinates relations among three or more states in accordance with generalized principles of conduct, will have different specific expressions depending on the type of institutionalized relations to which it pertains. Let us examine some instances. Common usage in the literature distinguishes among three institutional domains of interstate relations: international orders, international regimes, and international organizations. Each type can be, but need not be, multilateral in form.

The literature frequently refers to international economic orders, international security orders, international maritime orders, and so on. An "open" or "liberal" international economic order is multilateral in form, as is a maritime order based on the principle of *mare liberum*. The New Economic Order of the Nazis was not multilateral in form, for reasons that have already been suggested, and neither was the European security order crafted by Bismarck. The concept of multilateralism here refers to the constitutive rules that order relations in given domains of international life—their architectural dimension, so to speak. Thus, the quality of "openness" in an international economic order refers to such characteristics as the prohibition of exclusive blocs, spheres, or similar barriers to the conduct of international economic relations. The corresponding quality in an international security order—the quality that would cause it to be described as "collective"—is the condition of equal access to a common security umbrella. To the extent that the characteristic condition or conditions are met, the order in question may be said to be multilateral in form. In short, multilateralism here depicts the character of an overall order of relations among states; definitionally it says nothing about *how* that order is achieved.

A regime is more concrete than an order. Typically, the term "regime" refers to a functional or sectoral component of an order. Moreover, the concept of

37. Bilateral balancing need not imply equality; it simply means establishing a mutually acceptable balance between the parties, however that is determined in practice. For an extended discussion of this difference, see Karl Polanyi, "The Economy as Instituted Process," in Karl Polanyi, Conrad M. Arensberg, and Harry W. Pearson, eds., *Trade and Market in the Early Empires* (Glencoe, Ill.: Free Press, 1957), pp. 243–70.

38. Keohane, "International Institutions."

regime encompasses more of the "how" question than does the concept of order in that, broadly speaking, the term "regime" is used to refer to common, deliberative, though often highly asymmetrical means of conducting interstate relations. That much is clear from common usage. But while there is a widespread assumption in the literature that all regimes are, ipso facto, multilateral in character, this assumption is egregiously erroneous. For example, there is no reason not to call the Schachtian schemes for organizing monetary and trade relations international regimes; they fully meet the standard criteria specified by Stephen Krasner and his colleagues.[39] Moreover, it is entirely possible to imagine the emergence of regimes between *two* states—superpower security regimes, for example, were a topic of some discussion in the 1980s[40]—but such regimes by definition would not be multilateral either. In sum, what makes a regime a *regime* is that it satisfies the definitional criteria of encompassing principles, norms, rules, and decision-making procedures around which actor expectations converge. But in and of themselves, those terms are empty of substance. What makes a regime *multilateral* in form, beyond involving three or more states, is that the substantive meanings of those terms roughly reflect the appropriate generalized principles of conduct. By way of illustration, in the case of a multilateral trade regime, these would include the norm of MFN treatment, corresponding rules about reciprocal tariff reductions and the application of safeguards, and collectively sanctioned procedures for implementing the rules. In the case of a collective security regime, they would include the norm of nonaggression, uniform rules for use of sanctions to deter or punish aggression, and, again, collectively sanctioned procedures for implementing them.

Finally, formal international organizations are palpable entities with headquarters and letterheads, voting procedures, and generous pension plans. They require no conceptual elaboration. But, again, their relationship to the concept of multilateralism is less self-evident than is sometimes assumed. Two issues deserve brief mention. The first issue, though it may be moot at the moment, is that there have been international organizations that were not multilateral in form. The Comintern and the Cominform come to mind; they were based explicitly on Leninist principles of organization, which were quite different from their multilateral counterparts.[41] Along the same lines, the recently collapsed Soviet–East European system of organizations differed from multilateral forms in ways that students of international organization never fully came

39. Krasner, *International Regimes.*
40. Steve Weber predicted the emergence of a superpower security regime in "Realism, Detente, and Nuclear Weapons," *International Organization* 44 (Winter 1990), pp. 55–82. Robert Jervis discussed the possibility in two of his works: "Security Regimes," in Krasner, *International Regimes*, pp. 173–94; and "From Balance to Concert: A Study of International Security Cooperation," *World Politics* 38 (October 1985), pp. 58–79.
41. See Franz Borkenau, *World Communism: A History of the Communist International*, with an introduction by Raymond Aron (Ann Arbor: University of Michigan Press, 1962).

to grips with.[42] The second issue is more problematic even today. There is a common tendency in the world of actual international organizations, and sometimes in the academic community, to equate the very phenomenon of multilateralism with the universe of multilateral organizations or diplomacy. The preceding discussion makes it clear why that view is in error. It may be the case empirically that decisions concerning aspects of international orders or, more likely, international regimes in fact are made in multilateral forums. The EC exhibits this empirical pattern most extensively; the failed quest by developing countries for a New International Economic Order in the 1970s exhibits the desire to achieve it; and decisions on most international trade and monetary matters fall somewhere in between. But definitionally, "multilateral organization" is a separate and distinct type of institutionalized behavior, defined by such generalized decision-making rules as voting or consensus procedures.

In sum, the term "multilateral" is an adjective that modifies the noun institution. What distinguishes the multilateral form from other forms is that it coordinates behavior among three or more states on the basis of generalized principles of conduct. Accordingly, any theory of international institutions that does not include this qualitative dimension of multilateralism is bound to be a fairly abstract theory and one that is silent about a crucial distinction within the repertoire of international institutional forms. Moreover, for analytic purposes, it is important not to (con)fuse the very meaning of multilateralism with any one particular institutional expression of it, be it an international order, regime, or organization. Each can be, but need not be, multilateral in form. In addition, the multilateral form should not be equated with universal geographical scope; the attributes of multilateralism characterize relations within specific collectivities that may and often do fall short of the whole universe of nations. Finally, it should be kept in mind that these are formal definitions, not empirical descriptions of actual cases, and we would not expect actual cases to conform fully to the formal definitions. But let us turn now to some actual historical cases exhibiting the multilateral form.

Multilateralism in history

The institutional form of multilateralism has now been defined. What can we say about its specific expressions over time, their frequency distribution, and some possible correlates? A brief historical survey will situate the phenomenon better and help us begin to answer these questions. To organize the discussion,

---

42. See Gerard Holden, "The End of an Alliance: Soviet Policy and the Warsaw Pact, 1989–90," *PRIF Reports* (Peace Research Institute, Frankfurt), no. 16, December 1990.

I adapt a standard typology of institutional roles from the literature: defining and stabilizing international property rights, solving coordination problems, and resolving collaboration problems.[43]

Property rights

Not surprisingly, the earliest multilateral arrangements instituted in the modern era were designed to cope with the international consequences of the novel principle of state sovereignty. The newly emerged territorial states conceived their essence, their very being, by the possession of territory and the exclusion of others from it. But how does one possess something one does not own? And, still more problematic, how does one exclude others from it?

The world's oceans posed this problem. Contiguous waterways could be shared, administered jointly, or, more than likely, split down the middle; the international property rights of states thereby were established bilaterally. The oceans were another matter. States attempted to project exclusive unilateral jurisdiction, but they failed. Spain and Portugal tried a bilateral solution, whereby Spain claimed a monopoly of the western trade routes to the Far East and Portugal claimed the eastern routes. But they, too, failed. All such efforts failed for the simple reason that it is exceedingly difficult if not impossible in the long run to vindicate a property right that is not recognized as being valid by the relevant others in a given community, especially when exclusion is as difficult as it was in the oceans. Attempts to do so lead to permanent challenge and recurrent conflict. A multilateral solution to the governance of the oceans, therefore, was inescapable. The principle which was first enunciated by Hugo Grotius at the beginning of the seventeenth century and which states slowly came to adopt was one that defined an international maritime order in two parts: a territorial sea under exclusive state control, which custom eventually set at three miles because that was the range of land-based cannons at the time; and the high seas beyond, available for common use but owned by none.[44] Under this arrangement, all states were free to utilize the high seas, provided

43. The distinction between coordination and collaboration was proposed by Arthur Stein in "Coordination and Collaboration: Regimes in an Anarchic World," in Krasner, *International Regimes,* pp. 115–40. See also Duncan Snidal, "IGO's, Regimes, and Cooperation: Challenges for International Relations Theory," in Margaret P. Karns and Karen A. Mingst, eds., *The United States and Multilateral Institutions* (Boston: Unwin Hyman, 1990), pp. 321–50; and Lisa Martin, "Interests, Power, and Multilateralism," *International Organization,* forthcoming. The international property rights of states invariably are taken for granted, however, even though their stable definition is logically and temporally prior to the other two collective action problems. I have therefore added this dimension.

44. For a brief review of this subject and an interesting discussion of how global warming and rising sea levels may affect these practices, see David D. Caron, "When Law Makes Climate Change Worse: Rethinking the Law of Baselines in Light of a Rising Sea Level," *Ecology Law Quarterly,* vol. 17, no. 4, 1990, pp. 621–53.

only that they did not thereby damage the legitimate interests of others.[45] And each state had the same rules for all states, not one rule for some and other rules for others.

An even more profound instance of delimiting the property rights of states—more profound because it concerned internal, as opposed to external, space—was the invention of the principle of extraterritoriality as the basis for organizing permanent diplomatic representation. As Garrett Mattingly put it in his magisterial study of the subject: "By arrogating to themselves supreme power over men's consciences, the new states had achieved absolute sovereignty. Having done so, they found they could only communicate with one another by tolerating within themselves little islands of alien sovereignty."[46] Instituting those little islands of alien sovereignty in the end required a multilateral solution, though differential arrangements based on the religious preferences and social status of rulers were tried first. And their maintenance came to be seen as being necessary to the very existence of a viable political order among states.[47] As a result, grave breaches of the principle of extraterritoriality are, ipso facto, deemed to be a violation against the entire community of states.[48]

Until quite recently, neither regimes nor formal organizations played significant roles in the definition and stabilization of international property rights. Conventional practice and episodic treaty negotiations sufficed to establish multilateral orders of relations.

Coordination problems

States have strong and conflicting preferences about international property rights. In the case of the oceans, for example, coastal states were favored over landlocked states by the allocation of *any* territorial sea; different coastal states ended up with differentially sized territorial seas by virtue of the length of their coastlines; coastal states nevertheless would have preferred no limit at all to the territorial sea; and so on. There also exists a class of problems in international relations wherein states are more or less indifferent in principle to the actual

---

45. It took until the early eighteenth century before piracy, frequently state-sponsored, came to be generally defined as being inherently damaging to the legitimate interests of states. See Robert C. Ritchie, *Captain Kidd and the War Against the Pirates* (Cambridge, Mass.: Harvard University Press, 1986).

46. Garrett Mattingly, *Renaissance Diplomacy* (Baltimore, Md.: Penguin Books, 1964), p. 244.

47. On the emergence of the perception that extraterritoriality played a systemic role, see Adda B. Bozeman, *Politics and Culture in International History* (Princeton, N. J.: Princeton University Press, 1960), especially pp. 479–80.

48. Note in this connection that UN Security Council Resolution 667 *"strongly* condemns" Iraq for *"aggressive acts perpetrated.*.. against diplomatic premises and personnel in Kuwait," whereas Resolution 660, passed in response to Iraq's invasion of Kuwait, merely "condemns" the invasion, without embellishment. The full texts are contained in UN Security Council, S/RES/667, 16 September 1990, and S/RES/660, 2 August 1990; emphasis added.

outcome, provided only that all accept the same outcome. These are typically referred to as coordination problems.[49]

A paradigmatic case of a coordination problem in the mid-nineteenth century was posed by electronic telegraphy and concerned what would happen to a message as it came, for instance, to the border between France and the Grand Duchy of Baden. The following procedure was instituted: "A common station was established at Strasbourg with two employees, one from the French Telegraph Administration, the other from Baden. The French employee received, for example, a telegram from Paris, which the electric wires had transmitted to him with the speed of light. This message he wrote out by hand onto a special form and handed it across the table to his German colleague. He translated it into German, and then sent it again on its way."[50] However, with the intensification of trade, the desire for the latest stock market information from London, Paris, and Berlin, and important diplomatic messages that governments wished to send to one another, this arrangement became untenable. Its costs in profits lost, opportunities foregone, and administrative resources expended mounted rapidly. The initial response was to negotiate a series of bilateral treaties. But in the dense communications complex of the European continent, bilateral solutions soon also proved inadequate. Several multilateral arrangements were therefore constructed and were subsequently combined in 1865, when the International Telegraph Union was established.

The multilateral arrangement for telegraphy consisted of three parts. First, the parties devised rules concerning the network of telegraph lines that were to connect countries within Europe (and, later, in other parts of the world), the codes to be used, the agreed priorities of transmission, the languages that were permissible, the schedule of tariffs to be levied, the manner in which proceeds would be divided, and so on. Second, they established a permanent secretariat to administer the day-to-day implementation of these rules and to coordinate the technical operations of the system. And, third, they convened periodic conferences to make any such revisions in the basic system as became necessary over time.

Much the same kind of arrangement had already been anticipated in the domain of European river transport, as on the Rhine and the Danube, typically consisting of commissions, secretariats, and judicial bodies—and, in some instances, even uniforms for officials.[51] Later in the nineteenth century, similar multilateral arrangements were instituted in the field of public health.[52]

In situations exhibiting coordination problems, the incentives are high for

---

49. Stein, "Coordination and Collaboration."
50. International Telecommunications Union (ITU), *From Semaphore to Satellite* (Geneva: ITU, 1965), p. 45.
51. J. P. Chamberlain, *The Regime of International Rivers* (New York: Carnegie Endowment for International Peace, 1923).
52. Ernst B. Haas, *Beyond the Nation State* (Stanford, Calif.: Stanford University Press, 1964), pp. 14–17.

states to order their relations on the basis of generalized principles of conduct. At least in the long run, therefore, the desire to reduce transaction costs tends to become a driving factor. Not surprisingly, historically the highest incidence of multilateral regimes and organizations is found in this domain.

Collaboration problems

Where the definition and stabilization of at least some international property rights is concerned, there appears to exist an ultimate inevitability to multilateral solutions, although "ultimate" may mean after all possible alternatives, including war, have been exhausted. In cases of coordination problems, there appears to exist an ultimate indifference as to which one of several outcomes is selected, although "ultimate" here may mask such concrete problems as sunk investments that individual states may have in the "equally acceptable" outcome that did not get adopted.

Between the two extremes of inevitability and indifference lies the domain of mixed-motive, conflict of interest situations. Even in this domain, however, cooperation occurs. And sometimes it occurs on a multilateral basis. Before 1945, however, it did not do so very often.

In the security realm, the most celebrated case is the Concert of Europe, a case in which students of international relations have paid far more attention to the issue of whether or not it constituted a security regime than to the fact that it exhibited elements of the multilateral form. Charles and Clifford Kupchan have recently provided us with a useful continuum of collective security arrangements, with the "ideal" form at one end and concerts at the other. We have already examined the formal attributes of the "ideal" model. According to the Kupchans, the concert version is characterized by the dominance of the great powers, decisions taken by informal negotiations and consensus, and no explicit specification of the mechanisms for implementing collective action. But—and this is what puts it in the class of collective security mechanisms—a concert nevertheless is "predicated on the notion of all against one."[53] That is, a concert is predicated on the indivisibility of peace among its members and on their nondiscretionary obligation to respond to acts of aggression.

Between the Napoleonic and the Crimean wars, from 1815 to 1854, peace in Europe was maintained, in Henry Kissinger's words, by an institutional "framework" that was regarded by participants as being "legitimate," so that

---

53. See Kupchan and Kupchan, "Concerts, Collective Security, and the Future of Europe," p. 120. Note also the following analysis of the Treaty of Paris (1815) offered by historian Richard Langhorne in "Reflections on the Significance of the Congress of Vienna," *Review of International Studies* 12 (October 1986), p. 317: "There appeared at clause 6, in what was certainly Castlereagh's drafting, [a shift in] emphasis from a specific guarantee to a scheme for the continuous management of the international system by the great powers."

"they sought adjustment within [it] rather than in its overthrow."[54] In doing so, according to Robert Jervis, they "behaved in ways that sharply diverged from normal 'power politics.' "[55]

As Jervis describes it, the five leading powers—Austria, Great Britain, Prussia, Russia, and a French monarchy restored with the aid of the other four—refrained from seeking to maximize their relative power positions vis-à-vis one another, instead moderating their demands and behavior; they refrained from exploiting one another's temporary weaknesses and vulnerabilities; and they threatened force sparingly and used it rarely as a means to resolve differences among them—except, Kal Holsti adds, that they "were clearly of the opinion that force could be used individually or collectively for enforcing certain decisions and for coercing those who threatened the foundations of the order or the system of governance."[56]

How were these feats achieved? The five powers constituted themselves as "an executive body" of the European international system,[57] convening extensive multilateral consultations through which they acted on matters that could have undermined the peace. For example, they collectively created and guaranteed the neutrality of Belgium and Greece, thereby removing those territories from the temptations of bilateral partition or competition. As Rene Albrecht-Carrie has argued, the "Eastern question" in general—that is, the problem of how to secure orderly change and national independence in the wake of the irreversible decay of the Ottoman Empire—"provides many illustrations of an authentic common preference for orderly and peaceful procedure, more than once successfully implemented."[58]

What could account for this unusual institutional development? It seems that the threat posed by Napoleon's imperial ambitions to the very principle of the balance of power proved weightier than the usual risks and uncertainties that plague cooperation in the security realm. Moreover, the threat posed by the French revolutionary wars to the very principle of dynastic rule seems to have proved weightier than the differences in domestic social formations, such as those existing between liberal and protestant England on the one hand and the more conservative and catholic Austria and orthodox Russia on the other. These two threats helped crystalize the norm of systemic stability—the

54. See Henry A. Kissinger, *A World Restored* (New York: Universal Library, 1964), p. 5. Kissinger concentrates on the *Congress* system, a subset of the Concert of Europe, which ended by about 1823, but my commentary holds for the entire concert system.

55. See Robert Jervis, "Security Regimes," p. 178. See also Jervis, "From Balance to Concert"; and Richard B. Elrod, "The Concert of Europe: A Fresh Look at an International System," *World*

"repose" of Europe was the term the five preferred[59]—that the concert was geared to sustain. They emboldened states to place a *collective* bet on their future. And the multilateral consultations instituted via the concert limited the extent of cheating on that bet by providing a forum within which intelligence could be shared, actor intentions questioned, and justifications for actions proferred and assessed.

The Concert of Europe gradually eroded not only because the memory of the initial threats faded but also because over time the parameters of the situation were transformed. Above all else, the revolutions of 1848 seriously shook the prevailing concept of legitimate political order from within, and the sense of international cohesion diverged sharply thereafter. "I do not see Europe anymore," a French foreign minister lamented at the time.[60] In the second half of the nineteenth century, multilateral consultation and self-restraint yielded to the striving for unilateral advantage checked only by external constraints, while bilateral alliance formation was raised to a new level of sophistication by Bismarck.

In the economic realm, the nineteenth century witnessed what economists consider to be paradigms, if not paragons, of multilateralism: free trade and the gold standard. By free trade is meant two things: a minimum of barriers to trade, including tariff and nontariff barriers; and nondiscriminatory treatment in trade. An international gold standard exists when two sets of conditions are approximated. First, the major countries must maintain a link between their domestic money supply and gold at substantially fixed ratios. Second, in principle they must allow the outflow of gold to liquidate an adverse balance of current obligations and must accept a corresponding inflow in case of a favorable balance. These conditions also establish the convertibility of currencies at relatively fixed rates, and they facilitate international adjustment insofar as the initial imbalance in the current account in principle will be rectified automatically in both surplus and deficit countries by the appropriate domestic measures that follow from the inflow and outflow of gold.

By the mid-nineteenth century, Great Britain—the front-runner in the Industrial Revolution, the foremost importer of raw materials and exporter of manufactured products, and the enthusiastic occupant of the doctrinal house built by Adam Smith and David Ricardo—was prepared to move toward free trade on a unilateral basis. Prime Minister Robert Peel declared in Parliament that "if other countries choose to buy in the dearest market, such an option on their part constitutes no reason why we should not be permitted to buy in the cheapest."[61] Indeed, Britain did liberalize trade unilaterally, culminating in the

59. Holsti, "Governance Without Government," p. 4.
60. The French official is cited by F. H. Hinsley in *Power and the Pursuit of Peace* (Cambridge: Cambridge University Press, 1963), p. 243.
61. Robert Peel, in *Parliamentary Debates,* House of Commons, London, 29 June 1846; cited by Jagdish N. Bhagwati and Douglas A. Irwin in "The Return of the Reciprocitarians," *The World Economy* 10 (June 1987), p. 114.

abolition of the Corn Laws in 1846. Others, however, did not follow the British example as Britain had expected. Reluctantly, therefore, and in part also inspired by broader diplomatic considerations, Britain commenced with a series of bilateral tariff negotiations with other countries, and those other countries did the same with third parties, and this had the effect of significantly lowering tariff barriers. The model was the Cobden-Chevalier Treaty between Britain and France, concluded in 1860.[62] Although this was a bilateral treaty, it had multilateral *consequences* because it contained an unconditional MFN provision: it committed Britain and France to extend to each other any subsequent concessions obtained from agreements with any third party. Bismarck, Louis Napoleon, and Cavour all viewed such trade treaties primarily as instruments of traditional bilateral diplomacy and less as the means to multilateralize trade. But they negotiated them, and they included the MFN provision. The inclusion of this provision in a series of trade treaties had the effect of multilateralizing the trading order.[63]

As it did in international trade, Britain followed the rules of the gold standard more closely than anyone else. It thereby provided the world economy with a pillar of financial stability in the pound sterling, making multilateral convertibility and adjustment that much easier to achieve.[64] Britain's policies may have been conducive to multilateralism in two other ways as well. As the world's largest creditor country, Britain did not exploit its position to accumulate large gold stocks but instead made those surpluses available for additional overseas investments and loans. The international economy as a result functioned more smoothly and grew more steadily than would otherwise have been the case. In addition, Britain always allowed debts to Britain incurred by other countries to be cancelled by credits they earned elsewhere. That in turn facilitated the multilateral clearing of payments balances.[65]

The multilateralism of free trade and the international gold standard appears to have been created and sustained by two sets of factors. Although it may appear paradoxical, these paragon cases of multilateralism were not achieved by multilateral means. The decisive factor seems to have been

62. For an excellent heterodox treatment of these developments, see Stein, "The Hegemon's Dilemma."
63. See Jacob Viner, "The Most-Favored-Nation Clause," in Jacob Viner, *International Economics* (Glencoe, Ill.: Free Press, 1951). The United States continued to reject unconditional MFN provisions in its trade treaties until 1923.
64. Barry Eichengreen, "Conducting the International Orchestra: Bank of England Leadership Under the Classical Gold Standard," *Journal of International Money and Finance*, vol. 6, no. 1, 1987, pp. 5–29.
65. According to Briggs, "The key equations of multilateralism were that the United Kingdom itself had a credit balance in its dealings with the primary producing countries, and that they settled their balance of indebtedness by an export surplus to the continental countries and to the United States. The continental countries in their turn financed import surpluses with the primary producing countries and with the United States by export surpluses to the United Kingdom." See Asa Briggs, "The World Economy: Interdependence and Planning," in *The New Cambridge Modern History*, 2d ed. (Cambridge: Cambridge University Press, 1968), vol. 12, p. 42.

Britain's unilateral move toward free trade and the gold standard and its bilateral dealings to achieve both goals. Britain thereby signaled its willingness to bear the costs of an open trading order and a stable monetary order and thus reduced the distributive and strategic uncertainties of these arrangements for others.[66] In that sense, free trade and the gold standard can be said to have been less "regime-ish" than was the Concert of Europe. Another critical factor was a permissive domestic political environment. As Arthur Bloomfield has pointed out with regard to the monetary realm, "The view, so widely recognized and accepted in recent decades, of central banking policy as a means of facilitating the achievement and maintenance of reasonable stability in the level of [domestic] economic activity and prices was scarcely thought about before 1914, and certainly not accepted, as a formal objective of monetary policy."[67] Indeed, many countries lacked the institutional capacity to pursue such a monetary policy, in some cases including even a central bank itself. The second of these conditions collapsed well before the first.[68]

This brief overview of multilateralism prior to the twentieth century suggests several broad generalizations that shed further light on the character of the multilateral institutional form. First, the strategic task environment has an impact on the form that agreements take. Defining and delimiting the property rights of states is as fundamental a collective task as any in the international system. The performance of this task on a multilateral basis seems inevitable in the long run, although in fact states appear to try every conceivable alternative first. Moreover, in the past the multilateral arrangements that did emerge in this domain were monopolized by states and essentially codified state practice into prevailing orders of relations. At the other extreme, limiting transaction costs by solving coordination problems is institutionally neither complex nor particularly demanding, and it was the domain in which multilateralism in all three institutional expressions—orders, regimes, and organizations—flourished in the nineteenth century. Between these two lies the problematic terrain of significant conflict of interest situations, in which states *sometimes,* but prior to the twentieth century not often, construct multilateral arrangements *even though* alternatives are available and viable. The major powers could have selected bilateral alliances in the early nineteenth century and selected discriminatory economic arrangements in the mid-nineteenth century, as they had done before and as they would do again subsequently. But at those particular points in time, they did not. Why not? Presumably, multilateralism was in their interest. But what, concretely, does that mean? How and why did states come to define their interests in a manner that yielded such an unusual institutional outcome? As noted above, it seems that the Concert of Europe

66. Stein, "The Hegemon's Dilemma."

67. Arthur I. Bloomfield, *Monetary Policy Under the International Gold Standard* (New York: Federal Reserve Bank of New York, 1959), p. 23.

68. Peter Gourevitch, *Politics in Hard Times* (Ithaca, N. Y.: Cornell University Press, 1986), chap. 3.

was due in part to exogenous shocks to both the international system and the system of domestic rule. Free trade and the gold standard in part seem to have been due to the willingness and the capability of Great Britain to take the lead. Both cases also were made possible by the existence of compatible or at least permissive domestic settings.

Second, as was alluded to earlier, it seems that successful instances of multilateralism come to exhibit "diffuse reciprocity."[69] For example, what was crucial to the success of the Concert of Europe, according to Jervis, "is that 'self-interest' was broader than usual [and] also longer-run than usual. . . . For this system to work, each state had to believe that its current sacrifices would in fact yield a long-run return, that others would not renege on their implicit commitments when they found themselves in tempting positions."[70]

Third, the record shows that prior to the twentieth century, very few instances of multilateralism generated formal organizations. The Concert of Europe never went beyond great power consultations, while free trade and the international gold standard were instituted and sustained by even more ad hoc bilateral and unilateral means. The multilateral organizations that did exist functioned exclusively in the domain of coordination problems, where the task at hand was to devise mutually acceptable rules of the road and to change them as technology and other such factors changed. And the role of these organizations was strictly circumscribed by the overall normative structure within which they existed.

The twentieth-century discontinuity

An important break in this third pattern occurred with the twentieth-century "move to institutions," as the critical legal theorist David Kennedy has described it—by which he means a move to formal organizations.[71]

Above all, a completely novel form was added to the institutional repertoire of states in 1919: the multipurpose, universal membership organization, instantiated first by the League of Nations and then by the UN. Prior international organizations had but limited membership, determined by power, function, or both, and they were assigned specific and highly circumscribed tasks. In contrast, here were organizations based on little more than shared aspirations, with broad agendas in which large and small had a constitutionally mandated voice. Moreover, decision making within international organizations increasingly became subject to the mechanism of voting, as opposed to treaty drafting or customary accretion; and voting itself subsequently shifted away in most instances from the early unanimity requirement that was consistent with the traditional mode of conducting international proceedings. Finally, the

69. Keohane, "Reciprocity in International Relations."
70. Jervis, "Security Regimes," p. 180.
71. David Kennedy, "The Move to Institutions," *Cardozo Law Review* 8 (April 1987), pp. 841–988.

move amplified a trend that had begun in the nineteenth century, a trend toward multilateral as opposed to merely bilateral diplomacy, especially in the form of "conference diplomacy."[72]

This move to institutions produced several important consequences for the status of multilateralism. First, it complicated, and in some instances actually reversed, the straightforward ends-means relation that previously prevailed between the goals embodied in multilateral arrangements and whatever formal organizational mechanism may have existed to serve them. Or, to put it differently, it created principal-agent problems that had not existed before. Any form of organizational mediation is capable of affecting outcomes, of introducing elements into the substance or process of decision making that previously were not present. A multipurpose, universal membership organization complicates that situation by involving itself even in areas where no normative consensus exists; aspects of both the League of Nations and the UN illustrate that problem in spades. Second, multilateral forums increasingly have come to share in the agenda-setting and convening power of states. For example, such forums increasingly drive the international conference diplomacy game. Third, and perhaps most important, multilateral diplomacy has come to embody a procedural norm *in its own right*—though often a hotly contested one—in some instances carrying with it an international legitimacy not enjoyed by other means.

In short, as a result of the twentieth-century move to institutions, a multilateral political order that is "capable of handling at least some collective tasks in an *ex ante* co-ordinated manner" has emerged.[73] I might add in conclusion that while numerous descriptions of this "move to institutions" exist, I know of no good explanation in the literature of why states should have wanted to complicate their lives in this manner. And I would think it particularly difficult to formulate any straightforward explanation within the currently ascendant logic of instrumental rationality.

The United States and postwar multilateralism

The preceding discussion makes it abundantly clear that multilateralism was not invented in 1945. It is a generic institutional form in the modern state system, and incipient expressions of it have been present from the start. However, the breadth and diversity of multilateral arrangements across a broad array of issue-areas increased substantially after 1945. Quite naturally, therefore, one associates the change with the postwar position of the United States.

72. For a brief though excellent review, see Volker Rittberger, "Global Conference Diplomacy and International Policy-Making," *European Journal of Political Research,* vol. 11, no. 2, 1983, pp. 167–82.

73. Ibid., pp. 167–68.

According to the theory of hegemonic stability, hegemonic powers are alike in their quest to organize the international system. Hegemonic stability theory is right only up to a point. To the extent that it is possible to "know" these things, historical counterfactuals suggest that the likeness among hegemons stops short of the *institutional form* by which they choose to organize the system.[74] For instance, had Nazi Germany or the Soviet Union ended up as the world's leading power after World War II, there is no indication whatsoever that the intentions of either country included creating anything remotely like the international institutional order that came to prevail. Politically, Germany pursued an imperial design in the European core, complete with tributary states on the periphery. Economically, the Nazi scheme of bilateral, discriminatory, and state-controlled trade pacts and monetary clearing arrangements no doubt would have been extended geographically to complement Germany's political objectives. The Soviet Union presumably would have sought political control through a restored Comintern while causing the modes of production in its subject economies to be socialized and the relations among those economies to be administered on a planned and discriminatory basis.

In point of fact, and this we can say with greater assurance, things would have differed in some respects even if Britain had become hegemon. Colonialism as a political institution would have continued longer. And while monetary relations probably would have been organized similarly, merely based on sterling instead of the U. S. dollar,[75] British imperial preferences would have remained a central feature of international trade, possibly forcing others to carve out regional trading blocs for themselves.[76]

Finally, Europe certainly would have been "integrated" by a German or a Soviet hegemony—but in a markedly different fashion than exists via the EC today. And in a British-run system, Europe most probably would have returned to prewar multipolarity and the continued existence of separate national economies.

Thus, all hegemonies are not alike. The most that can be said about a hegemonic power is that it will seek to construct an international order in *some* form, presumably along lines that are compatible with its own international

---

74. The counter to my argument, of course, would be that "systemic factors" determine or at least shape the preferences and behavior of hegemons. That, too, is plausible as a hypothesis. As it concerns this particular instance, however, I attach greater credibility to the actual postwar plans of the Third Reich and to what, since 1917, we knew Leninist world order designs to be than I do to the explanatory or predictive value of systemic theory. For general methodological discussions of counterfactuals, see Philip Nash, "The Use of Counterfactuals in History: A Look at the Literature," *Newsletter of the Society for Historians of American Foreign Relations*, no. 22, March 1991; and James D. Fearon, "Counterfactuals and Hypothesis Testing in Political Science," *World Politics* 43 (January 1991), pp. 169–95.

75. The consensus on the basic contours of a desirable postwar monetary order was quite strong and widespread beyond the Axis powers and the Soviet Union. See League of Nations [Ragnar Nurkse], *International Currency Experience: Lessons of the Inter-War Period* (Geneva: League of Nations, 1944), especially pp. 66–112.

76. Gardner, *Sterling-Dollar Diplomacy in Current Perspective*, chaps. 5–8.

objectives and domestic structures. But, in the end, that really is not saying much.

For American postwar planners, multilateralism in its generic sense served as a foundational architectural principle on the basis of which to reconstruct the postwar world. Take first the economic realm. During the war, when planning for the postwar era began, the Nazi economic order was the focal point of American antipathy.[77] It had effectively excluded nonparticipants, which according to U. S. officials not only limited American trade opportunities but also triggered economic conflicts that readily spilled over into the security realm. "Nations which act as enemies in the market-place cannot long be friends at the council table," warned the assistant secretary of state for economic affairs, William Clayton, echoing a favorite refrain of his boss, Cordell Hull.[78]

The defeat of Germany and the allied occupation of its Western sector afforded the United States an opportunity to help implant the domestic social bases for a markedly different form of foreign economic policy by the new West German state. Much of the negotiating energy expended by the United States on the creation of the postwar economic order, therefore, was directed toward undoing the more benign but still vexing British position. It consisted of a commitment to imperial preferences on the part of the Tories and to extensive controls on international economic transactions by the Labour party as part of its objective to institute systematic national economic planning. Both were inherently discriminatory. The United States sought to substitute in their place a global version of the "open door."[79] Discriminatory trade barriers and currency arrangements were to be dismantled, tariffs reduced, and decolonization supported. But nowhere would domestic politics sustain a mere return to the nineteenth-century laissez-faire of unrestricted trade and the gold standard, wherein the level of domestic economic activity was governed by the balance of payments. Even for the relatively more liberal United States, the international edifice of the "open door" had to accommodate the domestic interventionism of the New Deal.[80]

---

77. This is quite clear from the provisions of the Anglo-American Atlantic Charter, promulgated in August 1941.

78. William Clayton, cited by Pollard in *Economic Security and the Origins of the Cold War,* p. 2.

79. Gardner, *Sterling-Dollar Diplomacy in Current Perspective,* part 1.

80. For a depiction of the subsequent economic regimes along these lines, see John Gerard Ruggie, "International Regimes, Transactions, and Change: Embedded Liberalism in the Postwar Economic Order," in Krasner, *International Regimes,* pp. 195–231. For additional documentation, see G. John Ikenberry, "A World Economy Restored: Expert Consensus and the Anglo-American Postwar Settlement," *International Organization* 46 (Winter 1992), pp. 289–321. The historian of the Marshall Plan, Michael Hogan, similarly has argued that U. S. postwar planners "married Hull's free-trade dictums to the new theories of economic regulation and countercyclical stabilization." See Michael J. Hogan, "One World into Two: American Economic Diplomacy from Bretton Woods to the Marshall Plan," unpublished manuscript, Ohio State University, Columbus, n. d., p. 7.

There is little debate in the literature about the role of multilateralism in organizing the postwar economic order; the consensus is that its role was substantial. There has been little debate about its role in the security domain either—but here for the very different reason that students of international relations have assumed that there was none. That interpretation is not supported by the historical record if we think of multilateralism in its broad generic sense rather than merely in the form of multilateral organizations.

As World War II drew to a close, President Roosevelt faced an institutional problem. The United States must not retreat back into a "fortress America," Roosevelt insisted, or else it would once again have won the war only to lose the subsequent peace. Winning the peace, Roosevelt felt, would require active U.S. international involvement. But at the same time, the American public would not accept international involvement via "entangling alliances."[81] Hence, some other form would have to be found. To complicate matters further, as John Gaddis puts it, Roosevelt favored a policy of "containment by cooptation" toward the Soviet Union and felt that a stable postwar security order required "offering Moscow a prominent place in it; by making it, so to speak, a member of the club."[82] That in turn required a club to which both belonged.

Given that combination of objectives, Roosevelt had little alternative but to move toward some form of collective security organization. But it was to be a modified form in the sense that it stripped away the Wilsonian aspiration that collective security somehow be *substituted for* balance-of-power politics. That was too wild and wooly a notion for the depression- and war-hardened U. S. officials in 1945. Instead, they sought to make the two compatible, so that the collective security mechanism would have a basis in the balance of power but also mute the more deleterious effects of balance-of-power politics. Thus was the UN born: at its core, an enforcement mechanism "with teeth," but subject to great power veto.[83]

81. See Dallek, *Franklin D. Roosevelt and American Foreign Policy,* pp. 406–41. Woodrow Wilson had confronted a similar dilemma at the end of World War I—though, unlike Roosevelt, Wilson sought to transcend what he termed "the evil machinations" of balance-of-power politics in the process of resolving it. "We still read Washington's immortal warnings against 'entangling alliances' with full comprehension and an answering purpose," he proclaimed in a 1918 speech. "But only special and limited alliances entangle; and we recognize and accept the duty of a new day in which we are permitted to hope for a general alliance which will avoid entanglements and clear the air of the world for common understandings and the maintenance of common rights." Wilson is cited by Ambrosius in *Woodrow Wilson and the American Diplomatic Tradition,* p. 46.

82. See John Lewis Gaddis, *Strategies of Containment* (New York: Oxford University Press, 1982), p. 9. See also Dallak, *Franklin D. Roosevelt and American Foreign Policy,* p. 508. According to Dallek, for Roosevelt "a United Nations would not only provide a vehicle for drawing Russia into extended cooperation with the West, but would also assure initial American involvement in postwar foreign affairs."

83. For a good discussion of this compromise, see Dallek, *Franklin D. Roosevelt and American Foreign Policy,* pp. 442–82. On the Kupchans' continuum (as outlined in their "Concerts, Collective Security, and the Future of Europe"), the UN design may be described as a concert placed within a collective security organization.

Once the iron curtain went down and Europe was split, containing Moscow by exclusion became the dominant U.S. objective, and the UN became marginalized to core U.S. security concerns.[84] But the American problem of simultaneously avoiding both a retreat into fortress America and an entrance into entangling alliances still had to be resolved vis-à-vis a threatened Europe. As Steve Weber reminds us, the United States repeatedly turned back requests from its European friends to form bilateral alliances with them.[85] Instead, the United States initially pursued a strategy of "economic security," of providing the Europeans with the economic wherewithal to take care of their own security needs.[86] By 1947, bilateral economic assistance to Europe gave way to the more comprehensive Marshall Plan, which required the Europeans to develop a multilateral framework for their own postwar reconstruction in return for receiving aid. Moreover, the United States was an early advocate and strong supporter of European efforts to achieve economic and political integration.[87]

But European security demanded more. Driven by *"la grande peur"* of 1948, the Europeans came to feel that "it was [also] necessary to have some measure of military 'reassurance,' " as Michael Howard argues.[88] Still, the United States continued to resist bilateral deals and avoid military commitments of any kind.[89] Eventually, the State Department relented, but not until succeeding in its insistence that the United States would only aid a European-initiated collective self-defense effort. The Belgians under Paul-Henri Spaak took the lead. In March 1948, the Benelux countries, France, and Britain signed a mutual assistance treaty. But how could they tie the United States to this framework? The British played the critical swing role in defining an indivisible security perimeter from Scandinavia to the Mediterranean and, with Canadian

84. The UN with U. S. support acquired a more modest collective security role in the form of peacekeeping in the 1950s and acquired a nuclear nonproliferation role via International Atomic Energy Agency safeguards and the nonproliferation treaty in the 1960s.

85. Weber, "Shaping the Postwar Balance of Power."

86. Pollard, *Economic Security and the Origins of the Cold War.*

87. The requirement that the Europeans cooperate in reconstruction on a multilateral basis produced the Organization for European Economic Cooperation in 1948; it eventually became the Organization for Economic Cooperation and Development (OECD)—the chief mechanism through which economic bureaucrats of all the advanced capitalist countries coordinate the conduct of day-to-day policies. As for European integration, by 1947 the idea had gained strong support in U. S. media and political circles. Senator Fulbright and Representative Boggs went so far as to introduce identical resolutions into the Congress that year, asking it to endorse "the creation of a United States of Europe within the framework of the United Nations." The bills were passed overwhelmingly. European integration was seen as a more promising idea for European economic recovery than individual national efforts alone, and it offered safeguards for the reindustrialization of Germany, which in turn was increasingly seen as being necessary for European recovery and for the success of the newly articulated U. S. policy of containing the Soviet Union. See Michael J. Hogan, *The Marshall Plan: America, Britain, and the Reconstruction of Europe* (New York: Cambridge University Press, 1987).

88. Michael Howard, "Introduction," in Olav Riste, ed., *Western Security: The Formative Years* (Oslo: Universitetsforlaget, 1985), p. 14.

89. Gaddis, *The Long Peace,* pp. 48–71.

help, getting it to reach across to the Western hemisphere.[90] The concept of the "North Atlantic" emerged as the spatial image that helped tie the knot. Its formulation and acceptance perhaps were facilitated by the recent revolution in military cartography, whereby the "airman's view," and thus the polar proximity of the Soviet Union to the United States, came to shape U.S. strategic planning.[91] The North Atlantic Treaty was concluded in 1949. "The signing of the NATO Alliance," Howard has said, "provided a sense that now at last all were for one and one was for all."[92] And this, of course, is what the notion of collective security has always meant.

Indeed, NATO was conceived and justified as an expression of the collective self-defense provision of the UN Charter. There is a direct path from the negotiations over Article 51 of the UN Charter, endorsing an inherent right of individual and collective self-defense, to the drafting of the North Atlantic Treaty.[93] The same cast of characters who negotiated the UN provision at San Francisco, Gladwyn Jebb on the British side and Senator Arthur Vandenberg on the American side, also sought to ensure that the North Atlantic Treaty would be compatible with it. That accomplishment allowed the United States to operate "within the Charter, but outside the [Soviet] veto," as the Senator liked to say.[94] What is more, Article 51 was *not* drafted with a future NATO in mind; it was instigated by the Latin Americans to allow for a Latin American regional security organization that was beyond the reach of the U. S. veto in the UN Security Council.

To underscore the obvious, the United States did not seek to endow formal international organizations with extensive independent powers; that was not its multilateralist agenda. The Americans insisted on a veto in the UN Security Council every bit as much as the Soviets did. Voting in the international financial institutions was and remains weighted, the United States still having the largest single share. GATT barely exists as a formal organization (it was supposed to have been folded into the International Trade Organization that never came into being), and until recently State Department funding for it came out of an account for ad hoc international conferences. And the "O" in

90. Martin H. Folly, "Breaking the Vicious Circle: Britain, the United States, and the Genesis of the North Atlantic Treaty," *Diplomatic History* 12 (Winter 1988), pp. 59–77.

91. Alan K. Henrikson, "The Map as an 'Idea': The Role of Cartographic Imagery During the Second World War," *The American Cartographer* 2 (April 1975), pp. 19–53 and 88.

92. Howard, "Introduction," p. 16.

93. On Article 51, see J. Tillapaugh, "Closed Hemisphere and Open World? The Dispute over Regional Security at the U. N. Conference, 1945," *Diplomatic History* 2 (Winter 1978), pp. 25–42. On the Vandenberg resolution, which paved the domestic political way for the eventual negotiations of the North Atlantic Treaty, and its explicit link to Article 51, see Daryl J. Hudson, "Vandenberg Reconsidered: Senate Resolution 239 and American Foreign Policy," *Diplomatic History* 1 (Winter 1977), pp. 46–63.

94. Arthur Vandenberg, cited by Hudson in "Vandenberg Reconsidered." Those who assume that Vandenberg's expressed concerns amounted to nothing more than window dressing have not made a case for why a Republican senator, who had only recently been converted from isolationism, should have thought it necessary to expend so much energy for so puny a purpose.

NATO never has and does not now determine the collective security of its members.

The American postwar multilateralist agenda consisted above all of a desire to restructure the international order along broadly multilateral lines, at the global level, and within Western Europe and across the North Atlantic. (In East Asia, on the other hand, the potential was lacking to construct anything but the bilateral security ties on which the United States turned its back in Europe.[95]) Secondarily, the United States occasioned the creation of several major multilateral regimes, as in the fields of money and trade, and also helped establish numerous formal international organizations to provide technically competent or politically convenient services in support of those objectives.[96]

To be sure, the United States hardly acted against its self-interests. But the fact that U. S. behavior was consistent with its interests does not explain the behavior. Nor was multilateralism what some would call "a consumption good" for the United States, an end in itself. So how do we explain U. S. actions? One possible source of explanation for the American multilateralist agenda is the international system itself. System-level theories of international relations, much favored in the discipline at the moment, essentially are of two sorts. One is structural, the other functional. Both offer parsimonious and often powerful first-cut explanations. Structural accounts of the postwar multilateralist posture of the United States would focus either on U. S. hegemony or on strategic bipolarity as the independent variable.[97] The problem with using hegemony— *tout court*—as an explanation has already been addressed: other hegemons would have done it differently, and so subsequent history would have been different. Hence, we still require insight into why this particular hegemon did things in this particular way.

Invoking bipolarity as an explanation is much more promising—once bipolarity exists.[98] But it is not without problems for the earliest postwar years, when bipolarity was just in the process of becoming, even as some of the multilateral developments described above were taking place. Indeed, it took policymakers and analysts quite some time to grasp the fact of bipolarity. Serious postwar planning by the United States began in 1942. William Fox's book, *The Super-Powers*, published in 1944, still assumed that there would be

---

95. See Marc S. Gallicchio, *The Cold War Begins in Asia* (New York: Columbia University Press, 1988); Gaddis, *The Long Peace*, pp. 72–103; and Pollard, *Economic Security and the Origins of the Cold War*, chap. 8.

96. For example, *The New York Times* described the April 1943 Hot Springs conference on food and agriculture, a conference that led eventually to the creation of the Food and Agriculture Organization of the UN, as "a prologue—a kind of dress rehearsal—preparatory to the world organization [Washington] hoped to set up after the war." Cited by Craig Alan Wilson in "Rehearsal for a United Nations: The Hot Springs Conference," *Diplomatic History* 4 (Summer 1980), p. 264.

97. While the work of Robert Gilpin exemplifies the first, that of Kenneth Waltz exemplifies the second.

98. Joanne Gowa, "Bipolarity, Multipolarity, and Free Trade," *American Political Science Review* 83 (December 1989), pp. 1245–56.

three of them.[99] The Bretton Woods conference was held that year, with the Soviets in attendance. Moreover, the option of dividing the world into three spheres of influence for the purposes of conflict management had not yet been entirely discarded in 1944. By 1945, it had been discarded, but in favor of the universal UN.[100] In his 1946 "long telegram" and again in his 1947 "Mr. X" article, George Kennan warned about the emerging Soviet sphere of influence, but he explicitly expected multipolarity to reemerge from the devastation of the war before long, and he designed his proposed containment strategy in order to achieve that goal.[101] Moreover, as late as 1947, trade negotiators were trying to square circles to devise a multilateral trade regime that could accommodate socialist state trading countries.[102] Even more important, also in 1947, Lucius Clay, the U. S. military governor in Germany, initially blamed the French, not the Soviets, for impeding quadripartite government there when it was still doable; the failure to achieve it resulted ultimately in the bizonal division of Germany that became emblematic of the cold war.[103]

Admittedly, actor perceptions do not matter much in structural theories. Nevertheless, it does seem more than a little awkward to retroject as incentives for actor behavior structural conditions which had not yet clearly emerged and were not yet fully understood and which in some measure only the subsequent behavior of actors helped to produce.[104]

Functional theories of international institutions, as we noted at the outset, thus far have focused largely on undifferentiated "cooperation" and "institutions," not the specific form of multilateralism. Their limited utility on this count has already been commented on. Moreover, functional theories have been concerned largely with such factors as the desire to minimize transaction costs, information costs, and similar institutional inefficiencies. This rationale, too, has limits. First, although our historical cases are too few to make a strong case, they do suggest that the drive to limit institutional inefficiencies of this

99. William T. R. Fox, *The Super-Powers: The United States, Britain, and the Soviet Union* (New York: Harcourt, Brace, 1944).
100. Dallek, *Franklin D. Roosevelt and American Foreign Policy*, chaps. 14–15.
101. For a discussion of Kennan's strategy, see Gaddis, *Strategies of Containment*, pp. 25–53.
102. See Viner, "Conflicts of Principle in Drafting a Trade Charter"; and Feis, "The Conflict Over Trade Ideologies."
103. See Jean Edward Smith, *Lucius D. Clay: An American Life* (New York: Henry Holt, 1990), especially pp. 423–49. Smith's overall assessment of U. S.–Soviet relations as seen on the ground in Germany is this: "The question of erecting a counterpoise to the Soviet Union did not enter Clay's thinking until late 1947, and until then his relations with the Russians were warm and cordial" (p. 7).
104. Jervis has pointed out that the decisive event in instituting the peculiar form of bipolarity known as the cold war was the Korean War. High U. S. defense budgets, a large U. S. armed presence in Europe to back the North Atlantic Treaty security guarantees, and anticommunist commitments all across the globe took hold only after that war. What is more, Jervis argues, "there were no events on the horizon which could have been functional substitutes for the war"—and which, therefore, would have been capable of producing those features of the international security environment. See Robert Jervis, "The Impact of the Korean War on the Cold War," *Journal of Conflict Resolution* 24 (December 1980), p. 563.

kind is most decisive in the realm of coordination problems. When it comes to shedding blood or institutionalizing hopes for lasting peace, the calculus of countries appears to draw on a different universe of discourse. Second, it also seems that what constitutes institutional inefficiencies or costs is not entirely independent of the attributes of the states making the calculation. For example, it is difficult to imagine an institutional arrangement that imposed higher transaction costs on all concerned than the Nazi trade and monetary regimes. But given the overall strategic objectives of the German state at the time, the price of administering those arrangements was seen as an investment, not an expenditure to be minimized. The domestic mechanisms that shape the Japanese foreign trade posture today, with all their reputed institutional "inefficiencies," may pose an analogous conceptual problem.[105]

In short, to determine why *this* particular institutional agenda was pursued, it is inescapable at some point to look more closely at *this* particular hegemon. That in turn requires not only examining the hegemon's international situation but also delving into its domestic realm.

It seems clear that across a broad array of social and economic sectors, the United States after World War II sought to project the experience of the New Deal regulatory state into the international arena.[106] According to Anne-Marie Burley, this endeavor entailed two distinct dimensions.[107] The first was a belief that the long-term maintenance and success of domestic reform programs required a compatible international order. The second was a commitment at the international level to institutional means which had already been tried domestically and which grew out of the legal and administrative revolution that accompanied the New Deal. The combination of the two translated into an active U. S. effort to institutionalize a multilateral international economic and social order.

In the security realm, a count of the domestic political noses led President Roosevelt to believe that isolationist tendencies could not be neutralized by having the United States form bilateral alliances with or against the very European states that kept dragging it into war—which is how the isolationists viewed the world. Accordingly, the notion was foremost in Roosevelt's mind that only by "binding" the United States to a more permanent multilateral institutional framework, which promised to *transform* traditional international

---

105. The so-called Gang of Four (Chalmers Johnson, Clyde Prestowitz, Karel van Wolferen, and James Fallows) has insisted that Japan is different in this regard; see "Beyond Japan-Bashing: The 'Gang of Four' Defends the Revisionist Line," *Business Week,* 7 May 1990. For a dispassionate empirical analysis, which does not reach radically different conclusions, see Edward J. Lincoln, *Japan's Unequal Trade* (Washington, D. C.: Brookings Institution, 1990).

106. See Michael J. Hogan, "Revival and Reform: America's Twentieth-Century Search for a New Economic Order Abroad," *Diplomatic History* 8 (Fall 1984), pp. 287–310; and Anne-Marie Burley, "Regulating the World: Multilateralism, International Law, and the Projection of the New Deal Regulatory State," in Ruggie, *Multilateralism Matters.* While Hogan stresses the economic interest group dimension, Burley focuses on the administrative and legal dimensions.

107. Burley, "Regulating the World."

politics, could a relapse into isolationism be avoided.[108] By 1947, the Truman administration discovered anticommunist rhetoric to be a useful tool toward that same end.[109]

More generally, Peter Cowhey has advanced the provocative thesis that the very structure of the U. S. polity enhanced the credibility of America's postwar commitment to multilateralism.[110] The problem of "defection" that is explored at length in the literature focuses not on the hegemon but, rather, on the other states, potential free riders one and all. But multilateralism is an extremely demanding institutional form, and the fact is that the hegemon has far more unilateral and bilateral options available to it than any other state. So how does the hegemon make its own commitment to multilateralism credible? How can the other states be assured that the hegemon will not defect if it should change its mind or recalculate its short-term interests, leaving them in the lurch? Ironically, Cowhey attributes the credibility of the American commitment to multilateralism to the very features of the U.S. polity that are often said to hamper its effective conduct of foreign policy. These include the institutional consequences of an electoral system geared to the median voter; a division of powers making reversals of fundamental policy postures difficult; and greater transparency of and access to the domestic political arena even on the part of foreign interests. No potential *Pax Nipponica* today, Cowhey concludes, would instill a sufficient level of confidence; it lacks the appropriate domestic base. Cowhey's thesis and the comparison deserve more extensive study.

In sum, in one crucial sense the origins of multilateralism in the postwar era reiterate the record of prior periods. Between the deep level of defining and stabilizing the international property rights of states and the relatively superficial level of solving coordination problems, a pronounced shift toward multilateralism in economic and security affairs requires a combination of fairly strong international forces and compatible domestic environments. If that is so, then it was the fact of an *American* hegemony that was decisive after World War II, not merely American *hegemony*. And this in turn makes the role of multilateralism in the current international transformation of even greater interest.

Multilateralism and transformation

The issue of whether the United States is in relative decline and, if so, whether it is taking the international order along with it has been debated in the

---

108. See Dallek, *Franklin D. Roosevelt and American Foreign Policy.*

109. See Thomas G. Paterson, *Meeting the Communist Threat: Truman to Reagan* (New York: Oxford University Press, 1988), pp. 3–158.

110. Peter F. Cowhey, "Elect Locally, Order Globally: Domestic Politics and Multilateral Cooperation," in Ruggie, *Multilateralism Matters.*

literature for nearly two decades.[111] More recently, the end of bipolarity has been adduced as a cause for similar alarm.[112] The new institutionalists were the first to question any direct relationship between international power shifts and institutional unraveling. They provided several functional reasons why states would, under some circumstances, remain committed to existing institutions even "beyond hegemony," focusing on such factors as institutional inertia, sunk costs, the services that institutions continue to provide, and the common objectives that they may continue to pursue.[113]

But as we saw at the outset of our discussion, the situation today, especially but not exclusively in Europe, is not simply one of past multilateral arrangements hanging on for dear life. There are numerous instances of active institutional adaptation and even creation. Again, there is not much in the theoretical literature that provides ready explanations. The definitional and historical analysis of multilateralism presented here, however, does suggest several factors that may be at work.

One such factor is logically implied by the definition of multilateralism itself. Ironically, the very features that make it strategically difficult to establish multilateral arrangements in the first place may enhance the durability and adaptability of these arrangements once they are in place. I pointed out earlier that successful multilateral arrangements in the past have come to exhibit expectations of diffuse reciprocity. It seems plausible to hypothesize that as long as that expectation continues to hold, as long as each party does not insist on being equally rewarded on every round, the sustainability of the arrangement should be enhanced because it makes both cross-sectoral and intertemporal trade-offs and bargains feasible. Cooperation with the EC seems most clearly to exhibit this pattern. It may have benefited from or perhaps even required active U. S. encouragement at the start, but obviously it has long since taken off on a self-sustaining institutional path.[114]

Similarly, all other things being equal, an arrangement based on generalized organizing principles should be more elastic than one based on particularistic interests and situational exigencies. It should, therefore, also exhibit greater continuity in the face of changing circumstances, including international power shifts. A collective security arrangement more readily absorbs such shifts, as

111. The debate was triggered by Charles Kindleberger's book, *The World in Depression, 1929–1939* (Berkeley: University of California Press, 1973), which also made popular the analogy between the 1930s and subsequent decades—first the 1970s, then the 1980s, and now the 1990s?

112. See, for example, Mearsheimer, "Back to the Future."

113. See Krasner, *International Regimes;* and Keohane, *After Hegemony.*

114. In his contribution to our project, Garrett analyzes the most far-reaching instance of multilateralism ever: the EC members' adoption and implementation of the Single European Act. He describes his story as being entirely consistent with a "rationalist" view of institutions. If he is correct, it would suggest that, given a certain set of incentives to collaborate and given a certain institutional framework for collaboration, beyond some point no extra push from any "extraneous" forces, symbols, or aspirations may be necessary to achieve integrative solutions. See Geoffrey Garrett, "International Cooperation and Institutional Choice: The European Community's Internal Market," *International Organization* 46 (Spring 1992), pp. 533–60.

does a trade regime based on MFN treatment. It is hard to imagine the discriminatory order of the Nazis surviving the hegemony of the Third Reich, however. And even in the case of traditional alliances, the major means of adjustment is simply to abandon the prevailing dyadic ties. Although the cases no doubt are overdetermined, the ready adaptation of NATO at least as a transitional arrangement versus the total collapse of the Warsaw Pact nevertheless may help illustrate this point.

The durability of multilateral arrangements, the analysis presented here suggests, is also a function of domestic environments. For example, there was no shift in multipolarity around the mid-nineteenth century that could have accounted for the final collapse of the Concert of Europe and the reemergence of competitive alliances, but domestic environments did diverge sharply after the revolutions of 1848. The erosion of the gold standard and free trade to some extent may be overdetermined in that both sets of factors changed; but even before Britain declined appreciably as a world power, governments were politically compelled to intervene in their domestic economies in ways that were incompatible with the two multilateral arrangements. In fact, even Charles Kindleberger's climacteric case of the 1933 London Economic Conference—when "the British couldn't and the United States wouldn't"—does not lend itself to a straightforward systemic account. What the United States "wouldn't" was to support the *prevailing form* of economic multilateralism: the laissez-faire kind, the London and New York bankers' kind, and Herbert Hoover's kind. But no one, including President Roosevelt, had yet figured out a viable and mutually acceptable alternative.[115] As Arthur Schlesinger notes in his classic account, "This difference [between the United States and Britain] was too great to be bridged by any form of economic or diplomatic legerdemain. The London Conference did not create the difference. It simply came along too late—or too early—to do anything about it."[116] No domestic divergence that stark exists among the major powers today. The collapse of the Soviet Union and the domestic changes in Eastern Europe have eliminated the international significance of the socialist economic model. The domestic economic structure of Japan may pose a remotely comparable problem, but it is hardly of the same magnitude.[117]

115. See Herbert Feis, *1933: Characters in Crisis* (Boston: Little, Brown, 1966).

116. See Arthur M. Schlesinger, *The Coming of the New Deal*, vol. 2 of *The Age of Roosevelt* (Boston: Houghton Mifflin, 1958), p. 229. For a game-theoretic rendering of this case, which not only supports Schlesinger's conclusion but also sheds considerable light on the broader debate, see the following works of Kenneth A. Oye: "The Sterling-Dollar-Franc Triangle: Monetary Diplomacy, 1929–1937," *World Politics* 38 (October 1985), pp. 173–99; and "On the Benefits of Bilateralism: Lessons from the 1930s," paper prepared for the Workshop on Change in the International System, University of Southern California, Los Angeles, 5–6 May 1989.

117. Gilpin raises this, correctly in my judgment, as one potential factor that could undermine the embedded liberalism compromise on which the postwar economic regimes have rested. See Robert Gilpin, *The Political Economy of International Relations* (Princeton, N. J.: Princeton University Press, 1987).

Furthermore, by and large actual multilateral arrangements with well-defined tasks simply have not lived up to the bad billing they get in some of the literature as unwieldy expressions of the law of large numbers. This is so for several reasons. First of all, most major multilateral arrangements in practice are governed by subsets of states—the "k-groups" that Duncan Snidal, following Russell Hardin, suggests attenuate many international collective action problems.[118] Miles Kahler shows empirically what Snidal postulates theoretically: the major postwar global regimes have been governed by what he terms "minilateralist" groupings within them.[119] Thus, the regimes were not mere expressions of hegemony, and they thereby avoided obvious legitimacy problems. Nor did they operate purely on the basis of egalitarian decision-making rules, however. Decolonization began to strain this "minilateralist" solution in the 1960s and 1970s. Nevertheless, whether in the subsequent Law of the Sea negotiations, GATT rounds, or drafting of global environmental conventions, Kahler finds little evidence that states have encountered insuperable difficulties in devising institutional mechanisms which, at one and the same time, accommodate larger numbers of participants while retaining their capacity to reach decisions. Even in the extraordinarily complex and more "democratic" context of the UN Conference on the Law of the Sea, as Barry Buzan has shown in great detail, the institutional inventiveness of states to accommodate large numbers was impressive, and the failure to obtain a ratified treaty resulted from fundamental conflicts of interest, not from any mechanical problem of size.[120]

A final factor to be considered in explanations for the adaptability of multilateral arrangements is that in some instances the twentieth-century "move to institutions" clearly has kicked in. Indeed, much of the institutional inventiveness within multilateral arrangements today is coming from the institutions themselves, from platforms that arguably represent or at least speak for the collectivities at hand. Again, the EC offers the most dramatic illustration, whether it concerns plans for orchestrating EC relations with the European Free Trade Area, the East European states, or the future of the Community itself.[121] Patrick Morgan goes so far as to argue that West European actors today are explicitly applying to Eastern Europe some of the institutional lessons that they derived from their own earlier postwar experience with the United States, not only in the economic realm but also in the security realm.[122] Beyond Europe, the

118. See Snidal, "The Limits of Hegemonic Stability Theory"; and Russell Hardin, *Collective Action* (Baltimore, Md.: Johns Hopkins University Press, 1982).

119. Kahler, "Multilateralism with Small and Large Numbers."

120. Barry Buzan, "Negotiating by Consensus: Developments in Technique at the U. N. Conference on the Law of the Sea," *American Journal of International Law* 75 (April 1981), pp. 324–48.

121. See "Western Europe Moves to Expand Free-Trade Links," *The New York Times,* 8 December 1989, pp. 1 and D5; "All Europe's a Stage," *The Economist,* 16 March 1991, p. 48; and "Inner Space," *The Economist,* 18 May 1991, pp. 53–54.

122. See Patrick M. Morgan, "Multilateralism and Security Prospects in Europe," in Ruggie, *Multilateralism Matters.* See also Kupchan and Kupchan, "Concerts, Collective Security, and the Future of Europe."

convening- and agenda-setting power of multilateral organizations is perhaps best illustrated in the area of the commons. There would be no plan to try to salvage the Mediterranean were it not for multilateral players, as Peter Haas has shown.[123] Similarly, multilateral players kept first the ozone issue and now global warming on the negotiating table even when major powers, including the United States, were reluctant participants at best.[124]

In sum, parts of the international institutional order today appear quite robust and adaptive. The above discussion suggests that the reason is not simply that these are institutions and that institutions are "in demand." The reason is also that these institutions are multilateral in form and that this form, under certain circumstances, has characteristics which may enhance its durability and ability to adapt to change. This, at any rate, is the central notion that the exploration of the concept of multilateralism presented here advances for further scrutiny. Discovering precisely what those circumstances are and why the picture is far from being uniform across issue-areas is clearly a necessary next step in this line of inquiry.

Conclusion

This article was written with two sets of protagonists in mind. The first are those theorists of international relations for whom institutions matter little. It may be true, as these theorists insist, that they do not purport to explain everything but that what they do explain is important.[125] It does not follow from that truth, however, that what they leave unexplained is unimportant. And institutions, clearly, are not unimportant.

The second set of protagonists are those of my fellow institutionalists for whom the form that institutions take is left unexplored. Their focus is on institutions in a generic sense or on cooperation even more generally. Much can be learned about international relations from that perspective. But at the same time, too much is left unsaid. And what is left unsaid—the form that institutions assume—affects vitally the role that institutions play on the world stage today. Above all else, policymakers groping for alternatives amidst rapid change, hoping to grasp the flow of events and channel it in desirable directions, do not deal in generic choices; their choices are palpably concrete.

123. Peter M. Haas, *Saving the Mediterranean* (New York: Columbia University Press, 1990).

124. See Peter M. Haas, "Banning Chlorofluorocarbons: Epistemic Community Efforts to Protect Stratospheric Ozone," *International Organization* 46 (Winter 1992), pp. 187–223; James K. Sebenius, "Crafting a Winning Coalition: Negotiating a Regime to Control Global Warming," in Richard Elliot Benedick et al., *Greenhouse Warming: Negotiating a Global Regime* (Washington, D. C.: World Resources Institute, 1991); and Mark W. Zacher, "Multilateral Organizations and the Institution of Multilateralism: The Development of Regimes for the Non-Terrestrial Spaces," in Ruggie, *Multilateralism Matters.*

125. This has been Waltz's standard response; see, for example, Kenneth Waltz, "Reflections on *Theory of International Politics:* A Response to My Critics," in Robert O. Keohane, ed., *Neorealism and Its Critics* (New York: Columbia University Press, 1986), pp. 322–45.

A core and concrete feature of current international institutional arrangements is their multilateral form. Why both the conventional literature on international relations and the literature on institutions should remain relatively silent on it may well have something to do with the atomistic ontology of the one and the instrumental-rationalist epistemology of the other, as James Caporaso and Friedrich Kratochwil, in different ways, suggest.[126] Be that as it may, I hope that the present article has established, at minimum, that it is worth investigating seriously the issue that form matters.

No theory has been advanced in the present article; no theory was vindicated or even tested. We cannot explain what we have not first described. And conceptual explication is a requisite for theoretically informed description, leading ultimately to theory building itself. My main objective here has been to explicate the concept of multilateralism, both analytically and historically, and to offer some preliminary guiding hypotheses about what may and may not explain its incidence and correlates and about how and why it matters.

---

126. See Caporaso, "International Relations Theory and Multilateralism"; and Friedrich V. Kratochwil, "Multilateralism and the Rationalist/Reflectivist Divide: A Unilateral Plea for Communicative Rationality," in Ruggie, *Multilateralism Matters.*

[5]

CREDIBILITY, COSTS, AND INSTITUTIONS
Cooperation on Economic Sanctions

By LISA L. MARTIN*

I N December 1981 the Polish government imposed martial law. The Reagan administration, believing that the Soviet Union had played a key role in this action, imposed economic sanctions against both Warsaw and Moscow. The most significant U.S. sanction was an embargo of the oil and gas equipment needed to build a natural gas pipeline from Siberia to Western Europe. Unilateral U.S. sanctions would have had little impact on completion of the pipeline, however, since European firms—many of them subsidiaries of American firms or acting under contract from them—were to supply most of the necessary materials. Hence, the United States pressured European governments to prevent their firms from fulfilling contracts with the Soviet Union. When the Europeans refused to comply with these demands, the U.S. tried to improve extraterritorial application of the law in an attempt to stop European firms from completing their deliveries.[1] The governments of Britain, West Germany, France, and Italy intervened to force firms to meet their contractual obligations. This precipitated a crisis in the NATO alliance, as the United States threatened to blacklist any firms not complying with the embargo. The situation was on the verge of an all-out trade war between the United States and Western Europe when the Reagan administration backed down. It did not impose the threatened countersanctions and indeed even lifted the restrictions on sales by American firms, thus ending the crisis.

* My sincere thanks go to Jeff Frieden, Jim Alt, Kimberly Elliott, Jim Fearon, Geoff Garrett, Robert Keohane, Gary King, Arthur Lupia, Michael Mastanduno, Jim Morrow, Richard Rosecrance, Duncan Snidal, Debora Spar, and George Tsebelis for valuable discussions and comments on this research. Any remaining deficiencies are solely my responsibility. I also gratefully acknowledge the support of the Social Science Research Council's Advanced Foreign Policy Fellowship Program and the Hoover Institution's National Fellows Program.
[1] Bruce Jentleson, *Pipeline Politics: The Complex Political Economy of East-West Energy Trade* (Ithaca, N.Y.: Cornell University Press, 1986); Antony J. Blinken, *Ally versus Ally: America, Europe, and the Siberian Pipeline Crisis* (New York: Praeger, 1987); Beverly Crawford and Stefanie Lenway, "Decision Modes and International Regime Change: Western Collaboration on East-West Trade," *World Politics* 37 (April 1985); David A. Baldwin, *Economic Statecraft* (Princeton: Princeton University Press, 1985), 278–89.

World Politics 45 (April 1993), 406–32

This story contrasts sharply with developments in the Persian Gulf in 1990 and 1991. After the Iraqi invasion of Kuwait in August 1990, the United States again took the lead in imposing economic sanctions. In this case, however, the Bush administration achieved an unprecedented level of international cooperation, even from countries for whom a boycott of Iraqi oil was expected to prove especially difficult. International acquiescence in the boycott was so extensive that Saddam Hussein's sales of oil began to suffer immediately, and sanctions continued even after Iraq's military defeat. While numerous factors distinguish these two cases from one another, they nevertheless also exemplify a pattern deserving explanation as levels of international cooperation on economic sanctions vary widely. Beyond posing this intriguing puzzle, cooperation has become an important substantive problem, since it is typically necessary for sanctions to be effective.

In examining international cooperation on economic sanctions, this article seeks to identify factors that influence the level of cooperation. The availability of data on many cases of sanctions allows testing of theories of international cooperation. The findings here support theories that focus on the credibility of commitments. The first section presents the cooperation problem, arguing that the leading sender's credibility is the key to explaining the level of cooperation achieved. The second section discusses the concept of audience costs, how they establish credibility, and the types of actions that would force the leading sender to incur audience costs if it did not live up to its threats and promises. The third section presents a simple game to formalize these insights and develop testable hypotheses. The final section uses data on ninety-nine cases of post-1945 economic sanctions to test the central hypotheses—that self-imposed costs and international institutions will increase the level of international cooperation. Because measurement of the dependent variable is problematic, I develop statistical models using two different proxies for cooperation. The results of these two models are consistent with one another and with the hypotheses developed here. In every case costs and institutions have a strong positive relationship with the level of cooperation achieved. Thus, the results support the notion that credibility is a central problem in the organization of cooperation on sanctions and that costly measures accompany credible commitments by the leading sender. These findings suggest that international institutions can promote cooperation by establishing credible issue-linkages in situations with heterogeneous actors.

The Sanctions Problem

Analysts of economic sanctions have often pointed to the importance of gaining international cooperation if sanctions are to work.[2] The reasoning behind this proposition is straightforward. States considering the use of export sanctions rarely have unilateral control over the goods they wish to deny to the target. Likewise, for states considering import sanctions, only a monopsonist would be able to deny a market to the target without international cooperation. Many unsuccessful cases, such as U.S. sanctions against Cuba or attempts to impose a grain embargo against the Soviet Union in 1980, are attributed to a failure to gain international cooperation. Unilateral sanctions may force the target to bear some transition costs as it finds new trading partners; it may have to pay higher prices for imports or accept lower prices for exports. Unless states achieve a significant level of international cooperation, however, market forces tend to make these effects transient and small in size.

Thus, states considering the use of economic sanctions attempt to generate support and promises of complementary actions from other potential sanctioners. The process of organizing multilateral sanctions typically occurs under conditions of significant asymmetry of interests among potential sanctioners, with one state having a strong interest in seeing sanctions imposed and thus assuming an entrepreneurial role in organizing the multilateral effort. In the most comprehensive study of economic sanctions to date, Hufbauer, Schott, and Elliott have clearly identified a "leading sender" in each of the more than one hundred cases they study.[3] While the leading sender attempts to organize sanctions, other states often appear willing to free ride on its efforts and need extensive persuasion before they will agree to cooperate. This cooperation problem diverges significantly from the symmetrical Prisoners' Dilemma or coordination problems assumed in many theories of international cooperation.

A number of factors give rise to an asymmetry of interests between the leading sender and other potential sanctioners. Particularly between 1945 and 1989, many cases of sanctions arose in the context of the East-West conflict and thus took on the character of a conflict between NATO

---

[2] Klaus Knorr, "International Economic Leverage and Its Uses," in Knorr and Frank N. Trager, eds., *Economic Issues and National Security* (Lawrence: University Press of Kansas, 1977); Robert L. Paarlberg, "Food, Oil, and Coercive Resource Power," *International Security* 3 (Fall 1978); Otto Wolff von Amerongen, "Economic Sanctions as a Foreign Policy Tool?" *International Security* 5 (Fall 1980).

[3] Gary Clyde Hufbauer, Jeffrey J. Schott, and Kimberly Ann Elliott, *Economic Sanctions Reconsidered: History and Current Policy*, 2d ed., 2 vols. (Washington, D.C.: Institute for International Economics, 1990).

and the Warsaw Pact. In this situation, the United States in its role as the leader of the NATO alliance faced high incentives to take the lead in confronting Moscow. Having the highest level of military commitment to NATO, low levels of trade with the Soviet bloc, and a unique position within cold war institutions such as NATO, Washington had little choice but to respond to perceived Soviet provocations. Domestic political pressures sometimes further pushed the government to take an active stance.[4]

In cases of sanctions outside the East-West context, other contingencies gave rise to similar asymmetries in the pattern of interests. Some of these cases, such as the sanctions directed by Britain against Argentina during the Falklands War of 1982, arose from former colonial associations.[5] Others took place in the context of regional rivalry, where neighbors or regional hegemons felt forced to respond. Indonesian sanctions against Malaysia in the 1960s illustrate regional power considerations.[6] In other cases, the leading sender responded to a specific provocation, such as expropriation of property, or to domestic demands for action, as in U.S. sanctions against Latin America in response to human rights violations.[7] Empirically, we find that this asymmetry of interests, with one state taking the lead in implementing and organizing sanctions, is a robust pattern.[8] For the reasons discussed above, the leading sender will prefer multilateral to unilateral sanctions. However, even without international cooperation, the leader may be prepared to act, preferring unilateral sanctions to none at all.[9]

The last decade has seen the growth of a large literature on international cooperation. A predominant strand in this literature, labeled "neoliberalism," focuses on the collective action problems faced by states and the structural conditions that facilitate solutions of such problems.[10] Neo-

[4] See Alan P. Dobson, "The Kennedy Administration and Economic Warfare against Communism," *International Affairs* (Autumn 1988); Paula Stern, *Water's Edge* (Westport, Conn.: Greenwood Press, 1979); Alexander Haig, *Caveat: Reagan, Realism, and Foreign Policy* (New York: Macmillan, 1984), 248–52.

[5] Lisa L. Martin, "Institutions and Cooperation: Sanctions during the Falkland Islands Conflict," *International Security* 16 (Spring 1992).

[6] Hufbauer, Schott, and Elliott (fn. 3), 2:247–59.

[7] Lars Schoultz, *Human Rights and United States Policy toward Latin America* (Princeton: Princeton University Press, 1981), chaps. 5–7.

[8] This result may be due in part to selection bias that results from only examining realized cases of economic sanctions. There may have been cases in which such asymmetry did not obtain, no state took the lead in imposing sanctions (in hopes that someone else would), and no sanctions were imposed. Given this kind of collective action problem, it is possible that sanctions never get organized without a leading sender even if they are Pareto-superior to no action. If this is so, situations without a leading sender will never make it into a data set on economic sanctions, which yields the empirical pattern found in studies of sanctions.

[9] Baldwin (fn. 1), 174–89.

[10] Robert O. Keohane, *After Hegemony: Cooperation and Discord in the World Political Economy* (Princeton: Princeton University Press, 1984); Kenneth A. Oye, ed., *Cooperation under*

liberal theories, which emphasize the role of international institutions, common interests, and uncertainty, developed in response to the perceived failure of the major realist explanation of international cooperation—hegemonic stability theory.[11] Realists have responded by elaborating an approach to international cooperation that focuses on power, the possibility of conflict, and distributional issues.[12] On economic sanctions, states do not appear to have a symmetrical pattern of interests, with similar preference orderings, that would allow them to achieve mutual gains assumed by most neoliberal theories. Instead, the fact that the leader has a dominant strategy creates problems of issue-linkage and credibility, the kinds of problems traditionally found in realist analyses. I do not argue, however, that relative gains or other distributional conflicts explain patterns of cooperation on economic sanctions. Rather, I focus on factors that allow states to establish credibility.[13]

Theoretically, we can begin to understand the dynamics of international cooperation on economic sanctions by considering dichotomous decisions about whether to impose sanctions made by each of two states, a leading sender (State A) and another potential sanctioner (State B). After this initial decision, they have to consider what kind of sanctions to impose, for what duration, and so on. Recognizing that states prefer cooperation to unilateral action for the reasons discussed above, we can put restrictions on the preference orderings for each state. First, it is

Anarchy (Princeton: Princeton University Press, 1986); Robert Axelrod, *The Evolution of Cooperation* (New York: Basic Books, 1984); Stephen D. Krasner, ed., *International Regimes* (Ithaca, N.Y.: Cornell University Press, 1983); Arthur A. Stein, *Why Nations Cooperate: Circumstance and Choice in International Relations* (Ithaca, N.Y.: Cornell University Press, 1990). For a review of the literature on cooperation, see Helen Milner, "International Theories of Cooperation among Nations: Strengths and Weaknesses," *World Politics* 44 (April 1992).

[11] Charles P. Kindleberger, *The World in Depression, 1929–1939* (Berkeley: University of California Press, 1973); Stephen D. Krasner, "State Power and the Structure of International Trade," *World Politics* 28 (April 1976); Robert O. Keohane, "The Theory of Hegemonic Stability and Changes in International Economic Regimes, 1967–1977," in Ole Holsti et al., *Change in the International System* (Boulder, Colo.: Westview Press, 1980); Duncan Snidal, "The Limits of Hegemonic Stability Theory," *International Organization* 39 (Autumn 1985); Bruce Russett, "The Mysterious Case of Vanishing Hegemony: Or, Is Mark Twain Really Dead?" *International Organization* 39 (Spring 1985).

[12] Joseph M. Grieco, *Cooperation among Nations: Europe, America, and Non-Tariff Barriers to Trade* (Ithaca, N.Y.: Cornell University Press, 1990); Stephen D. Krasner, "Global Communications and National Power: Life on the Pareto Frontier," *World Politics* 43 (April 1991).

[13] In addition to the work of political scientists on credibility, there is a large economic literature on this subject. See, e.g., Michael Spence, *Market Signaling* (Cambridge: Harvard University Press, 1974); Torsten Persson and Guido Tabellini, *Macroeconomic Policy, Credibility and Politics* (New York: Harwood Academic Publishers, 1990); Alberto Alesina, "Credibility and Policy Convergence in a Two-Party System with Rational Voters," *American Economic Review* 78 (September 1988); David M. Kreps, "Corporate Culture and Economic Theory," in James E. Alt and Kenneth A. Shepsle, eds., *Perspectives on Positive Political Economy* (New York: Cambridge University Press, 1990).

reasonable to assume that whatever its own decision, each state wants the other to impose sanctions. Thus, each prefers bilateral sanctions to unilateral sanctions, and free riding to no action. Second, at least one of the two—the leading sender—prefers bilateral sanctions to none at all. These restrictions rule out certain types of games, such as coordination games.[14] I assume that State A, the leading sender, prefers to free ride over acting alone, letting State B act unilaterally. However, A has a dominant strategy to sanction due to its preference for bilateral sanctions and reluctance to let the crisis pass without any action. So while in the abstract it is possible for neither A nor B to impose sanctions, I consider only cases where at least one will.

Given State A's dominant strategy, State B finds itself in a happy position. B, as a potential sanctioner, wants to see some action taken but prefers to avoid bearing the cost of sanctions; it is quite happy to free ride on State A's efforts. Given this configuration of interests, and knowing that State A will sanction regardless of B's actions, State B can achieve its highest possible payoff by simply refusing to impose sanctions. The leading sender finds itself imposing unilateral sanctions, even though it would prefer bilateral action or free riding on B's efforts.[15] However, within the isolated context of the sanctions game, A cannot credibly threaten to make its actions contingent on B's cooperation. State A's dominant strategy to impose sanctions means that regardless of how B acts, A is better off sanctioning than not. Thus, the only way for A to gain B's cooperation is to change the nature of the game through issue-linkage so that B will come to prefer bilateral sanctions to free riding.

Issue-linkage to convince B to impose sanctions can take one of two forms. One is the use of side payments or inducements.[16] With this tactic, State A attempts to increase B's payoff from bilateral sanctions sufficiently that B prefers cooperation to free riding, thus making bilateral sanctions an equilibrium. Essentially, side payments involve a transfer of benefits from State A to State B. In this way A achieves the preferred outcome of bilateral sanctions, but at a price. These benefits must be contingent on B's cooperation. During the course of sanctions against Iraq, we find significant use of this tactic with the United States offering

[14] Lisa L. Martin, *Coercive Cooperation: Explaining Multilateral Economic Sanctions* (Princeton: Princeton University Press, 1992), chap. 2.

[15] Arthur A. Stein, "The Politics of Linkage," *World Politics* 33 (October 1980).

[16] Robert D. Tollison and Thomas D. Willett, "An Economic Theory of Mutually Advantageous Issue Linkage in International Negotiations," *International Organization* 33 (Autumn 1979); James K. Sebenius, "Negotiation Arithmetic: Adding and Subtracting Issues and Parties," *International Organization* 37 (Spring 1983).

reluctant states, such as Jordan and Egypt, goods such as debt relief in an attempt to enhance the level of cooperation.

Threats constitute the second type of tactical issue-linkage that could be used to gain B's cooperation.[17] In the language of economic sanctions, these threats are called countersanctions. State A uses them to decrease B's payoff from free riding to the level where B prefers bilateral sanctions. Carrying out such threats is costly for State A as well as for State B. Threats differ from side payments in that they are carried out if B refuses to cooperate, and they do not improve B's welfare.[18] In the case of threats, unlike that of side payments, issue-linkage is not mutually advantageous but instead leaves B aggrieved. However, State A may prefer this tactic because if it is successful, threats do not have to be carried out. Thus, they can be a cheaper means of gaining B's compliance. In the 1982 pipeline crisis, the United States relied on threats of countersanctions to gain European cooperation. It declared that it would blacklist any firms that did not comply with the U.S. embargo.

Whether State A chooses to use side payments or threats, the credibility of this tactical issue-linkage is central to B's response.[19] State B, under pressure to impose sanctions it would prefer to avoid, must assess A's commitment to carry out threats or come through with side payments. Since either is costly, and B's cooperation rarely coincides with the implementation of promises or threats, A would prefer to gain B's cooperation and then renege on the issue-linkage. Beyond this incentive for defection, other factors intensify the credibility problem. Often, A requires a domestic political consensus to provide inducements or carry out threats. For example, when a U.S. president threatens countersanctions or promises increases in foreign assistance, these linkages either require legislation or can be overridden by legislative action. Thus, without congressional support, the administration may be subject to "involuntary defection."[20] This occurred in the 1982 pipeline crisis, as Congress made it clear that it was not willing to bear the costs of President Reagan's threatened trade war with Europe.[21]

[17] Kenneth A. Oye, "The Domain of Choice: International Constraints and Carter Administration Foreign Policy," in Oye, Donald Rothchild, and Robert J. Lieber, eds., *Eagle Entangled: U.S. Foreign Policy in a Complex World* (New York: Longman, 1979).

[18] Robert Axelrod and Robert O. Keohane, "Achieving Cooperation under Anarchy: Strategies and Institutions," in Oye (fn. 10), 240.

[19] Ibid.; Thomas C. Schelling, *The Strategy of Conflict* (New York: Oxford University Press, 1960), 31–32; Ernst B. Haas, "Why Collaborate? Issue-Linkage and International Regimes," *World Politics* 32 (April 1980), 372.

[20] Robert D. Putnam, "Diplomacy and Domestic Politics," *International Organization* 42 (Summer 1988).

[21] Firms lobbied their representatives heavily to decrease the stringency of sanctions, which suggests that escalating the conflict to a trade war would not receive legislative support. In

The problems of delays in carrying out threats and promises and the need for political approval create a credibility problem about the leading sender's commitment to issue-linkages. In order to gain B's cooperation, A must rely on some kind of commitment mechanism. In the domestic context, considerations of reputation and repeated play often make such commitment among domestic actors relatively easy, as the prevalence of logrolling behavior in legislative bodies demonstrates. However, the international context lacks the infrastructure of strong institutions and rule-governed behavior, which makes credible commitments more difficult to establish. In the following section, I argue that taking steps that would force the leading sender to bear audience costs if it reneges constitutes a potential commitment mechanism in international politics, but one that is available only under specific conditions.

Audience Costs and Credibility

In attempting to convince other potential sanctioners to cooperate in imposing sanctions rather than to free ride, the leading sender has to demonstrate a credible commitment to the threats and/or promises it uses to change the nature of the game. A viable commitment mechanism will raise A's costs of reneging on threats or promises, so that A will bear the costs of side payments or countersanctions. In many cases, the high cost of reneging is a function of domestic support for sanctions and a willingness by the relevant veto groups to bear costs. Here, I argue that two mechanisms that accompany credible commitments are the initial imposition of high-cost sanctions and the use of international institutions. Each of these mechanisms enhances the leading sender's credibility by increasing the "audience costs," that is, the domestic political costs or loss of reputation in international settings that it would have to bear if it failed to make good on threats or promises.[22]

The following discussion and model are purely a commitment story; they analyze both the conditions under which the leading sender's threats are credible and the equilibrium strategies and outcomes in a commitment game. Thus, the analysis assumes complete information on

---

fact, bills were introduced calling for an end to the unilateral U.S. measures. See *Congressional Record*, 97th Cong., 2d sess., July 22, 1982, p. E3429; *Congressional Quarterly*, August 14, 1982, p. 1961; *Congressional Record*, 97th Cong., 2d sess., September 29, 1982, pp. H7927–30; *Congressional Quarterly*, October 2, 1982, p. 2467.

[22] For a rigorous development of a similar argument about audience costs in the context of deterrence and the original development of the concept of audience costs, see James D. Fearon, "Deterrence and the Spiral Model: The Role of Costly Signals in Crisis Bargaining" (Paper presented at the annual meeting of the American Political Science Association, San Francisco, August 30–September 2, 1990).

the part of both the leading sender and another potential sanctioner. What follows is development and solution of a complete information commitment game, not a signaling game. Because the second player knows precisely the leading sender's payoffs from different types of sanctions, countersanctions, and audience costs, the leading sender cannot bluff or try to send signals about its willingness to carry through with threats. Instead, this willingness is common knowledge and determined by the relationship between audience costs and the costs of countersanctions, as explained below. While signaling games could give rise to propositions consistent with those developed and tested here, I find the complete information commitment game a more useful tool since it leads to precise, testable empirical hypotheses.

The leading sender plays simultaneously to both domestic and international audiences. On the domestic level, the costliness of sanctions initially imposed reduces the incentives to back down from issue-linkages. Assume that the leading sender is the United States and that the president is attempting to gain the cooperation of other countries by threatening countersanctions. To carry out such threats, the president will have to obtain the acquiescence of Congress and possibly of other groups as well. When the president initially imposes sanctions against the target, the options include many types of sanctions, with widely varying costs. Some sanctions, such as purely symbolic moves or reducing foreign aid, are costless or may actually incur negative costs. Cutting foreign aid, for example, saves the leading sender some money. On the other end of the scale, some sanctions are quite expensive. The grain embargo against the Soviet Union, for example, was very costly for American farmers, and the government compensated them.[23] By contrast, the costs of the pipeline sanctions in 1982 fell on just a few firms, which did not receive similar compensation.

The initial use of sanctions has domestic consequences that vary with the nature of those sanctions. Imposition of high-cost sanctions involves a significant exertion of political leverage—that is, the expenditure of a lot of political capital—to forge a domestic coalition in support of them. This refers especially to Congress if the United States is the leading sender.[24] The imposition of symbolic or low-cost sanctions will, by contrast, face much lower resistance and therefore not require as much active support. In the process of imposing costly sanctions, the administration must convince skeptics that sanctions are worth the cost. To this end

---

[23] Paarlberg (fn. 2).
[24] Barry E. Carter, *International Economic Sanctions: Improving the Haphazard U.S. Legal Regime* (New York: Cambridge University Press, 1988), 3.

it must advance credible arguments that the target's actions are egregious or threatening enough to warrant a vigorous response. Building a domestic coalition for costly sanctions also requires convincing the groups that bear the costs that international cooperation will be forthcoming. Exporters, for example, will be especially unwilling to assume those costs if other countries are thereby given an opportunity to claim markets in the target.

These considerations imply that the process of building domestic support for costly sanctions is one that cannot be reversed without political costs. An administration that justifies the use of costly sanctions by going to great lengths to persuade reluctant legislators and economic actors that vital interests are at stake will face high domestic costs if it then backs down from threats of countersanctions. Having committed itself to a particular policy, such reneging would call into question its initial arguments and damage its reputation. Thus, because the process of building such domestic support increases the costs of reneging, it also enhances the credibility of threats and promises used against other countries. If the administration is unable to build a coalition in support of costly sanctions, the credibility of threats to carry out costly countersanctions or make good on promises of side payments is severely undermined.

In a recent analysis of leadership in the formation of international regimes, Oran Young has similarly noted the role of domestic coalitions in creating credible leadership.[25] Arguments about the relationship between costs and credibility are a staple of the literature on security affairs, particularly the study of deterrence.[26] Thomas Schelling, in particular, has pointed out that in international politics actions speak louder than words precisely because actions involve incurring some cost, thus making them irrevocable.[27] Merely declaring one's commitment to a particular course of action carries little weight with other governments.[28] However, a course of action that actually imposes costs on the government indicates resolve.[29] According to David Baldwin, this logic suggests that economic

---

[25] Oran R. Young, "Political Leadership and Regime Formation: On the Development of Institutions in International Society," *International Organization* 45 (Summer 1991), 291–92.

[26] Fearon (fn. 22).

[27] Thomas C. Schelling, *Arms and Influence* (New Haven: Yale University Press, 1966), 150.

[28] However, when state interests are not as conflictual as in the case under consideration here, "cheap talk" may have a significant effect on outcomes. See James D. Morrow, "Modeling International Regimes" (Paper presented at the annual meeting of the American Political Science Association, San Francisco, August 30–September 2, 1990).

[29] The model developed here focuses on a rational-choice approach to costs and credibility. This subject has also received attention from those adopting a psychological approach. See Robert Jervis, *The Logic of Images in International Relations* (Princeton: Princeton University Press, 1970); Deborah Welch Larson, "Order under Anarchy: The Emergence of Convention

sanctions are valuable tools in international politics, precisely because they force those who impose them to bear some costs.[30]

Such arguments imply that a refusal or inability to forge a domestic coalition in support of costly sanctions indicates low credibility for threats of countersanctions. The 1982 pipeline case illustrates such a dynamic. In 1982 Reagan was constrained by electoral considerations from imposing a grain embargo, which forced him instead to take actions that were of relatively low cost for the United States. Other potential sanctioners noticed this and correctly surmised that the Reagan administration would not be able to carry through with countersanctions.[31] Thus, the Europeans called Reagan's bluff, and he backed down from threats to cut off their access to American technology.

To continue with the U.S. example, the administration must take account of international audiences as well. Thus, if the administration can create conditions for audience costs on the international level, its issue-linkages should be more credible. Above, I argued that credibility is a more serious problem in the international context than in the domestic context. However, many credibility dilemmas are mitigated when international bargaining takes place within the context of formal international institutions. Making threats and promises within an institutional framework significantly increases the audience costs of reneging.

Many theorists have argued that institutions perform functions that facilitate cooperation among states facing mixed-motive games.[32] The neoliberal paradigm argues that institutions allow states to overcome market failures by such means as providing information about others' incentives and actions, increasing the iterative nature of interaction, and setting standards by which to evaluate behavior. The argument advanced here recognizes these functions of institutions but applies them to a different context. If cooperation results from successful threats of countersanctions, it does not imply mutual adjustment of policies to achieve mutual gains. Instead, where both states impose sanctions, the cooperative outcome is coercive in nature. The leading sender uses threats or side payments to force other potential sanctioners to take actions they would

---

in U.S.-Soviet Relations" (Paper presented at the annual meeting of the American Political Science Association, Atlanta, Ga., August 31–September 3, 1989); Margaret G. Hermann, Charles F. Hermann, and Gerald L. Hutchins, "Affect," in Patrick Callahan, Linda P. Brady, and Margaret G. Hermann, eds., *Describing Foreign Policy Behavior* (Beverly Hills, Calif.: Sage Publications, 1982).

[30] Baldwin (fn. 1), 107–8.

[31] Jonathan Stern, *East European Energy and East-West Trade in Energy* (London: Policy Studies Institute, 1982), 78.

[32] Keohane (fn. 10); Axelrod and Keohane (fn. 18), 226–54.

prefer to avoid. Thus, a credible threat of retaliation leads to a cooperative outcome, but relative to the prelinkage situation this is not an outcome that benefits all participants. The use of inducements rather than threats more closely fits a neoliberal model, as both players can benefit. However, even inducements constitute a more asymmetrical situation than that typically considered in neoliberal models, since the leading sender makes the decision to use side payments unilaterally.

Thus, the cooperation problem under consideration here differs in significant ways from the paradigmatic problem considered by neoliberals. Nevertheless, institutions can facilitate cooperation in the more asymmetric context of sanctions as well. Some of the functions noted above, particularly the provision of information and setting of standards, may continue to be relevant in some coercive games. However, an additional dimension of institutionalization—the forging of issue-linkages—also matters when states face the problem of making credible threats. Economists studying credibility problems have identified steps that governments can take to enhance their credibility; these include reducing possible future incentives to reverse policies and making it more difficult to change policies in the future if the temptation arises.[33] These insights can be applied directly to the political problem of cooperation on economic sanctions, to suggest ways in which international institutions as well as self-imposed costs enhance credibility.

The leading sender can reduce incentives to renege by taking the sanctions issue to an international institution. Analogous to reasoning about domestic audience costs, achieving the support of the members of an institution requires the expenditure of political or economic resources that will raise the costs of changing course. For example, when Britain coordinated European Community sanctions against Argentina in 1982, it provided side payments to EC members on other Community issues.[34] In this context, Britain would have been subject to high audience costs in the form of damage to its reputation within the Community if it had not come through with the promised side payments. Reneging on this particular issue would have made EC members more skeptical about Britain's ability to live up to other Community deals, thus threatening the benefits Britain gained by participation in the EC. Audience costs would have taken the form of reduced British ability to achieve favorable deals in the EC.

[33] Dani Rodrik, "Credibility of Trade Reform: A Policy Maker's Guide," *World Economy* 12 (March 1989).
[34] Martin (fn. 5); Latin American Bureau, *Falklands/Malvinas: Whose Crisis?* (London: Latin American Bureau, 1982), 112.

By reducing incentives to change policies in midstream, the public, long-term forum of an institution thus increases audience costs. Charles Lipson has argued that formal agreements are more reliable than informal ones precisely because they involve a state's reputation.[35] Taking sanctions to such a forum involves a public commitment to action by the leading sender: having taken this step, its reputation within the institution would be damaged by backing down. As Robert Keohane has noted, by "rais[ing] the costs of deception and irresponsibility," institutions allow states to make credible commitments.[36] This effect results from the array of issue-linkages generated by international institutions. These structures provide benefits to states across a range of issues, and these benefits depend on members demonstrating that they can be trusted to live up to their institutional commitments. Once the leading sender has made a public institutional commitment to sanctions and countersanctions or side payments, reversing this policy would tend to decrease the level of benefits derived from other dimensions of the institution. In this way, an institutional commitment will reduce the leading sender's incentives to reverse course and hence will enhance its credibility.

Thus, to the extent that they perform some of the functions recognized by analysts of international regimes, institutions can increase the leading sender's credibility. Regime theorists have noted that once these structures are in place, they can increase members' influence over the behavior of others.[37] Work in economics supports this observation, by recognizing the role of institutions in establishing commitment and reducing incentives to renege on agreements. Thomas Schelling has argued that in order to establish credibility, states require "an occasion, an object, and a means of communication."[38] In the context of multilateral economic sanctions, institutions fulfill these functions. Like the process of imposing high-cost sanctions against the target, the process of generating the approval of an international institution for sanctions raises the future costs of reneging. In thus reducing the incentives to renege, the process makes commitments to tactical issue-linkages credible. These effects can be summarized by noting the impact of domestic and international audience costs on the leading sender's incentives. The next section uses a simple extensive-form game (1) to formalize the impact of audi-

[35] Charles Lipson, "Why Are Some International Agreements Informal?" *International Organization* 45 (Autumn 1991), 509. See also Baldwin (fn. 1), 108.
[36] Keohane (fn. 10), 97.
[37] Stephen D. Krasner, "Regimes and the Limits of Realism: Regimes as Autonomous Variables," in Krasner (fn. 10), 364; Robert O. Keohane and Joseph S. Nye, *Power and Interdependence* (Boston: Little, Brown, 1977), 55.
[38] Schelling (fn. 19), 51.

CREDIBILITY, COSTS, AND INSTITUTIONS   419

ence costs on the level of cooperation achieved under the strategic conditions discussed here and (2) to generate testable hypotheses.

THE BILATERAL SANCTIONS GAME

Figure 1 illustrates the sanctions game. The first player and leading sender, State A, begins by deciding whether to adopt a low-cost or high-cost strategy. Since State A's dominant strategy is to impose sanctions, the only decision is what type of sanctions to impose. In this framework, a low-cost strategy would involve imposing low-cost sanctions, such as symbolic moves, embargoes on imports of luxury goods, and reductions in foreign aid. Such moves usually encounter little domestic resistance and do not require extensive coalition building by those who favor sanctions. In addition, a low-cost strategy means that the leading sender does not expend the necessary effort to gain the support of an international institution for sanctions. Such efforts are generally costly and difficult, as was demonstrated by U.S. attempts to introduce human rights concerns into the deliberations of multilateral development banks.[39]

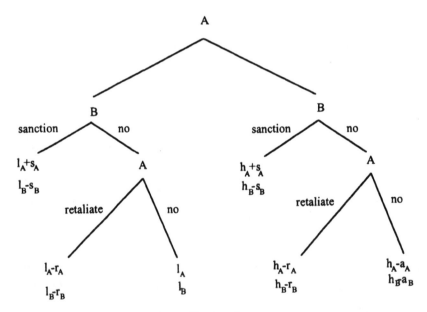

FIGURE 1
THE COUNTERSANCTIONS GAME

[39] Jonathan E. Sanford, *U.S. Policy and the Multilateral Banks: Politicization and Effectiveness,* Staff Report to the U.S. Senate Foreign Relations Subcommittee on Foreign Assistance, May 1977; Schoultz (fn. 7), chap. 7.

State B moves next and decides whether to impose sanctions. If B joins A in sanctions, the game ends here. If B does not impose sanctions, State A decides whether to impose countersanctions.[40] If A retaliates, both A and B bear costs of retaliation. If, however, A takes the high-cost route in the first round and does not retaliate, then it bears audience costs. In Figure 1, h represents the payoff to each player when A chooses high-cost sanctions, and l represents the payoff for low-cost sanctions. The benefits or costs of State B's sanctions are given by s. The costs of retaliation are given by r, and the audience costs by a.

Drawing on the above analysis, we can impose reasonable conditions on the ordering of these payoffs. State A, being the leading sender, derives high benefits from bilateral sanctions. Thus, the payoff from bilateral sanctions $(h_A + s_A)$ is greater than the payoff from unilateral low-cost sanctions (l_A). I also assume that audience costs are significant, so that the payoff from refusing to retaliate once a high-cost strategy has been adopted $(h_A - a_A)$ is lower than the payoff from unilateral low-cost sanctions. Together, these conditions imply that $h_A + s_A > l_A > h_A - a_A$. For State B, I assume that the threatened countersanctions would be more costly than cooperation, so that $r_B > s_B$. Thus, if A's threat is credible, B will prefer to impose sanctions. B prefers to free ride but loses more if A carries out countersanctions than if it (B) imposes sanctions.

This game has two equilibria, depending on State A's audience costs and the costs of retaliation against B. If retaliation is more costly than the audience costs A would have to bear from reneging $(r_A > a_A)$, State A cannot credibly threaten to retaliate even if it has imposed high-cost sanctions in its first move. Therefore, B will not cooperate if $r_A > a_A$. In this case, the only equilibrium is for A to adopt a low-cost strategy and for B to refuse to cooperate. State A has no incentive to impose high-cost sanctions, since it would then be forced to bear audience costs, and $l_A > h_A - a_A$. In this equilibrium, which results when the costs of carrying out countersanctions would be high, we expect to see a low-cost strategy by the leading sender—low-cost sanctions and no use of international institutions—and no cooperation from State B.

A second equilibrium results when the relation between audience costs and retaliation costs is reversed. In this case, where retaliation is relatively cheap $(a_A > r_A)$, State A's threats of countersanctions are credible. Knowing this, and given the fact that State B would lose more from countersanctions than by cooperating, B also imposes sanctions. Thus, when audience costs are greater than retaliation costs, the equilibrium

---

[40] This game could also be modeled with State A deciding whether to make side payments if B does impose sanctions. The equilibria are similar to those in this threat game.

outcome is for State A to impose high-cost sanctions and for State B to cooperate. The outcome with low-cost sanctions and no cooperation is not an equilibrium when audience costs are higher than the cost of countersanctions. If A were to choose low-cost sanctions, it would incur no audience costs from reneging. Knowing this, B will never cooperate when A chooses low-cost sanctions. Therefore, when the costs of countersanctions are relatively low, A will maximize its payoff by imposing high-cost sanctions so as to gain B's cooperation. We also see that in equilibrium retaliation is never actually carried out.[41]

Overall, we find two equilibria in the commitment game. In the first, by imposing high-cost sanctions and/or using international institutions, the leading sender undertakes a high-cost strategy and gains the cooperation of the other potential sanctioner. In the second, the leading sender adopts a low-cost strategy and does not gain the cooperation of others. The choice between the two depends on the relationship between audience costs and the costs of retaliation. The results suggest that in looking at cases of economic sanctions, we should find a high correlation between high-cost strategies, such as bearing high domestic costs and using institutions, and the level of cooperation actually achieved. If the model here captures the fundamental dynamics of cooperation on economic sanctions, we should find relatively few cases where a low-cost strategy coincides with cooperation, or where retaliatory threats are actually carried out. One case in which the United States apparently came close to carrying out threats was the 1982 pipeline crisis mentioned above. In this case, when European firms refused to comply, the Reagan administration blacklisted some of them. However, when blacklisting did not induce other firms to cooperate, the administration backed down and dropped countersanctions.[42] In the next section, I present an empirical test of the model based on data from post-1945 cases of economic sanctions.

TESTING THE IMPACT OF COSTS AND INSTITUTIONS

If the analysis of the above sections is correct, states can use self-imposed costs and international institutions to increase audience costs and thus make credible commitments. In equilibrium, we should see an increase in the level of international cooperation when the leading sender bears

---

[41] This is one conclusion that clearly differs from what we would find in a signaling game. With incomplete information, one usually finds some equilibria that include the carrying out of threats.

[42] *New York Times*, September 1, 1982, p. A1.

high costs and when sanctions have been organized within the confines of an institution. This section subjects these hypotheses to a preliminary test by looking for aggregate relationships between these factors and the level of cooperation in ninety-nine post-1945 cases of economic sanctions.

For this analysis, I use data collected primarily by Hufbauer, Schott, and Elliott. They use these data—covering virtually all cases of economic sanctions for the end of World War II through 1989—to explain the impact of sanctions on target country policies.[43] For the purposes of this analysis, in which cooperation is the dependent variable, I eliminate two cases from their data set, sanctions against Rhodesia and South Africa. These two cases are extreme outliers that exhibit a much higher level of cooperation than any other case in this period. Elimination of these cases is justified not because of their score on the dependent variable but because they are substantively unique: both involve global protests against white minority rule, in which international consensus far exceeded that on other issues that have led to sanctions. Inclusion of these two cases has a strong effect on the results. In particular, when we include Rhodesia and South Africa we find that the impact of institutions is much larger than when these two cases are eliminated.

We are interested in two independent variables: institutions and the costs borne by the leading sender. Hufbauer, Schott, and Elliott have coded the level of costs in each of their cases, assigning each a value ranging from 1, sanctions that actually result in a net economic benefit for the leading sender, to 4, sanctions that involve very high costs. Sanctions coded $COST = 1$ typically involve the cutoff or reduction of foreign economic or military assistance to the target, steps that cost the leading sender nothing. A value of $COST = 4$ might be assigned, for example, to sanctions that involved an oil embargo or other significant reduction in vital economic relations with the target.

---

[43] Although it is the most comprehensive descriptive study of sanctions to date, *Economic Sanctions Reconsidered* (fn. 3) has been criticized for some of its methods. Other students of economic sanctions have questioned in particular the definition and measurement of success. Hufbauer, Schott, and Elliott define success narrowly as a desired policy change in the target country; they constructed a 16-point scale that captures varying degrees of success. Baldwin, for one, disagrees with this definition; see Baldwin (fn. 1), 130–34. The 16-point scale also takes into account the contribution of sanctions to the observed change in policy, which perhaps is better left as a separate variable. *Economic Sanctions Reconsidered* also exhibits some weaknesses from a statistical perspective. Because the 16-point success scale is constructed by the multiplication of two 4-point scales, it is impossible for any case to achieve certain values, such as 7, 13, 14, and so forth. The results also do not meet the usual standards of statistical significance and examine only bivariate rather than multivariate relationships, so that correlations among the independent variables make the observed relationships unreliable. In this study, I do not use the success score but use only Hufbauer, Schott, and Elliott's measures of some independent variables, along with additional variables added to their data set. I also develop statistical techniques appropriate for the kinds of data used, rather than relying on bivariate correlations.

CREDIBILITY, COSTS, AND INSTITUTIONS   423

Thus, COST appears to be a good measure of the concept we are interested in testing, the self-imposed costs of sanctions to the leading sender.[44] However, we face one difficulty in using COST in this form—it is an ordinal-level rather than interval-level variable. The models used here assume that the independent variables are measured at an interval level, at a minimum. Thus, I have recoded COST to make it a dichotomous variable, COSTD, by combining the categories COST = 2, 3, and 4 into one. COSTD = 1 now reflects cases in which the leading sender bore negative or negligible costs, while COSTD = 2 reflects cases where sanctions imposed at least minimal costs on the leading sender.

The other independent variable I wish to test is the involvement of international institutions. I have created the variable INST to measure this dimension. INST is a dummy variable, with INST = 0 if no international organization called on its members to impose sanctions, and INST = 1 if some organization did. This variable clearly does not capture many of the dimensions of institutionalization of interest, which may be accessible only through detailed case studies. However, it will allow us to make some generalizations about the impact of institutions in the aggregate.

The following analyses control for four other factors that may be expected to have an impact on cooperation on sanctions: international assistance to the target (ASSIST), the political stability and economic health of the target (TARGET), whether the sanctions were imposed across East-West lines (COLDWAR), and the goals of sanctions (GOAL). The coding of these variables is described in the appendix. They are included to control for alternative explanations of cooperation. If common interests resulting from East-West competition or assistance to the target account for cooperation, COLDWAR or ASSIST should have significant effects. Likewise, if cooperation is simply a function of the demand for multilateral action, GOAL and TARGET should have an impact.

The next problem is to develop a measure of international cooperation that is applicable across the array of cases in this data set. Although the last few years have seen the development of an extensive literature on international cooperation, this work lacks attempts to operationalize cooperation in ways that fit more than a few specific cases. Here, I suggest two potential measures of cooperation. Each has its strong points as well as its weaknesses, and neither is a perfect measure of cooperation. Thus, rather than relying on just one measure, I develop statistical models appropriate for the analysis of each, assuming that these measurements are

---

[44] Note that COST is not intended as a direct measure of audience costs. Instead, it is an indicator of the strategy adopted by the leading sender, with higher levels of COST indicating a higher-cost strategy. This is assumed to lead to higher audience costs in case of reneging.

different realizations of an unobservable variable. In spite of the inherent difficulties of measurement, therefore, consistent results across the different models should increase our confidence in their validity.

Hufbauer, Schott, and Elliott have developed one measure of cooperation. They assign each sanctions episode a cooperation score, which can range from 1, indicating no cooperation, to 4, for significant international cooperation.[45] "No cooperation" means that only one country imposes sanctions. Many instances of U.S. sanctions against Latin American countries, such as Paraguay from 1977 to 1981, exemplify a cooperation score of 1. A value of 2 indicates "minor cooperation," typically meaning that the major sender is able to get some rhetorical support and possibly symbolic measures from other countries. The 1982 pipeline sanctions receive a score of 2. Hufbauer, Schott, and Elliott code "modest cooperation" as a 3, indicating that more than one state has imposed actual economic restraints but that they are limited in scope and duration. U.S. sanctions against Iran in 1979 over the taking of hostages receive a score of 3. Finally, a cooperation value of 4 indicates "significant cooperation," in which important trading partners of the target endeavor to restrict trade to a major degree, although enforcement of sanctions may not be perfect. The early years of CoCom, when the United States and its allies were pursuing a form of economic warfare against the Soviet Union, illustrates a case with a cooperation score of 4. I call this variable COOP.

COOP is a reasonable measure of cooperation that is susceptible to analysis with ordinal probit techniques. However, one of its drawbacks is that it is somewhat subjective. A more objective measure of cooperation might be simply a count of the number of countries imposing sanctions. I call this variable NUMBER, and use a variation of Poisson regression to analyze it. NUMBER is not a perfect measure of cooperation, since countries are not equally significant when it comes to their contribution to a multilateral effort. However, if the results from this independent measure of cooperation are consistent with those from COOP, they are clearly robust. In addition, this variable allows us to explore one other dimension of the sanctions problem, the contingent nature of decisions to cooperate.

ORDERED PROBIT ANALYSIS

The first analysis uses COOP as the measure of cooperation. COOP is an ordinal variable, reflecting an order but not an interval-level measurement. An appropriate method for analyzing a variable of this type, such

---

[45] Hufbauer, Schott, and Elliott (fn. 3), 1:35.

as COOP, is ordered probit analysis.[46] Ordered probit analysis estimates threshold values for the points at which the underlying continuum of cooperation is divided into categories and produces estimates of the placement of each case on this unobserved cooperation scale. Table 1 presents the results of the ordered probit model.

I have marked coefficients significant at the .05 level with an asterisk. The coefficients of COSTD and INST are positive, as expected, and statistically significant at the .05 level. This indicates that increases in the cost to the major sender lead to greater cooperation, as does the involvement of an international institution. These findings are what we expect from the above discussion and analysis. When the leading sender bears high costs or gains the approval of an international institution, the level of cooperation it achieves increases significantly. This is the pattern we would expect if the leading sender needs to establish credibility through creating the potential for high audience costs in order to convince other countries to cooperate.

Table 2 presents fitted values for various combinations of COSTD and INST, holding COLDWAR and ASSIST fixed at 1, TARGET at 2, and GOAL at 0.[47]

TABLE 1
ORDINAL PROBIT ANALYSIS
(COOP AS DEPENDENT VARIABLE)

Independent Variable[a]	Estimated Coefficient	Standard Error	t-Statistic
Constant	−1.15	0.482	−2.39
COLDWAR	0.404	0.290	1.39
ASSIST*	0.946	0.304	3.12
TARGET	−0.190	0.183	−1.04
COSTD*	0.641	0.302	2.12
INST*	1.68	0.297	5.66
GOAL	−0.439	0.271	−1.62
Thresh 1*	1.05	0.175	5.99
Thresh 2*	2.47	0.306	8.07
Log Likelihood	−86.3		
Percent Correctly Predicted	62.6		
Number of Observations	99		

[a] Asterisks indicate variables statistically significant with $p < .05$.

[46] Richard McKelvey and William Zavoina, "A Statistical Model for the Analysis of Ordinal Dependent Variables," *Journal of Mathematical Sociology* 4, no. 1 (1975).

[47] Ordered probit assumes that the dependent variable, cooperation, is an unobserved linear function of the independent variables. While the precise level of cooperation is unobserved, ordered probit assumes that we can split the cooperation continuum into four parts

TABLE 2
FITTED VALUES
(PROBIT MODEL)

COSTD	INST	*Fitted Value*	COOP
1	0	− 0.461	2
1	1	2.14	3
2	0	1.10	3
2	1	2.78	4

As these results show, both costs and institutions have a significant positive impact on cooperation as measured by COOP. INST appears to have a larger substantive impact, increasing the expected level of cooperation by 1.68 points, while COSTD increases cooperation by 0.641 points. Overall, they support the hypotheses about the factors that enhance credibility and therefore cooperation.

EVENT COUNT ANALYSIS

Above, I proposed a straightforward count of the number of countries imposing sanctions as a possible measure of cooperation. Analyzed in isolation, NUMBER is probably not an adequate direct measure of cooperation; it does seem plausible, however, that it is positively correlated with the level of cooperation. Thus, if we think about the process by which NUMBER is generated from an unobservable variable, we can develop a model that uses NUMBER to estimate the underlying level of cooperation. I adopt this approach to develop the event count analysis of this section.[48]

As in the probit analysis, I begin by assuming that there is some unobservable underlying continuous level of cooperation. We could think of cooperation as the rate at which countries decide to impose sanctions, λ. While we cannot directly observe λ, we can count up the number of countries imposing sanctions and use this number as an estimate of the underlying variable. In this framework, the decision to impose sanctions is an event, and the only data we have are the number of events during each sanctions episode.

Researchers have typically estimated event counts using a Poisson dis-

---

and observe in which of the four each case lies. See Gary King, *Unifying Political Methodology: The Likelihood Theory of Statistical Inference* (New York: Cambridge University Press, 1989), 115–17. Thus, the third column in Table 2 refers to the expected score on the unobserved cooperation scale, while the fourth column translates this score into an expected value for the observed variable COOP.

[48] Gary King, "Event Count Models for International Relations: Generalizations and Applications," *International Studies Quarterly* 33 (June 1989).

tribution. Here, I use a variation of the Poisson distribution, the negative binomial distribution. This distribution differs from the Poisson in that it includes an additional parameter, γ, which measures the amount of "contagion" in the data.[49] The Poisson distribution results from an accumulation of a series of independent events. Formally, this means that the probability of an event occurring at time $t + 1$ is independent of what has happened up to time t. In this case, a Poisson distribution relies on the assumption that the probability of one country imposing sanctions is independent of the decisions of all other countries. The assumption of independence, which results in the specification of variance equal to λ_t for all observations, is clearly incorrect in this case. In fact, the theoretical framework underlying the hypotheses being tested here assumes strategic interdependence—that states make their decisions based in part on what other states do.

We could think of strategic interdependence as "contagion" among states. Positive contagion resembles a situation of bandwagoning. Here, a decision by one state to impose sanctions will *increase* the probability that others will take a similar step. Likewise, a refusal to sanction will be followed by similar decisions from other states. In repeated trials this process of positive contagion would lead to relatively many cases where an unusually large or small number of states impose sanctions; extreme results would occur more frequently than under independent decision making. In other words, the variance of Y_t (the number of events occurring) will increase, so that $\text{Var}(Y_t) > \lambda_t$; in the Poisson, $\text{Var}(Y_t) = \lambda_t$. Thus, we set $\text{Var}(Y_t) = \lambda_t \exp(\gamma)$.[50] Independence of decision making will result in $\gamma = 0$ and positive contagion in positive values of γ. The process generating sanctions is specified as:

$$E(Y_t) = \lambda_t = \exp(x_t\beta), \qquad (1)$$

where x_t is a vector of explanatory variables and β is a parameter vector, indicating the effect of each explanatory variable on the underlying rate of cooperation, λ.

The probit model estimated above suffers from one weakness: it did not correct for selection bias present in the data. This bias results from the fact that there are no cases of zero sanctions in the data set. That is, I have not been able to include cases where no country has decided to impose sanctions. This kind of selection on the dependent variable creates a downward bias in the resulting estimates of the effects of explanatory variables. One gets an intuitive sense for why this would be so from

[49] King (fn. 47), 218–20.
[50] Ibid., 126–29.

a consideration of the impact of INST. It is reasonable to assume that cases where no country imposed sanctions would be positively correlated with the variable INST, since it is unlikely that we would see institutional involvement if no countries imposed sanctions at all. Theoretically, we should expect very few cases in which an international institution called for sanctions but no country imposed them, because the act of getting sanctions on an institution's agenda requires that at least one country have a strong interest in sanctions. Thus, when these "noncases" are excluded from the sample, we will tend to underestimate the actual effect of international institutions.

The negative binomial distribution can be modified to take into account the fact that the data have been truncated at zero, so that the event counts are always positive integers. Table 3 shows the results of the truncated-at-zero negative binomial model.

Gamma has an estimated value of 0.872, indicating that a significant amount of positive contagion is likely to be present in the data. This finding is consistent with a hypothesis that sanctions episodes tend to show bandwagoning behavior, where states jointly decide either to impose or not to impose sanctions. It fits the model developed here, where cooperation is dependent on a credible commitment to economic sanctions by the leading sender. Other potential sanctioners will cooperate only if they believe that the leading sender has a serious commitment to sanctions, reflected in high audience costs of reneging. Thus, we should expect a certain amount of positive contagion. An example may help to clarify the meaning of a positive value for gamma. In the case of inde-

TABLE 3
TRUNCATED NEGATIVE BINOMIAL RESULTS
(NUMBER AS DEPENDENT VARIABLE)

Independent Variable	Estimated Coefficient	Robust Std. Error	t-Statistic
Constant	0.214	0.295	0.725
COLDWAR	0.0326	0.187	0.174
ASSIST*	0.300	0.191	1.57
TARGET	−0.0520	0.102	−0.510
COSTD*	0.351	0.152	2.31
INST*	1.29	0.187	6.90
GOAL	0.0832	0.170	0.489
Gamma*	0.872	0.225	3.88
Log Likelihood	371.03		
Number of Observations	99		

pendence, $\mathrm{Var}(Y_t) = \lambda_t$. Thus, if $E(Y_t)$, the expected number of sanctioning countries for some particular set of circumstances, were 4, the standard deviation of the distribution of Y_t would be the square root of 4, or 2. However, the negative binomial model estimates gamma at .872, so that $\mathrm{Var}(Y_t) = \lambda_t(e^\gamma) = 9.57$. The standard deviation of Y_t thus would increase to 3.09, one and a half times greater than for the case of independent decision making. Substantively, this means that strategic independence has increased the variance in the expected number of countries participating in sanctions, making the outcome less predictable than it would have been if states made decisions independently of one another.

COSTD and INST both have significant positive effects, as in the probit model. Table 4 presents fitted values for values of COSTD and INST, holding the other independent variables fixed as above.[51]

As this table shows, if the leading sender bears low costs and does not involve an international institution, we expect approximately one additional country to impose sanctions, for a total expected NUMBER of 2.21. If the leading sender gains the approval of an institution, an additional six countries would be expected to come along, while bearing higher costs would persuade one additional country, on average, to impose sanctions. If the leading sender bears high costs and gets institutional approval, the expected number of sanctioners jumps to over eleven. These results reflect the nonlinear nature of the event count model.[52] The negative binomial model thus supports the results of the probit analysis, by

TABLE 4
FITTED VALUES
(EVENT COUNT MODEL)

COSTD	INST	*Expected* NUMBER
1	0	2.21
1	1	8.03
2	0	3.14
2	1	11.4

[51] These values are calculated by substituting the estimated parameters and specified values of COSTD and INST into the systematic component of the negative binomial model as given in Equation 1.

[52] As discussed above, the positive coefficient of gamma indicates positive contagion, thus making precise predictions of the expected number of cooperating countries impossible. This is reflected in large confidence intervals around the expected value of NUMBER. For example, in all cases in Table 4, the lower bound of a 95% confidence interval would include NUMBER = 1. Thus, the fitted values should not be taken as precise estimates but only illustrative of the logic of the event count model. More important for interpretive purposes are the estimated parameter coefficients.

showing that self-imposed costs and international institutions have a positive relationship with cooperation.

Overall, these quantitative results provide strong evidence that cooperation on economic sanctions is positively related to the costs borne by the leading sender and the activities of international institutions. Two different specifications, necessary because of the difficulty of measuring cooperation, gave consistent results to this effect. Thus, we find general support for the model of credibility developed above. Of course, these results are not in themselves conclusive. It remains possible that the causal link between these independent variables and cooperation flows through some channel other than the leading sender's credibility. Such relationships are best examined through more detailed case studies.[53] However, this work provides a complement to such studies by showing the generalizable nature of these effects. In addition, the lack of any relationship between cooperation and the other independent variables controlled for here suggests that the credibility model performs better than alternatives. Cooperation has no relationship to COLDWAR, suggesting that common interests created by East-West competition do not explain cooperation. Lack of significance for TARGET and GOAL suggests that cooperation is not simply a function of the difficulty of the goals of sanctions. States cannot simply achieve cooperation when they need it but must establish credible commitments to the extent they are allowed by the constraints in which they interact.

CONCLUSION

The concept of credibility has occupied the attention of political scientists and economists in recent years. While theorists of international cooperation have noted credibility problems, their assumptions of symmetrical patterns of state interests do not seem appropriate to many cases of economic sanctions, where one state has a dominant strategy to act and others prefer to free ride. Instead, the sanctions situation is analogous to that studied by Schelling and other analysts of deterrence who have argued that the ability to take costly actions allows states to establish credible commitments. This paper finds that this insight applies to problems of international cooperation as well as to those of deterrence and conflict.

Credibility is as important to gaining international cooperation as it is to the eventual impact of sanctions on their target. The model of sanctions used here considers two states. The leading sender can only gain

[53] Martin (fn. 14), chaps. 5–8.

cooperation if it transforms the sanctions game through issue-linkage, using either threats or promises to change the payoffs of the other potential sanctioner. Regardless of the tactic used, the other potential sanctioner considers whether the leading sender will actually carry out threats or make side payments. One mechanism by which the leading sender can establish a commitment involves increasing the audience costs that it will bear for reneging on threats or promises. The leading sender can increase audience costs on either the domestic or international level by building a coalition in support of stringent sanctions.

Given these conditions, we find two equilibria in a complete information commitment game. In the first, the leading sender imposes low-cost sanctions, does not use institutions, and gains no cooperation. In the second, the leading sender bears high costs and does gain the cooperation of other potential senders. This suggests that we should find a strong positive relationship between the costs of sanctions or the use of institutions and the level of cooperation observed. Data on ninety-nine cases of post-World War II economic sanctions support these hypotheses.

States do not cooperate simply because they have a common interest in doing so. Rather, they build their cooperation on tactical issue-linkages, making credibility of commitments a powerful explanatory variable. Similarly asymmetric patterns of interests are likely to exist in many issue-areas, such as environmental problems including global warming and acid rain. If so, tactical issue-linkages and credibility will be central to successful resolution of some of the most pressing issues facing states today.

Theorists of international relations in general and of international cooperation in particular are engaged in a debate about the value of formal modeling techniques. Formal approaches have the virtue of forcing theorists to consider rigorously their assumptions about the incentives facing actors and the capabilities of those actors, as well as the internal logic of their hypotheses. However, in order to persuade more theorists to use them, formal models must also be shown to lead to clear-cut, empirically testable propositions. In the case of cooperation on sanctions, a formal model of the commitment problem satisfies these criteria and thus should add to the growing evidence that such approaches will contribute to the development of tested, internally consistent bodies of theory.

APPENDIX: CONTROL VARIABLES

International assistance to the target has been coded by Hufbauer, Schott, and Elliott, with a dummy variable I call ASSIST. ASSIST = 0 indicates that the target did not receive assistance in response to the imposition of sanctions, while ASSIST = 1 indicates that it did. The target received assistance in twenty-three out of ninety-nine cases. Hufbauer, Schott, and Elliott have also developed an indicator of the political stability and economic health of the target. This is a three-category variable I call TARGET. TARGET = 1 indicates that the target of sanctions was undergoing severe domestic stress prior to the imposition of sanctions; TARGET = 2 reflects a more stable, prosperous state, but one with significant problems; and TARGET = 3 indicates that sanctions were directed against a stable, relatively wealthy state. Like COST, TARGET is an ordinal-level variable. However, unlike COST, statistical analyses have shown that recoding TARGET into two dummy variables makes no significant difference in the results. The mean of TARGET in this data set is 2.09.

I include a dummy variable, COLDWAR, designed to reflect the nature of the conflict leading to economic sanctions. If sanctions were imposed by some Western allies on the Soviet bloc, as in the pipeline case, or vice versa, COLDWAR = 1. If not, COLDWAR = 0. For example, British sanctions against Argentina during the Falklands War or U.S. sanctions against Latin America for human rights violations are coded COLDWAR = 0. Twenty-six cases in this data set are coded as cold war cases. Finally, the variable GOAL represents Hufbauer, Schott, and Elliott's assessment of how ambitious the goals of sanctions were. GOAL is a dummy variable coded 0 for sanctions with modest goals, such as settlement of expropriation disputes or minor improvements in human rights conditions. Major goals are coded 1 and include attempts to change governments, reverse or deter military adventures, and so on. Half of the cases here had major goals.

Anarchy in international relations theory: the neorealist–neoliberal debate

Robert Powell

Robert O. Keohane, editor. *Neorealism and Its Critics.* New York: Columbia University Press, 1986.

David A. Baldwin, editor. *Neorealism and Neoliberalism: The Contemporary Debate.* New York: Columbia University Press, 1993.

Two of the most influential contemporary approaches to international relations theory are neorealism and neoliberalism. The debate between these two approaches has dominated much of international relations theory for the last decade. It is now commonplace for an article about some aspect of international relations theory to begin by locating itself in terms of this debate. These two approaches and the debate between them have failed to contribute as much as they might have to international relations theory. These approaches suffer from serious internal weaknesses and limitations that the neorealist–neoliberal debate often has tended to obscure rather than to clarify. Once we have exposed and clarified these weaknesses and limitations, we will be able to see several important directions for future theoretical work.

Two books, *Neorealism and Its Critics* and *Neorealism and Neoliberalism: The Contemporary Debate,* make significant contributions to this debate. The former offered a wide-ranging critique of neorealism when it was published in 1986. The latter, which has just been published, is more narrowly focused. It takes up where some of the critiques in *Neorealism and Its Critics* left off. A review of these two complementary volumes affords an excellent opportunity to begin to identify some of the weaknesses and limitations that the neorealist–neoliberal debate frequently has obscured.

I am grateful to Carol Evans, Jeffry Frieden, Joanne Gowa, Joseph Grieco, Ernst Haas, Peter Katzenstein, Robert Keohane, David Lake, James Morrow, John Odell, Janice Gross Stein, and Kenneth Waltz for their thoughtful comments and criticisms of an earlier draft. I also thank Greg Louden and Michael Sinatra for invaluable research assistance. I gratefully acknowledge the support of a grant from the National Science Foundation, no. SES-921959.

International Organization 48, 2, Spring 1994, pp. 313–44
© 1994 by The IO Foundation and the Massachusetts Institute of Technology

In this review, I discuss four broad avenues of criticism that these volumes take in evaluating neorealism and specifically Kenneth Waltz's formulation of it.[1] The first three avenues are the origins of states' preferences, the agent–structure problem, and Waltz's specific definition of political structure. These criticisms generally do not challenge the logical coherence of neorealism. They focus instead on the limitations of the theory. The first two center on what neorealism takes for granted, e.g., preferences and intersubjective meanings and understandings. The third criticism finds Waltz's definition of structure too confining. The fourth avenue of criticism challenges the internal logic of neorealism directly. It argues that conclusions claimed to follow from the assumptions of neorealism actually do not. The neorealist–neoliberal debate lies along this fourth avenue.

Three issues lie at the center of the neorealist–neoliberal debate. In reviewing these issues, I try to bring important implicit assumptions to the fore and show that those assumptions account for many of the important differences between the two theories. Moreover, many of the differences that have been thought to be significant, such as the difference between relative and absolute gains, are not. The first issue at the heart of the debate is the meaning and implications of anarchy. Although the notion of anarchy has served as a central organizing concept for much of international relations theory, the emphasis on anarchy is misplaced. What have often been taken to be the implications of anarchy do not really follow from the assumption of anarchy. Rather, these implications result from other implicit and unarticulated assumptions about the states' strategic environment.

The second central issue is the problem of absolute and relative gains. I argue that the controversy surrounding this problem generally has mistaken effects for causes and that this mistake has handicapped analysis of the problem of international cooperation. More specifically, I try to demonstrate that the international relations literature generally holds, if at times only implicitly so, that the extent to which a state is concerned about relative gains depends on its strategic environment, for example, the offense–defense balance and the intensity of the security dilemma. But if this is the case, then the degree to which a state is concerned about relative gains is part of the outcome to be explained: it is an effect and not a cause. The extent to which a state is concerned about relative gains, therefore, does not explain the level of international cooperation. This realization should refocus our attention on what determines the degree of a state's concern about relative gains.

The third issue is the tension between coordination and distribution. There are often many ways to realize the joint gains from cooperation, and these alternatives often lead to different distributions of those gains. Thus, the potential for joint gains usually creates distributional disputes that tend to impede cooperation. Although these distributional concerns only recently have

---

1. Kenneth Waltz, *Theory of International Politics* (Reading, Mass.: Addison-Wesley, 1979).

begun to receive attention in the debate between neorealism and neoliberal-ism, they hold the promise of clarifying some of the questions that actually do divide these two approaches.

Neorealism and the structural approach

Much of the neorealist–neoliberal debate can be seen as a reaction to Waltz's *Theory of International Politics* and a response to those reactions. A brief discussion of two of that book's primary objectives is essential to understanding the debate.[2] One objective was to reiterate, reinforce, and refine a line of argument Waltz began in *Man, the State, and War.*[3] There, he had underscored the importance of third-image explanations. First-image explanations locate the causes of international outcomes, say the cause of war, "in the nature and behavior of men. Wars result from selfishness, from misdirected aggressive impulses, from stupidity."[4] Second-image explanations locate causes in the internal structure of the state. Imperialism, for example, results from a particular internal economic structure like capitalism; similarly, international peace results from a particular form of government like democracy.[5] Appealing to Rousseau's stag hunt and alluding to the then recent development of game theory, Waltz argued that first- and second-image explanations were insuffi-cient.[6] In a situation entailing strategic interdependence, such as that of the great powers, an actor's optimal strategy depends on the other actors' strategies. If, therefore, we want to explain what the actors will do, then, in addition to looking at the attributes of the actors, we must also look to the constraints that define the strategic setting in which the actors interact. The third image locates causes "within the state system."[7]

A simple example from microeconomic theory illustrates the potential importance of third-image explanations. The price is higher and the output is lower in a monopolized market than in a competitive one. But first- and second-image accounts, which Waltz collectively calls reductive explanations in *Theory of International Politics,* do not explain these differences. In both markets, the attributes of the actors, which are firms in this case, are identical: every firm tries to maximize its profits and consequently produces the level of output at which marginal cost equals marginal revenue. What accounts for the variation in price and output between these markets is not variation in the attributes of the units but variation in the environments or market structures in which they act. This is the essence of the third image.

2. For a summary of Waltz's goals, see p. 323 of Kenneth Waltz, "Reflections on *Theory of International Politics,*" in Keohane, *Neorealism and Its Critics,* pp. 322–45.

3. Kenneth Waltz, *Man, the State and War* (New York: Columbia University Press, 1959).

4. Ibid., p. 16.

5. Ibid., pp. 80–164.

6. Ibid., pp. 172–86 and 201–5.

7. Ibid., p. 12.

It is important to emphasize two points about the division of explanations into reductive and systemic accounts. The first is an assumption inherent in this division: namely, that we can usefully conceive of the actors or units in a system as separate and distinct from the constraints that define the strategic setting in which the units interact. The second important point is the kind of conceptual experiment and explanation that naturally follows from this division. Once a system has been decomposed into units and constraints, it is natural to ask one of two questions; or, to put it differently, it is natural to consider two types of thought experiment. First, how would some aspect of the units' behavior, say the probability of starting a war, vary if we conceptually change some attributes of the units while holding the constraints constant? What, for example, would happen to the probability of war if a state's form of government were democratic rather than authoritarian? Fixing constraints and varying units' attributes comprise the essential conceptual experiment underlying reductive explanations. Second, how would behavior change if the attributes of the units remained constant and the constraints were changed? What, for example, would happen to the probability of war if the attributes of the units were unchanged but the distribution of power changed from bipolarity to multipolarity? Fixing the units' attributes and varying the constraints facing the units comprise the fundamental conceptual experiment underlying systemic explanations.

After emphasizing the general importance of third-image or systemic explanations, Waltz turns to a second objective in *Theory of International Politics*. He sees structure as a "set of constraining conditions."[8] But states may be constrained by many things—like the distribution of power, the nature of military technology, or the state's comparative economic advantage. A second goal for Waltz is to specify a restricted set of constraints that provide a way of conceiving of a political system and then to demonstrate the power of this formulation by showing that it tells "us a small number of big and important things."[9] He restricts this set to three elements, defining a political structure in terms of its ordering principle, the distribution of the units' capabilities, and the functional differentiation or nondifferentiation of the units.[10]

Two criteria seem to have guided the selection of these elements and this definition of political structure. The first is pragmatic. This definition appeared to lead to interesting insights, which, of course, is the goal of all positive theories. The second criterion is less general and reflected a trade-off. Waltz tried to define political structure so that "it would show us a purely positional picture."[11] The advantage of a positional picture is that many systems can be seen as similar regardless of the particular substantive context in which the units interact. "Structure, properly defined, is transposable."[12] Thus, firms

8. Waltz, *Theory of International Politics*, p. 73.
9. Waltz, "Reflections on *Theory of International Politics*," p. 329.
10. Ibid., pp. 79–101.
11. Kenneth Waltz, "A Response to My Critics," in Keohane, *Neorealism and Its Critics*, p. 330.
12. Ibid.

facing a high risk of bankruptcy in an oligopolistic market may be seen to be in an anarchical, self-help system in much the same way that states facing a high risk of war in the international system are in an anarchical, self-help system.[13] If, therefore, anarchy implies certain behavior, such as the tendency for balances of power to form, then we would expect to see this behavior obtain "whether the system is composed of tribes, nations, oligopolistic firms, or street gangs."[14] The potential advantage of a spare definition of a political structure is that it may help us see similarities in what initially appeared to be very different domains. The potential disadvantage of this spare definition is that if the three dimensions Waltz uses to characterize systems do not sufficiently constrain the units' interaction, then units in similar systems may not interact in similar ways. If this is the case, then we shall have to look elsewhere for explanations of these variations. Recognizing this trade-off, Waltz opts for a spare definition.

Four avenues of criticism

Structural theories decompose a system into units and constraints. This decomposition makes these theories vulnerable to two broad avenues of criticism. The first criticism accepts this decomposition but stresses the need for a theory of preference formation to supplement the structural theory. Because the units' preferences are exogenously specified in a structural theory, we need a theory that explains their origins. The second avenue rejects this decomposition. It emphasizes the agent–structure problem, arguing that agents and structure are inseparable. In addition to these first two broad avenues of criticism, any particular structural theory, like Waltz's formulation of neorealism, is also subject to a third and fourth avenue of criticism. The third focuses on and questions the specific definition of structure employed in the theory. The fourth questions whether the conclusions claimed to follow from the theory do indeed follow.

Preferences are given exogenously

The first avenue of criticism centers on preferences. Structural approaches take the units' preferences as given. That is, these preferences are exogenously specified. They become inputs into the analysis rather than the subject of analysis. This may be an important weakness of the structural approach. As Robert Jervis cautions, "By taking preferences as given, we beg what may be the most important question on how they were formed. . . . Economic theory treats tastes and preferences as exogenous. Analysis is therefore facilitated, but

13. Waltz, *Theory of International Politics,* pp. 105 and 111.
14. The quotation is from p. 37 of Kenneth Waltz, "Realist Thought and Neorealist Theory," *Journal of International Affairs* 44 (Spring/Summer 1990), pp. 21–37.

at the cost of drawing attention away from areas that may contain much of the explanatory 'action' in which we are interested."[15]

The first step in assessing the force of the criticism that structural approaches lack a theory of preferences is to clarify the criticism by distinguishing two types of preferences. The first type is preferences over outcomes; the second is preferences over actions or policies. To differentiate these two types, consider a game in payoff-matrix form. The cells in the matrix correspond to potential outcomes. The utilities that appear in each cell in the matrix represent the players' preferences over these potential outcomes. That is, a player's utilities reflect its preference ranking of the possible outcomes. Given its preferences over outcomes and its beliefs about what the other players are doing, a player can rank its potential actions from most to least preferred. In a two-person game, for example, the row player can rank its actions from best to worst given its payoffs and its beliefs about what the column player is doing. This induced ranking defines a player's preferences over actions.[16]

Structural theories do not try to explain preferences of one type but do try to explain preferences of the other type. Structural theories take the units' preferences over possible outcomes as given and, consequently, lack a theory of preferences over outcomes. But structural theories try to make predictions about the units' preferred actions by combining assumptions about the units' preferences over outcomes with other assumptions about the structural constraints facing the units. In this sense, structural theories claim to be a theory of preferences over actions. Game theory, for example, is a theory of preferences over actions. It attempts to predict the units' optimal actions based on their preferences over outcomes and the strategic setting in which they interact. Similarly, Waltz's formulation of neorealism takes the units' preferences as given. "In a microtheory, whether of international politics or of economics, the motivation of the actors is assumed rather than realistically described."[17] In particular, Waltz assumes "that states seek to ensure their survival" and then attempts to predict the units' actions, albeit in a very general way, on the basis of this assumption about the units' preferences and other assumptions about the political structure in which the units interact.[18]

The two types of preferences are frequently conflated. For example, after noting that "economic theory takes tastes and preferences as exogenous" and warning that we may be begging the most important questions by doing so, Jervis discusses some of the sources of these tastes and preferences over outcomes. These sources include transnational forces, ideologies, beliefs,

---

15. Robert Jervis, "Realism, Game Theory, and Cooperation," *World Politics* 40 (April 1988), pp. 324–25. For similar warnings, see Joseph Nye, "Neorealism and Neoliberalism," *World Politics* 50 (January 1988), p. 238.

16. The distinction between preferences over outcomes and over actions is useful, but it should not be pushed too hard. An outcome in one game may be seen as a policy choice in a larger game.

17. Waltz, *Theory of International Politics,* p. 91.

18. The quotation is drawn from ibid.

experience, and knowledge.[19] He also sees realism as a source or theory of preferences over outcomes, saying, "Sometimes we can deduce preferences from the structure of the system, as Realism suggests. But even a structural theory of international politics as powerful as Waltz's has trouble producing precise deductions."[20] Jervis confounds the two types of preferences here. He correctly observes that economic theory takes preferences over outcomes as given but then treats neorealism, which is a theory of preferences over actions, as a theory of preferences over outcomes. Robert Keohane similarly conflates the two types of preferences when he intends to criticize neorealism as a weak theory of behavior (that is, a weak theory of preferences over actions) but describes neorealism as a weak theory of preferences over outcomes.[21]

Conflating the two types of preferences has at least two negative effects. The first is to suggest that we cannot use structural or game-theoretic approaches, which take preferences as given, to study the effects on preferences of changes in beliefs, experience, or knowledge.[22] This suggestion is simply wrong if what we want to study is how changes in these factors affect preferences over actions or policies. Indeed, one of the primary uses of incomplete-information games is to study how interaction affects players' beliefs and, through these beliefs, their preferred actions. Andrew Kydd, for example, develops an interesting incomplete-information model of arms races that he uses to study Jervis's spiral model of escalation.[23] The basic issue in Kydd's game is whether a state will change from preferring not to arm to preferring to arm because it interprets another state's arms increase as a sign of hostility rather than of insecurity. Kydd uses this model to study the circumstances in which two states that have no hostile intent might arm and eventually go to war because they fear that the other is hostile. The formal study of dynamic interactions and the learning and signaling inherent in them is at an early stage in international relations theory. Many legitimate criticisms can be made of this work.[24] But the claim that this work has nothing to say about learning and changes in preferences (over

19. Jervis, "Realism, Game Theory, and Cooperation," pp. 324–29.

20. Ibid., p. 325.

21. Robert Keohane, "Theory of World Politics," in Keohane, *Neorealism and Its Critics,* pp. 175–76. One factor contributing to this conflation may be that both Jervis and Keohane focus primarily on the prisoners' dilemma. There is no strategic interdependence in a one-shot prisoners' dilemma: a player always does strictly better by playing D rather than C regardless of what the other player does. In cases in which a player's optimal action is independent of what others do, a theory of preferences over outcomes also serves as a theory of preferences over actions. The distinction between the two types of preferences is meaningful only if the game entails a situation of strategic interdependence in which a player's optimal strategy depends on what it believes others will do.

22. Jervis, "Realism, Game Theory, and Cooperation," p. 327.

23. Andrew Kydd, "The Security Dilemma, Game Theory, and World War I," paper presented at the annual meeting of the American Political Science Association, Washington, D.C., 2–5 September 1993. For Jervis's insightful discussion of the spiral model, see his *Perception and Misperception in International Politics* (Princeton, N.J.: Princeton University Press, 1977).

24. For an excellent review of some of the limitations of this approach, see David Kreps, *Game Theory and Economic Modelling* (New York: Oxford University Press, 1990).

actions) because it takes preferences (over outcomes) as given is not one of these criticisms.

The second negative effect of conflating the two types of preferences is that doing so confounds two objections to structural approaches that need to be evaluated separately. The first objection is that these approaches take the units' preferences as given. The second is that these approaches offer at best very weak theories of preferences over actions and at worst misleading theories. As will be seen, the first objection is not very important to the neorealist–neoliberal debate, while the second objection lies at the heart of it.

The significance of taking the units' preferences as given in a theory or model depends very much on the theory or model and the purposes for which it has been constructed. In some models of nuclear crisis bargaining, for example, there are only three outcomes: a state prevails in the crisis, it backs down but avoids a nuclear exchange, or the crisis ends in nuclear war.[25] Preferences over these outcomes are exogenously given in these models, but it would seem bizarre not to assume that a state prefers the first outcome to the second and the second to the third. Many situations, however, are much more complicated and what to assume about preferences over outcomes is not obvious. It is not clear, for example, what to assume about a state's preferences over possible trade arrangements. Here the work of Jeffry Frieden, Peter Gourevitch, Peter Katzenstein, David Lake, Helen Milner, Ronald Rogowski, and others in developing an understanding of the origins of preferences is very important.[26] Similarly, a state's preferences over potential national security arrangements, for example, possible arms control agreements, may not be obvious, and theories may be needed to explain these preferences.[27]

That neorealism takes the units' preferences as given is of little consequence for the neorealist–neoliberal debate. As will be developed more fully below, this debate largely focuses on the likelihood of cooperation in anarchy and on the role of institutions in facilitating cooperation. Neorealism maintains that cooperation will be difficult in an anarchic system composed of units that prefer survival over extinction. Neoliberalism questions this conclusion but not the

---

25. See, for instance, the models of nuclear brinkmanship in Robert Powell, *Nuclear Deterrence Theory* (Cambridge: Cambridge University Press, 1990).

26. See Jeffry Frieden, "Invested Interests," *International Organization* 45 (Autumn 1991), pp. 425–51; Peter Gourevitch, *Politics in Hard Times* (Ithaca, N.Y.: Cornell University Press, 1986); Peter Katzenstein, ed., *Between Power and Plenty* (Madison: University of Wisconsin Press, 1978); David Lake, *Power, Protection, and Free Trade* (Ithaca, N.Y.: Cornell University Press, 1988); Helen Milner, *Resisting Protectionism* (Princeton, N.J.: Princeton University Press, 1988); and Ronald Rogowski, *Commerce and Coalitions* (Princeton, N.J.: Princeton University Press, 1989).

27. For example, Adler uses the concept of epistemic communities to explain American preferences about arms control agreements. See Emanual Adler, "The Emergence of Cooperation," *International Organization* 46 (Winter 1992), pp. 101–46. For attempts to explain a state's preferences over military doctrines and the importance of civil–military relations in determining those preferences, see Barry Posen, *The Origins of Military Doctrine* (Ithaca, N.Y.: Cornell University Press, 1984); Jack Snyder, *The Ideology of the Offensive* (Ithaca, N.Y.: Cornell University Press, 1984); and Stephen Van Evera, "The Cult of the Offensive and the Origins of the First World War," *International Security* 9 (Summer 1984), pp. 58–107.

assumption that units are minimally motivated to survive. Indeed, it would seem bizarre not to assume that units prefer survival over extinction. Thus, the criticism that these preferences are specified exogenously is unimportant to the debate about the likelihood of cooperation in anarchy. The potentially important criticism is that the conclusions claimed to follow from neorealism's spare assumption about units' preferences and about the political structure in which these units interact actually do not follow. This is the fourth avenue of criticism, which will be discussed below.

The inseparability of agents and structure

The structural approach decomposes a system into units and the constraints facing them. The second avenue of criticism denies the separability of agents and structure. Drawing on structurationist theories in sociology, Alexander Wendt argues that agents and structure are "mutually constitutive yet ontologically distinct entities. Each is in some sense an effect of the other; they are 'co-determined.' "[28]

If agents and structure were conceptually inseparable, two consequences would follow. First, the two conceptual experiments underlying the structural approach from which this approach derives its explanatory power would become problematic. We would no longer be able to study the constraining effects of structure by theoretically holding the units and their preferences constant while varying the structure in which they interact. If units and structure are inseparable so that each is at least partly the effect of the other, then variation in the structure will also change the units.

Second, challenging the separability of units and structure makes the units an object of inquiry and directs our attention to systemic change and transformation. If units and structure are mutually constitutive, then it is natural to ask, How do they evolve, and How do they interact over time? Thinking of the units as being endogenous shifts our attention away from a positional model to what David Dessler calls a transformational model. In a positional model like Waltz's formulation of neorealism, "structure is an *environment* in which action takes place. Structure means the 'setting' or 'context' in which action unfolds."[29] Structure is, in other words, a set of constraints. In a transformational theory, "structure is a medium of activity that in principle can be altered through activity."[30] Structure shapes action and is shaped by action. The goal, therefore, of a transformational theory is to explain how structure and agent interact. To do this, Robert Cox, Dessler, John

---

28. See p. 360 of Alexander Wendt, "The Agent–Structure Problem in International Relations Theory," *International Organization* 41 (Summer 1987), pp. 335–70.

29. The quotation is from p. 426 of David Dessler, "What's at Stake in the Agent–Structure Debate," *International Organization* 43 (Summer 1989), pp. 441–70, emphasis original.

30. Ibid., p. 461.

Ruggie, Wendt, and others have emphasized identities, interests, rules, roles, and intersubjective understandings and meanings.[31]

As with the first avenue of criticism, the force of the second avenue depends very much on the particular theory or model being criticized. Cox's distinction between problem-solving theories and critical theories is helpful here.[32] The former uses the ceteris paribus assumption to restrict the statement of a specific problem "to a limited number of variables which are amenable to a relatively close and precise examination."[33] Among the many things that problem-solving theories may exclude by taking them as given and unproblematic are intersubjective understandings and expectations. The ceteris paribus assumption effectively freezes and thereby assumes away the interaction of units and structure.

It seems entirely appropriate to assume away this interaction in a problem-solving theory *as long as* the applicability or domain of the theory is understood to be bounded by the ceteris paribus assumption. Structurationists rightly argue that intersubjective understandings are part of what is being taken as given or unproblematic in this assumption. If these understandings and meanings differ significantly from those presumed in the ceteris paribus assumption, then theories predicated on that assumption may be of little use. Of course, the ceteris paribus conditions—be they about interests and identities or about the many other factors left out of a specific theory—are never strictly satisfied. We do not know a priori whether differences in interests and identities or in the other excluded factors are important. The best we can do is try to determine the domain of applicability of problem-solving theories by using them in different settings. Powerful theories will work in a large domain because the excluded factors subsumed in the ceteris paribus assumption generally are insignificant. Weak theories will have a very limited domain. The sociological approach makes a serious and important criticism and contribution in stressing the importance of intersubjective meanings and understandings and the interaction between agents and structure.

The sociological approach stresses the inseparability of units and structure. But it is important not to identify this criticism with this particular approach. A second line of research is also predicated on the interaction of units and structure or, more precisely, the interaction of states and the international structure. The essence of Gourevitch's second-image-reversed argument is that

---

31. See Robert Cox, "Social Forces, States, and World Orders," in Keohane, *Neorealism and Its Critics,* pp. 204–54; Dessler, "What's at Stake in the Agent–Structure Debate?"; John Ruggie, "Continuity and Transformation in World Polity," in Keohane, *Neorealism and Its Critics;* John Gerard Ruggie, "Territoriality and Beyond," *International Organization* 47 (Winter 1993), pp. 139–74; Wendt, "The Agent–Structure Problem in International Relations Theory"; and Alexander Wendt, "Anarchy is What States Make of It," *International Organization* 46 (Spring 1992), pp. 391–425.
32. Cox, "Social Forces, States, and World Orders," p. 208.
33. Ibid., p. 208.

the international structure shapes domestic institutions and states' preferences: states and structure interact.

This second form of the criticism that agents and structure are inseparable is important for two reasons. First, it shows that the agent–structure problem may arise even in rationalist approaches that take interests and identities as given and assume that the units act in their own narrow self-interest. Second, the existing literature illustrates a way of trying to deal with this form of the agent–structure problem. The potential solution is to redefine the units in the system. Rather than treating states as unitary actors, states are decomposed into more basic units. The hope here is that we will be able to separate these more basic units from the constraints facing them.

To illustrate this approach to dealing with the interaction of states and the international structure, consider Rogowski's work on the effects of international trade on domestic political alignments and states' preferences.[34] At the risk of doing the subtlety of his analysis grave injustice, Rogowski decomposes a country into three groups or units: landowners, capitalists, and labor. A state's preferences emerge through competition among these units. Moreover, anything that significantly affects the terms of international trade shifts the distribution of domestic political power among the units. For example, technological or political changes, like the advent of railroads and steamships or the rise of British hegemony, reduce the cost or risk of international trade. These changes favor and enrich domestic groups that benefit from greater trade. By assumption, benefited groups become more powerful and the state's preferences generally become more reflective of the preferences of these favored groups.[35]

Rogowski's analysis illustrates a rationalist version of the agent–structure problem or, more accurately, the state–structure problem. Capital, land, and labor in Rogowski's argument are acting in their own material self-interest. Changing intersubjective meanings and understandings are not at issue here. Nevertheless, we cannot decompose the international system into units and structure if we treat states as the units. For example, a change in the international system, like the rise of British hegemony, that reduces the risk and therefore increases the expected return to international trade will also

34. Rogowski, *Commerce and Coalitions.*
35. Rogowski readily acknowledges that he is making assumptions about the domestic political process and does not have a theory of the state. He also emphasizes that although changes in the terms of trade may make some domestic groups more powerful, they still may lose in the domestic political struggle (ibid., pp. 4–5). The power of Rogowski's analysis, of course, lies in its ability to identify the groups that will benefit from greater trade and the domestic cleavages that greater trade will tend to create. Appealing to the Stolper–Samuelson theorem, Rogowski argues that greater trade favors the domestic group that controls the relatively abundant factor. So, for example, land was abundant and capital and labor were scarce in the United States in the latter part of the nineteenth century, while labor was abundant and capital and land were relatively scarce in Germany. Accordingly, agriculture in the United States and labor in Germany should have supported greater openness, while capital and labor in the United States and capital and land in Germany should have united in support of protectionism (pp. 3–20).

tend to change states' preferences. States and structure are interdependent; each is in part an effect of the other.

This brief illustration also suggests a way of trying to deal with this version of the agent–structure problem: namely, to decompose the system into different units that hopefully can be separated from the structure constraining them. In effect, we enlarge the game by trying to break what we previously took to be a unitary actor, namely the state, into more basic units.[36] Of course, enlarging the game to include the interaction between domestic and international politics makes any analysis much more difficult. Needless to say, an approach to dealing with the inseparability of states and structure is not a theory of their interaction. Much important work remains to be done on the interaction of states and structure.[37]

In sum, theories that take intersubjective meanings and understandings as given assume away one form of agent–structure interaction. Structural theories that take the state to be a unitary actor also assume away a rationalist form of agent–structure interaction. These theoretical simplifications may be appropriate for some questions and not for others. We need to do more to identify those domains in which this interaction can be disregarded and those in which it cannot.

Waltz's definition of structure

The first and second avenues of criticism are directed at the structural approach in general. The third and fourth avenues of criticism apply more specifically to neorealism and to Waltz's particular formulation of it. The third criticism focuses on Waltz's spare definition of structure and generally argues that other elements be included in the description of a system's structure.

Waltz defined a political structure by its ordering principle, the distribution of capabilities, and the functional differentiation or nondifferentiation of the units. This definition thus implies that the nuclear revolution in military technology is a unit-level change and not a structural change.[38] Joseph Nye finds it "particularly odd to see nuclear technology described as a unit characteristic."[39] He and Keohane argue that such factors as "the intensity of international interdependence or the degree of institutionalization of international rules do not vary from one state to another on the basis of their internal characteristics . . . and are therefore not unit-level factors."[40] They conclude

---

36. Clearly this approach does nothing to address the important concerns raised in the sociological approach to the agent–structure problem.

37. For suggestive discussions of the interaction between states and structure in different substantive contexts, see Brian Downing, *The Military Revolution and Political Change* (Princeton, N.J.: Princeton University Press, 1993); Katzenstein, *Between Power and Plenty;* and Charles Tilly, *Capital and Coercion* (New York: Blackwell, 1990).

38. Waltz, "Reflections on *Theory of International Politics,*" p. 327.

39. Nye, "Neorealism and Neoliberalism," p. 243.

40. Joseph Nye and Robert Keohane, "*Power and Interdependence* Revisited," *International*

that "making the unit level the dumping ground for all unexplained variance is an impediment to the development of theory."[41]

It is clear why Waltz would not want to include military technology in his definition of structure. Recall that one of his goals in fashioning his definition was to give a purely positional picture of a system so the notion of structure would be transposable from one substantive context to another. One can readily transpose the idea of the distribution of capabilities from the international system where states are the units to, for example, an oligopolistic market where firms are the actors. But what is the analogue to having a secure, second-strike force for a firm in an oligopoly? Including military technology in the definition of structure would seem to make the concept less transposable. Of course, greater transposability comes at a cost. Waltz's theory cannot account for variations in outcomes like the probability of war that may be due to the nuclear revolution. To understand those effects, we have to look to other theories.

Although it is evident why Waltz would not want to include dimensions like military technology in his notion of structure given his goal of transposability, why should the distribution of capabilities across states "be included in the definition and not other characteristics of states that could be cast in distributional terms?"[42] The answer seems to be a pragmatic one. Waltz believes that state "behavior varies more with differences of power than with differences in ideology, in internal structure of property relations, or in governmental form."[43] That is, Waltz believes that a definition of structure based on the distribution of capabilities rather than on the distribution of something else seems more likely to have greater explanatory power.[44] In evaluating the theory based on this definition, part of what is being evaluated is the usefulness of focusing on the distribution of capabilities.

Notwithstanding the prevalence of criticisms of Waltz's spare definition of structure, there is often a certain hollowness to debates about the proper definition of structure. Surely the effects of, say, the nuclear revolution on international politics do not depend on whether we attach the appellation "structural" or "unit-level" to this change. Putting a high value on transposability, Waltz opted for a definition that made the concept of structure more readily transposable. Other theorists working on other questions may value transposability less and may define structure differently. The important issue, however, is not whether the consequences of the nuclear revolution, different forms of property relations, varying degrees of institutionalization, or changes

---

Organization 41 (Autumn 1987), pp. 725–53, and especially p. 746, from which the quotation is drawn.

41. Ibid.
42. Waltz, "Reflections on *Theory of International Politics*," p. 329.
43. Ibid.
44. Buzan, Jones, and Little make a similar point in Barry Buzan, Charles Jones, and Richard Little, *The Logic of Anarchy* (New York: Columbia University Press, 1993), pp. 54–56.

in other sets of constraints are called "structural" or something else. The issue is to develop theories that explain these consequences.[45] When we debate what to call these changes rather than develop and test theories about the consequences of these changes, we appear to believe that the name implies the consequences.

Neorealism and its implications

The neorealist–neoliberal debate develops primarily along the fourth avenue of criticism. This criticism questions the conclusions claimed to follow from Waltz's assumptions and those of neorealism more generally. Neorealism, for example, claims that international institutions play a minimal role in shaping international politics and that the prospects for cooperation in anarchy are bleak.[46] Neoliberalism questions these claims in two ways. First, it challenges the logical coherence of the neorealist argument by trying to show that there is a mistake in the logic. Second, neoliberalism argues that the explanatory power of neorealism is weak when compared to neoliberalism. I trace the development of this criticism and the neorealist–neoliberal debate in the remainder of this section. I examine three major disputes in the debate in the next section.

In his contribution to *Neorealism and Its Critics,* Keohane surveys the neorealist research program and questions its predictive power.[47] He then describes what a "modified structural research program" would look like. It would "pay much more attention to the roles of institutions and rules than does Structural Realism. Indeed, a structural interpretation of the emergence of international rules and procedures, and of obedience to them by states, is one of the rewards that could be expected from this modified structural research program."[48]

Keohane challenges neorealism more directly and develops an institutional approach more fully in his work, *After Hegemony.*[49] The central question is, "Under what conditions can independent countries cooperate in the world political economy?"[50] Can, for example, states cooperate in the absence of a hegemon? Keohane begins his analysis of this question "with Realist insights about the role of power. . . . [Keohane's] central arguments draw more on the Institutionalist tradition, arguing that cooperation can under some conditions develop on the basis of complementary interests and that institutions, broadly defined, affect the patterns of cooperation that emerge."[51] In short, institutions

45. For a recent effort to do this, see ibid.
46. Joseph Grieco, "Anarchy and the Limits of Cooperation," in Baldwin, *Neorealism and Neoliberalism,* pp. 116–42 and pp. 118–19 in particular.
47. Keohane, "Theory of World Politics."
48. Ibid., p. 194.
49. Robert Keohane, *After Hegemony* (Princeton: Princeton University Press, 1984).
50. Ibid., p. 9.
51. Ibid., p. 9.

may be a significant factor in promoting international cooperation in ways that neorealism has failed to appreciate.

Keohane challenged both the logical coherence and the explanatory power of neorealism. Attacking the logic, Keohane writes, "I propose to show, on the basis of their own assumptions, that the characteristic pessimism of Realism does not follow. I seek to demonstrate that Realist assumptions about world politics are consistent with the formation of institutionalized arrangements, containing rules and principles, which promote cooperation."[52] In sum, Keohane intends to start with the same set of core assumptions that neorealism does and then show that cooperation is compatible with these assumptions.

Keohane attempts this demonstration in the context of the repeated prisoners' dilemma. There are two steps to the demonstration. The first is to argue that the repeated prisoners' dilemma is a reasonable model for the international system envisioned in neorealism, that is, that this model is compatible with realism's central assumptions about the international system. Although he does not develop this point at length, Keohane claims, "Not all situations in world politics or international political economy take the form of Prisoner's Dilemma, but many do."[53] As further support for the claim that the repeated prisoners' dilemma is generally seen to be compatible with realism's basic assumptions, he might also have referred to Jervis's belief that this game is an appropriate model for studying the security dilemma.[54] The second step in Keohane's argument is to appeal to the Folk theorem, which shows that the mutually cooperative outcome can occur in equilibrium in an infinitely repeated prisoners' dilemma if the actors do not discount the future too much.[55] These two steps taken together imply that cooperation is compatible with realism.

Writing in 1983, Keohane believed his neoliberal institutional approach would prove to have greater explanatory power than neorealism. But, a definitive test of his institutional approach was not yet possible because the world was "only just entering the posthegemonic era."[56] It was too soon to test the explanatory power of an argument that predicted that international institutions and cooperation would persist despite the absence of a hegemon. Instead of a test, Keohane offered a "plausibility probe" of his institutional approach in the cases of international trade, finance, and petroleum.[57]

One can envision two general types of response to Keohane's neoliberal challenge to neorealism. The first addresses Keohane's challenge to the logic of

52. Ibid., p. 67.
53. Ibid., p. 68.
54. Robert Jervis, "Cooperation Under the Security Dilemma," *World Politics* 30 (January 1978), pp. 167–214 and p. 170 in particular.
55. Drew Fudenberg and Eric Maskin, "The Folk Theorem in Repeated Games with Discounting or with Incomplete Information," *Econometrica* 54 (October 1986), pp. 533–54.
56. Keohane, *After Hegemony*, p. 218.
57. See Robert Keohane, "Institutionalist Theory and the Realist Challenge After the Cold War," in Baldwin, *Neorealism and Neoliberalism,* pp. 269–301, and particularly p. 292; and Keohane, *After Hegemony.*

neorealism's analysis of the problem of international cooperation. This response would show that Keohane had really not based his argument on the same set of core assumptions that neorealism does. If this were the case, then Keohane's argument that neorealism's conclusions about the prospects of international cooperation do not follow from its assumptions would be invalid. If, more specifically, the repeated prisoners' dilemma is incompatible with neorealism's core assumptions about the international system, then showing that cooperation in this game is possible would say nothing about what follows from neorealism's assumptions.

The second type of response is more empirical. It would say that neorealism never claimed that international cooperation was logically incompatible with neorealism's assumptions. So, showing that cooperation is possible given these assumptions does not contradict neorealism. The real question is how much international cooperation exists and whether neorealism or neoliberalism does a better job of accounting for the observed pattern of international cooperation. This response would then go on to compare the relative explanatory power of these two approaches.

Joseph Grieco developed both types of response to the institutionalist challenge.[58] He argued that Keohane had not started with the same assumptions neorealism does. In using the repeated prisoners' dilemma, Keohane implicitly had assumed that states try to maximize their absolute gains. According to Grieco, however, neorealism requires a state's utility function to reflect a concern for relative gains.[59] Consequently, Keohane does not "show, on the basis of their [realists'] own assumptions, that the characteristic pessimism of Realism does not follow," as he claimed.[60] In *Cooperation Among Nations,* Grieco tried to assess the relative explanatory power of neorealism and institutionalism. He considers the case of negotiations over nontariff barriers during the Tokyo Round of the General Agreement on Tariffs and Trade, a case that he believes poses a hard test for realism, and concludes that realism explains this case better than does institutionalism. The latest round of the debate between realism and liberalism was now fully engaged.[61]

David Baldwin brings a number of previously published contributions to this debate together in *Neorealism and Neoliberalism.*[62] Baldwin provides an

58. See the following works of Joseph Grieco: "Anarchy and the Limits of Cooperation"; "Realist Theory and the Problem of International Cooperation," *Journal of Politics* 50 (Summer 1988), pp. 600–624; and *Cooperation Among Nations* (Ithaca, N.Y.: Cornell University Press, 1990).
59. Grieco, "Anarchy and the Limits of Cooperation," p. 129. Gowa made the same criticism of Axelrod's use of the repeated prisoners' dilemma [Robert Axelrod, *The Evolution of Cooperation* (New York: Basic Books, 1984)] when he used this game to model international politics. See Joanne Gowa, "Anarchy, Egoism, and Third Images," *International Organization* 40 (1986), pp. 167–86 and particularly pp. 172–79.
60. Keohane, *After Hegemony,* p. 67.
61. See Nye, "Neorealism and Neoliberalism," and the references cited therein for an introduction to earlier rounds of this debate.
62. These contributions are: Robert Axelrod and Robert Keohane, "Achieving Cooperation

overview of the debate, and Grieco and Keohane offer their reflections and appraisals of the debate in new essays. This volume complements and extends some of the lines of analysis developed in *Neorealism and Its Critics*. *Neorealism and Its Critics* includes both internal and external critiques of neorealism. The former share neorealism's problem-solving approach, while the latter adopt a critical approach.[63] The scope of *Neorealism and Neoliberalism* is narrower, more focused, and wholly internal. All of the contributions exemplify the problem-solving approach and address various facets of the neorealist–neoliberal debate. Three issues have dominated this debate, and an assessment of it requires an examination of each.

At issue

The three issues at the center of neorealist–neoliberal debate are the meaning and implications of anarchy, the problem of absolute and relative gains, and the tension between cooperation and distribution. In what follows, I make three points about these issues. First, although anarchy is often taken to be a fundamental organizing concept in international relations theory, the emphasis on anarchy is misplaced. What have often been taken to be the implications of anarchy do not really follow from that assumption. Rather, these implications result from other implicit and unarticulated assumptions about states' strategic environment. Second, the controversy over the problem of absolute and relative gains generally has mistaken effects for causes in its analysis of the prospects for international cooperation. Finally, although the debate only recently has begun to consider distributional concerns, the analysis of these concerns may help to clarify the differences that do divide neorealism and institutionalism.

The meaning and implications of anarchy

Much of the neorealist–neoliberal debate centers on the meaning and implications of anarchy. According to Grieco, neorealism entails five proposi-

---

Under Anarchy," *World Politics* 38 (October 1988), pp. 226–54; Grieco, "Anarchy and the Limits of Cooperation"; Stephen Krasner, "Global Communications and National Power," *World Politics* 43 (April 1991), pp. 336–66; Charles Lipson, "International Cooperation in Economic and Security Affairs," *World Politics* 37 (October 1984), pp. 1–23; Michael Mastanduno, "Do Relative Gains Matter?" *International Security* 16 (Summer 1991), pp. 73–113; Helen Milner, "The Assumption of Anarchy in International Relations Theory," *Review of International Studies* 17 (January 1991), pp. 67–85; Robert Powell, "Absolute and Relative Gains in International Relations Theory," *American Political Science Review* 85 (December 1991), pp. 1303–20; Duncan Snidal, "Relative Gains and the Pattern of International Cooperation," *American Political Science Review* 85 (September 1991), pp. 701–26; and Arthur Stein, "Coordination and Collaboration," *International Organization* 36 (Spring 1982), pp. 294–324.

63. For an example of the former, see Keohane, "Theory of World Politics"; for one of the latter, see Richard Ashley, "The Poverty of Neorealism," in Keohane, *Neorealism and Its Critics*, pp. 255–300; and Cox, "Social Forces, States, and World Orders."

tions. He defines the last three of these as "Third, international anarchy is the principle force shaping the motives and actions of states. Fourth, states in anarchy are preoccupied with power and security, are predisposed towards conflict and competition, and often fail to cooperate even in the face of common interests. Finally, international institutions affect the prospects for cooperation only marginally."[64] The point of departure for Keohane's analysis in *After Hegemony* was to use the prisoners' dilemma to show that anarchy did not imply a lack of cooperation. Grieco responded by arguing that Keohane's model was misspecified because he neglected states' concerns for relative gains. Duncan Snidal then tried to show that anarchy does not imply a lack of cooperation even if states are concerned with relative gains.[65]

A review of the neorealist–neoliberal debate about the meaning and implications of anarchy shows that our continuing emphasis on anarchy is misplaced. Many of the purported implications of anarchy may be more usefully traced to other assumptions about the constraints facing the units. This suggests that we should focus less attention on anarchy and much more attention on characterizing the strategic settings in which the units interact.

In reviewing the debate about anarchy, it is necessary to begin by distinguishing between two formulations of anarchy. The first is that anarchy means the "lack of a common government" that can enforce agreements among the states or more generally among the units.[66] Robert Art and Jervis together explain that "international politics takes place in an arena that has no central governing body. No agency exists above individual states with authority and power to make laws and settle disputes. States can make commitments and treaties, but no sovereign power ensures compliance and punishes deviations. This—the absence of a supreme power—is what is meant by the anarchic environment of international politics."[67]

It is important to emphasize that this formulation of anarchy says nothing about the means the units have at their disposal as they try to further their ends. It says only that no higher authority exists that can prevent them from using the means they have. Thus, for Waltz, firms facing a high risk of bankruptcy may be in an anarchic self-help system even though the means available to them to further their interests, like cutting prices or forming alliances to distribute the

---

64. Grieco, "Anarchy and the Limits of Cooperation," pp. 118–19.
65. Snidal, "Relative Gains and the Pattern of Cooperation." For Grieco's critique of Snidal's analysis and Snidal's response, see Joseph Grieco, Robert Powell, and Duncan Snidal, "The Relative Gains Problem for International Cooperation," *American Political Science Review* 87 (September 1993), pp. 729–43.
66. The quotation is from p. 226 of Axelrod and Keohane, "Achieving Cooperation Under Anarchy." Also see Kenneth Oye, "Explaining Cooperation Under Anarchy," in Kenneth Oye, ed., *Cooperation Under Anarchy* (Princeton, N.J.: Princeton University Press, 1986), particularly pp. 1–2.
67. Robert Art and Robert Jervis, *International Politics,* 3d ed. (Boston: Harper Collins), p. 1.

costs of research and development, have nothing to do with the use of military force, which is one of the means available to states in the international system.[68]

One advantage of defining anarchy without reference to the means available to the units is that it makes the concept of anarchy readily transposable to different substantive domains. As discussed above, Waltz weighed this advantage heavily in constructing his formulation of structure, so it is hardly surprising that he would adopt this first definition of anarchy. But he certainly is not alone, as Milner's survey of different concepts of anarchy shows.[69]

The second notion of anarchy refers to the means available to the units. In "Coordination and Collaboration," Arthur Stein begins by observing that many international relations scholars use anarchy to describe "the classic characterization of international politics as relations between sovereign entities dedicated to their own self-preservation, ultimately able to depend only on themselves, and prepared to use force."[70] In effect, this second formulation adds another dimension to the lack of a central authority: namely, that one of the means available to the units is the use of force.

The addition of this second dimension has two consequences. First, it makes the transposability of the concept of anarchy more problematic. What, for example, is the analogue to using force for a firm facing a high risk of bankruptcy? If there is no analogue, then a group of firms facing a high risk of bankruptcy would not form an anarchic system according to this definition. If we want to argue that there is an analogue, what are the criteria for establishing that one of the means open to a firm is analogous to a state's ability to resort to force? Of course, a definition of anarchy that reduces its transposability may have compensating advantages. Whether these potential advantages outweigh the disadvantage of a less transposable definition will be discussed below.

Second, adding another dimension raises important questions for international relations theory. Do the patterns of behavior generally associated with anarchic systems, such as the tendencies for balances of power to form and—at least for neorealists—the limited prospects for international cooperation, result from the lack of a central authority? Or, are these patterns more heavily influenced by implicit and unarticulated assumptions about, say, the nature of military force that are subsumed in the second definition of anarchy?

Two arguments suggest that our emphasis on anarchy has been misplaced if by anarchy we mean the lack of a central authority. These arguments suggest that conclusions often claimed to follow from the absence of a central authority do not. These conclusions require other supporting assumptions. The first argument is really an empirical observation. Keohane notes in his assessment of the debate between neorealism and neoliberalism that the modern state

68. Waltz, *Theory of International Politics,* pp. 105 and 111.
69. Milner, "The Assumption of Anarchy in International Relations Theory."
70. Stein, "Coordination and Collaboration," p. 30.

system, conventionally dated from 1648, has always been anarchic in the sense that it lacked a common government.[71] Thus, anarchy, while perhaps a necessary condition, is certainly not sufficient to explain any of the variation in international politics during the modern era. In particular, anarchy cannot account for whatever variation in the level of international cooperation and institutionalization there has been.

The second argument is more theoretical and begins with a recent attempt to formalize the classic guns-versus-butter problem.[72] To summarize the model, there are two states. In each period a state must decide how much of its output to consume, how much to allocate to its military sector, and whether or not to attack the other state. Each state's utility is the discounted sum of its consumption in each period. As long as neither state attacks, the game continues. If a state attacks at some time, the game effectively ends in one of two ways. Either one state or the other will prevail by conquering the other. The odds that a state will prevail are simply the ratio of its military allocation to the other state's military allocation. The fact that a state's probability of victory depends on its military allocation creates a trade-off between current and expected future consumption. The more a state consumes today, the smaller its military allocation, and the higher the probability of defeat. Because defeat means a loss of future consumption, consuming more today reduces expected future consumption. The formal analysis of the game determines each state's equilibrium level of consumption and military spending that balances this trade-off.

The guns-versus-butter model shows that our emphasis on anarchy is misplaced. Neorealism expects balance-of-power politics to prevail whenever the system is anarchic and the units want to survive.[73] The guns-versus-butter model indicates that this expectation is too broad. Whether or not the states balance in the model depends on an assumption about military technology. Generalizing beyond this model, whether units balance or not depends as much on other features defining the strategic situation in which they interact as it does on the presence of anarchy.

To see that balancing depends on underlying assumptions about military technology, note that the guns-versus-butter game presumes a conventional military technology in which the probability of victory or defeat depends on the relative sizes of the opposing military forces. Given this stylized assumption about military technology, the states balance against each other in the way we would expect the units to do in an anarchic system.[74] Now suppose that

---

71. Keohane, "Institutionalist Theory and the Realist Challenge After the Cold War."

72. Robert Powell, "Guns, Butter, and Anarchy," *American Political Science Review* 87 (March 1993), pp. 115–32. The present discussion extends some of the observations made in that essay (see pp. 126–27).

73. Waltz, *Theory of International Politics*, p. 121.

74. External balancing through alliances is impossible when there are only two states. Rather, the states engage in internal balancing. For a discussion of internal and external balancing, see Waltz, *Theory of International Politics*, p. 168.

the states' strategic setting is different. Formalizing and stylizing the nuclear revolution in military technology, assume that there is, to use Bernard Brodie's term, an absolute weapon.[75] The probability of victory no longer depends on the relative size of the states' military forces. Rather, once both states have attained secure second-strike forces, war is certain to take a toll far higher than any potential gain. If we solve the model based on this assumption about military technology, the states will spend enough to acquire second-strike forces. But they will not spend more even if the other state does. There is no balancing here even though the system remains anarchic and the units still seek to survive.[76] The first notion of anarchy, albeit very transposable, does not imply balancing.

The guns-versus-butter model, like many models, makes many stark simplifications and, accordingly, must be used cautiously. On the plus side, models, in part because of these simplifications, let us vary one factor while holding everything else constant. Models thereby permit us to isolate the effects of different factors in ways that historical cases rarely do. When we use the guns-versus-butter model to isolate the effects of anarchy, we find that conclusions claimed to follow from the assumption of anarchy depend at least as much on other unarticulated assumptions about the units' strategic environment.

The first definition of anarchy is in some sense too transposable, while the second definition is not transposable enough. As we have seen, if defined as the absence of a central authority, anarchy encompasses systems in which states do and do not balance. Conversely, if we define anarchy by adding the notion of the potential use of force to the lack of a central authority, we find the transposability of the concept to be greatly limited, even if units generally will balance in such a system. The disadvantages of this very limited notion of anarchy are quite high. In particular, this notion does not apply to systems in which the use of force is for all intents and purposes not at issue. Even if neorealism's expectations about anarchic systems in which the use of force is a serious potential concern are correct, the arguments underlying these expectations cannot be transposed to systems in which the use of force among units is not at issue. Neorealist expectations about these systems may of course still prove to be correct, but they lack theoretical foundations.

75. Bernard Brodie, *Strategy in the Missile Age* (Princeton, N.J.: Princeton University Press, 1959). For other discussions of the effect of the nuclear revolution, see Robert Jervis, *The Meaning of the Nuclear Revolution* (Ithaca, N.Y.: Cornell University Press, 1989); Robert Powell, *Nuclear Deterrence Theory* (Cambridge: Cambridge University Press, 1990); Thomas Schelling, *Arms and Influence* (New Haven, Conn.: Yale University Press, 1966); and Glenn Snyder, *Deterrence and Defense* (Princeton, N.J.: Princeton University Press, 1961).

76. Buzan, Jones and Little reach the same conclusion in *The Logic of Anarchy*. They and Morrow offer the expansion of the Roman empire as an important example of the failure of balances to form. See James Morrow, "Social Choice and System Structure," *World Politics* 41 (October 1988), pp. 75–97.

The absence of a definition that is less transposable than the first and more transposable than the second poses an important problem for international relations theory after the cold war. The problem is evident in some recent efforts to use neorealism's analysis of anarchy and the problem of absolute and relative gains to outline the post–cold war contours of international politics. The neorealist analysis argues that states will start competing and balancing over economic issues after the cold war much as they competed and balanced over security issues during the cold war. Samuel Huntington, for example, bases his assessment of the continued importance of U.S. primacy on a neorealist analysis.[77] Yet, he and others also believe that the prospects of "military conflict between major states is unlikely."[78] The discussion of transposability shows that neither definition of anarchy provides adequate theoretical support for the neorealist analysis of international politics if the use of force is not a relevant concern. The first notion of anarchy can be transposed readily to a system in which the use of force is not at issue. But as we have seen, this definition does not support the neorealist claims that anarchy implies balance-of-power politics.[79] The second notion of anarchy, while it may imply balancing when force is at issue, cannot be transposed to a domain in which force is presumed not to be at issue.

Huntington, believing that the politics of international economics is more like a system with conventional military technology, argues for the importance of international primacy. Jervis, believing that the politics of international economics is more like a system with an absolute weapon, questions the importance of international primacy.[80] In either case, the neorealist–neoliberal debate's emphasis on the lack of a central authority is misplaced. As Charles Lipson puts it in his contribution to the Baldwin volume, "The idea of anarchy is, in a sense, the Rosetta stone of international relations. . . . But what was once a blinding insight—profound and evocative—has ossified and become blinding in the other sense of the word—limiting and obscuring."[81] We need to develop a more careful specification of the strategic settings in which units interact if we are to be able to explain the pattern of their interactions. Characterizing this structure is an important open question for international relations theory.

The problem of absolute and relative gains

The second major issue at the center of the debate between neorealism and institutionalism is the problem of absolute and relative gains. In what follows, I

77. Samuel Huntington, "Why International Primacy Matters," *International Security* 17 (Spring 1993), pp. 68–83. See also Robert Jervis, "International Primacy," *International Security* 17 (Spring 1993), pp. 52–67; and Kenneth Waltz, "The Emerging Structure of International Politics," *International Security* 18 (Fall 1993), pp. 44–79. Jervis uses a neorealist perspective to frame his discussion, but his conclusions differ from Huntington's.
78. Huntington, "Why International Primacy Matters," p. 93.
79. For a different view, see Waltz, "The Emerging Structure of International Politics," especially p. 74.
80. Jervis, "International Primacy," pp. 57–59.
81. Lipson, "International Cooperation in Economic and Security Affairs," p. 80.

first briefly summarize some aspects of the debate about this problem. Then I argue that in a narrower methodological sense this debate reflects a basic misunderstanding of the role of models. More broadly, the debate surrounding absolute and relative gains generally has mistaken effects for causes and, therefore, contributed little to the analysis of the problem of international cooperation. Once we separate causes from effects, we again see the need to focus our attention on a more elaborate characterization of the strategic settings confronting states.

To review the debate, neorealism assumes that states are concerned with relative gains. For Waltz, "states that feel insecure must ask how the gain will be divided. They are compelled to ask not 'Will both of us gain?' but 'Who will gain more?' "[82] In mounting his institutional challenge in *After Hegemony,* Keohane assumes that states are trying to maximize their absolute gains, that is, the states' preferences "are based on their assessments of their own welfare, not that of others."[83] He then analyzes the problem of cooperation in terms of the repeated prisoners' dilemma. Grieco in turn criticizes Keohane's assumption that states attempt to maximize their absolute gains. Grieco asserts that "realism expects a state's utility function to incorporate *two distinct terms*. It needs to include the state's individual payoff . . . reflecting the realist view that states are motivated by absolute gains. Yet it must also include a term integrating both the states' individual payoff . . . and the partner's payoff . . . in such a way that gaps favoring the state add to its utility while, more importantly, gaps favoring the partner detract from it."[84] In sum, the debate about absolute and relative gains became a debate about what to assume about states' utility functions.

The key to understanding this debate is to distinguish between two possibilities. The first is that a state's concern or, more precisely, the degree of its concern for relative gains is the product of the strategic environment in which the state finds itself. If so, then the degree of concern is likely to vary as the environment, say the intensity of the security dilemma, varies. In this case, the strategic setting facing the state induces a concern for relative gains. The second possibility is that a state's degree of concern does not vary and is the same regardless of its environment.

Both neorealism and neoliberalism appear to agree that this concern is induced. Grieco, for example, believes that a state's sensitivity to relative gains "will be a function of, and will vary in response to, at least six factors."[85] These include the fungibility of power across issues, the length of the shadow of the future, and whether the relative gains or losses occur over military or economic matters.[86] Neoliberalism also assumes that the degree of concern varies. Indeed, Keohane emphasizes that both neorealism and neoliberalism presume

82. Waltz, *Theory of International Politics,* p. 105. See also Waltz, *Man, State, and War,* p. 198.
83. Keohane, *After Hegemony,* p. 66.
84. Grieco, "Anarchy and the Limits of Cooperation," p. 129, emphasis original.
85. Grieco, "Realist Theory and the Problem of International Cooperation," p. 610.
86. Ibid., pp. 610–11.

that the concern for relative gains is conditional in his appraisal of the neorealist–neoliberal debate.[87]

Two important implications follow from the conclusion that the degree of a state's concern for relative gains is conditional and varies from situation to situation. The first is that the debate about what to assume about a state's preferences or utility function is largely irrelevant and reflects a basic misunderstanding of the role of models. We can formally induce a concern for relative gains in two ways. First, we can explicitly represent the constraints that lead to this concern in the model. This is the approach I followed in analyzing the absolute and relative gains problem.[88] I assumed that states were trying to maximize their absolute gains. But the strategic setting in which they were attempting to do so induced a concern for relative gains. The second way to induce a concern for relative gains is to represent this concern in the state's utility function. When done in this way, the model is in effect a reduced form for some more complicated and unspecified model in which the strategic constraints would induce this concern. Grieco's analysis may be seen as an attempt to work with a reduced form. Rather than specifying a model that explicitly represents the six factors he believes induce a concern for relative gains, he abbreviates the influences of these factors through his specification of the states' utility functions.[89]

Which approach to modeling a state's concern is better? I do not believe there is an a priori answer to this question. Models are tools and asking which approach is better is akin to asking whether a hammer or a saw is better. The answer depends on whether the task at hand is driving nails or cutting wood. One advantage of a reduced form is that it is likely to be simpler and easier to use analytically. A disadvantage is that as long as the more complicated underlying model remains unspecified, we cannot analyze the purported link between the constraints that are believed to induce a concern and the realization of this concern. The link thus remains problematic. Whether the balance of advantages and disadvantages favors an approach based on a reduced form or on a more explicit structural form depends on the model as a whole and on the substantive problem. Thus, debates about what to assume about preferences cannot be resolved without reference to an overall evaluation of the entire model and the substantive problem being modeled. By focusing solely on what to assume about preferences and not evaluating this

87. Keohane, "Institutionalist Theory and the Realist Challenge After the Cold War," pp. 418–25.

88. Powell, "Absolute and Relative Gains in International Relations Theory."

89. See Grieco, "Anarchy and the Limits of Cooperation," as well as his "Realist Theory and the Problem of International Cooperation," and *Cooperation Among Nations.* Although Grieco's model may be seen as a reduced form, it is not clear that he sees it as such. His assertion that a state's utility function must incorporate a term reflecting its concern for absolute gains and one reflecting its concern for relative gains may be true of a particular model, but it does not hold for all models. His apparent claim that it is true for all models suggests that he does not interpret his model as a reduced form.

assumption in the overall context of the entire model, the neorealist–neoliberal debate about states' preferences seems largely irrelevant. It reflects a basic misunderstanding of the role of models.

A second important implication follows from the conclusion that the degree of a state's concern for relative gains depends on, or is a function of, its strategic environment. This dependency means that the concern for relative gains is part of the outcome and not part of the explanation. A concern for relative gains is an effect and not a cause. We cannot explain the presence or absence of international cooperation because of the presence or absence of significant concerns for relative gains. Cooperation and concern for relative gains may co-vary, but one does not cause the other. The causes for both are the underlying features of the states' strategic environment that jointly induce a concern for relative gains and thereby make cooperation difficult.

Existing work in international relations theory has to varying degrees recognized first that relative gains concerns do not explain the level of cooperation and second the need to look to the underlying strategic environment. Lipson, for example, tries to relate differences in the strategic environments inherent in military and economic issues to differences in states' discount factors and, through the differences in those discount factors, to the likelihood of international cooperation in military and economic affairs.[90] Jervis explicitly recognizes this need: "The conditions under which states seek to maximize their relative as opposed to their absolute gains need more exploration."[91]

A possible explanation of the concern for relative gains might at first seem to be anarchy: a lack of a central authority leads to balancing and a concern for relative gains. This answer, however, fails for at least two reasons. Anarchy has been a constant feature of the modern international system. It cannot therefore account for variation in the degree of a state's concern for absolute gains. And, as we have seen above, anarchy does not imply balancing.

As emphasized above, models often must be judged in light of the problem they are designed to address. If we want to study the problem of international cooperation and its relation to concerns for relative gains, modeling that concern in terms of state preferences seems likely to prove a poor approach. The reduced form would be leaving implicit and unspecified precisely what we want to know more about, i.e., the link from the states' strategic environment to their concern for relative gains and the prospects for cooperation. Trying to make this link more explicit by elaborating a state's strategic setting and the connection between this setting and the induced concern for relative gains seems likely to prove a more fruitful approach. As in our discussion of anarchy, we are led to the need to focus our attention on a more sophisticated characterization of the strategic situations confronting the units.

---

90. Lipson, "International Cooperation in Economic and Security Affairs." See also Joanne Gowa and Edward Mansfield, "Power Politics and International Trade," *American Political Science Review* 87 (June 1993), pp. 408–20.

91. Jervis, "Realism, Game Theory, and Cooperation."

In sum, the debate surrounding the problem of absolute and relative gains has betrayed a fundamental methodological misunderstanding of the role of models. The debate has also mistaken effects for causes. Unfortunately, the methodological misunderstanding has reinforced the substantive mistake. By focusing on what to assume about states' preferences, the debate has made it more difficult to correct the mistake of seeing effects as causes. In a reduced form in which the concern for relative gains is represented in the states' utility functions, the degree of this concern is formally an independent variable. Thus, it is easy to imagine holding everything else constant and asking how changes in the degree of this concern would affect cooperation. The difficulty is, of course, that if the degree of concern is really an effect, then one cannot hold everything else constant while varying this concern. Although formally independent in the reduced form, the degree of this concern is substantively dependent. The reduced form thus masks this dependence and makes it more difficult to correct the mistake of seeing effects as causes. Once we separate effects from causes, we also appreciate the need for a more careful specification of the units' strategic setting.

Coordination and distribution

The debate between neorealism and neoliberalism recently has focused on a third issue. A central contention of the neoliberal approach is that institutions matter. In particular, they can help states cooperate: "institutions, broadly defined, affect the patterns of cooperation that emerge."[92] In analyzing how institutions matter, Keohane emphasizes market failures and explains that institutions can help independent actors overcome these failures by providing information and reducing transactions costs.[93] In short, institutions may make it possible to realize joint gains and move out toward the Pareto frontier. But there are often many ways to realize these gains, with some ways giving a larger share to one state and other ways giving a larger share to another state. "There are," as Stephen Krasner observes in his contribution to the Baldwin volume, "many points along the Pareto frontier."[94] These multiple ways of achieving the joint gains from cooperation can create conflicts over how those gains will be distributed. As Geoffrey Garrett observes of the Single European Act, "the EC [European Community] members shared the common goal of increasing the competitiveness of European goods and services in global markets. It is apparent, however, that there were also substantial differences in national preferences within this broad rubric."[95] Reflecting on the debate, Keohane

92. Keohane, *After Hegemony*, p. 9.
93. Ibid., p. 246.
94. Krasner, "Global Communications and National Power," p. 235.
95. The quotation is from p. 535 of Geoffrey Garret, "International Cooperation and Institutional Choice," *International Organization* 46 (Spring 1992), pp. 533–60. For another discussion of conflicting interests, see Andrew Moravcsik, "Negotiating the Single European Act," *International Organization* 45 (Winter 1991), pp. 19–56.

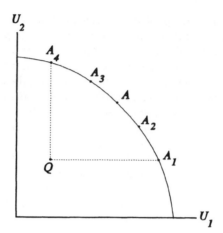

FIGURE 1. *Distributional conflicts: U_1 = the utility of state 1 (S_1); U_2 = the utility of state 2 (S_2); Q = status quo; A_1 through A_4 = possible agreements along the Pareto frontier*

now believes that he underemphasized "distributive issues and the complexities they create for international cooperation" in *After Hegemony*.[96] I will suggest that a careful analysis of the tension between cooperation and distribution can illuminate the debate between neorealism and neoliberalism by clarifying some of the differences that actually do divide these two approaches.

The distributive problem arises because there are many ways to divide the cooperative gains. Figure 1 illustrates this problem when two states, S_1 and S_2, are trying to cooperate. S_1's utility is measured along the horizontal axis, and S_2's utility is measured along the vertical axis. Q is the status quo. A_1 through A_4 are possible agreements that lie along the Pareto frontier. Both A_2 and A_3 lie on the Pareto frontier and are Pareto-superior to Q; i.e., both S_1 and S_2 prefer A_2 to Q and A_3 to Q. A_2 and A_3 are different ways of realizing the joint gains from cooperation. But, S_1 prefers A_2 to A_3 because A_2 yields a higher utility. Similarly, S_2 prefers A_3. Thus, there is a distributive conflict over A_2 and A_3. More generally, S_1 prefers agreements closer to A_1 and S_2 prefers agreements closer to A_4.

Krasner recently has used these distributional issues to challenge the neoliberal approach.[97] The thrust of Krasner's criticism is that "the nature of institutional arrangements is better explained by the distribution of national

96. Keohane, "Institutionalist Theory and the Realist Challenge After the Cold War," pp. 446–47.

97. Krasner, "Global Communications and National Power." See also James Morrow, "Modeling International Regimes," *International Organization,* forthcoming.

power capabilities than by efforts to solve problems of market failure."[98] In terms of Figure 1, the more powerful S_1, the greater will be its share of the joint gain and the closer the agreement will be to A_1.

Viewing the question of whether institutions matter in terms of distributional issues helps refine and clarify that question. If cooperation can take many different forms and these alternative forms have distributional consequences, then the arrangements themselves can become the object of negotiation. Indeed, given the absence of a supranational authority, the states cannot bind themselves to any particular initial institutional arrangement and corresponding allocation of cooperative benefits. The institutional structure is always subject to renegotiation if a state believes it worthwhile.

The perpetual possibility of renegotiation raises an important dynamic question that must be separated from a more static issue. That is, institutions might matter in either or both a static and a dynamic way. The static way that institutions might matter is that they might be a *means* of overcoming market failures or, more generally, of realizing joint gains from cooperation. As a means to an end, the structure of the institution becomes something to be explained. In his explanation of institutional structure, Keohane emphasizes monitoring and reducing uncertainty. In emphasizing these factors, he is trying to explain how institutions can serve as a means to achieving the joint gains from cooperation. Krasner focuses on another aspect of the explanation of institutional structure. He argues that the actual institutional arrangement that will emerge from the set of potential institutional arrangements that fulfill the functions Keohane describes will tend to reflect the desires of the more powerful actors. Thus, Keohane's and Krasner's analyses of the static issue complement each other.

There is also a second, more dynamic way that institutions may matter. If institutions do matter in this second sense, then they would be part of an explanation and not part of the outcome to be explained. Figure 1 can be used to illustrate this second way. Suppose that at some time t_0 two states are at Q. Both states want to move out to the Pareto frontier. To this end, they create an institution that reduces transaction costs and uncertainty in the way Keohane describes. In this way the institution is a means to the end of realizing the joint gains of cooperation. But there are also distributional conflicts, so both states also use their political power to shape the institutional arrangements in order to obtain a larger share of the joint gains. Assume that S_1 is more powerful and, as Krasner argues, the institution through which the states realize the joint gains will give S_1 a larger share of the benefits. In particular, suppose the arrangement moves them from Q to A_2. At A_2, S_1 receives a larger share of the joint gains, which reflects its greater power. A_2 thus reflects Keohane's and Krasner's complementary analyses of the static dimension of the way that institutions may matter.

98. Krasner, "Global Communications and National Power," p. 235.

To examine the dynamic aspect, suppose further that at some later time, say t_1, the balance of power has shifted in favor of S_2. Indeed, assume that if the institution created at time t_0 did not exist and that the states were trying to create an institution de novo at t_1, then S_2's greater power would mean that the institution that would be created would move the states from Q to A_3. At A_3, S_2 obtains more of the gains, presumably reflecting its greater power.

But the states are not creating a new institution at t_1, for they created an institution at t_0 that moved them from Q to A_2. How does the fact that an institution already exists at t_1, when the states must deal with a new distribution of power, affect the institutional arrangements and distribution of benefits that will be devised at that time? There are two possibilities.

First, the institutional arrangements existing at t_0 are irrelevant. Institutions adjust smoothly so that the distribution of benefits always reflects the underlying distribution of power. In terms of Figure 1, the states will be at A_3 at t_1 regardless of the existence of an institution at t_0. In brief, history does not matter.

The second possibility is that the institutional arrangements that exist at t_0 affect those that prevail at t_1. To illustrate this possibility, let A in Figure 1 denote the arrangements and associated distribution of benefits that exist at t_1 given the arrangements existing at t_0. Then A will in general differ from A_3, which is what would have prevailed had there been no preexisting institution or if institutions adjusted smoothly. Intuitively, the farther A is from A_3, the more current arrangements are shaped by past arrangements.[99] A more concise way of describing this second way that institutions may matter is that history matters.[100] In terms of Figure 1, the neoliberal claim that institutional history matters in international relations means that A will often be very different from A_3. Moreover, the fact that the states originally cooperated means that cooperation is less likely to collapse and A is more likely to lie on the Pareto frontier. Cooperation will often continue in the face of a change in the underlying distribution of power.

The possibility that institutions may not adjust smoothly and that the existing institutional arrangements and distribution of benefits may not reflect the underlying distribution of power is a recurrent theme in international politics. Robert Gilpin, for example, sees this as the cause of hegemonic war. A hegemon establishes an international order and associated distribution of benefits that favors the hegemon. Over time, the hegemon's relative power declines because of uneven economic growth, and the existing order and distribution of benefits no longer reflect the distribution of power. This sets the

99. To simplify matters, I have assumed that institutions are efficient in that they move the states out to the Pareto frontier. Of course, institutions need not be efficient. For a discussion of institutions and efficiency, see Douglass North, *Institutions, Institutional Change, and Economic Performance* (New York: Cambridge University Press, 1990).
100. North analyzes the problem of institutional change and stability in ibid.

scene for another hegemonic conflict.[101] Similarly, a disparity between the distributions of benefits and power is inherent in Krasner's metaphor of tectonic plates.[102] When regimes are first created, they generally reflect the underlying distribution of power. But the pressure to change the regime builds over time as the distribution of power changes. In the tectonic plate metaphor, this pressure does not lead to a smooth adjustment. Rather, the pressure grows until it is suddenly relieved in an earthquake in which the regime alters in a way that realigns it with the distribution of power.

In the neorealist–neoliberal debate, Keohane generally emphasizes market failures, transaction costs, uncertainty, information, and institutions as important means of cooperation. But he also argues that international institutional history matters. Once institutions or regimes are established, actors behave in ways that, whether deliberately or not, make it costly to change the regime or build a new one. Thus, even if the original distribution of power underlying the regime shifts, the now more powerful states will not change the regime unless the distribution of power has shifted to such an extent that the benefits of a new regime, which would reflect the new distribution of power, outweigh the cost of changing the existing regime. The cost of changing or constructing new regimes thus gives existing regimes some resilience to shifts in the balance of power. "The high costs of regime-building help existing regimes persist."[103]

In contrast, Krasner argues that regimes and institutions do not matter at least in the case of global communications:

> In recent years distributional questions have precipitated conflict over the allocation of the radio spectrum and over international telecommunications. The outcome of these disputes has been determined primarily by the relative bargaining power of the states involved. *Whereas previous institutional choices had not imposed much constraint,* new interests and power capabilities conferred by new technologies have led to new institutional arrangements.
>   This is not to say that institutional arrangements were ever irrelevant: indeed, they were necessary to resolve coordination problems and to establish stability. Without regimes all parties would have been worse off. There are, however, many points along the Pareto frontier: the nature of institutional arrangements is better explained by the distribution of national power capabilities than by efforts to solve problems of market failure.[104]

In brief, institutions may serve as a means of achieving the joint gains of cooperation. But institutional history does not matter. Previous institutional

101. Robert Gilpin, *War and Change in World Politics* (Cambridge: Cambridge University Press, 1981).

102. Stephen Krasner, "Regimes and the Limits of Realism," in Stephen Krasner, ed., *International Regimes* (Ithaca, N.Y.: Cornell University Press, 1983), pp. 355–68.

103. Keohane, *After Hegemony,* p. 103.

104. Krasner, "Global Communications and National Power," p. 235, emphasis added.

choices do not constrain or significantly affect the future institutional arrangements and the future distribution of benefits.

The neorealist–neoliberal debate leaves us with contrasting claims about the
importance of institutional history. These claims in turn pose two questions for
future research. First, do institutions or regimes actually adjust smoothly to
changes in the distribution of power. Does institutional history matter? Second,
what factors affect the stability or rigidity of a regime or institution and the
rates at which it adjusts? In particular, are there factors in the international
environment that make international regimes and institutions less stable than,
for example, the institution of the medieval law merchant, the Declaration of
Rights and associated institutional changes following the Glorious Revolution
in England, or the current efforts to establish constitutional governments in
Russia and Eastern Europe?[105] Douglass North and others offer many
examples in which institutional history seems to be profoundly important.[106]
We need a better understanding of the conditions under which institutional
history matters and the extent to which the international system satisfies these
conditions. Work on these questions holds the promise of a more unified
understanding of institutions and cooperation.

Before this work can be done, however, two obstacles must be overcome.
First, we need a way of measuring or assessing the constraining effects of
institutions. Figure 1 helps us visualize the issue, but much more than a
visualization is required. Second, we need more powerful theories that make
more specific claims about the extent to which institutions shape future
decisions and actions than neorealism or neoliberalism presently does.

Conclusion

Although the neorealist–neoliberal debate sometimes has obscured as much as
it has clarified, this debate has forced us to examine the foundations of some of
our most influential theories of international politics more carefully. This is an
important contribution. Such examinations deepen our understanding of these
theories by clarifying their strengths and weaknesses. These clarifications in
turn may suggest important directions for future work and ultimately lead to
better theories with greater explanatory power.

As we have seen, both neorealism and neoliberalism see the effects of
anarchy and the degree of concern about relative gains to be conditional. The

---

105. See Paul Milgrom, Douglass North, and Barry Weingast, "The Role of Institutions in the
Revival of Trade: The Law Merchants, Private Judges, and the Champagne Fairs," *Economics and
Politics* 2 (March 1990), pp. 1–23; Douglass North and Barry Weingast, "Constitutions and
Commitment," *Journal of Economic History* 49 (December 1989), pp. 803–32; and Barry Weingast,
"The Political Foundations of Democracy and the Rule of Law," manuscript, Hoover Institution,
February 1993.
106. North, *Institutions, Institutional Change, and Economic Performance.*

task ahead is to specify these conditions more precisely. We must also explain more satisfactorily how these conditions lead to particular outcomes like balancing behavior and a concern for relative gains. Grieco makes a useful start in this direction by identifying six factors that may affect the degree of a state's concern for relative gains.[107] The next step is to develop a more explicit characterization of the strategic settings that yield outcomes like balancing and relative-gains concerns.

When we look beyond the narrowness of the neorealist–neoliberal debate about anarchy and the relative-gains problem, we see that this debate has focused our attention on a very broad and important set of issues. These are the absence of central authority, the potential for joint or cooperative gains, the distributional conflict these potential gains engender, and the roles of coercion and institutions in realizing and allocating these joint gains. This nexus of issues also lies at the heart of the expanding literatures on constitutional design, governing the commons, and state formation.[108] That a core of common issues underlies these seemingly disparate substantive concerns makes it possible to imagine moving beyond what has become a rather sterile debate between neorealism and neoliberalism in a way that draws on and contributes to these other literatures.

---

107. Grieco, "Realist Theory and the Problem of International Cooperation," pp. 611–13. See also Gowa and Mansfield, "Power Politics and International Trade."

108. See, for example, Barry Weingast, "Constitutions as Governance Structures," *Journal of Institutional and Theoretical Economics* 149 (March 1993), pp. 286–311; Elinor Ostrom, *Governing the Commons* (New York: Cambridge University Press, 1990); and Tilly, *Capital and Coercion.*

[7]

Modeling the forms
of international cooperation:
distribution versus information

James D. Morrow

F02 F53

Two pairs of matched problems obstruct international cooperation. One pair, sanctioning and monitoring problems, plagues the enforcement of cooperative arrangements. Sanctions may be needed to penalize those who renege on cooperative arrangements; what is the optimal way to penalize defectors? Monitoring is needed to determine whether defection has occurred; are sanctions needed? These problems exacerbate one another. Applying the proper sanctioning strategy is problematic when compliance is difficult to monitor, and monitoring is more difficult when sanctions and uncooperative behavior are similar.[1]

This pair of problems is well-known, but a second pair—problems of distribution and information—also impedes international cooperation.[2] Distri-

Earlier versions of this article were presented at the annual meeting of the American Political Science Association, San Francisco, 30 August–2 September 1992, and the annual meeting of the Public Choice Society, New Orleans, La., 20–22 March 1992. I thank Bruce Bueno de Mesquita, Randy Calvert, Jim Fearon, Hein Goemans, Robert Keohane, Jochen Lorentzen, and Robert Powell for their comments on this article. This article benefitted from seminar presentations at: the Politics and Organizations Seminar at Stanford University, Washington University, the University of Rochester, the University of California at Berkeley, the PIPES seminar at the University of Chicago, and at the University of Illinois at Urbana-Champaign. I retain all responsibility for all interpretations and any errors herein.

1. For discussions of the interaction between sanctioning and monitoring problems, see Jonathan Bendor, "In Good Times and Bad: Reciprocity in an Uncertain World," *American Journal of Political Science* 31 (August 1987), pp. 531–58; and George W. Downs and David M. Rocke, *Tacit Bargaining, Arms Races, and Arms Control* (Ann Arbor: University of Michigan Press, 1990).

2. My distinction between sanctioning and monitoring on one hand and distribution and information on the other parallels Stein's distinction between collaboration and coordination. Sanctioning and monitoring are problems of collaboration, and distribution and information are problems of coordination. See Arthur A. Stein, *Why Nations Cooperate: Circumstance and Choice in International Relations* (Ithaca, N.Y.: Cornell University Press, 1990). Lisa Martin adds problems of suasion and assurance to Stein's two problems in "Interests, Power, and Multilateralism," *International Organization* 46 (Autumn 1992), pp. 765–92. The model here addresses both of Martin's problems. Suasion is a special case of coordination, and assurance is captured in the both-prefer games described below.

International Organization 48, 3, Summer 1994, pp. 387–423

© 1994 by The IO Foundation and the Massachusetts Institute of Technology

butional and informational problems arise when the actors select precisely how they will cooperate from a set of possible solutions.[3] These problems precede sanctioning and monitoring problems: if the actors cannot agree on how they will cooperate, there is nothing to enforce. A distributional problem arises when the actors have different preferences over the solutions. An informational problem occurs when the actors are uncertain of the value of the available solutions and can benefit by sharing their knowledge. These two problems confound one another when combined. Distributional interests prevent the honest sharing of information.

Any issue that is a candidate for international cooperation presents a mixture of all four problems; sanctioning, monitoring, distribution, and information. Negotiations to cooperate address all four issues. This article focuses on the interaction of distributional and informational problems by themselves. I am not arguing that sanctioning and monitoring problems are unimportant for understanding international cooperation. Instead, I focus on distribution and information for analytical purposes. I examine why actors adopt different arrangements to address varied combinations of distributional and informational problems.

Actors bargain in an effort to resolve these problems. Successful negotiations require the parties to share some expectations about the solution to the problem over which they are bargaining. Actors adopt standardized negotiating procedures to assist the formation of such expectations. International regimes provide forums for negotiations and are believed to assist international cooperation by facilitating the convergence of actor expectations.[4] The institutions, norms, and practices of a regime assist the actors in anticipating one another's actions in a negotiation. The actors can then choose actions that make mutually desirable solutions more likely. Commonly accepted forms of negotiation can assist coordination of actions between actors. This article examines how such forms of cooperation can deal with the problems of distribution and information.

The model elaborates the classic two-by-two game of coordination known as the "battle of the sexes." The players in that game try to coordinate on one of two solutions. Both players are better off if they cooperate, but they disagree about which solution is preferable. That game represents the essence of a distributional problem. It is also the simplest model of the bargaining problem. The battle of the sexes game does not capture all the problems that face

3. For discussions of some of the problems of reaching agreement on how to cooperate, see Stephen D. Krasner, "Global Communications and National Power: Life on the Pareto Frontier," *World Politics* 43 (April 1991), pp. 336–66; and James K. Sebenius, "Challenging Conventional Explanations of International Cooperation: Negotiation Analysis and the Case of Epistemic Communities," *International Organization* 46 (Winter 1992), pp. 323–365.

4. See Robert O. Keohane, *After Hegemony: Cooperation and Discord in the World Political Economy* (Princeton, N.J.: Princeton University Press, 1984); and Stephen D. Krasner, "Structural Causes and Regime Consequences: Regimes as Intervening Variables," in Stephen D. Krasner, ed., *International Regimes* (Ithaca, N.Y.: Cornell University Press, 1982), pp. 1–21.

international cooperation. I do not use it as the sole model of international cooperation. Instead, international cooperation requires solving distributional problems, and battle of the sexes is the simplest representation of a distributional problem.

The model adds an informational problem to the distributional problem in battle of the sexes. The players are uncertain about which solution is preferable, and they hold private information about that uncertainty. The players both are better off in some situations if they share their private information honestly.

I examine how certain forms of formal communication between the players can increase the chance of cooperation between them.[5] The players must agree on the form and understanding of messages for communication to increase the chance of cooperation. These forms of communication help coordinate actions although they have no coercive power over any of the players. They alter the players' expectations about one another's actions by creating the opportunity to exchange meaningful messages. Successful communication requires both a forum for the exchange of messages and a shared interpretation of those messages.

In the model, the equilibria of the game provide a set of descriptions of stable behavior under a successful form of cooperation.[6] An equilibrium specifies what messages the players send to one another about the game, how they interpret those messages, and what actions they take after interpreting the messages. A regime fails when its members have incentives to deviate from the behavior that guides their convergent expectations. Because equilibria are self-enforcing, they are candidates for persistent forms of cooperation and model the incentives and behavior in such cooperation. The model has multiple equilibria. The relative importance of distribution and information influences the choice among the equilibria.

The model demonstrates five points. First and foremost, the combination of distributional and informational problems impedes the solution of either. Actors can solve either of these problems in isolation, but the combination of the two prevents a complete solution to both. Second, leadership solutions to coordination problems always exist, but leadership here is very different from

5. The work here draws heavily on work in economics on "cheap talk"—cost-free, nonbinding messages. See Joseph Farrell, "Cheap Talk, Coordination, and Entry," *Rand Journal of Economics* 19 (Spring 1987), pp. 34–39; and Joseph Farrell and Robert Gibbons, "Cheap Talk Can Matter in Bargaining," *Journal of Economic Theory* 48 (June 1989), pp. 221–37. For a discussion of the signaling game framework and an analysis of how signals can aid cooperation, see Vincent P. Crawford and Joel Sobel, "Strategic Information Transmission," *Econometrica* 50 (November 1982), pp. 1431–51. For an analysis of how different forms of communication assist in coordination problems in which there is limited information, see Jeffrey S. Banks and Randall L. Calvert, "A Battle-of-the-Sexes Game with Incomplete Information," *Games and Economic Behavior*, vol. 4, no. 2, 1992, pp. 347–72.

6. Schotter develops the view that social institutions, of which regimes are an example, are equilibria of a game. See Andrew Schotter, *The Economic Theory of Social Institutions* (New York: Cambridge University Press, 1981).

hegemonic provision of public goods. Third, actors can cooperate in the face of anarchy even without a shadow of the future. Fourth, diffuse reciprocal strategies arise naturally in coordination problems through the actors' pursuit of their own interest.[7] Fifth, norms and institutions are intertwined within a successful regime. The model also predicts how the forms of cooperation vary with the relative importance of distributional and informational problems.

The model provides a way to begin to formalize how regimes help actors share information and knowledge to create shared understandings of their situation. In this way, it suggests the view of regimes as mechanisms of communication associated with Ernst Haas and with John Ruggie.[8] Their arguments generally have led to interpretive approaches to understanding regimes and the associated claim that rational models cannot explain the role of such shared understandings.[9] In this model, effective communication requires shared understandings between rational actors. This article suggests then that we can use rational models to explain the role of such shared understandings. Further, the approach here allows us to connect such understandings directly to the actors' choices and knowledge. We can see how behavior differs across disparate shared understandings.

The article first examines an example of continuing international coopera-tion, the International Telegraph Union (ITU), and then discusses existing formal models of international cooperation. It presents the limited information model and the different forms of cooperation within it, and then compares them to one another. Some examples illustrate how the combination of distributional and informational problems have been addressed. The article discusses the literature on cooperation in the light of the results of the model, then concludes by explaining the limits of the model.

The International Telegraph Union: an example of continuing international cooperation

The development of electric telegraphy in the mid-nineteenth century created the need for common standards for international messages. At first, bilateral agreements regulated messages across pairs of nations. As international traffic that crossed several borders grew, there was a clear need for multilateral standards. In 1865, Emperor Napoleon III of France convened the Paris

---

7. For a discussion of diffuse reciprocity, see Robert O. Keohane, "Reciprocity in International Relations," *International Organization* 40 (Winter 1986), pp. 1–27.

8. See Ernst B. Haas, "Why Collaborate? Issue-Linkage and International Regimes," *World Politics* 32 (April 1980), pp. 357–405; Ernst B. Haas, "Words Can Hurt You; or, Who Said What to Whom About Regimes," in Krasner, *International Regimes*, pp. 23–59; and John Gerard Ruggie, "International Regimes, Transactions, and Change: Embedded Liberalism in the Postwar Economic Order," in ibid., pp. 195–231.

9. See for example, Alexander Wendt, "Anarchy is What States Make of It: The Social Construction of Power Politics," *International Organization* 46 (Spring 1992), pp. 391–425.

Telegraph Conference, which led to the creation of the ITU. Numerous conferences were held following the Paris conference to update the regulations for international telegraphic messages. These conferences changed the regulations in response to changes in the technology and economics of telegraphy.

For example, the Saint Petersburg conference of 1875 considered the question of the unit size for billing telegrams. The existing unit size was twenty words; therefore, charges were assessed for every twenty words (rounded up) in a message. Extra-European members wished to reduce the unit size to single words in order to encourage more traffic. Charges on extra-European traffic were quite high to cover the high fixed cost of laying both undersea cable and cable in less developed areas. The unit size of twenty words was prohibitive for most extra-European traffic. Billing by the word would reduce the cost of sending short messages, and so encourage additional extra-European traffic. Many European states objected to reducing the unit size because it would cut their revenues from international messages. European members used international traffic to subsidize their domestic service, including governmental traffic. They believed that the additional traffic that cheaper rates would encourage would not compensate for the revenue loss and the increased cost of additional traffic, including the crowding out of governmental traffic as a nonmonetary cost. The members settled on a twenty-word unit size for European traffic and a one-word unit size for extra-European traffic at Saint Petersburg. However, the argument of the extra-European members proved to be correct; the unit size for European messages was reduced to one word in 1885.[10]

The ITU served as a forum for its members to resolve a host of issues facing international telegraphy. For example, in 1895 Germany proposed simplifying rates, billing, and accounting to encourage additional traffic and cut administrative costs. The proposed reform would have increased the share of transit charges that Germany collected by paying just the first transit nation in an international message. The regulation of acceptable codes for shortening messages was addressed, and an official codebook eventually was adopted. Codes were commonly used in the United States, who was not a member of the ITU because it had not nationalized its telegraph services. As cross-Atlantic traffic grew, arrangements were needed to regulate and encourage this traffic, and a common code was a central facet of the agreement.[11]

The issues the ITU addressed had four common characteristics. First, several solutions are always possible for each issue. The unit-size problem could have been solved many ways. The choice was not just between one-word and twenty-word units. The solution adopted in 1875 combined both sizes. Second, the actors are all better off if they coordinate on one solution than if they adopt different solutions. International telegraphy required international

---

10. George A. Codding, Jr., *The International Telecommunications Union: An Experiment in International Cooperation* (Leiden: E.J. Brill, 1952), pp. 60–61.
11. Ibid., pp. 61–75.

agreement on standards. Telegrams could not be sent if the sending agency did not know what rate to charge or if the receiving agency could not interpret the code of the message. All were better off adopting the same standard than leaving the ITU. Third, actors are often uncertain about which solution they prefer, and each possesses some information about which might be preferable. The consequences of the unit size on traffic and revenues was unclear in 1875. The European unit was changed to one word in 1885 because experience proved that the additional traffic generated enough revenue to cover both the loss of revenue on shorter messages and the cost of the added traffic. But that result was not obvious in 1875. Fourth, actors frequently have divergent preferences over which solution they prefer, given the constraint of their uncertainty. European members opposed the one-word unit because they feared it would reduce their revenues; extra-European members favored it because they wanted the additional traffic it would generate. The ITU solved a string of issues with these four characteristics over time. New problems emerged that required new agreements.[12] The unit size, accounting standards, and acceptable codes were just three of the standards needed for international telegraphy. The ITU provided a regular forum for negotiating agreements on standards.

These characteristics are not unique to the problems addressed by the ITU. Consider two other examples. One comprises the means by which the major money banks coordinate their actions when they organize a debt rescheduling.[13] Each debt rescheduling requires a new agreement about how much money is required and how nonperforming loans will be handled. Many possible refinancing packages are possible, but the banks need to coordinate on one plan. No one can know whether a particular rescheduling program will succeed. Even with this uncertainty, the banks disagree about the amount of "new money" required and how nonperforming loans should be treated. Issues of enforcing the agreement arise only after those two issues are resolved.

The problem of the pollution of the Mediterranean Sea, addressed by the Mediterranean Action Plan (Med Plan), also exhibits the four characteristics described above.[14] New agreements on different types of pollution have been negotiated as the Med Plan regime has developed. The different economic costs of various emission control levels of pollutants create disagreements about which level of pollution control should be established. The economic and

---

12. If the actors must reach an agreement that will persist over time, agreement may be difficult in the face of distributional interests. Fearon shows that long "shadows of the future" make reaching such agreements more difficult. See James Fearon, "Cooperation and Bargaining Under Anarchy," paper presented at the annual meeting of the Public Choice Society, New Orleans, La., 19–21 March 1993.

13. See pp. 206–14 of Charles Lipson, "Bankers' Dilemmas: Private Cooperation in Rescheduling Sovereign Debts," in Kenneth A. Oye, ed., *Cooperation Under Anarchy* (Princeton, N.J.: Princeton University Press, 1986), pp. 200–225.

14. Peter M. Haas, "Do Regimes Matter? Epistemic Communities and Mediterranean Pollution Control," *International Organization* 43 (Summer 1989), pp. 377–403.

environmental consequences of different controls cannot be known for certain before international regulations are adopted. Several actors, particularly Algeria, have reversed their positions on the Med Plan as the consequences of Mediterranean Sea pollution have become clearer. A dilemma of continuing cooperation occurs when actors face a string of problems with the four characteristics above.

These four characteristics address the problems of reaching an agreement. Problems of enforcement still exist even after an agreement is reached. However, there is nothing to enforce without an agreement.

All such international issues entail two problems on which the actors must cooperate to solve. The first is the *problem of distribution:* which solution will actors adopt in the face of their divergent preferences over the possible solutions? The second is *problem of information:* is there a solution that is best for all of them and if so, which solution? Because each actor has some, but not perfect, information on the value of different solutions, all actors have a joint incentive to pool their information to determine whether they agree that one solution is preferable to another. These two problems work against one another. Distributional problems create incentives to misrepresent one's private information in the hope of gaining what is likely to be a more favorable solution; yet, the actors require accurate communication messages to solve an informational problem.

The limits of other formal models of international cooperation

Formal models have spawned two major approaches to understanding international regimes. However, both focus on the sanctioning problem (and to a much lesser extent, the monitoring problem) at the expense of problems of distribution and information. The first draws on the public goods literature.[15] In this view, the provision of international order is seen as a public good. In the absence of coercion and selective incentives, public goods are underprovided unless one actor chooses to bear the burden of providing the public good alone. Hegemons provide international regimes as a means to establish order, which they and other states find beneficial.

This view generally has slighted an important distributional question in the provision of public goods.[16] Actors typically disagree about which form of

15. Charles P. Kindleberger, *The World in Depression, 1929–1939,* 2d ed. (Berkeley: University of California Press, 1986), pp. 288–305. Also see Duncan Snidal, "The Limits of Hegemonic Stability Theory," *International Organization* 39 (Autumn 1985), pp. 579–614, for a critique of this view.
16. Similarly, externalities create distributional problems. The Coase theorem states that such problems can be resolved by private negotiation if property rights are already defined, and the actors have perfect information and do not face transaction costs. But the adoption of a property rights regime creates a distributional problem. Keohane discusses the Coase theorem and international cooperation in *After Hegemony,* pp. 85–87.

provision of public goods is best. Hegemons desire a regime that produces the form of order that they prefer. Other actors may prefer an alternative regime, creating a distribution problem. Those other actors then have an incentive to misrepresent their interest in cooperating under the regime advanced by the hegemon.

Regimes also are seen as a means of communicating information to enhance the efficacy of reciprocal strategies of sanctioning. This view begins with Robert Axelrod's presentation of the value of the "tit-for-tat" strategy in open-ended iterated prisoners' dilemmas.[17] The tit-for-tat strategy is a simple reciprocal strategy of playing whatever move the opponent played in the prior round. Axelrod, drawing on the logic of the Folk theorem, shows that tit-for-tat forms a Nash equilibrium with itself that produces a higher payoff for both players than the strategy "defect on every round."[18]

If this result characterizes the world, institutions and regimes are unnecessary because the simple application of tit-for-tat leads to cooperative outcomes. But implementing this strategy requires knowledge of the other player's prior move. If noise in monitoring leads the players to misjudge the other's prior move, tit-for-tat quickly loses its desirable characteristics. Robert Axelrod and Robert Keohane suggest that institutions and regimes can enhance the chance of cooperation by reducing noise, which renders reciprocal strategies more effective at enforcing cooperation and avoiding mistaken feuds.[19] Axelrod and Keohane do not, however, analyze how institutions promote accurate communication. If a regime just publicizes information collected from its members, members may have an incentive to dissemble in their reports. The consequence is an informational problem.

Solving monitoring and sanctioning problems is important for the maintenance of regimes.[20] But some solutions to these problems create informational and distributional problems. Sanctioning creates a distributional problem if it is not known which actor of many must carry out a costly punishment. Different forms of sanction impose different patterns of costs across actors, leading to disagreement about which form of sanction should be invoked. An actor's compliance with monitoring requests from a regime can be threatened by

17. See Robert Axelrod, *The Evolution of Cooperation* (New York: Basic Books, 1984). Prisoners' dilemma is the two-by-two game with a dominant strategy equilibrium, typically labeled D for "defect," that is not Pareto-optimal. In single-shot play or iterated games with a fixed end point, D is the dominant strategy of the game on all rounds. The outcome produced by the other strategy, typically labeled C for "cooperate," improves both players' payoff over DD.

18. Tit-for-tat is not a perfect equilibrium of the open-ended iterated prisoners' dilemma because it requires suboptimal behavior if one side defects; see Eric Rasmusen, *Games and Information* (Cambridge: Basil Blackwell, 1989), p. 91. Actors are better off if they do not carry out the punishments dictated by tit-for-tat.

19. Robert Axelrod and Robert O. Keohane, "Achieving Cooperation Under Anarchy: Strategies and Institutions," in Oye, *Cooperation Under Anarchy*, pp. 226–54.

20. James E. Alt, Randall L. Calvert, and Brian D. Humes, "Reputation and Hegemonic Stability: A Game-Theoretic Analysis," *American Political Science Review* 82 (June 1988), pp. 445–66.

Player 2

		A	B
Player 1	A	(a,1)	(0,0)
	B	(0,0)	(1,a)

FIGURE 1. *Payoff matrix for battle of the sexes, with payoffs being given for player 1 first and player 2 second and assuming that a (the degree of distributional conflict) > 1*

incentives to distort both its own reports and its interpretation of others' reports. Such incentives to dissemble create an informational problem if it is not clear what actions constitute defections from the regime. Consequently, regimes may be unable to provide accurate information to their members.

The use of the prisoners' dilemma as the underlying model assumes away problems of distribution and information in favor of monitoring and sanctioning. There is only one way to cooperate in prisoners' dilemma; there are many ways to cooperate in the real world. To produce cooperation when distributional problems exist, actors must agree on how they will cooperate. If individual actors are uncertain about which solution is best, sharing their information about the value of candidate solutions can assist in achieving an outcome all would prefer. If problems of both distribution and information exist, an actor may be motivated to misrepresent its information about the value of solutions in the hope of producing an outcome it believes is better for itself. The distribution problem interferes with solving the information problem. A stylized model can help us understand these problems of continuing cooperation in the abstract and how regular forms of cooperation could address them.

A model of coordination under uncertainty

Regimes help actors solve dilemmas of continuing cooperation. I model those dilemmas with a variation of the classic two-person game, battle of the sexes. Battle of the Sexes, also known as a coordination game, is the two-by-two game shown in Figure 1. Its name is based on a story described by R. Duncan Luce and Howard Raiffa:

A man, player 1, and a woman, player 2, each have two choices for an evening's entertainment. Each can either go to a prize fight [strategy *A*] or to a ballet [strategy *B*]. Following the usual cultural stereotype, the man much prefers the fight and the woman the ballet; however, to both it is more important that they go out together than that each see the preferred entertainment.[21]

Both players are better off playing the same move, but they have conflicting preferences over the efficient outcomes.[22] Player 1 prefers they both play move *A* and player 2, move *B*. The magnitude of *a* (*a* > 1) gives the intensity of this distributional disagreement. The greater *a* is, the more strongly each prefers that they coordinate on its preferred move. I refer to "*a*" as the degree of distributional conflict. The degree of distributional conflict reflects the risks the actors are willing to accept to gain their preferred outcome. As *a* increases, the actors become more interested in securing their preferred solution at the expense of guaranteeing that they agree on some solution. The degree of distributional conflict does not reflect the relative capabilities of the actors in any fashion.

Battle of the sexes has three Nash equilibria, two in pure strategies: (*A*;*A*) and (*B*;*B*); and one in mixed strategies: [$a/(a + 1)A$, $1/(a + 1)B$]; [$1/(a + 1)$ *A*, $a/(a + 1)$ *B*]. The mixed-strategy equilibrium is read as (player 1's mixed strategy; player 2's mixed strategy). I separate the moves within each player's strategy with commas and players' strategies from one another with semicolons. The probabilities of each move in a mixed strategy are given within brackets. For example, Player 1 plays *A* with probability $a/(a + 1)$ in this equilibrium. In equilibrium, no player has an incentive to change its move unilaterally. Each equilibrium forms a stable and self-enforcing combination of strategies. The pure strategy equilibria guarantee that the players coordinate their strategies with one player receiving a payoff of *a* and the other player a payoff of 1. In the mixed-strategy equilibrium, the players choose the same move with a probability of $2a/(a + 1)^2$, and each has an expected payoff of $a/(a + 1)$.

Actors negotiate to coordinate their policies when they cooperate. Battle of the sexes captures the motivations underlying negotiations and is the simplest model of the negotiation problem. Imagine a buyer and seller negotiating over the sale of a house. There are only two prices available, high and low, and both parties are willing to trade at either price. Both the buyer and the seller are

21. R. Duncan Luce and Howard Raiffa, *Games and Decisions* (New York: John Wiley, 1957), p. 91. Snidal and Stein each also argue that battle of the sexes exhibits elements of the problem of international cooperation that the prisoners' dilemma does not. See Duncan Snidal, "Coordination Versus Prisoners' Dilemma: Implications for International Cooperation and Regimes," *American Political Science Review* 79 (December 1985), pp. 923–42; and Arthur A. Stein, "Coordination and Collaboration: Regimes in an Anarchic World," in Krasner, *International Regimes*, pp. 115–40, respectively.

22. I use the term "move" rather than "strategy" to describe each player's choice in a particular round. Strategies in game theory are complete plans to play the game. A strategy here specifies what moves should be played and what messages—if any—should be sent in any possible round. For an introduction to game theory, see James D. Morrow, *Game Theory for Political Scientists* (Princeton, N.J.: Princeton University Press, 1994).

better off agreeing on a price than not, but they disagree about which price is best. The buyer prefers the low price and the seller, the high price. The moves in battle of the sexes correspond to the negotiating positions of the parties; the negotiations break down if the players adopt different positions.[23] The two different possible agreements correspond to the two pure strategy equilibria of battle of the sexes.

Battle of the sexes does not reflect all the aspects of a negotiation or a problem of international cooperation. But the limitations of battle of the sexes as a model of bargaining parallel the limitations of prisoners' dilemma as a model of defection from agreements. There is a wide range of possible agreements in a negotiation, and there are many different ways to defect from an agreement. Battle of the sexes allows only two possible agreements, and prisoners' dilemma has only one way to defect. Both in negotiations and after defection, either side can revise its position, and these revisions can go on indefinitely. In both of the simplified models, the players have only one move. They cannot revise their positions in response to the other side's position. I use battle of the sexes because it is the simplest representation of a distributional problem.

For many international issues, states may be somewhat uncertain about the value of outcomes. This is the problem of information. To represent such uncertainty in the model, I add the possibility that the players are playing another game in which both prefer the same move. Neither player knows for certain which game they are playing, but both have some private information about it. The players' situation parallels that of actors in international politics described by Keohane: "perceptions of self-interest depend both on the actors' expectations of the likely consequences that will follow from particular actions and on their fundamental values."[24] Sometimes, the players do not know the consequences of their actions in the model, but they do have some expectations about those consequences. Further, they can disagree about the possible consequences of any move. The resulting game played under circumstances of limited information captures the conditions of a dilemma of continuing cooperation.

The players are playing one of three two-by-two games. The first is battle of the sexes. The second and third games are shown in Figure 2. The players in the latter two games still face a coordination problem but now prefer to coordinate on the same move. These games also have three Nash equilibria, two in pure strategies, $(A;A)$ and $(B;B)$, and one in mixed strategies, wherein each player plays the preferred move with probability $1/(a + 1)$ and the other move with

---

23. Alternatively, one can assume that the parties agree to a middle price halfway between the two prices if the buyer proposes a high price and the seller, a low price. This variation does not change the strategic logic of battle of the sexes. There are still two pure strategy equilibria, $(A;A)$ and $(B;B)$, and a symmetric mixed-strategy equilibrium. The probabilities of each move in the mixed-strategy equilibrium do change.

24. Keohane, *After Hegemony*, p. 63.

Player 2

	A	B
A	(*a,a*)	(0,0)
B	(0,0)	(1,1)

Player 1

Both prefer move *A*

Player 2

	A	B
A	(1,1)	(0,0)
B	(0,0)	(*a,a*)

Player 1

Both prefer move *B*

FIGURE 2. *Payoff matrices for both-prefer coordination games, with payoffs being given for player 1 first and player 2 second and assuming that* a *(the degree of distributional conflict)* > 1

probability $a/(a + 1)$. I refer to these games as "both prefer move A" and "both prefer move B" as given in Figure 2 and the two together as the "both-prefer" games.[25] These both-prefer games provide a simple model of situations in which the parties may need to negotiate to coordinate their actions, even though they do not disagree about what outcomes are preferable.[26]

To model uncertainty about the state of affairs, a round of the game begins with a random draw, not observed by either player, that determines which of

25. Both-prefer games are also known as "stag hunt" or an assurance game; see Martin, "Interests, Power, and Multilateralism," and Stein, *Why Nations Cooperate.*

26. The model is symmetric because all three games are symmetric. Both players have the same payoff for the three possible outcomes: more preferred coordination, less preferred coordination, and no coordination. This symmetry has no effect on the equilibria of the game, as I discuss later.

the three games they are playing. I refer to the game actually selected in a particular round as "the game being played." The probability of each of the three games varies with a parameter p. Battle of the sexes occurs with probability $1 - p$, and each of the both-prefer games with probability $\frac{1}{2}p$. The parameter p reflects the degree of similarity in the players' payoffs across the two strategies. When $p = 0$, both players know they are playing battle of the sexes and so know that they disagree about which move is preferable. When $p = 1$, they know they are playing either of the other two games and so have identical preferences over the two moves. I assume the players know the value of p but not the outcome of the random draw. They have a common belief about how likely it is that they share preferences over the strategies. I refer to p as the "probability of identical interest." The nature of the issue about which the actors are trying to cooperate determines this probability.

After the game they are playing has been selected, each player receives private information about that game in the form of a "signal." Each player receives its signal privately; each can observe only the signal it receives. Signals can be thought of as each players' current knowledge about the value of the two possible solutions. Such knowledge could be the result of research on the consequences of different policies or existing beliefs about the efficacy of policies. The players consult their own experts on policy in the area (e.g., scientists or economists) to learn what solution is better before entering negotiations on which solution to adopt. The experts provide a recommendation that one type of solution, $(A;A)$ or $(B;B)$, is better for the player. Each player uses its expert's recommendation to judge which solution is better for it. However, the experts are not always correct. The players discount the experts' recommendations in light of their accuracy. Unlike the literature on signaling games, I make a distinction between "signals," which give private information about the game being played, and "messages," which the players can send to one another after receiving their signals. This distinction is made purely because a player's type—the signal it receives—does not always allow it to know its preferred outcome.[27]

In this model, two signals are possible, signal 1 and signal 2. If battle of the sexes is the game being played, each has a one-half chance of receiving signal 1 and a one-half chance of receiving signal 2. If both prefer move $A(B)$ is the game being played, both players receive the same signal (either signal 1 or signal 2).[28]

These signals create different expectations between the players about the game they are playing. If player 1 receives a signal of 1, it knows it is playing

27. For a review of signaling games and their application to political science, see Jeffrey S. Banks, *Signaling Games in Political Science* (New York: Gordon and Breach, 1991).

28. The symmetry of equal chances of each game being played and each signal does not influence the set of equilibria for the model. Changing these probabilities alters the mixed strategies in each equilibrium.

either battle of the sexes or both prefer move *A*. It knows then that it prefers coordinating on (*A;A*) to (*B;B*) for that round of the game because (*A;A*) produces payoff *a* for player 1 and (*B;B*), payoff 1 in both games. But if player 1 receives a signal of *2*, it does not know whether it prefers (*A;A*) to (*B;B*). It could be playing either battle of the sexes or both prefer move B. Similarly, player 2 prefers (*B;B*) to (*A;A*) if it receives a signal of *2* and cannot tell if it receives a signal of *1*. I refer to signal *1* for player 1 and signal *2* for player 2 as "favorable signals." Signal *2* for player 1 and signal *1* for player 2 are "unfavorable signals."

This uncertainty about payoffs creates a mutual interest in sharing information. If one player has received signal *1* and the other signal *2* and if the players share that information honestly, they would know that they must be playing battle of the sexes. If they have both received the same signal, they cannot be certain they are playing the corresponding both-prefer game, but their confidence that they are rises. Because the experts are not always correct, the players can benefit by sharing their recommendations.

The model captures the combination of distributional and informational problems that complicate international cooperation. Regardless of which game they are playing, both players are better off if they can agree to coordinate on one solution. But coordination is easier if they are playing one of the both-prefer games because they prefer the same solution. In contrast, when they are playing battle of the sexes they are better off if they coordinate, but they do not agree on which solution is better. The possibility that they are playing battle of the sexes creates a distributional problem, while the fact that neither player can determine which game they are playing creates an informational problem. If they share their knowledge about the game being played, their beliefs about which outcome they prefer may change. I use "knowledge" here in the way Ernst Haas does in his approach to regimes—it is a guide to the solution that is better for the actors.[29]

Even if the players accurately report their private information to each other, there is still some chance that they are playing battle of the sexes. They cannot eliminate the distributional problem. Both players always possess some incentive, then, to dissemble about their private information. If the game being played is battle of the sexes, such dissembling might convince the other player to coordinate on their preferred outcome. Increasing the degree of distributional conflict (*a*) heightens the intensity of these problems, since the risk each side will accept to achieve its preferred outcome rises. This magnifies the distributional problem. The importance of solving the informational problem also rises because the value of the jointly preferred solution is greater relative to the less-preferred solution. Increasing the probability of identical interest (*p*) raises the importance of the informational problem relative to the distributional problem. As *p* increases, it becomes more likely that the game

---

29. E. Haas, "Why Collaborate?" pp. 367–70.

being played is a both-prefer game. The players would like to share information to increase their confidence that they are playing a both-prefer game.

Regimes assist coordination of action by structuring communication among actors.[30] I model communication by adding a move whereby the players can inform one another about the signal they have received. I refer to the reports the players exchange as "messages" and formalize them as message 1 and message 2. Actors send messages after they have received their signals but before choosing their move for that round. The exchange of messages corresponds to the exchange of views in negotiations. The opportunity to exchange messages gives the players a chance to negotiate which solution they will adopt. The form of those negotiations affects the chance that the players will succeed in adopting a solution. When the players fail to coordinate, the negotiations have failed. As we will see later, there are different ways for the players to use the messages to coordinate their actions. These different uses correspond roughly to different forms of bargaining.

To represent the repeated aspect of international cooperation, the model consists of a series of "rounds." Each round begins with a new random draw of the game being played. The players receive their signals based on the game they are playing in the round. They select their "moves," either move A or move B, simultaneously, after receiving their signals. Their moves and the game being played are revealed and payoffs rewarded. The game can repeat beginning with a new draw for a known finite number of times. Any communication between the players takes place after they have received their signals about the game being played but before they select their moves. Figure 3 presents the sequence of a round of the model. Each round of the model can be thought of as a particular agreement that the players could make on an issue of the moment. Multiple rounds model a string of possible agreements the players could reach.

I focus on stationary strategies of the model rather than on conditional punishment strategies. A conditional punishment strategy selects moves based in part on the prior play of the game, as in tit-for-tat. A stationary strategy does not condition its moves on play in prior rounds of the game. I focus on stationary strategies for several reasons. First, the well-known results of tit-for-tat in the iterated prisoners' dilemma have drawn much attention to the efficacy of punishment strategies. I show that stationary strategies can also be effective in producing cooperation between rational actors with divergent interests. Second, punishment strategies require indefinite iteration (either infinite with discounted payoffs or random chances of ending the game), which may be a tenuous assumption in some cases. The strategies for producing cooperation that I discuss here work for finite plays of the model as well as for indefinitely repeated plays. Third, the Folk theorem shows that large ranges of

---

30. Keohane adds that regimes assist cooperation by changing transaction costs to favor mutually beneficial trades. See *After Hegemony*, pp. 89–92.

(1) Nature selects randomly the game being played in that round. Selection probabilities are as follows:

Game	Probability
Battle of the sexes	$1 - p$
Both prefer move A	$1/2\,p$
Both prefer move B	$1/2\,p$

(2) Each player receives either signal *1* or signal *2* from nature based on the game being played. The probabilities of each signal being given in each game are as follows:

Game	Probability of receiving signal 1	Probability of receiving signal 2
Battle of the sexes	1/2	1/2
Both prefer move A	1	1
Both prefer move B	0	0

(3) Any communication between the players occurs.

(4) Each player selects its move, A or B for this round.

(5) Moves and the game being played are revealed. Payoffs (a, 1, or 0) are awarded based on the moves and the game being played. (Figures 1 and 2 provide payoff matrices for each game.)

FIGURE 3. *Sequence of one round of the model*

behavior can be supported in equilibrium using punishment strategies. Any outcome where both players receive at least as much as their minmax value in the stage game can be supported by a punishment strategy provided that discount factors are not too high.[31] It is difficult to derive testable hypotheses from models based on the Folk theorem because many types of behavior are possible in such models.[32]

The following section presents the equilibria of the model. These equilibria give stable arrangements for sending and understanding messages and selecting moves based on those messages. Neither player has an incentive to defect from an equilibrium once both understand they are playing that equilibrium. The set of equilibria are the candidates for regimes that could persist over time. A variety of forms of cooperation—stable arrangements that assist coordination—are possible. Different values of the degree of distributional conflict and probability of identical interest make different regimes preferable.

31. See James Friedman, "A Noncooperative Equilibrium for Supergames," *Review of Economic Studies* 38 (January 1971), pp. 1–12; and Drew Fudenberg and Eric Maskin, "The Folk Theorem in Repeated Games with Discounting or with Incomplete Information," *Econometrica* 54 (May 1986), pp. 533–54.

32. Robert Pahre, "A Model of Economic and Security Cooperation and the Case of Postwar Europe," University of Rochester, Rochester, N.Y., 1991.

The equilibria of the model

The model has four different types of equilibrium.[33] The four equilibria are distinguished by how the actors use the information in their messages. The first type of equilibrium, a "babbling equilibrium," lacks any effective regime. In a babbling equilibrium, each player always sends the same message regardless of the signal it has received. The actors adopt equivalent actions and receive equal expected payoffs, making this equilibrium symmetric.[34] The players' messages convey no meaning whatsoever (hence, the name). Neither player can learn anything about the other player's upcoming move from these messages.

The players choose their moves in a babbling equilibrium based on the signals they have received. When the probability of identical interest (p) is high, the actors follow the lead of the signal they receive; they choose move A if they receive signal 1 and move B if they receive signal 2.[35] When it is unlikely they have identical interests— formally when $p < (a - 1)/(3a - 1)$—both players follow the lead of a favorable signal (e.g., player 1 plays move A if it receives signal 1) but mix moves between A and B when they receive an unfavorable signal. The probability of cooperation and the players' expected payoffs rise with the probability of identical interests in the babbling equilibrium. When they cannot have identical interests ($p = 0$), both players know they are playing battle of the sexes and play its mixed-strategy equilibrium. When they must have identical interests ($p = 1$), the signal each receives suffices to coordinate their actions on the superior move.

The babbling equilibrium is analogous to the absence of a working regime. Without some mechanism to create expectations about what the other player will do, both players must proceed on their own. Even without structured communication, the actors in the model often coordinate their actions for their mutual benefit. Nonetheless, success in achieving cooperative outcomes is not necessarily evidence of successful cooperation. To understand what evidence

---

33. I examine perfect Bayesian equilibria of the model. Actors act rationally at each move given their beliefs in a perfect Bayesian equilibrium; see Morrow, *Game Theory for Political Scientists,* chap. 6. In this model, the actors' beliefs are the probability of the game they are playing given the information the actor has at that moment. Sequential rationality requires that the actors' messages and moves are optimal given their beliefs when those messages are sent and moves made and that their beliefs are calculated from their equilibrium strategies using Bayes's law whenever possible.

34. The model also has asymmetric equilibria without communication. In such an asymmetric equilibrium, the actors always coordinate on one move—A or B—leading to different expected payoffs. Because the game is symmetric, there is no a priori way to distinguish the players. Harsanyi and Selten argue that in the absence of any way to distinguish the players in a symmetric game, only symmetric equilibria are plausible; see John C. Harsanyi and Reinhart Selten, *A General Theory of Equilibrium Selection in Games* (Cambridge, Mass: MIT Press, 1988), pp. 70–71. I ignore the asymmetric equilibria of the game. Without some mechanism to explain how the players share mutual expectations that they will always play one move, we cannot explain how the players can play an asymmetric equilibrium. I discuss later a regime with communication that produces asymmetric payoffs for the players.

35. For specifications of all equilibria and proofs, please see the appendix.

would allow us to determine when actors cooperate, we must compare the babbling equilibrium to equilibria with meaningful communication.

A functioning regime elicits messages that allow the players to form expectations about one another's upcoming move. The second type of equilibrium, the "pure coordination equilibrium," addresses only the distributional problem. The players make no use of their private information and communicate purely to coordinate their moves. Each actor sends one of the two messages. If the messages match, they both play move *A*; if they do not match, they both play *B*. Using these messages, coordination is always achieved, and both players expect the same payoff $[(a + 1)/2]$ from a round of the model. Each player has an incentive to play the move suggested by the messages because it expects the other player also to play that move. Neither player has any preference over sending one message over another because the outcome on which they coordinate depends upon both players' messages.

The pure coordination equilibrium produces gains over the babbling equilibrium when the distributional problem looms larger than the informational problem (that is, when *p* is small); in other words, it focuses solely on the distributional problem at the expense of the informational problem. The pure coordination equilibrium ignores whatever information the signals convey about the game being played. It selects both solutions with equal probability, even when the actors are playing one of the both-prefer games. It can lead the actors to outcomes that are Pareto-suboptimal ex post facto—when they coordinate on the inferior outcome in a both-prefer game.

If the players know they are playing battle of the sexes, the pure coordination equilibrium solves the distributional problem of that game. The players always coordinate their moves. Thus, distributional issues are not sufficient to explain a lack of cooperation. The pure coordination equilibrium is analogous to accepting the principle of "splitting the difference" in all negotiations. Splitting the difference insures that neither party is cheated and avoids any chance that negotiations will fail. But that rule forgoes the opportunity to search for a solution that both actors might prefer to an equal division of the current issue, such as a deal that links new issues into the deal.

Regimes that address the informational problem require messages that convey information about what signals each player has seen. In the third type of equilibrium, a "communicative equilibrium," the players' messages correspond to the signals they have received.[36] Such messages, however, create an incentive for the players to dissemble. An actor can benefit sometimes by sending the

---

36. By assuming that messages honestly report information unless the players have incentives to dissemble, I follow Rabin's concept of "credible message" equilibrium; see Matthew Rabin, "Communication Between Rational Agents," *Journal of Economic Theory* 51 (June 1990), pp. 144–70. There are equilibria that mirror those discussed in the text, i.e., wherein the messages mean the opposite of the observed signal. As Rabin cogently argues, agents agree on forms of communication that can be used to refine the set of equilibria of a game. Equilibrium behavior depends not only on the incentives of the game but also on forms of communication between the players.

message that it has received a favorable signal when in fact it has received an unfavorable signal. Players receiving messages discount them based on the possibility that the sender is lying about its signal. How the actors interpret messages and which move they then play varies with the degree of distributional conflict (a) and the probability of identical interest (p). These "interpretations" prescribe what move each player should play in response to each combination of messages. Some interpretations and the moves they recommend cannot be supported in equilibrium.

When it is likely that the players have identical interests ($p > \frac{1}{2}$), an "honest communicative equilibrium" exists. Both players accurately report the signals they receive. If both players send message 1, then they both play move A. If both players send message 2, they play B. If one player sends message 1 and the other message 2, they follow the procedure used in the pure coordination equilibrium to determine which move to play. The honest communicative equilibrium always produces coordination and each player expects the same payoff [$ap + \frac{1}{2}(1 - p)(a + 1)$]. If this equilibrium can be sustained, no other equilibrium produces a greater total payoff for both players.

When it is likely that the players do not have identical interests ($p < \frac{1}{2}$), the players lose the incentive to report their signals honestly given the interpretation of the honest communicative equilibrium. Actors who receive unfavorable signals would prefer lying to sending an honest message if they believe the interpretation of the honest communicative equilibrium is in effect. When each actor expects the other to send a dishonest message, a "dishonest communicative equilibrium" is possible. The actors discount one another's messages of favorable signals in dishonest communicative equilibria. One interpretation that does so directs the actors to play A if both send message 1, to play B if both send message 2, to use the pure coordination equilibrium if player 1 sends message 2 and player 2 sends message 1, and to play the babbling equilibrium if player 1 sends message 1 and player 2 sends message 2. This equilibrium rewards both players with successful coordination when they both send honest messages of unfavorable signals. Both sides protect themselves against the possibility of dishonest messages by playing the babbling equilibrium when they both send messages of favorable signals. Playing the dishonest communicative equilibrium entails a chance that the players will fail to coordinate, creating a cost for dishonest signals; but it also produces a penalty for honest messages of favorable signals.

The likelihood of coordination and the payoff the players expect from a dishonest communicative equilibrium depends upon the probability of identical interest (p). The lower p is, the greater the players' incentive to send dishonest messages when unfavorable signals are received. Dishonest communicative equilibria are less likely to produce coordination as the distributional problem looms larger than the informational problem. Increasing the degree of distributional conflict (a) also dwindles the probability of cooperation by exacerbating the distributional problem. If $\frac{1}{2} > p > (a - 1)/(3a + 1)$, players employ the babbling equilibrium, wherein strategies are dictated by the signals players have received. Players that receive unfavorable signals do not, however, always send honest messages, and the probability of a dishonest message rises with a. The probability of coordination under the dishonest communicative equilibrium is $\frac{1}{2} + \frac{1}{2}p + (1 - p) [a/(a + 1)^2]$, and each player's expected payoff is $ap + \frac{1}{4}(1 - p) (a + 2)$. Both are higher in the dishonest communicative equilibrium than in the babbling equilibrium.

When the probability of identical interest is low—that is, when $p < (a - 1)/(3a + 1)$—coordination becomes increasingly difficult to produce through a communicative equilibrium. In some cases, no communicative equilibrium is possible. Players receiving unfavorable signals always send dishonest messages in these cases, and the players find themselves in a babbling equilibrium. When players send the same message no matter what signals they have received, messages lose their ability to communicate information. Under these circumstances, the pure coordination equilibrium produces a higher expected payoff for both players than any possible communicative equilibrium. Thus, under these conditions actors prefer a pure coordination equilibrium to any communicative equilibrium. The problem of distribution overwhelms the problem of information.[37]

Negotiations occurring within communicative equilibria, both honest and dishonest, center on searching for the best possible deal for the players. When an honest communicative equilibrium can be supported, the likelihood of identical interest is sufficiently high that the players reveal their signals honestly. Dishonest communicative equilibria demonstrate the limits of negotiations as a mechanism to communicate information. The distributional problem is more significant here than under an honest communicative equilibrium. Both players have an incentive to misrepresent their signal to advance their interest if battle of the sexes is the game being played. Such incentives reduce the possibility of successful coordination because each player is less likely to take the other's message seriously. Each is more likely to interpret the other's negotiating stance to be self-interested rather than an indication of the true value of one of the solutions.

The equilibria considered so far are all symmetric; both players are treated identically. In the fourth type of equilibrium, a "leadership equilibrium," the players send their messages sequentially, giving them different roles. One player sends a message about its signal; the second player then tells the first which move it (the second) will play.[38] I refer to the latter player as the leader

---

37. The pure coordination equilibrium is also preferable to the dishonest communicative equilibrium when $p < a/(3a - 2)$, which is greater than $(a - 1)/(3a + 1)$. A later section discusses choosing among different possible equilibria.

38. There are other ways to send messages sequentially that have the same effect. For example, the first player's message indicates what move the players will coordinate on unless the second player objects to that move in its response. In all cases, the second message provides the cue that the players use to coordinate.

and the former as the follower. The follower always "babbles"—sends the same message regardless of the signal received—and so the leader cannot learn anything about the follower's private information from its message. The follower can never gain by sending a message that it has seen an unfavorable signal. If the leader has received a favorable signal, it always plays its preferred move regardless of the follower's message. If the leader has not received a favorable signal, the follower is always better off if it convinces the leader that it has received a favorable signal. The follower always says it has received a favorable signal, and the leader, knowing this, ignores its message. Once the leader has announced its chosen move, the dynamics of battle of the sexes and the both-prefer games drive both players to adopt the announced move. The players always succeed in coordinating their moves in a leadership equilibrium, but they cannot make use of the information in the follower's signal. Like the pure coordination equilibrium, a leadership equilibrium concentrates on the distributional problem at the expense of the informational problem.

The players' values for a leadership equilibrium depend upon the probability of identical interest. When it is unlikely that they have identical interests ($p < \frac{1}{2}$), the leader directs the follower to play the leader's preferred move in battle of the sexes—e.g., $(A;A)$ if player 1 is the leader—regardless of the signal it receives. The leader expects to receive a greater payoff than the follower: $a - \frac{1}{2}p(a - 1)$ versus $1 + \frac{1}{2}p(a - 1)$. If it is likely that the players have identical interests ($p > \frac{1}{2}$), the leader follows the signal it receives. If it receives a favorable signal, it orders the follower to play its preferred move in battle of the sexes; if it receives an unfavorable signal, it orders the follower to play the other move. Both players expect the same payoff in this case, namely, $\frac{1}{2}(1 - p + a + ap)$.

Leadership equilibria are inefficient because the follower's signal is ignored. This inefficiency always leads to losses for the leader and sometimes leads to losses for the follower. When $p < \frac{1}{2}$, the players coordinate on the inferior move when they play the game wherein both prefer the follower's preferred move. If $\frac{1}{3} < p < \frac{1}{2}$, the leader will change the move it orders if it knows the follower's signal. If $p > \frac{1}{2}$, the leader will always order its preferred move in battle of the sexes if it knows when both players receive unfavorable signals. This loss to the leader is a transfer to the follower rather than a joint loss to the pair.

None of these four equilibria solves both problems at the same time. The pure coordination and leadership equilibria coordinate the players' actions while neglecting the informational problem. Communicative equilibria fail to coordinate actions sometimes. Thus, it can be seen that problems of distribution and information interfere with one another. A form of cooperation can solve one, but not both, of these problems.

Four different ways to address the joint problems of information and distribution have been presented. In what follows I discuss how these solutions reflect the logic of bargaining and communication in international cooperation.

Regimes as forums for bargaining and communication

The equilibria of the model parallel behavior under effective regimes. A regime provides a forum for its members to negotiate solutions to recurring problems of coordination. A successful regime provides incentives for its members to engage in communication that coordinates their behavior; it promotes exchanges of information about its members' collective problems. This section compares how the equilibria defined above, on the one hand, and regimes, on the other, coordinate actions.

Equilibria in the model assist the actors in achieving cooperative outcomes by providing mechanisms for meaningful communication. How does communication coordinate the players' actions? Optimal play of all three games requires anticipation of the other player's move. If a player knows which move the other player will make, it should match that move. The equilibria help the players form those expectations. If the players believe they are playing a both-prefer game and they both know the other has that belief, coordinating on the mutually preferred move is easy. Communicative equilibria nurture these beliefs by allowing the players to share the information in their signals about the nature of the game. If the players believe they are playing battle of the sexes, coordination on one of the two moves is in both players' interest. The pure coordination equilibrium does this by creating mutual expectations about the move to be played. Once the leader announces its move in a leadership equilibrium, both players want to play that move. All the interpretations in these different equilibria produce such mutual expectations without imposing costs on the players.

The equilibria also produce norms of behavior. The actors' behavior in any equilibrium, except the leadership equilibrium, matches the norm of diffuse reciprocity. Diffuse reciprocity occurs when the players anticipate that they will be compensated for short-term losses in the long term, so they cooperate even when cooperation entails a short-term loss. In the model, the equilibrium resolves how the players will coordinate. Each is willing to play the other's preferred move in a round if the equilibrium dictates that outcome. But a player's willingness to make these concessions is not based on the expectation of compensation in the next round. Unlike the play of tit-for-tat in the iterated prisoners' dilemma, reciprocal rewards from the equilibria here are diffused over many rounds. An actor may have to accept playing the other's preferred move for several rounds, but going into any one round it expects at least one-half chance that they will coordinate on its preferred move. Obeying the recommendation of an accepted interpretation is in both players' short-run interest.[39] They act as if they are obligated to follow the equilibrium, a crucial

---

39. The self-enforcing feature of battle of the sexes contrasts with prisoners' dilemma, in which players always have a short-run incentive to defect. General reciprocal punishment strategies also produce behavior that looks like Keohane's diffuse reciprocity. See Bendor, "In Good Times and Bad," and Downs and Rocke, *Tacit Bargaining, Arms Races, and Arms Control.*

element of diffuse reciprocity according to Keohane.[40] In the long run, they expect their benefits to exceed any short-run relative losses.[41] *Ex ante* rationality in the model parallels the norm of diffuse reciprocity.

The players' expectations about one another's moves are analogous to norms within a regime. Strategies are complete plans for playing the model; they specify particular messages and moves for specific situations and histories of the model. Like norms, the players' cognizance of one another's equilibrium strategies allows them to determine when another player has deviated from suggested behavior. Norms then are generated by an equilibrium of the model. Some equilibria, like the honest communicative equilibrium, produce exacting norms, honesty in this case. Others can support only weak norms of behavior. Regimes produce norms that help the actors create expectations about one another's future behavior. Different regimes produce norms of varying strength, just as the different equilibria in the model do.

Institutions have no immediate parallel in the model. In successful regimes, institutions help the players implement the real-world analog of an interpretation. An interpretation in the model assists the coordination of the players' moves only if they both agree to accept that interpretation before a round begins. The form and interpretation of messages must be common knowledge for them to coordinate actions. Frequent changes in interpretations undermine that common knowledge. Institutions obstruct players from changing the interpretation from round to round to suit their immediate ends. Institutions increase the cost of changing the interpretation and help routinize the form and exchange of messages. Because the parameters (a and p) of the model are fixed, how the players change from one equilibrium to another as conditions vary cannot be addressed by this model.

Just as regimes require both norms and institutions, an equilibrium intertwines strategies and interpretations so that both are required.[42] Strategies and their interpretations each depend on the other. Without an interpretation, the strategies followed would not be optimal. Without the corresponding strategies, an interpretation produces misleading expectations.

To see how the logic of the model reflects some aspects of reality, let us return to the three examples of continuing international cooperation mentioned above. The ITU helped coordinate policy on international telegraphy by providing a regular forum for negotiating changes in regulations. Those negotiations addressed both the distributional and informational issues of such policies. However, merely arguing that efficiency could be improved by a

---

40. Keohane, "Reciprocity in International Relations," pp. 20–21.

41. In the leadership regime, there is no reciprocity for the follower. The follower does the leader's bidding because following the leader's directives is in its short-run interest. Still, the leadership equilibrium does produce an equal expected distribution of the total payoff when $p > \frac{1}{2}$. This equality results because the follower denies the leader the information that the leader needs to exploit the follower.

42. Keohane, *After Hegemony,* p. 59.

change in policies was not always sufficient to bring about that change. The German proposal in 1895 to simplify the accounting and billing procedures was not adopted in part because of its distributional consequences. In that sense, the ITU reflects the dishonest communicative equilibrium. Other nations discounted the efficiency gains of the German proposal because of its obvious effect of increasing German revenues since Germany served as a transit carrier of telegrams. The distributional issue confounded the transmission of information through the negotiations.

How major money banks determine the funds they will require to reschedule a debt also displays the characteristics of a dishonest communicative equilibrium.[43] After it becomes apparent that a state's debts must be rescheduled, banks establish a creditor committee that collects information on the situation from each participating bank. This information is not easily available and is needed to determine how much "new money" is needed. The banks differ about this figure based on their own exposure in that country and their domestic regulatory structure, producing an incentive to dissemble when providing information to the creditor committee. The greater a bank's existing loans to a country, the greater the loss it will absorb in the rescheduling of those loans. Restructuring affects the profits of U.S. banks more than those of German banks because the former do not have so-called hidden reserves to cover their losses and so treat those loans as nonperforming. Strategic misrepresentation surfaces in the discussion of which loans should be included in the total of "old money." The more old money a bank has in a country, the more new money it will have to provide. Each bank has an incentive, then, to argue that some of its loans do not belong in the pool of old money. But if all member banks do so, the ability of the creditor committee to determine the magnitude of the problem and how much new money the banks should provide would be compromised. The banks then face a problem of both information and distribution. They need to know how much old money is at risk, but they disagree about how much new money is needed once they agree on the figure for old money. Member banks help solve the informational problem by treating all loans equally—with some notable exceptions like officially guaranteed loans and short-term trade credits. This general standard eliminates the problem of negotiating how the different classes of loans will be treated in each case. The banks can also anticipate their exposure at the beginning of a rescheduling and know that they will not be singled out to provide an excessive amount of new money. The system does extract accurate information from the member banks.

Peter Haas's discussion of the Med Plan, a regime for marine pollution control, may provide an example of an honest communicative equilibrium.[44] The essential problem of controlling pollution of the Mediterranean is ascertaining its extent and consequences. Enforcement of the regime's man-

43. Lipson, "Bankers' Dilemmas."
44. P. Haas, "Do Regimes Matter?"

International Institutions in the New Global Economy

dates has not been problematic. The Med Plan has used its resources to fund studies of the consequences of pollution and has collected accurate information on emissions by publishing only total figures, rather than potentially embarrassing national emission figures. The epistemic community of ecologists plays a large role in this regime. They are the source of the information needed to determine what should be done. The regular meetings sponsored by the Med Plan provide a setting for scientists to exchange research on the consequences of different pollutants. These exchanges lead to common views on what regulations are needed and how national policies should enact those regulations in the face of the economic costs of emission controls. Like an honest communicative equilibrium in the model, the Med Plan has concentrated on the exchange of information among actors.

There are also problems of enforcement in each of these three cases. My brief discussions here address just the problems of distribution and information, how they interact, and how they have been dealt with in the three cases of successful international cooperation described above. A complete discussion of these cases also would have to address how the problems of enforcement were handled.

Choosing among forms of cooperation

The players are always better off adopting an equilibrium other than the babbling equilibrium, even if they expect the model to last just one round. Unlike tit-for-tat in the iterated prisoners' dilemma, these tools of cooperation can succeed even if there are no future rounds of the model. Egoists can cooperate under anarchy even if there is no future.[45] The self-enforcing nature of the three games guarantees compliance once the players have agreed how they should cooperate.

But which equilibrium should the players adopt? Figure 4 presents a graphical comparison of the expected payoff to each player from each equilibrium as p, the probability of identical interest, varies. The choice between communicative and coordination equilibria reflects the twin problems of information and distribution. Both players prefer a communicative equilibrium to a pure coordination equilibrium when $p > a/(3a - 2)$. Coordination equilibria are more attractive as the informational problem wanes in importance relative to the distributional problem (as p declines). Leadership equilibria pose a distributional problem. Leaders are always best off in a leadership equilibrium. Followers are better off in a pure coordination equilibrium when $p < \frac{1}{2}$ and as well off in an honest communicative equilibrium when $p > \frac{1}{2}$. Followers almost always prefer a communicative equilibrium to a leadership equilibrium (except when p is small).

45. For the claim that the "shadow of the future" is necessary for cooperation among egoists, see Axelrod, *The Evolution of Cooperation.*

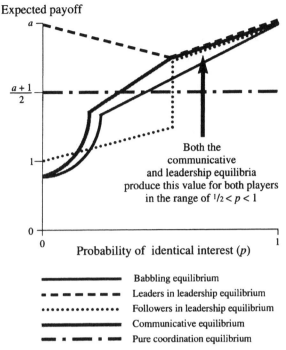

FIGURE 4. *Players' expected payoffs from the various equilibria, where* a = *degree of distributional conflict*

When will the players adopt one equilibrium over the others? For middling values of p, that is when $a/(3a - 2) < p < \frac{1}{2}$, both players prefer a dishonest communicative equilibrium. Although the leader does better in a leadership equilibrium, the follower can offer a side-payment to the leader to adopt the communicative equilibrium, yielding a better result for both players. For smaller values of p, either a pure coordination or a leadership equilibrium is likely. Both produce the same total payoff, differing only in their distribution of that payoff. For all but small values of p, the follower is better off in the babbling equilibrium than in a leadership equilibrium. A threat by the follower to refuse a leadership equilibrium may be sufficient to force the leader to accept a pure coordination equilibrium here. For large values of p, the honest communicative and leadership equilibria produce the same value for both players. In summary, communicative equilibria occur when the probability of identical interest is substantial, while lower values of p give rise to pure coordination equilibria. Leadership equilibria are possible either when p is small or large, but some symmetric equilibria can produce the benefits of leadership. Leadership equilibria cannot occur for middling values of p because the followers are better off with no regime than they are under such an equilibrium.

These choices among the equilibria lead directly to testable hypotheses about when we should expect different forms of cooperation. Issues differ in the relative importance of distributional problems to informational problems. Issue-areas in which information is the more prominent problem should produce cooperation like the communicative equilibrium. Negotiations focus first on exchanging information and seeking a consensus about what solutions are best. When distributional issues are more important than informational ones, pure coordination and leadership equilibria are more likely. Split-the-difference bargaining and other types of formulaic negotiations that attempt to guarantee fairness are more likely in those settings. These hypotheses, of course, address how cooperation deals with these two issues. Regimes could address enforcement differently, even if they use similar mechanisms to reach agreement.

But regimes are not always adopted; why not? First, the actors may expect a regime to produce asymmetrical benefits as the leadership equilibrium does. The follower would object to any regime that reduced its payoff below what it would receive without a regime. Even if the disadvantaged player benefitted from a biased regime, it might withdraw from that regime to try to force a redistribution of benefits. If the regime produces a Pareto-optimal outcome, any increase in the disadvantaged player's payoff must cause the other player's payoff to decrease. Expected asymmetry in the distribution of benefits could lead to an attempt to renegotiate the terms of the regime. If the negotiations were to fail, the regime would collapse.

Second, actors might see close ties between the establishment of a regime and the outcome of several rounds of the model. A regime is more difficult to establish when the actors can predict its distributive consequences. The mutual interest in regimes in the model depends on the players' inability to predict what outcome the regime will produce in any given round of the model. If the players can foresee the immediate consequences of a regime, the relative losers may be less interested in its adoption. Once again, they might hold out for a distribution of benefits of a regime more favorable to their immediate interests.[46]

Third, some situations pose problems beyond the problems of distribution and information analyzed here. It is widely believed that regimes have difficulties resolving security issues.[47] Security issues do reflect some of the

---

46. Oran R. Young, "The Politics of International Regime Formation: Managing Natural Resources and the Environment," *International Organization* 43 (Summer 1989), pp. 349–75 and specifically pp. 361–62 and 367.

47. Jervis argues that the Concert of Europe functioned as a regime during the period 1815–22 and that other examples of security regimes can be found. However, he concedes that security regimes are rare. See his essays, "Security Regimes," in Krasner, *International Regimes*, pp. 173–94; and "From Balance to Concert: A Study of International Security Cooperation," in Oye, *Cooperation Under Anarchy*, pp. 58–79.

features of the model: each side has a preferred solution to the issue, and generally both sides prefer either solution to not coordinating on a solution—war. It is unlikely that they have identical interests, however (p is close to 0). The pure coordination equilibrium should render both actors better off. However, there is one very important difference between most security issues and the model. In the model, both sides must cooperate for either to receive its most preferred outcome; in security issues, one actor may be able to secure its most preferred outcome by force.[48] Even when neither side believes it can use force successfully, it cannot exclude the possibility that the other believes it can win through force. The inability to exclude the option of force undermines both communication and coordination. It destroys both sides' incentive to follow the equilibrium.

Knowledge and cooperation

The equilibria require intersubjective knowledge that a particular equilibrium exists in order to facilitate communication and coordination. This mutual acknowledgment could be reached either through agreement or by the emergence of convention. Vincent Crawford and Hans Haller have shown that actors can develop methods of coordinating strategies in coordination games without focal points.[49] According to their definition of a coordination game, the "players have identical preferences over strategy combinations, with two or more (Nash equilibrium) combinations at which each player's strategy choice is a unique best reply if the other player correctly anticipates it, but not in general otherwise."[50] Actors facing a combined informational and distributional problem could then develop an interpretation of messages over time in the absence of an explicit agreement.

Viewed in this way, the model suggests the view of regimes as mechanisms of communication associated with Ernst Haas and with Ruggie.[51] The actors are uncertain about their preferences over strategies, and they use intersubjective understandings to assist their communication of relevant knowledge about the problem they face. As Ruggie argues, the "normative framework" of a regime, which corresponds to the interpretation and the expected strategies it produces in the model, is as essential to a successful regime as its "instruments" (i.e., rules and procedures).[52]

---

48. See James D. Morrow, "A Continuous-Outcome Expected Utility Theory of War," *Journal of Conflict Resolution* 29 (September 1985), pp. 473–502; and James D. Morrow, "Capabilities, Uncertainty, and Resolve: A Limited Information Model of Crisis Bargaining," *American Journal of Political Science* 33 (November 1989), pp. 941–72.

49. Vincent P. Crawford and Hans Haller, "Learning How to Cooperate: Optimal Play in Repeated Coordination Games," *Econometrica* 58 (May 1990), pp. 571–95.

50. Ibid., p. 571.

51. See E. Haas, "Why Collaborate?"; E. Haas, "Words Can Hurt You"; and Ruggie, "International Regimes, Transactions, and Change."

52. Ruggie, "International Regimes, Transactions, and Change," p. 200.

The idea of "knowledge" formalized here is quite limited. Policy coordination requires not only international agreement but also shared understandings about the consequences of policies. For example, international macroeconomic cooperation relies on economic theory that explains how policies affect economic conditions. Because economic theory changes and no one theory can be accepted as definitive and final, actors may disagree about the consequences of proposed policies. In a very uncertain world, enduring cooperation requires shared understandings about the consequences of policies or at least what consequences each actor expects from each possible policy. Otherwise, actors cannot form the expectations of one another's policies needed for successful coordination. In game theory, such shared understandings are called "common knowledge." Something is common knowledge if everyone knows it, if everyone knows that everyone knows it, and so on in an infinite regress. Regimes can be thought of as assisting the creation of common knowledge. In the model, the players' payoffs for the two forms of cooperation are *not* common knowledge. By exchanging private information, the players increase their common knowledge about their payoffs, which can increase the likelihood of coordination.

Hegemony versus leadership

The leadership equilibrium contrasts with the role that many identify with hegemony in the establishment and maintenance of regimes. There are two versions of hegemonic stability theory, one theorizing benevolent and the other self-interested hegemons. In the former view, the hegemon benevolently shoulders the burden of establishing a regime.[53] Free trade illustrates this view. Although all nations benefit from loosening trade restrictions, hegemons—like Great Britain in the nineteenth century and the United States in the twentieth century—prefer minimal restrictions. Other states, like the followers in the model, prefer some restrictions on trade to protect nascent industries. In the other view of hegemonic stability, hegemons are not benevolent; they simply establish the order they prefer.[54]

The idea of leadership in the model neatly combines both views. The follower does better in a leadership equilibrium than in the babbling equilibrium when the probability of identical interest is small or large (when p is close to 0 or $> \frac{1}{2}$). These cases parallel the benevolent view of hegemons; both sides are better off under a leadership equilibrium. But like the version that views hegemons as self-interested, the leader always gets the outcome it believes is best when it issues its directives.[55] Both sides are generally better off with a leader, but leadership advances the leader's interests as it perceives them.

53. Kindleberger, *The World in Depression,* pp. 288–305.

54. Stephen D. Krasner, "State Power and the Structure of International Trade," *World Politics* 28 (April 1976), pp. 317–47.

55. We cannot say that the leader benefits more than the follower because that statement makes an interpersonal comparison of utilities.

Leadership in the model does not require superior capabilities. The mutual recognition that one actor is a leader is sufficient by itself to sustain leadership. Leadership equilibria work because they create stable expectations about what the actors will do. An advantage in capabilities is irrelevant to successful leadership in the model. A leader in the model has power; it achieves the outcomes that it prefers by eliciting supportive actions from the follower. Then actors can have power in the model even without asymmetry in capabilities.

The observation that capabilities may not be necessary for leadership raises two questions for hegemonic stability theory. First, why would relative decline in the hegemon's capabilities cause a regime to fail? Because capabilities are not necessary for leadership, such equilibria should not fail as the leader declines. Keohane's question about how international cooperation is sustained as the hegemon's capabilities decline is irrelevant in the model.[56] Keohane's answer to his own question, however, is correct: an operating hegemonic equilibrium creates self-sustaining expectations. Regimes under leadership persist because they are in both actors' interest.

Second, how is leadership achieved? Here the model provides no clue. Advantages in capabilities, either economic or military, are beside the point. Capabilities do not affect either the probability of identical interest (p) or the degree of distributional conflict (a). All that is needed to establish a leadership equilibrium is a shared understanding that one actor is the leader. It may be that preponderance in capabilities furthers these expectations in the follower. In that case an argument—and even better a model—that shows how these expectations arise should be advanced.

These points mirror the observation that the qualifications for hegemony have never been made explicit.[57] Is it size of economy, military power, or something else? Does relative or absolute size matter?[58] Without such a definition, we cannot test hegemonic stability theory. This conceptual vagueness leads to the confusion underlying the debate on whether U.S. hegemony has passed.[59] If we do not know what characterizes hegemony, we can hardly tell whether it has passed.

To be fair to hegemonic stability theory, many reasons why hegemony fosters regimes have been advanced. This model alone cannot address all these

---

56. Keohane, *After Hegemony*.
57. Timothy J. McKeown, "Hegemonic Stability Theory and Nineteenth Century Tariff Levels in Europe," *International Organization* 37 (Winter 1983), pp. 73–91.
58. Snidal shows that the public goods argument for hegemony relies on absolute rather than relative size of economy. See Snidal, "The Limits of Hegemonic Stability Theory," p. 589.
59. See Jacek Kugler and A.F.K. Organski, "The End of Hegemony?" *International Interactions*, vol. 15, no. 2, 1989, pp. 113–28; Bruce Russett, "The Mysterious Case of Vanishing Hegemony; or Is Mark Twain Really Dead?" *International Organization* 39 (Spring 1985), pp. 207–31; and Susan Strange, "The Persistent Myth of Lost Hegemony," *International Organization* 41 (Autumn 1987), pp. 551–74. All argue that the United States is still a hegemon.

arguments. For example, hegemonic stability theory sees the sanctioning problem as more central than informational and distributional problems. James Alt, Randall Calvert, and Brian Humes focus on the sanctioning problem and produce a similar result to the model here.[60] Hegemony can be sustained in their model even as the hegemon becomes weaker (as the probability that punishment is costly to the hegemon, w, increases) if the allies begin with a sufficiently strong belief about the willingness of the hegemon to punish defection—$\beta/(\alpha + \beta)$ in their model. But how strong such a belief must be depends upon the benefits to the follower of unchallenged defection (b in their model). Even if we focus on the sanctioning problem, it is not clear that a decline in the hegemon's capabilities leads to a weakening of regimes. Hegemonic stability theory requires explicit models that explain how hegemony fosters and supports regimes. The existing models of hegemonic stability do not provide a sufficient explanation.

The leadership equilibria provide a crude way to formalize the effects of hegemonic leadership apart from the effects of hegemonic capabilities. Leadership in the model reflects some characteristics of leadership in the literature. Oran Young discusses how three types of political leadership—structural, entrepreneurial, and intellectual—assist in the creation of regimes.[61] Although the model discussed here addresses how regimes operate rather than how they are established, leadership in the model parallels elements of entrepreneurial and intellectual leadership. Entrepreneurial leadership shapes issues so that all parties to a negotiation see benefits for themselves in a deal. Intellectual leadership provides a system of thought that allows all to see the benefits of an agreement. Both types of leadership rely on the ability to provide information that creates common interests by shaping how states perceive their interests. Once the follower knows which move the leader will play, playing that same move is always in its interest.

Leadership in the model also displays a simple idea of the "second and third faces of hegemony" discussed by Scott James and David Lake.[62] The first face is the direct use of sanctions; the second face is the use of policy to alter others' incentives internally; the third face is the use of ideology to alter others' perceptions of their interests. Like the second and third faces, leadership in the model provokes the follower to obey the leader by changing its interests. This formal understanding of leadership is rudimentary, but it provides a way to connect leadership clearly to the follower's choices.

60. Alt, Calvert, and Humes, "Reputation and Hegemonic Stability."

61. Oran R. Young, "Political Leadership and Regime Formation: On the Development of Institutions in International Society," *International Organization* 45 (Summer 1991), pp. 281–308.

62. Scott C. James and David A. Lake, "The Second Face of Hegemony: Britain's Repeal of the Corn Laws and the American Walker Tariff of 1846," *International Organization* 43 (Winter 1989), pp. 1–29.

Conclusion

This article has presented a way to formalize cooperation in the face of problems of distribution and information. The model examines situations in which the actors must balance these twin problems. Both actors face uncertainty about which move is preferable within a round of the model. Arrangements to share information can increase the probability of coordinating action by assisting the convergence of the actors' expectations about one another's moves. These arrangements require prior agreement between the actors about their specific form. Several different equilibria are possible; the most advantageous equilibrium depends upon the relative importance of the two problems.

The model demonstrates that first, leadership solutions to coordination problems always exist—but the idea of leadership here is very different from the concept of hegemonic provision of public goods. Second, institutions without any power of enforcement can help actors coordinate. They achieve cooperation in the face of anarchy even without a shadow of the future. Third, diffuse reciprocal strategies arise naturally in these equilibria through the actors' pursuit of their own interests. Fourth, norms and institutions are intertwined within a functioning regime. Fifth, communicative equilibria are more likely than coordination equilibria as the probability of identical interest increases. Finally, problems of distribution and information cannot be solved simultaneously.

Any stylized model has limitations. This model analyzes the problem of distribution and information isolated from problems of sanctioning and monitoring. This model does not address the latter problems at all. Real issues involve all four problems. Sanctioning and monitoring problems must also be addressed. The creation and implementation of regimes may be substantially more difficult than the model suggests because of these problems. The equilibria here are self-enforcing; actors follow the recommendations of the interpretation because it is in their immediate interest to do so. When defection can be profitable in the short run, sanctions may be needed to enforce cooperation. Effective sanctioning may not be possible if defection is difficult to detect.

Second, this model is highly stylized. It should not be taken as a model of any particular instance of cooperation. Instead, the model focuses on the interaction between distribution and information in the abstract. This abstraction helps us to see that distributional and informational problems cannot be solved simultaneously.

One stylization in the model is not an issue. The model is symmetric; the payoffs of the players are identical, and they face the same strategic problem. Real issues are not symmetrical. Introducing asymmetry in the payoffs does change the exact strategies used in each equilibrium, but it does not change the character of the equilibria. All four equilibria are possible with asymmetric payoffs.

International cooperation calls for some answer to the problems of distribution and information. Multiple solutions are possible, and actors have divergent preferences over those solutions. Because economic and political issues are complex, actors cannot always have clear preferences over which courses of action produce the most desirable outcomes. Communication can help to alleviate the collective problem of lack of knowledge of the consequences of different actions. Further, these two problems exacerbate one another. The distributional problem hinders solutions to the informational problem. Creating and implementing regimes that can assist cooperation depends on addressing them successfully.

Appendix

This appendix presents proofs of the various equilibria presented in the text. I denote an equilibrium as: (player 1's move if signal *1* is received, player 1's move if signal *2* is received; player 2's move if signal *1* is received, player 2's move if signal *2* is received).

Babbling equilibrium

I begin by calculating a player's beliefs about what game is being played after the player receives its signal. Because I am solving for a babbling equilibrium, I need only solve for one player's strategy, say player 1. (Player 2's strategy can be found by exchanging 1 and 2 and *A* and *B* in the following calculations.) Let "battle of the sexes is game being played" be abbreviated as *BotS*, "both prefer move A (B) is game being played" be abbreviated as *BPMA* (*BPMB*), and "signal *1* (*2*) received" be abbreviated as *1* (*2*), we have the following conditional probability from Bayes's theorem:

$$p(BotS| \pm 1) = \frac{p(BotS)p(1|BotS)}{p(BotS)p(1|BotS) + p(BPMA)p(1|BPMA) + p(BPMB)p(1|BPMB)}$$

$$= \frac{\frac{1}{2}(1-p)}{\frac{1}{2}(1-p) + 1(\frac{1}{2}p) + 0(\frac{1}{2}p)} = 1 - p$$

Similarly, $p(BPMA|1) = p$, $p(BPMB|1) = 0$, $p(BotS|2) = 1 - p$, $p(BPMA|2) = 0$, and $p(BPMB|2) = p$.

First, I find the conditions under which the players will follow their signals, that is, when $(A,B;A,B)$ is an equilibrium. Any player receiving a favorable signal [i.e., player 1 (2) receives signal *1* (*2*)] always prefers playing its preferred strategy—*A* for player 1 and *B* for player 2. Let "player 2 plays *A* (*B*)" be abbreviated as *2A* (*2B*) and "player 1's utility for the *AA(BB)* outcome" be abbreviated as $u_1(AA)$ [$u_1(BB)$]. Given player 2's equilibrium strategy, $p(2 A|BotS) = p(1|BotS) = \frac{1}{2}$, and $p(2A|BPMA) =$

$p(1|BPMA) = 1$. Player 1's optimal strategy given its signal and player 2's strategy is then calculated:

$$u_1(A|1) = p(BotS|1)p(2A|BotS)u_1(AA|BotS)$$

$$+ p(BPMA|1)p(2A|BPMA)u_1(AA|BPMA)$$

$$+ p(BPMB|1)p(2A|BPMB)u_1(AA|BPMB)$$

$$= (1-p)\tfrac{1}{2}(a) + p(1)(a) + (0)(0)(1) = \tfrac{1}{2}a(1+p)$$

$$u_1(B|1) = p(BotS|1)p(2B|BotS)u_1(BB|BotS)$$

$$+ p(BPMA|1)p(2B|BPMA)u_1(BB|BPMA)$$

$$+ p(BPMB|1)p(2B|BPMB)u_2(BB|BPMB)$$

$$= (1-p)\tfrac{1}{2}(1) + (p)(0)(1) + (0)(1)(a) = \tfrac{1}{2}(1-p)$$

As $u_1(A|1) \geq u_1(B|1)$, player 1 will always play A if it receives a signal of 1. Now the values of p such that player 1 will play B if it receives signal 2 can be found:

$$u_1(A|2) = p(BotS|2)p(2A|BotS)u_1(AA|BotS)$$

$$+ p(BPMA|2)p(2A|BPMA)u_1(AA|BPMA)$$

$$+ p(BPMB|2)p(2A|BPMB)u_1(AA|BPMB)$$

$$= (1-p)\tfrac{1}{2}(a) + (0)(1)(a) + (p)(0)(1) = \tfrac{1}{2}a(1-p)$$

$$u_1(B|2) = p(BotS|2)p(2B|BotS)u_1(BB|BotS)$$

$$+ p(BPMA|2)p(2B|BPMA)u_1(BB|BPMA)$$

$$+ p(BPMB|2)p(2B|BPMB)u_1(BB|BPMB)$$

$$= (1-p)\tfrac{1}{2}(1) + (0)(0)(1) + (p)(1)(a) = \tfrac{1}{2}(1-p) + ap$$

Player 1 prefers playing move B to move A when $u_1(B|2) \geq u_1(A|2)$; substituting the above values and solving for p, we arrive at $p \geq (a-1)/(3a-1)$.

For $p < (a-1)/(3a-1)$, players who receive unfavorable signals play a mixed strategy. We can solve for this mixed strategy by finding the probability q that 2 plays B

when it receives signal *1* that makes player 1 indifferent between playing move *A* and move *B* when it receives signal 2:

$$u_1(A|2) = (1 - p)(\tfrac{1}{2}q)(a) + p(0)(1) = \tfrac{1}{2}aq(1 - p)$$

$$u_1(B|2) = (1 - p)(1 - \tfrac{1}{2}q)(1) + p(1)(a) = ap + (1 - p)(1 - \tfrac{1}{2}q)$$

Setting the two expected utilities above equal and solving for *q*, we obtain

$$q = \frac{2(1 - p + ap)}{(a + 1)(1 - p)}$$

The babbling equilibrium without communication when $p < (a - 1)/(3a - 1)$ is $\{A, [qA, (1 - q)B]; [(1 - q)A, qB], B\}$ for *q* above.

Pure coordination equilibrium

To show that the pure coordination equilibrium indeed is an equilibrium, begin with play after messages have been exchanged. Whenever one player expects the other to play *A* (or *B*), it should play *A* (or *B*) regardless of which game is being played. Because both players understand what strategy they are to play after the messages are revealed, their behavior at this stage is self-enforcing.

At the message stage of the game, both players send each message with a probability of ½, making each other indifferent between sending either of the messages. If one player sends a message with a probability greater than ½, the other can increase its payoff by sending the corresponding message (the matching message for player 1, the other message for player 2). Then the strategy pairing is an equilibrium.

Communicative equilibria

In the honest communicative equilibrium, each player's message reports accurately the signal it has received and the combination of the messages determines on which equilibrium players coordinate. If both send message 1 (or 2), they both play *A* (or *B*, respectively). If the messages do not match, they send a second set of messages using the pure coordination equilibrium above, producing (*A*;*A*) one-half of the time and (*B*;*B*) the other half. At the stage of playing moves, this equilibrium is self-enforcing. I determine the conditions under which the players send honest messages.

Both players report favorable signals accurately. The question of honesty lies with players receiving unfavorable signals. Let "player 1 sends message 1" be abbreviated as 1*s*1. Player 1's expected utility for sending each type of message, given that it has received a signal of 2, is thus calculated:

$$u_1(1s1|2) = p(BotS|2)[p(2s1|BotS)u_1(AA|BotS) + p(2s2|BotS)u(\frac{1}{2}AA, \frac{1}{2}BB|BotS)]$$

$$\cdot p(BPMA|2)[p(2s1|BPMA)u_1(AA|BPMA)$$

$$+ p(2s2|BPMA)u_1(\frac{1}{2}AA, \frac{1}{2}BB|BPMA)]$$

$$\cdot p(BPMB|2[p(2s1|BPMB)u_1(AA|BPMB)$$

$$+ p(2s2|BPMB)u_1(\frac{1}{2}AA, \frac{1}{2}BB|BPMB)]$$

$$= (1 - p)\{\frac{1}{2}(a) + \frac{1}{2}[\frac{1}{2}(a + 1)]\} + 0[(1)(a) + (0)(1)] + (p)[(0)(1) + (1)(a)]$$

$$= \frac{1}{2}(a - 1)(1 - p)$$

$$u_1(1s2|2) = (1 - p)\{\frac{1}{2}[\frac{1}{2}(a + 1)] + \frac{1}{2}(1)\} + (0)[(1)(a) + (0)(1)] + (p)[(0)(1) + (1)(a)]$$

$$= \frac{1}{2}p(a - 1)$$

Setting the two expected utilities above equal, $p = \frac{1}{2}$. For $p \geq \frac{1}{2}$ then, the strategies of the honest communicative equilibrium form an equilibrium.

For $p < \frac{1}{2}$, honest reporting of players receiving unfavorable signals cannot be supported in equilibrium. One interpretation that can be supported is described in the text. Message pairs of (1,1), (2,1), and (2,2) are treated as in the honest communicative equilibrium, but (1,2) directs the players to play the babbling equilibrium of the game without communication where the players follow their signals [i.e., $(A,B;A,B)$]. Again the strategies are self-enforcing at the stage of playing moves, so only the signaling stage is checked. If r is the probability that player 2 sends message 2 when it receives signal *1*, the expected values for player 1 of sending messages of 1 and 2 if signal *2* is received can then be calculated:

$$u_1(1s1|2) = \frac{1}{2}(1 - p)(1 - r)a + \frac{1}{2}(1 - p)r(0) + \frac{1}{2}(1 - p)(1) + p(a)$$

$$= \frac{1}{2}(1 - p)(1 + a - ar) + ap$$

$$u_1(1s2|2) = \frac{1}{2}(1 - p)(1 - r)[\frac{1}{2}(a + 1)] + \frac{1}{2}(1 - p)r(1) + \frac{1}{2}(1 - p)(1) + p(a)$$

$$= \frac{1}{4}(1 - p)(3 + a + r - ar) + ap$$

Setting the two expected utilities equal and solving for r, $r = (a - 1)/(a + 1)$. Further, the babbling equilibrium without communication can only be supported if player 1's updated probability that one of the both-prefer games is being played after receiving signal *1* and observing messages (1,2), $p[BPMB|(1,2)]$, is greater than or equal to $(a - 1)/(3a - 1)$. Otherwise, $(A,B;A,B)$ is not an equilibrium.

$$p[BPMB|(1, 2)] = \frac{p(2s2|BPMB)p(BPMB)}{p(2s2|BPMB)p(BPMB) + p(2s2|BotS)p(BotS)}$$

$$= \frac{(1)(p)}{(1)(p) + (\frac{1}{2} + \frac{1}{2}r)(1 - p)} = \frac{p}{p + \frac{1}{2}(1 + r)(1 - p)}$$

Setting this equal to $(a - 1)/(3a - 1)$, substituting for r, and solving for the original probability p, I obtain $p \geq (a - 1)/(3a+1)$.

For $p < (a - 1)/(3a + 1)$, a dishonest communicative equilibrium can be supported using the other babbling equilibrium without communication. However, the pure coordination equilibrium Pareto dominates that equilibrium, so I omit it.

Leadership equilibria

Once the leader announces its intended move, both players have an incentive to play that move. I concentrate then on showing first, which move the leader will announce and second, why the follower always sends the same message regardless of what signal it has received. Assume for convenience that player 1 is the leader. Then the leader prefers playing *A* if the game is *BotS*. If it receives signal *1* (a favorable signal), it knows it is playing either *BotS* or *BPMA*, implying it is always better off coordinating on *A*. If it receives signal *2*, it knows it is playing either *BotS* or *BPMB* with probabilities p and $1 - p$, respectively. The leader's expected utility for announcing moves *A* and *B* are as follows:

$$u_1(A|2) = (a)p(BotS|2) + (1)p(BPMB|2) = ap + 1 - p$$

$$u_1(B|2) = (1)p(BotS|2) + (a)p(BPMB|2) = p + a - ap$$

When $p = \frac{1}{2}$, these values are equal; when $p < \frac{1}{2}$, player 1 prefers *A;* and when $p > \frac{1}{2}$, player 1 prefers *B*.

To see that player 2 always sends the same message, note that player 1 announces move A if it receives signal *1* regardless of player 2's message. Then player 2's message can influence player 1 only when player 1 receives signal *2*. But then the players are playing either *BotS* or *BPMB* and player 2 always prefers move *B* regardless of which signal it has received. Player 2 always sends the same message regardless of which signal it has received.

[8]

Why States Act through Formal International Organizations

KENNETH W. ABBOTT

Graduate and International Studies

Northwestern University School of Law

DUNCAN SNIDAL

Department of Political Science

University of Chicago

States use formal international organizations (IOs) to manage both their everyday interactions and more dramatic episodes, including international conflicts. Yet, contemporary international theory does not explain the existence or form of IOs. This article addresses the question of why states use formal organizations by investigating the functions IOs perform and the properties that enable them to perform those functions. Starting with a rational-institutionalist perspective that sees IOs as enabling states to achieve their ends, the authors examine power and distributive questions and the role of IOs in creating norms and understanding. Centralization and independence are identified as the key properties of formal organizations, and their importance is illustrated with a wide array of examples. IOs as community representatives further allow states to create and implement community values and enforce international commitments.

- When the United States decided to reverse the Iraqi invasion of Kuwait, it did not act unilaterally (although it often does). It turned to the United Nations (UN) Security Council.
- When the Security Council sought to learn the extent of chemical, biological, and nuclear arms in Iraq, it did not rely on U.S. forces. It dispatched inspectors from the International Atomic Energy Agency (IAEA).
- When the international community sought to maintain the suspension of combat in Bosnia, it did not rely only on national efforts. It sent in peacekeeping units under the aegis of the UN and North Atlantic Treaty Organization (NATO).
- When states liberalized trade in services and strengthened intellectual property protection in the Uruguay Round, they were not content to draft rules. They created the World Trade Organization (WTO) and a highly institutionalized dispute settlement mechanism.

Formal international organizations (IOs) are prominent (if not always successful) participants in many critical episodes in international politics. Examples in addition

AUTHORS' NOTE: We are grateful for valuable comments from Lea Brilmayer, Judith Goldstein, Charles Lipson, Andrew Moravcsik, James Morrow, Anne-Marie Slaughter, and seminar participants at the University of California at Berkeley, Harvard University Law School, New York University Law School, Princeton University, and the Program on International Politics, Economics and Security (PIPES) at the University of Chicago. For financial support, Abbott thanks the Russell Baker Fund, the Charles C. Linthicum Fund, and the Northwestern Summer Research Grant program.

JOURNAL OF CONFLICT RESOLUTION, Vol. 42 No. 1, February 1998 3-32

to those above include the following: Security Council sanctions on Libya, IAEA inspectors in North Korea, UN peacekeepers in the Middle East, and so forth. The UN secretary-general's 1992 Agenda for Peace sets out an even broader range of current and proposed UN functions in situations of international conflict: fact finding, early warning, and preventive deployment; mediation, adjudication, and other forms of dispute resolution; peacekeeping; sanctions and military force; impartial humanitarian assistance; and postconflict rebuilding. But IO influence is not confined to dramatic interventions like these. On an ongoing basis, formal organizations help manage many significant areas of interstate relations, from global health policy (the WHO) to European security (OSCE and NATO) to international monetary policy (IMF). What is more, participation in such organizations appears to reduce the likelihood of violent conflict among member states (Russett, Oneal, and Davis in press).

IOs range from simple entities like the APEC secretariat, with an initial budget of $2 million, to formidable organizations like the European Union (EU)[1] and the World Bank, which has thousands of employees and multiple affiliates and lends billions of dollars each year. Specialized agencies like the ILO, ICAO, and FAO play key roles in technical issue areas. New organizations like UNEP, the EBRD, and the International Tribunal for the former Yugoslavia are regularly created. Older IOs like NATO and the Security Council are rethought and sometimes restructured to meet new circumstances.[2] As the examples illustrate, moreover, even the most powerful states often act through IOs. In short, "it is impossible to imagine contemporary international life" without formal organizations (Schermers and Blokker 1995, 3).

Why do states so frequently use IOs as vehicles of cooperation? What attributes account for their use, and how do these characteristics set formal organizations apart from alternative arrangements, such as decentralized cooperation, informal consultation, and treaty rules? Surprisingly, contemporary international scholarship has no clear theoretical answers to such questions and thus offers limited practical advice to policy makers.

We answer these questions by identifying the functional attributes of IOs across a range of issue areas. Although we are concerned with the concrete structure and operations of particular organizations, we also see IOs as complex phenomena that implicate several lines of international relations (IR) theory. From this vantage point, we identify two functional characteristics that lead states, in appropriate circumstances, to prefer IOs to alternate forms of institutionalization. These are *centralization* and *independence*.

IOs allow for the centralization of collective activities through a concrete and stable organizational structure and a supportive administrative apparatus. These increase the

---

1. Although we discuss certain of its operations, we deliberately de-emphasize the EU because some would regard it as an exceptional case of institutionalization.

2. A discussion of IOs is an exercise in acronyms. The ones not identified in the text, in order, are the World Health Organization (WHO), Organization for Security and Cooperation in Europe (OSCE), International Monetary Fund (IMF), Asia-Pacific Economic Cooperation forum (APEC), International Labor Organization (ILO), International Civil Aviation Organization (ICAO), Food and Agriculture Organization (FAO), United Nations Environment Program (UNEP), and European Bank for Reconstruction and Development (EBRD).

efficiency of collective activities and enhance the organization's ability to affect the understandings, environment, and interests of states. Independence means the ability to act with a degree of autonomy within defined spheres. It often entails the capacity to operate as a *neutral* in managing interstate disputes and conflicts. IO independence is highly constrained: member states, especially the powerful, can limit the autonomy of IOs, interfere with their operations, ignore their dictates, or restructure and dissolve them. But as in many private transactions, participation by even a partially autonomous, neutral actor can increase efficiency and affect the legitimacy of individual and collective actions. This provides even powerful states with incentives to grant IOs substantial independence.

The broad categories of centralization and independence encompass numerous specific functions. Most IOs perform more than one, though each has its own unique combination. We do not enumerate every such function or provide a comprehensive typology. Instead, we highlight several of the most important. We focus especially on the active functions of IOs—facilitating the negotiation and implementation of agreements, resolving disputes, managing conflicts, carrying out operational activities like technical assistance, elaborating norms, shaping international discourse, and the like—that IR theory has only sparingly addressed. Rational states will use or create a formal IO when the value of these functions outweighs the costs, notably the resulting limits on unilateral action.

Distinguishing formal IOs from alternative forms of organization is important from several perspectives. For IR scholars, who largely abandoned the study of formal IOs in the move from the legal-descriptive tradition to more theoretical approaches, developing such distinctions should "open up a large and important research agenda" with institutional form and structure as central dependent variables (Young 1994, 4; see also Koremenos et al. 1997). This will complement emerging work on international legalization, a closely related form of institutionalization (Burley and Mattli 1993; Abbott and Snidal 1997; Keohane, Moravcsik, and Slaughter 1997). Such research will also benefit practitioners of conflict management and regime design (Mitchell 1994). The policy implications of our analysis are significant as well. Many states, notably the United States, now resist the creation of IOs and hesitate to support those already in operation, citing the shortcomings of international bureaucracy, the costs of formal organization, and the irritations of IO autonomy. This is an ideal time for students of international governance to focus on the other side of the ledger.

The next section spells out our theoretical approach, drawing lessons from the ways in which different schools of theory have dealt with (or have failed to deal with) the questions posed above. It is followed by an analysis of the organizational attributes of centralization and independence and the functions they make possible—especially in contexts of cooperation and nonviolent conflict. The final section explores two composite functions that challenge conventional views of IO capabilities and demonstrate the complementarity of prevailing theories: developing, expressing, and carrying out community norms and aspirations and enforcing rules and commitments. We conclude with the example of the Security Council in the Gulf War, which draws together these themes in the context of violent conflict.

PUTTING IOs INTO THEORY
AND THEORY INTO IOs

Our primary approach is rationalist and institutionalist. We assume, for simplicity, that states are the principal actors in world politics and that they use IOs to create social orderings appropriate to their pursuit of shared goals: producing collective goods, collaborating in prisoner's dilemma settings, solving coordination problems, and the like. We start with the pursuit of efficiency and employ the logic of transaction costs economics and rational choice (Snidal 1996), using analogies with business firms and medieval trading institutions. Decentralized cooperation theory and, especially, regime theory provide a strong deductive basis for this analysis.

Regime theory (Krasner 1983; Keohane 1984) represents a major advance in understanding international cooperation. It is self-consciously theoretical and focuses directly on the institutional organization of international cooperation. But it has several shortcomings. Most important, regime scholars embrace an earlier turn in IR, which unnecessarily coupled a move to theory with a move away from consideration of IOs themselves. This resulted in "the steady disengagement of international organization scholars from the study of organizations, to the point that today one must question whether such a field even exists any longer except in name only" (Rochester 1986, 783-84). Indeed, regime theory deals with institutions at such a general level that it has little to say about the particular institutional arrangements that organize international politics. Our focus on the concrete operations of formal IOs not only brings them into regime theory but also provides a broader opportunity for IR theory to differentiate among institutional forms and recapture institutional details. We draw on the legal-descriptive literature to accomplish this.

Furthermore, regime theory has been rightly criticized for paying insufficient attention to issues of power and distribution in international politics. We draw on realist considerations to supplement our institutionalist approach in this regard. Finally, although regime theory has paid increasing attention to the role of ideas and norms in international politics (Goldstein and Keohane 1993), it has only begun to incorporate these important considerations. Here, we draw on constructivist theory for guidance. In sum, we enrich our primarily rationalist approach with important insights from several different traditions, which we see as complementary rather than competitive.

Decentralized cooperation theory takes as the problematic of international governance the existence of coordination and collaboration problems requiring collective action (Oye 1986; Stein 1983; Snidal 1985a). It assumes anarchy, often depicted in game models, and analyzes how states cooperate in that spare context through strategies of reciprocity and other forms of self-help. The dependent variable is typically cooperation in the abstract, and much of the research in this tradition has been directed to disproving the realist assertion that cooperation in anarchy is unlikely. There is no nuanced account of the forms of cooperation because the anarchy assumption makes IOs and other institutions largely irrelevant. However, the strong assumptions that underlie the theory, such as the need for high-quality information, suggest that cooperation is unlikely without an adequate institutional context—although the theory is only beginning to analyze that context (Morrow 1994). For our purposes, however, it performs a useful service by emphasizing that institutional capacities other than centralized enforcement are crucial in mediating interstate relations.

Regime theory, in contrast, deals explicitly with institutional factors affecting cooperation, and regime scholars frequently mention IOs. But they downplay the distinctive institutional role(s) of IOs, perhaps in continued reaction against the earlier preoccupation with formal organizations. For example, Martin (1992) depicts the European Economic Community (EEC) and the Coordinating Committee for Export Controls (COCOM) as important but nevertheless quite rudimentary forums for intergovernmental bargaining; Weber (1994) emphasizes the broad political and symbolic goals of the EBRD. Neither discusses the organizations' primary operational roles. Keohane's (1984) *After Hegemony* also emphasizes intergovernmental bargaining, arguing that regimes help states reach specific agreements by reducing transaction costs, improving information, and raising the costs of violations. But this valuable analysis also excludes many significant operational activities of IOs.[3] In all these works, furthermore, regime scholars treat international institutions as passive. Regimes are seen, for example, as embodying norms and rules or clarifying expectations (Keohane 1984; Yarbrough and Yarbrough 1992; Garrett and Weingast 1993), functions also performed by treaties and informal agreements. Regimes are also seen as forums in which states can interact more efficiently: like Keohane and Martin, Moravcsik's (1991) analysis of the Single European Act treats IOs as sites of, but not as agents in, cooperation. Indeed, the canonical definition of *regime* (Krasner 1983) encompasses only norms and collective choice procedures, making no provision for the active and independent IO functions—and the corresponding institutional forms— that we emphasize below.

Legal scholarship continues to offer descriptive accounts of the history and institutional architecture of IOs, as well as doctrinal analysis of norms and texts, especially the normative output of organizations such as ILO treaties or General Agreement on Tariffs and Trade (GATT)/WTO panel decisions (Bowett 1982; Kirgis 1993). More important for present purposes, another strand of doctrinal theory addresses the constitutional law of IOs, including membership and voting rules, external relations, finance, and the authority of specific organs (Amerasinghe 1994; Sohn 1950, 1967; Dupuy 1988; Shihata 1991, 1995). The best of this work is comparative, examining how common problems of organization and operation are addressed in the constitutive documents and practices of various IOs (Schermers and Blokker 1995; Chayes and Chayes 1995). Unfortunately, "in the land of legal science, there is no strongly established tradition of developing theories on IOs" (Schermers and Blokker 1995, 8; see also Brownlie 1990, 679). Nevertheless, legal scholarship— like some earlier work in IR, notably Cox and Jacobson (1973)—carefully differentiates among institutional forms and emphasizes institutional details, an important contribution that we use in our analysis.

---

3. Keohane (1984) does discuss monitoring, but Glaser (1995) argues that regime theorists do not explain why monitoring must be done centrally.

Realist theory finds both legal and regime scholarship naive in treating IOs as serious political entities. Realists believe states would never cede to supranational institutions the strong enforcement capacities necessary to overcome international anarchy. Consequently, IOs and similar institutions are of little interest; they merely reflect national interests and power and do not constrain powerful states (Mearsheimer 1995; Strange 1983; for a more nuanced view, see Glaser 1995). We accept the realist point that states are jealous of their power and deeply concerned with the distributive consequences of their interactions. Yet, realists underestimate the utility of IOs, even to the powerful. The United States, at the peak of its hegemony, sponsored numerous IOs, including GATT, IMF, and NATO; these organizations have provided "continuing utility . . . as instruments . . . for regime and rule creation" (Karns and Mingst 1990, 29). Even the Soviet Union, the very model of a modern repressive hegemony, used the Council for Mutual Economic Assistance to organize economic relations within the eastern bloc. We argue that powerful states structure such organizations to further their own interests but must do so in a way that induces weaker states to participate. This interplay is embedded in IO structure and operations.

Finally, Kratochwil and Ruggie (1986) argue that only *constructivist* (interpretivist) *theory*—focusing on norms, beliefs, knowledge, and understandings—can satisfactorily explain formal organizations. We accept the insight that social constructions are fundamental elements of international politics (Wendt 1992, 1995; Barnett 1993) and agree that IOs are—in part—both reflections of and participants in ongoing social processes and prevailing ideas (Finnemore 1996; Kennedy 1987). But the role of IOs is best understood through a synthesis of rationalist (including realist) and constructivist approaches. States consciously use IOs both to reduce transaction costs in the narrow sense and, more broadly, to create information, ideas, norms, and expectations; to carry out and encourage specific activities; to legitimate or delegitimate particular ideas and practices; and to enhance their capacities and power. These functions constitute IOs as agents, which, in turn, influence the interests, intersubjective understandings, and environment of states (McNeely 1995). Potentially, these roles give IOs an influence well beyond their material power, which is trivial on conventional measures. Indeed, IO activities may lead to unintended consequences for member states, a fear often expressed by U.S. politicians. Yet, IO autonomy remains highly constrained by state interests, especially those of the powerful—a fact often demonstrated by U.S. politicians.

Although we adopt a predominantly rationalist theoretical approach, we are concerned with highlighting the importance of formal IOs as empirical phenomena rather than with maintaining a particular theoretical dogma. None of the individual approaches mentioned adequately explains why states use formal IOs; each holds key insights. In identifying formal IOs as an important category of institutionalization to be explained, therefore, we proceed in a more interpretive mode, drawing on different strands of argumentation to highlight ways in which formal IOs function to manage interstate cooperation and conflict.[4]

---

4. On the use of rational choice as an interpretive device, see Ferejohn (1991), Johnson (1991), and Snidal (1985b).

THE FUNCTIONS OF IOs:
CENTRALIZATION AND INDEPENDENCE

Two characteristics distinguish IOs from other international institutions: centralization (a concrete and stable organizational structure and an administrative apparatus managing collective activities) and independence (the authority to act with a degree of autonomy, and often with neutrality, in defined spheres).[5] The very existence of a centralized secretariat implies some operational autonomy, but this is often limited to administrative and technical matters and subject to close supervision by governments. In other situations—sometimes involving the same organizations—substantive autonomy and neutrality are essential. The range and potential importance of these activities lead us to treat independence as a separate category.

Centralization and independence enhance efficiency. An analogy to private business firms is instructive. The firm replaces contractual relations among suppliers, workers, and managers; it substitutes a centralized, hierarchical organization for the horizontal, negotiated relations of contract. In Coase's (1937) theory, firms are formed when the transaction costs of direct contracting are too high for efficient operation. Similarly, the move from decentralized cooperation to IOs occurs when the costs of direct state interaction outweigh the costs of international organization, including consequent constraints on unilateral action (Trachtman 1996).

Centralization and independence represent different forms of transaction cost economizing. Small businesses draw mainly on the centralization benefits of formal organization, interposing a legal entity with the ability to manage employees hierarchically and the capacity to contract, sue, and be sued. The owners still manage the business directly, though their interactions are more highly structured. Investors in larger firms additionally benefit by granting autonomy and supervisory authority to professional managers; in Berle and Means's (1968, 5) famous phrase, there is a "separation of ownership and control." The situation is similar in complex IOs, in which member states grant some authority to IO organs and personnel but supervise them through structures resembling the corporate shareholders meeting, board of directors, and executive committee. Introducing these new actors changes the relations among states and allows them to achieve goals unattainable in a decentralized setting.

Centralization and independence produce political effects beyond mere efficiency. In these respects, IOs resemble governments and private associations more than business firms. Independence, in particular, enables IOs to shape understandings, influence the terms of state interactions, elaborate norms, and mediate or resolve member states' disputes. The acts of independent IOs may be accorded special legitimacy, and they affect the legitimacy of members' actions. Even centralization, seemingly more mechanical, can alter states' perceptions and the context of their interactions.

---

5. Centralization and independence are matters of degree, not only among IOs but even between IOs and related institutions. For example, the Group of Seven is not a formal IO but merely a negotiating forum. Its organizational practices (e.g., a rotating chair) nevertheless provide some centralization benefits, and it partakes of some autonomy, as in legitimating members' actions.

CENTRALIZATION

It is no great theoretical insight that an established organizational structure and centralized administrative support can render collective activities more efficient: even students of international governance are not content to communicate by e-mail; they form the International Studies Association and the International Law Association. This simple insight goes far to explain the proliferation of IOs in this century in a period of increasing issue complexity and a growing number of states. The (inter)subjective effects of centralization are less apparent, though equally important. We consider the benefits of centralization under two headings—support for direct state interaction (the principal focus of regime theory) and operational activities (the traditional focus of IO studies). Here, we emphasize concrete activities in which governments remain closely involved; the following section introduces broader functions also requiring IO autonomy.

SUPPORT FOR STATE INTERACTIONS

The organizational structure of IOs enhances even the passive virtues recognized by regime theory. An established organization provides a stable negotiating forum, enhancing iteration and reputational effects. Such a stable forum also allows for a fast response to sudden developments. The Security Council, for example, is organized so that it can function on short notice, with each member required to maintain continuous representation at UN headquarters. A permanent organization also reinforces accepted norms: the most favored nation (MFN) principle instantiated in the WTO provides a sounder basis for state expectations than any informal arrangement.

In other ways too, centralization shapes the political context of state interactions. IOs provide neutral, depoliticized, or specialized forums more effectively than almost any informal or decentralized arrangement. This enables a broader range of behavior: the superpowers could discuss technical nuclear issues within the IAEA without the intrusion of high politics, even at the height of the cold war. IOs also serve as partisan forums for political coalitions: the United Nations Conference on Trade and Development (UNCTAD) for developing countries, the Organization for Economic Cooperation and Development (OECD) for industrialized states. Finally, IOs strengthen issue linkages by situating them within common organizational structures, as the WTO has done for goods, services, and intellectual property rights.

Formal organizations further embody the precise terms of state interaction. Representation and voting rules "constitutionalize" balances among states having different levels of power, interest, or knowledge. States with advanced nuclear technology and large supplies of nuclear raw material are guaranteed seats on the IAEA Board of Governors; states with major shipping and carrier interests have equal representation on the International Maritime Organization (IMO) Council. Such decision structures frequently guarantee disproportionate influence for powerful states. Yet, they may also constitutionalize protection for weaker states and hold the powerful accountable to fixed rules and procedures. For example, both the Security Council and the EU Council are structured so that the most powerful members can block affirmative actions but, even if united, cannot approve actions without support from smaller powers.

Such considerations often lead to elaborate organizational structures. The substantive work of many IOs takes place in specialized committees staffed by their secretariats. The OECD uses more than 200 committees and working groups; the IMO prepares treaties in substantive groupings like the maritime safety and marine environmental protection committees. Such committees are often formally open to all members, but specialization occurs naturally because of differences in interest, expertise, and resources. Delegation can also be encouraged institutionally: in the third UN law of the sea conference (UNCLOS III), the chairs of open-ended committees sometimes scheduled meetings in rooms capable of holding only 30 people![6]

Organizational structure influences the evolution of interstate cooperation as conditions change. For example, several environmental agreements were facilitated by appointing UNEP as secretariat and the World Bank as financial administrator, obviating the need for new institutions. These institutional links are often contested because of their distributional implications. The advanced countries fought to locate new intellectual property rules in the WTO (rather than in the World Intellectual Property Organization [WIPO]) so they could enforce their rights more effectively. In other cases, organizational structures create vested interests that impede change or politicize issues, as in the United Nations Education, Scientific, and Cultural Organization (UNESCO) during the 1970s. More generally, because IOs are designed for stability, they may not adapt smoothly to changing power conditions, as the continuing makeup of the Security Council attests. Yet, the gradual reduction of U.S. voting power in the IMF, mandated by its declining share of capital contributions, illustrates how organizational structure can facilitate such adaptation.

Most IOs include a secretariat or similar administrative apparatus. In simple *consultative* organizations, the secretariat need only assist with the mechanics of decentralized interaction. The 1985 Vienna Ozone Convention assigned the following functions to its secretariat: "(a) To arrange for and service meetings . . . ; (b) To prepare and transmit reports based upon information received . . . ; (d) To prepare reports on its activities . . . ; (e) To ensure the necessary coordination with other relevant international bodies . . . ; (f) To perform such other functions as may be determined" ("Vienna Convention" 1985, 1532). The secretariat for the Convention on Long-Range Transboundary Air Pollution (LRTAP) performed similar functions with only five professionals. Levy (1993, 84) notes that the staff had "little time to do anything else but keep the meetings running smoothly."

Even such modest activities can strengthen international cooperation. Here, we draw on the analogy to the medieval law merchant and the corresponding theoretical literature (Milgrom, North, and Weingast 1990; Calvert 1995; Morrow 1994). Informal consultations produced sufficient information on the identity of untrustworthy traders to support a substantial volume of trade. Yet, modest efforts by central administrators at commercial fairs to collect and relay additional information created a new equilibrium at a higher level of exchange.

6. Personal communication from Bernard Oxman, member of the U.S. delegation, 21 May 1997.

12   JOURNAL OF CONFLICT RESOLUTION

Most IOs perform more extensive *supportive* functions. Law-making conferences like UNCLOS III or the Rio conference on the environment and development rely heavily on their secretariats. IO personnel coordinate and structure agendas, provide background research, and promote successful negotiations. They keep track of agreements on particular issues, trade-offs, and areas of disagreement, periodically producing texts that consolidate the current state of play. They also transmit private offers or assurances, improving the flow of information.

IO staffs support decentralized cooperation between major conferences. The large, expert OECD secretariat collects, produces, and publishes information relevant to national economic policy coordination. The WTO secretariat assists in numerous negotiations, from the settlement of disputes to sectoral talks under the services agreement. IO staffs also support the decentralized implementation of norms. UNEP, secretariat for the Basel convention on the transboundary movement of hazardous wastes, provides information states need to manage activities under the treaty; the ILO receives, summarizes, and circulates national reports on treaty implementation.

Experience under the international trade regime testifies to the importance of organizational structure and administrative support. The original GATT was a normative and consultative arrangement; almost all organizational features were removed at the instance of the United States. Yet, member states soon needed more extensive organizational structure and support. As membership expanded and complex new issues appeared on the agenda, GATT began its metamorphosis into the WTO, a true IO.

MANAGING SUBSTANTIVE OPERATIONS

IOs do more than support intergovernmental negotiations; they manage a variety of operational activities. A prototypical operational organization is the World Bank, which finances massive development projects, borrows on world capital markets, reviews state investment proposals, provides technical assistance and training in many disciplines, generates extensive research and publications, and performs other substantive activities. Operational organizations normally have sizable budgets and bureaucracies, complex organizational structures, and substantial operational autonomy.[7]

Member states of an IO like the World Bank use the institution as an agent, taking advantage of its centralized organization and staff to carry out collective activities. The analogy of the large business corporation, with its dispersed owner-investors and professional managers, is apt. Compared with a decentralized approach based on ad hoc contracting, a formal organization provides efficiency gains that outweigh the accompanying costs in terms of money, human resources, and constraints on unilateral action. Especially when participating states differ in power, centralized operations will have significant distributional consequences.

---

7. We reserve for the following section discussion of those functions that turn directly on independence and neutrality.

IO operations also significantly influence the capabilities, understandings, and interests of states. This is most apparent with outputs such as information and rules. But it is also true of more material activities like technical assistance and joint production. Indeed, virtually all of the activities discussed below promote certain norms and practices among states, often in unanticipated ways.

Pooling

Many IOs are vehicles for pooling activities, assets, or risks. Some pooling can be accomplished on a decentralized basis, as in a business partnership, but a separate entity with a stable organizational structure and specialized staff can greatly reduce transaction costs while providing additional advantages.

Consider the World Bank again. As in other international financial institutions (IFIs), members pool financial resources through capital contributions and commitments. Pooling provides a solid cushion of capital that enables the World Bank to make credible financial commitments to borrowers, who rely on them for costly planning and investment decisions, and to world capital markets, in which the bank borrows at advantageous rates. In addition, this common effort promotes burden sharing in providing a collective good and may limit the competition for influence that characterizes some bilateral assistance. Similarly, by combining development loans in a common portfolio, bank members pool, and thereby reduce, their individual risk.

Pooling enables the World Bank to achieve economies of scale by carrying out a large volume of activities, establishing uniform procedures and building up a common body of data. These economies allow it to develop greater technical expertise on various aspects of country and project assessment than could most states and to innovate in emerging areas like "basic needs." Finally, the bank's broad jurisdiction creates a horizontal advantage akin to economies of scope: by dealing with virtually all needy countries, the bank can target global priorities while avoiding duplication and gaps in coverage.[8]

The largest states, especially the United States, could mobilize sufficient capital to accomplish their international financial objectives unilaterally.[9] They are unwilling to do so, however, for international and domestic political reasons and because of competing priorities. Indeed, the United States is actively working to strengthen the IFIs, in part because their broad membership and assessment structures encourage wide cost sharing.[10] In the meantime, although the G-7 countries bear most of the costs of the IFIs, they also retain the greatest share of voting power and influence on management. During the cold war, they successfully excluded the Soviet bloc and the People's Republic of China. Yet, the United States has been unable consistently to dictate IFI decisions on specific transactions.

8. Of course, as Kratochwil (1996) notes, large-scale centralized operations may not be necessary or desirable in all cases. The Maastricht Treaty's subsidiarity principle adopts this view, while authorizing supranational activity when the scale of the problem makes that appropriate.

9. The desire to benefit from pooling is nevertheless reflected in U.S. Treasury Secretary Rubin's lament that the "United States cannot be the lender of last resort to the world" (quoted in Sanger 1995).

10. The G-7 countries also benefit from IFI independence, as discussed below.

Nonfinancial IOs provide similar advantages. The public health activities of WHO, like other UN-specialized agencies, are based on the pooling of national contributions and cost sharing (though the industrialized countries bear the bulk of the costs); economies of scale provide operational efficiencies. The WHO smallpox campaign illustrates the horizontal benefits of centralization: a single global campaign against a contagious disease is more effective than decentralized efforts because global scope avoids gaps in coverage. (The IAEA nuclear safeguards system offers a similar advantage.) In addition, the stable organizational structure of WHO and the reputation-staking effect of membership encourage participation. Free-rider problems remain, but the organization can alleviate them by using its own resources. WHO also provides effective technical assistance by pooling financial and technical resources and accumulating expertise; its global scope diffuses new technologies and allows rational prioritization of needs. By enhancing the development and transmission of ideas, technical activities of specialized organizations have significantly shaped the interests and identities of states. At the same time, they have helped less developed states acquire capacities essential to both national policy making and international activity.

An example of the limits of pooling illustrates these effects and the importance of realist and constructivist considerations. UNESCO's scientific arm was intended to promote the public goods aspects of scientific research by pooling international scientific facilities and creating a central clearinghouse. The organization was initially oriented toward the needs of scientists: executive board members did not represent governments. With the cold war, however, state interests asserted themselves. The board was reorganized to represent states, and UNESCO's orientation shifted to national science. Finnemore (1996) documents how UNESCO technical assistance subsequently promoted national science programs even in states where there was little need for them. Thus, UNESCO helped shape states' identities, interests, and capabilities in the area of science policy even though its initial global objectives were frustrated by interstate rivalries.

Joint Production

Alchian and Demsetz's (1972) theory of the firm suggests that a centralized organization is particularly important when workers, managers, and other "inputs" must work in teams, producing a joint output. In these situations, the hierarchical organization of the firm makes it easier for managers, themselves beholden to the owners ("residual claimants"), to monitor, reward, and discipline employees. IO personnel engage in similar teamwork and thus are typically organized hierarchically, with supervision by and on behalf of member states.

Beyond this, states themselves sometimes form multinational "teams" to engage in production activities. Experts from several European states cooperate in subatomic research through the European Organization for Nuclear Research (CERN), an IO that operates a nuclear laboratory; the Airbus project is a similar example. In addition to holding participants responsible, these organizations pool resources and risks, achieve economies of scale, avoid duplication and unproductive competition, and ensure that the outputs, including technological externalities, are shared. Projects like CERN and Airbus resemble business firms even more than the typical IO. Indeed, Airbus, originally created as a partnership under French law, is being transformed into a private corporation to better coordinate the participants.

Perhaps the best example of interstate joint production is the NATO military alliance. Common war plans, specialization of military tasks, joint exercises, common equipment and interchangeable parts, and, of course, the conduct of battle are examples of teamwork par excellence. NATO's integrated command—operating hierarchically on behalf of member states as residual claimants—organizes, monitors, and disciplines participants in the joint activities of the alliance, probably the most successful in history.[11]

Norm Elaboration and Coordination

States arrange cooperative relationships through agreements. As Williamson (1985, 1994) and others have pointed out, bounded rationality and high transaction and information costs make it difficult for states—like the parties to any contract—to anticipate and provide for all possible contingencies. The longer and more complex the relationship, the more significant the contingencies; the greater the investment in specific assets, the greater the uncertainty and risk of opportunism. The domestic legal system helps alleviate these problems by supplying missing terms and decision rules, but the international institutional context is comparatively thin. "First, in international law, there is not a very complete body of law that can be applied to supply missing terms. . . . Second, . . . there is generally no dispute resolution tribunal with mandatory jurisdiction. . . . The alternative, of course, is to write comprehensive contracts" (Trachtman 1996, 51-54).

There is another alternative: to create procedures for the elaboration of norms within an IO. Decentralized procedures do not address the problems of transaction costs and opportunism. Even with coordination issues—in which equilibria can sometimes be reached without communication—these problems can stymie cooperation when there are many actors, complex problems, and distributive conflicts. The stable organizational structure of IOs addresses both issues. Established procedures for elaborating rules, standards, and specifications enhance cooperation even when member states retain the power to reject or opt out—as they do even in IOs with relatively advanced legislative procedures, like the ILO. Nonbinding recommendations can become de facto coordination equilibria, relied on by states and other international actors. This gives IOs some power to affect international norms and state behavior and potentially much greater power with the backing of key states.

As always, powerful states exert disproportionate influence over norm elaboration and structure legislative processes to ensure their influence. Here, too, however, protection for weaker states may be the price of their participation, and the effective-

11. The analogy is imperfect. NATO's organization differs from that of a firm. Nevertheless, team analysis suggests why a formal IO is valuable, whereas the standard public goods analogy reduces the problem simply to one of individual (under)provision. See Olson and Zeckhauser (1966).

ness of an established rule-making procedure requires that powerful states respect those arrangements. For example, powerful states often limit IO jurisdiction to technical areas with limited distributional impact; as a result, IO legislative procedures may go forward—up to a point, at least—less influenced by narrow national interests and differential power than direct intergovernmental bargaining.

Many IOs engage in norm elaboration, especially of a technical kind. The EU, most notably, has issued a huge number of directives, regulations, and other legislative acts—affecting everything from franchise agreements to telecommunication interconnectivity standards to tax policy—though many important issues have been addressed through interstate agreements and mutual recognition. The preparation of proposed legislation is housed exclusively in the commission to facilitate a depoliticized and expert approach.

Many other IOs carry out extensive legislative programs, frequently focusing on coordination rules. The ICAO promulgates international "rules of the air"; the International Telecommunications Union (ITU) coordinates national broadcasting standards; the Customs Cooperation Council implements common customs rules; and the Codex Alimentarius Commission harmonizes food standards. Although technical, these standards have important effects on (and within) states, as the concern over privileging Codex standards under the North American Free Trade Agreement (NAFTA) demonstrated. Although the associated IOs are quite weak, their influence is strengthened by the self-enforcing nature of coordination equilibria.

INDEPENDENCE

Although centralization often requires some operational autonomy, many valuable IO functions require more substantive independence. The participation of an IO as an independent, neutral actor can transform relations among states, enhancing the efficiency and legitimacy of collective and individual actions. These functions require a delicate balance among short- and long-term collective and distributional interests. Powerful states will not enter an organization they cannot influence, yet undermining the independence of an organization performing the functions discussed here will simultaneously reduce its effectiveness and their own ability to achieve valued ends.

Analogies from the business firm and the law merchant illustrate the point. Shareholders in a large corporation must monitor managers to limit agency costs. Yet, if major shareholders cause managers to favor their interests unduly, others may refuse to invest. If shareholders generally assert excessive control, moreover, they lose the advantages of professional management. The law merchant analogy is even sharper. Powerful princes granted monopoly privileges to independent guilds of foreign merchants, enabling them to embargo the princes themselves if they took advantage of the merchants (Grief, Milgrom, and Weingast 1994). By eliminating princes' incentives to cheat, these arrangements enabled them to make the binding commitments necessary to induce mutually beneficial trade. The princes could withdraw the guilds' privileges, of course, but were constrained from doing so by the resulting loss of trade.

SUPPORT FOR DIRECT STATE INTERACTION

Independent IOs promote intergovernmental cooperation in more proactive ways than those discussed earlier; they are *initiating* as well as supportive organizations. The governing body is often authorized to call together member states to consider current problems. IO personnel also influence negotiation agendas. On a high political plane, UNEP kept ozone protection alive when interstate negotiations deadlocked and built support for the Montreal Protocol. The UN secretary-general may put before the Security Council any matter that, in his opinion, threatens international peace and security. At the administrative level, the ILO governing body sets the General Conference agenda with assistance from the International Labor Office. At the technical level, IO and conference officials advance specific proposals and suggest linkages or trade-offs: the president of UNCLOS III was authorized to defer contentious votes to forge a consensus during deferment; the negotiating text advanced by GATT Director-General Dunkel during the Uruguay Round catalyzed the faltering negotiations and helped bridge substantive differences.

IO officials are also prominent members of the epistemic communities that develop and transmit new ideas for international governance (Haas 1992). Drake and Nicolaïdis (1992, 76) document the role of IOs in developing the concepts behind the liberalization of trade in services: a "comparatively small number of experts in the GNS [Group on Negotiation in Services] and on the GATT, UNCTAD and OECD staffs [were] the main source of the specific kinds of new ideas needed to carry the policy project to a conclusion." The UN Economic Commission on Latin America is well known as the source of many ideas regarding economic development that rallied the Group of 77. Such autonomous efforts can modify the political, normative, and intellectual context of interstate interactions. These factors are not purely exogenous, as in structural theories or constructivist approaches that locate them in general societal trends, but are tied to the agency and interests of IOs (Ness and Brechin 1988; Scott 1992).

Independence is equally important in implementation. The ILO committee of experts—a group of private individuals—comments on national reports. Some ILO organs use these comments to highlight noncompliance with ILO conventions and recommendations and to invite governments to submit additional information. Other IOs report on state compliance in addition to, or in lieu of, national reports. IO officials further monitor state conduct, in more or less intrusive ways, although enforcement remains decentralized. For example, the WTO regularly reviews the general effects of national trade policies.

MANAGING SUBSTANTIVE OPERATIONS

In the above examples, IOs facilitate interstate collaboration by pushing negotiations forward. This role could be played by, say, a dominant state, but suspicions of bias might impede cooperation; an independent IO may be more acceptable because it is neutral. For many substantive IO operations, however, it is the existence of a truly independent third party, not the absence of bias per se, that enables states to achieve their ends.

Laundering

Laundering has a negative connotation from its association with running ill-gotten gains through seemingly independent financial institutions until they come out clean, having lost their original character and taint. Without necessarily adopting that connotation, we use the term advisedly because the process at work in IOs is similar: activities that might be unacceptable in their original state-to-state form become acceptable when run through an independent, or seemingly independent, IO. The concept should be familiar to IR scholars who are reluctant to accept Central Intelligence Agency funds but eagerly accept National Science Foundation grants overseen by independent academic panels.

Appropriately enough, the World Bank, IMF, and other IFIs provide clear examples. States may prefer development assistance from an independent financial institution over direct aid from another state, especially a former colonial power or one seeking political influence. IFI restrictions on national autonomy (e.g., on project design or broader economic policies) may not carry the same domestic political implications of dependence and inferiority as would conditions imposed directly by, say, the United States or France. These considerations may make IFI conditions a superior means of promoting domestic reforms.

IFIs equally serve a laundering function for donor states seeking to avoid domestic and international controversies. The World Bank's charter requires, for example, that development loans be made without regard for the "political character" of the recipient; disregard of this factor is difficult within the United States, where financial assistance budgets require congressional approval. The United States called on the IMF to manage the 1980s debt crisis, keeping the issue less politicized and more technical. Similarly, the Soviet Union laundered subsidies to subordinate states in Eastern Europe through Council for Mutual Economic Assistance (CMEA) trading practices, muting domestic opposition to these political and economic arrangements both at home and in recipient states (Marreese 1986). IFIs also inhibit domestic special interests from distorting policy for other purposes, as in the case of tied aid.

Although the obligation to participate in IFIs may be strong, doing so helps donor states curtail aid recipients' expectations, thus preserving flexibility. Although international intermediaries diminish a donor state's leverage over recipient states, this factor is offset by decreases in other states' leverage and in competition for leverage among donors. Donor states as a group, of course, retain control over the IFIs. But it is the fund, not the United States or Germany, that imposes austerity on borrowers.

The autonomy needed for successful laundering gives IOs influence over the substance of their activities. For example, IFI staff have significant input into lending criteria and adjustment policies and, increasingly, into social, environmental, and other related policies. Robert McNamara was able to broaden development discourse beyond economic growth to include social factors and to reorient World Bank policy (Finnemore 1996; Sanford 1988). The point should not be overstated. McNamara's reforms were hardly radical, and Western countries were largely receptive. Subsequently, the Reagan administration pushed the World Bank partially back toward market policies. Thus, IO autonomy remains bounded by state interests and power, as reflected in institutional arrangements.

Such interventions can cause IOs to be perceived as politicized, responding to the interests of certain states or to issues beyond their regular purview. This occurred in the 1960s and 1970s, when the World Bank withheld loans from states that expropriated foreign property without compensation (Lipson 1985, 138-39); recently, the United States linked support for World Bank lending to human rights in cases, including China and Malawi (Kirgis 1993, 572-75). Whatever their justification, such measures reflect a partial failure we label *dirty laundering*. Powerful states face a tension between the immediate advantages of dirty laundering versus the long-run costs of jeopardizing IO independence.

Laundering is not limited to financial organizations. UN peacekeeping allows powerful states to support conflict reduction without being drawn into regional conflicts and discourages other powers from taking advantage of their inaction. This simultaneously reassures small countries that the conflict will not be enlarged. The IAEA performs two different laundering functions. First, recipients may prefer technical assistance from an independent agency rather than a particular nuclear state, even though nuclear states as a group dominate the agency. Direct assistance may create dependence, reduce policy flexibility, and be domestically controversial. IAEA technical assistance programs also distance provider states from recipient nuclear programs and inhibit the commercial rivalry among suppliers that otherwise facilitates proliferation. Second, states subject to nuclear safeguards may be more willing to admit independent international monitors into sensitive nuclear facilities than to permit entry by representatives of another state. Interestingly, when the United States transferred bilateral safeguard responsibilities to the IAEA in 1962, some recipients resisted the new arrangement, fearing that nationals of various states on the IAEA staff would conduct covert intelligence missions. This suggests, however, not that the logic of laundering is false but that it turns on the perceived independence of the organization.

Laundering thus has significant implications for the constitutive rules of IOs. Although member states retain ultimate control, organizations must be structured—from their organs of governance down to their personnel policies—to create sufficient independence for laundering to succeed. A failing of the UN secretariat is that its personnel are viewed as retaining their national identities; by contrast, the "Eurocrat" is seen as having loyalties beyond his or her individual state.

Neutrality

Neutrality adds impartiality to independence. It enables IOs to mediate among states in contested interactions, including disputes and allocation decisions. UN neutrality underlies most of the functions discussed in the secretary-general's Agenda for Peace, from fact-finding and other forms of preventive diplomacy through dispute resolution and peacekeeping to postconflict consolidation of peace. Even more than laundering, neutrality demands that institutions be buffered from direct pressures of states.

IO as neutral information provider. Regime theory recognizes the importance of information but does not emphasize differences in its quality. Information created or verified by an independent, neutral IO is more reliable than that provided by states because it is free of national biases. Consider the air pollution monitoring stations established in Europe under LRTAP. Data supplied by Sweden or Russia could be perceived as biased, but a neutral source of information was more credible and could support greater cooperation. The convention protecting Antarctic seals incorporated an existing institution, the Scientific Commission on Antarctic Research, as a neutral source and verifier of information on the status of seals and state activities. Based on this information, the parties attained a rather high degree of cooperation. Similar conventions without neutral sources of information, such as that concerning Antarctic marine living resources, have been less successful. Finally, the 1991 General Assembly declaration on fact finding strengthens the UN secretary-general's role as a neutral information source in politically charged situations; the General Assembly has similarly encouraged the secretary-general to develop early-warning systems for international disputes and humanitarian crises.

International monitoring organizations, notably those operating under multilateral arms control treaties, provide outstanding examples of neutral information production. From the perspective of many participants, the neutrality of these organizations is their most important feature. Impartial information not only deters cheating by others but also helps states assure others of their own compliance (Abbott 1993). Although the literature on informal cooperation and the U.S.-Soviet arms control experience suggest that states can perform these functions on their own (Glaser 1995), the widespread use of IOs testifies to the advantages of third-party neutrals.

IO as trustee. In private commercial dealings, neutral parties often hold assets belonging to persons who cannot be trusted with possession until a transaction is completed. The escrow agent, for example, protects assets until all elements of the transaction are ready for closing, while the trustee holds assets on behalf of owners who cannot take title immediately.

Such arrangements are not common in IR, but notable examples exist. The Security Council held Iraq responsible for losses caused by its invasion of Kuwait. It required Iraq to contribute a percentage of its oil export revenues to a UN compensation fund from which payments would be made. A compensation commission (whose governing council includes representatives of Security Council members) administers the fund as trustee for claimants. Subsequently, concerned about humanitarian needs in Iraq, the council authorized states to import limited amounts of Iraqi oil with payments to be made directly into a special escrow account for purchases of food and medicine. Similarly, an international oil pollution compensation fund is part of the IMO regime governing oil spills in territorial waters.

Building on the League of Nations mandate system, the UN charter established an international trusteeship system. Individual states were typically designated as trustees for various territories, with mixed results. But the charter did establish standards for trustees and a trusteeship council to monitor them. It even contemplated that the UN itself would perform the trustee function directly, an extraordinary example of the IO as a neutral party.

Traditional UN peacekeeping also illustrates the trustee function: UN forces patrol or even control territory to separate combatants, prevent conflict, and supervise negotiated cease-fires. UN neutrality also allows major powers to support peacekeeping without choosing sides among friendly states, as in Cyprus. Blue-helmet neutrality is crucial and guaranteed in multiple ways: operations are voluntary and require continuing consent of all parties, peacekeepers are from countries with no stake in the conflict and under UN command, operations are financed through general assessments, and troops are unarmed (observers) or lightly armed for self-defense to prevent uses of force inconsistent with neutrality. But these restrictions can limit the effectiveness of peacekeeping operations in some conflictual environments—as has been evident in Bosnia. To deal with these limitations, the secretary-general's Agenda for Peace proposes a preventive trustee function: UN-administered demilitarized zones, established in advance of actual conflict to separate contending parties and remove any pretext for attack.

Neutral activities must be keenly attuned to the realities of international power. U Thant's quick withdrawal of the United Nations Emergency Force (UNEF) at Egypt's request in 1967 was based on the legal principle requiring consent for UN operations but equally reflected the reality that two contributing countries had threatened to withdraw troops if Egyptian wishes were not respected. Nevertheless, like an escrow agent, peacekeeping is effective when it furthers state interests in limiting conflict.

The Acheson-Lilienthal (Baruch) Plan would have created an international agency to manage fissile material, contributed by the United States and the United Kingdom, the existing nuclear powers. This institutional arrangement (which was not, of course, adopted) resembled a trusteeship with the world community as beneficiary. It reflected the vital interests of donor states in preventing destabilizing proliferation, but the plan required a neutral trustee. The sponsors would not have been trusted to hold the material themselves.

Similarly, under the "common heritage" principle of UNCLOS III, the convention declares that rights to seabed resources are "vested in mankind as a whole, on whose behalf the Authority shall act." The powers of the Seabed Authority were limited to accord better with market principles and U.S. interests, but it retains its basic institutional structure, including important trustee characteristics that may evolve over time.

IO as allocator. A neutral party often allocates scarce resources among claimants to avoid paralyzing negotiating standoffs and lingering resentment: the parent, not the children, slices the birthday cake. IOs also serve this function.

The IAEA, for example, assists peaceful national nuclear programs. It necessarily evaluates proposed projects and allocates financial and personnel resources. Only a neutral body could be entrusted with such responsibility in a sensitive area. IFIs also allocate scarce resources according to project worthiness. The World Bank's charter tries to guarantee its neutrality by requiring that it ignore the political character of potential borrowers. The perception that the World Bank promotes promarket policies on behalf of the Western powers and punishes governments that pursue other goals such as equity reduces its effectiveness. The World Bank defends its neutrality by presenting its policies as driven by technical analyses rather than value judgments. It has retained a sufficient aura of neutrality to be entrusted with allocating funds under the Global Environment Facility, the Ozone Trust Fund, and the climate change convention.

IO as arbiter. According to Morgenthau (1967, 272), "despite . . . deficiencies [in] . . . the legislative function [in international politics], a legal system might still be capable of holding in check the power aspirations of its subjects if there existed judicial agencies that could speak with authority whenever a dissension occurred with regard to the existence or the import of a legal rule." Few international institutions are truly designed to restrain state power, yet many help states resolve legal (and political) disputes. Neutrality is essential for such institutions, just as for a judge in the law merchant system (Milgrom, North, and Weingast 1990), the European Court, or a domestic court.

In *facilitative intervention*, an IO operates as "honest broker" to reduce transaction costs, improve information about preferences, transmit private offers, and overcome bargaining deadlocks. Chapter VI of the UN charter requires states to use traditional measures—including good offices, mediation, conciliation and fact finding—to resolve disputes that threaten international peace and security. The secretary-general frequently provides these services. The Human Rights Committee provides its good offices in interstate disputes and may appoint ad hoc conciliation commissions to propose possible settlements. Numerous international conventions, from the Antarctic to the NATO treaties, provide for similar measures if direct negotiations fail. Even the highly legalized WTO understanding on dispute settlement allows members to request mediation or conciliation by the director-general.

In *binding intervention*, international institutions issue legally binding decisions with the consent of all parties. The mere possibility of binding external intervention may bring recalcitrant states to the bargaining table and make negotiating positions more reasonable. The most common dispute resolution mechanism of this kind is arbitration. Participating states agree on arbitrators, procedures, and jurisdiction and agree to be bound by the arbitrators' decision. When agreement on these matters cannot be reached, other neutral IOs sometimes fill the gap—as when the Permanent Court of Arbitration selected the president of the U.S.-Iran claims tribunal.

Arbitral tribunals resolve disputes on an ad hoc basis, as in the 1941 U.S.-Canada *Trail Smelter* arbitration, a leading precedent in international environmental law, or in the secretary-general's "Rainbow Warrior" arbitration between France and New Zealand. They also handle classes of disputes such as the famous *Alabama Claims* arbitration following the Civil War, the special claims commission for allied property claims following World War II, and the Iran-U.S. claims tribunal. The following comment on the Rainbow Warrior dispute applies to most of these cases: "This solution is not without critics in both countries. . . . However, . . . the settlement proved much more acceptable—precisely because of its unimpeachable source—than would have been the same, or any other, solution arrived at solely by the parties themselves. Neither government . . . could be accused by its internal critics of having yielded to the other" (Franck and Nolte 1993, 166).

Many international agreements, from bilateral commercial treaties to the law of the sea convention, rely on arbitration through ad hoc panels or more permanent institutions. The GATT-WTO dispute resolution process is similar to arbitration. In the interest of neutrality, the director-general maintains a roster of qualified panelists, suggests panelists to disputants, and names the panel if the parties cannot agree. NAFTA incorporates several arbitration procedures, including an innovative one whereby arbitrators review national antidumping and countervailing duty decisions to ensure that national law was followed. The International Centre for the Settlement of Investment Disputes (ICSID), affiliated with the World Bank, provides neutral facilities for arbitrations between private investors and host governments.

The principal international judicial authority is the International Court of Justice (ICJ). Unlike domestic courts, it must be granted jurisdiction by parties to a dispute. Most cases have arisen under treaties that include submission to ICJ jurisdiction. The ICJ also issues advisory opinions to UN organs and specialized agencies. The court has issued a number of decisions of significance but has not been heavily used by states; GATT panels, for instance, have issued many more decisions than the ICJ. A relatively small number of states have accepted compulsory jurisdiction, and efforts to use the court during high-profile disputes led France and the United States to terminate their acceptance, although not without cost. The European Court of Justice and the European Court of Human Rights (which also requires acceptance of jurisdiction) have been more successful. Indeed, the former—whose judges are chosen "from persons whose independence is beyond doubt"—approaches the authority of the judicial institutions Morgenthau had in mind. Its judges have played a leading (independent) role in promoting European legal integration (Burley and Mattli 1993). Other international institutions, including the WTO appellate body, may also develop into successful judicial agencies.

IO AS COMMUNITY
REPRESENTATIVE AND ENFORCER

In this section, we consider broader and more controversial functions of formal IOs, some of which go beyond a simple state-centric approach. We examine how states structure and use formal organizations to create and implement community values and norms and to assist in the enforcement of international commitments. This discussion demonstrates further how the study of IOs forces different theoretical schools to engage one another. We discuss these two functions separately, then together in a brief examination of the role of the UN in the Gulf War—an example that also illustrates the significance of IOs in situations of violent conflict.

THE IO AS COMMUNITY REPRESENTATIVE

States establish IOs to act as a representative or embodiment of a community of states. This was a central aspiration in the postwar organizational boom and remains an important, if only partially fulfilled, aspect of IO operations today.

Community institutions take several forms. They may be inclusive bodies such as the General Assembly, the town square of international politics, created as a forum in which common issues can be addressed. Within such institutions, states work out and express their common interests and values. The process may be largely consensual, as when states consider some problem of common concern such as environmental change or the behavior of a rogue state, or it may entail one set of states pressuring another to accept new principles such as human rights, the oceans as a commons, or democracy. Other community institutions, such as the Security Council, are representative bodies. These incorporate the major actors (as realism would predict) as well as states representing other interests. These smaller bodies instantiate political bargains in their representation rules while providing a more efficient forum in which to deal with issues, especially those requiring operational responses. Finally, community institutions such as the ICJ are structured to promote independence and neutrality, their actions constrained by a charge to act in the common interest. All three types can advance community interests with special legitimacy.

The UN, established by the Allies when they had unchecked dominance, was undoubtedly intended to serve their own purposes. It was also based on a conception of shared interests and values that went well beyond laundering or even neutrality. The charter's broad goals presupposed a direct relation between national welfare, conditions around the globe, and the peaceful working of the international community as a whole. The principal goal was to maintain international peace and security, and UN organs were authorized to intervene—not just mediate—in interstate disputes that threatened peace. Other goals were to develop friendly relations among states based on the principles of equal rights and self-determination, to promote fundamental freedoms, and to promote cooperation on a wide range of global problems. Shared interests in many of these areas—human rights, democracy, and liberal economic relations—are still developing.

Perhaps the most important function of community organizations is to develop and express community norms and aspirations. Although the General Assembly lacks the Security Council's power of action, it can have substantial impact on international politics by expressing shared values on issues like human rights, apartheid, decolonization, and environmental protection in ways that legitimate or delegitimate state conduct. The Universal Declaration of Human Rights is a striking example. Although the declaration cannot be enforced, its explicit and sweeping formulation of standards has significantly affected state behavior. Its norms have been included in binding treaties, and the declaration itself has been incorporated into some national constitutions, thereby influencing the character and preferences of states and, thus, of the international system itself. Although smaller states have been disproportionately held to account on this issue, even large states like the former Soviet Union and reputed nuclear states like South Africa have been affected.

Similarly, although GATT (unlike the WTO) was intentionally created with as few attributes of an independent IO as possible, its contracting parties and council have formulated important policies for the trading community, including "differential and more favorable treatment" for developing countries. Although contested, this principle has been reflected in subsequent trade negotiations and the generalized system of preferences.

Courts as independent institutions also formulate and express community policy. By enunciating, elaborating, and applying rules publicly, they educate the community and strengthen underlying norms (Abbott 1992). A highly unusual IO, the UN tribunal dealing with war crimes in the former Yugoslavia, combines these public judicial roles with the closely related public role of prosecutor. But states have not fully embraced the community functions of courts. Even the ICJ is structured to minimize its community role: its jurisdiction rests on party consent, and its decisions have no formal status as precedents. Yet, ICJ decisions are regularly relied on, and the court has on important occasions acted as expositor of fundamental community values, as in the Iranian hostages case and, many would say, Nicaragua's suit against the United States. These decisions have important moral authority even when they cannot be enforced in the traditional sense. Similar functions are performed by the European and Inter-American Commissions and Courts of Human Rights, and even by quasi-judicial bodies like the ILO governing body.

The most controversial example of community representation is the Security Council's "primary responsibility for the maintenance of international peace and security." The council is empowered to investigate any situation that might lead to international friction and recommend means of resolving the conflict, including terms of settlement. It is further empowered under Chapter VII to "take action" against any threat to peace. When using armed force, however, the council has proceeded much as with economic sanctions, calling on members to give effect to measures it has approved.

An IO with these powers could overcome free-rider problems hampering decentralized efforts to maintain peace. But the Security Council has the deeper rationale of representing the community. Because local disputes might spill over and disrupt the larger community, they affect the general welfare. Such disputes should not be dealt with exclusively by the parties themselves, or by third states intervening for their own private interests, but by collective bodies that consider the effects of the dispute and of external intervention on the general welfare. Chapter VIII of the charter even authorizes regional organizations like the Organization of American States (OAS) to deal with local disputes, although they only take "enforcement action" with council approval, lest such action itself threaten the peace of the larger community. Finally, situating private disputes in terms of community interests and institutions brings a heightened level of political and moral pressure to bear on disputants and potential intervenors.

The creation and development of IOs often represent deliberate decisions by states to change their mutually constituted environment and, thus, themselves. IOs can affect the interests and values of states in ways that cannot be fully anticipated. Yet, it is important to stress that these processes are initiated and shaped by states. Furthermore, IOs are constrained by institutional procedures—including financial contributions and leadership appointments—that are controlled by states and, ultimately, by the ability of (some) states to withdraw, albeit at some cost. These possibilities and limitations make IOs an important window into the relation between rationalist and constructivist analysis.

IOs AS MANAGERS OF ENFORCEMENT

The role of IOs in ensuring compliance with international commitments can best be understood by integrating managerial and enforcement views of the process. Observing high levels of compliance with international agreements, even though strong enforcement provisions are rarely included or used, the managerial school concludes that IR has focused too heavily on coercive enforcement. In this view, noncompliance typically results not from deliberate cheating but from ambiguity in agreements, insufficient state capacity, or changing international and domestic circumstances (Chayes and Chayes 1995; see also Mitchell 1994; Young 1994). Resolution of such problems lies not in stronger enforcement but in better management of compliance. Downs, Rocke, and Barsoom (1996) counter that, without enforcement, states will cheat on agreements and that observed compliance levels largely reflect shallow agreements that require little change in state behavior.

An overly sharp distinction between managerial and enforcement functions is misleading. For many significant day-to-day activities—especially ones involving coordination—incentives to defect are relatively small compared with the benefits of cooperation; here, the managerial approach is sufficient. In other cases, some enforcement may be necessary, at least potentially. IOs support both kinds of activities. More important, the strictly decentralized models that underpin the enforcement view do not apply strictly to the richer environment of international politics, especially when states are numerous and face significant informational problems. In these more complex settings, IOs can manage enforcement activities to make them more effective and to limit their adverse side effects.

Many IO functions identified earlier are valuable in implementing the managerial approach. Ambiguity can be resolved through dispute resolution and other third-party procedures, including fact finding, good offices, interpretation of international agreements, and mediation. State incapacity is addressed directly by financial and technical assistance. Emerging compliance problems due to changing circumstances can be managed by IO political and judicial organs with authority to interpret and adapt agreements and elaborate norms.

When enforcement is needed, IOs can facilitate decentralized action. They increase the prospect of continued interaction, often across issues, and generalize reputational effects of reneging across members of the organization. Some IOs directly monitor state behavior, producing credible neutral information necessary for effective enforcement. IOs further provide forums in which suspicious actions can be explained, lowering the risk that misperceptions will upset cooperation, and in which pressure can be brought on transgressor states. In these ways, international legal discussions about "mobilization of shame" can be understood not in the moral sense of creating guilt among states but in an instrumental sense of enhancing reputational and other incentives to abide by commitments.

IOs also have some direct avenues of enforcement. These include requirements of national reporting—wherein failure to report itself indicates improper behavior—and the issuance of findings by the IO itself. The ILO has issued such reports with respect to labor practices, even in the case of powerful states such as the Soviet Union and Britain. A less frequent sanction occurs through resolutions criticizing state behavior. Such practices pressure, states to change their behavior both by impairing their international standing and by empowering private groups to pressure national governments, thus increasing "audience costs" (Fearon 1994). Currently, the G-7 states are working to empower the IMF to make findings on national economic policies and to issue public criticism with precisely these goals in mind.

A second means of direct enforcement is withholding IO benefits, as the IAEA suspended technical assistance after Israel bombed an Iraqi nuclear reactor. The IMF's "conditionality" requirements and the World Bank's requirements on development loans have expanded over the postwar period, and these agencies have frequently had strong effects on the policies of member states.

Finally, IOs play an important role as managers of enforcement, authorizing and giving meaning to retaliation, thus ensuring that enforcement activities are not excessively disruptive to the larger international community. This possibility is differentially developed. The GATT only once authorized retaliation, whereas WTO practice is still emerging; the Security Council, by contrast, has authorized economic sanctions on numerous occasions. Martin (1992, 245) finds IOs important in managing economic sanctions because they provide a framework for side payments among retaliating states and increase incentives to cooperate in sanctions so as not to jeopardize the "broad functional benefits these organizations provided."[12] Furthermore, such validation is akin to laundering: when an IO legitimates retaliation, states are not vigilantes but upholders of community norms, values, and institutions. The IO imprimatur clarifies retaliatory behavior so that it will be seen by the target state for what it is, not as noncooperation by the retaliating state, while reassuring third parties that the retaliating state is acting appropriately. (Again, influential states might seek IO approval to disguise their noncooperative acts as retaliation, a form of dirty laundering, but this practice is limited by its self-defeating character and IO independence.) IO approval frequently limits the severity and duration of state retaliation, as the WTO does by limiting the amount of retaliation and the economic sectors targeted. Indeed, the IO may negotiate a response with the retaliating state to maximize third-party support for the action. Such managerial activities counteract "echo effects" and are improvements over strictly decentralized enforcement.

CHAPTER VII: THE USES AND LIMITS OF DIRECT ENFORCEMENT

The Security Council's experience with Chapter VII illuminates the role of the community representative in constructing interests, the possibility of more forcible

---

12. Martin (1992, 245) also finds it important that the leading "sender" be willing to bear extra costs, suggesting a possible limitation to IO enforcement capacity in the absence of "leadership."

methods of direct enforcement, and, equally important, their limitations. As noted above, the original conception of Chapter VII involved independent action by the Security Council on behalf of the community of states, using military units provided "on its call" by member states and guided by a military staff committee. This was direct enforcement except that the units to be deployed, even the members of the committee, were to be provided by states. This distinguishes Chapter VII from, say, the independent ability of the IMF to cut off funds to a country that violates its financial commitments. Moreover, Chapter VII has never operated as originally intended. In the two principal episodes in which military force has been used—Korea and the Gulf War—the council instead authorized national military actions, led in both cases by the United States. How are these episodes to be understood?

In the more cynical view, both are examples of dirty laundering. By obtaining Security Council approval, the United States cast essentially unilateral action as more legitimate collective action. The same interpretation can be applied to various OAS enforcement actions against Castro's Cuba. Arguably, the organizations were not sufficiently independent of U.S. influence to convert the measures taken into genuine community action. In the Gulf War, these measures were transparently national: the council simply called on other states to cooperate with the United States, which was already operating in the Gulf theater, and coalition forces were visibly dominated by the United States, whose troops even retained their own uniforms and commanders.

Yet, these episodes can also be seen in a more affirmative light. The institutional underpinnings essential to the original vision of Chapter VII had never been put in place: there were no agreements for the provision of national forces, no emergency units standing by, no military staff committee. Lacking appropriate institutional arrangements, the council carried out its community responsibilities in the only practicable way, by shifting from direct to indirect enforcement, lending its institutional authority to legitimate action by willing nations. Its membership structure and voting rules made the council sufficiently independent and representative to perform a genuine laundering function.[13] The United States, after all, assiduously courted council approval (partly by moving more cautiously) for reasons of both domestic and international politics. The imprimatur of the council was essential to other participants: Middle Eastern states, for example, needed it to justify cooperation with the coalition. In this episode, just as Claude (1966, 74) put it more than 30 years ago, "proclamations of approval or disapproval by organs of the United Nations, deficient as they typically are in . . . effective supportive power, are really important. . . . [S]tatesmen, by so obviously attaching importance to them, have made them important."[14]

The affirmative view sees the council, especially during the Gulf War, as representing the community of states. This representative status, not simply the formal procedures of Chapter VII, led the United States and other states to seek council action:

13. The current debate over the composition of the council reflects the idea that such an institution should be more representative of the community on behalf of which it acts.

14. See also Haas (1958) and, for a more skeptical view, see Slater (1969).

Security Council resolutions on Iraq carried unique political weight because they came from the established community institution with primary responsibility for international peace and security. Resolutions condemning the Iraqi invasion of Kuwait as unlawful, declaring void the incorporation of Kuwaiti territory into Iraq, denouncing human rights and environmental abuses by Iraqi forces, authorizing member states to cooperate with U.S. forces, forcing the destruction of Iraqi weapons, and holding Iraq financially responsible for its actions are clear expressions of the shared moral and legal sense of organized international society. The IO was the locus for giving meaning to state action. The United States, even as the clearly dominant power in coercive activity, had good reasons to act not simply from might but from persuasion.

Thus, realist, constructivist, and rational-regime arguments come together in consideration of the role of IOs in the Gulf crisis. Although some might prefer to find a singular "winner" among the three explanations, we believe each explains a significant part of the episode and that any unidimensional explanation would be incomplete. In any event, IOs provide an important laboratory in which to observe the operation of these different aspects of international politics.

CONCLUSION

For several decades, states have taken IOs more seriously than have scholars. Whereas formal IOs have been seriously neglected in the theoretical study of international regimes, they have played a major role in many, if not most, instances of interstate collaboration. By taking advantage of the centralization and independence of IOs, states are able to achieve goals that they cannot accomplish on a decentralized basis. In some circumstances, the role of IOs extends even further to include the development of common norms and practices that help define, or refine, states themselves. At the same time, because issues of power and distribution are pervasive, states are wary of allowing IOs too much autonomy. Thus, we do not claim that IOs are supplanting the states system. We do claim that IOs provide an important supplement to decentralized cooperation that affects the nature and performance of the international system. Scholars must take IOs more seriously if they are to understand interstate relations.

Although we have presented the case for the importance of formal institutions in international cooperation, the shortcomings of many actual organizations go without saying. In addition, in emphasizing the possibilities for formal organizations, we should not ignore the difficulty and even impossibility of some of the tasks that are presented to them. Despite these severe limitations, the fact that IOs have not been abandoned by states is testimony to both their actual value and their perhaps greater potential. A better theoretical and empirical understanding of formal organizations should help improve their performance.

30   *JOURNAL OF CONFLICT RESOLUTION*

REFERENCES

Sanger, David E. 1995. Big powers plan a world economic bailout fund. *The New York Times,* 8 June, D1.

Abbott, Kenneth W. 1992. GATT as a public institution: The Uruguay Round and beyond. *Brooklyn Journal of International Law* 31:31-85.

———. 1993. Trust but verify: The production of information in arms control treaties and other international agreements. *Cornell International Law Journal* 26:1-58.

Abbott, Kenneth W., and Duncan Snidal. 1997. The many faces of international legalization. Draft paper presented at the Conference on Domestic Politics and International Law, June, Napa Valley, CA.

Alchian, Armen, and Harold Demsetz. 1972. Production, information costs and economic organization. *American Economic Review* 62:777-95.

Amerasinghe, C. F. 1994. *The law of the international civil service.* 2d rev. ed. Oxford, UK: Clarendon.

Barnett, Michael. 1993. Institutions, roles and disorder: The case of the Arab states system. *International Studies Quarterly* 37:271-96.

Bowett, D. W. 1982. *The law of international institutions.* 4th ed. London: Stevens.

Berle, Adolf A., and Gardiner C. Means. 1968. *The modern corporation and private property.* Rev. ed. New York: Harcourt, Brace & World.

Brownlie, Ian. 1990. *Principles of public international law.* 4th ed. New York: Oxford University Press.

Burley, Anne-Marie, and Walter Mattli. 1993. Europe before the court: A political theory of legal integration. *International Organization* 47:41-76.

Calvert, Randall L. 1995. Rational actors, equilibrium and social institutions. In *Explaining social institutions,* edited by Jack Knight and Itai Sened, 57-94. Ann Arbor: University of Michigan Press.

Chayes, Abraham, and Antonia Handler Chayes. 1995. *The new sovereignty: Compliance with international regulatory agreements.* Cambridge, MA: Harvard University Press.

Claude, Inis Jr. 1966. Collective legitimization as a political function of the United Nations. *International Organization* 20:367-79.

Coase, R. H. 1937. The nature of the firm. *Economica* 4:386-405.

Cox, Robert W., and Harold K. Jacobson, eds. 1973. *The anatomy of influence.* New Haven, CT: Yale University Press.

Downs, George W., David M. Rocke, and Peter N. Barsoom. 1996. Is the good news about compliance good news about cooperation? *International Organization* 50:379-406.

Drake, William, and Kalypso Nicolaïdis. 1992. Ideas, interests and institutionalization. *International Organization* 46:37-100.

Dupuy, Rene Jean, ed. 1988. *A handbook on international organisations.* Hingham, MA: Kluwer Academic.

Fearon, James. 1994. Domestic political audiences and the escalation of international disputes. *American Political Science Review* 88:577-92.

Ferejohn, John. 1991. Rationality and interpretation: Parliamentary elections in early Stuart England. In *The economic approach to politics,* edited by Kristen R. Monroe, 279-305. New York: HarperCollins.

Finnemore, Martha. 1996. *National interests in international society.* Ithaca, NY: Cornell University Press.

Franck, Thomas M., and Georg Nolte. 1993. The good offices function of the UN secretary-general. In *United Nations, divided world: The UN's role in international relations,* 2d ed., edited by Adam Roberts and Benedict Kingsbury, 143-82. Oxford, UK: Clarendon.

Garrett, Geoffrey, and Barry Weingast. 1993. Ideas, interests and institutions: Constructing the European Community's internal market. In *Ideas and foreign policy: Beliefs, institutions and political change,* edited by Judith Goldstein and Robert O. Keohane, 173-206. Ithaca, NY: Cornell University Press.

Glaser, Charles. 1995. Realists as optimists: Cooperation as self-help. *International Security* 19:50-93.

Goldstein, Judith, and Robert O. Keohane, eds. 1993. *Ideas and foreign policy: Beliefs, institutions and political change.* Ithaca, NY: Cornell University Press.

Grief, Avner, Paul Milgrom, and Barry R. Weingast. 1994. Merchant gilds. *Journal of Political Economy* 102:745-76.

Haas, Ernst. 1958. *Beyond the nation-state.* Stanford, CA: Stanford University Press.

Haas, Peter M., ed. 1992. Knowledge, power and international policy coordination. *International Organization* 46 (Special issue): 1-390.

Johnson, James D. 1991. Rational choice as a reconstructive theory. In *The economic approach to politics*, edited by Kristen R. Monroe, 113-42. New York: HarperCollins.

Karns, Margaret, and Karen Mingst, eds. 1990. *The United States and multilateral institutions*. Boston: Unwin Hyman.

Kennedy, David. 1987. The move to institutions. *Cardozo Law Review* 8:841-988.

Keohane, Robert O. 1984. *After hegemony*. Princeton, NJ: Princeton University Press.

Keohane, Robert O., Andrew Moravcsik, and Anne-Marie Slaughter. 1997. A theory of legalization. Draft paper presented at the Conference on Domestic Politics and International Law, June, Napa Valley, CA.

Kirgis, Frederic L. Jr. 1993. *International organizations in their legal setting*. 2d ed. St. Paul, MN: West.

Koremenos, Barbara, Charles Lipson, Brian Portnoy, and Duncan Snidal. 1997. Rational international institutions. Paper presented at the American Political Science Association Meetings, 28-31 August, Washington, DC.

Krasner, Stephen D., ed. 1983. *International regimes*. Ithaca, NY: Cornell University Press.

Kratochwil, Friedrich. 1996. International organization(s): Globalization and the disappearance of "publics." Unpublished manuscript.

Kratochwil, Friedrich, and John Gerard Ruggie. 1986. The state of the art on the art of the state. *International Organization* 40:753-75.

Levy, Mark A. 1993. European acid rain: The power of tote-board diplomacy. In *Institutions for the Earth: Sources of effective international environmental protection*, edited by Peter M. Haas, Robert O. Keohane, and Marc A. Levy, 75-132. Cambridge, MA: MIT Press.

Lipson, Charles. 1985. *Standing guard: Protecting foreign capital in the nineteenth and twentieth centuries*. Berkeley: University of California Press.

Marreese, Michael. 1986. CMEA: Effective but cumbersome political economy. *International Organization* 40:287-327.

Martin, Lisa L. 1992. *Coercive cooperation*. Princeton, NJ: Princeton University Press.

McNeely, Connie L. 1995. *Constructing the nation-state: International organization and prescriptive action*. Westport, CT: Greenwood.

Mearsheimer, John. 1995. The false promise of international institutions. *International Security* 19:5-49.

Milgrom, Paul R., Douglass C. North, and Barry R. Weingast. 1990. The role of institutions in the revival of trade: The law merchant, private judges, and the champagne fairs. *Economics and Politics* 2 (1): 1-23.

Mitchell, Ronald. 1994. Regime design matters: Intentional oil pollution and treaty compliance. *International Organization* 48:425-58.

Moravcsik, Andrew. 1991. Negotiating the Single European Act: National interests and conventional statecraft in the European Community. *International Organization* 45:19-56.

Morgenthau, H. 1967. *Politics among nations*. 4th ed. New York: Knopf.

Morrow, James D. 1994. The forms of international cooperation. *International Organization* 48:387-424.

Ness, Gary D., and Steven R. Brechin. 1988. IOs as organizations. *International Organization* 42:245-74.

Olson, Mancur, and Richard Zeckhauser. 1966. An economic theory of alliances. *Review of Economics and Statistics* 48:266-79.

Oye, Kenneth A., ed. 1986. *Cooperation under anarchy*. Princeton, NJ: Princeton University Press.

Rochester, J. Martin. 1986. The rise and fall of international organization as a field of study. *International Organization* 40:777-813.

Russett, Bruce, John R. Oneal, and David R. Davis. In press. The third leg of the Kantian tripod for peace: International organizations and militarized disputes, 1950-85. *International Organization* 42.

Sanford, Jonathon. 1988. The World Bank and poverty: The plight of the world's impoverished is still a major concern of the international agency. *American Journal of Economics and Sociology* 47:257-765.

Schermers, Henry, and Niels Blokker. 1995. *International institutional law: Unity within diversity*. 3d rev. ed. Cambridge, MA: Kluwer Law International.

Scott, W. Richard. 1992. *Organizations: Rational, natural and open systems*. 3d ed. Englewood Cliffs, NJ: Prentice Hall.

Shihata, Ibrahim F. I., ed. 1991. *The World Bank in a changing world*. Vol. 1. Norwell, MA: Kluwer Academic Publishers.

———, ed. 1995. *The World Bank in a changing world*. Vol. 2. Cambridge, MA: Kluwer Law International.

Slater, Jerome. 1969. The limits of legitimation in international organizations: The Organization of American States and the Dominican crisis. *International Organization* 23:48-72.

Snidal, Duncan. 1985a. Coordination versus prisoners' dilemma: Implications for international cooperation and regimes. *American Political Science Review* 79:923-42.

———. 1985b. The game *theory* of international politics. *World Politics* 38:25-57.

———. 1996. Political economy and international institutions. *International Review of Law and Economics* 16:121-37.

Sohn, Louis. 1950. *Cases and other materials on world law*. Brooklyn, NY: Foundation.

———. 1967. *Cases on United Nations law*. 2d rev. ed. Brooklyn, NY: Foundation.

Stein, Arthur. 1983. Coordination and collaboration: Regimes in an anarchic world. In *International regimes*, edited by Stephen D. Krasner, 115-40. Ithaca, NY: Cornell University Press.

Strange, Susan. 1983. *Cave! Hic dragones*: A critique of regime analysis. In *International regimes*, edited by Stephen D. Krasner, 337-54. Ithaca, NY: Cornell University Press.

Trachtman, Joel P. 1996. The theory of the firm and the theory of international economic organization: Toward comparative institutional analysis. Unpublished manuscript.

Vienna convention for the protection of the ozone layer. 1985. *International Legal Materials* 26:1529-40.

Weber, Steven. 1994. The European Bank for reconstruction and development. *International Organization* 48 (1): 1-38.

Wendt, Alex. 1992. Anarchy is what states make of it: The social construction of power politics. *International Organization* 46:391-425.

———. 1995. Constructing international politics. *International Security* 20:71-81.

Williamson, Oliver. 1985. *The economic institutions of capitalism*. New York: Free Press.

———. 1994. *The mechanisms of government*. Oxford, UK: Oxford University Press.

Yarbrough, Beth V., and Robert M. Yarbrough. 1992. *Cooperation and governance in international trade*. Princeton, NJ: Princeton University Press.

Young, Oran R. 1994. *International governance*. Ithaca, NY: Cornell University Press.

[9]

Bargaining, Enforcement, and International Cooperation
James D. Fearon

Introduction

A cluster of arguments referred to as "cooperation theory" or "neoliberal institutionalism" stands as one of the more interesting and important developments in international relations theory in the last fifteen years.[1] Focused on the problems of whether and how states might cooperate for mutual advantage despite the absence of supranational government (anarchy), these arguments may be summarized as follows.

Cooperation theorists argued that different international issues and issue domains—trade, finance, arms control, the environment, and so on—may have different strategic structures, and these crucially affect the prospects for international cooperation and the nature of the specific problems states must overcome to achieve it. The different strategic structures have typically been characterized by reference to simple 2×2 matrix games such as Prisoners' Dilemma, Chicken, Harmony, Deadlock, Stag Hunt, and Pure Coordination.[2] Analysts have focused primarily on Prisoners' Dilemma problems and, to a much lesser degree, on coordination problems.

Scholars working in the realist tradition had already suggested that cooperation may occur when states are "playing a coordination game" such as allying against a common threat or choosing telecommunications standards. They argued, however, that cooperation is more difficult in Prisoners' Dilemma–like situations, which they imply are more prevalent and more fundamental in international politics.[3] In re-

An earlier version of this article was presented at the 1993 Public Choice Meetings in New Orleans, Louisiana. For valuable comments, I wish to thank Dale Copeland, Matthew Evangelista, Charles Glaser, Joanne Gowa, Robert Keohane, Lisa Martin, Ken Oye, Stergios Skaperdas, Stephen Walt, and seminar participants at Harvard University and the University of Chicago.

1. See in particular Axelrod 1984; Keohane 1984; Lipson 1984; Oye 1986a; Snidal 1985; and Stein 1982.

2. See Oye 1986a for a description of these games in an international relations context.

3. See in particular Jervis 1978 and Waltz 1979 (for example, 107–11). Specific issue domains that have been characterized as having a Prisoners' Dilemma-like structure are arms levels and force structures (for example, Downs, Rocke, and Siverson 1986; and Waltz 1979, 110); competitive alliance formation (Snyder 1984); arms levels within alliances (Olson and Zeckhauser 1966); imperialism and territorial

International Organization 52, 2, Spring 1998, pp. 269–305

sponse, cooperation theorists observed that if states interact repeatedly on a particular issue—which they typically do— cooperation in Prisoners' Dilemma–like situations might be sustained by mechanisms of conditional retaliation such as Tit-for-Tat. For example, mutually beneficial cooperation in satellite reconnaissance might be sustained by the implicit threat that "if you try to shoot down our spy satellites, we will shoot down yours." A key condition for such mechanisms to work is that the "shadow of the future" be long enough—the states have to care sufficiently about future payoffs and expect that future interactions are likely enough for the threat of retaliation to deter cheating. Cooperation theorists further suggested that international institutions might serve to extend the shadow of the future by regularizing interactions and to facilitate the information flows and monitoring necessary to make mechanisms of conditional retaliation work.

In this article I develop two main arguments bearing on these central propositions of cooperation theory. First, while conceiving of different issue domains in terms of different strategic structures may be heuristically useful for some purposes, doing so misunderstands the problem of international cooperation as state leaders typically face it. I argue that understanding problems of international cooperation as having a common strategic structure is more accurate and perhaps more theoretically fruitful. Empirically, there are always many possible ways to arrange an arms, trade, financial, or environmental treaty, and before states can cooperate to enforce an agreement they must bargain to decide which one to implement. Thus, regardless of the substantive domain, problems of international cooperation typically involve first a bargaining problem (akin to various coordination games that have been studied) and next an enforcement problem (akin to a Prisoners' Dilemma game). To specify and explore this conception analytically, I develop a game-theoretic model that depicts problems of international cooperation as having two linked phases. In the first phase, states bargain over the particular deal to be implemented in the second, "enforcement phase" of the game, which is modeled as a repeated Prisoners' Dilemma.

Second, using this model I show that the bargaining and enforcement problems can interact in an interesting way that cuts against the received wisdom of cooperation theory. Whereas cooperation theorists argued that a longer shadow of the future makes cooperation sustainable and so more likely, the analysis here suggests that though a long shadow of the future may make *enforcing* an international agreement easier, it can also give states an incentive to *bargain harder,* delaying agreement in hopes of getting a better deal. For example, the more an international regime creates durable expectations of future interactions on the issues in question, the greater the incentive for states to bargain hard for favorable terms, possibly making cooperation

aggrandizement (for example, Jervis 1976, 66; Howard 1972 is consistent with this interpretation as well); tariff and nontariff barrier policies in trade (for example, Brander and Spencer 1984; and Conybeare 1987); competitive exchange-rate manipulation (Caves, Frankel, and Jones 1993, 549–50); intervention and efforts to dominate peripheral and buffer states (Larson 1987); first-strike incentives and "the security dilemma" (Jervis 1978; and Van Evera 1984); and global commons problems (Hardin 1968).

harder to reach. The shadow of the future thus appears to cut two ways. Necessary to make cooperative deals sustainable, it nonetheless may encourage states to delay in bargaining over the terms.[4]

These arguments and the model are presented in the second and third sections of the article. In the fourth section I briefly assess empirical implications of these theoretical claims, arguing in particular that the theory may make better sense of the early Cold War arms competition than received cooperation theory can. The conclusion compares the bargaining problem to the relative-gains problem and notes some implications for understanding international regimes.

Strategic Structure and Problems of International Cooperation

Whether the goal is to control arms racing, reduce the risk of preemptive war, limit global environmental damage, stabilize exchange rates, or reduce protectionism in trade, state leaders need to coordinate state policies and the actions of the relevant state bureaucracies if they wish to gain various benefits of cooperating. Cooperation theorists proposed that such diverse problems might be usefully analyzed by focusing on the *strategic structure* of the decision problem faced by state leaders contemplating cooperation. As exemplified by the 1985 *World Politics* volume titled "Cooperation Under Anarchy," strategic structures were understood in terms of simple 2 × 2 games, which include a description of two policy choices available to each state (typically labeled "cooperate" and "defect"), an outcome associated with each of the four combinations of policy choices, and preferences for each state over the four outcomes.[5]

As noted earlier, the various arguments making up cooperation theory advance two, not entirely consistent, propositions. First, different issue domains have different strategic structures with different consequences for the likelihood of international cooperation. Second, many or even most domains have the structure of a repeated Prisoners' Dilemma and so may allow international cooperation by means of a Tit-for-Tat-like regime if state leaders perceive a long enough shadow of the future. Because it more directly challenges the realist claim that cooperation under anarchy is very difficult, the second proposition has attracted the most attention and controversy, chiefly in the form of the relative-gains debate.[6] In addition, empirical work drawing

---

4. Discussing the possible effects of iteration on play in a simultaneous-move coordination game, Duncan Snidal (1985, 36) suggested that a longer shadow of the future could give states "incentives to be more concerned with the exact distributional consequences of particular coordination outcomes," although he argued that "these considerations will still typically be dominated by the overall stability of the coordination situation." Oye (1986a, 14) makes a related conjecture about the effect of repetition on play in Chicken games.

5. The 1985 *World Politics* issue was reprinted as Oye 1986a.

6. See Jervis 1988, however, for a broader range of criticisms that generally equate both game theory and cooperation theory with the study of repeated Prisoners' Dilemmas. See also Gowa 1986 and Milner

on cooperation theory has generally attempted to characterize different international issue domains and problems as repeated Prisoners' Dilemmas,[7] while empirical instances of coordination problems have been relatively neglected.[8]

Despite the greater attention paid to the second argument, I would argue that the first set of propositions is integral to the way that cooperation theory envisions international politics. Further, the "different strategic structures" argument has (often unwittingly) shaped the major questions asked by scholars working in this research program.

Regarding the importance of the argument, two of the earliest theoretical articles in cooperation theory maintained that empirically, states face two types of problems of international cooperation, labeled "coordination versus collaboration" by Arthur Stein and "coordination versus Prisoner's Dilemma" by Duncan Snidal.[9] Both Stein and Snidal argued that differences in international regimes could be explained according to whether they focused on solving a problem of coordination or collaboration (Prisoners' Dilemma), which was held to depend on the nature of the issues in question. For example, Stein saw the Strategic Arms Limitation Talks (SALT) agreements, market-sharing arrangements like the International Coffee Agreement, and international "commons" dilemmas as regimes addressing Prisoners' Dilemma–like problems, whereas product standardization agreements and international radio and airplane traffic conventions were cited as instances of regimes focused on problems of coordination.[10]

The same thesis is very much in evidence in the "Cooperation Under Anarchy" volume, where Kenneth Oye and other contributors made the "payoff structure" in different 2×2 games one of their three major independent variables for explaining variation in cooperation across cases and issue domains.[11] Oye in fact ranged the several 2×2 games used by the authors on a rough scale reflecting the degree to which the strategic structure in question was hypothesized to favor cooperation.[12]

The idea that different international issues and issue domains have different strategic structures has had at least three important consequences for the evolution of research on international cooperation. First, by leading scholars to ask "Which 2×2 game best characterizes the specific empirical case that I am interested in?", the idea of different strategic structures inevitably led scholars to focus on the question "What are the preferences?", understood as how the states in question would rank the four

1992. For the relative-gains debate, see Grieco 1988 and Baldwin 1993. Glaser (1994–95) argues that, rightly understood, neorealism predicts the international cooperation under some circumstances.

7. For a few examples, see Downs and Rocke 1990, 1995; Evangelista 1990; Keohane 1984, 1986; Larson 1987; Rhodes 1989; and Weber 1991.

8. Important exceptions include Krasner 1991; Garrett 1992; Sebenius 1992; and Morrow 1994.

9. See Stein 1982; and Snidal 1985.

10. See Martin 1992 and 1993b for more recent applications of this approach to explaining cooperation in economic sanctioning and variation in the design of multilateral institutions.

11. An influential earlier example of this approach was Snyder and Diesing 1977, who had argued that variation in bargaining behavior in international crises could be understood in terms of different strategic structures in 2×2 games.

12. Oye 1986a, 6–11; see also Snidal 1991, 707.

outcomes deemed possible by the theoretical setup. But cooperation theory provided no guidance here, and the problem of how to assign preferences often seems so difficult or controversial as to render the exercise pointless—most of the "action" of the theory is loaded into the arguments about what the right preferences are and how exactly to characterize what "cooperate" and "defect" mean in a particular setting.[13] Mainly due to this problem of assigning preferences, analysis of problems of international cooperation in terms of different 2 × 2 games has not blossomed, although on the plus side the problem helped lead researchers to look more carefully at how multiple domestic actors with diverse goals interact to influence the foreign policy preferences and strategies of the "chief of government."[14] As I will argue, one reason that assigning preferences to define the "right" 2 × 2 game is so difficult as an empirical matter may be that such games are simply bad models of the strategic problem that leaders typically confront when they are contemplating international cooperation.

A second significant consequence of the "different strategic structures" idea has been a running debate over the relative empirical importance of Prisoners' Dilemma and coordination problems as obstacles to international cooperation. This is seen most clearly in Stephen Krasner's "Global Communications and National Power," where he argues that coordination problems such as the 2 × 2 game Battle of the Sexes are empirically more prevalent than problems of "market failure," a reference to Prisoners' Dilemma–like problems of cheating and enforcement.[15] This framing suggests an either/or choice in characterizing which strategic structure, coordination or Prisoners' Dilemma, is most common and important in international relations. The idea of "coordination versus Prisoners' Dilemma" also appears among proponents of the relative-gains argument, whom Krasner cites as providing supporting evidence for his thesis and who cite Krasner in turn, thus establishing a loose (and, as I later argue, dubious) association between coordination problems and the relative-gains argument.[16]

The third significant consequence of the "different strategic structures" idea is the most relevant for the argument of this article. By defining the realm of interesting possibilities as coordination and Prisoners' Dilemma games, cooperation theorists fostered considerable confusion about how international relations scholars should think about international *bargaining*. The confusion is due to the fact that bargaining problems are not well represented by any 2 × 2 game. Indeed, coordination games such as Chicken and Battle of the Sexes are such minimal models of the bargaining problem that in the international relations literature they generally are not understood

13. Snidal (1991, 704) notes that "Choosing among such different [strategic structures] . . . poses a tough problem at the foundations of IR theory."

14. See, in particular, Putnam 1988; Evans, Jacobson, and Putnam 1993; and Keohane and Milner 1996. For recent work drawing on the 2 × 2 game approach, see Aggarwal 1996; Conybeare 1987; Martin 1992, 1993b; and Weber 1991. Evangelista (1990, 526) explicitly argues that his study "reinforces criticisms of game theoretic approaches that posit the state as a unitary actor."

15. Krasner 1991.

16. See Krasner 1991, 362, 365; and Grieco 1993, 320.

as being about bargaining at all.[17] For this reason and because of the "either coordination or Prisoners' Dilemma" framing, many scholars using cooperation theory treated repeated Prisoners' Dilemma inappropriately as a model of international bargaining, when it is better understood as a model of the problem of enforcing a particular agreement given short-run incentives to renege.

In the classic theoretical sense elaborated by John Nash and Thomas Schelling, a bargaining problem refers to a situation where there are multiple self-enforcing agreements or outcomes that two or more parties would all prefer to no agreement, but the parties disagree in their ranking of the mutually preferable agreements.[18] As an empirical matter, a second characteristic feature of bargaining problems is that they are dynamic. They are resolved, if at all, through time, in sequences of offers and counteroffers or with one or both parties "holding out" in hope that the other will make concessions.[19] A final empirically significant aspect of bargaining problems is that they typically involve uncertainty or private information about what the other side's true "bottom line" is and thus possibilities for bluffing and misrepresentation.

Given this understanding of the nature of a bargaining problem, it is immediately apparent that virtually all efforts at international cooperation must begin by resolving one. Regardless of whether the specific domain is arms control, trade talks, exchange-rate coordination, or environmental regulation, there will almost invariably be *many* possible ways of writing the treaty or agreement that defines the terms of cooperation, and the states involved will surely have conflicting preferences over some subset of these various possibilities. Further, in practice the resolution of such a bargaining problem will take place, if at all, in a series of offers and counteroffers or with states holding out for their preferred option. And of course uncertainty about the minimum that the other side would accept is often important in international negotiations.[20]

At the same time, most efforts at international cooperation also involve issues of monitoring and enforcement. Once a deal is struck on the terms of cooperation—as at a GATT round or an IMF negotiation, for example—the next task is typically to implement, monitor, and enforce the agreement. A very few international agreements (such as air traffic control guidelines) may be largely self-implementing and self-enforcing without any special arrangements. But in the majority of cases, the parties involved recognize that there may be incentives for them to renege in various ways

17. For example, Krasner groups Chicken with Prisoners' Dilemma as an example of a "market failure problem" rather than one of coordination with conflicting interests, as most game theorists see it. He also observes, more justifiably, that in the international relations literature "Battle of the Sexes is hardly noted at all as a possible payoff matrix" (1991, 361).

18. See Nash 1950; and Schelling 1960, chap. 2. Chicken and Battle of the Sexes are thus minimal models of such a problem. Technically, folk theorems (for example, Fudenberg and Tirole 1991, chap. 5) imply that practically all infinitely repeated "mixed motive" games can be bargaining problems in this most basic sense, although the extensive forms of games such as repeated Prisoners' Dilemma are difficult to interpret as models of a bargaining process.

19. The first successful formalization of the dynamic aspect of bargaining is Rubinstein 1982. For applications in international relations, see Powell 1996; Fearon 1995; and Wagner 1996.

20. See, for examples, Morrow 1989; Powell 1990; and Fearon 1992, 1994a, 1995.

on aspects of the deal, and they set up governance structures—regimes—of varying complexity to cope with this.[21]

It follows, then, that the empirical problem faced by states contemplating international cooperation cannot be grasped by a theoretical apparatus that poses an either/or distinction between coordination and collaboration problems. In a broad range of empirical settings, getting to international cooperation involves first a bargaining problem and, second, issues of monitoring and enforcement. This simple observation is obscured by the theoretical apparatus of received cooperation theory. In the next section I consider a model in which the problem of bargaining (coordination with conflicting interests) and enforcement are combined in sequence in order to examine how they interact.[22]

Before developing this conception, a further distinction should be made, one that is also unclear in received cooperation theory. Empirically, problems of international cooperation may involve either (1) bargaining over the division of *new* or potential benefits; or (2) attempts to *renegotiate* an existing cooperative arrangement, where one party threatens to revert to noncooperation if the present terms are not adjusted. In the first class of cases, something happens to "open up" a set of deals that both or all parties would prefer to the status quo. For example, new ideas or more consensual scientific knowledge may lead state leaders to see potential benefits from cooperation on environmental problems, as with the Mediterranean Plan, the 1979 Convention on Long-Range Transboundary Air Pollution (LRTAP), the Montreal Ozone Protocol, or certain aspects of the Law of the Sea Treaty.[23] Alternatively, a change in domestic political circumstances may lead government leaders to see new potential gains from collaboration, as when a political party with stronger commitments to liberalizing trade comes to power or the costs of arms racing or agricultural price supports generate new domestic political pressures.[24] And, of course, technological and economic changes can produce new benefits obtainable by international cooperation, as when the globalization of capital markets creates gains for international macroeconomic and exchange-rate coordination, or when satellite technology makes possible arms control monitoring that in turn makes mutually beneficial arms treaties newly feasible.

In the second type of problem the states involved have already negotiated, tacitly or explicitly, a cooperative arrangement, and some change leads one or more to want to renegotiate the terms. In recent years, threatened trade wars among the OECD countries provide the most striking examples—one state (typically the United States)

---

21. Governance structures may also be desired as means for handling unforeseen contingencies, which are often problematic because they render unclear what constitutes reneging. See Hart 1995; and Williamson 1975.

22. The effort parallels that of Morrow (1994), who showed how distributional conflicts might interfere with mutually advantageous pooling of information in regimes. Garrett (1992) and Garrett and Weingast (1993) have also stressed that questions of distribution and enforcement both appear in typical problems of international cooperation.

23. See E. Haas 1980; and P. Haas 1990, 1992.

24. See Paarlberg 1997, 419–20, for an interesting example concerning farm policies and the Uruguay Round.

threatens to begin a mutually damaging trade war by unilaterally imposing tariffs or other protective measures unless the others renegotiate more favorable terms of market access.[25] In terms of strategic structure, problems of this sort are similar to cases of international crisis bargaining in which one state threatens military action and war (mutually costly noncooperation) in the event of failed efforts at renegotiation.[26] It should be noted, however, that once the phase of "trade war" or costly noncooperation has begun, problems of international renegotiation are structurally similar to problems of dividing up new benefits. Although the model developed in the next section depicts the first type of problem—bargaining over newly available benefits—it can also be understood as a model of renegotiation once the "trade war" or other costly conflict has begun. In addition, note that after an initial agreement is reached, bargaining problems may recur as circumstances change or relative power shifts, leading to efforts at renegotiation. Indeed, some international regimes build in formal arrangements for periodic renegotiation of prior agreements, and to an extent they might even be identified with these institutions of renegotiation.[27]

Saying that diverse international issue domains can be productively viewed as having a common strategic structure does not imply that bargaining and enforcement issues arise in the same manner in all issue areas if these are considered at a lower level of generality. My point is simply that reflection on the empirical problem faced by states wishing to cooperate suggests that, taken as dichotomous alternatives, coordination games and Prisoners' Dilemma-type games are misleading theoretical models. Almost regardless of the substantive domain, states will face *both* a bargaining problem *and* problems of enforcement, and it is natural to expect that the two problems will interact. To ask "which is more common empirically?" or to treat a model of enforcement (repeated Prisoners' Dilemma) as a model of bargaining is to start with a theoretical apparatus ill-suited for the empirical matter at hand.

A Model in Which States Bargain to Determine
Which Agreement to Enforce

I will consider a model in which two states must bargain to decide which of two possible deals they will implement before they can begin cooperating. The states are assumed to have conflicting preferences over the two deals. Both would prefer coordinating on either one of the two packages to noncooperation, but they differ over their most preferred package. Once the states reach agreement in the bargaining phase, they begin the enforcement phase, in which the deal they agreed to establishes

25. For analyses of cases of this sort, see Bhagwati and Patrick 1990; Conybeare 1986; Odell 1993; Noland 1997; and Rhodes 1989.

26. For theoretical work that understands crisis bargaining in these terms, see Fearon 1992, 1994a; Morrow 1989; Nalebuff 1986; and Powell 1990. On a related problem concerning economic sanctions, see Martin 1993a.

27. Koremenos (1996) gives examples along with an analysis of state motivations for renegotiation and how its anticipation affects regime design.

the payoffs for mutual cooperation. In the enforcement phase the states have a short-run incentive to defect, to renege on the agreement while the other side cooperates. Thus in the enforcement phase the states engage in a classical repeated Prisoners' Dilemma.

By restricting attention to the simplest case of two possible cooperative deals, I can model the bargaining phase as a war of attrition, a simple bargaining model that has a number of appealing features. In the classical war of attrition, two parties choose lengths of time to hold out for the prize in question (here, the better cooperative deal), and holding out is costly. The first player to quit the contest cedes the prize to the other side. As an international politics example, we might think of the United States and France each refusing to back down over whether the French will make a specific trade concession.[28] Delay is costly here for two main reasons. First, delay means more time spent without the benefits an agreement would bring; second, as time passes there may be some growing risk that one side will break off negotiations entirely and look for other trading partners (for example, drop GATT in favor of a regional trade bloc).

As an empirical matter, international bargaining often takes the appearance of a war of attrition—two sides holding out, waiting in the hope that the other will make some significant concession first. This holds true at least for international crises, U.S.-Soviet arms control bargaining, and bargaining in GATT rounds; so there is some justification for using a war-of-attrition model for the bargaining phase.[29] However, it should be stressed that the issues states bargain over are typically divisible in many more ways than two. Something more like "continuous offer" bargaining is normally possible in principle, and if states do not make smooth sequences of offers (as in, say, bargaining over the price of a car), this is because for some reason they choose not to. For example, states are not really unitary actors, and the need to forge a domestic consensus among relevant bureaucracies and interest groups may make it very costly for state leaders to generate new offers. I will discuss the possible consequences of allowing for continuous-offer bargaining at the end of the section.

The Model

There are two states, 1 and 2, that attempt in the first phase of the game to select a particular cooperative deal from a set of possible deals. Let the interval $X = [0, 1]$ be the policy space, with each point in X representing the terms of a particular cooperative agreement. Let state 1's utility for the deal $z \in X$ be z, while state 2's is $1-z$. Thus the states have conflicting preferences over the deals in X. State 1 likes deals closer to

---

28. See, for example, Roger Cohen, "Culture Dispute with Paris Now Snags World Accord," *New York Times* , 8 December 1993, A1.

29. On crises as attrition contests, see Nalebuff 1986; and Fearon 1994a. On arms control and trade bargaining, see the examples discussed later. Interestingly, in the econometric literature on labor strikes, war-of-attrition models tend to do better empirically than other, more "continuous" bargaining models. See Kennan and Wilson 1989.

	Cooperate	Defect
Cooperate	$z, 1-z$	$-b, a$
Defect	$a, -b$	$-c_1, -c_2$

Note: $a > 1, b > c_i$ $(i = 1,2)$, $z \in [0,1]$, and $a - b < 0$.

FIGURE 1. *Per-unit-time payoffs in the enforcement phase (a prisoners' dilemma)*

1, state 2 likes deals closer to 0. For concreteness we could think of $z \in X$ as some measure of state 2's trade openness to state 1's products.

As discussed earlier, I will assume that for whatever reason only two deals in X can actually be implemented or that coming up with alternative proposals is prohibitively costly. Let this set of feasible agreements be $A = \{x, y\}$, where $x > y$. Thus state 1 prefers agreement x, whereas 2 prefers y. To illustrate, we could take x to be a trade deal in which state 2 lowers its barriers to a particular product produced mainly by state 1, and y to be the same deal without this concession.

The enforcement phase of the game will be described first. If the states manage to agree on a particular deal $z \in A$ in the bargaining phase, they will play a continuous-time Prisoners' Dilemma with payoffs per unit of time represented in Figure 1.[30] The deal agreed to establishes the per-unit-time payoffs for the mutual cooperation outcome. $a > 1$ is the per-unit-time gain from defecting while the other player cooperates, and $b > 0$ is the per-unit-time cost of being "the sucker."[31] c_1 and c_2 are the states' per-unit-time costs for mutual defection (assume that b is greater than both c_1 and c_2). Finally, in order to make it possible for a state to gain by defecting, assume that if a state switches strategies at time t, the other state is unable either to detect or to respond to this switch for a length of time $\Delta > 0$. The term Δ represents the *detection lag*. If states could instantaneously detect and respond to defection by another state, there would be no short-term gain from reneging and so no problem of enforcement. Thus Δ is naturally interpreted as a measure of how easy or difficult it is to monitor the terms of an agreement, with smaller Δ's implying greater efficacy of monitoring arrangements.

I now describe the bargaining phase that precedes the enforcement phase. The game starts at time $t = 0$. A pure strategy for a state in this phase is a choice of a "quit time" $t_i \geq 0$ $(i = 1, 2)$. This is the time at which state i will concede the better deal if the other side has not already done so.[32] Thus a state's quit time t_i determines how long it will incur the costs of noncooperation, holding out in hope of getting the

---

30. I would prefer to use a discrete-time repeated Prisoners' Dilemma, as does the international relations literature, but unfortunately the war-of-attrition bargaining phase is more conveniently modeled in continuous time.

31. Further, assume that $a-b < 0$ so that mutual cooperation is Pareto efficient for all $z \in X$.

32. Assume that if both states "quit" at the same time, the deal implemented is chosen by a fair lottery.

better deal. For example, if $t_1 < t_2$, the states will move at time t_1 to the enforcement phase with y as the cooperative deal to be implemented—state 2 gets its preferred deal because state 1 "caved in" first. It is natural to say that the longer a state plans to hold out (the bigger t_i), the tougher its bargaining strategy.

While the states hold out in the bargaining phase, they incur per-unit-time costs c_1 and c_2. The idea is that before they reach an agreement about how to cooperate, both suffer the costs of noncooperation. Finally, in both phases the states discount payoffs according to a constant discount rate $r > 0$. When r is close to zero, the states discount future payoffs very little so that the shadow of the future is long. The greater r, the more states discount future payoffs, and the shorter the shadow of the future.

Thus there are *two* costs for delay in the bargaining phase. First, there is the usual discount rate, or shadow of the future, assumed to affect both players. Second, there is the opportunity cost of living with the status quo relative to a cooperative agreement, which varies with the cost terms c_1 and c_2. Differences in costs for noncoopera- tion can be thought of as reflecting the *states' relative power* on the specific issue in question. It is natural to say that the state with lower costs for noncooperation is more powerful, because it has less to lose from not cooperating.

Analysis

Clearly, expectations about what will happen in the enforcement phase will affect how the states bargain. Suppose, for example, that the states expect that neither agreement (x or y) would be enforceable, so that the "both defect" outcome would prevail in the second phase. Then there is no incentive to bargain seriously. A state may as well hold out forever or concede the better deal at any time with no intention of observing the agreement. An interesting substantive implication follows. If states anticipate that obstacles to monitoring and enforcement would make any cooperative agreement in an issue area unstable, they have no incentive to negotiate or to negoti- ate seriously. Thus there is a potentially important *selection effect* behind cases of international negotiations aimed at cooperation. We should observe serious attempts at international cooperation in cases where the monitoring and enforcement dilem- mas are probably resolvable. Other obstacles to cooperation, such as bargaining inef- ficiencies, may then *appear* to be the more significant constraints in the cases we actually observe.[33]

Under what conditions will a particular agreement $z \in X$ be enforceable? The answer depends on the specific "punishment regime" that states expect to govern relations in the enforcement phase. Of many possibilities (Tit-for-Tat is a well- known example), for the rest of the article I will use the simple and severe "grim trigger" regime. In this strategy profile, if during the enforcement phase either player

---

33. Downs, Rocke, and Barsoom (1996) make a closely related point; see later discussion. For analyses of selection effects in international disputes, see Fearon 1994c, 1995.

is ever observed to have defected for any length of time, both then defect forever afterwards. This regime is employed purely for convenience—no substantive results depend critically on its choice.[34]

I show in the appendix that an agreement $z \in X$ will be enforceable by trigger strategies when the following condition holds:

$$r\Delta \leq \min \left\{ \ln \frac{a + c_1}{a - z}, \ln \frac{a + c_2}{a - (1 - z)} \right\} \tag{1}$$

Loosely, this means that it is more likely that an agreement will be enforceable the longer the shadow of the future (that is, smaller r); the better the technology for monitoring and response to violations (smaller detection lag Δ); the lower the short-run benefits of defection, a; and the greater the costs of noncooperation, c_1 and c_2.

These results are familiar and unsurprising. Greater interest attaches to the nature of the agreement, z, about which two points emerge. First, it is easily shown that the longer the shadow of the future (the smaller r), the larger the set of enforceable agreements. Second, consider the case of two "equally powerful" states that have the same fixed costs for delay ($c_1 = c_2$). Then condition (1) is more easily satisfied the more symmetric the agreement—that is, the closer z is to 1/2. Asymmetric agreements are harder to enforce because the state getting the raw end of the deal is more tempted to renege. This temptation is less, of course, the greater the costs of noncooperation for this state (that is, the less powerful it is). Thus the less powerful a state is, the more it is willing to live with relatively asymmetric deals that disadvantage it, because the option of noncooperation is relatively worse.

For a given pair of feasible agreements x and y, condition (1) determines which of three cases is relevant, namely, whether both, one, or neither of the two agreements is enforceable in the second phase of the game. The case where neither agreement can be enforced has just been discussed; here, the states have no incentive to bargain seriously. Similarly, in the case where only one of the two agreements is enforceable, there is in effect nothing to bargain over. If the preferred deal of state i is the only enforceable one, in any efficient equilibrium state j will concede this immediately at time $t = 0$. Relative power may matter in this case, however. Greater power means lower costs for noncooperation, and condition (1) implies that the lower c_i, the less willing state i is to abide by an asymmetric agreement that disadvantages it. Thus the lower a state's costs for noncooperation, the more likely it is that only agreements favoring this state will be enforceable and so the subject of negotiations.

In the most interesting case, the shadow of the future is long enough that both cooperative agreements are enforceable. Here there is something to bargain over, namely the "prize" represented by the present value of the difference between the better and the worse deals, $(x - y)/r$. When both agreements are enforceable, the game

---

34. More precisely, the statement is true if we assume that players do not condition the nature of the punishment regime on what happens in the negotiating phase. I make this assumption for the rest of the

proves to have multiple subgame perfect equilibria.[35] Even so, all equilibria that involve some chance of delay in the bargaining phase have a common feature, described in the following proposition.

PROPOSITION: *Consider any subgame perfect equilibrium of the game in which (1) the agreement reached in the first phase (either x or y) will be successfully enforced in the second phase; and (2) there is positive probability that the bargaining phase will last longer than time $t = 0$. In any such equilibrium, the probability that a state will concede in an instant of time dt conditional on having "stood firm" until time $t > 0$ is constant and approximately equal to*

$$\frac{r(1 - x + c_2)}{x - y} dt$$

for state 1, and

$$\frac{r(y + c_1)}{x - y} dt$$

for state 2. Moreover, for small enough r, subgame perfect equilibria of this form exist.

Proof: See the appendix.

As in other complete information wars of attrition, this game has a family of equilibria involving a chance of delay before one side concedes the prize. These are "mixed strategy" equilibria, which may be interpreted as follows. Neither side knows exactly when the other side will quit, but in equilibrium each knows the probability distribution that describes the other side's likely behavior. Holding out poses a trade-off. The longer one holds out, the greater the chance of receiving the prize, but at the same time the costs will be greater if the other side does not back down. In a mixed strategy equilibrium this trade-off is perfectly balanced—the states are always indifferent between conceding at time t and waiting any further length of time. This proves to imply equilibrium probability distributions in which the conditional probability that a state will quit in the next instant is constant.

Using some probability theory, the expressions in the proposition imply that in any equilibrium, if the dispute is not resolved immediately (at $t = 0$), then the expected time until agreement is always

$$\bar{t} = \frac{x - y}{r[1 + c_1 + c_2 - (x - y)]}.$$

---

35. This is true even given the restriction to trigger strategies in the second phase. For a full description of the set of equilibria in the classic (complete information) war of attrition, see Hendricks, Weiss, and Wilson 1988.

Notice that as r approaches 0, $\bar{t}$ approaches infinity. Thus, *as the shadow of the future lengthens, both states choose tougher and tougher bargaining strategies on average, implying longer and longer delay till cooperation begins.*

The rationale behind this result is straightforward. When states care a lot about future payoffs, the expected long-run benefits of getting the better deal are very large [$(x - y)/r$ approaches infinity as r approaches 0]. Thus the potential benefits of holding out increase. At the same time, when a state values future payoffs almost the same as current payoffs, conceding today is little better than conceding tomorrow—thus the costs of holding out are lower as well. With the benefits of holding out rising and the costs falling as the shadow of the future lengthens, equilibrium is maintained only if *both* states adopt tougher bargaining strategies, yielding more delay before agreement.[36]

This logic generalizes easily to another set of empirically relevant cases where the states expect to cooperate not indefinitely but rather for a finite amount of time. For example, arms control treaties, trade agreements, and agreements establishing international regimes are frequently expected to bind for the foreseeable future. By contrast, an agreement among central bankers to coordinate intervention to stabilize a currency has a clear object that will or will not be achieved within a certain length of time. Discount rates do not adequately capture the difference between these sorts of cases. With respect to the model, it is more like saying that there is a time $T > 0$ at which point the gains from cooperating on this issue will disappear, and that this T can vary from small (the exchange-rate case) to very large (regimes rules, and so on). The preceding result generalizes to this case as follows: The smaller T, the more quickly will states reach agreement in the bargaining phase (on average).[37] Thus, if less time is available for states to take advantage of the gains from cooperation, it makes less sense to waste time holding out for a better deal. Likewise, the longer states expect today's agreement to be relevant in the future, the more reason they have to delay agreement by bargaining hard over distributional advantage.

An Incomplete-Information Version

In the complete-information version of the game, the states know exactly how the other side values cooperative versus noncooperative outcomes. This is an implausibly strong assumption. In addition, many economic theorists have argued that uncertainty about another party's value for an agreement can cause inefficient delay in

---

36. Another implication of the mixed-strategy equilibrium given in the proposition is that the greater the difference in the two deals, x and y, the lesser the likelihood that states will concede at any given instant. When the two deals are close to identical ($x \approx y$), the players place close to zero weight on holding out. Thus greater distributional conflict implies greater delay and more difficulty in reaching a mutually advantageous deal, as intuition suggests.

37. Of course, fixing a horizon in the present model would raise the issue of the "last-period effect" undermining cooperation altogether in the enforcement phase. Little substantive importance should be attached to this problem, however, since last-period effects in repeated Prisoners' Dilemma are not robust against small changes in the specification of the game, such as assuming that the date of the last period is not common knowledge (see, for example, Kreps, Milgrom, Wilson, and Roberts 1982).

bargaining.[38] For example, in bargaining on agricultural policy, a state may "hold out" in an effort to convince the other side that it has high costs for cooperation and so must be offered favorable terms if a deal is to be struck.

To consider the impact of incomplete information, suppose that the states know their own values for noncooperation (c_1 and c_2), but that they know only the distribution of their opponent's value. To keep things manageably simple, I consider a symmetric case where the feasible agreements are $x = 1$ and $y = 0$, and both states' cost terms, c_1 and c_2, are initially drawn from uniform distributions on the interval [1, 2]. Each state is informed of its own cost for noncooperation at the start of the game but not of its opponent's.

A strategy in the bargaining phase now says how long a state will hold out as a function of its privately known cost c_i for noncooperation. In the appendix, I show that the following strategy forms a symmetric Bayesian equilibrium in the bargaining phase: If the state's cost for noncooperation is $c \in [1, 2]$, the state holds out in the bargaining phase until time

$$t(c) = \frac{1}{r} \ln \frac{c}{2(c - 1)}. \tag{2}$$

This expression implies that the lower a state's cost for noncooperation, the longer it will hold out for the better deal. Thus "more powerful" types adopt tougher bargaining strategies and are more likely to prevail in the bargaining phase.[39] The catch is that ex ante, the states are uncertain about who is more powerful, in the sense of having lower opportunity costs for no agreement. Indeed, it is precisely this uncertainty that leads them to engage in a costly war of attrition. Willingness to hold out, bearing the costs of noncooperation, acts as a costly signal in the bargaining phase that credibly reveals a state's "power" on the issue in question.

Expression (2) also shows that the main result for the complete information model holds up in the incomplete information case, namely that the expected delay before agreement increases as the shadow of the future lengthens. When states care more about future payoffs (that is, the discount rate r is smaller), all types choose tougher bargaining strategies. The ex ante expected time till agreement in this equilibrium is $[(\ln 8) - 1]/r$, or approximately $1/r$. Thus as the discount rate approaches zero, the expected time till agreement approaches infinity.

Bargaining with Many Possible Agreements

Probably the most restrictive assumption made in these models is that there are only two feasible agreements. Although international bargaining about how to cooperate

---

38. See Kennan and Wilson 1993.

39. The derivative of $t(c)$ is negative for costs $c > 1$, so that types with larger costs for delay quit sooner. This property holds in any Bayesian equilibrium of the game—incentive compatibility conditions imply that if $c' < c$, then type c' chooses a quit time at least as large as that chosen by type c. See Fudenberg and Tirole 1991, 216–17, for a proof in a standard war of attrition.

often takes the appearance of a war of attrition—two sides waiting for the other to back down—in principle states can usually offer compromise deals, attempts to "split the difference," and so on. Would the main result in the preceding models hold up if such offers could be made? In particular, if the bargaining phase allowed for continuous offers, would a longer shadow of the future be associated with greater delay before agreement?

In its present condition, bargaining theory does not allow an unambiguous answer. In complete-information bargaining models that allow for continuous offers, agreement typically occurs immediately, independent of the discount rate.[40] With incomplete information, however, multiple equilibria usually exist that may or may not have the property observed in the attrition games. Recently, much interest in the theoretical literature on bargaining has been in the validity of the "Coase conjecture" —the proposition that as the costs of delay go to zero, trade will occur immediately between rational, though incompletely informed, bargainers.[41] (Note that this is the exact opposite of the result given earlier, based on an attrition game.) The Coase conjecture holds under some fairly restrictive conditions; namely, bargaining in which one side makes all the offers, only the receiver of the offers has private information, and it is common knowledge that there are gains from exchange. However, it may or may not hold in different equilibria of alternating offer games in which one or both sides has private information. In fact, in some equilibria the *opposite* of the Coase conjecture holds: As the discount rate approaches zero, the expected time till agreement approaches infinity.[42] Even when bargainers can "divide the pie" in an infinite number of ways, equilibria with attrition dynamics may exist. Tough types hold out longer than weak types, using delay to signal that they must be given a good deal. When the costs of delay are low, more delay is necessary to send the same signal. So although the option of dividing the "pie" in many ways may reduce the likelihood of costly standoffs with attrition dynamics, this possibility remains even with such "continuous offer" bargaining.[43]

Empirical Implications

Received cooperation theory suggests that in domains where states have long shadows of the future and adequate monitoring capabilities, they should have little trouble

---

40. This is the result for the classic alternating-offer model of Rubinstein 1982. Motty Perry and Philip Reny (1993) have shown that if players are allowed to choose when and whether to make an offer, nontrivial delay may occur in subgame perfect equilibria if it takes time to react to offers.

41. Named for arguments in Coase 1972, the Coase conjecture should not be confused with the better known "Coase theorem."

42. See Fudenberg and Tirole 1991, 422–23, especially note 34. For the result supporting the Coase conjecture, see Gul, Sonnenschein, and Wilson 1986. For contrary equilibria, see Bikhchandani 1992; and Cramton 1992.

43. The strongest results here are given by Abreu and Gul (1994), who show that if players are uncertain about each others' bargaining strategies rather than about their valuations for the good or time, then, almost regardless of the specific bargaining protocol, all equilibria converge to one with attrition dynamics as the time between offers gets small.

arranging mutually beneficial international cooperation. Following the repeated Prisoners' Dilemma analogy, they need only agree to move to the "cooperate-cooperate" option and then enforce this with implicit threats of retaliation for defection. The theory predicts that we should observe new cooperation when something happens to reduce states' discount rates, increase monitoring abilities and information flows, or open up new benefits for coordination in an area where states' shadow of the future is long and monitoring is feasible.

When we distinguish between bargaining and enforcement phases and analyze them together, we obtain a more nuanced and rather different set of predictions.

First, in cases where effective monitoring is thought infeasible or the shadow of the future too short, state leaders will expect that no bargained agreement will be enforceable due to incentives to renege in the enforcement phase. Thus we should observe either (1) discussions about how to make monitoring and enforcement feasible; (2) nonserious bargaining, where states "commit" to vague agreements for various political purposes (in some instances they might make "framework agreements" to structure further discussions); or (3) no bargaining at all. Especially in the last case, a selection effect results. If we observe states bargaining seriously over the terms of cooperation in some issue area, they probably expect that monitoring and enforcement problems are not insuperable. And because the empirical literature on international cooperation typically samples cases by looking for serious bargaining, it may be biased against finding that concerns about reneging and enforcement are important. George Downs, David Rocke, and Peter Barsoom make this point in a different way. They argue that in constructing international agreements states can choose the "depth" of cooperation, and that they will choose to go only as deep as they expect they can successfully enforce.[44]

To some extent we might avoid the selection-effect problem if we sample cases by issue area rather than by looking at serious efforts to construct agreements or the functioning of completed agreements. For example, if we examined the problem of arms control over a span of time rather than specific negotiations and agreements, we could ask, first, whether monitoring and enforcement concerns precluded serious negotiations and mutually beneficial "deeper" cooperation, and, second, how monitoring concerns compared to the bargaining problem as an obstacle over the whole period. Later I briefly sketch such an analysis for U.S.-Soviet arms control in the 1950s and 1960s.

The second prediction is that we should sometimes observe costly, noncooperative standoffs in precisely those circumstances where received cooperation theory would predict cooperation (that is, when the shadow of the future is long and there are potential mutual gains from agreement). Note that the theoretical results given earlier do not predict a long stalemate in every such case. Even in the war-of-attrition model, agreement will often be reached fairly quickly. For example, if success in the distributional struggle is 20 percent better than getting the worse deal ($x = 1$, $y = 0$, $c_1 =$

---

44. Downs, Rocke, and Barsoom 1996.

$c_2 = 5$) and the states' leaders discount future payoffs by 10 percent each year, agreement will be reached within one year about 63 percent of the time in the most inefficient equilibrium of the game. In other, more efficient equilibria the average delay will be less.[45] Allowing for "continuous offer" bargaining, or for the fact that for some issues there may be salient "focal points," might make for quicker agreements still.[46] The prediction is not that a long shadow of the future will make for a costly standoff in every case, but only in some.

The results can be pushed further on this point—they yield comparative-statics predictions about the circumstances under which costly standoffs are more or less likely. First, and most intuitively, the greater the day-to-day opportunity cost of going without agreement, relative to size of the distributional stake at issue, the less the incentive to engage in a costly stalemate. Second, if the gains from cooperation will be available for a fixed amount of time (as in, say, coordinated intervention to stabilize exchange rates), the bargaining problem should be less problematic the shorter the time horizon for cooperation. Third, and most surprisingly from the perspective of existing theory, the bargaining problem should pose a greater obstacle the longer states' "shadow of the future."[47]

Lacking the space for an extensive empirical test, I will use this section to sharpen these general hypotheses and to give a preliminary assessment where possible. I consider each set of general predictions in turn, concentrating most on the first set.

Before beginning, I should stress that the mechanism identified here is clearly not the only reason that international bargaining over how to cooperate is sometimes protracted, contentious, and prone to failure. Other obstacles to agreement include the sheer complexity of many international issues (for example, in the Law of the Sea and the GATT negotiations), scientific and technical disagreements about the likely effects of different cooperative policies, and the time necessary to piece together domestic political coalitions in favor of a particular offer.[48] I focus here on the effects of the shadow of the future because of the interesting way in which it is predicted to effect both the enforcement and the bargaining problem, and because of its importance in the literature.

---

45. More efficient equilibria in the war of attrition involve one side conceding with positive probability at $t = 0$. See Hirshleifer and Riley 1992, 381ff.

46. See Garrett and Weingast 1993, who argue that policy "ideas" can make particular agreements focal; and Weber 1991, who analyzes three cases of U.S.-Soviet arms policy as repeated Prisoners' Dilemmas (antiballistic missile systems, MIRV warheads, and antisatellite weapons). I would argue that in each case Weber takes "focal point" resolutions of issues that might be resolved in many ways as the mutual cooperation outcomes in his Prisoners' Dilemmas.

47. The incomplete-information model also yields predictions about the influence of relative power. In brief, the more powerful state (the one with lower costs for noncooperation) gets its preferred outcome in bargaining, because it holds out longer. This supports Krasner's (1991) argument.

48. On complexity as a source of delay, see Winham 1977. On scientific and technical obstacles (which can interact in interesting ways with the bargaining problem; see Morrow 1994), see E. Haas 1990, P. Haas 1992. Domestic political obstacles to agreement are the subject of a large literature; for some examples, see Evans, Jacboson, and Putnam 1993.

Bargaining Versus Enforcement Problems

As argued, if we observe states attempting to craft an international agreement, the states' shadow of the future is probably not so short as to make cooperation infeasible due to fears of reneging. Thus the model predicts that bargaining problems will often *appear* to be more salient obstacles to international cooperation than will monitoring and enforcement problems in observed cases of international negotiations.

This hypothesis seems supported by the extensive literature examining the run-ups to international agreements. In the first place, a number of authors note a relative absence of concerns about reneging. Abram Chayes and Antonia Handler Chayes suggest that the "cooperation under anarchy" literature greatly overemphasizes the fear of deliberate cheating as an obstacle to existing international agreements. They state that "It is not conceivable that foreign ministries and government leaders could devote time and energy on the scale they do to preparing, drafting, negotiating, and monitoring treaty obligations unless there is an assumption that entering into a treaty commitment ought to and does constrain the state's own freedom of action and an expectation that the other parties to the agreement will feel similarly constrained."[49] In their analysis of macroeconomic coordination at the 1978 Bonn summit, Robert D. Putnam and Nicholas Bayne "find little evidence that the negotiations were hampered by mutual fear of reneging," and argue more generally that "As a practical matter, it seems unlikely that the fear of intentional defection can explain all, or even most, of the unconsummated opportunities for mutually beneficial cooperation, particularly among Western nations."[50] Michael C. Webb argues that "The record of international macroeconomic adjustment policy coordination . . . suggests that the key issue in international negotiations has been determining how burdens of adjustment . . . will be distributed among countries, not overcoming obstacles to cooperation posed by the fear of cheating in an anarchic world."[51] Downs, Rocke, and Barsoom describe "the bedrock of the managerial school" as "the finding that state compliance with international agreements is generally quite good and that enforcement has played little or no role in achieving and maintaining that record."[52]

Second, numerous case studies find not only that major concerns about enforcement do not predominate in observed cases, but also that the question of "who backs down?" is often at least as or more difficult for states than "will the other side renege on the deal?" Studies of missed cooperation over arms, trade, and finance frequently find states failing to cooperate not because of problems arranging credible commitments but rather due to apparent "deadlock" in bargaining—the failure to find terms acceptable to both sides.[53]

49. Chayes and Chayes 1993, 186–87.
50. Putnam and Bayne 1989, 101, 102. See also Kenen 1989, 31.
51. Webb 1995, 46–47.
52. Downs, Rocke, and Barsoom 1996, 380, who also provide references to the "managerial school."
53. On arms control, see Evangelista 1990; and Downs, Rocke, and Siverson 1986. On trade, see Conybeare 1986; Grieco 1990; and Mastanduno 1991. On finance, see Oye 1986b; and Webb 1995. Citing Harrison Wagner, Oye (1986a, 7) offers the general caution, "When you observe conflict, think Deadlock—the absence of mutual interest—before puzzling over why a mutual interest was not realized." (It is

Analysts have responded to such results in two ways, saying either that there must not have been any mutual benefits at issue ("Deadlock") or that "relative-gains problems" explain the missed opportunities. The former explanation may be valid in some cases, but the possibility of bargaining delay—states rejecting current offers in hopes of getting a better deal in the future—needs to be considered. The case evidence given in these studies suggests both that nonagreement entailed costs for the states involved (implying a likelihood of some mutual interest), and that bargaining hard for relative advantage played a major role in making cooperation more difficult.[54]

This is equally true of case studies that explain noncooperation by reference to the "relative-gains problem." A relative-gains problem exists if, for all divisions of a flow of benefits from mutual cooperation, at least one state prefers not to cooperate for the following reason: the state fears that its short-run gains will be outweighed by long-run losses due to future economic or military actions by the other state, which is anticipated to grow stronger due to "relative gains" from the original agreement. Demonstrating that negotiations stalemate due to relative-gains fears rather than a bargaining problem entails showing that at least one state's leaders feared that a specific distributional disadvantage would translate in the future into military danger or state-led economic extortion. Correctly understood, the "relative-gains problem" is a problem of credible commitment rather than a bargaining problem—the inefficiency arises from states' inability to commit not to take advantage of greater relative power in the future.[55]

While Joseph Grieco and Michael Mastanduno have shown the United States, the EC, and Japan all bargaining hard for relative advantage in trade deals, the evidence that this was motivated primarily by fears that the other side might use its "relative gains" for military threats or economic extortion is slim, particularly in Grieco's case of U.S.-EC nontariff barrier negotiations and implementation.[56] Grieco seems to accept that military considerations were not at issue in his cases, and for his evidence Mastanduno says explicitly that "The immediate concern was not military security, but economic well-being."[57] Concerning economic well-being, both authors effectively count any evidence of worries about differential economic growth as confirming the relative-gains hypothesis. But such worries should count only if leaders fear future economic coercion and extortion by the partner–adversary, rather than if they are simply worried about the long-run (absolute) welfare of their countries' high-technology firms in industries marked by increasing returns to scale. If cooperation fails on the latter account, this is not a case of a relative-gains problem, but rather a more simple matter of bargaining for relative advantage within a deal.

---

worth noting that if there really is no mutual interest in "cooperation," then "conflict" is actually a good thing from a normative standpoint.)

54. I reconsider Evangelista's case along these lines later.

55. This point is further developed in the conclusion.

56. See Grieco 1990; and Mastanduno 1991. For this criticism, see also Keohane 1993, 280–83; Snidal 1991, 723n1; and especially Liberman 1996, 155–58.

57. See Grieco 1993, 316, 325; and Mastanduno 1991, 109.

Finally, case studies of international negotiations that ultimately *did* yield successful agreement frequently find state agents concentrating far more on bargaining problems than on enforcement and monitoring issues. To give some examples from trade,[58] the major obstacles to the conclusion of each of the last three GATT rounds were not intractable problems of monitoring, commitment, enforcement, or information flows to make enforcement possible. Instead, negotiations have regularly stalemated on questions of who would make the concessions necessary to conclude an agreement. Deadlines declared by the negotiators have been largely useless for eliciting "bottom-line" offers. The key concessions yielding agreement in the Kennedy Round were made only on the eve of a more credible deadline—the expiration of the U.S. executive's negotiating authority granted by Congress. John W. Evans observes that

> It was . . . no coincidence that the apparent settlement in May [1967] came at so nearly the last possible minute. . . . [T]he American negotiators had reason to put off a final compromise until they were certain that no further concessions could be extracted from others, especially the EEC [European Economic Community]. As for other negotiators, the conviction that the United States could not afford to let the Kennedy Round fail must have encouraged the belief that the American negotiators would finally be forced . . . to increase their own concessions. . . . In the days just before May 15, however, any hope that the Community or others may have had of exploiting the American need for a successful Kennedy Round must have faded. The failure of the U.S. administration to ask for an extension of the Trade Expansion Act authority may have provided the most convincing evidence.[59]

Evans concludes that the effect of delay in multilateral trade negotiations is to increase the political costs to any one state for appearing to be the cause of failure, and that such delay is necessary to gain agreements.[60]

In the Uruguay Round, even this U.S. Congress-imposed deadline was (thrice) let pass, as the United States and the EC waited and pushed for the other to back down or back off on the issue of agricultural subsidies. The Omnibus Trade and Competitiveness Act of 1988 expired in December 1990, just after talks on agriculture failed "spectacularly" in Brussels.[61] The Bush administration won an extension of negotiating authority in May 1991 to June 1993; this deadline again passed without agreement.[62] Consistent with the theoretical argument made earlier, it is the very fact that states expect to be bound by a GATT agreement (that is, that it will be largely enforceable) that gives them an incentive to bargain so hard over the precise terms.

58. For examples concerning telecommunications, see Krasner 1991.

59. Evans 1971, 276–77.

60. See also Preeg 1970, 74–76, 139–43, 146–50, chap. 11, esp. 189ff., 260–62; and Paarlberg 1997, 423, who observes that "serious bargaining in GATT does not begin to replace posturing until several years into the round." The "audience cost" mechanism described by Evans operates in other international bargaining contexts as well, such as international crises; see Fearon 1994a.

61. See Winham 1992, 73–74 (who termed the failure spectacular); and Destler 1992, 134–35.

62. *The Economist*, "Better Barter," 23 May 1993, 76. The 1990 deadline was perhaps less credible than that for the Kennedy Round; the 1988 act allowed for a two-year extension of fast-track authority, provided that no disapproval motion passed in Congress.

Which is the more significant obstacle to beneficial international agreements, bargaining problems or concerns about enforcement and reneging? The selection effect implies that case evidence like that just considered cannot provide an answer (though it can provide evidence about the salience of bargaining problems). As the equilibrium results given earlier suggest, by sampling on negotiations we may be missing cases where no serious bargaining occurs because both sides expect that all mutually beneficial deals would be unenforceable. Further, as Downs, Rocke, and Barsoom argue, the selection effect can operate even in the set of *observed* international agreements, since if states can choose the depth of cooperation on an issue, they will choose to go only as deep as they expect they can enforce.

To some degree, these problems can be addressed by (1) sampling on issue areas rather than negotiations or agreements, and (2) asking whether the state leaders in question believe that they are forgoing substantial benefits because of the enforcement problem and are seeking ways to improve monitoring and enforcement in order to gain greater cooperation (and thus welfare). On the latter point, note that if Downs, Rocke, and Barsoom are correct in their claim that "deep" cooperation—which, by hypothesis, would make all parties *much* better off—is rare due to the enforcement problem, we would expect state leaders to be very unhappy about this. They should recognize the (prisoners') dilemma they face and be actively engaged in seeking ways to resolve or ameliorate the enforcement problem that traps them in a bad collective outcome relative to what is ideally possible. In making their empirical case, Downs, Rocke and Barsoom argue that U.S.-Soviet arms control agreements did not dramatically alter the course of either side's arms policies, which is consistent with the claim that the superpowers achieved at best "shallow" cooperation. However, they do not argue or establish that U.S. and Soviet leaders saw themselves as forced to forgo highly beneficial "deep" cooperation due to the enforcement problem. I next consider the arms control issue area in the 1950s and 1960s, suggesting that although some evidence supports the view that monitoring and enforcement problems precluded deeper cooperation, the more significant obstacle in this instance was a bargaining problem that rendered moot the issue of gaining "deep" cooperation by better enforcement.

If an enforcement problem plagued arms control in the early Cold War, this probably had to do with monitoring difficulties rather than a short shadow of the future. For most of the Cold War, the shadow of the future was arguably long for both sides' leaderships. Until the later Mikhail Gorbachev years, neither U.S. nor Soviet leaders showed any great concern that the other side was too impatient or politically volatile to be trusted to stick to deals, and both sides surely expected a high probability of continued interactions. Monitoring, by contrast, would at first glance appear to have posed significant barriers to cooperation, especially in the 1950s. The Soviets rejected the idea of on-site inspections, and without this both the Harry Truman and Dwight Eisenhower administrations argued that disarmament and arms control proposals were unenforceable and thus dangerous.[63] It is worth noting that Soviet objec-

---

63. See, for example, Bundy 1988, 164, 297–98; and Evangelista 1990, 514–15.

tions to on-site inspections themselves stemmed from a political commitment (or enforcement) problem—the Soviets did not trust U.S. assurances that inspections would not be used for spying. Nikita Khrushchev put it nicely to Averell Harriman, when Harriman denied that the United States would use inspections for espionage: "You're trying to tell me that if there's a piece of cheese in the room and a mouse comes into the room that the mouse won't go and take the cheese. You can't stop the mouse from going for the cheese."[64]

As the model suggests when monitoring is thought infeasible, what arms control bargaining took place in the 1950s was not serious, especially on the U.S. side. John Foster Dulles in particular was more interested in using arms control bargaining to win the public opinion or propaganda battle than in gaining agreements on arms.[65] Consistent with the argument about selection effects, when serious bargaining finally did occur in the early 1960s, it focused on an issue for which the monitoring issues were resolvable given the technology of the time. One element of the appeal of the 1963 Limited Test Ban Treaty was that it was straightforwardly self-enforcing. Each state could easily determine if the other had resumed atmospheric testing and then reply in kind if necessary.[66]

Similarly, the development of satellite reconnaissance technology in the early 1960s solved monitoring problems that made it possible to bargain in SALT I over limiting antiballistic missile (ABM) systems and new offensive missile deployments. Still unwilling to grant U.S. inspectors ground access, the Soviets were willing to allow verification by "national technical means," as the euphemism used in the 1972 treaty put it.[67] Although questions of whether compliance could be adequately monitored did arise (particularly in the U.S. Senate and Joint Chiefs of Staff[68]), it would be hard to argue that enforcement issues posed the major obstacle to getting a SALT I agreement. Instead, as the model would predict for a case of high discount factors and adequate monitoring capabilities, questions of who would back down on specific demands concerning the number and placement of ABM systems, and more impor-

64. Cited in Seaborg 1981, 241.
65. See Bundy 1988, 296–302; and Evangelista 1990, 520–21.
66. By July 1963, when serious work on the limited test ban began, the United States and the Soviet Union had been bargaining over a comprehensive test ban treaty for six years. The major sticking points were the number of on-site inspections the Soviets would allow and the way these inspections would be conducted. Although the limited test ban treaty was perceived as "half a loaf" by Kennedy and probably by Khrushchev, what made it feasible was that it did not require the on-site monitoring that the Soviets rejected and U.S. senators demanded for a comprehensive ban. See Seaborg 1981, 240–42; and Bunn 1992, chap. 2.
67. Gaddis concludes that "virtually none of the limited progress the two countries have made in the field of arms control would have been possible had Americans and Russians not tacitly agreed to the use of reconnaissance satellites and other surveillance techniques to monitor compliance" (1987, 233). James A. Schear (1989, 275) suggests that technological advances in the monitoring capabilities "played a crucial role" in laying the groundwork for the SALT I negotiations. See also Bunn 1992, 107; Garthoff 1977, 16; and Newhouse 1973, 70–71, 174.
68. See Newhouse 1973, 162. As in the 1950s, U.S. military objections to SALT I on the grounds of monitoring problems were often just acceptable cover for not liking the terms of the deal.

tantly over which missiles would be counted and to what relative levels, were the principal obstacles to concluding the agreement.[69]

Thus, for the period before satellite reconnaissance, there is some evidence that perceived monitoring difficulties did prevent serious bargaining over cooperation and may have also limited the "depth" of what cooperation occurred. But this short account overstates the importance of monitoring issues as obstacles to U.S.-Soviet arms control agreements, especially for the 1950s. Several authors have argued that for important figures in the Eisenhower administration concerns about monitoring were significant but not crucial. Matthew Evangelista concludes that although in the 1950s most U.S. officials were skeptical about the prospects for verification, "they believed, in any case, that U.S. security would be better served by an arms buildup."[70] Dulles, for example, supported the "Open Skies" proposal made at the 1955 Geneva summit not because its acceptance would make "deeper" arms agreements possible by improving monitoring capabilities. Instead, Dulles saw it as a way to divert public and ally pressures for arms control while the U.S. pursued an arms race in which it was doing well.[71]

Evangelista concludes that U.S. officials in the 1950s had "Deadlock" preferences concerning the arms race: "Most American officials evidently preferred the risk of an unconstrained arms race to any conceivable agreement that could be reached with the USSR."[72] If attention is restricted to these specific arms negotiations it may be reasonable to characterize them as "Deadlock." The theory sketched earlier suggests what may be a more fruitful interpretation, however, which embeds the arms negotiations in a larger context of Cold War bargaining. In this larger context, Eisenhower and Dulles did not think of the Cold War in terms of "Deadlock" but rather as a costly standoff or war of attrition. They certainly perceived the arms race as costly, but they also believed that the United States could hold out in the broader Cold War bargaining game longer than the Soviets could, and that this would yield a future outcome worth waiting for. As Dulles put it in a remarkable memo written in June 1955, "The Soviet Bloc economy cannot indefinitely sustain the effort to match our military output. . . . The greater military potential of the United States . . . gives the United States its maximum bargaining power and this is a power which should not be cheaply relinquished."[73] This is a clear statement of war-of-attrition reasoning— Dulles argues in favor of "holding out" despite the costs of arms racing because he thinks the Soviets will have to "back down" first, and the diplomatic and strategic benefits will be worth the costs in the end.[74]

---

69. For good treatments of the bargaining, see Newhouse 1973; and Garthoff 1985.
70. Evangelista 1990, 514.
71. Bundy 1988, 298–301.
72. Evangelista 1990, 514.
73. Cited in Bundy 1988, 299.
74. Evangelista agrees that Eisenhower and Dulles viewed arms racing as costly but argues that the Joint Chiefs of Staff did not due to their institutional interests; Evangelista 1990, 524. Further, he maintains that they had "veto power" and could block concessionary policies by Eisenhower; ibid., 527. Although the Joint Chiefs' preferences certainly influenced Eisenhower, they are not formally empowered to veto presidential initiatives. They can, however, testify before Congress, which in particular circumstances may

The U.S.-Soviet arms race was a long-lived, costly standoff that is anomalous for received cooperation theory but not for the theory advanced here. As Evangelista suggests, the shadow of the future extended a long way for these two superpowers; so if the race were appropriately conceived as a repeated Prisoners' Dilemma, we would predict that "Both sides would have had an incentive to strengthen measures of verification and move toward cooperation rather than continue to compete indefinitely in a series of mutual defections."[75] Instead, cooperation was rejected. This may not have been because there was no mutual interest in ending the costly arms race but rather because of a bargaining problem— *on what terms* would the race be ended?

Costly Stalemates and Comparative Statics

The preceding section argued that at least one important case of international noncooperation—the early Cold War arms competition—might be usefully understood in terms of the model developed here. Though often described this way, the competition was not simply "like" a repeated Prisoners' Dilemma where the problem is to achieve cooperation despite incentives to renege. Rather, its dynamics turned crucially on the distributional problem of how or on what terms any mutually beneficial cooperation (an end to the arms race) might take place, a problem that must be resolved before enforcement and monitoring of a deal can begin. Consistent with the model's results, we observe a costly standoff in a case where both sides saw much at stake in the distributional conflict and (arguably) had a long shadow of the future.

Finding other cases of costly standoffs that have a war-of-attrition aspect is not difficult; for example border disputes in which two states incur the costs of arming or poor relations as they "stand firm" on the question of precisely where the border lies or who has sovereignty over which small island. The long-standing Russian–Japanese dispute over ownership of the Kuriles is a case in point, where the mutual costs have been investment, trade, and aid opportunities forgone, along with generally poor diplomatic relations.[76] Similarly, protracted civil wars, which are tragically common, can pose a puzzle for received cooperation theory.[77] There are clearly mutual gains to be had if the warring factions can agree on a constitution to regulate the political and economic life of the country they inhabit. Given that the shadow of the future is likely to be long due to the frequency and expected duration of interaction among the inhabitants of the territory, why do they not move straight away to the "cooperate-cooperate" option of common government and constitution? Although the problem of arranging credible commitments to observe a constitutional settlement's terms is indeed crucial,[78] the mechanism described here may sometimes be

---

give them an effective veto. If, in this instance, Eisenhower could not have prevailed over them, had he wanted to, then war-of-attrition bargaining was arguably a sufficient but not necessary cause of the policy.

75. Evangelista 1990, 523. Note that this point applies equally to Downs, Rocke, and Barsoom's analysis.

76. See Goodby, Ivanov, and Shimotamai 1995.

77. For data, see Licklider 1995; and Walter 1997.

78. See Fearon 1994b; and Walter 1997. Cooperation theory's Tit-for-Tat mechanism may be inapplicable in this context because a single "defection" by the faction that gains power can eliminate or perma-

relevant as well. Warring factions invariably have conflicting preferences over the terms of a settlement and may hold out for better terms for a long time in a (literal) war of attrition.

Insofar as such cases can be anomalous for received cooperation theory but explicable when we bring the bargaining problem in, this is a success for the theory. Nonetheless, we would like to go beyond this to test for the specific and perhaps counterintuitive dynamic predicted by the war-of-attrition model—that costly standoffs are more likely to occur in cases where state leaderships discount future payoffs relatively little.

To do so, we need to be able to interpret and measure leaders' discount rates empirically, a difficult task since the number of factors that might influence a leadership's value for present versus future benefits is large. Although the personal time preferences of leaders (that is, their impatience) probably explain little variation across states, discounting due to government instability, elections, random domestic political pressures for reneging, and random fluctuations in matters affecting the value of a particular agreement can all vary, whether across states, issue areas, or even specific issues subject to international bargaining.[79] Since all or several of these factors can operate in any specific case, comparing discount rates across cases is problematic. Further, since other things besides discount rates influence the probability of a costly standoff (even in the simple model considered earlier), any systematic effect of discount rates is unlikely to be observed in a small-N study.

Given these problems, the best I can do here is to make broad comparisons using a rough measure—states' expectations about the likely *duration* of an agreement, should an agreement be reached. If the parties expect that an agreement would be likely to govern relations for a long time to come, the parties must not expect exogenous random shocks of various sorts to lead to the termination of the arrangement—thus discounting is probably low. By contrast, if the parties expect that an agreement will probably be short-term because circumstances are likely to change so as to render the agreement irrelevant or unprofitable, their shadow of the future is probably relatively short.

For example, territorial settlements negotiated outside of war are typically expected to be obligatory and observed for a very long time. As noted earlier, for such cases we often observe long, costly stalemates with no agreement. The case of civil wars is similar. The factions involved in civil war know that the premise of a constitutional settlement is that it will govern relations for a long, possibly indefinite period. The model's prediction, then, is that conditional on civil war occurring, pro-

---

nently weaken opponents, rendering conditional retaliation ineffective for the policing of power-sharing agreements. Thus a commitment problem can make the object of contention (state power) effectively indivisible and so a prime candidate for war-of-attrition bargaining.

79. Simmons successfully uses measures of government instability to proxy for state discount rates in her study of interwar monetary cooperation, though she "recognize[s] that domestic time horizon is only likely to account for a small part of the overall variance in a cooperative outcome, since a large proportion of cases will surely be stable ones, and stable governments will nevertheless vary greatly in their willingness and ability to cooperate" (1994, 286n9).

tracted, costly standoffs should often be observed, which is consistent with empirical work on the subject.[80]

At the other end of the spectrum, states negotiate short-term international agreements regarding specific "issues of the day" all the time—agreements to intervene collectively in exchange markets, to intervene with military forces in peace-keeping missions, to coordinate public declarations regarding a hostage crisis, and so on. Such agreements, as in the monetary example, frequently oblige the continuous or repeated choices of cooperative actions by the states involved, even if the total duration of cooperation is not expected to be long. Further, states almost invariably face distributional conflicts in bargaining to such agreements. When agreement duration is expected to be short because of likely exogenous shocks, discount rates are low and the prediction is for quick settlement in the bargaining phase. When duration is expected to be short because some specific task is being accomplished (such as exchange-rate stabilization), incentives to stand firm in the bargaining phase are low also. In both cases, the theoretical prediction accords with what is typically observed—a relatively brief bargaining phase so that cooperation can begin while there are still expected benefits to be had.

The international agreements most studied by international political economy scholars—trade, arms, and environmental treaties or regimes—generally fall in between these extremes in terms of state expectations about likely duration. I will not hazard strong generalizations about typical discount rates in these cases, except to say that one might expect the bargaining problem to be worse when states are negotiating over the construction of a *regime* with significant distributional implications (like European monetary union, for instance) as opposed to specific agreements within a regime. Insofar as a regime is expected to govern relations for a long time, the states' distributional stakes are raised at the outset. If this is correct, then, paradoxically, the "stronger" states expect a regime to be, the more difficult it may be for them to reach agreement on its construction.

Counteracting this effect, however, is the fact that negotiations over regime construction typically involve more than two parties. So far I have said nothing about how the theoretical argument extends to problems of international cooperation negotiated and enforced in a multilateral setting. In multilateral bargaining (over, say, regime rules), there can be a new cost associated with holding out for a better deal— the risk that the other parties will cut their own deal, excluding the recalcitrant state. This risk acts very much like a discount rate, since a state's expected future benefits for delay have to be discounted by the probability of exclusion.[81] The theoretical argument made earlier would then suggest that, other things equal, the risk of exclusion in multilateral bargaining will constrain states' ability to engage in costly stand-

---

80. Empirical evidence on the intractability of civil conflicts is summarized in Walter 1997; see also Licklider 1995. As noted earlier, commitment problems can contribute to the problem by making political power hard to divide.

81. See, for example, Baron and Ferejohn's (1989) model of multilateral bargaining in a legislature, where the risk of being excluded from the winning coalition in the next period acts much like a discount factor in leading legislators to accept current proposals.

offs, or at least for states not essential to any agreement. For example, Geoffrey Garrett observes that in the bargaining over the Single European Act, "Threats by France and Germany to create some sort of free trade area between themselves were highly credible, and Mitterand and Helmut Kohl consistently raised this prospect when negotiations with Britain became bogged down."[82] This factor works in the opposite direction from the effect of the relative permanence of regime rules; so here I can only note the existence of these two potentially off-setting mechanisms.

Conclusion

Problems of international cooperation have a common strategic structure. Before states can implement, monitor, and enforce an international agreement, they must bargain to decide which of many possible agreements to implement. This simple point is obscured or misunderstood by the theoretical apparatus of cooperation theory and its critics. Received theory suggests that some problems of international cooperation are about coordination, whereas others are about monitoring and enforcement, or that in general one of these two options dominates.[83] The model proposed here more accurately and simply depicts the problem of international cooperation as states face it and yields some interesting theoretical implications as well. For example, posing the problem as "bargaining first, then enforcement" leads us to see that bargaining and enforcement problems may interact in a way that cuts against the standard argument about cooperation and the shadow of the future. The more states value future benefits, the greater the incentive to bargain hard for a good deal, possibly fostering costly standoffs that impede cooperation.

I conclude with a clarifying comment on the relationship between bargaining and relative-gains problems and a brief statement of implications for understanding international regimes.

Bargaining Versus Relative Gains

Since Grieco's influential framing of the problem in "Anarchy and the Limits of Cooperation," scholars have distinguished and argued the relative importance of two obstacles to international agreements—problems of monitoring, enforcement, and credible commitment to uphold a deal, and the "relative-gains problem."[84] This article has suggested that the bargaining problem represents a third important obstacle, distinct from the other two. Because relative-gains and bargaining problems are sometimes conflated, I should clarify how they differ.

A relative-gains problem blocks mutually advantageous international cooperation if two conditions are met. First, the states involved are unable to commit not to use

---

82. Garrett 1992, 547, who is citing Moravcsik 1991, 38. For more general theoretical arguments that turn on closely related mechanisms, see Gruber 1996; and Snidal 1996.
83. Some influential examples include Keohane 1984; Krasner 1991; Snidal 1985; and Stein 1982.
84. Grieco 1988. For studies of both problems and the debate, see Baldwin 1993.

relative gains accruing from an agreement to extort or extract further gains in the future. Properly understood, then, the relative-gains problem is a Prisoners' Dilemma–like problem of credible commitment, of the same family as those stressed by the cooperation theorists. It belongs, however, to a species of Prisoners' Dilemma–like problems that are not resolvable by the "Tit-for-Tat" mechanisms of conditional retaliation. In situations where today's interaction changes relative-bargaining power tomorrow, Tit-for-Tat strategies can be insufficient to gain cooperation, because retaliatory actions may be rendered ineffective in the future due to today's shift in bargaining power.[85]

Second, for a relative-gains problem to block cooperation, the states must be unable to divide the gains so that current relative-bargaining power will be preserved in the future. Although this condition is crucial, advocates of the relative-gains argument have not explained why or under what conditions it should be expected to hold.[86] If the answer is that the bargaining problem—distributional conflict over the terms of agreement—may prevent this, it seems that relative-gains problems *require* a bargaining problem to operate at all. An alternative possibility is that if the states are quite risk averse and are also uncertain about future relative gains resulting from any agreement, in principle states might prefer the noncooperative status quo to all divisions of expected relative gains.[87]

The bargaining and relative-gains problems are thus distinct. The latter should be understood as a problem of credible commitment (or anarchy) that may require, in addition, a bargaining problem to operate at all.

Bargaining Problems and International Regimes

Conceiving of problems of international cooperation primarily as analogous to repeated Prisoners' Dilemma games, cooperation theory understands international regimes primarily as institutional solutions to problems of monitoring and enforcement. Thus, in *After Hegemony*, Robert O. Keohane argued that states may create and maintain regimes because they increase information flows about state behavior and so facilitate monitoring and establishing valuable reputations.[88] Likewise, the explicit norms, principles, and rules that mark international regimes are argued to foster a common understanding about what actions constitute "defection," thus making the recognition of defection easier and possibly aiding the coordination of punishment strategies.[89] Finally, Keohane argued that by bundling issues together and regu-

---

85. For formal analyses of several settings where this sort of commitment problem appears, see Fearon 1994b, 1995, 1997; and Powell 1991.

86. Snidal 1991, 703, makes this point; see also Liberman 1996. In response, Grieco (1993, 321) simply asserts that "In the real world states can and sometimes do receive unequal gains," and that it is "implausible" to suppose that states might "as a matter of course" resolve relative-gains concerns by bargaining.

87. Snidal (1991, 723n3) seems to allude to this possibility and notes that it is not systematically developed in the relative-gains literature.

88. See Keohane 1984, chap. 6; and Keohane and Axelrod 1985.

89. Keohane 1984, 94, 106.

larizing interstate interactions over them, regimes may increase the shadow of the future and so raise the costs of being punished in the repeated Prisoners' Dilemma.[90]

To be fair, Keohane also suggested that states may construct and maintain regimes because these can lower "transaction costs," a large category that includes some costs related to bargaining. He argues that regimes "cluster" issues together, which facilitates side payments and issue linkages, in turn aiding in "the construction of mutually beneficial bargains."[91] Thus regimes might lower the likelihood of costly stalemates by increasing the ease of splitting the difference.

In line with the arguments presented earlier, I would suggest that regimes deserve greater attention as *forums for bargaining* rather than primarily as institutions that aid monitoring and enforcement.[92] Interstate bargaining increasingly takes place in the context of international regimes created by states. How do these regimes ease (or exacerbate) the problem of distributional conflict over the terms of interstate agreements?

Beyond Keohane's idea about side payments and issue linkage, the preceding analysis suggests three mechanisms. First, focal points and bargaining precedents are undoubtedly created by the experience of repeatedly negotiating certain sets of issues within the context of a regime. This is probably true of any repeated bargaining situation, but compare bargaining within a regime with ad hoc, possibly bilateral bargaining that takes place in no larger framework. Almost surely, both the propensity to create focal principles and the force of such principles will be greater in the case of explicit regimes. Regimes establish connections and parallels between different rounds of bargaining and may legitimize focal principles because regimes bear legitimacy as the concrete products of visions of world order. And, as Schelling argued, focal points and principles can be decisive in the resolution of distributional conflict in bargaining.[93]

Second, regimes put explicit structure on interstate bargaining processes; they may specify who can make what sort of offers, when, in what sequence, to whom, and so on. Keohane and others have already observed that such rules might facilitate complex bargaining in multilateral contexts. But bargaining theory suggests other influences as well. The institutions that structure bargaining can affect distributional outcomes and the probability of stalemate or "no agreement."[94]

Third, regimes may lessen the bargaining problem by raising the political costs of failure to agree, since a failure to agree can now have adverse implications for the regime. The examples from GATT rounds, discussed earlier, are emblematic here. As Evans argued, the effect of delay in GATT negotiations was to increase the political costs to any one state for appearing to cause a breakdown.[95] Beyond the Kennedy Round that Evans analyzed, impasse in GATT rounds has regularly been accompa-

---

90. Keohane 1984, 89–90, 103–107.
91. Keohane 1984, 91.
92. See also Morrow 1994, 408–11, for this view.
93. Schelling 1960.
94. See, for example, concerning the European Union, Garrett 1992; and Tsebelis 1994.
95. Evans 1971, 276–77.

nied by dire warnings in the business press about the possibility of a "collapse" of the whole trade regime. Although these warnings were no doubt exaggerations, they are indicative of how the existence of a formal, named, and highly articulated trade regime raised the costs of bargaining failure within the regime. Similar pressures for settlement were associated with the SALT talks, which were likewise played as drama for domestic political audiences.

Appendix

DERIVATION OF CONDITION (1). Suppose the enforcement phase begins at time T, with $(z, 1 - z)$ as the per-unit-time payoffs for mutual cooperation. Consider the following strategies for the subgame beginning at T: Each state cooperates for times $t \in [T, T + \Delta)$, and at all $t \geq T + \Delta$ provided that both states cooperated at all $t' \in [T, t - \Delta)$. If either state is ever observed to have deviated (say, at time $t' \geq t$), then both states defect at all times $t \geq t' + \Delta$ regardless of play after t'.

These trigger strategies will form a subgame perfect equilibrium in the subgame beginning at T if neither state has an incentive to deviate after any history following T. Abiding by these strategies yields a payoff of z/r for state 1 and $(1 - z)/r$ for state 2 (as assessed from time $t \geq T$). By deviating at time $t \geq T$, state 1 receives at most

$$\int_0^\Delta ae^{-rs}\,ds - \int_\Delta^\infty c_1 e^{-rs}\,ds = \frac{1}{r}[a(1 - e^{-r\Delta}) - c_1 e^{-r\Delta}],$$

assessed from time t on. Thus the condition for state 1 to be willing to abide by the equilibrium strategy is

$$\frac{z}{r} \geq \frac{1}{r}[a(1 - e^{-r\Delta)}) - c_1 e^{-r\Delta}],$$

or

$$r\Delta \leq \ln \frac{a + c_1}{a - z}.$$

A symmetric calculation establishes the relevant minimum $r\,\Delta$ for state 2 to be willing to stick with the equilibrium strategy.

PROOF OF THE PROPOSITION. The bargaining phase of the game can be redescribed as a standard complete-information war of attrition studied by John Maynard Smith, John Riley, and others.[96] In the present case, the prize V is the discounted value of the difference between the better and worse deals, $(x - y)/r$, while the per-unit-time cost of delay is the difference

---

96. See, for examples, Maynard Smith 1982; Fudenberg and Tirole 1991; and Hendricks, Weiss, and Wilson 1988.

between the worse deal and the state's value for noncooperation—that is, $y - (-c_1) = y + c_1$ for state 1, and $1 - x - (-c_2) = 1 - x + c_2$ for state 2. As Hirshleifer and Riley show, any equilibrium in which delay may occur involves both sides choosing mixed strategies such that each is indifferent between quitting at every time t and delaying for another instant of time dt.[97] This implies that the marginal benefit of delaying for the instant dt must equal the marginal cost. Let $F_2(t)$ be the cumulative distribution describing a mixed strategy for state 2. The marginal benefit of delay for state 1 is

$$\frac{F_2(t + dt) - F_2(t)}{1 - F_2(t)} \frac{x - y}{r},$$

where the first term is the conditional probability that state 2 will quit in the next instant, and the second term is the value of the prize. The marginal cost of delay for state 1 is $(y + c_1)dt$. Thus in any mixed equilibrium we have

$$\frac{F_2(t + dt) - F_2(t)}{1 - F_2(t)} \frac{x - y}{r} = (y + c_1)dt.$$

Rearranging and taking limits yields

$$\frac{f_2(t)}{1 - F_2(t)} = \frac{r(y + c_1)}{x - y},$$

where $f_2(t)$ is the density function for $F_2(t)$. This is the condition given in the proposition. Similar logic applies for the hazard rate of quitting for state 1. Q.E.D.

EQUILIBRIUM WITH INCOMPLETE INFORMATION. I will first show that the strategy $t(c)$ given in the text forms a symmetric Bayesian Nash equilibrium in the bargaining phase treated as a game by itself. I will next discuss the extension to the whole (two-phase) game.

The strategy

$$t(c) = \frac{1}{r} \ln \frac{c}{2(c - 1)},$$

is strictly decreasing for $c \in [1, 2]$, and so has an inverse $c(t)$, which gives the type c of a player that chooses to quit at time t in the proposed equilibrium. By time t, all types of each player with $c \in [c(t), 2]$ will have quit, if both states are following the strategy $t(c)$. Since, for each state, c is drawn from a uniform distribution on $[1, 2]$, the probability that one's opponent will quit by time t, $F(t)$, is thus $2 - c(t)$. Algebra indicates that $c(t) = 2/(2 - e^{-rt})$ and differentiation that the implied hazard rate for each state is

$$\frac{f(t)}{1 - F(t)} = \frac{-c'(t)}{c(t) - 1} = \frac{2r}{2 - e^{-rt}} \tag{3}$$

97. Hirshleifer and Riley 1992, chap. 10. For a more general analysis, see Hendricks, Weiss, and Wilson 1988.

A necessary condition for type c to wish to quit in equilibrium is that the marginal gain from holding out for another instant equals the marginal cost, or, for type c,

$$\frac{f(t)}{1 - F(t)} \frac{1}{r} = c \tag{4}$$

In other words, the t that solves equation (4) is the best reply for type c, given $F(t)$. (Since the hazard rate given by equation (3) strictly decreases in t, the second-order condition for a maximum that corresponds to equation (4) is satisfied.) Substituting equation (3) into equation (4) yields

$$\frac{2r}{2 - e^{-rt}} \frac{1}{r} = c,$$

or

$$\frac{2}{2 - e^{-rt}} = c.$$

But this is just the expression for $c(t)$ derived from the proposed equilibrium strategy $t(c)$ given in the text. Thus if each player expects the opponent to choose according to $c(t)$, then each player maximizes its expected utility by choosing according to $t(c)$, and we have a Bayesian Nash equilibrium for the bargaining phase of the game.[98]

The bargaining phase, however, is not the whole game, and we need to check whether there are profitable deviations for any type when both phases are considered together (and under the assumption that trigger strategies are employed in enforcement phase). In particular, we must consider the possibility that a state might wish to choose a delay time different from $t(c)$, and then defect in the enforcement phase. But it is immediately clear that if r is small enough, no such strategy could be sequentially rational for any type c: If this different delay time were reached, no type would have an incentive to defect in the enforcement phase since the payoff for complying ($y/r = 0$) will surely be larger than the payoff for defecting,

$$\frac{1}{r}[a(1 - e^{-r\Delta}) - ce^{-r\Delta}]$$

for small enough r.

References

Abreu, Dilip, and Faruk Gul. 1994. Bargaining and Reputation. Mimeo, Princeton University, Princeton, N.J., and Stanford University, Stanford, Calif.

98. As is typical in wars of attrition, the Bayesian Nash equilibrium strategies are also perfect, that is, they imply equilibrium behavior in all subgames. A demonstration is omitted, but see, for example, Fearon 1994a; and Fudenberg and Tirole 1991, 219n11.

Aggarwal, Vinod. 1996. *Debt Games*. Cambridge: Cambridge University Press.

Axelrod, Robert. 1984. *The Evolution of Cooperation*. New York: Basic Books.

Baldwin, David A., ed. 1993. *Neorealism and Neoliberalism*. New York: Columbia University Press.

Baron, David P., and John A. Ferejohn. 1989. Bargaining in Legislatures. *American Political Science Review* 83:1181–1206.

Bhagwati, Jagdish, and Hugh T. Patrick. 1990. *Aggressive Unilateralism*. Ann Arbor: University of Michigan Press.

Bikhchandani, Sushil. 1992. A Bargaining Model With Incomplete Information. *Review of Economic Studies* 59 (January):187–203.

Brander, James A., and Barbara J. Spencer. 1984. Trade Warfare: Tariffs and Cartels. *Journal of International Economics* 16:227–42.

Bundy, McGeorge. 1988. *Danger and Survival*. New York: Vintage.

Bunn, George. 1992. *Arms Control by Committee*. Stanford, Calif.: Stanford University Press.

Caves, Richard, Jeffrey Frankel, and Ronald Jones. 1993. *World Trade and Payments: An Introduction*. New York: Harper Collins.

Chayes, Abram, and Antonia Handler Chayes. 1993. On Compliance. *International Organization* 47:147–64.

Coase, Ronald. 1972. Durability and Monopoly. *Journal of Labor and Economics* 15:143–49.

Conybeare, John. 1986. Trade Wars. In *Cooperation Under Anarchy*, edited by Kenneth Oye, 147–72. Princeton, N.J.: Princeton University Press.

———. 1987. *Trade Wars*. New York: Columbia University Press.

Cramton, Peter. 1992. Strategic Delay in Bargaining with Two-sided Uncertainty. *Review of Economic Studies* 59 (January):205–25.

Destler, I. M. 1992. *American Trade Politics*. Washington, D.C.: IIE.

Downs, George, and David Rocke. 1990. *Tacit Bargaining, Arms Races, and Arms Control*. Ann Arbor: University of Michigan Press.

———. 1995. *Optimal Imperfection?* Princeton, N.J.: Princeton University Press.

Downs, George, David Rocke, and Peter Barsoom. 1996. Is the Good News about Compliance Good News about Cooperation? *International Organization* 50 (summer):379–407.

Downs, George, David Rocke, and Randolph Siverson. 1986. Arms Races and Cooperation. In *Cooperation Under Anarchy*, edited by Kenneth Oye, 118–46. Princeton, N.J.: Princeton University Press.

Evangelista, Matthew. 1990. Cooperation Theory and Disarmament Negotiations in the 1950s. *World Politics* 42 (July):502–28.

Evans, John W. 1971. *The Kennedy Round in American Trade Policy*. Cambridge, Mass.: Harvard University Press.

Evans, Peter B., Harold K. Jacobson, and Robert D. Putnam. 1993. *Double-Edged Diplomacy*. Berkeley: University of California Press.

Fearon, James D. 1992. Threats to Use Force: Costly Signals and Bargaining in International Crises. Ph.D. diss., University of California, Berkeley.

———. 1994a. Domestic Political Audiences and the Escalation of International Disputes. *American Political Science Review* 90:715–35.

———. 1994b. Ethnic War as a Commitment Problem. Paper presented at the 90th Annual Meeting of the American Political Science Association, 2–5 September, New York.

———. 1994c. Signaling versus the Balance of Power and Interests: An Empirical Test of a Crisis Bargaining Model. *Journal of Conflict Resolution* 38:236–69.

———. 1995. Rationalist Explanations for War. *International Organization* 49:379–414.

———. 1997. Bargaining over Objects that Influence Future Bargaining Power. Paper presented at the 93d Annual Meeting of the American Political Science Association, 28–31 August, Washington, D.C.

———. Forthcoming. Selection Effects and Deterrence. In Ken Oye, ed., *Deterrence Debates*.

Fudenberg, Drew, and Jean Tirole. 1991. *Game Theory* . Cambridge, Mass.: MIT Press.

Gaddis, John Lewis. 1987. *The Long Peace*. Oxford: Oxford University Press.

Garrett, Geoffrey. 1992. International Cooperation and Institutional Choice: The European Community's Internal Market. *International Organization* 46:533–60.

Garrett, Geoffrey, and Barry R. Weingast. 1993. Ideas, Interests, and Institutions: Constructing the European Community's Internal Market. In *Ideas and Foreign Policy*, edited by Judith Goldstein and Robert O. Keohane, 173–206. Ithaca, N.Y.: Cornell University Press.

Garthoff, Raymond. 1977. Salt I: An Evaluation. *World Politics* 31:1–25.

———. 1985. *Detente and Confrontation*. Washington, D.C.: Brookings Institution.

Glaser, Charles. 1994–95. Realists as Optimists: Cooperation as Self-Help. *International Security* 19:50–90.

Goodby, James E., Vladimir I. Ivanov, and Nobuo Shimotamai, eds. 1995. *"Northern Territories" and Beyond: Russian, Japanese, and American Perspectives.* Westport, Conn.: Praeger.

Gowa, Joanne. 1986. Anarchy, Egoism, and Third Images: *The Evolution of Cooperation* and International Relations. *International Organization* 40 (winter):167–86.

Grieco, Joseph. 1988. Anarchy and the Limits of Cooperation: A Realist Critique of the Newest Liberal Institutionalism. *International Organization* 42:485–507.

———. 1990. *Cooperation among Nations*. Ithaca, N.Y.: Cornell University Press.

———. 1993. Understanding the Problem of International Cooperation. In *Neorealism and Neoliberalism*, edited by David A. Baldwin, 301–38. New York: Columbia University Press.

Gruber, Lloyd. 1996. *Ruling the World: Power Politics and the Rise of Supranational Institutions*. Unpublished manuscript. University of Chicago.

Gul, Faruk, Hugo Sonnenschein, and Robert Wilson. 1986. Foundations of Dynamic Monopoly and the Coase Conjecture. *Journal of Economic Theory* 39 (June):155–90.

Haas, Ernst. 1980. Why Collaborate? Issue Linkage and International Regimes. *World Politics* 32 (April):357–405.

———. 1990. *When Knowledge Is Power*. Berkeley: University of California Press.

Haas, Peter. 1990. *Saving the Mediterranean: The Politics of International Environmental Cooperation*. New York: Columbia University Press.

Haas, Peter, ed. 1992. Knowledge, Power, and International Policy Coordination. *International Organization* 46 (winter). Special issue.

Hardin, Garret. 1968. The Tragedy of the Commons. *Science*, 13 December, 1243–48.

Hart, Oliver. 1996. *Firms, Contracts, and Financial Structure*. Oxford: Oxford University Press.

Hendricks, K., A. Weiss, and C. Wilson. 1988. The War of Attrition in Continuous Time with Complete Information. *International Economic Review* 29:663–80.

Hirshleifer, Jack, and John G. Riley. 1992. *The Analytics of Uncertainty*. Cambridge: Cambridge University Press.

Howard, Michael. 1972. *The Continental Commitment*. London: Temple Smith.

Jervis, Robert. 1976. *Perception and Misperception in International Politics*. Princeton, N.J.: Princeton University Press.

———. 1988. Realism, Game Theory, and Cooperation. *World Politics* 40:317–49.

Kenen, Peter B. 1989. *Exchange Rates and Policy Coordination*. Ann Arbor: University of Michigan Press.

Kennan, John, and Robert Wilson. 1989. Strategic Bargaining Models and the Interpretation of Strike Data. *Journal of Applied Econometrics* 4 (December):S87–130.

———. 1993. Bargaining with Private Information. *Journal of Economic Literature* 31 (March):45–104.

Keohane, Robert. 1984. *After Hegemony*. Princeton, N.J.: Princeton University Press.

———. 1986. Reciprocity in International Relations. *International Organization* 40 (winter):1–27.

———. 1993. Institutionalist Theory and the Realist Challenge. In *Neorealism and Neoliberalism*, edited by David A. Baldwin, 301–38. New York: Columbia University Press.

Keohane, Robert, and Robert Axelrod. 1985. Achieving Cooperation Under Anarchy. In *Cooperation Under Anarchy*, edited by Kenneth Oye, 226–45. Princeton, N.J.: Princeton University Press.

Keohane, Robert, and Helen Milner, eds. 1996. *Internationalization and Domestic Politics*. Cambridge: Cambridge University Press.

Koremenos, Barbara. 1996. The Duration of International Agreements. Paper presented at the 36th Annual Meeting of the International Studies Association, San Diego, California.

Krasner, Stephen D. 1991. Global Communications and National Power: Life on the Pareto Frontier. *World Politics* 43:336–66.

Kreps, David, Robert Wilson, Paul Milgrom, and John Roberts. 1982. Rational Cooperation in a Finitely Repeated Prisoner's Dilemma. *Journal of Economic Theory* 245–52.

Larson, Deborah. 1987. Crisis Prevention and the Austrian State Treaty. *International Organization* 41: 27–60.

Liberman, Peter. 1996. Trading with the Enemy: Security and Relative Economic Gains. *International Security* 21:147–75.

Licklider, Roy. 1995. The Consequences of Negotiated Settlements in Civil Wars, 1945–1993. *American Political Science Review* 89:681–90.

Lipson, Charles. 1984. International Cooperation in Economic and Security Affairs. *World Politics* 37:1–23.

Martin, Lisa. 1992. *Coercive Cooperation*. Princeton, N.J.: Princeton University Press.

———. 1993a. Credibility, Costs, Institutions: Cooperation on Economic Sanctions. *World Politics* 45:406–32.

———. 1993b. Interests, Power, and Multilateralism. *International Organization* 46:765–92.

Mastanduno, Michael. 1991. Do Relative Gains Matter? America's Response to Japanese Industrial Policy. *International Security* 16 (summer):73–113.

Maynard Smith, John. 1982. *Evolution and the Theory of Games*. Cambridge: Cambridge University Press.

Milner, Helen. 1992. International Theories of Cooperation Among Nations: Strengths and Weaknesses. *World Politics* 44:466–96.

Moravscik, Andrew. 1991. Negotiating the Single European Act: National Interests and Conventional Statecraft in the European Community. *International Organization* 45:19–56.

Morrow, James D. 1989. Capabilities, Uncertainty, and Resolve: A Limited Information Model of Crisis Bargaining. *American Journal of Political Science* 33:941–72.

———. 1994. Modeling the Forms of International Cooperation. *International Organization* 48:387–423.

Nalebuff, Barry. 1986. Brinkmanship and Nuclear Deterrence: The Neutrality of Escalation. *Conflict Management and Peace Science* 9 (spring):19–30.

Nash, John F. 1950. The Bargaining Problem. *Econometrica* 18:155–62.

Newhouse, John. 1973. *Cold Dawn*. New York: Holt, Rinehart and Winston.

Noland, Marcus. 1997. Chasing Phantoms: The Political Economy of the USTR. *International Organization* 51:365–88.

Odell, John S. 1993. International Threats and Internal Politics: Brazil, the European Community, and the United States, 1985–87. In *Double-Edged Diplomacy*, edited by Peter B. Evans, Harold K. Jacobson, and Robert D. Putnam, 233–64. Berkeley: University of California Press.

Olson, Mancur, and Richard Zeckhauser. 1966. An Economic Theory of Alliance. *Review of Economics and Statistics* 48 (August):266–79.

Oye, Kenneth, ed. 1986a. *Cooperation Under Anarchy*. Princeton, N.J.: Princeton University Press.

———. 1986b. The Sterling-Dollar-Franc Triangle: Monetary Diplomacy 1929–1937. In *Cooperation Under Anarchy*, edited by Kenneth Oye, 173–99. Princeton, N.J.: Princeton University Press.

Paarlberg, Robert. 1997. Agricultural Policy Reform and the Uruguay Round: Synergistic Linkage in a Two-Level Game? *International Organization* 51:413–44.

Perry, Motty, and Phillip Reny. 1993. A Non-Cooperative Bargaining Model with Strategically Timed Offers. *Journal of Economic Theory* 59:50–77.

Powell, Robert. 1990. *Nuclear Deterrence Theory: The Problem of Credibility*. Cambridge: Cambridge University Press.

———. 1991. The Problem of Absolute and Relative Gains in International Relations Theory. *American Political Science Review* 85 (December):1303–20.

———. 1996. Bargaining in the Shadow of Power. *Games and Economic Behavior* 15:255–89.

Preeg, Ernest H. 1970. *Traders and Diplomats*. Washington, D.C.: Brookings Institution.

Putnam, Robert D. 1988. Diplomacy and Domestic Politics: The Logic of Two-Level Games. *International Organization* 42:427–60.

Putnam, Robert D., and Nicholas Bayne. 1989. The Bonn Summit of 1978: A Case Study in Coordination. In *Can Nations Agree? Issues in International Economic Cooperation*, edited by Richard Cooper. Washington, D.C.: Brookings Institution.

Rhodes, Carolyn. 1989. Reciprocity in Trade: The Utility of a Bargaining Strategy. *International Organization* 43:273–300.

Rubinstein, Ariel. 1982. Perfect Equilibrium in a Bargaining Model. *Econometrica* 50:97–109.

Schear, James A. 1989. Verification, Compliance, and Arms Control: The Dynamics of Domestic Debate. In *Nuclear Arguments*, edited by Lynn Eden and Steven E. Miller, 264–321. Ithaca, N.Y.: Cornell University Press.

Schelling, Thomas. 1960. *The Strategy of Conflict*. Cambridge, Mass.: Harvard University Press.

Seaborg, Glenn T. 1981. *Kennedy, Khrushchev, and the Test Ban*. Berkeley: University of California Press.

Sebenius, James K. 1992. Challenging Conventional Explanations of International Cooperation: Negotiation Analysis and the Case of Epistemic Communities. *International Organization* 46:323–66.

Simmons, Beth A. 1994. *Who Adjusts?* Princeton, N.J.: Princeton University Press.

Snidal, Duncan. 1985. Coordination Versus Prisoner's Dilemma: Implications for International Cooperation and Regimes. *American Political Science Review* 79:23–42.

———. 1991. Relative Gains and the Pattern of International Cooperation. *American Political Science Review* 85:701–26.

———. 1996. Membership Has Its Privileges. Mimeo, University of Chicago.

Snyder, Glenn. 1984. The Security Dilemma in Alliance Politics. *World Politics* 36:461–95.

Snyder, Glenn, and Paul Diesing. 1977. *Conflict Among Nations*. Princeton, N.J.: Princeton University Press.

Stein, Arthur. 1982. Coordination and Collaboration: Regimes in an Anarchic World. *International Organization* 36:299–324.

Tsebelis, George. 1994. The Power of the European Parliament as a Conditional Agenda Setter. *American Political Science Review* 88:128–42.

Van Evera, Stephen. 1984. Causes of War. Ph.D. diss., University of California, Berkeley.

Wagner, R. Harrison. 1996. Bargaining and War. Mimeo, University of Texas, Austin.

Walter, Barbara. 1997. The Critical Barrier to Civil War Settlement. *International Organization* 51:335–64.

———. 1979. *Theory of International Politics*. Reading, Mass.: Addison-Wesley.

Webb, Michael C. 1995. *The Political Economy of Policy Coordination*. Ithaca, N.Y.: Cornell University Press.

Weber, Steve. 1991. *Cooperation and Discord in U.S.-Soviet Arms Control*. Princeton, N.J.: Princeton University Press.

Williamson, Oliver. 1975. *Markets and Hierarchies*. New York: Free Press.

Winham, Gilbert R. 1977. Negotiation as a Management Process. *World Politics* 30:87–114.

———. 1992. *The Evolution of International Trade Agreements*. Toronto: University of Toronto Press.

[10]

THE KANTIAN PEACE
The Pacific Benefits of Democracy, Interdependence, and International Organizations, 1885–1992

By JOHN R. ONEAL and BRUCE RUSSETT*

JUST over two hundred years ago Immanuel Kant suggested that "republican constitutions," a "commercial spirit" of international trade, and a federation of interdependent republics would provide the basis for perpetual peace. The alternative, even starker in the nuclear era than in 1795, would be peace of a different sort: "a vast grave where all the horrors of violence and those responsible for them would be buried."[1] Consequently, Kant declared, we have a duty to work for peaceful international relations. Though he emphasized the absolute character of this moral imperative, he was no idealist; rather, he believed that natural processes based on self-interest impelled individuals to act in ways that would eventually produce a lasting and just peace. Kant was also realistic. He acknowledged that war was inherent in the anarchic international system and therefore cautioned that nations must act prudently until the federation of interdependent republics was established. But he also knew that the mechanisms of power politics produce only temporary respite from conflict, not lasting solutions.

Over the past half century much of the world has been at peace. Understanding that phenomenon, its causes and trajectory, is the fundamental challenge for international relations scholars today. We seek to show that Kant's realistic statement of liberal theory provides useful guidance for this task. Most political scientists now agree that the contemporary peacefulness can be traced in part to the so-called democratic peace, wherein established democratic states have fought no

* We thank the Carnegie Corporation of New York, the Ford Foundation, and the National Science Foundation for financial support; Zeev Maoz for comments; and Jennifer Beam, Margit Bussmann, Soo Yeon Kim, Yury Omelchenko, Brian Radigan, and Jacob Sullivan for data collection and management.

[1] Kant, *Perpetual Peace: A Philosophical Sketch*, in *Kant's Political Writings*, ed. Hans Reiss (Cambridge: Cambridge University Press, 1970), 105. See also James Bohman and Matthias Lutz-Bachmann, eds., *Perpetual Peace: Essays on Kant's Cosmopolitan Ideal* (Cambridge: MIT Press, 1997).

2   WORLD POLITICS

international wars with one another and the use or threat of force among them, even at low levels, has been rare.[2] This view is incomplete, however, because it fails to recognize the pacific benefits of the other liberal elements of Kant's program for peace. Moreover, the term hides the vigorous theoretical controversy about the processes underlying this separate peace—over whether democracy is really even its cause and over the degree to which the empirical phenomenon existed in other eras.

These theoretical and empirical concerns are linked. If, for example, peaceful relations among democracies during the cold war era were simply a consequence of their shared security interests vis-à-vis the opposing alliance system in a bipolar world, then their peacefulness would be spuriously related to the character of their regimes. The same conclusion would result if the democratic peace could be attributed to the hegemonic power of the United States to suppress conflict among its allies or to East-West differences in preferences unrelated to underlying differences in regimes.[3] One would not then expect to find a separate peace among democratic states in other periods evincing different patterns of interstate relations. We address these questions by reporting analyses covering 1885–1992, to show that peaceful relations among democracies existed throughout the twentieth century.[4] Extending the historical domain also allows us to assess the effect of the changing character of the international system on interstate relations.[5]

---

[2] By convention in the social science literature, war is defined as a conflict between two recognized sovereign members of the international system that results in at least one thousand battle deaths. The most complete data on militarized international disputes (MIDs), compiled by Stuart Bremer and his colleagues, are available at http://pss.la.psu.edu/MID_DATA.HTM. The democracy data we employ were compiled by Keith Jaggers and Ted Robert Gurr, "Tracking Democracy's Third Wave with the Polity III Data," *Journal of Peace Research* 32, no. 4 (1995), available at http://isere.colorado.edu/pub/datasets/polity3/politymay96.data. Both data sets are produced independently from the democratic peace research program, and the initial codings, from the 1980s, precede it. Reviews of the program include Steve Chan, "In Search of Democratic Peace: Problems and Promise," *Mershon International Studies Review* 41, no. 1 (1997); James Lee Ray, "Does Democracy Cause Peace?" *Annual Review of Political Science* 1 (1997); and Bruce Russett and Harvey Starr, "From Democratic Peace to Kantian Peace: Democracy and Conflict in the International System," in Manus Midlarsky, ed., *Handbook of War Studies*, 2d ed. (Ann Arbor: University of Michigan Press, forthcoming).

[3] Henry Farber and Joanne Gowa, "Common Interests or Common Polities?" *Journal of Politics* 57, no. 2 (1997); Gowa, *Ballots and Bullets: The Elusive Democratic Peace* (Princeton: Princeton University Press, 1999); Douglas Lemke and William Reed, "Regime Types and Status Quo Evaluations," *International Interactions* 22, no. 2 (1996); Erik Gartzke, "Kant We All Just Get Along? Opportunity, Willingness and the Origins of the Democratic Peace," *American Journal of Political Science* 42, no. 1 (1998).

[4] The MIDs data (fn. 2) are unavailable after 1992, and data on dyadic trade are sparse and unreliable before 1885. In any event the further back one goes into the nineteenth century, the rarer are instances of democracy, intergovernmental organizations, and high levels of economic interdependence. The MIDs data include only disputes between recognized states and not, for example, extrasystemic (i.e., colonial) actions, covert operations, or domestic military interventions in support of a recognized government.

[5] We will not here offer a new theory on why democracy produces peaceful relations. A recent statement is Bruce Bueno de Mesquita et al., "An Institutional Explanation of the Democratic Peace," *American Political Science Review* 93, no. 4 (1999).

In keeping with the Kantian perspective, we expand our analysis beyond the democratic peace, incorporating the influence of economically important trade and joint memberships in international organizations. The classical liberals of the eighteenth and nineteenth centuries expected interdependence as well as popular control of government to have important pacific benefits. Commercial relations draw states into a web of mutual self-interest that constrains them from using force against one another. Thus interdependence and democracy contribute to what we have called the "liberal peace." Kant emphasized, in addition, the benefits of international law and organization. Our previous analyses of the cold war era indicate that, during those years at least, trade and networks of intergovernmental organizations did reduce the number of militarized interstate disputes; these effects were on top of the benefits of democracy.[6] We show here that they also operated in earlier and later years.

Our Objectives and Method

Although the liberal and realist perspectives are often considered antithetical, in keeping with Kant's philosophical analysis we conduct our tests of the Kantian peace while taking into account important realist influences. We believe, as Kant did, that both perspectives matter, as

[6] John R. Oneal and Bruce Russett, "The Classical Liberals Were Right: Democracy, Interdependence, and Conflict, 1950–1985," *International Studies Quarterly* 40, no. 2 (1997); Russett, Oneal, and David R. Davis, "The Third Leg of the Kantian Tripod: International Organizations and Militarized Disputes, 1950–85," *International Organization* 52, no. 3 (1998); Oneal and Russett, "Assessing the Liberal Peace with Alternative Specifications: Trade Still Reduces Conflict," *Journal of Peace Research* 36, no. 4 (1999). Here we extend this line of research in three ways: (1) providing a conceptual synthesis of Kantian and realist theories that treats conflict as inherent but subject to important constraints; (2) extending the temporal domain for trade and IGOs into the nineteenth century; and (3) assessing realist theories regarding the role of the hegemon and Kantian theories about systemic influences in a way that addresses, among others, constructivist and evolutionary perspectives on the international system. Note that the Kantian influences may be mutually reinforcing in a dynamic system of feedback loops, as suggested by Wade Huntley, "Kant's Third Image: Systemic Sources of the Liberal Peace," *International Studies Quarterly* 40, no. 4 (1996); and Russett, "A Neo-Kantian Perspective: Democracy, Interdependence, and International Organizations in Building Security Communities," in Emanuel Adler and Michael Barnett, eds., *Security Communities in Comparative Perspective* (New York: Cambridge University Press, 1998).

We and others have begun to address some of these links, such as greater trade between democracies, the possibility that trade is diminished between conflicting states, the effect of democracy, trade, and peace in increasing membership in international organizations, and the effect of conflict on democracy. On the first, see Harry Bliss and Russett, "Democratic Trading Partners: The Liberal Connection," *Journal of Politics* 58, no. 4 (1998), and James Morrow, Randolph Siverson, and Tessa Tabares, "The Political Determinants of International Trade: The Major Powers, 1907–90," *American Political Science Review* 92, no. 3 (1998); on the second, see Soo Yeon Kim, "Ties That Bind: The Role of Trade in International Conflict Processes" (Ph.D. diss., Yale University, 1998); on the third, see Russett, Oneal, and Davis (this fn.); and on the last, see Oneal and Russett, "Why 'An Identified Systemic Model of the Democratic Peace Nexus' Does Not Persuade," *Defence and Peace Economics* 11, no. 2 (2000).

4   WORLD POLITICS

both consider conflict and the threat of violence to be inherent in an anarchic world of sovereign states. The Hobbesian element of this understanding is central to realist theory, but it is also deeply embedded in the liberal tradition. Kant accepted Hobbes's description of a state of war among nations and believed that a balance of power could prevent war; but history has shown all too clearly, as most realists acknowledge, that this "peace" is tenuous. Kant, however, was convinced that a genuine, positive peace could be developed within a "federation" of liberal republics that rested more on the three Kantian supports—democracy, interdependence, and international law and organizations—than on power politics. The pacific federation envisioned by Kant is not a world state but a federation whose members remain sovereign, linked only by confederational or collective security arrangements. Liberalism, that is, sees democratic governance, economic interdependence, and international law as the means by which to supersede the security dilemma rooted in the anarchy of the international system. For states not much linked by these ties, however, the threat of violence remains. In addition, liberal states must fear those illiberal states that remain outside the Kantian confederation.[7]

Thus we begin by assuming that the international system is anarchic and power is important. Yet despite the inherent possibility of violence, states do not fight all others or at all times even where realist principles dominate. Rather, they are constrained by power, alliances, and distance. States must be concerned with the balance of power and the coincidence of national interests expressed in alliances. Many states, moreover, are irrelevant to these calculations: in general, the farther apart two states are, the fewer are the issues over which to fight and the less the threat they pose to one another. Ultimately therefore realists are concerned only with states that have the opportunity and incentive to engage in conflict.[8] Accordingly because these constraints provide a baseline against which to assess the additional impact of the Kantian influences, we incorporate them as central features of our theoretical model. To the realist variables we add measures for the three Kantian constraints, hypothesizing that (1) democracies will use force less frequently, especially against other democracies; (2) economically important trade creates incentives for the maintenance of peaceful relations;

[7] Michael W. Doyle, *Ways of War and Peace* (New York: W. W. Norton, 1997), chap. 8; David Lake, "Powerful Pacifists: Democratic States and War," *American Political Science Review* 86, no. 4 (1992).

[8] Birger Heldt, "Inherency, Contingency, and Theories of Conflict and Peace" (Manuscript, Yale University, 1998); Benjamin Most and Harvey Starr, *Inquiry, Logic, and International Politics* (Columbia: University of South Carolina Press, 1989), chap. 2.

and (3) international organizations constrain decision makers by promoting peace in a variety of ways. Since the modern international system is far from a pacific federation of democratic states, we expect both realist and Kantian factors to affect interstate relations. We explicitly consider how realist and liberal influences at both the dyadic and the systemic level have altered the functioning of the international system, addressing the role of the leading state and the influence of the changing Kantian variables over time.

Evidence for the pacific benefits of economic interdependence and membership in intergovernmental organizations (IGOs) is less widely accepted than is that for the democratic peace, and it has been subjected to less extensive critical scrutiny. We alone have assessed the effect of IGOs on conflict at the dyadic level of analysis. Moreover, theoretical expectations regarding the impact of trade and IGOs are more diverse than those concerning democracy. No one hypothesizes that democracies are *more* likely to fight each other than are other polities; but the liberal view of the pacific effects of trade is contradicted by those who expect conflict over the division of the gains from trade and by the dependency school and its intellectual predecessors and descendants, who expect conflict between large and small states.[9] As for IGOs, a plausible view might be that states form or join international organizations to manage—albeit often without success—disputes with their adversaries, the UN being an example. More commonly, realists regard international institutions as nearly irrelevant to the security issues at the heart of high politics, with no effect independent of existing power relations.[10] Even among those who hold that trade or IGOs play a positive role in promoting peace, the reasons advanced vary. Rational choice theorists emphasize political actors' complementary economic interests in maintaining peaceful interstate relations—interests that are reflected in the decisions of national leaders. Fearful of the domestic political consequences of losing the benefits of trade, policymakers avoid the use of force against states with which they engage in economically important trade. But one can also devise constructivist explanations about how the communication associated with trade builds cross-national sentiments of shared identity.[11]

---

[9] A useful review is Susan McMillan, "Interdependence and Conflict," *Mershon International Studies Review* 41, no. 1 (1997).

[10] John Mearsheimer, "The False Promise of International Institutions," *International Security* 19 (Winter 1994–95).

[11] Emanuel Adler and Michael Barnett, "Security Communities in Theoretical Perspective," in Adler and Barnett (fn. 6); Alexander Wendt, *Social Theory of International Politics* (New York: Cambridge University Press, 1999). For microlevel evidence that trading contacts expand elites' views of

Even realists acknowledge that international institutions like NATO help to preserve peace among their members by supplementing the deterrent effect of sheer military power. Liberals emphasize the potential of institutions for communicating information and facilitating bargaining,[12] while constructivists see institutions as instruments for expanding people's conceptions of identity, relatedness, and self-interest. Because IGOs vary widely in their functions and capabilities, any or all of these explanations may be correct in a particular instance.[13] As with the consequences of democratic institutions, we do not attempt to resolve these theoretical debates here. Instead we seek to offer an empirical assessment of the effect of the Kantian influences on interstate relations.

In expanding the historical domain of the Kantian peace, one encounters hurdles (and opportunities) that arise from marked changes in the nature of political regimes, the importance of international trade, and the role of international organizations. As measured by the standard data on political regimes, Polity III,[14] the average level of democracy in the international system has risen since the early 1800s, in a pattern that is sporadic and wavelike.[15] Similarly, the mean level of economic interdependence as measured by the ratio of bilateral trade to gross domestic product fell after World War I but rose again in subsequent years. Most clear is the growth in the number of IGOs, though those associated with the creation and sustenance of a truly global economy largely emerge only after World War II. These trends for the 1885–1992 period are shown in Figure 1.[16] Higher levels of democracy, interdependence, and IGO membership should, of course, reduce conflict for the pairs of countries affected; but we also expect that as the number of democracies increases, trade grows, and IGOs proliferate, there will be important systemic influences on other pairs of states as well. The effect of the Kantian influences should, we hypothesize, be apparent over time as well as cross-nationally.

---

their self-interest, see Daniel Lerner, "French Business Leaders Look at EDC," *Public Opinion Quarterly* 24, no. 1 (1956); and Bruce Russett, *Community and Contention: Britain and America in the Twentieth Century* (Cambridge: MIT Press, 1963), chap. 9.

[12] Robert O. Keohane and Lisa Martin, "The Promise of Institutionalist Theory," *International Security* 20, no. 1 (1995); Lisa Martin and Beth Simmons, "Theories and Empirical Studies of International Institutions," *International Organization* 52, no. 4 (1998).

[13] For a review of some relevant hypotheses and findings, see Russett, Oneal, and Davis (fn. 6).

[14] Jaggers and Gurr (fn. 2).

[15] Samuel P. Huntington, *The Third Wave: Democratization in the Late Twentieth Century* (Norman: University of Oklahoma Press, 1991).

[16] For graphing purposes the scale for bilateral trade/GDP has been increased by two orders of magnitude and that for IGO membership has been reduced by one order of magnitude.

KANTIAN PEACE   7

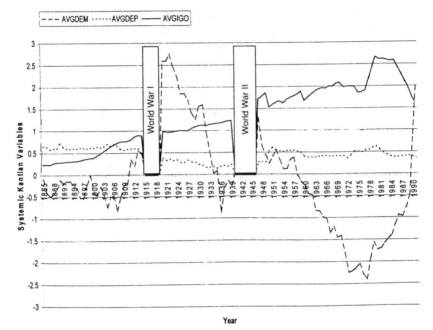

FIGURE 1
KANTIAN VARIABLES

Our statistical method—pooled cross-sectional time-series regression analysis of data regarding pairs of states (dyads) observed annually —is well suited to the purposes at hand. It considers variance in states' involvement in militarized disputes across dyads in each year and in dyadic relations through time. Consequently we can determine the likelihood of conflict as a function of differences across thousands of pairs of states annually and of changes in dyadic relations or in the international system from year to year over a period of more than one hundred years. By measuring change in the Kantian variables through time, we can begin to disentangle their systemic effects from their strictly dyadic influences.

Changes over time in the average level of democracy, interdependence, and IGO involvement capture important elements of the norms and institutions of the international system. Wendt, for instance, contends that world politics has slowly evolved from Hobbesian anarchy to a Lockean system wherein the security dilemma is ameliorated by norms recognizing the right of sovereign states to exist; these, in turn effectively limit the use of force.[17] Thus, states are no longer subject to elimination: whereas twenty-two internationally recognized states were forcibly occupied or absorbed during the first half of the twentieth century, no state has lost its formal sovereignty through conquest since World War II.[18] The emergence of a Kantian subsystem of states, within which the unprovoked use of force is illegitimate, may have contributed directly to this evolutionary development and affected the probability that force will be used primarily by states that are not particularly democratic, interdependent, or involved in international organizations.

If democracies are more likely than are autocracies to win their wars, then the latter will have to be concerned about the security implications of weakening themselves in war, whether with democracies or other autocracies, especially as the number of democracies in the international system grows.[19] If most great powers are democratic, their peaceful relations should reduce the incentive for war for all states across their spheres of influence. If globalization increases and stimulates economic growth among interdependent states, nonliberal states will have to be concerned lest they be punished by global markets and trading states for instigating international violence that disrupts trade and investment; even antagonistic dyads with little mutual trade may find it prudent to avoid conflict.[20] If international norms and institutions for

---

[17] Wendt (fn. 11). On some systemic effects of a high proportion of democracies, see Huntley (fn. 6); Nils Petter Gleditsch and Havard Hegre, "Peace and Democracy: Three Levels of Analysis," *Journal of Conflict Resolution* 41, no. 2 (1997); Sara McLaughlin Mitchell, Scott Gates, and Havard Hegre, "Evolution in Democracy-War Dynamics," *Journal of Conflict Resolution* 43, no. 6 (1999); and Lars-Erik Cederman, "Back to Kant: Reinterpreting the Democratic Peace as a Collective Learning Process" (Manuscript, Political Science Department, University of California at Los Angeles, December 1998).

[18] For dates of independence, see Bruce Russett, J. David Singer, and Melvin Small, "National Political Units in the Twentieth Century: A Standardized List," *American Political Science Review* 62, no. 3 (1968). Germany and Japan temporarily lost sovereignty after World War II, but soon regained it (Germany as two states). Kuwait was briefly occupied in 1990–91; but a large, diverse coalition of states under the aegis of the United Nations forced Iraq to withdraw in order to protect the sovereignty of established states. South Vietnam is an exception to this generalization if one regards its unification with North Vietnam in 1976 as the result of external conquest rather than of an internationalized civil war. Whereas state extinction as a consequence of international war has become rare, the ideology of ethnic self-determination has led to the breakup of many states and empires.

[19] A counterhypothesis would be that as democracies become more numerous and more confident in their individual and collective strength, they may become emboldened to pursue coercive relationships with those autocracies that remain. For evidence that democracies do win most of their wars, see Bruce Bueno de Mesquita, Randolph Siverson, and Gary Woller, "War and the Fate of Regimes: A Comparative Analysis," *American Political Science Review* 86, no. 3 (1992); Lake (fn. 7); and Allan C. Stam III, *Win Lose or Draw* (Ann Arbor: University of Michigan Press, 1996).

[20] Thomas L. Friedman, *The Lexus and the Olive Tree* (New York: Farrar, Straus, and Giroux, 1999); and Stephen G. Brooks, "The Globalization of Production and International Security" (Ph.D. diss., Yale University, forthcoming).

resolving disputes grow, even nonliberal states may be impelled to use regional or international organizations to help settle their disputes rather than accept the political, military, and economic costs imposed by the liberal community as penalties for using military force. Thus increases in the Kantian influences at the system level may have beneficial effects on the behavior of dyads that are not particularly democratic, economically interdependent, or involved in international organizations.

This is not an ecological fallacy.[21] We do not make inferences about dyadic conflict from information about conflict at the systemic level. In all our analyses we address the incidence of militarized disputes among pairs of states. We investigate the consequences of purely dyadic characteristics for dyadic behavior, but we also do consider the effects of evolutionary changes in the international system. To capture the effects of such systemic changes, we use the annual mean scores of democracy, bilateral trade as a proportion of gross domestic product (GDP), and joint memberships in IGOs graphed in Figure 1. They effectively gauge the pervasiveness of changes in international norms and institutions and document the example of the success of liberal states in the competition among nations. We also consider the influence of the leading state, the hegemon, on interstate relations. We investigate this aspect of leading realist theories with measures of the relative power of the hegemon, states' satisfaction with the status quo, and the hegemon's sense of its own security.

HISTORICAL DOMAIN, KEY VARIABLES, AND SOURCES OF DATA

As our analysis spans the years 1885 to 1992, it enables us to examine the effects of democracy, economic interdependence, and international organizations over a long period before the cold war and for a few years after. Realists often contrast the dynamics of bipolar and multipolar systems, though there is disagreement over their consequences for interstate relations. By Waltz's criteria, the international system was multipolar for the centuries preceding 1945 but bipolar during the cold war.[22] And the current, post-Soviet world is neither bipolar nor multipolar but perhaps is best understood as unipolar, at least as measured by

---

[21] Identified by W. S. Robinson, "Ecological Correlations and the Behavior of Individuals," *American Sociological Review* 15, no. 3 (1950). On how some inferences can be made, see Gary King, *A Solution to the Ecological Inference Problem* (Princeton: Princeton University Press, 1997).

[22] Kenneth Waltz says that it is the power of the units (states) themselves that defines polarity and not the number or power of the alliances they lead; see Waltz, *Theory of International Politics* (Reading, Mass.: Addison-Wesley, 1979), 98–99. Thus the formation of two opposing alliance systems prior to World War I did not change the structure of the multipolar system. Waltz's emphasis on the systemic

the relative power of the United States (in its capabilities if not in its will to control or shape events). These theoretically based distinctions require us to consider the effects of the Kantian variables within different international structures, though evaluation of the post–cold war era necessarily remains tentative.

We omit from our analyses all but the first year of both World War I and World War II, because bilateral trade data for those years are fragmentary, as they are for the immediate postwar years, 1919–20 and 1946–49. Omitting all but the first year of the world wars, which consisted of conflicts between democracies and autocracies or between two autocracies, biases our results against finding evidence of the democratic peace, but it also provides assurance that our results are not determined by these dramatic but atypical events.[23] Most of our variables and data are discussed in previous publications. Here we concentrate on what is new.

DEPENDENT VARIABLE: INVOLVEMENT IN MILITARIZED DISPUTES

We use the Correlates of War (COW) data on interstate disputes (MIDs). We code each year that a dyad was involved in a dispute in which one or both states threatened to use force, made a demonstration of force, or actually used military force against the other. The variable DISPUTE equals 1 if a dispute was ongoing and 0 if not. Some researchers urge that only the initial year of a dispute be noted since a dispute in one year increases the chances that the dyad will experience a dispute in subsequent years.[24] This procedure eases some problems but raises others. If leaders are rational, as all our theories assume, they will frequently reevaluate their positions, whether to escalate, deescalate, or maintain the existing strategy. We agree with Blainey: "The beginning of wars, the prolonging of wars and the prolonging or shortening of pe-

---

effects of nuclear weapons would also imply a break between 1945 and all previous years of modern history. Dating the end of the bipolar cold war system is more problematic. Waltz's definition would argue for a break at the end of 1991, when the Soviet Union was dissolved. But William Dixon and Stephen Gaarder show a decisive shift in the pattern of Soviet-American conflict in 1988; see Dixon and Gaarder, "Presidential Succession and the Cold War: An Analysis of Soviet-American Relations, 1948–1992," *Journal of Politics* 54, no. 1 (1992).

[23] Farber and Gowa (fn. 3) express this concern.

[24] Stuart A. Bremer, "Dangerous Dyads: Conditions Affecting the Likelihood of Interstate War," *Journal of Conflict Resolution* 36, no. 1 (1993); Katherine Barbieri, "International Trade and Conflict: The Debatable Relationship" (Paper presented at the annual meeting of the International Studies Association, Minneapolis, Minn., February 1998); Nathaniel Beck, Jonathan Katz, and Richard Tucker, "Taking Time Seriously in Binary Time-Series-Cross-Section Analysis," *American Journal of Political Science* 42, no. 4 (1998). See, however, our comment in fn. 49 below.

riods of peace all share the same causal framework. The same explanatory framework and the same factors are vital in understanding each
state in the sequel of war and peace."[25] Moreover, we investigated 166
multiyear disputes during the post–World War II era and found that
more than half involved a change in the level of force employed over
the course of the dispute or that a new dispute arose as the first was
concluding. Thus we report analyses of states' involvement in disputes
rather than of just their onset; but as in earlier studies of the cold war
era,[26] we reestimated key analyses using only the first year of disputes
without finding material differences from those reported below.

DYADIC INDEPENDENT VARIABLES

We lag all independent variables by one year to ensure that they were
not affected by a dispute to be explained. For some explanatory
variables this precaution is clearly important; for example, conflict may
limit trade just as trade may constrain conflict. A similar reciprocal
relationship can be imagined for international organizations and
conflict, as many IGOs—though hardly all—are formed among states
that maintain peaceful relations. For other variables such considerations
are irrelevant. Geographically proximate countries are prone to conflict,
but the frequency of their disputes does not affect their proximity. To be
consistent, however, we lag all the independent variables. This
precaution does not put to rest all questions about the direction of
causality, but it is a reasonable step at this time.[27] All the variables are
listed by their acronyms in the appendix.

DEMOCRACY

We use the Polity III data to compute a summary measure of the
political character of regimes, subtracting every country's score on the
autocracy scale from its score on the democracy scale. The resulting
variable (DEM_i) ranges from −10 for an extreme autocracy to +10 for
the most democratic states. Because a dispute can result from the
actions of a single state, the likelihood of conflict is primarily a function
of the degree of constraint experienced by the less constrained state in
each dyad. As that state is the weak link in the chain of peaceful

[25] Geoffrey Blainey, *The Causes of War*, 3d ed. (New York: Free Press, 1988).

[26] Oneal and Russett (fn. 6, 1999).

[27] Kim (fn. 6), using a simultaneous equation model, finds that the effect of trade on conflict is much
stronger than the reciprocal one. Russett, Oneal, and Davis (fn. 6) construct a model for predicting
IGO membership that includes, among other factors, the absence of conflict. There is an effect, but it
is weaker than the influence of IGOs on conflict.

relations,[28] we expect that the less democratic state (DEM$_L$) in a dyad is the stronger determinant of interstate violence. Conversely, the more democratic that state, the more constrained it will be from engaging in a dispute and the more peaceful the dyad. In previous analyses we found, as Kant had expected, that the *difference* between states' political regimes also affects the likelihood of conflict. Democratic-autocratic dyads were the most conflict-prone in the cold war era; two autocracies were less likely to fight, and two democracies were the most peaceful. We reconsider these findings below.

The Polity III regime scores exhibit some problems of comparability over time. Until 1918 about 40 percent of British males (disproportionately working class) were disfranchised by residence requirements; female suffrage was granted partially in 1918 and fully only in 1928.[29] In the United States women obtained the vote only in 1920, and blacks were systematically excluded until the 1960s. Swiss women achieved the franchise only in 1971. Some of these changes are reflected in the Polity data and hence in rising levels of democracy in the international system. For example, the United Kingdom goes from 6 to 7 on the democracy scale in 1880, to 8 in 1902, and jumps to 10 only in 1922. But Switzerland is coded at 10 from 1848, as is the United States from 1871. The consequences of these restrictions on political participation for foreign policy may not be trivial. In the contemporary United States, for example, women are significantly more averse to the use of military force than are men and vote in part on this basis.[30] Thus the exclusion of women from the franchise in earlier periods could have profoundly reduced the tendency of even the most "democratic" states to avoid conflict.

---

[28] William J. Dixon, "Democracy and the Peaceful Settlement of International Conflict," *American Political Science Review* 88, no. 1 (1994).

[29] Trevor Wilson, *The Myriad Faces of War: Britain and the Great War, 1914–1918* (Cambridge, England: Polity Press, 1986), 660–61; Kenneth MacKenzie, *The English Parliament* (Harmondsworth: Penguin, 1950), 106.

[30] Carole Kennedy Chaney, R. Michael Alvarez, and Jonathan Nagler, "Explaining the Gender Gap in U.S. Presidential Elections," *Political Research Quarterly* 51, no. 2 (1998). To take such changes into account, Zeev Maoz uses an adjusted threshold of democracy for all countries that shifts upward in 1870 (for general male suffrage) and 1920 (female suffrage); see Maoz, *Domestic Sources of Global Change* (Ann Arbor: University of Michigan Press, 1996), 54. Our use of unadjusted democracy scores thus leans against our hypothesis of democratic peace before World War I. Kristian Gleditsch and Michael Ward note that our continuous measure, Democracy minus Autocracy score, has the virtues of being symmetric and transitive; but the relative importance of its components is unstable over time; see Gleditsch and Ward, "Double Take: A Re-examination of Democracy and Autocracy in Modern Polities," *Journal of Conflict Resolution* 41, no. 3 (1997). For the period 1880–1969 this aggregated measure is largely influenced by the degree of competition for executive recruitment; subsequently constraints on the executive are the main determinant. Fortunately the relatively stable earlier period covers all the pre–cold war years we add here. As no analysis of the democratic peace after World War II has yet addressed the 1969 break, we too leave that for later investigation.

ECONOMIC INTERDEPENDENCE

For most of the post–World War II era the measurement of this Kantian variable is straightforward, because the International Monetary Fund reports statistics regarding bilateral trade. Since trade is expected to influence dyadic relations only if it is economically important, we divide the sum of a country's exports and imports with its partner by its GDP, as reported in the standard references for the years after 1950.[31] As with the influence of democratic institutions, we expect the likelihood of a dispute to be primarily a function of the freedom of the less constrained state to use force, that is, the bilateral trade-to-GDP measure of the state less dependent economically on trade with its dyadic partner $(DEPEND_L)$. We also report tests for a positive effect of asymmetric dependence on conflict, as proposed by dependency theorists.

When we move back to the years before World War II, however, national economic data become more problematic. During the years 1920–38 the League of Nations compiled contemporary data on bilateral trade in current values, along with exchange rates.[32] While the accuracy and the comparability of these data are undoubtedly less than in the later IMF reports, they are the best available. There are no institutional compilations of trade data for the years of the two world wars, nor for the period before 1914. Before World War I the annual editions of *The Statesman's Yearbook*[33] offer the closest approximations, but these data are less standardized, the appropriate exchange rates for converting the data to a common unit are less certain, and more data are missing.[34]

---

[31] International Monetary Fund, *Direction of Trade (ICPSR 7623)* (Washington, D.C.: IMF, 1993; distributed by Ann Arbor, Mich.: Inter-University Consortium for Political and Social Research). Robert Summers et al., *The Penn World Table (Mark 5.6a)* (Cambridge, Mass.: National Bureau of Economic Research, 1995). Due to missing data for trade and/or GDP, the great majority of dyads involved in the Korean and Vietnam Wars are omitted, as are most Arab-Israeli dyads. Since most of those are conflicting democratic-autocratic dyads with no trade, our analysis is likely to be biased against the liberal hypotheses. Because these conflicts spanned several years, excluding these cases mitigates the problem of temporal dependence in the time series, as does omitting all but the first year of the world wars. Also omitted are roughly 2,500 communist dyad-years: non-IMF members. These states traded among themselves but did not report it to the IMF and generally had little conflict. Had we been able to include them, the post–1950 sample would have been increased by only about 2 percent.

[32] League of Nations, *International Trade Statistics* (Geneva: League of Nations, annual volumes).

[33] Martin Epstein, ed., *The Statesman's Yearbook, 1913* (London: Macmillan, 1913), and earlier annual editions by other editors.

[34] We took several steps to minimize missing trade data in this period. We used information regarding one state's exports to another to infer its partner's imports; we interpolated between known values of trade and used the average value of a dyad's trade to extrapolate; and we assumed, for those states for which we had data, that there was no trade between any two if neither reported any exports or imports with the other. As a result we have trade data for 61 percent of the dyads 1885–1913 and 1920–38. We conducted several tests to see if these methods might have biased our results. First we dropped all zero values of trade, and then we dropped all interpolations and extrapolations. Analyses with the remaining "real" data, 1885–1940, revealed little change in the results. We also determined

Because of these difficulties we collected alternative estimates for bilateral trade in the 1885–1949 period, compared them with the data from *The Statesman's Yearbook* and the League of Nations, and adjusted the data from our principal sources as appropriate.[35]

Information on dyadic trade, the numerator of the dependence measure, is only half of the problem for the pre-1950 era, however. To calculate the economic importance of trade we need estimates of nations' gross domestic products. No comprehensive collection of GDP data exists, but Maddison provides estimates in constant dollars for fifty-six countries in all regions of the world for 1870–1992.[36] We used these in a two-step procedure to estimate the GDPs in current dollars for a large number of countries. First, we regressed Maddison's constant dollar GDP estimates on states' total annual energy consumption, the region where they were located, the year, and various interactive terms. Annual energy consumption, collected by the Correlates of War (COW) project, is a good correlate of the size of national economies, as Morgenstern, Knorr, and Heiss noted twenty-five years ago.[37] More than 93 percent of the variance in Maddison's GDPs was explained. Based on the coefficients in this analysis, we were able to estimate the constant dollar GDPs for a large number of other countries. Second, we converted these constant dollar estimates to current dollars, using Maddison's U.S. dollar GDP deflator.

JOINT IGO MEMBERSHIPS

The influence of international organizations on interstate conflict, the last Kantian variable, is assessed by the number of IGOs in which both

---

that the sample of dyads for which we have trade data is unlikely to be biased. To do this, we created a variable (MISSING) that equaled 1 if $DEPEND_L$ was missing and 0 otherwise and then changed all missing values of $DEPEND_L$ to zero. We then estimated equation 1 below with the variable MISSING added. It was not statistically significant, indicating that the incidence of disputes among the dyads for which trade (or GDP) data are missing does not differ from that for the dyads for which data are available.

[35] These include volumes by Brian R. Mitchell for each region of the world and for the United Kingdom (Cambridge: Cambridge University Press, various years); U.S. Department of Commerce, *Historical Statistics of the United States: Colonial Times to 1970* (New York: Basic Books, 1976); and Katherine Barbieri's data posted at http://pss.la.psu.edu/TRD_DATA.htm. Exchange rates come from U.S. Federal Reserve Bank sources, *The Statesman's Yearbook*, and Global Financial Data Company, www:globalfindata.com.

[36] Angus Maddison, *Monitoring the World Economy, 1820–1992* (Paris: Organization for Economic Cooperation and Development, 1995). His U.S. dollar GDP deflator is found in Maddison, "A Long Run Perspective on Saving" (Manuscript, Institute of Economic Research, University of Groningen, October 1991).

[37] Oskar Morgenstern, Klaus Knorr, and Klaus P. Heiss, *Long Term Projections of Power: Political, Economic, and Military Forecasting* (Cambridge, Mass.: Ballinger, 1973); and also John R. Oneal, "Measuring the Material Base of the East-West Balance of Power, *International Interactions* 15, no. 2 (1989).

states in a dyad share membership, as reported by the *Yearbook of International Organizations*.[38] Simply counting joint memberships (ranging from 0 to over 130 for some dyads in recent years) is far from an ideal measure of the importance and effectiveness of international organizations. It includes organizations that are weak and strong, regional and global, functional and multipurpose. Ideally the total should be broken down and some organizations given special weight, but this is hard to do as a practical matter and there is little theory to guide the attempt. For now we use the simple count of joint memberships in intergovernmental organizations; this variable is labeled IGO.

CAPABILITY RATIO

The first of the realist constraints on states' use of military force is relative power, specifically the balance of power within a dyad. The idea that an equal balance of power may deter conflict has deep historical roots, as does the idea that a preponderance of capabilities is more likely to preserve the peace by reducing uncertainty as to which side would win a contest of arms. Recent empirical work suggests, however, that it is preponderance that deters military action.[39] Our index of relative power (CAPRATIO) is the natural logarithm of the ratio of the stronger state's military capability index to that of the weaker member in each dyad. We make these calculations using the COW data on population, industry, and military forces.[40]

ALLIANCE

Allies are generally thought to fight each other less than other states because they share common security interests. They often share other political and economic interests as well. We control for this influence using a variable (ALLIES) that equals 1 if the members of a dyad were linked by a mutual defense treaty, neutrality pact, or entente; it equals 0 otherwise.[41]

---

[38] We extended the data from the sources in Russett, Oneal, and Davis (fn. 6).

[39] Bremer (fn. 24); Jacek Kugler and Douglas Lemke, eds., *Parity and War: Evaluations and Extensions of the War Ledger* (Ann Arbor: University of Michigan Press, 1996). Waltz (fn. 22), 117–23, reviews the balance of power literature and states his own version.

[40] Data are from J. David Singer and Melvin Small, *National Military Capabilities Data* (Ann Arbor: University of Michigan, Correlates of War Project, 1995); the date of final modification of the data was December 28, 1994.

[41] We updated J. David Singer, *Alliances, 1816–1984* (Ann Arbor: University of Michigan, Correlates of War Project, 1995), with material from N. J. Rengger, with John Campbell, *Treaties and Alliances of the World*, 6th ed. (New York: Stockton, 1995).

CONTIGUITY AND DISTANCE

The potential for interstate violence exists when at least one member of a dyad can reach the other with effective military force. For most states the ability to do so is determined foremost by geographic proximity, especially as one goes farther back in history. Furthermore, neighbors are likely to have the most reasons to fight—over territorial boundaries, natural resources, the grievances of cross-border ethnic groups, and so on. Thus the constraint of distance reduces the capability to fight and most of the incentives to do so as well; this finding is extremely strong in previous research.

Accordingly, we include two different terms in our regression analyses to capture this effect as fully as possible. DISTANCE is the natural logarithm of the great circle distance in miles between the capitals of the two states (or between the major ports for the largest countries); using the logarithm acknowledges a declining marginal effect. Additionally we include NONCONTIG, a measure that equals 1 if two states are not directly or indirectly contiguous (via colonies or other dependencies). It equals 0 if they share a land boundary or are separated by less than 150 miles of water. Because of the widespread nature of colonial empires, these two measures are not highly correlated ($r^2 = 0.21$), especially up to World War II. The effect of distance in constraining conflict, however, is less for the great powers: those with the land, sea, or (in the last half-century) air capability to deliver substantial forces or destructive power globally. The COW project has identified these major powers on the basis of a consensus of historians. To give full consideration to realists' concerns, we add a third variable, MINORPWRS, coded 1 if a dyad is composed of minor powers and 0 for those that include at least one great power. (To be consistent with our view that conflict is endemic but subject to constraints, we reverse the terminology and coding of the last two variables from those in previous research reports where we used CONTIG and MAJOR. This has no effect on our statistical analyses, other than to reverse the sign of the coefficients. Note that some contiguous dyads also include one or two major powers.)

In most of the analyses below, we include all possible pairs of states for which information is available, using COW data regarding membership in the international system to generate these cases. Thus we do not limit our study to the politically relevant dyads, identified as contiguous states and dyads containing at least one major power. We continue to believe that such a restriction makes good theoretical sense, however. These dyads are much more likely to engage in military disputes. Politically relevant dyads constitute just 22 percent of all the dyads for which we have data; nevertheless they account for 87 percent of all the disputes. In other words, the politically relevant dyads are twenty-four times more likely to experience a militarized dispute than are those we have deemed to be "irrelevant." And some disputes among these other dyads are contagion effects of being drawn into conflicts through alliance commitments. We include all dyads in most of the analyses reported below to be sure we are not ignoring the causes of these other disputes, [42] but we also explore the consequences of including the nonrelevant pairs.

Systemic Independent Variables

Kantian Systemic and Relative Dyadic Measures

To clarify the influence of the international system on the likelihood of dyadic conflict, we create three system-level Kantian variables and three realist variables, the latter designed to capture the hegemon's effect on interstate relations. The three Kantian variables are straightforward derivations of our basic measures: we simply computed the means of DEM, DEPEND, and IGO for each year. These are the measures (omitting the years of the world wars) graphed in Figure 1. In the analyses below, they are identified as AVGDEM, AVGDEPEND, and AVGIGO. We hypothesize that the greater these systemic measures, the more the global system will reflect the normative and institutional constraints associated with democracy, interdependence, and the rule of law. It is also possible to assess the standing of each dyad in each year relative to our three annual Kantian averages. Thus we calculated three relative dyadic measures: $\text{RELDEM}_L = (\text{DEM}_L - \text{AVGDEM})$ / the standard deviation of DEM; $\text{RELDEPEND}_L = (\text{DEPEND}_L - \text{AVGDEPEND})$ / the standard deviation of DEPEND; and $\text{RELIGO} = (\text{IGO} - \text{AVGIGO})$ / the standard deviation of IGO. These measures identify the dyads that were most democratic, interdependent, and involved in intergovernmental organizations at each point in time. By dividing by the standard deviations, we can directly compare these estimated coefficients. Combining systemic and relative measures in a single equation allows us to compare the effect of changing values of the Kantian variables through time versus the standing of dyads cross-sectionally relative to

[42] As recommended by William Reed, "The Relevance of Politically Relevant Dyads"(Paper presented at the annual meeting of the Peace Science Society [International], New Brunswick, N.J., October 1998).

18 WORLD POLITICS

the annual means. We expect the systemic and relative variables to make independent contributions to the frequency of dyadic disputes.

REALIST SYSTEMIC MEASURES

Hegemony. We also create three systemic variables associated with prominent realist theories regarding the hegemon's influence on international relations. Hegemonic-stability theory postulates that the most powerful state in the system, the hegemon, has the ability to constrain weaker states from resorting to violence.[43] This power to keep the peace might be manifested as dominance within the hegemon's sphere of influence and the ability to deter adversaries from using military force in a way detrimental to its interests. A crude but reasonable measure of the power of the leading state is its share of all the major powers' capabilities in each year. As before, we use COW data to make this calculation.

Identification of the hegemon is not obvious in all cases. Through much of recent history it is not clear whether any state was truly hegemonic.[44] It is generally agreed that in the thirty years before World War I the United Kingdom was closer than any other country to being hegemonic, although its power relative to both Germany and the United States was declining. During the interwar era the United States clearly had greater economic strength and military potential than the United Kingdom; but its actual military power was only about equal. Moreover, its geographic position and isolationist policy limited its involvement in the Central European system. Consequently, we accept Organski and Kugler's judgment that Britain was the hegemon in the interwar period as well.[45] In the post–World War II years, if any state can be said to have been hegemonic, it is the United States. Hence we use the proportion of capabilities held by the United Kingdom as the measure of the hegemon's power in the first sixty years analyzed and that of the U.S. after 1945. Our systemic indicator (HEGPOWER) has reasonable face validity, declining from 33 percent in 1885 to 14 percent in 1913, and dropping under 11 percent by 1938. America's hegemony is manifest immediately following World War II, when it controlled 52 percent of the major powers' capabilities. This declined

---

[43] Robert Gilpin, *War and Change in World Politics* (Cambridge: Cambridge University Press, 1981).
[44] Bruce Russett, "The Mysterious Decline of American Hegemony, or, Is Mark Twain Really Dead?" *International Organization* 32, no. 2 (1985).
[45] A. F. K. Organski and Jacek Kugler, *The War Ledger* (Chicago: University of Chicago Press, 1980). On measurement, see David Sacko, "Measures of Hegemony" (Paper presented at the annual meeting of the Peace Science Society [International], New Brunswick, N.J., October 1998).

to 26 percent by the early 1980s but rose to 29 percent with the collapse of the Soviet Union.

Satisfaction with the status quo. The power-transition theory originally advanced by Organski consists of propositions not only about the constraining influence of an imbalance of power but also about the role played by states' satisfaction with the status quo. States rising in power will challenge a hegemon only if they are dissatisfied with the international system it dominates. Lemke and Reed extend this rationale in an effort to subsume the democratic peace within power-transition theory.[46] They contend that democracies have fought less historically because the hegemon has been democratic since the end of the Napoleonic Wars. First Britain and then the United States, it is argued, used its power to construct an international system that provided benefits to itself and its mostly democratic allies. Thus democracies' satisfaction with the status quo created by the most powerful democratic state and reinforced by its system of alliances accounts for the peace among democratic dyads. Like Lemke and Reed, we assess this view by computing a measure of each state's satisfaction with the status quo based on the correspondence between its portfolio of alliances and that of the hegemon, as indicated by the tau-b measure of statistical association. Then we multiply the scores of the two states in a dyad to create a measure of joint satisfaction (SATISFIED).[47] This measure indicates the degree to which each dyad is content with the distribution of benefits achieved under the leadership of the dominant state.

Hegemonic tensions. Both hegemonic-stability theory and power-transition theory hold that the international system will be more peaceful when the hegemon is strong relative to its principal rivals. The hegemon may also affect the system by transmitting concerns for its own security to other states. International tensions involving the hegemonic power are likely to have consequences for its allies, its rivals, its rivals' allies, and even neutral states. "When elephants fight, the grass gets trampled," as the adage goes. It is also possible, to extend the metaphor, that when small animals fight, big ones will be drawn in. Large states may intervene in ongoing conflicts because they see an opportunity to achieve gains or avoid losses. Either way, international ten-

---

[46] Lemke and Reed (fn. 3).

[47] We added 1 to each state's tau-b score to make it positive. The tau-b index of the similarity of alliance portfolios was introduced by Bruce Bueno de Mesquita, "Measuring Systemic Polarity," *Journal of Conflict Resolution* 19, no. 2 (1975). It was adapted as a dyadic measure of satisfaction by Woosang Kim, "Alliance Transitions and Great Power War," *American Journal of Political Science* 35 (1991), and subsequently used by Lemke and Reed (fn. 3).

sions may be contagious. To assess this view, we created a measure of the hegemon's sense of its own security, calculating its defense spending as a share of its GDP (HEGDEF).[48] We hypothesize that the global system will experience more numerous disputes when the hegemon is committing more of its resources to the military. In such times, the hegemon presumably perceives greater threats to its interests. To assess the scope of contagion, we consider whether involvement in disputes rises mostly for the hegemon itself, for the hegemon and its allies, or for unallied states.

RESULTS

We evaluate the Kantian peace, 1885–1992, employing logistic regression analysis. First we assess the effects of democracy, interdependence, and IGOs using a simple dyadic specification. In this view the likelihood of conflict is primarily determined by the state less constrained economically or politically. We also consider the degree to which the political and economic characteristics of the other member of a dyad affect the likelihood of a militarized dispute. Next we disentangle the systemic and cross-sectional influences of the Kantian variables on dyadic conflict. We consider the effects of trends in the underlying variables and each dyad's degree of democracy, interdependence, and involvement in IGOs relative to these annual systemic averages. Finally we investigate central realist tenets regarding the role of the leading state in the international system.

We examine the involvement in militarized interstate disputes of nearly 6,000 pairs of states observed annually, for a total of almost 150,000 observations. Because of the lagged variables the analysis begins with disputes in the year 1886 that are explained by reference to conditions in 1885. As noted earlier, we do not consider the two world wars after the first year of conflict or the immediate postwar years; that is, we exclude disputes for 1915–20 and 1940–46.

Unless otherwise indicated, we estimate the coefficients in our regression equations using the general estimating equation (GEE) method. We adjust for first-order autoregression (AR1) and estimate statistical significance using robust standard errors that take into account the clustering of our data by dyads. Thus we respond to the con-

---

[48] Military expenditure is a component of the COW index of militarily relevant capabilities. On the validity of our measure, see John R. Oneal and Hugh Carter Whatley, "The Effect of Alliance Membership on National Defense Burdens, 1953–88," *International Interactions* 22, no. 2 (1996). Changes in this index for the hegemon's military burden correlate highly with changes in the average military burden for all the major powers.

KANTIAN PEACE   21

cerns raised by Beck, Katz, and Tucker. We rely on GEE rather than on their recommended solution for temporal dependence because of doubts about its appropriateness, especially given the strong, theoretically specified relation between trade and the time elapsed since a dyad's last dispute.[49] We have, however, reestimated our key equations using their method as a check on our findings. Because our hypotheses are directional and we have corrected for these violations in the assumptions underlying regression analysis, we report one-tailed tests of statistical significance.

EVALUATING THE KANTIAN PEACE USING THE
    WEAK-LINK SPECIFICATION

Our first test is the simplest. We expect the likelihood of conflict to be primarily a function of the degree to which the less constrained state along each of several dimensions is free to use military force. This is the weak-link assumption that this state is more likely to precipitate a break in the peace: the less the political or economic constraints on that state's use of force, the greater the likelihood of violence. Consequently we include the lower democracy score and the lower bilateral trade-to-GDP ratio. The number of joint memberships in international organizations is inherently a dyadic measure; it completes the Kantian specification. We include in the regression equation a measure of the dyadic balance of power and an indicator of whether the members of a dyad are allied. We also control for the distance separating the two states, whether or not they are contiguous, and whether both are minor powers.[50] Our first equation then takes the form:

$$\text{DISPUTE} = \text{DEM}_L + \text{DEPEND}_L + \text{IGO} + \text{ALLIES} + \text{CAPRATIO}$$
$$+ \text{NONCONTIG} + \text{DISTANCE} + \text{MINORPWRS} \quad (1)$$

The results of estimating equation 1, found in the first column of Table 1, provide strong support for the pacifying influence of democ-

---

[49] On GEE, see Peter J. Diggle, Kung-Yee Liang, and Scott L. Zeger, *Analysis of Longitudinal Data* (Oxford: Clarendon Press, 1994). We used the computing algorithms in StataCorp, *Stata Statistical Software*, Release 5.0 (College Station, Tex.: Stata Corporation, 1997). For Beck, Katz, and Tucker's methods, see fn. 24. We express our doubts that the effects of the theoretical variables and of time are separable, as Beck, Katz, and Tucker's method requires, in Oneal and Russett (fn. 6, 1999). GEE allows for temporal dependence in the time series but gives the theoretical variables primacy in accounting for interstate disputes. Beck, Katz, and Tucker introduce the PEACEYRS variables into the estimation process as coequals of the theoretical variables. See also D. Scott Bennett, "Parametric Methods, Duration Dependence, and Time-Varying Data Revisited," *American Journal of Political Science* 43, no. 1 (1999).

[50] Our recent specifications are found in Oneal and Russett (1997); and Russett, Oneal, and Davis (fn. 6). The controls, from Oneal and Russett (fn. 6, 1999), draw on Barbieri (fn. 24).

TABLE 1

MODELS OF THE KANTIAN PEACE, 1886–1992: PREDICTING INVOLVEMENT IN MILITARIZED DISPUTES

Variable	1. 1886–1992 Simplest, All Dyads	2. 1886–1992 Peaceyears Correction	3. 1886–1939 All Dyads	4. 1886–1992, Politically Relevant Dyads
Lower democracy	−0.0658***	−0.0628***	−0.0568***	−0.0595***
(DEM_L)	(0.0106)	(0.0093)	(0.0106)	(0.0106)
Trade/GDP	−57.8650***	−31.0726**	−43.2490**	−35.2394**
($DEPEND_L$)	(15.4901)	(10.6036)	(16.2861)	(12.3044)
International organizations	−0.0010	0.0160#	0.0068	−0.0068*
(IGO)	(0.0379)	(0.0042)	(0.0068)	(0.0039)
Capability ratio	−0.2337***	−0.1913***	−0.3638***	−0.2747***
($CAPRATIO$)	(0.0502)	(0.0401)	(0.0664)	(0.0516)
Alliances	−0.2511	−0.3691**	−0.1727	−0.2822*
($ALLIANCES$)	(0.1659)	(0.1574)	(0.1905)	(0.1677)
Noncontiguity	−2.0038***	−1.5864***	−1.3357***	−1.118***
($NONCONTIG$)	(0.1836)	(0.1532)	(0.1844)	(0.1724)
Log distance	−0.4647***	−0.3615***	−0.3536***	−0.2610***
($DISTANCE$)	(0.0571)	(0.0498)	(0.0620)	(0.0605)
Only minor powers	−1.8392***	−1.7208***	−1.8342***	−0.6754***
($MINORPWRS$)	(0.1706)	(0.1351)	(0.1904)	(0.2082)
Constant	−1.9349***	−1.6174***	−2.2235***	−1.5765***
	(0.4731)	(0.4060)	(0.5316)	(0.4992)
Chi²	1354.80	1920.45	494.98	193.43
P of Chi²	0.0000	0.0000	0.0000	0.0000
Log Likelihood		−5732.4260		
Pseudo R²		0.284		
N	149,373	149,404	33,346	33,334

*p<.05; **p<.01; ***p<.001, one-tailed tests; #p<.001, one-tailed test but wrong sign

racy and trade: the more democratic the less democratic state in a dyad and the more economically important is trade, the greater is the likelihood of peace. The lower democracy and dependence measures are both significant at the .001 level. The number of joint memberships in IGOs, however, does not have a statistically significant effect on conflict in this specification (p < .40). This is a consequence of two things: the inclusion of all possible dyads in the analysis (not just those thought to be politically relevant) and the rapid growth in the number of international organizations over time. The realist variables perform generally as expected, though the indicator of alliance is only significant at the .07 level: (1) a preponderance of power rather than a balance deters conflict; (2) contiguous states are prone to fight, as are those whose homelands are geographically proximate; and (3) major powers are involved in disputes more than are smaller states. All these variables are significant at the .001 level.[51] Using the onset (or first year only) of a dispute as the dependent variable produced nearly identical results.

Column 2 of Table 1 shows the results of estimating equation 1 using Beck et al.'s correction for temporal dependence in the time series. The coefficients and significance levels are usually similar. The most notable exception involves the variable IGO. Its coefficient is now not only positive but nearly four times its standard error.[52]

To see if the pacific benefits of the Kantian variables are limited to the cold war era, we first reestimated equation 1 for just the early years, 1886–1914 and 1921–39 using GEE. The results appear in column 3. Comparing them with column 1 shows much the same pattern as the analysis for all years. Both the lower democracy score (p < .001) and the smaller bilateral trade-to-GDP ratio (p < .004) are highly significant.

---

[51] To test the robustness of these results, we estimated separate regressions for each theoretically interesting variable with just the controls for distance, contiguity, and major-power status. The signs and significance levels were consistent with those in the multivariate regressions, with one exception. Joint IGO memberships significantly (p < .001) reduced conflict in the restricted analysis. We also reestimated equation 1 after dropping the measure of economic interdependence because this variable has the most missing values. The pacific benefits of democracy remained strong (p < .001). Joint membership in IGOs, too, was significantly associated with a reduction in conflict (p < .02) when DEPEND$_L$ was omitted. Not surprisingly, interdependent states share memberships in international organizations.

[52] We suppress coefficients for the four spline segments to save space. All are significant (p < .001). In this equation, and others presented subsequently, the coefficients for IGOs are the only ones not robust to the different methods for adjusting for temporal dependence. As our results suggest, joint membership in IGOs is most correlated of the three Kantian variables with the years of peace since a dyad's last dispute. Our methodological preference for GEE preceded our work on IGOs. We also estimated equation 1 using conditional or fixed effects logistic regression. Greater democracy (p < .001) and interdependence (p < .05) continued to be associated with peaceful dyadic relations, as was the existence of an alliance. Joint membership in IGOs and a greater capability ratio increased the prospects of conflict. These results are based on the 20,289 observations for dyads that experienced at least one dispute; 129,092 cases were dropped because the dependent variable always equaled zero.

Democracy and interdependence had strong peace-inducing effects during the multipolar period after 1885 and before the cold war. The benefits of democracy are strongest in the interwar years, but, as Gowa[53] also reports, by the decade leading to World War I democracies had become less likely to engage in militarized disputes with each other—an important shift that is obscured by using the years 1886–1914 as the period of analysis. In light of this evidence, the absence of democratic peace in the nineteenth century—not its presence in the cold war era—becomes the anomoly to be explained. The answer may lie more in the lower inclusiveness of democratic politics in that century than in characteristics of the international system.

Our measure of joint memberships in IGOs is insignificant for the period 1885–1939. The other coefficients in equation 1 are reasonably similar for the early years and the entire period. The effect of alliances before 1940 is even weaker ($p < .19$) than when all years are considered.

We also estimated equation 1 after creating an indicator for the 1989–92 post–cold war years and forming interactive terms with each of the three Kantian variables. The results indicate that the influence of democracy has not changed in this short span of time and the benefits of interdependence have been reduced, but IGOs are more important constraints on the threat or use of force.

In the past we limited our analyses to the politically relevant states, in the belief that the relations of most other dyads are not importantly influenced by the political and economic influences we have modeled. To see how including all possible pairs of states affects our results, we reestimate equation 1 using just the contiguous pairs of states and those that contain at least one major power—the politically relevant dyads—for all years, 1885–1992. This excludes dyads that in the great majority of cases had no reasonable opportunity to engage in armed conflict because the states were too far apart and had few issues over which to fight.

The last column of Table 1 provides strong support for the pacific benefits of all three elements of the Kantian peace. For the dyads most prone to conflict, joint membership in international organizations does reduce the likelihood of conflict ($p < .04$). The benefits of democracy ($p < .001$) and interdependence ($p < .002$) remain apparent. These results for the extended period, 1886–1992, are consistent with those in Russett, Oneal, and Davis, where only the years 1950–85 were considered; and they are more significant statistically.[54]

[53] Gowa (fn. 3), 98–100.
[54] Oneal, Russett, and Davis (fn. 6). Farber and Gowa (fn. 3), 409, analyze lower-level MIDs for 1816–1976 and find that democracy significantly affects the likelihood of conflict only after 1919.

Our tests with all possible pairs understate the pacific benefits of
IGOs because most of these dyads do not have significant political-
military relations. The probability that a nonrelevant dyad will become
involved in a dispute is only 1/18 that of a major-power pair; it is 1/44
that of a contiguous dyad. Democracy, interdependence, and involvement in IGOs constrain states from using force; but if there is no realistic possibility of two states engaging in conflict, then the absence of
these constraints will not increase the incidence of violence. With all
dyads included a large number of false negatives obscures the hypothesized relationship. The theoretically interesting variables in equation 1
are simply irrelevant in explaining the state of relations, such as they
are, between Burma and Ecuador, for example. Including numerous irrelevant dyads can bias the results, as we have recently shown with regard to trade.[55]

With logistic regression, the easiest way to show the substantive effects of the variables is to estimate the probability of a militarized dispute for various illustrative dyads. The same procedure is often used in
epidemiological studies. For example, epidemiologists report the effect
of various risk factors on the probability that an individual will contract
lung cancer. As in our analyses, some of their independent variables are
not subject to intervention (for example, age, heredity, gender; and for
us distance and contiguity), while others are amenable to some degree
of "policy" control (for example, diet, exercise, smoking; and for us alliances, democracy, interdependence, and IGOs). By statistical inference
they, and we, can estimate the reduction in the probability of an event
occurring if any one risk factor for a typical individual were different by
a given amount.

For this, we calculated a baseline probability against which to make
comparisons. We assumed the dyad is contiguous, because these states

---

However, using interactive terms for years, we find evidence of democratic peace by 1900. Earlier than
that even the most democratic states were not democratic by contemporary standards. As democracy
developed, the common interests of democracies and their antagonisms with authoritarian states may
have become more substantial. Support for the benefits of democracy in Farber and Gowa's analyses is
weakened by their decision to exclude consideration of all years of the world wars. Due to possible si-
multaneity problems, they do not control for alliances. Since alliances show little impact in our analyses, this may not matter. For results for trade that agree with ours, see Christopher Way, "Manchester
Revisited: A Theoretical and Empirical Evaluation of Commercial Liberalism" (Ph.D. diss., Stanford
University, 1997). For results that differ from ours, see Barbieri (fn. 24); and idem, "Economic Interdependence: A Path to Peace or a Source of Interstate Conflict?" *Journal of Peace Research* 33, no. 1
(1996). Our analyses to date indicate that this is primarily due to our different measures of interdependence: Barbieri does not weight trade by its contribution to GDP. The results reported in Oneal and
Russett (fn. 6, 1999) show that the pacific benefits of trade, 1950–92, are robust to several alternative
specifications, samples, and estimation procedures.
[55] Oneal and Russett (fn. 6, 1999).

are particularly prone to conflict. Then we set each continuous variable at its mean value for the contiguous dyads, except that the lower dependence score was made equal to its median value, which is more representative. We postulated that the pair of states is not allied and does not include a major power. We then estimated the annual probability that this "typical" dyad would be involved in a militarized dispute using the coefficients reported in columns 1 and 4 in Table 1. Next we changed the theoretically interesting variables in succession by adding a standard deviation to the continuous measures or by making the dyad allied.

The first two columns of Table 2 give the percentage increase or decrease in the annual risk of a dyad being involved in a dispute under these various conditions. Column 1 is based on the coefficients estimated using all dyads, and column 2 is produced with the coefficients for just the politically relevant subset of cases.[56] Looking at the results in column 1, it is apparent that democracy and interdependence dramatically reduce the likelihood of conflict. Compared with the typical dyad, the risk that the more democratic dyad will become engaged in a dispute is reduced by 36 percent. If the dyad is more autocratic, the danger of conflict is increased by 56 percent. A higher dyadic trade-to-GDP ratio cuts the incidence of conflict by 49 percent. A larger number of joint memberships in IGOs has little effect on a dyad's likelihood of conflict if all pairs of states are used in the estimation process. When analysis is limited to the politically relevant dyads, however, the benefit of joint memberships in IGOs is clear. If the number of common memberships is fifty-three rather than thirty-two, the likelihood of conflict is reduced by 13 percent. And when the analysis is limited to politically relevant pairs, the effects of democracy and economic interdependence are somewhat less than when all dyads are considered.

The substantive importance of the Kantian variables is confirmed if their effects are compared with the results of changing the realist variables. Consider again the second column of Table 2. If a state's preponderance of power is a standard deviation higher, that reduces the probability of a dispute by 31 percent, but that result would require a fourfold increase in the capabilities of the stronger state. An alliance lowers the incidence of interstate violence by 24 percent. This is substantially less than when the dyad is more democratic or with a standard deviation higher level of bilateral trade.

---

[56] This baseline probability is .031 among all dyads and .055 for the politically relevant pairs.

TABLE 2

PERCENTAGE OF CHANGE IN RISK FOR ANNUAL INVOLVEMENT IN A
MILITARIZED DISPUTE FOR CONTIGUOUS DYADS[a]
(1886–1992)

	Based on		
	1. Equation 1 (All Dyads)	2. Equation 1 (Politically Relevant Dyads)	3. Equation 2 (All Dyads)
DEM_L increased by 1 std. dev.	−36	−33	
DEM_L decreased by 1 std. dev.	+56	+48	
$DEPEND_L$ increased by 1 std. dev.	−49	−33	
IGO increased by 1 std. dev.	−2	−13	
CAPRATIO increased by 1 std. dev.	−27	−31	−33
ALLIES equals 1	−22	−24	−22
$RELDEM_L$ increased by 1 std. dev.			−30
$RELDEPEND_L$ increased by 1 std. dev.			−36
RELIGO increased by 1 std. dev.			−18
$AVGDEM_L$ increased by 1 std. dev.			−26
$AVGDEPEND_L$ increased by 1 std. dev.			−33
AVGIGO increased by 1 std. dev.			+3

[a] In each case other variables are held at baseline values.

We have argued that the characteristics of the less constrained state largely account for the likelihood of dyadic conflict, but the potential for violence may be significantly affected by the nature of the other dyadic member.[57] Democracies are more peaceful than autocracies at the national (or monadic) level as well as dyadically; but in our previous research we found, as Kant expected, that democracies and autocracies are particularly prone to fight one another because of the political distance separating them. Other analysts think that asymmetric interdependence may lead to conflict.[58] To evaluate these hypotheses we considered the influence of the higher democracy score and trade-to-GDP ratio, adding these variables to equation 1 both individually and as interactive terms with the lower democracy score or trade-to-GDP ratio.[59]

[57] Maoz (fn. 30); Oneal and Russett (fn. 6, 1997); Oneal and James Lee Ray, "New Tests of the Democratic Peace Controlling for Economic Interdependence, 1950–1985," *Political Research Quarterly* 50, no. 4 (1997).

[58] Robert O. Keohane and Joseph S. Nye, *Power and Interdependence: World Politics in Transition* (Boston: Little Brown, 1997); John A. Kroll, "The Complexity of Interdependence," *International Studies Quarterly* 37 (September 1993); Immanuel Wallerstein, "The Rise and Future Demise of the World Capitalist System," *Comparative Studies in Society and History* 16, no. 4 (1974); Barbieri (fnn. 24 and 54).

[59] If the effect of one variable (DEM_L, $DEPEND_L$) is thought to depend on the value of another (DEM_H, $DEPEND_H$), the test should include their interactive terms ($DEM_L{}^* DEM_H$ and $DEPEND_L{}^*$

The results, not reported in a table but available from the authors, indicated that the conflict-prone character of mixed pairs—one democracy and one autocracy—was limited to the post–World War II era. Plausibly the special institutional and ideological animosities between democrats and communists, solidified by the cold war, account for that. In the multipolar period, 1885–1939, dyads consisting of two democracies were the most peaceful after about 1900. Autocratic pairs and mixed dyads had similar rates of conflict. We found no evidence that asymmetric interdependence raised the likelihood of a militarized dispute. Increasing trade had significant pacific benefits whatever the relative size of the states involved. We did find a declining marginal utility for high levels of economic interdependence.[60]

DISENTANGLING THE SYSTEMIC AND CROSS-NATIONAL INFLUENCES OF THE KANTIAN MEASURES

Estimating equation 1 indicates that the likelihood of a dispute among all dyads is a function of the lower democracy score and the lower trade-to-GDP ratio in a dyad but not of states' joint memberships in international organizations. We suggested that the failure of the IGO variable to perform as expected results partly from including large numbers of irrelevant pairs of states that have no significant political relations and lack a realistic possibility of becoming engaged in a dispute. By contrast, limiting the analysis to contiguous dyads and those containing a major power highlights the benefits of international organizations. We also noted that our measure of joint IGO membership increases rather steadily over time. This may obscure the contribution of international organizations to peaceful interstate relations by making comparisons across time less meaningful, as with nominal GDPs in periods of inflation.

The influence of IGO membership can be reconsidered by distinguishing between the frequency of states' participation in international organizations through time and the standing of individual dyads relative to this annual measure at each point in time. We decompose each Kantian variable—the lower democracy score, the lower trade-to-GDP

DEPEND$_H$). See Robert J. Friedrich, "In Defense of Multiplicative Terms in Multiple Regression Equations," *American Journal of Political Science* 26, no. 4 (1982).

[60] Analyses in which we modeled the effect of interdependence as a hyperbola suggest that the benefits of trade increase rapidly and then approach a limit asymptotically. See Mark Gasiorowski and Solomon Polachek, "East-West Trade Linkages in the Era of Detente," *Journal of Conflict Resolution* 26, no. 4 (1982).

ratio, and the number of joint IGO memberships—into a systemic measure, the average value of states' democracy score, level of interdependence, or joint membership in IGOs (Figure 1), and a cross-sectional measure that ranks dyads relative to this annual average. The annual average of the number of joint IGO memberships (AVGIGO), for example, captures the prominence through time of international organizations, while the degree of involvement of individual dyads relative to this average (RELIGO) identifies those states that are more (or less) linked through the network of IGOs in each year.

To distinguish between the systemic and cross-sectional Kantian influences, we substitute in equation 1 AVGDEM and $RELDEM_L$ for DEM_L, AVGDEPEND and $RELDEPEND_L$ for $DEPEND_L$, and AVGIGO and RELIGO for IGO. Our second equation becomes:

$$\begin{aligned}
\text{DISPUTE} = {} & \text{RELDEM}_L + \text{RELDEPEND}_L + \text{RELIGO} + \text{AVGDEM} \\
& + \text{AVGDEPEND} + \text{AVGIGO} + \text{ALLIED} + \text{CAPRATIO} \\
& + \text{NONCONTIG} + \text{DISTANCE} + \text{MINORPWRS}
\end{aligned} \tag{2}$$

Column 1 of Table 3 reports the results of estimating equation 2 using all pairs of states. All the relative and systemic Kantian variables except the annual average of states'involvement in IGOs have a negative sign, indicating that increasing values reduce the likelihood of a militarized dispute; all but AVGIGO are very significant statistically. As explained in the last section, we standardized the three relative measures to permit direct comparison of their estimated coefficients. These indicate that economically important trade has the greatest conflict-reducing benefits, followed by democracy and joint memberships in international organizations. Two of the three Kantian systemic variables also affect the incidence of dyadic disputes: the likelihood of conflict drops when there are more democracies in the system and trade is more important economically; with both variables significant at the .001 level.[61] The influences of the other variables in the equation are

---

[61] There is a mild downward trend in the likelihood of a dispute over the period 1885–1992. To insure that the systemic Kantian variables were not simply collinear with this secular trend toward decreasing rates of disputes, we included in each of the equations reported in Table 3 an indicator of time, which equals the year minus 1884. The coefficients of the Kantian variables changed very little, and the average democracy score and trade-to-GDP ratio remained significant at the .001 level; the measure of time was never significant at the .05 level in these tests. If equation 2 is estimated for just the 1885–1939 period, the coefficient of the average level of interdependence becomes statistically insignificant, primarily because the level of trade at the outset of World War I was higher than it was during the interwar years; the average level of democracy remained significant at the .001 level.

TABLE 3
MODELS OF THE KANTIAN PEACE, 1886–1992:
PREDICTING INVOLVEMENT IN MILITARIZED DISPUTES
(DYADIC AND SYSTEMIC INFLUENCES, ALL DYADS)

Variable	1. Only Kantian Systemic Variables	2. Systemic Kantian, Heg. Power, Satisfaction	3. Systemic Kantian, Heg. Defense Burden
Relative lower democ.	−0.3688***	−0.3576***	−0.4102***
(RELDEM$_L$)	(0.0680)	(0.0677)	(0.0703)
Relative trade/GDP	−0.7270***	−0.7045**	−0.5149**
(RELDEPEND$_L$)	(0.2333)	(0.2412)	(0.2132)
Relative IGO	−0.1304**	−0.1060*	−0.1602***
(RELIGO)	(0.0500)	(0.0512)	(0.0502)
Average democracy	−0.2383***	−0.2485***	−0.2702***
(AVGDEM)	(0.0412)	(0.0412)	(0.0423)
Average dependence	−292.4397***	−260.3094***	−355.5549***
(AVGDEPEND)	(36.4178)	(48.7066)	(39.7875)
Average IGOs	0.0043	0.0102	−0.0440***
(AVGIGO)	(0.0109)	(0.0115)	(0.0136)
Capability ratio	−0.2897***	−0.2787***	−0.3125***
(CAPRATIO)	0.0518	(0.0521)	(0.0135)
Alliances	−0.2554	−0.2186	−0.3330*
(ALLIES)	(0.1625)	(0.1665)	(0.1636)
Noncontiguity	−2.0080***	−2.0423***	−1.9225***
(NONCONTIG)	(0.1803)	(0.1828)	(0.1802)
Log distance	−0.4915***	−0.4637***	−0.5202***
(DISTANCE)	(0.0567)	(0.0597)	(0.0569)
Only minor powers	−2.0230***	−2.0073***	−2.0694***
(MINORPWRS)	(0.1893)	(0.1941)	(0.1911)
Hegemonic power		−1.5339	
(HEGPOWER)		(0.9502)	
Joint satisfaction		−0.0893	
(SATISFIED)		(0.1057)	
Heg. defense burden			17.9704***
(HEGDEF)			(1.9906)
Constant	−0.7345	−0.7113	−0.3735
	(0.4850)	(0.5075)	(0.4975)
Chi²	1559.82	1530.24	1529.38
P of Chi²	0.0000	0.0000	0.0000
N	149,372	147,963	149,372

*p < .05; **p < .01; ***p < .001, one-tailed tests

relatively unchanged. Preponderant power reduces the likelihood of a dispute, as do distance, an alliance, or the absence of a major power in the dyad. Using the onset of a dispute as the dependent variable produced nearly identical results.

The results of estimating equation 2 are important for three reasons. First, they show that dyads relatively more involved in international organizations at any point in time tend to be more peaceful, supporting the Kantian hypothesis regarding IGOs. Second, the results indicate that the statistical significance of democracy and the trade-to-GDP ratio in equation 1 is the consequence of temporal as well as cross-sectional variation. This is valuable assurance of the robustness of the pacific benefits of these Kantian influences. We now have explicit justification for believing that states can modify their circumstances by policies that increase democracy, interdependence, and, given the significance of the relative IGO measure, participation in international organizations. Third, it supports the view that there are systemic consequences of increasing democracy and trade for all pairs of states, not just for the liberal dyads.

The estimated coefficients for equation 2 allow us to compare the substantive importance of the relative and cross-sectional measures. We again calculate the probabilities of conflict for various hypothetical dyads. In calculating the baseline risk, we assume as before that the dyad is contiguous and set each continuous variable at its mean (or median for the trade ratio) for this subset of cases. We make the dyad unallied and assume it does not include a major power. We estimate the annual probability that this representative dyad would be involved in a dispute using the coefficients in column 1 of Table 3. Then one at a time we change each continuous variable by a standard deviation; finally we make the dyad allied.

Column 3 of Table 2 gives the annual probabilities of a dyad being involved in a dispute under these conditions. The effects of the cross-sectional Kantian variables, which rank dyads according to their position relative to the annual systemic averages, are again substantial. For dyads with a higher relative democracy score the risk of conflict is 30 percent below the baseline rate; a standard-deviation increase in relative dependence means a 36 percent lower probability of conflict; and when states' participation in IGOs is higher the likelihood of conflict is reduced by 18 percent. The substantive significance of the Kantian variables for interstate relations again emerges by comparing these effects with those that result from changing the realist variables.

A higher capability ratio means lowering the danger of violence by a third, and when two states are allied the probability of conflict is lower by 22 percent. Note also the effects of the Kantian systemic variables. The risk of a dispute drops by 26 percent if the systemic average of the democracy score increases by a standard deviation (from −0.47 to +1.26); it falls 33 percent if the systemic average of the trade-to-GDP ratio rises by a standard deviation (about 30 percent to .006). There is effectively no change if the systemic average for states' participation in IGOs grows. Thus, two of the Kantian systemic variables have powerful effects throughout the international system. By normative or institutional means, an increase in the number of liberal states constrains the use of force even by dyads that are not democratic or interdependent.[62] The effect of IGOs is limited, however, to those states that participate jointly in more of these international forums relative to other pairs.

Assessing the Hegemon's Influence on Dyadic Conflict

In our last analyses we investigate the role of the hegemon. We first evaluate a central claim of the theory of hegemonic stability and power-preponderance theory.[63] Both of these realist theories predict that conflict becomes more likely as the power of the leading state declines relative to its principal rivals. At the same time, we also address the argument that it has been the power of the (democratic) hegemon to reward its allies that accounts for the democratic peace. In a final test we consider whether the hegemon's sense of its own insecurity, as indicated by the ratio of its military expenditures to its gross domestic product, is associated with a heightened danger of conflict globally.

We assess the importance of the hegemon's relative power and states' satisfaction with the status quo by adding two terms to equation 2: HEGPOWER, the proportion of the major powers' capabilities held by Britain (through 1939) and the U.S. (after 1945); and SATISFIED, our measure of joint satisfaction, based on the similarity of each dyadic member's portfolio of allies to that of the leading power. It is appropriate theoretically to include both in the same equation. If the hegemon is able to regulate the level of conflict in the international system, then

---

[62] To insure that the effects of the annual averages of the democracy score and trade ratio were truly systemic and not confined to only those dyads that were relatively democratic or interdependent, we added three interactive terms (AVGDEM*RELDEM$_L$, AVGDEPEND*RELDEPEND$_L$, and AVGIGO*RELIGO) to equation 2. The results indicated that the effects of the systemic Kantian variables are not confined to just those dyads that rank high relative to the annual averages.

[63] A. F. K. Organski, *World Politics* (New York: Knopf, 1968); George Modelski, ed., *Exploring Long Cycles* (Boulder, Colo.: Lynne Rienner, 1987); Gilpin (fn. 43); Kugler and Lemke (fn. 39); K. Edward Spiezio, "British Hegemony and Major Power War, 1815–1939: An Empirical Test of Gilpin's Model of Hegemonic Governance," *International Studies Quarterly* 34, no. 2 (1990).

its influence should be greatest with those states with which it is most closely allied. At the same time the advantages for a state of aligning itself closely with the hegemon should be greatest when the power of the leading state is relatively large vis-à-vis its principal rivals; the hegemon in that situation should be most able to confer benefits upon its supporters.

Column 2 of Table 3 suggests that the strength of the leading state relative to its principal rivals does matter. The measure of hegemonic power is nearly significant ($p < .06$). Strong hegemony seems to reduce violence in the international system. This apparent effect stems, however, from the inability of a weakened hegemon (Britain) to prevent the outbreak of systemwide wars. In an analysis not reported in the table, the coefficient of our measure of hegmonic power reversed signs when the first year of each of the world wars was dropped: hegemony was then positively related to the incidence of disputes in the system ($p < .003$). Apparently the pacific benefits of hegemonic strength do not apply during normal periods of international relations. By contrast, we found no evidence in these analyses that states' satisfaction with the status quo accounts for the democratic peace. The measure of joint satisfaction in column 2 of Table 3 is far from statistical significance, while the significance of relative and systemic democracy is little changed.[64]

Finally we consider whether the hegemon's sense of its own security, as indicated by the proportion of GDP it devotes to military expenditures (HEGDEF), is related to the likelihood of dyadic conflict. We add our measure of the hegemon's defense burden to equation 2. The results of this test are reported in column 3. As seen there, the defense burden of the leading state is positively associated ($p < .001$) with the likelihood of dyadic disputes. There are wide-ranging consequences when the hegemon feels endangered. Nor is the heightened danger of conflict limited to the world wars, as with hegemonic power, or significant only for the hegemon or its allies. In a separate analysis not reported in the table, we confirmed that other states, too, experience more disputes when the hegemon has increased the proportion of its resources committed to the military. Our systemic and relative Kantian variables nonetheless remain important. Even the systemic measure of states' participation in international organizations is now significant at the .001 level. The effectiveness of IGOs may depend in part upon the

---

[64] We tested alternative specifications in evaluating the role played by states' satisfaction with the status quo. We adopted the weak-link assumption, adding the smaller of the tau-b measures of satisfaction to equation 2, and investigated whether two dissatisfied states might also be peaceful; but these terms were not statistically significant.

major powers not feeling a need to develop, and presumably use, independent military means for protecting and promoting their interests.

A KANTIAN SYSTEM? PAST AND FUTURE

Our analyses for the years 1885–1992 indicate that Kant was substantially correct: democracy, economic interdependence, and involvement in international organizations reduce the incidence of militarized interstate disputes. The pacific benefits of the Kantian influences, especially of democracy and trade, were not confined to the cold war era but extend both forward from that era and back many decades. Moreover, these benefits are substantial. When the democracy score of the less democratic state in a dyad is higher by a standard deviation, the likelihood of conflict is more than one-third below the baseline rate among all dyads in the system; a higher bilateral trade-to-GDP ratio means that the risk of conflict is lower by half. The pacific benefits of democracy in the twentieth century are clear, and the change from the nineteenth century is consistent with an evolutionary view: democratic institutions matured, and the suffrage was extended. In addition, as Kant believed, states may learn from the success and failure of their policies.

The benefits of joint membership in intergovernmental organizations are more modest but nevertheless significant for the politically relevant dyads—contiguous states and dyads containing at least one major power. For these particularly dangerous dyads, the probability of a dispute drops by 13 percent when the number of joint memberships in IGOs is greater by a standard deviation. The pacific benefits of international organizations are also apparent when the trend in this variable is eliminated: among all dyads, pairs of states more involved by a standard deviation in IGOs relative to the annual systemic average are 18 percent less likely to become embroiled in interstate violence.

By distinguishing the influences of the Kantian systemic averages from the standings of each dyad relative to the annual means, we also showed benefits of democracy and trade over time as well as cross-sectionally. The effects of the systemic Kantian influences on dyadic conflict are important. The international system is more peaceful when there are more democracies and when trade is greater. *All* dyads—even those not democratic or interdependent—become less dispute-prone when those systemic Kantian variables increase. The constraining effect of norms and institutions that emerge when there are more democracies and when trade is economically important for many states holds even for those that participate to only a limited degree in the Kantian subsystem.[65]

Over the period 1885–1992 states' participation in IGOs rose steadily, but there is little evidence of a trend toward increased democracy or economic interdependence over the complete span of time. A long trend toward greater interdependence may be masked by two aspects of our data. First, the sample changes over time. Less developed and more peripheral states are probably underrepresented before World War I. Only with the establishment of the IMF and UN agencies does information on states' wealth and dyadic trade become reasonably complete. Thus, the average level of bilateral interdependence may be overstated in the early years. Second, decolonization in the late 1950s and the 1960s created dozens of new states that were less democratic and less integrated into the global economy than the states already in the system, lowering the average scores for democracy and interdependence. And as noted, the codings of democracy that we use overstate the democratic character of states in much of the nineteenth century before suffrage was extended to women and those without property.

Both democracy and interdependence do show a marked jump after World War II. The number of democracies has grown steadily since the late 1970s, especially after the cold war ended. Trade grew rapidly in the 1970s. Since 1987 these phenomena have been followed by a precipitous drop in the number of interstate wars, despite the entry of many new states into the system.[66] Our results for the early post–cold war years cover only 1989–92, but they indicate that the beneficial effects of democracy, interdependence, and IGOs continued past the end of the cold war. Moreover, our analyses of the 1885–1992 period suggest that the relative peace of the past decade owes less to the systemic effects of power and hegemony than to growing Kantian influences.

As for the realist influences, some of the dyadic characteristics—chiefly distance, power preponderance, and minor power status—also reduce the likelihood of disputes. This is not surprising, though the lack of a robust effect for alliances is. The Kantian influences have not abolished power politics. Realist variables at the systemic level also make a difference in the incidence of dyadic conflict. Both world wars occurred when Britain, the hegemonic state, was weak. Yet hegemony does not always work as hypothesized. During more normal periods of

[65] See the references in fnn. 17 and 19 and the textual discussion accompanying them.
[66] Monty G. Marshall, *Third World War* (Lanham, Md.: Rowman, Littlefield, 1999).

international relations, there were more militarized disputes when the hegemon was powerful than when it was weak; and when the hegemon felt threatened (as evidenced by higher military spending relative to its gross domestic product), the likelihood of disputes rose throughout the system.

Democracies fought two world wars side by side, along with some autocracies that shared their strategic interests. Was the democracies' common alignment purely a result of strategic interests? It is more likely that shared interests in democracy and economic freedom played an important role. By contrast, alliances had no systematic dispute-inhibiting influence prior to the cold war. For the post-1945 era, when a reasonably strong effect of alliances is evident, it strains belief to attribute that effect primarily to strategic interests. Of course the cold war was substantially about national security as understood by realists. But it was also about a clash of two fundamentally different political and economic systems. The governments, dominant classes, and peoples of the free-market democracies felt not only that their physical security and national independence were threatened but also that their prosperity and especially their political and economic liberties were at stake. Hence they allied with one another to preserve their common way of life.[67]

The post–cold war era is full of affirmations about the importance of democracy, freedom, and prosperity built on interdependent markets. Some may be just rhetoric, but sophisticated global economic actors understand the role that interdependence plays in their prosperity. In 1999 NATO fought a war against Serbia in the name of democracy and human rights in Europe, against a dictatorial government that did not constitute a strategic threat. In time we shall see whether peace will hold among democracies and interdependent states, but to call the democratic peace "a byproduct of a now extinct period in world politics"[68] sounds very like a premature report of its death.

Analytically, we are progressing toward a synthesis of Kantian and realist influences and of dyadic and systemic perspectives. Kant argued that three naturally occurring tendencies operate to produce a more peaceful world. Individuals desire to be free and prosperous, so democracy and trade will expand, which leads to the growth of international law and organizations to facilitate these processes. Peace, therefore,

---

[67] By controlling for states' interests, we have tried to show that the democratic peace is not an artifact of the cold war; see Oneal and Russett, "Is the Liberal Peace Just an Artifact of Cold War Interests? Assessing Recent Critiques," *International Interactions* 25, no. 3 (1999).

[68] Gowa (fn. 3), 114.

does not depend upon a moral transformation of humanity as long as even devils are self-interested and can calculate.[69] For Kant, a child of the Enlightenment, this was evidence of an ordered universe and, perhaps, of providential design. Yet he did not think that the process was mechanical or the outcome certain: reason would not always prevail, and states and individuals would not always act in conformity with their enlightened interests. Human agents must learn from experience, including that of war, and change behavior.

The current unipolar character—inevitably transitory—of our world, with no other state close to the power of the United States, provides an opportunity to build a peace based not only on military force but also on Kantian principles. Hegemony does not last forever. Consequently, democracy should be extended and deepened, the "cosmopolitan law" of commerce expanded, and international law and respect for human rights institutionalized. Kant would say this is a moral imperative.

Appendix: Variables

ALLIES: 1 if dyad members linked by defense treaty, neutrality pact, or entente
AVGDEM: average democracy score for all states in a year
AVGDEPEND: average dyadic trade to GDP ratio for all states in a year
AVGIGO: average number of dyadic shared IGO memberships
CAPRATIO: logarithm of ratio of higher to lower power capability in a dyad
DEM_H: higher democracy score in a dyad
DEM_L: lower democracy score in a dyad
$DEPEND_H$: higher dyadic trade-to-GDP ratio in a dyad
$DEPEND_L$: lower dyadic trade-to-GDP ratio in a dyad
DISPUTE: involvement in dyadic dispute
DISTANCE: logarithm of dyadic distance in miles between capitals or major ports
HEGDEF: ratio of leading state's military spending to its GDP
HEGPOWER: leading state's proportion of the capabilities of all major powers
IGO: number of international organization memberships shared by a dyad
MINORPWRS: 1 if dyad does not include a major power
NONCONTIG: 1 if dyad is not contiguous by land border or less than 150 miles of water
$RELDEM_L$: DEM_L − AVGDEM/standard deviation of DEM
$RELDEPEND_L$: $DEPEND_L$ − AVGDEPEND/standard deviation of $DEPEND_L$
RELIGO: IGO − AVGIGO/standard deviation of IGO
SATISFIED: tau-b measure of similarity of dyad members' alliance portfolios to that of the leading state

[69] Kant (fn. 1), 112.

[11]

THE HIGH POLITICS OF IMF LENDING

By STROM C. THACKER*

INTRODUCTION

CONSIDERING the degree of scrutiny given to the role of the International Monetary Fund (IMF, or Fund) in the international economy, we know little about the underlying causes of the IMF's behavior.[1] During the 1980s, the IMF became a "lender of last resort" for many developing country governments that had been cut off from private credit markets and faced destabilizing imbalances of payments. After private capital began to return voluntarily to what were called the emerging markets in the early 1990s, the anticipated erosion of the Fund's role in the developing world did not materialize. Faced with recurrent payments' imbalances, pressures for currency devaluation, and the macroeconomic instability associated with crises in Latin America, Asia, and Russia, the developing nations have turned with increasing frequency to IMF credits and stabilization plans. Despite the growing body of research on the IMF's critical role in international finance, we still have few explanations of and only patchy empirical data on why the IMF approves loans to some countries but not others. As the Fund delves further into the management of balance of payments and currency crises around the world, both theoretical and practical imperatives dictate that we specify more fully and test more systematically

*A preliminary version of this paper was presented at the 1997 annual meeting of the American Political Science Association in Washington, D.C. I would like to thank Tim McKeown, Patrick Conway, William Bernhard, Mary Matthews, Dane Rowlands, the participants in the faculty research seminar in the Department of International Relations at Boston University, and the anonymous *World Politics* referees for their insightful comments and suggestions. Yvonne Ochoa and Jaya Badiga provided able research assistance. The usual disclaimers apply.

[1] The literature on the IMF is extensive. For useful surveys, see Graham Bird, "The International Monetary Fund and the Developing Countries: A Review of the Evidence and Policy Options," *International Organization* 50, no. 3 (1996); idem, *IMF Lending to Developing Countries: Issues and Evidence* (London: Routledge, 1995); Sebastian Edwards, "The International Monetary Fund and the Developing Countries: A Critical Evaluation," NBER Working Paper, no. 2909 (1989); Tony Killick, *IMF Programs in Developing Countries: Design and Impact* (London: Routledge, 1995); John Williamson, ed., *The Lending Practices of the International Monetary Fund* (Washington, D.C.: Institute for International Economics, 1982); and idem, *IMF Conditionality* (Washington, D.C.: Institute for International Economics, 1983).

World Politics 52 (October 1999), 38–75

competing explanations of IMF behavior. What factors influence the IMF's decisions to lend? Are these decisions based on technical economic criteria, or do they reflect the political preferences of the Fund's more powerful members? What are those preferences, and how do they affect the IMF's relationship with its developing country clients? In other words, does politics matter? More importantly, *how* does politics matter?

The literature on international institutions and multilateralism suggests that the operation of multilateral economic organizations like the IMF will assume growing importance in a posthegemonic international order.[2] This body of theory raises several important questions: To what extent do multilateral institutions modify the interests or constrain the behavior of their member states? Can the more powerful states use these organizations as effective instruments of national foreign policy, or are such pressures diluted or transformed in passing through multilateral channels? Finally, what underlying political interests drive the behavior of the large powers within the multilateral institutions, and how do they do so? On the practical side, Gallarotti has shown that poorly managed international organization not only can be ineffective but also can destabilize the international system.[3] The debates surrounding proposed increases in Fund resources and recent loan packages negotiated with South Korea, Indonesia, Russia, and Brazil demonstrate the growing popular recognition of these kinds of problems, but scholarly research has yet to address these questions adequately.

Economists have made inroads in isolating the economic bases of IMF lending, but they are the first to point out that their models remain incomplete. Researchers have found statistically significant results for

[2] For effective treatments of these and related issues, see Robert O. Keohane, *After Hegemony: Cooperation and Discord in the World Political Economy* (Princeton: Princeton University Press, 1984); idem, *International Institutions and State Power: Essays in International Relations Theory* (Boulder, Colo.: Westview, 1989); idem, "Multilateralism: An Agenda for Research," *International Journal* 45, no. 1 (1990); John Gerard Ruggie, ed., *Multilateralism Matters: The Theory and Praxis of an Institutional Form* (New York: Columbia University Press, 1993); Stephen D. Krasner, ed., *International Regimes* (Ithaca, N.Y.: Cornell University Press, 1983); and Kenneth A. Oye, ed., *Cooperation under Anarchy* (Princeton: Princeton University Press, 1986).

International institutions and multilateralism are not necessarily equivalent. The IMF fits Ruggie's definition in *Multilateralism Matters* of multilateral organization as "defined by such generalized decision-making rules as voting or consensus procedures" (p. 14). On IMF decision-making procedures, see Frank Southard, "The Evolution of the International Monetary Fund," Princeton Essays in International Finance, no. 135 (1979); and Frederick K. Lister, *Decision-Making Strategies for International Organizations*, vol. 20, *World Affairs* (Denver, Colo.: Graduate School of International Studies, University of Denver, 1984).

[3] Giulio M. Gallarotti, "The Limits of International Organization: Systematic Failure in the Management of International Relations," *International Organization* 45, no. 2 (1991).

the impact of a number of economic variables on IMF lending, but the low overall explanatory power of the econometric models reviewed by Bird suggests that "there are probably a range of other non-economic factors which still need to be delineated."[4] One likely source of noneconomic factors is politics, but political scientists have not yet been able to demonstrate the systematic impact of political variables on IMF lending.[5] Several case studies offer suggestive, but not generalizable, evidence of the political bases of IMF lending. Fewer studies have attempted to construct a systematic political explanation of Fund behavior. This paper attempts to fill some of those gaps in the literature and proposes answers to those questions by developing and testing statistically a political explanation of IMF lending patterns.

The IMF's stated decision-making procedures prohibit the consideration of political factors. Loans are made strictly on the basis of the monetarist "Financial Programming" model and a "Doctrine of Economic Neutrality" that is blind to such factors as international politics and the nature of developing country regimes.[6] The Fund may impose strict lending requirements, but it applies them fairly to all countries. The meetings of the IMF executive board, which approves all Fund programs, are highly secretive.[7] The specific considerations that determine the board's deliberations and decisions are therefore not available in the public domain. For its part, the Fund staff publicly maintains the position of economic neutrality, but evidence presented in numerous case studies leaves open the possibility that political factors play an important role.

There are at least three reasons to suspect that politics matters in the IMF. First, several studies have found extremely low rates of borrower compliance with Fund conditionality, yet the IMF continues to lend to many of these problem debtors even after earlier programs have been canceled for noncompliance.[8] Finch, a former IMF staff member, suggested in the late 1980s that economic factors could not explain these

---

[4] Bird (fn. 1, 1995), 124.

[5] Dane Rowlands, "Political and Economic Determinants of IMF Conditional Credit Arrangements: 1973–1989" (Manuscript, Norman Paterson School of International Affairs, Carleton University, Ottawa, Ont., 1995).

[6] Jacques J. Polak, "Monetary Analysis of Income Formation and Payments Problems," IMF Staff Papers, no. 6 (1957), cited in Edwards (fn. 1); and idem, "The Changing Nature of IMF Conditionality," Princeton Essays in International Finance, no. 184 (1991); and Richard Swedberg, "The Doctrine of Economic Neutrality of the IMF and the World Bank," *Journal of Peace Research* 23 no. 4 (1986).

[7] R. S. Eckaus, "How the IMF Lives with Its Conditionality," *Policy Sciences* 19 (October 1986).

[8] Southard (fn. 2), 13; Edwards (fn. 1); C. David Finch, "The IMF: The Record and the Prospects," Princeton Essays in International Finance, no. 175 (1989); and John Spraos, "IMF Conditionality: Ineffectual, Inefficient, Mistargeted," Princeton Essays in International Finance, no. 166 (1986).

patterns: "Because decisions were no longer based on compatibility with repayment terms, lending was guided increasingly by the political preferences of the leading industrial countries."[9] Second, each country's representative on the Fund's executive board is appointed by his or her home government (Treasury, in the case of the United States). Thus it should come as no surprise that the positions of those representatives within the Fund reflect the political interests of the national governments they serve.[10] As Smith puts it, "The IMF is itself a political institution. It is managed by politically appointed individuals from member nations, and the political interests of its members influence its decisions."[11] Although the staff is less directly linked to national governments, the executive board must approve all proposed programs. The familiarity of Fund staff members with the preferences of the executive board discourages them from submitting loan packages that the board is likely to veto.[12]

Finally, weighted voting and the decision-making procedures of the Fund also leave room for politics. As of April 1995, the U.S. controlled 17.83 percent of the voting power in the IMF, followed by Germany and Japan with 5.5 percent each, and France and the United Kingdom with 5.0 percent each.[13] An evolving system of special majorities has helped the U.S. maintain its influence beyond that dictated by its gradually decreasing voting share.[14] An 85 percent majority is required for the most important Fund decisions, giving the U.S. alone, and other groups of countries together, veto power. The U.S. can also push through favored programs, which it might not be able to do based on its votes alone. Although the managing director has traditionally been a European, he rarely acts against U.S. preferences.[15] That is not surprising since he is appointed through a process over which the U.S. has veto power.[16] But

[9] Finch (fn. 8), 2.

[10] Lars Schoultz, "Politics, Economics, and U.S. Participation in Multilateral Development Banks," *International Organization* 36, no. 3 (1982); Benjamin J. Cohen, "International Debt and Linkage Strategies: Some Foreign Policy Implications for the United States," in Miles Kahler, ed., *The Politics of International Debt* (Ithaca, N.Y.: Cornell University Press, 1986).

[11] Fred L. Smith, "The Politics of IMF Lending," *Cato Journal* 4 (Spring/Summer 1984). The U.S. representative is "ordered by law to clear his or her decisions with the Secretary of the Treasury." Swedberg (fn. 6), 379.

[12] Kendall W. Stiles, *Negotiating Debt: The IMF Lending Process* (Boulder, Colo.: Westview, 1991).

[13] *IMF Annual Report* (Washington, D.C.: IMF, 1995), 216.

[14] See Lister (fn. 2).

[15] Samuel Lichtensztejn and Mónica Baer, *Fondo Monetario Internacional y Banco Mundial: Estrategias y Políticas del Poder Financiero* (Mexico City: Ediciones de Cultura Popular, 1987), 60–61.

[16] Miles Kahler notes that the U.S. has in the past refused to support a renewal of the managing director's tenure when his "accomplishments did not meet American expectations." Kahler, "The United States and the International Monetary Fund," in Margaret P. Karns and Karen A. Mingst, eds., *The United States and Multilateral Institutions* (Boston: Unwin Hyman, 1990), 94.

that power rarely needs to be wielded openly. The managing director typically makes decisions based on a "sense of the meeting," derived from the comments of the various participants and their relative voting power.[17] Other powers can be reluctant to speak against the U.S. for fear that the U.S. will later retaliate by exercising its veto power over their own favored programs.[18] Finally, the U.S. and its like-minded allies together can effect international monetary cooperation by forming subsets, or "k-groups," of countries to push through certain packages that single parties cannot.[19]

Given the possibility that political factors influence IMF decisions, several scholars have argued that the Fund's more powerful members manipulate it to further their own political and economic interests.[20] The U.S. government, for its part, "has repeatedly told foreign governments that it will not intervene in negotiations between the Fund and member governments."[21] Kahler notes, however, that "the U.S. (and other major countries) can still influence programs for friends and clients at the margin."[22] Others suggest that American politicization of Fund lending is more widespread. A series of case studies conducted for a project directed by Killick and Bird reveals that at least one-third of the seventeen countries studied secured favorable loan terms on their IMF programs due to the intervention of major shareholding countries on their behalf.[23] Stiles concludes that in only one of seven cases examined did the Fund adopt a politically neutral, technocratic approach to lending.[24]

Such case studies have been useful for providing the kind of rich detailed data that are unavailable by other means, for formulating testable hypotheses, and for providing initial evidence of the role of politics in IMF lending. Despite these advances, we are still unable to say much more than that politics *seems* to matter, at least in some cases. This

[17] The origins of this procedure date back to the Fund's early years, when the U.S. executive director went to great lengths to muffle the strong voice of U.S. power, which nevertheless was decisive. See Southard (fn. 2), 5–6, 19–20.

[18] Eckaus (fn. 7), 237; Stiles (fn. 12), 37.

[19] Ruggie (fn. 2), chap. 1; James A. Caporaso and Miles Kahler attribute part of the postwar economic cooperation to this type of "minilateralism." The creation of the Bretton Woods monetary order through U.S. and British coordination and the subsequent adjustments made by the G-7 after its breakdown (for example, the Plaza and Louvre accords) can be profitably understood in these terms. Caporaso, "International Relations Theory and Multilateralism: The Search for Foundations," and Kahler, "Multilateralism with Small and Large Numbers," in Ruggie (fn. 2).

[20] Cheryl Payer, *The Debt Trap: The International Monetary Fund and the Third World* (New York: Monthly Review Press, 1974); and Swedberg (fn. 6).

[21] Kahler (fn. 16), 110.

[22] Ibid.

[23] Killick (fn. 1), 118–19.

[24] Stiles (fn. 12), 196–97.

paper aims to accomplish two essential tasks. First, it attempts to provide the first systematic quantitative evidence for whether politics affects IMF behavior. Second, it proposes a dynamic explanation of how political factors affect interactions of multilateral organizations with their member states, and tests the statistical formulation of that argument in the case of the IMF. I first propose a simple macroeconomic model and a political explanation of IMF lending. I then operationalize these hypotheses together and report the results of a series of statistical tests conducted on them jointly. I conclude with a discussion of the limitations and broader implications of this research.

A SIMPLE MACROECONOMIC MODEL

Economists have isolated several important demand- and supply-side macroeconomic determinants of IMF lending. Rather than attempt to replicate such studies, I take them as a starting point for my political analysis. Conway has modeled participation in IMF programs as a function of a country's economic environment and its past economic performance.[25] He finds statistically significant negative results for lagged variables representing the ratio of foreign exchange reserves to imports, the growth rate of real gross national product, the ratio of the current account to GNP, the terms of trade, and the real rate of interest.[26] Variables capturing level of development (proxied by the share of output from the agricultural sector) and long- and short-term debt stocks did not attain conventional levels of statistical significance.

Lindert tests the impact of several variables on the interest rate charged on official creditor lending to fifty-one countries in 1985.[27] He obtained statistically significant results for only two variables—the log of absolute nominal public and publicly guaranteed debt in 1981 and the log of per capita income—each with a positive coefficient. None of the other variables—the share of debt held by official creditors, the ratio of debt service to GNP, the ratio of reserves to imports, money stock growth, prior default, prior rescheduling, and years since first rescheduling—approached conventional levels of statistical significance.

Summarizing his own and others' research, Bird identifies statistically significant regression results with negative coefficients for balance

---

[25] Patrick Conway, "IMF Lending Programs: Participation and Impact," *Journal of Development Economics* 45, no. 2 (1994).

[26] He finds statistically significant positive results for prior participation and the percentage of available funds drawn down. A series of dummy variables for each year had generally significant results.

[27] Peter H. Lindert, "Response to Debt Crisis: What Is Different about the 1980s?" in Barry J. Eichengreen and Lindert, eds., *The International Debt Crisis in Historical Perspective* (Cambridge: MIT Press, 1989).

of payments, per capita income, current account, and reserves.[28] Collectively, these studies find statistically significant positive regression coefficients for inflation, access to private bank credit,[29] domestic credit growth, and government spending. With the exception of Conway, the low predictive power of these models suggests that they are underspecified. Rather than attempt to test the validity of distinct competing macroeconomic models, this paper draws upon the large body of existing research to identify the putative economic determinants of Fund activities. First, the balance of payments position of a country is the initial baseline upon which its participation in IMF programs is evaluated. An improvement in the balance of payments is the stated primary goal of most IMF lending programs,[30] and without a payments deficit, a country should neither need nor be eligible for Fund lending.[31] When faced with a payments deficit, a country can either run down its reserves or borrow internationally.[32] In the context of the debt crisis, running down reserves was not a viable long-term solution, and the most reliable source of international borrowing was the IMF. Specifically, deterioration in the balance of payments is expected to increase the chances of receiving a loan from the IMF.

Second, a country's debt position should affect its demand for and the supply of an IMF loan for distinct reasons. On the demand side, a heavier debt burden increases developing countries' need for external finance to service that debt. In terms of supply, some have argued that the more heavily indebted countries have more bargaining leverage over the IMF because of their importance to global financial stability.[33] In addition, some view IMF loans as a payoff to foreign creditors.[34] Assuming that those lenders wield influence within the executive board, IMF loans more likely will go to countries where creditors are more heavily exposed. Lindert found that the more heavily indebted countries did receive official creditor loans, but at higher interest rates than the smaller debtors, due to the reluctance of Northern taxpayers to finance more

---

[28] Bird (fn. 1, 1995).

[29] This result supports the catalytic impact of IMF lending as providing a "seal of approval" that encourages private banks to resume lending to a country that has negotiated an agreement with the Fund. Bird (fn. 1, 1995), 122. A negative result would suggest a substitution effect between IMF and private lending.

[30] Spraos (fn. 8); and Finch (fn. 8).

[31] Bird (fn. 1, 1995), 109.

[32] Ibid., 23.

[33] See Jahangir Amuzegar, "The IMF under Fire," *Foreign Policy* 64 (Fall 1986).

[34] See Walden Bello and David Kinley, "The IMF: An Analysis of the International Monetary Fund's Role in the Third World Debt Crisis, Its Relation to Big Banks, and the Forces Influencing Its Decisions," *Multinational Monitor* 4 (1983).

concessionary terms.[35] For the purposes of this study, the fact that the larger debtors were more likely to receive loans is of primary interest.

Third, the level of per capita income of a country also may influence its ability to secure Fund assistance. Killick notes that the IMF's historically narrow focus on balance-of-payments considerations has given way in recent years to a broader view that acknowledges the relationship between the balance of payments and growth.[36] Lindert reports that official favoritism for poor countries resulted in lower interest rates on official loans, and Bird argues that poorer countries are less likely to borrow on private capital markets and therefore to have a higher relative demand for IMF loans.[37] Countries with lower per capita incomes should be more likely to request and receive a loan from the IMF.

Fourth, if the Doctrine of Economic Neutrality is followed, a poor credit history should decrease the chances of receiving a loan. After the massive defaults of the 1930s, the debtor nations were effectively cut off from credit for several years. Many have argued that we should expect similar outcomes now.[38] Specifically, past failures to uphold IMF loan requirements should make it more difficult to receive additional loans.

Finally, both neomarxist and modern political economy interpretations would suggest two additional macroeconomic indicators that should affect Fund decisions due to the influence of "low politics": the trade and investment exposure of firms based in the IMF's major principal shareholder, the U.S. Authors grouped loosely within a neomarxist (or dependency) perspective argue that capitalists in the core states, especially the U.S., dictate IMF policy at the expense of the nations of the periphery.[39] A political economist more concerned with the impact of domestic politics on foreign economic policy might also posit, without necessarily adopting the concomitant exploitation argument, that well-organized export enterprises and multinational corporations (MNCs) pressure the U.S. government to protect their interests on the executive board. Neomarxism suggests that higher levels of U.S. exposure lead to a greater likelihood of receiving an IMF loan because the attendant pol-

---

[35] Lindert (fn. 27), 245.

[36] Killick (fn. 1).

[37] Lindert (fn. 27), 243; Bird (fn. 1, 1995), 112.

[38] Barry Eichengreen has questioned the impact of the "default penalty" on future credit access. Eichengreen, "The U.S. Capital Market and Foreign Lending, 1920–1955," in Jeffrey D. Sachs, ed., *Developing Country Debt and the World Economy* (Chicago: University of Chicago Press, 1989), 247. Cf. Jonathan Eaton and Mark Gersovitz, "Debt with Potential Repudiation: Theoretical and Empirical Analysis," *Review of Economic Studies* 48 (April 1981).

[39] See E. A. Brett, "The World's View of the IMF," in Latin America Bureau, ed., *The Poverty Brokers: The IMF and Latin America* (London: Latin America Bureau, 1983); Manuel Pastor, "The Effects of IMF Programs in the Third World: Debate and Evidence from Latin America," *World Development* 15 (Fall 1987); and Swedberg (fn. 6).

icy conditionality promotes the expansion of global capitalism. A less explored, domestic-politics interpretation yields more ambiguous expectations. The inflow of foreign exchange and the restoration of international creditworthiness would be expected to benefit U.S. exporters and foreign investors, while the demand-reduction components of the typical IMF program would suggest a negative impact for these variables.[40]

HIGH POLITICS AND THE IMF

The international political aspects of IMF lending have received far less rigorous analysis. Two rudimentary strands of thought comprise this genre, but neither has been fully developed nor adequately tested. I label the first, more common strand the "political proximity" hypothesis. Simply put, political friends of the U.S. are more likely to receive loans than are its enemies. In addition to the case studies described above, Bello and Kinley argue that the U.S. disregarded the Fund's economic criteria and pressured the Fund to approve loans to politically friendly South Africa, El Salvador, and Haiti.[41] The IMF has also denied loans to economically worthy political enemies of the U.S., such as Vietnam.[42] In sum, the more closely a country aligns with the U.S., the higher the probability it will receive a loan from the IMF.

These arguments have not yet been fully developed conceptually nor thoroughly tested empirically. To illustrate an intuitive analytical foundation for this argument and to facilitate its testing, I construct a continuous voting space, scaled from 0 to 1, where 1 represents total agreement and 0 complete discord with the United States on a single broad dimension of foreign policy affinity (such affinity could be easily measured by votes in a majority-rule international voting arena, such as the United Nations General Assembly). Figure 1 is a graphic representation of this space and a schematic portrayal of the political proximity hypothesis. Countries at point A, at the far left-hand side of the voting space, have little chance of receiving a loan, while those at point C, at the far right, are much more likely to receive Fund support. Alignment near the middle, at point B, has little or no effect.

---

[40] The net effect of DFI exposure may depend on the sectoral location of the investment. If it serves primarily the domestic market, a negative result might be expected. If it serves mostly export markets, a positive result would be more likely. The impact of export exposure may depend on whether the product exported is a final consumption good (negative) or an input into the export sector (positive).

[41] Bello and Kinley (fn. 34), 14.

[42] Susumu Awanohara, "Fiscal Interdiction: U.S., Japan Block IMF Effort to Support Vietnam," *Far Eastern Economic Review*, September 28, 1989.

HIGH POLITICS OF IMF LENDING   47

A	B	C

	A	B	C
Voting scale	0	0.5	1
Impact on loan probability	(−)	(neutral)	(+)

FIGURE 1
THE POLITICAL PROXIMITY HYPOTHESIS

Despite the existence of plentiful case studies, previous research has not effectively evaluated this argument. Furthermore, several studies have documented numerous cases where U.S. "enemies" are rewarded or "friends" punished. In many instances the Fund has made loans to leftist governments, such as Manley's in Jamaica in 1979 and the East European Soviet bloc countries of Hungary, Yugoslavia, and Romania, each of which ranked among the top fifteen IMF loan recipients from 1952 to 1984.[43] This evidence seems to paint a picture of IMF lending as an apolitical technocratic process, economic neutrality at its best. But these loans may not have been justifiable on purely economic grounds, either. Assetto compares the results of a regression equation designed to predict the size of IMF loans based solely on economic criteria with the size of the actual loans received by the three East European countries to conclude that actual lending exceeded predicted lending by a significant margin.[44]

A less static interpretation of these anomalies introduces the "political movement" hypothesis, the less-developed second strand of the political argument. Movement toward or away from the U.S. on international political issues may be at least as important as the absolute political alignment of a particular country. Hinting at this idea, Horowitz asks whether the IMF should use loans to entice countries like Romania and Hungary away from the Soviet bloc.[45] This notion is consistent with the cases of Hungary, Yugoslavia, and Romania, all of whom distanced themselves politically from the Soviet Union (that is, moved closer to the U.S.). In contrast, neither Czechoslovakia nor

[43] Amuzegar (fn. 33); Valerie J. Assetto, *The Soviet Bloc in the IMF and the IBRD* (Boulder, Colo.: Westview, 1988).

[44] Ibid., 50.

[45] Irving Louis Horowitz, "The 'Rashomon Effect': Ideological Proclivities and Political Dilemmas of the IMF," in Robert J. Myers, ed., *The Political Morality of the International Monetary Fund* (New Brunswick, N.J.: Transaction Books, 1987), 96.

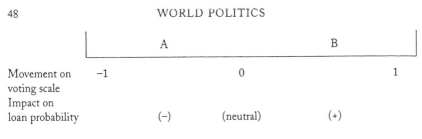

FIGURE 2

THE POLITICAL MOVEMENT HYPOTHESIS

Poland, more consistently faithful Soviet allies, received any IMF funding during this period.[46]

Frey applies Hirschman's neutrality model to formulate a model of the bilateral aid-giving process in a bipolar world where aid recipients can play the two superpower donors off one another.[47] On a more general level, McKeown models the aid relationship formally as a sequential bargaining game between the lending principal and borrower.[48] The lender exchanges aid for political realignment by a developing country toward the position of the lender. The borrower moves from its "ideal" point to a new equilibrium point where the marginal utility of additional aid received equals the domestic political loss incurred by another move away from its ideal position. I adapt and extend these central insights to hypothesize that political movement toward the U.S. increases a country's probability of receiving a loan from the IMF.

I portray the lending process as a dynamic game between each borrower and a single lender. I do not model this interaction in formal game-theoretic terms, nor do I model the relationship between the U.S. and IMF. Rather, I assume the U.S. plays the role of principal within the IMF, generate testable hypotheses about the relationship between the Fund and borrowing countries, and evaluate them empirically. If the data confirm these hypotheses, it would strongly suggest, but not directly confirm, a predominant U.S. presence in an increasingly important multilateral organization. Such a conclusion would have important implications for the study of international institutions and regimes, as well as for the multilateral management of the international economy.

[46] Assetto (fn. 43), 184.

[47] Bruno S. Frey, *International Political Economics* (London: Basil Blackwell, 1984), chap. 5; Albert O. Hirschman, "The Stability of Neutralism: A Geometrical Note," *American Economic Review* 54 (March 1964).

[48] Timothy J. McKeown, "Resolving the 'Conditionality Paradox' in U.S. Bilateral Foreign Aid" (Manuscript, University of North Carolina, Chapel Hill, n.d.).

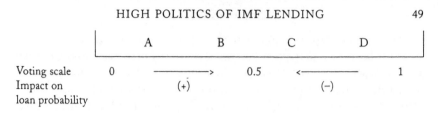

FIGURE 3
THE IMPACT OF POLITICAL MOVEMENT OVER TIME

Figure 2 captures the basic argument of the political movement hypothesis. For simplicity's sake, I present this as a linear relationship, though future research might loosen this assumption. It is based on the same 0–1 voting space. Rather than measure a country's absolute political alignment, however, it charts the change (or realignment) in that position from one time period to another. The maximum distance a country can move vis-à-vis the lender is ±1.0. Countries that make large movements toward the U.S., such as at point B, have a greater chance of receiving IMF credit than those that make movements away from the U.S., such as at point A. Figure 3 brings the spatial and temporal sides of the story together to illustrate the effect of political realignment from one voting cycle to the next. A country shifting from point A to point B has a better chance of receiving a loan than one moving from point D to point C, even though point C is still closer to the lender's position than is point B.

OPERATIONALIZATION OF THE HYPOTHESES

Because theory tells us that both economic and political factors affect IMF lending, a model that excludes either category is, by definition, misspecified. A combined political economy approach addresses one of Bird's main concerns:

> [S]ome countries may be able to muster more support amongst the membership of the Executive Board than others. The problem is that such [political] factors are difficult to model formally and include in econometric estimation, but their exclusion may explain why demand functions which rely exclusively upon economic characteristics will leave much of the story untold.[49]

It may be difficult to model and test political factors econometrically, but it is certainly possible.

[49] Bird (fn. 1, 1995), 149–50.

The analysis focuses not on the size of the loans, the interest rate, or other conditions but simply on the decision to lend. The structure of the Fund leaves more room for political factors to enter into the process of loan approval than into the formation of the terms of the loans themselves. The politically appointed executive board generally votes yes or no on a complete package that has been assembled by the staff, based largely upon market conditions and its own modeling and forecasting. Furthermore, Fund rules on confidentiality make data collection on most of the terms and conditions of loan packages impossible.[50]

This section presents the hypotheses introduced above in the form of a pooled logit model of IMF lending to eighty-seven developing countries from 1985 to 1994.[51] The dichotomous nature of the dependent variable requires the use of logit estimation, which treats the relationship between a categorical dependent variable (the probability of receiving a loan) and the continuous independent variables as a nonlinear one that approaches both 0 and 1 asymptotically.[52]

The basic logit can be expressed symbolically as:

$$\ln[(P(L = 1)_{it})/(1-(P(L = 1)_{it})] = b_0 - b_1(\text{BalPay}) + b_2(\text{Debt})$$
$$- b_3(\text{PerCapY}) - b_4(\text{Default}) + b_5(\text{USX}) + b_6(\text{USDFI})$$
$$+ b_7(\text{PolProx}) + b_8(\text{PolMove})$$

L is a dichotomous variable coded 1 if country i received an IMF Stand-by Arrangement (SBA) or Extended Fund Facility (EFF) loan during the calendar year t, 0 if it did not.[53] $P(L = 1)_{it}$ is the estimated

[50] Regressions were run on the amount of the loan divided by GNP, and the general results were similar to those reported here, particularly for the political variables.

[51] This figure represents all of the developing countries, as defined by the IMF, for which data were available. See IMF, *Annual Report* (Washington, D.C.: IMF, 1986), 162. Data for the indicator of political alignment used here are not available before 1983. For some countries, data are available only for certain years. See Appendix B for a list of countries used in the data analysis.

[52] See John H. Aldrich and Forrest D. Nelson, *Linear Probability, Logit, and Probit Models* (Beverly Hills, Calif.: Sage, 1984).

[53] Two other IMF lending programs, the Structural Adjustment Facility (SAF) and the Enhanced Structural Adjustment Facility (ESAF), are not included in this analysis for a number of reasons. First, only low-income developing countries qualify for SAF and ESAF loans. A large number of countries in the sample would therefore not qualify for these programs, while all are eligible for SBA and EFF packages. Second, the SAF and ESAF are structural adjustment rather than economic stabilization programs. To include them in the analysis would require a different underlying macroeconomic model than that specified for SABs and EFFs. Third, 1987 was the first full year of operation for the SAF and 1988 for the ESAF. Only SBA and EFF programs were operational throughout the entire time period examined here. See Polak (fn. 6, 1991); and Susan Schadler, Adam Bennett, Maria Carkovic, Louis Dicks-Mireaux, Mauro Mecagni, James H. J. Morisink, and Miguel A Savastano, "IMF Conditionality: Experience under Stand-By and Extended Arrangements. Part I: Key Issues and Findings," IMF Occasional Paper, no. 128 (1995). Compared to the number of SBAs and EEFs, there have been few SAF and ESAF loans

HIGH POLITICS OF IMF LENDING   51

probability that a country will receive a loan in year t.[54] b_0 is the intercept term. "BalPay" is the balance of payments position; "Debt" is the debt burden; "PerCapY" is per capita income; "Default" is a measure of credit history; "USX" is the amount of U.S. exports to the country; "USDFI" is the amount of U.S. direct foreign investment in the country; "PolProx" is political proximity to the U.S. in the international voting space described above; and "PolMove" is political movement toward the U.S. within the same space. The economic variables are lagged by one year and the political variables by one to two years to establish the direction of causality.

To pose a more challenging test for the political model, I isolate a number of critical macroeconomic factors expected to affect Fund behavior and select several statistical proxies for them. The balance of payments is operationalized into several different variables. BOP_{it-1} is the overall balance of payments of a country in year $t-1$.[55] ΔBOP_{it} is the change in the overall balance of payments from $t-1$ to t. $PCBOP_{it-1}$ and $\Delta PCBOP_{it}$ are per capita balance of payments and change in per capita balance of payments, respectively.[56] $CACCT_{it-1}$ is the current account, and $\Delta CACCT_{it}$ is the change in the current account. $CACCT/GNP_{it-1}$ and $\Delta CACCT/GNP_{it}$ capture the ratio of the current account to GNP and the change in that ratio.[57] Since higher payments deficits are thought to increase the chances of receiving a loan, all coefficients should be negative.

A country's debt burden is measured by the following variables: $DEBT_{it-1}$ is the level of absolute public and publicly guaranteed debt in year $t-1$, and $\Delta DEBT_{it}$ is the change in that level of debt from $t-1$ to t. $PCDEBT_{it-1}$ and $\Delta PCDEBT_{it}$ compute per capita debt figures. A se-

made. Regressions run on a variable including all of these programs together yielded results generally consistent with those reported in the following section.

[54] Logit transforms this variable, which has a nonlinear relationship to the independent variables, into the log-odds of receiving a loan, which has a linear relationship to the independent variables. The new dependent variable, or logit, is then regressed on the independent variables using maximum likelihood estimation (MLE). Data for this variable were gathered from IMF, *Annual Report* (Washington, D.C.: IMF, various issues).

[55] All economic variables except ratios are expressed in millions of 1990 U.S. dollars, using the 1990 U.S. GDP deflator reported in IMF, *International Financial Statistics Yearbook*. (Washington, D.C.: IMF, various issues).

[56] These variables make the figures for large and small countries more comparable. I also tested the ratio of balance of payments to GNP and the change in that ratio with the same substantive results. Data are from IMF, *International Financial Statistics Yearbook* (Washington, D.C.: IMF, various issues).

[57] The World Bank's debt ratios (DEBT/GNP, INT/GNP, and RES/DEBT) appear to have been multiplied by 100. To make comparisons across units consistent, I multiplied the CACCT/GNP ratios calculated from (but not listed in) World Bank data by 100. World Bank, *World Debt Tables* (Washington, D.C.: World Bank, various issues); and idem, *Global Development Finance* (Washington, D.C.: World Bank, various issues).

ries of ratios captures the debt service burden for each economy. $DEBT/GNP_{it-1}$ is the ratio of long-term total debt stocks (public and private) to GNP, and $\Delta DEBT/GNP_{it}$ tracks the change in that ratio. INT/GNP_{it-1} and $\Delta INT/GNP_{it}$ are the variables for the ratio of interest payments to GNP and its change, and $RES/DEBT_{it-1}$ and $\Delta RES/DEBT_{it}$ measure the ratio of reserves to GNP and the change in that ratio.[58] Because a heavy debt burden increases debtors' demand for loans and because the Fund is hypothesized to give greater supply consideration to the larger debtors,[59] all coefficients should be positive except those for $RES/DEBT_{it-1}$ and $\Delta RES/DEBT_{it}$, which are expected to be negative.

$PCAPY_{it-1}$ represents per capita GNP, computed from data reported in the World Bank's *World Debt Tables* and *Global Development Finance* and in the IMF's *International Financial Statistics*. Lower-income countries should be more likely to receive loans, so a negative coefficient is expected.

$DEFAULT_{it-1}$ is a dummy variable coded 1 if a country has had a prior IMF program canceled any time since 1975 (the first full year of the EFF program) through year $t-1$, 0 otherwise. Since a bad credit history should adversely affect the likelihood of future loans, its coefficient should be negative.[60]

USX_{it-1} is the level of U.S. exports to a country. According to the neomarxist hypothesis, it should be positively signed. The domestic-level political economy perspective has ambiguous expectations for the direction of this effect.[61]

$USDFI_{it-1}$ is the value of the stock of U.S. direct investment for all industries in a country. Expectations are similar to those for USX_{it-1}.[62]

The voting space depicted in Figures 1 to 3 is measured by $KVOTE_{it-2}$, an index of political agreement between country i and the U.S. in year $t-2$. Calculated as a decimal between 0 and 1, this variable measures the degree of coincidence between the votes of the sample

[58] These figures are from the World Bank, *World Debt Tables* (Washington, D.C.: World Bank, various issues); and idem, *Global Development Finance* (Washington, D.C.: World Bank, various issues); with population data taken from IMF, *International Financial Statistics Yearbook* (Washington, D.C.: IMF, various issues).

[59] Adequate data on the exposure of U.S. banks in particular countries are unavailable. In any event, the largest creditor banks are likely to be based in the U.S. and the IMF's other principal shareholder countries.

[60] A variable measuring the total number of cancellations that a country experienced from 1975 through $t-1$ did not yield statistically significant results. Data were gathered from IMF, *Annual Report* (Washington, D.C.: IMF, various issues).

[61] Data are from IMF, *Direction of Trade Statistics Yearbook* (Washington, D.C.: IMF, various issues).

[62] Data have been taken from the U.S. Department of Commerce, *Survey of Current Business*, various issues.

country and the U.S. in the United Nations General Assembly (UNGA) on the approximately ten to fifteen issues in each session that the U.S. Department of State has deemed key votes. Under Congressional mandate, the State Department has compiled the voting records of all UN member nations on these selected issues since the 1983 General Assembly in its annual publication, *Report to Congress on Voting Practices in the United Nations.*[63] Appendix A lists the key votes identified in this report for the years examined here. In accordance with the political proximity hypothesis, a positive coefficient is anticipated.[64]

Using UN voting patterns to measure international political alignment is one solution to the problem of testing political variables lamented by Bird. For its part, the U.S. government has proclaimed that examining UN votes makes it "possible to make judgments about whose values and views are harmonious with our own, whose policies are consistently opposed to ours, and whose practices fall in between."[65] But not all UN votes are equally important. In reference to the key votes, the same report states that the "only votes that can legitimately be read as a measure of support for the United States are those which we identified as important to us, and on which we lobbied other nations"[66] The validity of UNGA voting records has been debated extensively.[67] I

[63] Using these annual reports, I coded votes in agreement with the U.S. 1.0, votes in disagreement with the U.S. 0.0, and abstentions or absences by the sample country 0.5. I then added and divided these numbers by the total number of key votes each year to come up with the annual decimal measure for each country. This method differs slightly from the technique of discarding absences and abstentions from the total count of UNGA votes used in Charles W. Kegley Jr. and Steven W. Hook, "U.S. Foreign Aid and U.N. Voting: Did Reagan's Linkage Strategy Buy Deference or Defiance?" *International Studies Quarterly* 35 (September 1991). Rather than not count those nonvotes on "key" issues, I interpret them as neutral.

[64] The transmission of United States foreign policy preferences from the State Department is not necessarily direct in the case of the multilateral development banks and the IMF, where Treasury plays a critical role. See Schoultz (fn. 10). The (American) deputy managing director has typically been "a 'Treasury man,' reinforcing the close ties between that agency of the U.S. government and the IMF." Kahler (fn. 16), 94. Furthermore, Kahler argues that Treasury maintains tight control over U.S.-Fund relations and that "other agencies that might attempt to politicize the IMF for broader foreign policy goals tended to be excluded from direct access to it." Kahler (fn. 16) 94, 97. On the other hand, Joanne Gowa notes that Treasury has adopted an ordering of priorities that "subordinates the demands of the international monetary order to the imperatives of domestic economic policy and foreign security policy," suggesting some coordination—or at least compatibility—between different agencies within the executive branch. Gowa, *Closing the Gold Window: Domestic Politics and the End of Bretton Woods* (Ithaca, N.Y.: Cornell University Press, 1983). The present analysis of policy output (as opposed to interagency input) is an indirect test of these two competing hypotheses. Future work should address the interagency dynamics more directly.

[65] U.S. Department of State, *Report to Congress on Voting Practices in the United Nations* (1985), 2.

[66] Ibid., 4.

[67] See Soo Yeon Kim and Bruce Russett, "The New Politics of Voting Alignments in the United Nations General Assembly," *International Organization* 50, no. 4 (1996); Steven K. Holloway and Rodney Tomlinson, "The New World Order and the General Assembly: Bloc Realignment at the UN in the Post–Cold War World," *Canadian Journal of Political Science* 28, no. 2 (1995); Leona Pallansch and

adopt the self-identified measure of political alignment of the principal U.S. foreign policy decision-making body: UNGA key votes. There is also evidence that the State Department tracked such data in a similar manner previous to the Congressional mandate, that it considered UN votes a reliable indicator of alignment, and that the U.S. allocated aid on the basis of that alignment. In a 1964 memo to the director of the Food for Peace Program, Dick Reuter, Lansdale noted that "at critical moments in the world's recent history, the U.S. 'bought' votes subtly and indirectly to support its stand in the General Assembly. The 'buying' is in terms of U.S. assistance to the voting country."[68] Furthermore, Lansdale's analysis employed a measure of alignment similar to the current State Department use of key votes, charting only votes on cold war issues.

It also appears that at least some recipient countries take U.S. vigilance of UN voting seriously. Argentina, for example, previously a leader in the Non-Aligned Movement, modified its voting stance in the UNGA to reflect better its improved relations with the United States in the early 1990s.[69] In a 1997 interview, Carlos Escudé, a former adviser to Argentina's minister of foreign relations, revealed that "with respect to some important United Nations resolutions, there was direct contact between Argentina and the United States, and Argentina voted in a manner favorable to the United States."[70] More generally, between 1990 and 1991 Argentina altered its UN votes to move from the fourth, most anti-U.S. stance in the UN to a position similar to that of Turkey.[71]

MKVOTE$_{it-1}$ measures the movement in political alignment between the sample country and the U.S. within the voting space from

Frank Zinni Jr., "Demise of Voting Blocs in the General Assembly of the UN? A Multidimensional Scaling Analysis" (Paper presented at the annual meeting of the Southern Political Science Association, Atlanta, 1996); Brian W. Tomlin, "Measurement Validation: Lessons from the Use and Misuse of UN General Assembly Roll-Call Votes," *International Organization* 39, no. 1 (1985); and Kenneth J. Menkhaus and Charles W. Kegley Jr., "The Compliant Foreign Policy of the Dependent State Revisited: Empirical Linkages and Lessons from the Case of Somalia," *Comparative Political Studies* 21, no. 3 (1988).

[68] Ed Lansdale, "Memo Re: Long Range Impact FPF-II," April 24, 1964, National Archives, Record Group 59, Lot file 67D554, Under Secretary for Political Affairs, Records of the Special Assistant 1963–65, Box 2. I thank Tim McKeown for providing me with a transcription of this document.

[69] For example, Argentina sent troops to the 1991 Persian Gulf conflict. Carlos Escudé, "Entrevista a Escudé realizada por Lorena Kniaz" (1997), cited May 19, 1999, http://www.geocities.com/CapitolHill/Congress/4359/reporta.html.

[70] Ibid.

[71] Ibid.; Carlos Escudé, E-mail from the author, February 16, 1999.

HIGH POLITICS OF IMF LENDING 55

year *t-2* to year *t-1*, measured in UNGA key votes.[72] From the political movement hypothesis, I expect a positive coefficient.

FINDINGS AND INTERPRETATIONS

Table 1 presents the results of three different versions of the model. The combination of pooled data and a categorical dependent variable presents unique diagnostic challenges.[73] Column 1 presents the results for the basic logit model, with no correction for autocorrelation. It appears to provide a good overall fit: -2 times the log-likelihood ratio ($-2 \times$ LLR) for the model is 124.85, with p < 0.0001. We can reject the null hypothesis that none of the independent variables individually or collectively explain a significant amount of variation of the dependent variable.[74] The model correctly predicted 83.25 percent of the outcomes. In terms of individual coefficients, $PCAPY_{it-1}$ and $KVOTE_{it-2}$ are significant at the 0.90 level of confidence; BOP_{it-1} and $PCDEBT_{it-1}$ at 0.95; and $DEBT/GNP_{it-1}$, INT/GNP_{it-1}, $\Delta INT/GNP_{it}$, $RES/DEBT_{it-1}$, and $MKVOTE_{it-1}$ at 0.99; all with the anticipated signs.

To test and correct for autocorrelation, I employed the binary time-series-cross-section estimation technique formulated by Beck, Katz, and Tucker.[75] I constructed a series of nine (T–1) dummy variables coded 1 if it had been (1, 2, 3, . . . T–1) years since a country last received an IMF loan, 0 otherwise. If these nine variables collectively are significant in a log-likelihood ratio test, it is an indication of autocorrelation. The correction for autocorrelation is simply the inclusion of the temporal dummy variables in the estimation. Once corrected, the new coefficients for the original variables of interest should better satisfy the

---

[72] Because of the UNGA's voting calendar, the voting variables have a longer lag structure than the economic variables. The fact that UNGA votes are taken in the last four months of the calendar year means that there is a 67 percent chance that a given loan decision will be made before the UNGA meets in a given year. The chances that such a decision will be made before the session is complete and final votes are tallied approaches 100 percent. Conversely, movement at *t–1* occurs immediately before the next calendar year's loan cycle begins.

[73] James A. Stimson, "Regression in Space and Time: A Statistical Essay," *American Journal of Political Science* 29, no. 4 (1985); Nathaniel Beck, Jonathan N. Katz, and Richard Tucker, "Taking Time Seriously: Time-Series-Cross-Section Analysis with a Binary Dependent Variable," *American Journal Political Science* 42, no. 4 (1998).

[74] This assumes a Chi Square distribution for the $-2 \times$ LLR figure. While this assumption may not be entirely valid for individual level data, the strong results are still encouraging.

[75] Beck, Katz, and Tucker (fn. 73). This approach is designed for longitudinally dominant data with typically twenty or more time periods. The authors have not yet tested this exploratory method on shorter time periods like the one used here (T = 10). Richard Tucker, conversation with the author, August 1998. We may therefore have somewhat less confidence in a negative diagnostic for autocorrelation than in the positive one obtained here.

TABLE 1

LOGIT COEFFICIENT ESTIMATES OF IMF LENDING, 1985–94

Independent Variables	Basic Logit (1)	With Temporal Dummies (2)	Refined with Dummies (3)
BOP_{it-1}	$-1.907 \times 10^{-4**}$	$-2.091 \times 10^{-4**}$	$-1.277 \times 10^{-4***}$
	(0.911×10^{-4})	(0.926×10^{-4})	(0.583×10^{-4})
ΔBOP_{it}	-1.200×10^{-6}	1.580×10^{-6}	
	(79.600×10^{-6})	(84.000×10^{-6})	
$PCBOP_{it-1}$	6.642×10^{-4}	8.886×10^{-4}	
	(17.944×10^{-4})	(18.001×10^{-4})	
$\Delta PCBOPt_{it}$	-7.526×10^{-4}	-9.787×10^{-4}	
	(18.621×10^{-4})	(19.023×10^{-4})	
$CACCT_{it-1}$	-1.089×10^{-4}	-1.252×10^{-4}	
	$(.956 \times 10^{-4})$	(0.974×10^{-4})	
$\Delta CACCT_{it}$	0.920×10^{-4}	1.192×10^{-4}	$1.453 \times 10^{-4**}$
	(0.976×10^{-4})	(1.031×10^{-4})	(0.632×10^{-4})
$CACCT/GNP_{it-1}$	-0.020	-0.022	$-3.506*$
	(0.026)	(0.027)	(2.044)
$\Delta CACCT/GNP_{it}$	0.002	0.003	
	(0.024)	(0.025)	
$DEBT_{it-1}$	-2.400×10^{-6}	-6.600×10^{-6}	
	(11.000×10^{-6})	(11.400×10^{-6})	
$\Delta DEBT_{it}$	-3.320×10^{-5}	-4.760×10^{-5}	
	(6.63×10^{-5})	(6.730×10^{-5})	
$PCDEBT_{it-1}$	$9.960 \times 10^{-4***}$	$8.726 \times 10^{-4*}$	$8.319 \times 10^{-4*}$
	(4.58×10^{-4})	(4.655×10^{-4})	(4.340×10^{-4})
$\Delta PCDEBT_{it}$	5.641×10^{-4}	1.525×10^{-4}	
	(12.84×10^{-4})	(13.253×10^{-4})	
$DEBT/GNP_{it-1}$	$-0.011***$	$-0.010***$	$-0.010***$
	(0.003)	(0.003)	(0.003)
$\Delta DEBT/GNP_{it}$	0.001	0.002	
	(0.003)	(0.004)	
INT/GNP_{it-1}	$0.284***$	$0.274***$	$0.267***$
	(0.065)	(0.069)	(0.065)
$\Delta INT/GNP_{it}$	$0.503***$	$0.519***$	$0.516***$
	(0.100)	(0.102)	(0.099)
$RES/DEBT_{it-1}$	$-0.026***$	$-0.027***$	$-0.024**$
	(0.010)	(0.010)	(0.010)
$\Delta RES/DEBT_{it}$	-4.541×10^{-4}	10.000×10^{-4}	
	(0.021)	(0.022)	
$PCAPY_{it-1}$	$-3.638 \times 10^{-4*}$	-3.074×10^{-4}	$-3.453 \times 10^{-4*}$
	(02.112×10^{-4})	(2.122×10^{-4})	(2.052×10^{-4})
$DEFAULT_{it-1}$	$0.394*$	$0.412*$	$0.467**$
	(0.231)	(0.238)	(0.226)
USX_{it-1}	-4.800×10^{-6}	-2.500×10^{-6}	
	(65.300×10^{-6})	(67.300×10^{-6})	

continued overleaf

TABLE 1 *(cont.)*

Independent Variables	Basic Logit (1)	With Temporal Dummies (2)	Refined with Dummies (3)
USDFI$_{it-1}$	-9.940×10^{-5}	-8.870×10^{-5}	
	(8.800×10^{-5})	(8.880×10^{-5})	
KVOTE$_{it-2}$	1.247*	1.004	0.898
	(0.716)	(0.728)	(0.677)
MKVOTE$_{it-1}$	2.756***	2.858***	2.711***
	(0.795)	(0.856)	(0.827)
Intercept	-2.294***	-2.243***	-2.247***
	(0.476)	(0.522)	(0.490)
Correctly predicted (%)	83.25	82.98	82.98
Model χ^2	124.85	145.03	140.14
p-value	p < 0.0001	p < 0.0001	p < 0.0001
	24 d.f.	33 d.f.	21 d.f.

N = 746. Standard errors are in parentheses below the estimates. Coefficients for temporal dummies not reported.

  * Significant at p ≤ 0.10 level.
  ** Significant at p ≤ 0.05 level.
  *** Significant at p ≤ 0.01

assumption of error independence. This test revealed a high likelihood of autocorrelation (log-likelihood ratio = 20.18 with 9 d.f., p < 0.025). Columns 2 and 3 in Table 1 report the results of the full model and a more refined model correcting for autocorrelation.

Tests were also conducted for multicollinearity and heteroskedasticity. Neither revealed any indications of problems. Despite the presence of a large number of potentially overlapping economic variables, none of the variables in the model exhibited high degrees of collinearity with the other variables (either collectively or individually). To test for heteroskedasticity, I incorporated a variable for GNP to test the impact of country size and a series of eight dummy variables to capture the effect of geographic region. The results of these tests did not approach conventional levels of statistical significance, so I retained the assumption of homoskedasticity.

The parameter estimates of the corrected full model (Column 2) yield several interesting, albeit tentative, findings. The only significant balance of payments variable is the overall balance, BOP$_{it-1}$. As expected, its coefficient is negatively signed, suggesting that a country with an extra $100 million payments deficit increases its log-odds of receiving an IMF loan by about 0.02. The insignificant findings for the current account differ from others' results.[76] Controlling for the overall balance, the current account does not seem to matter. Similarly, with the current account controlled for, the negative impact of the balance of payments supports the argument that there is a substitution effect between IMF lending and other foreign capital inflows. Foreign capital inflows (an improvement in the balance of payments) in the year prior to the lending period lower the log-odds of receiving a loan from the IMF.

Several demand-side debt indicators were statistically significant.[77] In particular, the ratio of interest payments to GNP and the change in that ratio seem to have a strong positive impact on the log-odds of receiving a loan. The coefficients for the supply-side aggregate debt indicators $DEBT_{it-1}$ and $\Delta DEBT_{it}$ were not significant. These findings generally confirm the importance of debt in the borrowers' demand functions. They do not, however, support the argument that the IMF gives special treatment to large debtors, either because of their importance to global financial stability or as a payoff to the large creditor banks whose holdings may increase in value if an IMF loan is granted. Special treatment received by any particular debtors may be better explained by political factors than by their position in the international financial system or their relationship with creditor banks. This is a particularly interesting finding in light of the controversies surrounding the U.S.- and IMF-sponsored bailout packages in 1995 in Mexico and in 1997 and 1998 in Asia and Russia.[78]

Per capita income behaves as expected but is no longer significant in the corrected model ($p < 0.1475$). A country's history of default with the IMF is significant at the 0.90 level, but carries a positive sign. This contradicts the notion that economic neutrality drives Fund lending and confirms the pattern of recidivism observed by others.[79] Having had a previous IMF program canceled increases the log-odds of receiv-

[76] Conway (fn. 25).

[77] Per capita debt reached the 0.90 level of confidence, and the following variables attained the 0.99 level: the debt to GNP ratio, the interest to GNP ratio, the change in the interest to GNP ratio, and the ratio of reserves to debt. Curiously, the coefficient for debt to GNP is negative (all others are correctly signed). I have no explanation for this anomalous result, except to surmise that the impact of high relative levels of debt may be sensitive to the burden of repayment as captured by the interest to GNP ratio.

[78] On the Mexican crisis, see Riordan Roett, "The Mexican Devaluation and the U.S. Response: Potomac Politics, 1995-Style," in Roett, ed., *The Mexican Peso Crisis: International Perspectives* (Boulder, Colo.: Lynne Rienner, 1996).

[79] Bird (fn. 1, 1995).

HIGH POLITICS OF IMF LENDING 59

ing a new loan by 0.41.[80] The coefficients for U.S. exports and U.S. direct foreign investment do not attain statistical significance at conventional levels.[81] The neomarxist hypothesis is therefore not confirmed by these data. The potentially mixed interests of U.S. exporters and investors described above makes the domestic politics argument more difficult to assess. Some of the positive and negative impact of exports and investments in different sectors of the economy (for example, traded vs. nontraded, export vs. import competing, consumption vs. intermediate goods) would be expected to work at cross purposes to yield statistically insignificant results overall. Subtler model specification and future research may help clarify these issues.

Both political variables carry the correct sign, but the political proximity hypothesis is not confirmed in the serially corrected model (p < 0.1682). The results for the political movement hypothesis are strongly positive and significant at the 0.99 level. A movement toward the U.S. along the 0–1 UNGA key-vote continuum of 0.10 (for example, switching one vote out of ten) raises the log-odds of receiving a loan by 0.29. Politics does matter but not in the manner typically argued. These data suggest that movement toward the U.S. within the political space portrayed in this paper influences IMF decisions regardless of absolute alignment position. Additionally, the effects of these variables are robust to changes in the specification of the underlying macroeconomic model. I do not report the intermediate results here, but the addition and deletion of various economic variables had little effect on the parameter estimates or the standard errors of the political variables (see Table 1, Columns 2 and 3).

I added an interactive political variable, $KVOTE_{it-2}*MKVOTE_{it-1}$, in an attempt to capture some of the potential nonlinear effects of realignment by testing the hypothesis that the impact of a change in political alignment by a country is dependent on that country's starting position. A given movement toward the U.S. by an already tight American ally, whose allegiance is unquestioned by the American government, may not increase the probability of receiving a loan as much as the same degree of movement by a more politically distant country. Expectations for the interactive term were tentative, but a negative coeffi-

---

[80] This result may be spurious. Bird suggests that requesting a loan from the IMF has a threshold effect; once a country requests one loan, it is more likely to request additional loans. Since any country that has a loan canceled has already crossed this threshold, it may be more likely to receive loans in the future. Bird (fn. 1, 1995).

[81] Regressions were also run using each variable without the other, yielding similar negative results.

cient would be consistent with this discussion. I do not report those results here, but the coefficient for this variable was not significant at conventional levels and positively signed.[82] The data suggest that the impact of movement toward the U.S. is consistent across different starting points. This supports the argument depicted in Figure 3 that realignment toward the U.S. improves a country's chances of receiving a loan regardless of the starting position.

Table 1, Column 3, presents the results of a refined statistical model, which largely confirm the above interpretations with the exception of the current account and per capita income variables. I constructed this model by sequentially deleting any previously nonsignificant variables and conducting a series of log-likelihood ratio tests to determine if their inclusion significantly improved the overall fit of the model. With the exception of $KVOTE_{it-2}$, which I retained because of its intrinsic interest, I omitted all variables not meeting these criteria from the refined model.[83] The overall current account balance still does not seem to matter, but its improvement or decline and its weight in the economy do. We detect some impact for the current account by eliminating some potentially overlapping variables.[84] Per capita income is negatively signed and significant at the 0.90 level, a modest improvement from the full model.

Because the logit model is nonlinear, the relative effect of any single variable depends on the value of all the independent variables, which determine where on the curve an estimate lies. To make the parameter estimates more readily interpretable, Table 2 uses the refined model results to illustrate the impact of different values of political realignment on the probability of receiving a loan from the IMF in the hypothetical case where the values of all other independent variables in the model are set at their means. Two clear patterns emerge. First, even if we assume that absolute alignment position matters, a political realignment has a much stronger impact on the probability of receiving an IMF lend-

---

[82] There was a possible collinearity problem with this variable. Specifically, it correlated strongly with $MKVOTE_{it-1}$. Because the inclusion of the interactive term is likely to have inflated the standard error of the movement variable and because its inclusion did not significantly improve the model's fit, I did not retain it.

[83] Because of the potential for omitted variable bias and the negative diagnostic for multicollinearity in the original specification, I have greater confidence in the results of the full model. I therefore present the refined model results for the interested reader but focus most of the substantive interpretations on the full model.

[84] The change in the current account from *t–1* to t is significant at the 0.95 level, and the ratio of the current account to GNP is significant at the 0.90 level. The unexpectedly positive coefficient for the change in the current account from *t–1* to t could be due to the fact that an IMF loan at time *t* can itself cause an improvement in the balance of payments at time *t*.

HIGH POLITICS OF IMF LENDING 61

TABLE 2
THE EFFECT OF POLITICAL REALIGNMENT ON IMF LENDING[a]

	Original Position	New Position	Loan Probability
1.	0.0	0.0	0.065
2.	0.0	0.25	0.121
3.	0.0	0.50	0.213
4.	0.0	0.75	0.348
5.	0.0	1.0	0.513
6.	0.50	0.0	0.027
7.	0.50	0.25	0.053
8.	0.50	0.50	0.099
9.	0.50	0.75	0.178
10.	0.50	1.0	0.298
11.	1.0	0.0	0.011
12.	1.0	0.25	0.022
13.	1.0	0.50	0.042
14.	1.0	0.75	0.080
15.	1.0	1.0	0.147

Moments: $KVOTE_{it-2}$: mean = 0.5156, standard deviation = 0.1857;
$MKVOTE_{it-j}$: mean = 0.0082, standard deviation = 0.1555
[a] All other variables from Table 1, Column 3, held at their means.

ing package than the starting position.[85] Second, the patterns revealed in Table 2 are consistent with the scenario portrayed in Figure 3. A distant country that starts out at a key-vote index score of 0.0 and moves to 0.25 has a much better chance (p = 0.121) of receiving a loan than a country that moves away from perfect alignment with the U.S. (1.0) to a point (0.75) that is still much closer to the U.S. (p = 0.080) (Table 2, Lines 2 and 14). In fact, a country moving from discord to neutrality has a higher loan probability (p = 0.213) than a country that starts out and then remains in perfect alignment (p = 0.147) (Table 2, Lines 3 and 15).

Killick raises the possibility that changes in the structure of the international system alter the political dynamics treated here. Specifically, he suggests that the end of the cold war may dilute the effect of international politics on IMF behavior.[86] If no single power (for example, the USSR) lies at the other end of the 0–1 voting space, does the U.S. still reward political movement? *Does politics matter less after the cold war?*

[85] I retained absolute alignment position here to facilitate a clearer comparison of the hypothetical scenarios and to create more difficult conditions for demonstrating the strength of the impact of political realignment. Omitting $KVOTE_{it-2}$ would lower the probability for the static U.S. ally even more, relative to any country moving toward the U.S.
[86] Killick (fn. 1), 128.

TABLE 3
LOGIT COEFFICIENT ESTIMATES OF IMF LENDING, 1985–89 AND 1990–94

Independent Variables	Cold War (1)	Post–Cold War (2)	Cold War Refined (3)	Post–Cold War Refined (4)
BOP_{it-1}	-4.072×10^{-4}**	-1.08×10^{-4}	-4.331×10^{-4}**	-0.931×10^{-4}
	(1.736×10^{-4})	(1.623×10^{-4})	(1.72×10^{-4})	(1.596×10^{-4})
ΔBOP_{it}	-2.273×10^{-4}	-0.166×10^{-4}	-2.784×10^{-4}**	0.304×10^{-4}
	(1.468×10^{-4})	(1.378×10^{-4})	(1.317×10^{-4})	(1.235×10^{-4})
$PCBOP_{it-1}$	0.004	3.88×10^{-4}	0.005*	-2.057×10^{-4}
	(0.003)	(28.569×10^{-4})	(0.003)	(24.936×10^{-4})
$\Delta PCBOPt_{it}$	-0.002	0.002		
	(0.003)	(0.003)		
$CACCT_{it-1}$	-2.776×10^{-4}	-0.535×10^{-4}	-2.880×10^{-4}	-0.572×10^{-4}
	(1.855×10^{-4})	(1.529×10^{-4})	(1.777×10^{-4})	(1.523×10^{-4})
$\Delta CACCT_{it}$	3.040×10^{-4}	0.193×10^{-4}	3.023×10^{-4}	0.031×10^{-4}
	(1.857×10^{-4})	(1.311×10^{-4})	(1.844×10^{-4})	(1.274×10^{-4})
$CACCT/ GNP_{it-1}$	-0.046	-0.013	-0.054	-0.011
	(0.039)	(0.044)	(0.036)	(0.044)
$\Delta CACCT/ GNP_{it}$	-0.031	0.045	-0.042	0.053
	(0.035)	(0.043)	(0.031)	(0.042)
$DEBT_{it-1}$	-1.93×10^{-5}	2.144×10^{-5}	-2.110×10^{-5}	1.976×10^{-5}
	(2.12×10^{-5})	(1.62×10^{-5})	(2.13×10^{-5})	(1.61×10^{-5})
$\Delta DEBT_{it}$	-1.639×10^{-4}	0.856×10^{-4}	-1.591×10^{-4}*	0.875×10^{-4}
	(1.035×10^{-4})	(1.602×10^{-4})	(0.945×10^{-4})	(1.504×10^{-4})
$PCDEBT_{it-1}$	1.577×10^{-4}	0.002**	1.205×10^{-4}	0.002**
	(7.045×10^{-4})	(0.001)	(6.823×10^{-4})	(0.001)
$\Delta PCDEBT_{it}$	2.425×10^{-4}	0.001		
	(19.369×10^{-4})	(0.002)		
$DEBT/GNP_{it-1}$	-0.007	-0.016**	-0.007	-0.016**
	(0.005)	(0.005)	(0.005)	(0.005)
$\Delta DEBT/GNP_{it}$	-6.81×10^{-5}	0.001		
	(417.55×10^{-5})	(0.012)		
INT/GNP_{it-1}	0.362**	0.183	0.363***	0.197
	(0.094)	(0.142)	(0.092)	(0.135)
$\Delta INT/GNP_{it}$	0.530**	0.646**	0.530**	0.655***
	(0.153)	(0.184)	(0.151)	(0.173)
$RES/DEBT_{it-1}$	-0.056**	-0.009	-0.052**	-0.009
	(0.019)	(0.012)	(0.017)	(0.012)
$\Delta RES/DEBT_{it}$	-0.022	0.020		
	(0.044)	(0.028)		
$PCAPY_{it-1}$	-1.753×10^{-4}	-7.171×10^{-4}**	-1.288×10^{-4}	-7.021×10^{-4}**
	(3.345×10^{-4})	(3.188×10^{-4})	(3.096×10^{-4})	(3.16×10^{-4})
$DEFAULT_{it-1}$	0.447	0.345	0.438	0.350
	(0.322)	(0.404)	(0.320)	(0.400)

continued overleaf

HIGH POLITICS OF IMF LENDING   63

TABLE 3 *(cont.)*

Independent Variables	Cold War (1)	Post–Cold War (2)	Cold War Refined (3)	Post–Cold War Refined (4)
USX_{it-1}	1.757×10^{-4}	-1.041×10^{-4}	1.841×10^{-4}	-1.099×10^{-4}
	(1.141×10^{-4})	(1.508×10^{-4})	(1.131×10^{-4})	(1.528×10^{-4})
USDFI_{it-1}	-2.848×10^{-4}	-0.395×10^{-4}	-2.901×10^{-4}	-0.344×10^{-4}
	(1.972×10^{-4})	(1.036×10^{-4})	(1.997×10^{-4})	(1.02×10^{-4})
KVOTE_{it-2}	0.599	3.115¨	0.566	2.967¨
	(0.955)	(1.510)	(0.951)	(1.488)
MKVOTE_{it-1}	3.609¨	4.333¨	3.551¨	4.192¨
	(1.492)	(1.401)	(1.485)	(1.363)
Intercept	−1.949¨	−3.570¨	−2.008¨	−3.468¨
	(0.730)	(0.928)	(0.728)	(0.911)
Correctly predicted (%)	81.17	88.10	80.66	88.10
Model χ^2	96.75	72.04	95.81	70.64
p-value	p < 0.0001	p < 0.0001	p < 0.0001	p < 0.0001
	28 d.f.	28 d.f.	24 d.f.	24 d.f.

N = 393 for cold war, N = 353 for post–cold war. Standard errors are in parentheses below the estimates. All specifications include temporal dummy variables (coefficients not reported).
˙ Significant at $p \leq 0.10$ level.
¨ Significant at $p \leq 0.05$ level.
‥ Significant at $p \leq 0.01$ level.

Table 3 presents the full and slightly refined results (using the same re-fining technique as above) of separate analyses for the 1985–89 and 1990–94 periods. The model provides a good fit for each of the two subsamples, with $-2 \times \text{LLR}$ for all four scenarios yielding p < 0.0001. The model had a higher success rate in predicting outcomes in the second period, correctly predicting 88 percent of the outcomes in both the full and restricted versions versus approximately 81 percent in both specifications for the first period.

The underlying macroeconomic models appear to differ slightly for the two periods. Balance of payments considerations have a greater impact during the cold war years (Table 3, Columns 1 and 3). The overall balance is correctly signed and significant at the 0.95 level. In the refined model, the change in the balance of payments is also significant at the 0.95 level and correctly signed. The coefficients for the current account and the change in the current account approach but do not quite attain statistical significance at the 0.90 level in both cold war specifications. No balance of payments variables even approach statistical significance in the post–cold war period (Table 3, Columns 2 and 4). The relevant debt indicators for each subsample differ slightly, but both periods generally confirm the borrower need hypothesis with the exception of the incorrectly signed debt-to-GNP coefficient. The results for per capita income help clarify the ambiguous results for this variable in the full sample specifications by suggesting that while per capita GNP did not affect IMF decisions during the cold war, it has become more important in the post–cold war period. That confirms an apparent trend toward placing greater emphasis on economic growth in formulating IMF programs in recent years.[87] The default variable does not reach statistical significance in either period, possibly due to the smaller sample size. Again, the economic neutrality hypothesis is not confirmed. Finally, U.S. exports and U.S. direct foreign investment are not statistically significant in either subsample, though the USX_{it-1} variable comes reasonably close to attaining 90 percent confidence in the cold war period.

The differences between the impact of the economic variables across the two samples imply two tentative conclusions. First, similar models may produce divergent results if they are tested on different time periods. This may help explain the contradictory results of several seemingly similar econometric studies. Second, splitting larger time series into subsamples may be one good way to compare competing macroeconomic models and to chart their evolution over time.

The impact of politics also varies across the two subsamples but not in the way Killick anticipates. If anything, these results suggest that politics may be *more* important now than ever. The manner in which the U.S. treats its allies and potential allies within the Fund seems to have changed in important ways since 1990. The coefficient for alignment position does not approach statistical significance in the 1985–89 period, but movement is positively signed and statistically significant. Based on this sample, the U.S. appears to have been playing a cold war game of encouraging movement toward it without regard for original alignment position.

Since the end of the cold war, however, both alignment position and movement are statistically significant and positively signed. This suggests that the U.S. is both playing the realignment game as vigorously as ever and is rewarding the allegiance of those who stay close without necessarily moving any closer. Once a country reaches perfect agreement with the U.S., it cannot move any closer. These results imply that

---

[87] Killick (fn. 1).

during the cold war such a country would have had to move away from the U.S. and then back toward it to secure favorable treatment from the IMF. By rewarding such behavior, the United States may have encouraged countries to move toward the median voting position in the UN. Countries might also employ dual tactics of backscratching and blackmail to parlay political realignments and potential realignments into material gains.[88] Such maneuverings may no longer be necessary for close U.S. allies in the post–cold war period. More generally, these results suggest that the ability of the U.S. to influence IMF behavior to achieve its own political goals has not eroded. These goals may have simply shifted according to changes in the structure of the international system, and the U.S. still seems willing and able to exercise its weight within the executive board of the IMF to pursue them. The case of the IMF suggests that multilateralism, while useful for facilitating cooperation among a small number of like-minded states, may not be an effective buffer of U.S. power in the modern global political economy.

LIMITATIONS

This section highlights some of the limitations of this study's approach and data analysis with an eye toward future research. First and foremost, does voting in the UN General Assembly really matter, even on issues that the U.S. has deemed important? The UN itself has little power, and measures adopted within the UNGA in particular (as opposed to the Security Council) are largely symbolic.[89] In a similar vein, this study does not distinguish between countries according to their strategic and domestic characteristics. It could be argued that UN voting patterns are just a proxy for more fundamental variables. In particular, as countries democratize and open their economies to market forces, they may also be likely to alter their UN votes to reflect these underlying political and economic changes. The United States and IMF may be rewarding the political and economic shifts themselves, rather than the reflection of those shifts within the UNGA. This line of thinking is not necessarily inconsistent with the argument of this paper, but it merits further consideration. In fact, if UN voting does capture these more fundamental characteristics of countries, then it could be a very useful summary measure of them. I ran several new regressions to address these concerns empirically. I included commercial energy produc-

---

[88] See McKeown (fn. 48).

[89] Only one developing country (China) is a permanent member of the Security Council, so we cannot use Security Council votes to measure alignment.

tion (ENERGY$_{it-1}$) as a measure of strategic importance to explain why the U.S. might treat some countries differently from others. Measures of money supply (M/GDP$_{it-1}$), money supply growth (MGROW$_{it-1}$), budget deficits (DEFICIT$_{it-1}$), and trade openness (OPEN$_{it-1}$ = export plus imports, divided by GNP) captured the relative degree of "economic freedom."[90] Finally, several indicators of democracy, including the Polity III democracy (DEM$_{it-1}$) and authoritarianism (AUTH$_{it-1}$) scores and the Freedom House rankings on political rights (PR$_{it-1}$) and civil liberties (CL$_{it-1}$), helped assess the impact of regime type and democratization (change in regime type from one year to the next). Table 4 presents these results. Interestingly, none of these new variables yielded statistically significant results, and their inclusion in the estimation did not significantly alter the effects of the voting variables.[91] In sum, the model presented here appears robust to the inclusion of these factors.

Second, I have kept the underlying macroeconomic model as broad and simple as possible. This makes a direct comparison of theoretically distinct macroeconomic models more difficult, but the inclusion of a large number and wide range of economic variables raises the level of confidence in the statistical significance of the results obtained for the political variables, my more immediate concern. Further refinement or inclusion of additional economic variables could be undertaken if justified by other research.

Third, this paper treats the IMF essentially as an instrument of the U.S. government to test indirectly the proposition that relatively straightforward power considerations help explain the behavior of multilateral economic organizations. But the more powerful Fund members are likely to agree on many UNGA votes. Multidimensional scaling analyses conducted by Pallansch and Zinni suggest that the UNGA voting patterns of the G-7 countries tend to congregate together in a Euclidian space.[92] Future work should explore internal executive board politics and expand the focus to include Germany, Japan, France, and the United Kingdom. An approach centered around the formation and operation of subsets, or "k-groups," of countries within the organiza-

---

[90] Data from World Bank, *World Development Indicators 1998* (Washington, D.C.: World Bank, various issues); idem, *World Debt Tables* (Washington, D.C.: World Bank, various issues); and idem, *World Bank Global Development Finance* (Washington, D.C.; World Bank, various issues).

[91] The results for some of the economic variables differ from those in Table 1. Given the smaller number of cases used in Table 4 (a result of data availability), I base my substantive interpretations on the results presented in Tables 1 and 3. Several intermediate and refined specifications yielded similar results.

[92] Pallansch and Zinni (fn. 67).

tion could lead to a more complex specification of intraorganizational politics.[93]

Fourth, more careful consideration of the possible impact of U.S. domestic politics would help clarify and respecify those aspects of the problem. Specifically, the influence of domestic interest groups (for example, exporters and foreign investors) and the relations between different government agencies (particularly State and Treasury) merit further attention. Finally, I do not test directly for the impact of a country's past agreements with the IMF, nor do I exclude cases from the data sample that already have a program in effect. The former is partially captured by the default variable. The latter is much less of a problem than it appears because loans are often canceled and immediately replaced, suggesting that having a program in effect at a given moment does not exclude a country from the eligible sample.

IMPLICATIONS

This paper has two central goals: 1) to determine the degree to which high politics affects IMF lending patterns; and 2) to develop and test a more precise and more general explanation of *how* high politics influences the behavior of multilateral organizations. Most researchers of the politics of IMF lending argue that the U.S. punishes enemies and rewards friends via its influence within the Fund's executive board. Those who introduce a somewhat greater degree of complexity do not adequately develop nor test the dynamic impact of international political realignment. Previous research on foreign aid more generally has attempted but generally failed to find a statistically significant relationship between aid flows and political conditionality.[94] This paper provides the first systematic evidence that politics does affect IMF lending, and its conceptual framework and statistical analysis demonstrate the political factors that are most important, the mechanisms through which they influence Fund behavior, and the more general relationship between multilateral organizations and their member states. The results obtained here show that movement toward the United States within a defined international political space (like that measured by UN voting patterns) can significantly increase a country's chances of receiving a loan from the IMF. This suggests that the U.S. has been more concerned with attracting new allies and punishing defectors than reward-

[93] Ruggie (fn. 2).
[94] See McKeown (fn. 48).

TABLE 4
LOGIT COEFFICIENT ESTIMATES WITH CONTROL VARIABLES, 1985–94

Independent Variables	Using Polity III Measures (1)	Using Freedom House Measures (2)
BOP_{it-1}	-1.201×10^{-4}	-1.041×10^{-4}
	(1.184×10^{-4})	(1.192×10^{-4})
ΔBOP_{it}	6.235×10^{-5}	7.452×10^{-5}
	(11.02×10^{-5})	(11.19×10^{-5})
$PCBOP_{it-1}$	-0.002	-0.002
	(0.003)	(0.003)
$\Delta PCBOP_{it}$	-0.003	-0.003
	(0.003)	(0.003)
$CACCT_{it-1}$	9.496×10^{-5}	9.373×10^{-5}
	(13.09×10^{-5})	(13.14×10^{-5})
$\Delta CACCT_{it}$	2.163×10^{-4}	2.052×10^{-4}
	(1.332×10^{-4})	(11.327×10^{-4})
$CACCT/GNP_{it-1}$	$-0.082^{\cdot}$	$-0.089^{\cdot}$
	(0.049)	(0.049)
$\Delta CACCT/GNP_{it}$	-0.020	-0.021
	(0.043)	(0.043)
$DEBT_{it-1}$	1.933×10^{-5}	2.475×10^{-5}
	(2.01×10^{-5})	(2.00×10^{-5})
$\Delta DEBT_{it}$	-3.45×10^{-5}	-2.97×10^{-5}
	(8.35×10^{-5})	(8.21×10^{-5})
$PCDEBT_{it-1}$	0.001	$0.002^{\cdot}$
	(0.001)	(0.001)
$\Delta PCDEBT_{it}$	0.001	0.001
	(0.002)	(0.002)
$DEBT/GNP_{it-1}$	-0.014^{--}	-0.016^{--}
	(0.005)	(0.005)
$\Delta DEBT/GNP_{it}$	9.460×10^{-4}	6.491×10^{-4}
	(62.071×10^{-4})	(61.295×10^{-4})
INT/GNP_{it-1}	0.168	0.153
	(0.107)	(0.106)
$\Delta INT/GNP_{it}$	0.642^{--}	0.663^{--}
	(0.160)	(0.160)
$RES/DEBT_{it-1}$	$-0.030^{\cdot}$	$-0.026^{\cdot}$
	(0.018)	(0.017)
$\Delta RES/DEBT_{it}$	-0.026	-0.022
	(0.035)	(0.035)
$PCAPY_{it-1}$	$-4.716 \times 10^{-4\cdot}$	$-6.376 \times 10^{-4\cdot}$
	(4.072×10^{-4})	(3.833×10^{-4})
$DEFAULT_{it-1}$	$0.653^{\cdot}$	$0.684^{\cdot}$
	(0.361)	(0.364)
USX_{it-1}	1.079×10^{-4}	1.09×10^{-4}
	(0.928×10^{-4})	(0.897×10^{-4})

continued overleaf

TABLE 4 (cont.)

Independent Variables	Using Polity III Measures (1)	Using Freedom House Measures (2)
USDFI $_{it-1}$	-1.328×10^{-4}	-1.452×10^{-4}
	(1.03×10^{-4})	(1.037×10^{-4})
KVOTE $_{it-2}$	1.095	1.350
	(1.209)	(1.203)
MKVOTE $_{it-1}$	4.138***	4.464***
	(1.270)	(1.265)
ENERGY $_{it-1}$	-1.11×10^{-5}	-1.13×10^{-5}
	(0.86×10^{-5})	(0.85×10^{-5})
M/GDP $_{it-1}$	0.017	0.015
	(0.012)	(0.011)
MGROW $_{it-1}$	-1.032×10^{-4}	-0.715×10^{-4}
	(3.026×10^{-4})	(3.033×10^{-4})
DEFICIT $_{it-1}$	0.062	0.062
	(0.050)	(0.050)
OPEN $_{it-1}$	-0.538	-0.490
	(0.694)	(0.688)
DEM $_{it-1}$	-0.033	
	(0.103)	
AUTH $_{it-1}$	-0.055	
	(0.123)	
PR $_{it-1}$		0.099
		(0.168)
CL $_{it-1}$		-0.134
		(0.214)
Intercept	-2.253^{*}	-2.533^{**}
	(1.247)	(1.170)
Correctly predicted (%)	83.72	84.84
Model χ^2	99.94	106.79
p-value	p < 0.0001	p < 0.0001
	40 d.f.	40 d.f.

N = 436 for Column 1, N = 455 for Column 2. Standard errors are in parentheses below the estimates. Both specifications include temporal dummy variables (coefficients not reported).

  * Significant at $p \leq 0.10$ level.
  ** Significant at $p \leq 0.05$ level.
  *** Significant at $p \leq 0.01$ level.

ing loyal friends. It has been able to do so through multilateral chan-nels like the IMF.

The evidence presented here also suggests that changes in the struc-ture of the international system may have altered U.S. and IMF behav-ior but not in the predicted manner. In fact, these initial results suggest that the end of the cold war has been associated with the increasing politicization of the IMF by the U.S. There is evidence that the U.S. has been willing to reward friends and punish enemies only since 1990. During the cold war (at least in its last few years), unless they were moving closer to the U.S. politically, allies of the U.S. had no greater chance than its adversaries of receiving assistance from the Fund. Only in the post–cold war period have these countries been able to cash in on their political allegiance.

The demonstration of the systematic impact of international politics on IMF lending poses interesting methodological, theoretical, and practical implications. Methodologically, the use of key UNGA votes provides a more easily quantifiable and temporally sensitive alternative to traditional indicators of international political alignment, such as security alliances, military base locations, treaties, and content analysis. The use of this indicator may facilitate research in other areas of inquiry.

On a theoretical level, the evidence presented here suggests that multilateral organizations like the IMF, despite their enhanced influence in the developing world, are still most profitably analyzed within the parameters of an international political context shaped primarily by the industrialized nations. More specifically, there is strong evidence that the political interests of the United States drive much of the behavior of one of the most important multilateral organizations in the post-hegemonic global economy. I do not explore the reverse causal relationship—the impact of the IMF on U.S. interests and behavior[95]—but these results suggest more generally that the multilateral institutions are still quite sensitive to direct political pressures and influences from their more powerful member states. These influences translate into particular modes of behavior by the multilateral organizations themselves that can be analyzed conceptually, observed empirically, and tested statistically. The study of the role of international institutions and multilateral organizations must take into account not simply the fact that international political factors help determine their behavior on the input side. Such research should also view the operation of such entities as a tool used by the great powers to achieve specific, identifiable, political goals on the output side, such as realignment within the international system. The ability of the U.S. to employ such tools underscores the practical limits of multilateralism and confirms the rather dramatized fears of one of the original architects of the postwar international economic order, John Maynard Keynes:

[95] See Kahler (fn. 16), 93

> There is scarcely any enduringly successful experience of an international body
> which has fulfilled the hopes of its progenitors. Either an institution has become
> diverted to the instrument of a limited group or else it has been a puppet —
> sawdust through which the breath of life does not blow.[96]

On the practical side, the experience of the IMF suggests that Keynes's first fear has been partially realized. To an extent, the U.S. has been able to use the IMF to further its own international political agenda. On perhaps a more positive note, his second fear of irrelevance appears to be a distant one, despite the relative economic decline of the U.S. and the end of the cold war. While undermining the principle of multilateralism, the continued strength of national influence over Fund behavior may well help maintain the stability of great power support for the multilateral organizations if those powers continue to reap important gains from them that may be more economically or politically costly to obtain bilaterally.[97] Such conclusions could help allay the fears of those within the U.S. Congress who question U.S. support for the IMF based on concerns that it would strengthen multilateralism at the expense of U.S. power.

Finally, as a multilateral organization, the IMF is in a sense a difficult or crucial case for political theories of international finance. It is easy to see how bilateral capital flows could be subjected to the push and pull of international and domestic politics, but on the executive board of the IMF any single country's power is diluted by the presence of other principals within the decision-making body. The structure of the Fund leaves the door open, but a priori we would expect to see less of an impact for politics in the IMF than in bilateral financial flows. If high politics affects IMF lending, then it should have an even stronger impact on national policies. A confirmation of the impact of political realignment on IMF lending therefore provides stronger corroboration of this theory than that which could be obtained in a study of bilateral capital flows and suggests that such ideas may be fruitfully applied to other areas of international finance and international relations more generally.

---

[96] Cited in Nick Butler, *The IMF, Time for Reform* (London: Fabian Society, 1982), 24.
[97] Cf. Ruggie (fn. 2), chap. 1.

APPENDIX A
UNGA KEY VOTES AS IDENTIFIED BY THE DEPARTMENT OF STATE, 1983–93

Year	Issue	Resolution	Vote (Yes–No–Abstain–Absent)[a]
1983	Israeli credentials	Motion	79(U.S.)-43-19
	Middle East situation	38/180E	81-27(U.S.)-17
	Afghanistan	38/29	116(U.S.)-20-17
	Kampuchea	38/3	105(U.S.)-23-19
	Grenada	Motion	60-54(U.S.)-24
	Grenada	38/7	108-9(U.S.)-27
	Chemical and bacteriological weapons	38/187C	97(U.S.)-20-30
	Human rights in El Salvador	38/101	84-14(U.S.)-45
	Collaboration with South Africa	38/39G	122-9(U.S.)-17
	South Africa	38/39A	124-16(U.S.)-10
1984	Kampuchea	39/5	110(U.S.)-22-18
	Afghanistan	39/13	119(U.S.)-20-18
	Israeli credentials	Motion	80(U.S.)-41-22
	Chemical and bacteriological weapons	39/65A	99(U.S.)-14-13
	Military activities in dependent areas	39/412	62(U.S.)-47-24
	Apartheid	Motion	50-56(U.S.)-28
	Middle East	39/146	28(U.S.)-69-23
	Human rights in El Salvador	39/119	93-11(U.S.)-40
	Economic commission for Africa Conference Center	39/236 (III)	83-3(U.S.)-13
	Middle East situation	39/146A	69-39(U.S.)-26
1985	Kampuchea	40/7	114(U.S.)-21-16
	Afghanistan	40/12	122(U.S.)-19-12
	Human rights in Afghanistan	40/137	80(U.S.)-22-40
	Human rights in Iran	40/141	53(U.S.)-30-45
	Israeli credentials	Motion	80(U.S.)-41-20
	Chemical and bacteriological weapons	40/92C	112(U.S.)-16-22
	Namibia	Vote to retain 40/97B	54-63(U.S.)-29
	Middle East	Vote to retain 40/168A	64-33(U.S.)-41
	Central America	40/188	91-6(U.S.)-49
	Budget	40-253A	127-10(U.S.)-11
1986	Kampuchea	41/6	115(U.S.)-21-13
	Israeli credentials	Motion	77(U.S.)-40-16
	Nicaragua	41/31	94-3(U.S.)-47
	Afghanistan	41/33	122(U.S.)-20-11
	Libya	41/38	79-28(U.S.)-33
	Namibia	Vote to retain 41/39A	57-46(U.S.)-40
	Chemical and bacteriological weapons	41/58C	137(U.S.)-0-14
	Supplemental budget	41/211	122-13(U.S.)-10
	Human rights in Afghanistan	41/158	89(U.S.)-24-36

continued overleaf

APPENDIX A *(cont.)*

Year	Issue	Resolution	Vote (Yes–No–Abstain–Absent)[a]
	Middle East	Vote to retain 41/162A	66-38(U.S.)-41
1987	Israeli credentials	Motion	80(U.S.)-39-10-30
	Kampuchea	42/3	117(U.S.)-21-16-5
	Trade embargo against Nicaragua	42/176	94-2(U.S.)-48-15
	Afghanistan	42/15	123(U.S.)-19-11-6
	Human rights in Iran	42/136	64(U.S.)-22-45-28
	Apartheid	Vote to retain 42/23C	78-38(U.S.)-27-16
	Comprehensive system of international peace and security	42/93	76-12(U.S.)-63-8
	Program budget for the Biennium 1988–89	42/226	146-1-3(U.S.)-9
	Human rights in Afghanistan	42/135	94(U.S.)-22-31-12
	Middle East	Vote to retain 42/209B	64-33(U.S.)-41-21
1988	Israeli credentials	Motion	95(U.S.)-41-7-16
	Comply with International Court of Justice verdict in Nicaragua vs. U.S.	43/11	89-2(U.S.)-48-20
	Condemn foreign intervention in Cambodia	43/19	122(U.S.)-19-13-5
	Critical of human rights abuses in Iran	43/137	61(U.S.)-25-44-29
	Change name of PLO to "Palestine" in UN usage	43/177	104-2(U.S.)-36-17
	USSR resolution on international peace and security	43/89	97-3(U.S.)-45-14
	External debt crisis and development	43/198	150-1(U.S.)-1-7
	Foreign intervention in Afghanistan	43/20	Adopted by consensus[b]
	Genuine and periodic elections	43/157	Adopted by consensus[b]
	Program budget outline	43/214	Adopted by consensus[b]
1989	Israeli credentials	Motion	95(U.S.)-37-15
	Situation in Kampuchea	44/22	124(U.S.)-17-12
	Situation in the Middle East	Paragraph vote	63-35(U.S.)-47
	Situation in the Middle East: Palestine and International Peace Conference	44/40A	109-18(U.S.)-31
	Situation in the Middle East: Golan Heights	44/40B	84-22(U.S.)-49
	International Court of Justice judgment re: Nicaragua	44/43	91-2(U.S.)-41
	UNRWA: Assistance to Palestine refugees	44/47A	134(U.S.)-0-1

APPENDIX A *(cont.)*

Year	Issue	Resolution	Vote (Yes-No-Abstain-Absent)[a]
	Questions relating to information	44/50	127-2(U.S.)-21
	Cessation of all nuclear test explosions	44/105	136-3(U.S.)-13
	Amendment of the Limited Test Ban Treaty	44/106	127-2(U.S.)-22
	Prevention of an arms race in outer space	44/112	153-1(U.S.)-0
	Nuclear arms freeze	44/117D	136-13(U.S.)-5
	Indian Ocean Zone of Peace	44/120	137-4(U.S.)-14
	Enlargement of the Commission on Human Rights	44/167	151-2(U.S.)-2
	Trade embargo against Nicaragua	44/217	82-2(U.S.)-47
	Military intervention in Panama	44/240	75-20(U.S.)-40
1990	Comprehensive Nuclear Test Ban Treaty	45/51	140-2(U.S.)-6
	Bilateral nuclear arms negotiations	45/58H	99(U.S.)-0-50
	UNRWA: Assistance to Palestine refugees	45/73A	146(U.S.)-0-1
	Situation in the Middle East	Paragraph vote	52-37(U.S.)-49
	Situation in the Middle East: Palestine and International Peace Conference	45/83A	99-19(U.S.)-32
	Situation in the Middle East: Golan Heights	45/83B	84-23(U.S.)-41
	Periodic and genuine elections— UN electoral assistance	45/150	129(U.S.)-8-9
	Human rights in Occupied Kuwait	45/170	144(U.S.)-1-0
	Entrepreneurship	45/188	138(U.S.)-1-0
1991	IAEA report	Motion	88(U.S.)-25-26
	IAEA report	46/16	141(U.S.)-0-9
	Comprehensive Nuclear Test Ban Treaty	46/29	147-2(U.S.)-4
	Register of conventional arms transfers	46/36L	150(U.S.)-0-2
	UNRWA	46/46A	137(U.S.)-0-1
	Palestine—International Peace Conference	46/75	104-2(U.S.)-43
	Middle East—Palestinian question	46/82A	93-27(U.S.)-37
	Zionism/racism	Motion	34-96(U.S.)-13
	Zionism/racism	46/86	111(U.S.)-25-13
	Human rights in Occupied Kuwait	46/135	155(U.S.)-1-0
	Periodic and genuine elections	46/137	134(U.S.)-4-13
	Political and economic coercion	46/210	97-30(U.S.)-9
1992	Yugoslavia: UN membership	47/1	127(U.S.)-6-26
	IAEA report	47/8	146(U.S.)-0-5
	U.S. embargo of Cuba	47/19	59-3(U.S.)-71
	Comprehensive Nuclear Test Ban Treaty	47/47	159-1(U.S.)-4
	Maintenance of international security	47/60B	79(U.S.)-0-84
	Middle East—Golan Heights	47/63A	72-3(U.S.)-70
	Palestine—International Peace Conference	47/64D	93-4(U.S.)-60

continued overleaf

APPENDIX A *(cont.)*

Year	Issue	Resolution	Vote (Yes-No-Abstain-Absent)[a]
	UNRWA	47/69A	136(U.S.)-0-2
	Israeli practices	47/70A	83-5(U.S.)-55
	Situation in Bosnia and Herzegovina	47/121	102(U.S.)-0-57
	Periodic and genuine elections	47/138	141(U.S.)-0-20
	Human rights in Cuba	47/139	69(U.S.)-18-64
	Human rights in Sudan	47/142	104(U.S.)-8-33
	Human rights in Iraq	47/145	126(U.S.)-2-26
	Human rights in Iran	47/146	86(U.S.)-16-38
	External debt problems and development	47/198	158-1(U.S.)-0
1993	IAEA report	48/14	140(U.S.)-1-9
	U.S. embargo of Cuba	48/16	88-4(U.S.)-57
	Middle East peace process	48/58	155(U.S.)-3-1
	Middle East—Golan Heights	48/59B	65-2(U.S.)-83
	Israeli nuclear armament	48/78	53-45(U.S.)-65
	Situation in Bosnia and Herzegovina	48/88	109(U.S.)-0-57
	Periodic and genuine elections	48/131	153(U.S.)-0-13
	Human rights in Cuba	48/142	74(U.S.)-20-61
	Human rights in Iraq	48/144	116(U.S.)-2-43
	Human rights in Iran	48/145	74(U.S.)-23-51
	Human rights in Sudan	48/147	111(U.S.)-13-30
	Peaceful settlement of Palestine question	48/158D	92-5(U.S.)-51
	External debt problems of developing countries	48/182	164-1(U.S.)-0

SOURCE: U.S. Department of State, *Report to Congress on Voting Practices in the United Nations*, various years.

[a] U.S. vote shown in parentheses. Abstentions and absences combined from 1983–86. Only yes-no-abstain votes given for 1989–93.

[b] No records kept of which member states were present for consensus resolutions. Not included in voting index scores of countries.

APPENDIX B
COUNTRIES USED IN THE ANALYSIS

Algeria, Argentina, Bahamas, Bangladesh, Barbados, Benin, Bolivia, Botswana, Brazil, Burma/Myanmar, Burundi, Cameroon, Central African Rep., Chad, Chile, China, Colombia, Comoros, Congo, Costa Rica, Côte d'Ivoire, Cyprus, Dominican Rebublic, Ecuador, Egypt, El Salvador, Equatorial Guinea, Ethiopia, Fiji, Gabon, Gambia, Ghana, Grenada, Guatemala, Guyana, Haiti, Honduras, India, Indonesia, Jamaica, Jordan, Kenya, Lesotho, Liberia, Madagascar, Malawi, Malaysia, Mali, Malta, Mauritania, Mauritius, Mexico, Morocco, Nepal, Nicaragua, Niger, Nigeria, Oman, Pakistan, Panama, Papua New Guinea, Paraguay, Peru, Philippines, Romania, Rwanda, Senegal, Sierra Leone, Somalia, Sri Lanka, Sudan, Swaziland, Syria, Tanzania, Thailand, Togo, Trinidad and Tobago, Tunisia, Turkey, Uganda, Uruguay, Venezuela, Yemen Arab Republic, P.D. Republic of Yemen, Yugoslavia, Zaire, Zambia

[12]

An Economic Theory of GATT

By Kyle Bagwell and Robert W. Staiger *

We propose a unified theoretical framework within which to interpret and evaluate the foundational principles of GATT. Working within a general equilibrium trade model, we represent government preferences in a way that is consistent with national income maximization but also allows for the possibility of distributional concerns as emphasized in leading political-economy models. Using this general framework, we establish that GATT's principles of reciprocity and nondiscrimination can be viewed as simple rules that assist governments in their effort to implement efficient trade agreements. From this perspective, we argue that preferential agreements undermine GATT's ability to deliver efficient multilateral outcomes. (JEL F02, F13, F15)

The central role played by the General Agreement on Tariffs and Trade (GATT) in shaping postwar trade policy is widely accepted. Through the eight rounds of trade negotiations that have followed since the inception of GATT in 1947, average ad valorem tariffs on industrial goods have fallen significantly from over 40 percent to less than 4 percent. Over the same period of time, membership in GATT [and now its successor organization, the World Trade Organization (WTO)] has risen from 23 countries to well above 100. Despite the important role played by GATT in the world economy, however, economists have not yet developed a unified theoretical framework that interprets and eval-

uates the principles that form the foundation of GATT. Our purpose here is to propose such a framework.

We begin with a first and most basic question: What can governments gain from a trade agreement? We adopt the view that a trade agreement is appealing to governments if it offers them greater welfare than they would receive in the absence of the agreement. If in the absence of an agreement, governments set trade policies in a unilateral fashion, then a trade agreement is appealing provided that an inefficiency (relative to governments' preferences) exists under unilateral tariff setting. Viewed from this perspective, the role of a trade agreement is then to remove the inefficiency, so that member governments can enjoy higher welfare. The principles embodied in the trade agreement can then be interpreted and evaluated in this light.

What, then, is the inefficiency that trade agreements are designed to remedy? Working with models in which governments maximize national income, previous authors have established that the classic terms-of-trade externality creates an inefficiency in unilateral trade policies.[1] Intuitively, when a government imposes an import tariff, some of the cost of this

* Bagwell: Department of Economics, International Affairs Building, Columbia University, 420 West 118th Street, New York, NY 10027, and National Bureau of Economic Research; Staiger: Department of Economics, Social Science Building, University of Wisconsin, 1180 Observatory Drive, Madison, WI 53706, and National Bureau of Economic Research. We thank Jim Anderson, Jagdish Bhagwati, Alan Deardorff, Ronald Findlay, Ronald McKinnon, T. N. Srinivasan, three anonymous referees, and seminar participants at Boston University, Columbia University, the University of Michigan, Harvard University, the University of Toulouse, Stanford University, the University of Wisconsin, the World Trade Organization, and the 1997 NBER Summer Institute for helpful comments. This paper was written while Staiger was a Fellow at the Center for Advanced Study in the Behavioral Sciences. Staiger is also grateful for financial support provided by the National Science Foundation Grant No. SBR-9022192.

[1] For an early formal analysis of the terms-of-trade externality, see Harry G. Johnson (1953–1954). More recent discussions include John McMillan (1986, 1989), Avinash Dixit (1987), and Bagwell and Staiger (1990).

policy is shifted to foreign exporters, whose products sell at a lower world price (i.e., at less favorable terms of trade). This temptation to shift costs naturally leads governments to set unilateral tariffs that are higher than would be efficient. A trade agreement can then promote a more efficient outcome for its member governments, if it serves as a means to eliminate the terms-of-trade-driven restrictions in trade that arise when policies are set unilaterally. The assumption that governments maximize national income, however, stands in contrast to the manifest political constraints under which real governments operate. It is thus important to consider further the rationale for a trade agreement, within a richer model in which governments may have political concerns.

To this end, we construct a general model that allows for a wide class of government preferences. The economic environment is captured with a standard two-good general equilibrium model of trade between two countries, and we represent each government's welfare as a general function of the local and world prices that the tariff selections imply. This formulation allows us to associate a government's motivation to manipulate the terms of trade with the welfare gain that the government receives when its tariff choice changes the world price (holding fixed the local price). The government's preferences as to the local price are unconstrained and may reflect general economic and political (i.e., distributional) considerations. Our representation of government preferences thus includes the traditional case in which governments maximize national income as well as the possibility emphasized in leading political-economy models that governments are concerned with the distributional implications of their tariff choices.

Working with this general framework, we observe that political motivations influence the determination of the tariff policies to which governments aspire. For example, when governments have political motivations, free trade may not rest on the efficiency frontier. But it is the terms-of-trade externality—and this externality alone—that creates an inefficiency when governments set their trade policies unilaterally. For the class of government preferences that we entertain, we thus offer as our

first broad conclusion that trade agreements are appealing to governments solely as a means to remedy the inefficient terms-of-trade-driven restrictions in trade that arise when trade policies are set unilaterally. To establish this conclusion, we demonstrate that unilateral trade policies would be efficient in a hypothetical world in which governments pursued political goals but were not motivated by the terms-of-trade implications of their trade policies. In other words, if governments were not motivated by the terms-of-trade implications of their trade-policy selections, then there would be no reason for the creation of GATT.[2] This hypothetical experiment yields a set of *politically optimal* tariffs, which are efficient precisely because the motivation for such tariffs is separate from any cost-shifting incentive.[3]

Armed with this basic conclusion as to the purpose of trade agreements, we next interpret and evaluate the key principles on which GATT is founded. Following the legal literature on GATT (see, e.g., John H. Jackson, 1989 pp. 85–89), we interpret GATT as a "rules-based" institution whereby, prior to negotiating over trade policy, member governments agree to a set of rules or principles which describe the limits of acceptable behavior and thereby govern the "bargaining chips" that can be brought to the actual trade-policy negotiations that follow.[4] While GATT has a large number of specific articles, it is widely accepted that the two "pillars" of the GATT approach are the principles of reciprocity and nondiscrimination. The principle of reciproc-

---

[2] A political motivation for trade agreements might arise if governments seek such agreements to gain commitment relative to their private sectors. This possibility, which is not included in our modeling framework, is explored by Staiger and Guido Tabellini (1987), Staiger (1995), and Giovanni Maggi and Andres Rodriguez-Clare (1998). However, whether this commitment theory of trade agreements offers an interpretation of the basic principles of GATT is still an open question.

[3] The politically optimal tariffs correspond to reciprocal free trade when governments maximize national income.

[4] A separate question is how these rules are to be enforced. We abstract from the issue of enforcement in the body of the paper, but return to it in the concluding section.

ity is a GATT norm under which one country agrees to reduce its level of protection in return for a reciprocal "concession" from its trading partner. At the broadest level, this principle refers to the "ideal" of mutual changes in trade policy which bring about equal changes in import volumes across trading partners. The principle of nondiscrimination is a separate norm, under which a member government agrees that any tariff on a given product applied to the imports of one trading partner applies equally to all other trading partners. This discussion motivates our second question: Do the principles of reciprocity and nondiscrimination serve governments as simple rules of negotiation that promote efficiency, by "undoing" the terms-of-trade-driven inefficiency that arises in the absence of an agreement?

We begin with the principle of reciprocity. Our discussion here builds upon a key observation: mutual changes in trade policy that conform to the principle of reciprocity leave world prices unchanged. Recalling that trade-policy decisions are inefficient if and only if governments are motivated by their abilities to *change* the world price, we propose at a general level that the principle of reciprocity can be efficiency enhancing, since it neutralizes the terms-of-trade externality that underlies inefficient behavior. To develop this general proposal in a more concrete fashion, we then identify and consider the two specific applications of reciprocity that arise in GATT practice.

A first application arises when governments seek negotiated tariff reductions. While there is no formal requirement in GATT articles that governments exchange reciprocal tariff reductions in these negotiations, it has been observed that governments in fact seek a *balance of concessions* (i.e., tariff cuts). This emphasis on reciprocal tariff reductions contrasts sharply with the standard economic argument that unilateral free trade is the best policy for a (small) country, independent of the tariff selected by its trading partner, and this contrast has led many to conclude that governments approach trade negotiations from a mercantilist perspective that is driven by political forces and divorced from sound economic reasoning. We show instead that the principle of reciprocity as it arises in this application can be

given a rather direct economic interpretation: whatever their underlying political motivations, governments are driven to choose overly protective trade policies because of the cost-shifting effects of the world-price movements associated with their unilateral tariff choices, and they would therefore seek lower tariffs if the world-price implications of their liberalization could be neutralized—a feat that reciprocity achieves.

A second application of reciprocity in GATT practice occurs when a government decides to increase a previously "bound" (i.e., negotiated) tariff and invokes GATT's procedures for renegotiation. Here, GATT's reciprocity rules explicitly require moderation on the part of trading partners, who are permitted to withdraw *substantially equivalent concessions* of their own. In this case, the principle of reciprocity governs the manner in which tariffs may be *increased* as part of a renegotiation. In light of this possibility for renegotiation, an important issue is whether *any* efficient set of tariffs that might be agreed to in an original negotiation is in fact "renegotiation proof" under the rules of GATT. We show that GATT's insistence on reciprocity in renegotiations is indeed compatible with an efficient set of tariffs, and we further find that the only efficient tariffs that are impervious to renegotiation of this nature are the politically optimal tariffs. If governments seek an efficient outcome that will not be renegotiated as allowed under the principle of reciprocity, they therefore will negotiate to the politically optimal tariffs.

We then turn to the principle of nondiscrimination. Extending our framework to a multi-country setting, we begin by establishing an "affinity" between politically optimal tariffs and the principle of nondiscrimination: while there will in general be many points on the efficiency frontier that entail discriminatory tariffs, we show that politically optimal tariffs are efficient if and only if they conform to the principle of nondiscrimination. We next explore the implications of reciprocity in our multicountry setting, finding that an efficient multilateral trade agreement is impervious to renegotiation as allowed under the principle of reciprocity if and only if it is characterized by politically optimal tariffs that satisfy the principle of nondiscrimination. Thus, if a trade agreement permits renegotiation that conforms to the principle of reciprocity, then governments can achieve an efficient outcome only if the agreement also imposes the principle of nondiscrimination.[5]

The complementary relationship between the principles of reciprocity and nondiscrimination in generating efficient outcomes rests upon a simple intuition. As we have discussed above, the principle of reciprocity has the effect of neutralizing the world-price effects of a government's decision to raise tariffs, and so it can eliminate the externality that causes governments to make inefficient trade-policy choices provided that trade-policy externalities travel only through world prices. While externalities indeed travel only through world prices in the basic two-country model, when the modeling framework is extended to include multiple countries, there arises as well the possibility of a local-price externality. In particular, if a country discriminates when setting its trade policy, then, all else equal, it would prefer that a greater fraction of a given import volume be provided by the export source on whom it places the highest tariff. But the export volumes from trading partners are in turn determined in part by the local prices in these countries, and so a local-price externality is created. If the importing country adopts a policy of nondiscrimination, however, the preference for one export source over another is removed, and the only remaining externality is again the world-price externality, which the principle of reciprocity is well designed to neutralize.

Drawing on these findings, we offer as our second broad conclusion that the principles of reciprocity and nondiscrimination may be interpreted as simple negotiation rules that work hand in hand to assist governments as they attempt to undo the terms-of-trade-driven inefficiency that characterizes unilateral trade policies. In fact, we offer the more specific finding that these principles direct negotiation outcomes toward the tariffs that are both politically optimal and nondiscriminatory, and

hence toward the tariffs that governments would have chosen had they not been motivated by cost-shifting incentives in the first place. We interpret these results as establishing an efficiency-enhancing role for the two principles that form the pillars of the GATT architecture.

Finally, we consider the implications of a major exception to the principle of nondiscrimination that must be granted whenever GATT's member governments negotiate *preferential agreements.* This exception, embodied in Article XXIV of GATT, was controversial in its inception and has met with renewed controversy recently as many GATT members have increasingly exercised their rights under this article to negotiate preferential agreements. Against this backdrop, we use our modeling framework to address a third question: Will preferential agreements interfere with the efficiency properties of a multilateral trading system that is otherwise built upon the pillars of reciprocity and nondiscrimination?

In accord with Article XXIV, we consider two forms of preferential agreements: *free-trade areas,* in which member countries eliminate internal barriers to trade, and *customs unions,* in which members also adopt a common external tariff. Preferential agreements are inherently discriminatory, and so they revive the local-price externality described above. As a consequence, the principle of reciprocity typically does not deliver an efficient outcome when preferential agreements are in place. The only exception arises in the special case in which the preferential agreement takes the form of a customs union formed by members with sufficiently similar preferences. In this case, the customs union can be regarded as a "single" country with no internal tariff, and our previous results then imply that the principles of reciprocity and nondiscrimination can serve to deliver an efficient outcome. More generally, we offer as our third broad conclusion that preferential agreements pose a threat to the efficiency properties of the existing multilateral system.

This paper builds on the approach from Bagwell and Staiger (1996), in which we study the purpose of reciprocal trade agreements but do not interpret and evaluate the

---

[5] The principle of nondiscrimination is trivially satisfied in the basic two-country model described earlier.

principles of reciprocity and nondiscrimination as embodied in GATT practice. A more closely related paper is Bagwell and Staiger (1997a), where we adopt a partial equilibrium framework, impose a particular representation of political economy, and explore similar themes.

The remainder of the paper proceeds as follows. Section I presents our basic framework in a two-country setting and examines the purpose of reciprocal trade agreements. Section II then turns to an interpretation and evaluation of the principle of reciprocity. A multicountry extension of the modeling framework is developed in Section III, and the principle of nondiscrimination is analyzed. Preferential agreements are examined in Section IV. Next, in Section V we consider why governments might choose to design an institutional arrangement such as GATT that adopts a rules-based approach to trade negotiations. We argue that this approach can encourage participation of weaker countries in GATT, and we show that stronger countries might support the creation of such an institution for this reason. Finally, in Section VI, we conclude the paper with a discussion of evidence relating to our implicit hypothesis that governments have the ability and the desire to manipulate the terms of trade in a quantitatively significant fashion.

I. The Purpose of Reciprocal Trade Agreements

In this section, we develop a model of the economic environment for the case in which two countries trade two goods. Allowing for a wide range of government preferences, we then show that trade agreements are appealing to governments if and only if they serve as a means to remedy the inefficient terms-of-trade-driven restrictions in trade that arise under unilateral trade policies.

A. *The Economic Environment*

We begin with a description of the economic environment in which trade takes place. We work within a standard two-sector, two-country perfectly competitive general equilibrium trade model. Two countries, home (no *) and foreign (*), trade two goods, x and y, taken to be normal goods in consumption and

produced under conditions of increasing opportunity costs. Production takes place under perfect competition, facing tariffs on imports by each country. Let $x(y)$ be the natural import good of the home (foreign) country, and define $p \equiv p_x/p_y$ ($p^* \equiv p_x^*/p_y^*$) to be the local relative price facing home (foreign) producers and consumers. With $t(t^*)$ representing the home (foreign) ad valorem import tariff which we take to be nonprohibitive, and with $\tau \equiv (1 + t)$ and $\tau^* \equiv (1 + t^*)$, we have $p = \tau p^w \equiv p(\tau, p^w)$ and $p^* = p^w/\tau^* \equiv p^*(\tau^*, p^w)$, where $p^w \equiv p_x^*/p_y$ is the "world" (i.e., untaxed) relative price. The foreign (domestic) terms of trade are then measured by $p^w(1/p^w)$. We interpret $\tau > 1$ ($\tau < 1$) to be an import tax (import subsidy) and similarly for τ^*.[6]

Production in each country is determined by selecting the point on its production possibilities frontier at which the marginal rate of transformation between x and y is equal to the local relative price: $Q_i = Q_i(p)$ and $Q_i^* = Q_i^*(p^*)$ for $i \in \{x, y\}$. Consumption is a function of the local relative price—which defines the trade-off faced by consumers and determines the level and distribution of factor income in the economy—and of tariff revenue $R(R^*)$, which is distributed lump sum to domestic (foreign) consumers and which we measure in units of the local export good at local prices. We represent domestic and foreign consumption, respectively, as $D_i = D_i(p, R)$ and $D_i^* = D_i^*(p^*, R^*)$ for $i \in \{x, y\}$. Tariff revenue is defined implicitly by $R = [D_x(p, R) - Q_x(p)][p - p^w]$ or $R = R(p, p^w)$ for the domestic country, and similarly by $R^* = [D_y^*(p^*, R^*) - Q_y^*(p^*)][1/p^* - 1/p^w]$ or $R^* = R^*(p^*, p^w)$ for the foreign country, with each country's tariff revenue an increasing function of its terms of trade under the assumption that goods are normal. National consumption in each country can thus be written as $C_i(p, p^w) \equiv D_i(p, R(p, p^w))$ and $C_i^*(p^*, p^w) \equiv D_i^*(p^*, R^*(p^*, p^w))$.

---

[6] The Lerner symmetry theorem ensures that trade taxes or subsidies can be equivalently depicted as applying to exports or to imports in this two-sector general equilibrium setting.

220   THE AMERICAN ECONOMIC REVIEW   MARCH 1999

We next introduce notation for imports and exports, so that the trade balance and equilibrium conditions may be expressed. For the home country, imports of x are denoted as $M_x(p, p^w) \equiv C_x(p, p^w) - Q_x(p)$ and exports of y are represented as $E_y(p, p^w) \equiv Q_y(p) - C_y(p, p^w)$. Foreign country imports of y, M_y^*, and exports of x, E_x^*, are similarly defined. Home and foreign budget constraints imply that, for any world price, we have balanced trade:

$$(1) \quad p^w M_x(p(\tau, p^w), p^w)$$

$$= E_y(p(\tau, p^w), p^w);$$

$$M_y^*(p^*(\tau^*, p^w), p^w)$$

$$= p^w E_x^*(p^*(\tau^*, p^w), p^w),$$

where we now represent explicitly the functional forms of the local prices. Finally, the equilibrium world price $\tilde{p}^w(\tau, \tau^*)$ is determined by the y-market-clearing condition

$$(2) \quad E_y(p(\tau, \tilde{p}^w), \tilde{p}^w)$$

$$= M_y^*(p^*(\tau^*, \tilde{p}^w), \tilde{p}^w),$$

with market clearing for good x then implied by (1) and (2).

In summary, given an initial pair of tariffs, the equilibrium world price is implied by (2), and the equilibrium world price and the given tariffs then together determine the local prices. In this way, the initial tariffs imply local and world prices and thereby the levels for production, consumption, imports, exports, and tariff revenue. Finally, we add the standard restriction that $dp/d\tau > 0 > dp^*/d\tau^*$ and $\partial \tilde{p}^w / \partial \tau < 0 < \partial \tilde{p}^w / \partial \tau^*$, which ensures that the prices so determined do not succumb to the Lerner and Metzler paradoxes.

B. *Government Objectives*

We next offer a general representation of government preferences. While it is customary to represent a government's payoff (i.e., welfare) in terms of the underlying choice variables (i.e., tariffs), we choose instead to

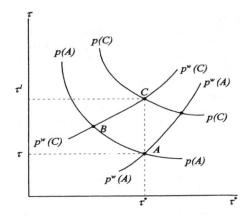

FIGURE 1. THE WORLD- AND LOCAL-PRICE EFFECTS OF A TARIFF CHANGE

represent each government's welfare as a function of the local and world prices that the tariffs imply, as this approach enables us to isolate the terms-of-trade externality that tariff selections generate. We thus represent the objectives of the home and foreign governments by the general functions $W(p(\tau, \tilde{p}^w), \tilde{p}^w)$ and $W^*(p^*(\tau^*, \tilde{p}^w), \tilde{p}^w)$, respectively.

The essential structure we place on W and W^* is that, holding its local price fixed, each government achieves higher welfare when its terms of trade improve:

$$(3) \quad \partial W(p, \tilde{p}^w)/\partial \tilde{p}^w < 0 \text{ and}$$

$$\partial W^*(p^*, \tilde{p}^w)/\partial \tilde{p}^w > 0.$$

Figure 1 illustrates. An initial tariff pair $A \equiv (\tau, \tau^*)$ is associated with a domestic iso-local-price locus, $p(A) \to p(A)$, and an iso-world-price locus, $p^w(A) \to p^w(A)$.[7] Also depicted is a second iso-world-price locus, $p^w(C) \to p^w(C)$, along which the world price is lower than at point A, indicating an improved terms of trade for the domestic country. A reduction in the world price that maintains the domestic

---

[7] Given the assumptions that Metzler and Lerner paradoxes are absent, the iso-local-price locus exhibits negative slope and the iso-world-price locus is positively sloped.

local price is thus achieved with the movement from point A to B, corresponding to a higher (lower) domestic (foreign) import tariff. We assume only that the implied income transfer from the foreign to the domestic country is valued by the domestic government.

This representation of government preferences is quite general, as it includes both the traditional possibility that governments maximize national income as well as the possibility that governments are also motivated by distributional concerns. With respect to the latter possibility, as Richard E. Baldwin (1987) observes, the political economy models of trade policy proposed by Mancur Olson (1965), Richard E. Caves (1976), William A. Brock and Stephen P. Magee (1978), Robert C. Feenstra and Jagdish Bhagwati (1982), Ronald Findlay and Stanislaw Wellisz (1982), and Arye L. Hillman (1982) can all be represented in this way. Similarly, the median-voter model of Wolfgang Mayer (1984), the lobbying models of Gene M. Grossman and Elhanan Helpman (1994, 1995) and Dixit et al. (1997), and the political-constraint model of Robert E. Baldwin (1985) fit within this framework.[8]

C. *The Purpose of Reciprocal Trade Agreements*

We assume that governments seek *reciprocal trade agreements* to achieve mutually beneficial changes in trade policy; that is, through a reciprocal trade agreement governments seek tariff changes that result in Pareto improvements for member countries (as measured by W and W^*) over what could be achieved by unilateral tariff setting. *Recipro-*

cal *trade liberalization* then refers to mutual reductions in tariffs implemented through a reciprocal trade agreement. Finally, if the tariffs negotiated under a reciprocal trade agreement reach the efficiency locus, defined by

$$(4) \quad [d\tau/d\tau^*]|_{dW=0} = [d\tau/d\tau^*]|_{dW^*=0},$$

then the governments have formed an *efficient reciprocal trade agreement*.

We begin our exploration of reciprocal trade agreements by considering the trade-policy inefficiencies that arise in their absence. To this end, we first suppose that each government sets its trade policy unilaterally, selecting a tariff to maximize its objective function taking the tariff choice of its trading partner as given. The resulting reaction functions are defined implicitly by

$$(5a) \quad \text{Home:} \quad W_p[dp/d\tau]$$

$$+ W_{p^w}[\partial\tilde{p}^w/\partial\tau] = 0,$$

$$(5b) \quad \text{Foreign:} \quad W_{p^*}^*[dp^*/d\tau^*]$$

$$+ W_{\tilde{p}^w}^*[\partial\tilde{p}^w/\partial\tau^*] = 0,$$

where subscripts denote partial derivatives.[9] Thus, with $\lambda \equiv [\partial\tilde{p}^w/\partial\tau]/[dp/d\tau] < 0$ and $\lambda^* \equiv [\partial\tilde{p}^w/\partial\tau^*]/[dp^*/d\tau^*] < 0$, (5a) and (5b) can be rewritten as

$$(6a) \quad \text{Home:} \quad W_p + \lambda W_{p^w} = 0,$$

$$(6b) \quad \text{Foreign:} \quad W_{p^*}^* + \lambda^* W_{\tilde{p}^w}^* = 0.$$

Each government's best-response tariff is therefore determined by the combined impact that the induced local- and world-price movements have on welfare.

The forces that determine best-response tariffs are illustrated in Figure 1. Consider an initial tariff pair represented by the point $A \equiv (\tau, \tau^*)$. Holding fixed τ^*, if the domestic government were to unilaterally increase its tariff from τ to τ^1, a new tariff pair corresponding to the point $C \equiv (\tau^1, \tau^*)$ would be induced.

---

[8] Baldwin (1985) proposes that a government has autonomous *ideological* concerns (e.g., it may be a "free trader") but faces a *political-support constraint* (e.g., export-sector support for proposed liberalization efforts must counterbalance import-competing-sector opposition) when pursuing these goals. To see that this case is included, let G be the objective of the domestic government and let the political-support constraint be given by the inequality restriction $S(p(\tau, \tilde{p}^w), \tilde{p}^w) \geq \bar{S}$. Then W is the Lagrangian $W(p(\tau, \tilde{p}^w), \tilde{p}^w) = G(p(\tau, \tilde{p}^w), \tilde{p}^w) + \rho[S(p(\tau, \tilde{p}^w), \tilde{p}^w) - \bar{S}]$, where the multiplier ρ depends also on $p(\tau, \tilde{p}^w)$ and $\tilde{p}^w$.

[9] We also assume throughout that second-order conditions are globally satisfied.

222   THE AMERICAN ECONOMIC REVIEW   MARCH 1999

This tariff pair lies on a new iso-local-price locus, given as $p(C) \to p(C)$, and also on a new iso-world-price locus, represented as $p^w(C) \to p^w(C)$. By increasing its tariff, the domestic government thus induces a local price that is higher and a world price that is lower. As Figure 1 illustrates and (6a) suggests, the overall movement from A to C can be disentangled into separate movements in the local and world prices, respectively. The movement from A to B isolates the world-price change. The welfare gain for the domestic government that is associated with this change is captured in (6a) with the term λW_{p^w}, which is strictly positive by (3). The movement from B to C then reflects the induced increase in the local price, and the effect of this change on the domestic government's welfare is represented in (6a) by the term W_p.

We now define *Nash equilibrium tariffs* as a pair of domestic and foreign tariffs (τ^N, τ^{*N}) which simultaneously satisfy (6a) and (6b).[10] Our first pair of results establish that a Pareto improvement from the Nash equilibrium can be achieved through a reciprocal trade agreement, but only if the agreement is characterized by reciprocal trade liberalization.

PROPOSITION 1: *Nash equilibrium tariffs are inefficient.*

PROPOSITION 2: *A reciprocal trade agreement must entail reciprocal trade liberalization.*

Proofs of these propositions are found in the Appendix.

These results reflect a familiar intuition. When a government imposes an import tariff, its terms of trade improve, and part of the cost of this policy is borne by its trading partners, whose products sell at a lower world price. This terms-of-trade externality implies that the government faces less than the full costs of protecting its import-competing sectors. As a consequence, governments oversupply policies directed toward import protection relative to the efficient intervention levels given their preferences, and a reciprocal trade agreement can therefore benefit all governments if it serves as a mechanism through which the protection levels of each country can be reduced. An implication of our analysis is that the benefits of reciprocal trade liberalization are quite robust, as they arise for a very general class of government preferences.

More strikingly, for the class of government preferences entertained here, we find that the terms-of-trade externality is the *only* inefficiency that a reciprocal trade agreement can remedy. To establish this conclusion, we consider a hypothetical world in which governments are assumed not to value the terms-of-trade effects that their unilateral tariff choices imply.[11] If under this hypothesis unilateral tariff choices are efficient, then we may conclude that the terms-of-trade externality is the only rationale for a trade agreement. With this experiment in mind, we define *politically optimal tariffs* as any tariff pair (τ^{PO}, τ^{*PO}) that simultaneously satisfies:

$$(7a) \qquad \text{Home: } W_p = 0,$$

---

[10] We postpone for now discussion regarding the existence and uniqueness of Nash equilibria, choosing instead to focus on statements that are true for any Nash equilibrium with positive trade that is not Pareto dominated by other Nash equilibria. An implication of this focus is that we ignore here and throughout the paper the possible gains from a reciprocal trade agreement that could come from coordinating across Pareto-ranked Nash equilibria. The emphasis placed on enforcement issues in actual trade agreements suggests that the achievement of coordination gains is not the primary purpose of such agreements. Similarly, we ignore for now issues associated with the existence and uniqueness of politically optimal tariffs, as defined in the text.

[11] The assumption here is not that governments fail to understand that their tariff choices affect the terms of trade; rather, the hypothetical situation we consider is that governments are not motivated by the world-price implications of their tariff choices. In terms of (6a), governments recognize that $\lambda < 0$, but we now consider the tariffs that they would select were their welfare functions such that $W_{p^w} \equiv 0$. Our thought experiment identifies the tariffs that would be chosen by governments with these hypothetical preferences and evaluates the efficiency properties of these tariffs with respect to actual government preferences.

(7b)   Foreign: $W_{p*}^* = 0$.

In the special case where the domestic and foreign governments seek to maximize national income, politically optimal tariffs correspond to reciprocal free trade.[12]

We now find that the terms-of-trade externality is indeed the only inefficiency that a trade agreement can remedy.

PROPOSITION 3: *Politically optimal tariffs are efficient.*

This proposition is proved in the Appendix, but the intuition follows from Figure 1. When choosing its tariff, the domestic government considers the domestic costs and benefits that a tariff increase has through the corresponding increase in the domestic local price (the movement from B to C), and it also considers the extent to which the costs associated with a higher local price are shifted onto its trading partner through the corresponding reduction in the world price (the movement from A to B). In the hypothetical case in which the domestic government does not value the world-price change that a tariff increase implies, however, it is motivated only by the former consideration. When both governments behave in this fashion, the resulting politically optimal tariffs are thus efficient.

Of course, the politically optimal tariffs are not the only efficient tariffs. To see this, we use (4) to recast the efficiency locus in the form

(8) $(1 - AW_p)(1 - A^*W_{p*}^*) = 1,$

where $A \equiv (1 - \tau\lambda)/(W_p + \lambda W_{p^w})$ and $A^* \equiv (1 - \lambda^*/\tau^*)/(W_{p*}^* + \lambda^*W_{p^w}^*)$, with $A \neq 0$ and $A^* \neq 0$ under the further assumption that the partial derivatives of the welfare functions are always finite. Observe that (8) is satisfied

when $W_p = 0 = W_{p*}^*$, confirming that politically optimal tariffs are efficient; however, (8) can also be satisfied if $W_p \neq 0$ and $W_{p*}^* \neq 0$, and politically optimal tariffs thus define only a particular point on the efficiency locus. Starting from the political optimum, other points on the efficiency locus can be reached by altering tariffs so as to generate local prices that are efficient given the new distribution of world income implied by the associated world-price movements.[13]

We now add some additional structure to the model and assume that: (i) a unique Nash equilibrium exists; (ii) a unique political optimum exists; and (iii) the political optimum lies on the contract curve (i.e., it corresponds to a point on the efficiency locus that yields mutual gains for each government relative to its Nash welfare).[14] These assumptions are imposed in Figure 2, which illustrates the three propositions of the section. As Proposition 1 indicates, the Nash tariffs (point N) lie off of the efficiency locus as defined by (8) (the curve $E \rightarrow E$). The figure also depicts the Nash iso-welfare curves for the domestic and foreign governments, and these curves illustrate the message of Proposition 2: relative to the Nash equilibrium, a trade agreement can increase the welfare of both governments only if the agreement calls for a reduction in both tariffs. Finally, as Proposition 3 requires, the politically optimal tariffs (point PO) lie on the efficiency locus. Notice that the iso-welfare

---

[12] When the domestic government maximizes the utility of a representative agent, its objective can be represented as $W(p, p^w) \equiv V(p, I(p, p^w))$, with V denoting the indirect utility of the representative domestic agent and with I denoting the domestic national income measured in units of y at local prices. With a similar expression for the foreign government, a direct application of Roy's identity indicates that $W_p = 0 = W_{p*}^*$ implies $\tau = 1 = \tau^*$.

[13] In the special case of national-income-maximizing governments, as Mayer (1981) shows, the efficiency locus is described by the set of tariffs that satisfy $\tau = 1/\tau^*$. In this case, along the efficiency locus, tariffs are adjusted so as to maintain equality in relative local prices across countries, with different efficient tariff pairs resulting in different world prices and thus different distributions of income across countries. In the more general formulation considered here, it remains true that the efficiency locus determines a relationship between domestic and foreign tariffs, but it need not be the case that this relationship equates relative local prices across trading partners.

[14] The political optimum lies on the contract curve if the countries are not too asymmetric. As Johnson (1953–1954), Mayer (1981), and John Kennan and Raymond G. Riezman (1988) show for the case in which governments maximize national income, when governments are sufficiently asymmetric, the political optimum (which is then free trade) need not offer Pareto gains relative to the Nash equilibrium for all governments.

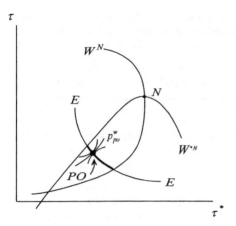

FIGURE 2. THE PURPOSE OF A RECIPROCAL TRADE
AGREEMENT

curves are tangent at every point along this locus. A novel feature of the politically optimal point is that the iso-welfare curves are also tangent to the iso-world-price locus. The bold portion of the efficiency locus corresponds to the contract curve.

More broadly, Figure 2 illustrates the general purpose of a reciprocal trade agreement. When governments interact unilaterally, the associated Nash tariffs are inefficient as a consequence of the terms-of-trade externality. A reciprocal trade agreement is then attractive to governments if it enables them to cooperate and replace the high Nash tariffs with lower tariffs that rest on the contract curve. While the rationale for a reciprocal trade agreement may be understood in these general terms, there remains an important practical issue: How is the trade agreement to be designed?

There are two basic approaches. In a "rules-based" approach, governments agree to certain principles under which subsequent negotiations will be undertaken. Alternatively, governments might adopt a "power-based" approach in which they bargain in a direct fashion that is not constrained by agreed-upon principles of negotiation. With the creation of GATT, governments chose to adopt a rules-based approach, and two foundational rules of GATT are reciprocity and nondiscrimination. We focus in the next two sections on the efficiency properties of these simple rules.

II. Reciprocity

In this section, we define and interpret GATT's principle of reciprocity. We then show that reciprocity can enhance efficiency, as it can guide governments toward the politically optimal tariffs.

A. *The Principle of Reciprocity*

We begin with a definition of reciprocity. At the broadest level, reciprocity refers to the "ideal" of mutual changes in trade policy that bring about equal changes in import volumes across trading partners.[15] We thus propose the following definition: a set of tariff changes $\Delta\tau \equiv (\tau^1 - \tau^0)$ and $\Delta\tau^* \equiv (\tau^{*1} - \tau^{*0})$ conforms to *the principle of reciprocity* provided that

$$\tilde{p}^{w0}[\, M_x(p(\tau^1, \tilde{p}^{w1}), \tilde{p}^{w1})$$

$$- M_x(p(\tau^0, \tilde{p}^{w0}), \tilde{p}^{w0})\,]$$

$$= [\, M_y^*(p^*(\tau^{*1}, \tilde{p}^{w1}), \tilde{p}^{w1})$$

$$- M_y^*(p^*(\tau^{*0}, \tilde{p}^{w0}), \tilde{p}^{w0})\,],$$

where $\tilde{p}^{w0} \equiv \tilde{p}^w(\tau^0, \tau^{*0})$, $\tilde{p}^{w1} \equiv \tilde{p}^w(\tau^1, \tau^{*1})$ and changes in import volumes are measured at existing world prices. Using the trade-balance condition (1) and the equilibrium condition (2), it is now direct to show that this expression reduces to

$$[\tilde{p}^{w1} - \tilde{p}^{w0}]M_x(p(\tau^1, \tilde{p}^{w1}), \tilde{p}^{w1}) = 0.$$

Hence, *mutual changes in trade policy that conform to reciprocity leave world prices unchanged.*

With this observation in hand, we may anticipate the general manner in which reciprocity can be efficiency enhancing. Intuitively, as we argued above, unilateral tariff choices are inefficient if and only if governments are mo-

---

[15] See, for example, Kenneth W. Dam (1970 pp. 58–61; 87–91) on the concept of reciprocity in GATT and the various ways in which reciprocity is measured in practice.

tivated by their abilities to *change* the world price. When governments negotiate tariffs under the rule of reciprocity, however, this terms-of-trade externality is neutralized, as the mutual tariff changes that occur under reciprocity leave the world price *fixed.* This feature of reciprocity, which can be seen transparently in our two-country, two-good model but which also extends beyond the 2 × 2 case, will play a central role in our analysis.[16]

To explore this general proposal more fully, we identify the two specific applications of reciprocity that occur within GATT practice. First, the principle of reciprocity is often associated with the informal idea that governments seek a "balance of concessions" (i.e., reciprocal tariff cuts) when they enter into trade negotiations. The emphasis that governments place upon reciprocity in this sense has attracted the interest of many economists, and we therefore pause and offer an economic in-

terpretation of this application in the next subsection. A second application of reciprocity can be found within the formal rules of GATT itself. We give this application primary emphasis, and it concerns the rules by which GATT members must abide when they renegotiate agreements. In the final subsection, we interpret and evaluate the agreements that governments can implement when they recognize that the principle of reciprocity governs any renegotiation process.

B. *Reciprocity and the Balance of Concessions*

When governments negotiate tariff reductions in a GATT round, they do so under GATT Article XXVIII bis. As the language therein makes clear, participation in negotiations is voluntary and suggests a desire to arrange "reciprocal and mutually advantageous" reductions in tariffs. At the same time, there is no formal requirement in GATT that negotiated tariff reductions conform to the principle of reciprocity as defined above. Rather, governments have developed an informal reliance upon this principle, as they typically seek a *balance of concessions* through a negotiated agreement.[17]

This informal principle of reciprocity appears to defy standard economic logic, which holds that unilateral free trade is the optimal policy for a country. Why should a government require a "concession" from its trading partner in order to do what is in any event best for its country? Indeed, the observation that governments seek reciprocity in negotiated agreements is sometimes interpreted as evidence that government negotiators adopt a mercantilist perspective that is inconsistent with economic reasoning and derives from political forces. For example, Paul R. Krugman (1991 p. 25) observes the following.

> To make sense of international trade negotiations, one needs to remember three simple rules about the objectives of the negotiating countries:

---

[16] To see that this property of reciprocity holds more generally, consider a two-country, *N*-good world economy. Let $(\mathbf{p}^{w0'}, \mathbf{p}^{0'}, \mathbf{E}^0)$ denote an initial triple consisting of a $(1 \times N)$ vector of equilibrium world prices, a $(1 \times N)$ vector of equilibrium local home country prices, and an $(N \times 1)$ vector of equilibrium trades with the *j*th element of *E* positive (negative) if good *j* is imported by the foreign (home) country. Similarly, let $(\mathbf{p}^{w1'}, \mathbf{p}^{1'}, \mathbf{E}^1)$ denote a second set of equilibrium prices and quantities that arise under an alternative set of trade policies. In analogy with our approach above, the view that reciprocity reflects mutual changes in trade policy which bring about equal changes in import volumes across trading partners can be represented with the restriction that tariff changes conforming to reciprocity lead to changes in trade volumes which satisfy $\mathbf{p}^{w0'}[\mathbf{E}^1 - \mathbf{E}^0] = 0$. Utilizing the balanced trade conditions $\mathbf{p}^{w0'}\mathbf{E}^0 = 0$ and $\mathbf{p}^{w1'}\mathbf{E}^1 = 0$ and proceeding as above, the restriction of reciprocity can be rewritten as $(\mathbf{p}^{w1'} - \mathbf{p}^{w0'})\mathbf{E}^1 = 0$. Thus, mutual changes in trade policy continue to satisfy the restriction of reciprocity if world prices are unchanged. In the many-good case, however, it is also possible that reciprocity can be satisfied even when world prices change. To evaluate this possibility, we note that the restriction of reciprocity can be further rewritten as $(\mathbf{p}^{w1'} - \mathbf{p}^{1'})\mathbf{E}^1 = (\mathbf{p}^{w0'} - \mathbf{p}^{1'})\mathbf{E}^1$. This indicates that any trade-policy adjustment giving rise to the price vectors $\mathbf{p}^{w1}$ and $\mathbf{p}^1$ results in the same aggregate tariff revenue as would an alternative tariff-policy adjustment that gave rise to the price vectors $\mathbf{p}^{w0}$ and $\mathbf{p}^1$, when each adjustment is consistent with the restriction of reciprocity. Since world prices affect welfare only through tariff revenue, we may therefore restrict attention to tariff-policy adjustments that preserve the world prices. These properties of reciprocity also extend naturally to a many-country setting.

[17] For a discussion of the informal application of reciprocity, see, e.g., Dam (1970 p. 59) and Bhagwati (1991).

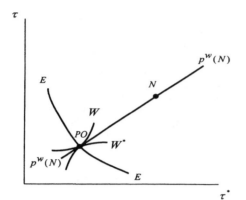

FIGURE 3A. LIBERALIZATION ACCORDING TO
RECIPROCITY — THE SYMMETRIC CASE

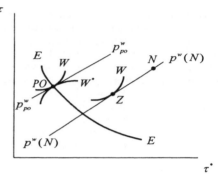

FIGURE 3B. LIBERALIZATION ACCORDING TO
RECIPROCITY — THE ASYMMETRIC CASE

(1) *Exports are good.*
(2) *Imports are bad.*
(3) *Other things equal, an equal increase in imports and exports is good.*

In other words, GATT-think is enlightened mercantilism.

By contrast, we argue next that the informal principle of reciprocity that characterizes actual trade negotiations admits a direct and simple economic interpretation.[18]

To develop this argument, we assume for the moment that governments begin at the Nash equilibrium point, and we show formally in the Appendix that reciprocal trade liberalization that satisfies the principle of reciprocity raises the welfare of each government in a monotonic fashion, at least if the liberalization effort does not proceed too far.

PROPOSITION 4: *Beginning at a Nash equilibrium, reciprocal trade liberalization that conforms to reciprocity will increase each government's welfare monotonically until this liberalization has proceeded to the point*

---

[18] Krugman (1997) develops more fully the view that GATT negotiations are incompatible with economic reasoning and reflect mercantilist logic. Some of the advantages of reciprocity described by McMillan (1986, 1989) and Bhagwati (1990 p. 15) are more in line with the results we discuss here.

where $\min[-W_p, W_{p*}^*] = 0$. *If countries are symmetric, this liberalization path leads to the politically optimal outcome.*

Intuitively, at a Nash equilibrium, each government would prefer more trade, if only it could achieve this increase without experiencing a decline in its terms of trade. For example, it is direct from (3) and (6a) that $W_p < 0$ at a Nash equilibrium, which indicates that the domestic local price is higher than the domestic government prefers, taking as given the Nash world price. The domestic government would thus prefer to reduce its tariff, lower the local price, and experience a corresponding increase in trade volume, if it could do so without reducing its terms of trade. While a unilateral liberalization effort is unappealing at the Nash equilibrium as a consequence of the associated deterioration in the terms of trade, a negotiated *mutual* reduction in tariffs that conforms to the principle of reciprocity results in a higher trade volume without a terms-of-trade loss for either government. Both governments thus benefit from reciprocal tariff reductions of this form, provided that the reciprocal liberalization effort does not proceed past the point at which $\min[-W_p, W_{p*}^*] = 0$, where one government obtains its preferred local price given the initial Nash world price.

Figures 3A and 3B illustrate the liberalization paths described in Proposition 4. In Figure 3A, the countries are symmetric, and so the iso-world-price locus that runs through the Nash point N also intersects the politically optimal point PO. In this case, as governments liberalize according to the principle of reciprocity, each government benefits until both simultaneously achieve their preferred local prices at the politically optimal tariffs. The case in which countries are asymmetric is depicted in Figure 3B, and the Nash iso-world-price locus now need not intersect the politically optimal point. As Proposition 4 indicates, it remains true that liberalization from the Nash point under reciprocity initially raises the welfare of each government; but in the asymmetric case, the mutual benefits from further liberalization terminate before the efficiency locus is reached. For instance, in Figure 3B, it is the domestic government that first achieves its preferred local price at the given Nash world price, and so the mutual benefits from further liberalization terminate at point Z.

It is convenient now to consider further the relationship between reciprocity and the politically optimal tariffs. As discussed in the previous section, under the hypothetical experiment in which the domestic government does not value movements in the terms of trade, the domestic government sets its tariff to satisfy $W_p = 0$. When both governments select tariffs in this fashion, the resulting tariffs are the politically optimal tariffs. Of course, there is no reason to expect that actual governments would be indifferent to terms-of-trade movements. The experiment is instructive, though. We may think of reciprocity as corresponding to a related experiment, in which governments ignore the terms-of-trade implications of their tariff selections, not because such a movement would be without value, but rather because the mutual adjustments in tariffs implied by reciprocity guarantee that the world price is, in fact, fixed. The domestic government's preferred tariff thus again satisfies $W_p = 0$, which is to say that reciprocity induces governments to act *as if* they did not value the terms-of-trade movements associated with their unilateral tariff selections.[19]

Finally, we return to Krugman's (1991) three rules of "enlightened mercantilism" that characterize actual negotiations, and we note that Propositions 1 through 4 provide a formal economic interpretation of these rules. Specifically, we find that: (1) governments enter into negotiations seeking more open export markets ("exports are good"), because a reduction in the import tariff levied by the trading partner serves to improve the terms of trade; (2) import liberalization is viewed by governments as a concession ("imports are bad"), because it implies reducing the import tariff below the best-response value and suffering a terms-of-trade decline; and (3) each government benefits from a concession at home that is balanced under reciprocity against an "equivalent" concession abroad ("other things equal, an equal increase in imports and exports is good"), because the balance of concessions so achieved serves to neutralize the terms-of-trade decline that would have made unilateral liberalization undesirable.[20]

C. *Reciprocity and the Withdrawal of Substantially Equivalent Concessions*

There is nothing in GATT which *requires* that the outcome of negotiations produce a balance of concessions; rather, reciprocity in this circumstance describes the broad manner in which governments seem to approach trade negotiations. Reciprocity also plays an important role in GATT in a second circumstance, however, and in this case GATT does require that countries comply with the rule of reciprocity. This second application of reciprocity concerns the manner in which countries may

---

[19] This discussion may be made more concrete with reference to (6a). As this equation makes clear, the domestic government's preferred tariff satisfies $W_p = 0$ when the term λW_{p^*} is zero. This would in fact be the case, either

if the government were hypothesized not to value a change in the terms of trade (i.e., if $W_{p^*} \equiv 0$) or if it were to expect a reciprocal tariff adjustment from its trading partner that would result in no change in the terms of trade (i.e., if $\lambda = 0$).

[20] It is interesting to note that, according to a popular political argument, the appeal of reciprocity is that it mobilizes export-sector support for liberalization. In fact, however, this political argument can be captured by our model. The key point is that the proposed export-sector support for reciprocity is ultimately tied to the anticipated economic benefits of a lower foreign import tariff, and these benefits travel through the world price. See also footnote 8.

lawfully *re*negotiate a previous agreement. Under GATT Article XXVIII (Dam, 1970 pp. 79–99; Jackson, 1989 p. 119; Alice Enders, 1999), a country may propose to modify or withdraw a tariff concession to which it had previously committed in a round of tariff negotiation. In the circumstance in which the country fails to reach agreement with its trading partners over a renegotiated tariff schedule, the country is free to carry out the proposed changes anyway, and the notion of reciprocity is used to moderate the responses of its trading partners, who are permitted to withdraw *substantially equivalent concessions* of their own.[21]

By requiring moderation on the part of trading partners, this second application of reciprocity ensures that the proposing country's unilateral decision to increase a previously bound tariff results in an offsetting tariff adjustment from its trading partner which preserves the original world price. Consequently, under GATT's rules, any agreement that leaves some government wanting less trade at the prevailing world price will be renegotiated. For the remainder of the paper, we will focus on reciprocity as it applies in this second circumstance, and we will consider the trade agreements that can be implemented when governments negotiate an initial set of tariff "bindings," where subsequently either government is free to increase its previously bound tariff with the understanding that the outcome of any renegotiation that follows will

preserve the world price implied by the previous agreement. We wish to characterize the set of trade agreements that can be implemented as the end result of this process, i.e., once no further renegotiation is desired by either government.

Formally, we consider a negotiation process that entails three stages. In the initial negotiation stage (corresponding to Article XXVIII bis), governments agree to bind their tariffs at specified levels.[22] The second stage is a renegotiation stage (corresponding to Article XXVIII), where any renegotiation satisfies the restriction of reciprocity as outlined above, and thus results in mutual changes in tariffs that preserve the world price from the first stage. Finally, to ensure that the renegotiation process achieves eventual resolution (and in line with Article XXVIII), we introduce a third stage that arises if governments fail to agree on a renegotiated set of tariffs. In this final stage, the tariffs that are implemented are those that achieve the greatest trade volume consistent with the restriction of reciprocity and the requirement that no country is asked to import a volume greater than is implied by its government's proposal in the renegotiation stage.

We begin our analysis with some definitions. Given a world price $\bar{p}^w$ that is determined in the first stage of negotiations, we will say that a renegotiated tariff pair (τ, τ^*) satisfies the *restriction of reciprocity* if the tariff pair preserves the original world price: $\bar{p}^w(\tau, \tau^*) = \bar{p}^w$. If in the renegotiation stage the domestic government proposes a domestic tariff $\hat{\tau}$ and the foreign government proposes a foreign tariff $\hat{\tau}^*$, then under the restriction of reciprocity the tariff proposed by one government

---

[21] In fact, it is in the context of Article XXVIII renegotiations that perhaps the clearest statement of the measurement of reciprocity in GATT practice has been given. In describing the "fairly well-established criteria" that were considered in determining what would constitute the withdrawal of substantially equivalent concessions, the Legal Adviser to GATT's Director-General observed (WTO, 1995 p. 949):

> The first criterion was the development of the imports during, normally, the three years before the renegotiations started. What was taken into account was not just a statistical average, but also the trend in the development of trade during that period. Furthermore, account was taken of the size of the tariff increase being negotiated. Moreover, an estimate was made of the price elasticity of the product concerned.

[22] Our purpose here is to examine the tariffs that *can* be implemented in the presence of renegotiation as formally allowed by GATT rules. Consistent with this objective and the formal content of GATT rules, we thus allow that governments are unconstrained with respect to the tariff bindings to which they initially agree. In particular, we depart from the focus of the previous subsection, in which negotiated tariffs are constrained (at least informally) to lie on the Nash iso-world-price locus. This focus served well to illustrate the point that the informal pursuit of reciprocity in trade negotiations has a direct economic interpretation, but it is an unduly restrictive focus in light of our present objectives.

will "imply" a world-price-preserving tariff for its trading partner. We thus define the domestic government's implied foreign tariff, $\tau^* = \tau^*(\hat{\tau}, \bar{p}^w)$, and the foreign government's implied domestic tariff, $\tau = \tau(\hat{\tau}^*, \bar{p}^w)$, by the requirements that $(\hat{\tau}, \tau^*(\hat{\tau}, \bar{p}^w))$ and $(\tau(\hat{\tau}^*, \bar{p}^w), \hat{\tau}^*)$ satisfy the restriction of reciprocity. We may then say that the proposed tariffs, $\hat{\tau}$ and $\hat{\tau}^*$, *agree* if they imply the same tariff pair along the iso-world-price locus: $(\hat{\tau}, \tau^*(\hat{\tau}, \bar{p}^w)) = (\tau(\hat{\tau}^*, \bar{p}^w), \hat{\tau}^*)$. When the proposed tariffs do not agree, the tariff pair (τ, τ^*) that is implemented in the final stage satisfies the *restriction of proposed import limits* if the domestic import volume under (τ, τ^*) is no greater than the implied import volume $M_x(p(\hat{\tau}, \bar{p}^w), \bar{p}^w)$ and the foreign import volume under (τ, τ^*) is likewise no greater than the implied import volume $M_y^*(p^*(\hat{\tau}^*, \bar{p}^w), \bar{p}^w)$. This final restriction formalizes the idea that neither government can be forced to import a volume greater than implied by its own proposal in the renegotiation stage.

We are prepared now to formally define the *Bilateral Negotiation Game:*

Stage 1.—Governments bargain over tariffs and a world price, $\bar{p}^w$, is determined.

Stage 2.—The domestic government proposes a domestic tariff, $\hat{\tau}$, at the same time that the foreign government proposes a foreign tariff, $\hat{\tau}^*$. If the tariff proposals agree, then they are implemented as the outcome of the negotiation.

Stage 3.— If the tariff proposals do not agree, then the tariffs that are implemented are those which achieve the greatest trade volume while satisfying the restrictions of reciprocity and proposed import limits.

Our approach is to first determine the tariffs that can be achieved under the representation of reciprocity given in stages 2 and 3, and then later provide a description of the stage-1 bargaining process that encompasses a range of possibilities.

While there are a variety of simple rules under which governments might negotiate, we will argue that an appealing feature of reciprocity is that this rule is compatible with an

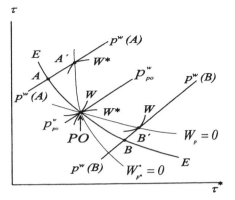

FIGURE 4. RENEGOTIATION UNDER RECIPROCITY

efficient outcome. In fact, renegotiation under reciprocity results in an efficient outcome if and only if tariffs are ultimately set at their politically optimal levels. The key intuition is again that the rule of reciprocity eliminates the ability of any government to shift costs onto its trading partner through a change in the world price. This rule therefore induces each government to behave as if it did not value world-price movements, a behavior which leads naturally toward the selection of politically optimal tariffs.

The main ideas can be developed more concretely with reference to Figure 4. There, we identify three pairs of efficient tariffs, labeled A, B, and PO. We represent as well the iso-world-price loci that run through each of the three tariff pairs. Finally, we also illustrate the loci that represent tariffs for which $W_p = 0$ and $W_{p*}^* = 0$, respectively. For illustrative purposes only, these loci are assumed downward sloping. According to (8), each locus intersects the efficiency frontier at the politically optimal point PO and nowhere else.[23]

Suppose now that the governments' initial agreement corresponds to point A. In this case, the foreign government would prefer to move up the associated iso-world-price locus to

---

[23] Using (8), efficiency is possible if and only if both $W_p = 0$ and $W_{p*}^* = 0$ (corresponding to the politically optimal point) or both $W_p \neq 0$ and $W_{p*}^* \neq 0$.

point A', where it achieves its preferred local price. The foreign government thus has incentive to propose the tariff $\tau^*(A')$, with the corresponding implied domestic tariff $\tau(A')$; in fact, for the bilateral negotiation game represented above, this proposal is a dominant strategy for the foreign government.[24] The efficient tariff pair at A is thus not "renegotiation proof" under GATT rules, since the foreign government would request a renegotiation to raise its tariff to $\tau^*(A')$, knowing that the domestic government would then withdraw a substantially equivalent concession that preserved the world price and delivered the point A'. Using a similar argument, it is apparent that the point B also fails the renegotiation test, although in this case it is the domestic government that withdraws its original concession in order to induce the point B'. It is now direct to see that there is exactly one efficient tariff pair which, if agreed to initially, would be impervious to the renegotiation process. This tariff pair is the politically optimal tariff pair, since this is the only point on the efficiency locus at which each government achieves its preferred local price for the given world price.[25]

We now say that a tariff pair (τ, τ^*) can be *implemented under reciprocity* if there exists a world price $\bar{p}^w$ such that the outcome of

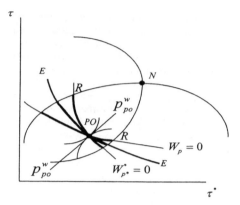

FIGURE 5A. THE LOCUS OF TARIFFS IMPLEMENTABLE UNDER RECIPROCITY

stages 2 and 3 of the Bilateral Negotiation Game is uniquely (τ, τ^*), when governments make dominant proposals. Arguing in this general fashion described above, we show formally in the Appendix that the following proposition obtains.

PROPOSITION 5: *An efficient trade agreement can be implemented under reciprocity if and only if it is characterized by tariffs which are set at their politically optimal levels.*

Thus, if governments recognize the potential for renegotiation as allowed by GATT rules, and if they seek an efficient outcome, then their negotiations will result in the politically optimal tariffs.

We turn now to Figure 5A and consider the stage-1 bargaining process in more detail. This figure illustrates the complete locus of reciprocal trade agreements that are implementable under reciprocity. With τ and τ^* on the vertical and horizontal axis, respectively, we depict there the efficiency locus (labeled $E \rightarrow E$), the contract curve (the bold portion of the efficiency locus), and the politically optimal point (labeled PO). The locus of tariff combinations implementable under reciprocity in a reciprocal trade agreement corresponds to the upper envelope of the portions of the $W_p = 0$ and $W_{p^*}^* = 0$ loci that lie inside the Nash welfare contours of the two governments, and we label this locus $R \rightarrow PO \rightarrow R$.

---

[24] The restriction of proposed import limits ensures that, if the proposals do not agree, the tariff pair that is implemented is the proposed tariff pair that is the "highest" (i.e., most restrictive) pair. Thus, if the domestic government proposes a tariff pair that is lower than A', then the foreign government's proposal is pivotal, and the foreign government achieves its preferred point on the given iso-world-price locus. On the other hand, if the domestic government proposes a tariff pair that is higher than A', then the foreign proposal is nonpivotal, and the foreign government's proposal would matter only if it were higher yet, which would result in an even worse (i.e., further above A') outcome for the foreign government.

[25] In the special case in which governments maximize national income, the political optimum corresponds to reciprocal free trade and the locus at which $W_p = 0$ ($W_{p^*}^* = 0$) is horizontal (vertical) out of this point. The efficiency locus passes through the reciprocal-free-trade point as well, but it otherwise lies below the loci at which $W_p = 0$ and $W_{p^*}^* = 0$. If governments maximize national income, therefore, the point of reciprocal free trade is the only point on the efficiency frontier that is impervious to renegotiation as allowed by GATT rules.

Figure 5B translates this information into welfare space, with the vertical (horizontal) axis measuring $W(W^*)$ and the origin representing the Nash welfare levels of each government. In this figure, the dashed curve represents the efficiency frontier, while the bold curve indicates the combinations of welfare achievable under reciprocity in a reciprocal trade agreement, corresponding to the welfare levels along the locus $R \to PO \to R$ in Figure 5A. As depicted in Figure 5B, reciprocity has the effect of shrinking the feasible set of bargaining outcomes to lie within the efficiency frontier at all but the politically optimal point.

With reference to Figure 5B, we may now understand the constraint of reciprocity more broadly as a rule of negotiation that has the effect of steering the stage-1 bargaining outcome toward the political optimum. To make this point, we consider any stage-1 bargaining process that can be represented in terms of the maximization of a general function, the iso-quantity contours of which are downward sloping and convex in the space of welfare. The objective function specified in the Nash bargaining solution is one example. The maximization is taken over a set of feasible tariff/welfare outcomes, and the feasible set is determined in turn by the bargaining format.

We compare two bargaining formats.[26] Suppose first that governments bargain directly in stage 1 over final tariff/welfare outcomes, without the possibility of subsequent renegotiation. The feasible set of welfare outcomes then corresponds in Figure 5B to those welfare levels that lie on or within the efficiency frontier. Assuming that the efficiency frontier is concave, the bargaining outcome is uniquely determined as a tangency between an iso-quantity contour and the efficiency frontier. We represent this solution as point A. The second format corresponds to the Bilateral Negotiation Game. In this case, the feasible set of welfare outcomes is represented in Figure 5B as those welfare levels that lie on or within the bold curve. If this curve is concave, the

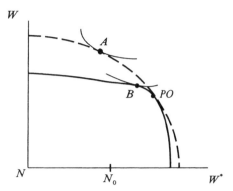

FIGURE 5B. THE FEASIBLE SET OF BARGAINING OUTCOMES IMPLEMENTABLE UNDER RECIPROCITY

bargaining solution is uniquely determined as a tangency between the iso-quantity contour and the bold curve. The solution under this second format is depicted at point B, where the stage-1 bargaining outcome is now closer to the political optimum.[27]

This discussion indicates that the restriction of reciprocity directs the bargaining outcome toward the political optimum. Intuitively, this restriction limits the extent to which one government can gain when the other government's welfare is diminished (relative to the political optimum), and this "efficiency penalty" ensures that governments will not venture too far from the political optimum in their stage-1 negotiations. Finally, we also observe that, as Proposition 5 states, the politically optimal outcome is itself necessary under any stage-1

---

[26] We explore the differences between these two formats at greater length in Section V, where we refer to the first (second) format as a power- (rules-) based approach.

[27] The details depicting the positions of points A and B in Figure 5B will depend on the specific stage-1 bargaining process adopted, but the general point illustrated by the figure—that each government's payoff lies closer to its politically optimal payoff under the second bargaining format—will hold in a variety of settings. For example, this will always be the case if countries are not too asymmetric, or with sufficient concavity of the reciprocity-constrained efficiency frontier relative to the unconstrained frontier. It will also hold if stage-1 bargaining is characterized by the generalized Nash bargaining solution with sufficiently large bargaining-power asymmetries, under the added regularity condition that the reciprocity-constrained frontier is globally more concave than the unconstrained frontier.

bargaining process, if this process is to deliver an efficient outcome for the Bilateral Negotiation Game. Hence, the politically optimal tariffs will be the outcome of negotiations under a wide range of stage-1 bargaining procedures when, for example, the ability of governments to make side payments is allowed.[28]

III. Nondiscrimination

Along with reciprocity, the principle of non-discrimination—as embodied in the most-favored-nation (MFN) clause—provides the second pillar of the foundation upon which GATT is built. We now extend our framework to a multicountry setting in order to assess the role of nondiscrimination in multilateral trade agreements.

A. *The Economic Environment*

We assume that there is one home country (no *) and three foreign countries (*).[29] The home country is a natural importer of x, and the three foreign countries are natural importers of y. We assume that the three foreign countries have no basis for trade among themselves in the absence of discriminatory tariffs. Furthermore, if tariffs are discriminatory, we assume that the "natural" flow of trade is not altered: discriminatory tariffs do not induce trade among the foreign countries, and they also do not reverse the pattern of trade between the home country and any of its foreign trading partners.[30] As such, each foreign country

[28] Government-to-government side payments are often considered in theoretical analyses of trade agreements (e.g., Grossman and Helpman, 1995; Eric W. Bond and Constantinos Syropoulos, 1996). The general relevance of such side payments in practice is less clear, though important cases are discussed in Carsten Kowalczyk and Tomas J. Sjostrom (1994) and John Whalley (1998).

[29] Three is the minimal number of foreign countries that will allow us to consider the role of nondiscrimination in a multilateral agreement when the domestic country is also a member of a preferential agreement. This topic is the subject of Section IV.

[30] These assumptions will be met if, for example, transportation costs between foreign countries are large as compared to the extent of discriminatory home tariffs. Their only role in our analysis is to ensure that it is possible for the home country to select discriminatory tariffs without

trades only with the home country, and the home country is thus the only country that has the opportunity to set discriminatory tariffs.

We now introduce some notation. The set of foreign countries is denoted by $\mathcal{N}^* \in \{1, 2, 3\}$, and we use $j \in \mathcal{N}^*$ as an index for foreign country j. We continue to define $p \equiv p_x/p_y$ as the home local relative price, and we now denote the local relative price in foreign country j as $p^{*j} \equiv p_x^{*j}/p_y^{*j}$. The ad valorem tariff levied by the home country on imports from foreign country j is denoted as t^j, and similarly t^{*j} is the ad valorem tariff imposed by foreign country j on imports from the home country. We assume these tariffs are nonprohibitive. Next, we define the "world" (untaxed) relative price for trade between the home country and foreign country j as $p^{wj} \equiv p_x^{*j}/p_y$. Defining $\tau^j \equiv (1 + t^j)$ and $\tau^{*j} \equiv (1 + t^{*j})$, we then have that $p = \tau^j p^{wj} \equiv p(\tau^j, p^{wj})$ and $p^{*j} = p^{wj}/\tau^{*j} \equiv p^{*j}(\tau^{*j}, p^{wj})$. Finally, we note that bilateral trades link world prices according to:

$$(9) \quad p^{wj} = [\tau^k/\tau^j] \cdot p^{wk}, \text{ for } j, k \in \mathcal{N}^*.$$

Thus, a home-country policy of MFN (i.e., $\tau^1 = \tau^2 = \tau^3$) implies a single world price: $p^{wj} \equiv p^w$. By contrast, tariff discrimination across imports from foreign countries j and k (i.e., $\tau^j \neq \tau^k$) implies different world prices: $p^{wj} \neq p^{wk}$.

Foreign production and consumption decisions can be characterized exactly as in our two-country model, since each foreign country j has only one trading partner, and so its terms of trade are given simply by p^{wj}. Thus, production, consumption, exports and imports for foreign country $j \in \mathcal{N}^*$ are denoted respectively by $Q_i^{*j} = Q_i^{*j}(p^{*j})$ for $i \in \{x, y\}$, $C_i^{*j}(p^{*j}, p^{wj})$ for $i \in \{x, y\}$, $E_x^{*j}(p^{*j}(\tau^{*j}, p^{wj}), p^{wj})$, and $M_y^{*j}(p^{*j}(\tau^{*j}, p^{wj}), p^{wj})$. The presence of multiple trading partners for the domestic country potentially complicates the expression of domestic quantities, as the home country may face different terms of trade with each of its trading partners. This complication does not affect the determination

prohibiting trade between it and its less-favored trading partners.

of domestic production, which is still represented as a function of local relative prices: $Q_i = Q_i(p)$ for $i \in \{x, y\}$. Likewise, domestic consumption of good i is still determined as a function of the local relative price and domestic tariff revenue: $D_i(p, R)$ for $i \in \{x, y\}$. But, in light of the possibility of discriminatory tariffs, domestic tariff revenue now depends both on the total volume of x imported by the domestic country and the composition of this given volume across the foreign trading partners.

To construct an expression for domestic tariff revenue, we let $\{p^{*j}\}$ and $\{p^{wj}\}$ denote the set of foreign local and world prices, respectively, and we define bilateral trade shares by

$$s_x^{*j}(\{p^{*j}\}, \{p^{wj}\})$$

$$\equiv E_x^{*j}(p^{*j}, p^{wj}) \bigg/ \left[\sum_{i \in \mathcal{N}^*} E_x^{*i}(p^{*i}, p^{wi}) \right].$$

We then define the domestic country's *multilateral* terms of trade by the trade-weighted average of the set of bilateral world prices:

$$T(\{p^{*j}\}, \{p^{wj}\})$$

$$\equiv \sum_{i \in \mathcal{N}^*} s_x^{*i}(\{p^{*i}\}, \{p^{wi}\}) \cdot p^{wi}.$$

With this definition in place, domestic tariff revenue is given implicitly by

$$R = [D_x(p, R) - Q_x(p)]$$

$$\times \sum_{i \in \mathcal{N}^*} s_x^{*i}(\{p^{*i}\}, \{p^{wi}\}) \cdot [p - p^{wi}]$$

$$= [D_x(p, R) - Q_x(p)] \cdot [p - T],$$

or $R = R(p, T)$.

We may now represent the domestic country's consumption as $C_i(p, T) \equiv D_i(p, R(p, T))$. It follows that home-country imports of x may be denoted as $M_x(p, T) \equiv C_x(p, T) - Q_x(p)$, while home-country exports of y may be represented as $E_y(p, T) \equiv Q_y(p) - C_y(p, T)$. Henceforth, we will refer to T simply as

the home country's terms of trade, and it will play a role analogous to p^w in the two-country model of the previous sections. In fact, as (9) indicates, if the home country adopts a MFN tariff policy, then $T = p^{wj} \equiv p^w$. However, a discriminatory tariff policy implies $T \neq p^{wj}$ for $j \in \mathcal{N}^*$.

We turn finally to the trade-balance and market-clearing conditions. Home and foreign budget constraints imply that, for any world prices, we have

$$(10) \quad T(\{p^{*j}\}, \{p^{wj}\})$$

$$\times M_x(p, T(\{p^{*j}\}, \{p^{wj}\}))$$

$$= E_y(p, T(\{p^{*j}\}, \{p^{wj}\}));$$

$$M_y^{*j}(p^{*j}, p^{wj})$$

$$= p^{wj} \cdot E_x^{*j}(p^{*j}, p^{wj}), \text{ for } j \in \mathcal{N}^*.$$

With $\{\tau^j\}$ and $\{\tau^{*j}\}$ representing the set of domestic and foreign tariffs, respectively, we denote the equilibrium world price for trade between the home and foreign country j by $\tilde{p}^{wj}(\{\tau^j\}, \{\tau^{*j}\})$. Equilibrium world prices are then determined by (9) and the market-clearing condition for good x:

$$(11) \quad M_x(p, T(\{p^{*j}\}, \{\tilde{p}^{wj}\}))$$

$$= \sum_{i \in \mathcal{N}^*} E_x^{*i}(p^{*i}, \tilde{p}^{wi}).$$

The equilibrium in the y-market is then assured by (10).

B. *Government Objectives*

We again represent the objectives of each government as a general function of its local price and terms of trade. Thus, the home government maximizes $W(p, T)$ while foreign government j maximizes $W^{*j}(p^{*j}, \tilde{p}^{wj})$. We assume only that, with local prices held fixed, each government strictly prefers an improvement in its terms of trade: $W_T(p, T) < 0$ and $W_{p^{wj}}^{*j}(p^{*j}, \tilde{p}^{wj}) > 0$.

The home-government welfare function embodies a novel pattern of externalities. As in the two-country model, the tariff level selected by a foreign government alters world prices, and this in turn affects the home country's terms of trade T and imparts a home-government externality through the consequent change in tariff revenue. In the multicountry model, however, the tariff level selected by the foreign government may also exert a home-government externality through the effect that the tariff has on the foreign local price and thereby the home country's terms of trade and tariff revenue. Intuitively, for any given total import volume for the home country, if the home country sets tariffs in a discriminatory fashion, then the home government receives greater tariff revenue when a larger fraction of imports emanates from the foreign country on whom it places the highest import tariff. The foreign export volumes, however, are determined in part by foreign local prices, and therefore foreign local prices impart a home-government externality when home tariffs are discriminatory. Importantly, this "local-price externality" disappears when the home government's tariffs satisfy MFN, since in that event the home country's terms of trade is independent of foreign local prices and is given simply by the (common) world price.

C. Tariff Policies

As in our analysis of the two-country model, we compare the Nash, politically optimal, and efficient tariffs. We begin with the Nash tariffs. Let the domestic government select a tariff policy, (τ^1, τ^2, τ^3), to maximize its welfare, W, at the same time that each foreign government j chooses its tariff policy, τ^{*j}, to maximize its welfare, W^{*j}. The resulting best-response conditions are

(12a)   Home: $W_p + \tilde{\lambda}^j W_T = 0$, for $j \in \mathcal{N}^*$,

(12b)   Foreign: $W^{*j}_{p^{*j}} + \tilde{\lambda}^{*j} W^{*j}_{p^{wj}}$

$\qquad\qquad = 0$, for $j \in \mathcal{N}^*$,

with $\tilde{\lambda}^j \equiv [dT/d\tau^j]/[dp/d\tau^j]$ and $\tilde{\lambda}^{*j} \equiv [\partial\bar{p}^{wj}/\partial\tau^{*j}]/[dp^{*j}/d\tau^{*j}]$. A set of tariffs $(\{\tau^j\}, \{\tau^{*j}\})$ for $j \in \mathcal{N}^*$ forms a *Nash equilibrium* if each government's tariff policy satisfies its best-response condition(s).

We next extend to our multicountry setting the definition of politically optimal tariffs. In analogy with our two-country model, we define *politically optimal tariffs* as a set of tariffs $(\{\tau^{jPO}\}, \{\tau^{*jPO}\})$ for $j \in \mathcal{N}^*$ that satisfies

(13a)   Home: $W_p = 0$,

(13b)   Foreign: $W^{*j}_{p^{*j}} = 0$, for $j \in \mathcal{N}^*$.

Notice that (13a) and (13b) comprise a set of four equations that must be met by a set of six tariffs (three domestic, three foreign). As such, in the multicountry setting, there are in general many combinations of tariffs that are politically optimal. However, if the additional restriction of MFN is imposed, the number of tariffs drops to four (one domestic, three foreign), and so it may be expected that there is a unique set of politically optimal tariffs that conform to MFN.

We consider next the set of *efficient tariffs*. To characterize this set, we may fix the welfare levels of each foreign government and determine the set of tariffs that maximizes the welfare of the domestic government. This defines a point on the efficiency locus. By varying foreign welfare levels over all feasible values, the entire efficiency locus can be described. We carry out this analysis in the Appendix, where we confirm that the Nash equilibrium tariffs are again inefficient. We establish as well the following proposition.

PROPOSITION 6: *Politically optimal tariffs are efficient if and only if they conform to MFN.*

This proposition thus reports an "affinity" between politically optimal tariffs and the principle of nondiscrimination. Intuitively, politically optimal tariffs are efficient provided that the externalities countries impose on one another in their tariff choices travel only through world prices. In a multicountry world, trade policy externalities indeed travel in this way if and only if tariffs conform to MFN.

Tariff discrimination complicates the transmission of externalities across trading partners by allowing bilateral trade volumes, and hence local prices, to transmit externalities as well. Finally, we note that nondiscrimination is not a general property of points on the efficiency frontier, but is rather a special property required by political optimality.

D. Reciprocity and Nondiscrimination

We now interpret and evaluate the role of nondiscrimination in the presence of reciprocity. To this end, we first adapt our earlier definition of reciprocity to a multicountry setting. Maintaining our interpretation of reciprocity as calling for equal changes in exports and imports across trading partners, we say that a set of tariff changes $\Delta\tau^j \equiv (\tau^{j1} - \tau^{j0})$ and $\Delta\tau^{*j} \equiv (\tau^{*j1} - \tau^{*j0})$ conforms to reciprocity provided that, for $j \in \mathcal{N}^*$,

$$\tilde{p}^{wj0} \cdot [\, E_x^{*j}(p^{*j}(\tau^{*j1}, \tilde{p}^{wj1}), \tilde{p}^{wj1})$$

$$- E_x^{*j}(p^{*j}(\tau^{*j0}, \tilde{p}^{wj0}), \tilde{p}^{wj0})\,]$$

$$= M_y^{*j}(p^{*j}(\tau^{*j1}, \tilde{p}^{wj1}), \tilde{p}^{wj1})$$

$$- M_y^{*j}(p^{*j}(\tau^{*j0}, \tilde{p}^{wj0}), \tilde{p}^{wj0}),$$

where we now make explicit the dependence of local prices on tariffs and the market-clearing world prices. Trade balance [condition (10)] implies that this expression can be reduced to

$$[\tilde{p}^{wj1} - \tilde{p}^{wj0}] \cdot E_x^{*j}(p^{*j}(\tau^{*j1}, \tilde{p}^{wj1}), \tilde{p}^{wj1})$$

$$= 0 \text{ for } j \in \mathcal{N}^*.$$

Hence, as before, mutual tariff changes that conform to reciprocity leave world prices unchanged.

Our next task is to develop the appropriate extension of the Bilateral Negotiation Game for the multicountry model. As before, we posit a three-stage negotiation process that begins with an initial stage in which tariffs are bound at specified levels, determining a set of bilateral world prices. In the second stage, governments make renegotiation proposals, where under the restriction of reciprocity the bilateral world prices must

be preserved. If governments fail to reach an agreement in this renegotiation stage, a third stage is entered in which tariffs are implemented that achieve the greatest multilateral trade volume consistent with the constraints that the tariffs satisfy the restriction of reciprocity and require no government to import a bilateral volume in excess of that implied by its proposal in the renegotiation stage.

We now develop a formal representation of the trade negotiation process. Letting $\{\tilde{p}^{wj}\}$ denote the set of bilateral world prices determined in the first stage, we say that a renegotiated set of tariffs $(\{\tau^j\}, \{\tau^{*j}\})$ satisfies the *restriction of reciprocity* if the tariff set preserves the bilateral world prices: $\tilde{p}^{wj}(\{\tau^j\}, \{\tau^{*j}\}) = \bar{p}^{wj}$ for each $j \in \mathcal{N}^*$. We now consider the foreign tariffs and bilateral trade volumes that are "implied" by the domestic government's proposal in the renegotiation stage, where the domestic proposal is a set $\{\hat{\tau}^j\}$ of domestic tariffs that satisfy (9) given $\{\bar{p}^{wj}\}$. In contrast to the two-country model, the proposed tariff set when combined with the fixed set of bilateral world prices $\{\bar{p}^{wj}\}$ does not uniquely imply domestic import volumes nor foreign tariffs.[31] We therefore assume that the domestic government also proposes the shares $\{\hat{s}_x^{*j}\}$ of its total import volume that are to come from each foreign trading partner, where these proposed shares are nonnegative and sum to one. When the domestic government proposes $\{\hat{\tau}^j\}$ and $\{\hat{s}_x^{*j}\}$, the implied foreign tariffs, $\tau^{*j} = \tau^{*j}(\{\hat{\tau}^j\}, \{\hat{s}_x^{*j}\}, \{\bar{p}^{wj}\})$, are defined by the requirements that the tariffs $(\{\hat{\tau}^j\}, \{\tau^{*j}\})$ satisfy the restriction of reciprocity and generate the proposed set of trade volume shares:

$$E_x^{*j}(p^{*j}(\tau^{*j}(\cdot), \bar{p}^{wj}), \bar{p}^{wj})$$

$$= \hat{s}_x^{*j} \cdot \sum_{i \in \mathcal{N}^*} E_x^{*i}(p^{*i}(\tau^{*i}(\cdot), \bar{p}^{wi}), \bar{p}^{wi})$$

for $j \in \mathcal{N}^*$,

---

[31] For a fixed set of domestic tariffs $\{\hat{\tau}^j\}$ and bilateral world prices $\{\bar{p}^{wj}\}$, the local domestic price $p(\tau^j, \bar{p}^{wj})$ is implied. In the multicountry model, however, this price alone is insufficient to determine domestic import volume, as T is affected by the set of foreign tariffs, $\{\hat{\tau}^{*j}\}$, when domestic tariffs are discriminatory. See equilibrium condition (11).

where $\tau^{*j}(\cdot)$ denotes the value $\tau^{*j}(\{\hat{\tau}^j\}, \{\hat{s}_x^{*j}\}, \{\bar{p}^{wj}\})$.[32]

We consider next the foreign trade volumes and domestic import tariffs that are implied by the proposals of the foreign governments in the renegotiation stage. We assume that, in this stage, each foreign government j proposes its tariff, $\hat{\tau}^{*j}$. Given the bilateral world price $\bar{p}^{wj}$, this proposal directly implies an import volume for foreign country j, which is given as $M_y^{*j}(p^{*j}(\hat{\tau}^{*j}, \bar{p}^{wj}), \bar{p}^{wj})$. In addition, the three foreign tariff proposals together imply a set of domestic tariffs, when the bilateral world prices are fixed.[33] Thus, if in the renegotiation stage each foreign government j proposes tariff $\hat{\tau}^{*j}$, then the set $\{\hat{\tau}^{*j}\}$ defines an implied set of domestic tariffs, with member $\tau^j = \tau^j(\{\hat{\tau}^{*j}\}, \{\bar{p}^{wj}\})$, by the requirement that the tariffs $(\{\tau^j\}, \{\hat{\tau}^{*j}\})$ satisfy the restriction of reciprocity.

We are now prepared to state two final definitions. First, we say that the proposals $(\{\hat{\tau}^j\}, \{\hat{s}_x^{*j}\})$ and $\{\hat{\tau}^{*j}\}$ *agree* if $(\{\hat{\tau}^j\}, \{\tau^{*j}(\cdot)\}) = (\{\tau^j(\cdot)\}, \{\hat{\tau}^{*j}\})$, where as above $\tau^{*j}(\cdot)$ denotes the implied value $\tau^{*j}(\{\hat{\tau}^j\}, \{\hat{s}_x^{*j}\}, \{\bar{p}^{wj}\})$ and where $\tau^j(\cdot)$ denotes the implied value $\tau^j(\{\hat{\tau}^{*j}\}, \{\bar{p}^{wj}\})$. Second, when the proposals do not agree, the tariff set $(\{\tau^j\}, \{\tau^{*j}\})$ that is implemented in the final stage is said to satisfy the *restriction of proposed import limits* if the domestic import volume from any foreign trading partner j under $(\{\tau^j\}, \{\tau^{*j}\})$ is no greater than the implied import volume from this partner $E_x^{*j}(p^{*j}(\tau^{*j}(\cdot), \bar{p}^{wj}), \bar{p}^{wj})$ and the import volume for any foreign country j under $(\{\tau^j\}, \{\tau^{*j}\})$ is no greater than the implied import volume $M_y^{*j}(p^{*j}(\hat{\tau}^{*j}, \bar{p}^{wj}), \bar{p}^{wj})$, for every $j \in \mathcal{N}^*$.

We now define the *Multilateral Negotiation Game*.

Stage 1.—Governments bargain over tariffs and a set of bilateral world prices, $\{\bar{p}^{wj}\}$, is determined.

Stage 2.—The domestic government proposes a set of domestic tariffs, $\{\hat{\tau}^j\}$, and trade-volume shares, $\{\hat{s}_x^{*j}\}$, at the same time that each foreign government j proposes a foreign tariff, $\hat{\tau}^{*j}$. If the proposals agree, then the tariffs are implemented as the outcome of the negotiation.

Stage 3.—If the proposals do not agree, then the tariffs that are implemented are those which achieve the greatest multilateral trade volume while satisfying the restrictions of reciprocity and proposed import limits.

As before, we concentrate on stages 2 and 3, in order to determine the tariffs that can be implemented when reciprocity is represented in this way.

We say that a tariff set $(\{\tau^j\}, \{\tau^{*j}\})$ can be *implemented under reciprocity* if there exists a set of bilateral world prices $\{\bar{p}^{wj}\}$ such that the outcome of stages 2 and 3 of the Multilateral Negotiation Game is uniquely $(\{\tau^j\}, \{\tau^{*j}\})$, when foreign governments choose dominant proposals and the proposal of the domestic government is a best response to the foreign proposals.[34] We can now state our next proposition.

PROPOSITION 7: *An efficient multilateral trade agreement can be implemented under reciprocity if and only if it is characterized by tariffs which conform to the principle of MFN and are set at their politically optimal levels.*

---

[32] Given $\{\bar{p}^{wj}\}$, $\{\hat{\tau}^j\}$, and $\{\hat{s}_x^{*j}\}$, foreign tariffs and bilateral trade volumes are implied as follows. First, p is determined as $p = p(\hat{\tau}^j, \bar{p}^{wi})$ while T is determined as $T = \Sigma_{i \in \mathcal{N}^*} \hat{s}_x^{*i} \cdot \bar{p}^{wi}$. Total import volume is then determined as $M_x = M_x(p, T)$, where under (11) we have $M_x = \Sigma_{i \in \mathcal{N}^*} E_x^{*i}$ as well. E_x^{*j} is then implied as $E_x^{*j} = \hat{s}_x^{*j} \cdot \Sigma_{i \in \mathcal{N}^*} E_x^{*i}$, and this in turn implies p^{*j} as $p^{*j} = p^{*j}(\tau^{*j}, \bar{p}^{wj})$, and hence a value for τ^{*j}, for each $j \in \mathcal{N}^*$.

[33] Given $\{\bar{p}^{wj}\}$ and $\{\hat{\tau}^{*j}\}$, we have that $\{p^{*j}\}$ is determined, and so the right-hand side of (11) is also determined. Furthermore, with $\{p^{*j}\}$ determined, we see that T is determined as well. Thus, satisfaction of (11) determines p. But this means that τ^j is implied as $\tau^j = \bar{p}^{wj}/p$.

[34] In the multicountry model, we no longer require that the domestic-government proposal is dominant. Intuitively, the domestic government will wish to choose its share proposal so as to trade as much as possible with the partners with whom it has the most favorable terms of trade. The optimal domestic share proposals are thus sensitive to the anticipated foreign proposals, as the latter bound the import volumes that the respective foreign partners will accept.

A proof of this proposition is provided in the Appendix.

Intuitively, nondiscrimination ensures that all international externalities are channeled through world-price movements, and the principle of reciprocity serves effectively to neutralize externalities of exactly this nature. Alternatively, if stage-1 bargaining results in discriminatory tariffs, then the tariff choices of each foreign country will impart externalities on the home country through both world price and foreign local-price effects, and reciprocity is ill suited to handle the latter. Reciprocity and nondiscrimination are thus simple rules that, when used together, can deliver an efficient outcome. Furthermore, these rules direct attention toward a particular set of tariffs—the politically optimal MFN tariffs—along the efficiency frontier.[35]

IV. Preferential Agreements

While the principles of reciprocity and nondiscrimination form the pillars of GATT, a major exception to the latter principle is allowed for the purpose of creating preferential agreements. As mentioned in the introduction, this exception, embodied in GATT Article XXIV, was controversial in its inception and has met with renewed controversy recently. In this section, we use our modeling framework to address a central question in this controversy: Will preferential agreements interfere with a multilateral trading system that is built upon the pillars of reciprocity and nondiscrimination?

In accord with Article XXIV, we consider two forms of preferential agreements. First, the domestic country forms a *free-trade area* with foreign country i if $\tau^i = 0 = \tau^{*i}$ and $\tau^j > 0$ for some $j \neq i$. As free-trade areas are

inherently discriminatory, the next result is a direct implication of Proposition 7.

PROPOSITION 8: *An efficient multilateral trade agreement can not be implemented under reciprocity in the presence of a free-trade agreement.*

Free-trade agreements are thus fundamentally at odds with a multilateral trading system that is built on the pillars of reciprocity and nondiscrimination. This is because, to deliver efficiency, reciprocity requires a world in which the transmission of externalities is contained within world-price movements, but externalities travel through local prices as well when tariffs are discriminatory.

A second preferential agreement is a *customs union*, in which members eliminate all internal trade barriers and adopt a common external tariff as well. Proposition 7 no longer directly applies to this case, since the creation of a customs union reduces the number of external tariff authorities from four to three. But Proposition 7 is instructive, in that it suggests that reciprocity might continue to deliver efficiency, provided that the union can be viewed as a single country in the previous analysis that sets its external tariffs at the politically optimal MFN levels.

To explore this possibility, we must define the objectives of the tariff authorities in the customs union. If the domestic country forms a customs union with foreign country i, we assume that the customs union sets external tariffs to maximize a function $U(W, W^{*i})$, where U is increasing in each argument. The elimination of internal barriers implies that $p = p^{*i} = \tilde{p}^{wi} \equiv p^{cu}$ and that the two countries experience a common external terms of trade, $T \equiv T^{cu}$. The objectives of the customs union may thus be represented further as $U(W, W^{*i}) = U(W(p^{cu}, T^{cu}), W^{*i}(p^{cu}, T^{cu})) \equiv W^{cu}(p^{cu}, T^{cu})$, with $W^{cu}_{T^{cu}} < 0$. With $W^{*j}(p^{*j}, \tilde{p}^{wj})$ still representing the objectives of each foreign government $j \neq i$, it follows from Proposition 7 that an efficient multilateral trade agreement between the customs union and the remaining foreign countries can be achieved under reciprocity if and only if the external tariffs of the customs union

---

[35] At this point it is useful to comment on the relation between the Bilateral and Multilateral Negotiation Games. In our analysis of the latter we have allowed for the possibility of discriminatory tariffs and have shown that MFN is required for efficiency. This possibility introduces some complications, as we then must consider share announcements and best-response choices by the domestic government. If we had instead imposed MFN from the outset, then the analysis would again be exactly analogous to the Bilateral Negotiation Game.

and the tariffs of all other countries conform to the principle of MFN and are set at their politically optimal levels.

This conclusion is appropriate if we define efficiency in terms of the welfare of the customs union itself and the remaining foreign countries. When we define efficiency in terms of the welfare of individual countries, however, we must determine as well whether it is internally efficient (i.e., with respect to W and W^{*i}) for members of the customs union to share a common local-market price. If the tariff revenue collected by the customs union can be divided among members in a way that achieves internal efficiency at this common price, we will call the two countries *natural integration partners*. This possibility is ensured if the political preferences and income levels of the two countries are sufficiently similar. We can now state the following proposition.

PROPOSITION 9: *An efficient multilateral trade agreement can be implemented under reciprocity in the presence of a customs union if and only if the members of the customs union are natural integration partners and the external tariffs of the customs union and the tariffs of all other countries conform to the principle of MFN and are set at their politically optimal levels.*

Together, Propositions 8 and 9 identify a rather limited set of circumstances under which preferential agreements can exist without compromising the effectiveness of the principles of reciprocity and nondiscrimination in delivering an efficient multilateral trading agreement.

V. Participation

GATT is a "rules-based" approach to trade negotiations. While there are all manner of rules that might be contemplated when designing a rules-based institution, an important feature of the GATT rules of reciprocity and nondiscrimination is that they steer negotiations toward a particular point on the efficiency frontier: the political optimum. As mentioned in Section I, an alternative negotiation approach is "power-based." Under this approach, governments negotiate directly over tariffs, without reference to any previously agreed-upon rules, and the outcome of the negotiations is thus especially sensitive to the "bargaining power" that the governments respectively possess. Natural formalizations of the power-based approach, such as the Nash bargaining solution, indicate that power-based negotiations may result in an agreement that rests on the efficiency frontier. Yet these negotiations, by favoring the more powerful country, would typically not deliver the political optimum. This raises a central question: How might governments choose between alternative institutional designs (e.g., rules-based versus power-based approaches)?

This is a fundamental question within the field of international relations, and we do not presume to provide a complete answer here. Some of the broader considerations involved are described below by Jackson (1989 pp. 85–86), who concludes that the history of international relations has witnessed a gradual evolution from a power-based to a rules-based approach:

> In broad perspective one can roughly divide the various techniques for the peaceful settlement of international disputes into two types: settlement by negotiation and agreement with reference (explicitly or implicitly) to relative power status of the parties; or settlement by negotiation or decision with reference to norms or rules to which both parties have previously agreed.
>
> For example, countries A and B have a trade dispute regarding B's treatment of imports from A to B of widgets. The first technique mentioned would involve a negotiation between A and B by which the most powerful of the two would have the advantage. Foreign aid, military maneuvers, or import restrictions on other key goods by way of retaliation would figure in the negotiation. A small country would hesitate to challenge a large one on whom its trade depends ...
>
> On the other hand, the second suggested technique—reference to agreed rules—would see the negotiators arguing about the application of the rule

... . During the process of negotiating a settlement it would be necessary for the parties to understand that an unsettled dispute would ultimately be resolved by impartial third-party judgements based on rules so that the negotiators would be negotiating with reference to their respective predictions as to the outcome of those judgments and not with reference to potential retaliation or actions exercising power of one or more of the parties of the dispute.

In both techniques negotiation and private settlement of disputes is the dominant mechanism for resolving differences; but the key is the perception of the participants as to what are the "bargaining chips." ...

All diplomacy, and indeed all government, involves a mixture of these techniques. To a large degree, the history of civilization may be described as a gradual evolution from a power-oriented approach, in the state of nature, toward a rule-oriented approach....[36]

While our simple modeling framework can not capture the breadth of themes to which Jackson alludes, it can be used to explore a pair of important issues that are associated with the choice between rules-based and power-based approaches to trade-policy negotiations.

The first issue concerns the sense in which GATT is a rules-based institution. Up to this point, we have regarded any negotiating approach as "rules-based," if the approach involves agreed-upon rules under which subsequent negotiations are undertaken. Certainly, GATT satisfies this standard. As Jackson's discussion above suggests, however, there is also a second standard that might be put forth: a rules-based agreement is designed so that the outcome of negotiations is insulated from the power positions of the par-

ties involved. While it is inevitable that real-world negotiations are influenced to some degree by the power positions of the participants, we argue that GATT also satisfies this second standard, since it is designed in a manner that reduces the effect of bargaining power on negotiation outcomes. In particular, the rule of reciprocity neutralizes power asymmetries and guides governments toward the political optimum, an outcome that is defined without reference to countries' relative power status. In this sense, our results confirm the widely held view that reciprocity is one "pillar" of GATT's architecture, with nondiscrimination then required as a second pillar that preserves the effectiveness of reciprocity in a multicountry world.

This discussion leads naturally to a second issue: Why would powerful countries agree to participate in GATT under the rule of reciprocity? In the remainder of the section, we offer one possible answer: by serving to moderate the lawful response of powerful countries in case of disagreement, GATT's rule of reciprocity may encourage weaker countries to participate in GATT negotiations without the fear of exploitation by their stronger trading partners.

To develop this point, we return to the Bilateral Negotiation Game described in Section II and consider the addition of a stage 0 in which each government decides whether or not to participate in negotiations in light of the bargaining format which follows. As with reference to Figure 5B, we may consider the possibility of two bargaining formats: a "power-based" format, in which governments bargain directly in stage 1 over final tariff/welfare outcomes without the possibility of subsequent renegotiation, and a "rules-based" format corresponding to the Bilateral Negotiation Game. As described in Section II, the power-based format gives rise to a negotiation outcome corresponding to the point labeled A in Figure 5B, while the rules-based format gives rise to the negotiation outcome labeled B in Figure 5B.

The question we now pose is whether the stage-0 participation decision might be influenced by the bargaining format. More specifically, we ask whether, in directing the bargaining outcome toward the political optimum, GATT's rule of reciprocity might

---

[36] As Jackson's discussion goes on to suggest, a separate issue is how agreements are to be enforced. Whether the agreement is over tariff levels directly or rather over rules within which governments agree to operate when determining their tariff policies, enforcement of the agreement is an issue which should not be ignored. We return to this important issue in our concluding section.

encourage weaker countries to participate in GATT negotiations without the fear of exploitation by their stronger trading partners. Essentially, the answer to this question is "yes," provided that there exists a distinction between stage-0 and stage-1 government preferences which leads to a difference between the Nash (disagreement) welfare levels as viewed from stage-1 negotiations (labeled N in Figure 5B) and the Nash welfare levels as viewed from the stage-0 participation decision (which we depict for illustrative purposes by the point labeled N_0 in Figure 5B). Here we briefly consider one way in which such a difference could arise: from sunk costs associated with the actions of private agents.[37]

If production requires irreversible investments, then private-sector decisions made in anticipation of negotiations to liberalize markets may alter the payoffs to governments should negotiations break down. John McLaren (1997 p. 404) has argued that this observation may be particularly relevant in describing the plight of a small country negotiating to gain access to the markets of a large trading partner, where "the rational investments undertaken by small-country citizens ... in anticipation of future bargaining can rob the small country of its flexibility ..." and make it worse off under the resulting bargain than if the opportunity to negotiate had never arisen. This point may be illustrated in the present context with the use of Figure 5B, if we think of the foreign government as representing the smaller country, and we think of the irreversible small-country investments in serving the large-country market as being determined between stages 0 and 1.

Consider first the possibility of a power-based bargaining format. The curves represented in Figure 5B will correspond to the situation as viewed in stage 1 (i.e., after the

decision to negotiate has been made and the investment decisions of the small country have been sunk), with the welfare levels at point N depicting the respective payoffs for the two governments in the event that stage-1 negotiations break down, and the point A reflecting the bargaining outcome under a power-based format. The point labeled N_0 depicts the respective payoffs for the two governments if either government decides in stage 0 not to participate in negotiations, and the payoff to the foreign government is larger at N_0 than at N as a result of the sunk investments associated with the latter. If, as depicted in Figure 5B, N_0 lies to the right of the outcome under the power-based bargain A, then the foreign country would do better to pass up the opportunity to negotiate a trade agreement with its large trading partner, much as McLaren's (1997) remarks suggest. As a result, negotiations do not occur, and governments receive the Nash payoffs associated with N_0 in this case.

Now consider the possibility of a rules-based bargaining format. In particular, suppose that the stage-0 participation decision is made with reference to the Bilateral Negotiation Game, whose outcome is depicted in Figure 5B by the point B. It is here that, by guiding countries toward the political optimum in their tariff negotiations, the introduction of a rule such as reciprocity can diminish power asymmetries, thereby relaxing the participation constraint for the weaker country and facilitating its entry into tariff negotiations. In terms of Figure 5B, the foreign government will agree to participate in negotiations under the rule of reciprocity provided that, as depicted, the point N_0 lies to the left of the rules-based negotiating outcome depicted at B. It is now apparent that, as long as B lies to the northeast of N_0, it will also be in the interest of the more powerful country to agree to a rule of reciprocity, so as to encourage the widest participation of its trading partners.

VI. Conclusion

Working within a general equilibrium model and adopting a representation of government trade-policy objectives that accom-

---

[37] An alternative way to generate a difference between *ex ante* (prior to initiating negotiations) and *ex post* government preferences would be to focus on changing political constraints associated with the resolution of uncertainty over the effects of liberalization, along the lines of Raquel Fernandez and Dani Rodrik (1991). See also footnote 8.

modates the major formulations of political economy motives, we have shown that governments can shift the cost of their intervention onto trading partners by altering world prices with their unilateral tariff choices, and that this is the source of the inefficiency which a reciprocal trade agreement must address. From this perspective, we have offered an interpretation of GATT's principles of reciprocity and non-discrimination as rules that work in concert to guide governments toward efficient multilateral trade agreements. While we establish circumstances under which customs unions are compatible with an efficient multilateral trading system built on these principles, we have shown that these circumstances are quite narrow, and that in addition free-trade agreements are fundamentally incompatible with such a system. As such, we offer support for the view that preferential agreements pose a threat to the multilateral trading system.

Our basic argument is developed in four main steps. First, we establish that governments' unilateral tariffs are higher than is efficient, because of the temptation to shift costs onto trading partners via the world-price externality. Second, utilizing the requirement of balanced trade, we find that the principle of reciprocity as practiced in GATT serves to neutralize the world-price implications of tariff negotiations. Reciprocity can thus assist governments in achieving efficient trade-policy outcomes. Third, we construct a multicountry model and observe that externalities then may travel to the home government both through world and foreign local prices. When the home government sets MFN tariffs, however, externalities travel only through the world price, and so the principle of reciprocity is again well suited to address the inefficiencies with which a trade agreement must contend. Finally, we observe that exceptions to MFN for the purpose of creating preferential agreements revive the local-price externality, thus frustrating the ability of a multilateral system governed by the principle of reciprocity to deliver an efficient outcome.

The empirical relevance of our theory requires that governments are able to shift the costs of their intervention onto trading partners and that the implications of such cost-shifting activities are quantitatively significant. The first requirement is met if governments are able to improve their terms of trade with their trade-policy choices, which is the case when foreign exporters incur some of the incidence of an import tariff (i.e., when the full tariff is not passed through to domestic consumers). Equivalently, the hypothesis that governments can improve their terms of trade with their tariff choices is supported if a reduction in the domestic import tariff is not fully passed through as a reduced price for domestic consumers. It is therefore relevant to refer to the study of GATT negotiations by Mordechai E. Kreinin (1961 p. 314), who suggests that "less than a third ... of the tariff concessions granted by the United States were passed on to the U.S. consumer in the form of reduced import prices, while more than two-thirds ... accrued to the foreign suppliers and improved the terms of trade of the exporting nations."[38] It is also relevant to note that a large empirical literature exists that documents imperfect pass-through of exchange-rate shocks. Presumably, if the cost increase to foreign exporters takes the form of a tariff increase as opposed to an exchange-rate shock, imperfect pass-through would once again occur, confirming that some of the incidence of the import tariff is borne by foreign exporters. Empirical support for this presumption is offered by Feenstra (1995).[39]

Evidence also exists that supports the requirement that the terms-of-trade effects of trade-policy choices influence the national cost

---

[38] A recent study which finds large terms-of-trade effects from regional liberalization is L. Alan Winters and Won Chang (1999).

[39] In this context, it is instructive also to mention the theoretical analysis of Daniel Gros (1987). He finds that even apparently small countries have some power over the terms of trade, provided that the industry is monopolitically competitive. We also stress that our theory does not require that all countries are able to alter the terms of trade. Our theory suggests that truly "small" countries should be extended MFN treatment under GATT without a requirement that they offer reciprocal liberalization of their own. (This is because the unilateral tariff policies of small countries impart no externality; see Bagwell and Staiger, 1996.) To some extent, this treatment is represented in GATT through MFN combined with the "principle supplier" rule (see Dam, 1970 p. 61) as it applies to reciprocal tariff negotiations.

of intervention in quantitatively important ways. In particular, this requirement is strongly supported in the empirical studies by Stephen T. Berry et al. (1995) and Pinelopi K. Goldberg (1995). In both studies, it is found that the terms-of-trade implications of the U.S. decision in the 1980's to restrict automobile imports from Japan with voluntary export restraints (VERs) (rather than tariffs) increased substantially the cost to the United States of achieving the reduced import volumes. Berry et al. report a particularly striking experiment. They compare the actual VER policy with a hypothetical equivalent-tariff policy and calculate that the equivalent-tariff policy would have yielded revenue sufficient to turn what was a losing trade policy in terms of U.S. national income into a policy that would have generated a net gain to U.S. national income of $12.5 billion. The study is relevant for our arguments, since the only difference between the two policies is that they generate distinct world prices. It is precisely this role of world prices to affect the incidence of the cost of intervention across trading partners that is the starting point of our theory.[40]

Finally, we note that relevance of cost-shifting motives for the purpose and design of trade agreements has been suggested as well by GATT legal scholars. For example, in discussing rationales for departing from a goal of free trade, Jackson (1989 p. 19) observes:

> More subtle is the possibility that a national consensus could explicitly opt for a choice of policies that would not maximize wealth (in the traditionally measurable sense, at least), but would give preference to other non-economic goals ... . It can be argued that when a nation

makes an "uneconomic" choice, it should be prepared to pay the whole cost, and not pursue policies which have the effect of unloading some of the burdens of that choice on to other nations. In an interdependent world, paying the whole cost is not often easy to accomplish.

We conclude by mentioning two caveats that apply to our analysis. First, we have interpreted reciprocity and nondiscrimination as principles that can help guide governments from inefficient unilateral outcomes to the efficiency frontier. In practice, however, enforcement difficulties at the international level (see, e.g., Dam, 1970) may preclude governments from eliminating fully the terms-of-trade driven restrictions in trade volume and arriving at the efficiency frontier. When this is the case, the efficiency properties of reciprocity and nondiscrimination may be weakened. For example, it then becomes possible that the formation of preferential agreements may enhance the efficiency of the multilateral trading system, by providing additional enforcement ability that results in multilateral tariffs that are closer to the efficiency frontier.[41]

Second, while the government welfare function that we have employed in our analysis is quite general, it does not capture all of the reasons that governments might pursue trade agreements in practice. For example, regional integration initiatives may reflect broader objectives, such as military security and political stability, which are not captured by local and world prices. This suggests that GATT's willingness to allow Article XXIV exceptions to MFN might be understood in terms of the broader benefits that regional integration may confer. Our framework also excludes the possibility that

---

[40] At the same time, the decision of the United States to "give away" such an amount might be taken as evidence that governments in fact do not care about the terms of trade, even when the associated implications for income are large. This inference, however, does not follow from the U.S. VER experience. The relevant policy alternative for the United States was not a set of unilateral tariff increases (corresponding to the equivalent-tariff policy above), which surely would have incited a retaliatory "trade war" with Japan, but rather a set of tariff changes from the United States and Japan that were consistent with GATT rules.

[41] As we show in other work (Bagwell and Staiger, 1999), however, the enforcement implications of preferential agreements for multilateral tariff cooperation are complex, and there is as yet no basis from which to conclude that such agreements are necessarily efficiency enhancing. See also Bond and Syropoulos (1996), Bond et al. (1996), and Bagwell and Staiger (1997b, d). Maggi (1999) offers a broader perspective as to the role of enforcement in the multilateral trading system.

governments seek trade agreements as a commitment device in a game with domestic agents. These and other possibilities are important topics for future research.

APPENDIX

PROPOSITION 1: *Nash equilibrium tariffs are inefficient.*

PROOF:

We begin by noting that

$$(A1) \quad \frac{d\tau}{d\tau^*}\bigg|_{dW=0}$$

$$= -\frac{\partial \tilde{p}^w/\partial \tau^*}{dp/d\tau}\left[\frac{\tau W_p + W_{p^w}}{W_p + \lambda W_{p^w}}\right];$$

$$\frac{d\tau}{d\tau^*}\bigg|_{dW^*=0} = -\frac{dp^*/d\tau^*}{\partial \tilde{p}^w/\partial \tau}$$

$$\times \left[\frac{W_{p^*}^* + \lambda^* W_{p^w}^*}{W_{p^*}^*/\tau^* + W_{p^w}^*}\right].$$

At a pair of Nash equilibrium tariffs (τ^N, τ^{*N}), $[d\tau/d\tau^*]|_{dW=0} = \infty > 0 = [d\tau/d\tau^*]|_{dW^*=0}$ by (6a), (6b), and (A1). Thus, by (4), the tariff pair (τ^N, τ^{*N}) is inefficient.

PROPOSITION 2: *A reciprocal trade agreement must entail reciprocal trade liberalization.*

PROOF:

We establish that a necessary condition for a tariff pair (τ^0, τ^{*0}) to yield welfare improvements for both the domestic and foreign government relative to the Nash tariffs (τ^N, τ^{*N}) is that $\tau^0 < \tau^N$ and $\tau^{*0} < \tau^{*N}$. To establish this we suppose that $\tau^0 > \tau^N$ and show that the foreign government must lose. The other case in which $\tau^{*0} > \tau^{*N}$ can be handled in an analogous way. First consider the impact of each country's tariff change on the welfare of its trading partner, given by $dW/d\tau^* = [\tau W_p + W_{p^w}][\partial \tilde{p}^w/\partial \tau^*]$ and $dW^*/d\tau = [W_{p^*}^*/\tau^* + W_{p^w}^*][\partial$

$\tilde{p}^w/\partial \tau]$, respectively. Recalling that (6a) and (6b) define, respectively, the domestic and foreign reaction functions $\tau^R(\tau^*)$ and $\tau^{*R}(\tau)$, we note that when the domestic or foreign government, respectively, is on its reaction function, the impact on its welfare of a rise in its trading partner's tariff is

$$dW/d\tau^* = [1 - \tau^R(\tau^*)\lambda]W_{p^w}[\partial \tilde{p}^w/\partial \tau^*]$$

$$< 0;$$

$$dW^*/d\tau$$

$$= [1 - \lambda^*/\tau^{*R}(\tau)]W_{p^w}^*[\partial \tilde{p}^w/\partial \tau] < 0.$$

These inequalities imply that, along each government's reaction function, its welfare is strictly declining in the tariff of its trading partner. With this we now have that $\tau^0 > \tau^N$ implies

$$W^*(p^*(\tau^{*0}, \tilde{p}^w(\tau^0, \tau^{*0})), \tilde{p}^w(\tau^0, \tau^{*0}))$$

$$\leq W^*(p^*(\tau^{*R}(\tau^0)), \tilde{p}^w(\tau^0, \tau^{*R}(\tau^0))),$$

$$\tilde{p}^w(\tau^0, \tau^{*R}(\tau^0))) < W^*(p^*(\tau^{*R}(\tau^N)),$$

$$\tilde{p}^w(\tau^N, \tau^{*R}(\tau^N))), \tilde{p}^w(\tau^N, \tau^{*R}(\tau^N)))$$

$$= W^*(p^*(\tau^{*N}, \tilde{p}^w(\tau^N, \tau^{*N})),$$

$$\tilde{p}^w(\tau^N, \tau^{*N})).$$

Thus, the foreign government must be hurt by any change in tariffs that involves increasing the domestic tariff from its Nash level.

PROPOSITION 3: *Politically optimal tariffs are efficient.*

PROOF:

Using (A1), we have $[d\tau/d\tau^*]|_{dW=0} = -[\partial \tilde{p}^w/\partial \tau^*]/[\partial \tilde{p}^w/\partial \tau] = [d\tau/d\tau^*]|_{dW^*=0}$ at politically optimal tariffs defined by (7a) and (7b), which therefore by (4) are efficient.

PROPOSITION 4: *Beginning at a Nash tariff equilibrium, reciprocal trade liberalization that conforms to reciprocity will increase each government's welfare monotonically until this liberalization has proceeded to the point where* $\min[-W_p, W^*_{p*}] = 0$. *If countries are symmetric, this liberalization path leads to the politically optimal outcome.*

PROOF:

Consider reciprocal reductions in τ and τ^* beginning from the Nash equilibrium and moving along the positively sloped iso-world-price locus that passes through (τ^N, τ^{*N}). With $dp^w = 0$, the impact of a small amount of reciprocal liberalization along this path on domestic government welfare W is just $-W_p(\partial p/\partial \tau)d\tau$ while the impact on foreign government welfare W^* is $-W^*_{p*}(\partial p^*/\partial \tau^*)d\tau^*$. Both are strictly positive around the Nash equilibrium, and both continue to be strictly positive until liberalization has proceeded down this path to the point where $\min[-W_p, W^*_{p*}] = 0$. If countries are symmetric, then both W_p and W^*_{p*} will reach zero at the same point on the iso-world-price locus through (τ^N, τ^{*N}), defining a pair of politically optimal tariffs by (7a) and (7b).

PROPOSITION 5: *An efficient trade agreement can be implemented under reciprocity if and only if it is characterized by tariffs which are set at their politically optimal levels.*

PROOF:

A tariff pair (τ, τ^*) can be implemented under reciprocity if there exists a world price $\bar{p}^w$ such that the outcome of stages 2 and 3 of the Bilateral Negotiation Game is uniquely (τ, τ^*), when governments make dominant proposals. Therefore, to prove the proposition, we must establish that politically optimal tariffs are the only tariffs on the efficiency frontier that can be implemented under reciprocity. Expression (8) characterizes the efficiency frontier, and along this frontier it is necessary that $W_p = 0 = W^*_{p*}$ or $W_p \neq 0 \neq W^*_{p*}$. Observe as well that the restriction of proposed import limits will bind in stage 3 at the highest proposed tariff from stage 2, and therefore that the mapping from tariff proposals to the tariffs $(\tilde{\tau}(\bar{p}^w), \tilde{\tau}^*(\bar{p}^w))$ that are actually implemented as the outcome of the Bilateral Negotiation Game is given by $\tilde{\tau}(\bar{p}^w) = \max\{\hat{\tau}, \tau(\hat{\tau}^*, \bar{p}^w)\}$ and $\tilde{\tau}^*(\bar{p}^w) = \tau^*(\tilde{\tau}(\bar{p}^w), \bar{p}^w)$. The proposition now follows once it is observed that, for any world price $\bar{p}^w$ determined in

stage 1 of the Bilateral Negotiation Game, it is a dominant strategy in the subgame corresponding to stages 2 and 3 for the domestic government to propose $\hat{\tau} = \tau^0(\bar{p}^w)$ and for the foreign government to propose $\hat{\tau}^* = \tau^{*0}(\bar{p}^w)$ where $\hat{\tau} = \tau^0(\bar{p}^w)$ satisfies $W_p(p(\tau, \bar{p}^w), \bar{p}^w) = 0$ and $\hat{\tau}^* = \tau^{*0}(\bar{p}^w)$ satisfies $W^*_{p*}(p^*(\tau^*, \bar{p}^w), \bar{p}^w) = 0$.

PROPOSITION 6: *Politically optimal tariffs are efficient if and only if they conform to MFN.*

PROOF:

We first characterize the efficiency locus. Define $\tilde{p}^{wj}(\tau^{*j}, \bar{W}^{*j})$ as the equilibrium world price for trade between the domestic country and foreign country j that would provide the government of country j with the welfare level $\bar{W}^{*j}$ when its tariff is set at τ^{*j}. This magnitude is defined implicitly by $W^{*j}(p^{*j}(\tau^{*j}, \tilde{p}^{wj}), \tilde{p}^{wj}) = \bar{W}^{*j}$. For simplicity we treat $\tilde{p}^{wj}(\tau^{*j}, \bar{W}^{*j})$ as a well-defined function of τ^{*j}, which it must be provided that W^{*j} is sufficiently close to a representation of national income. Cases where $\tilde{p}^{wj}$ is not uniquely defined can be handled with appropriate modifications without changing our results. For future reference we note that

(A2) $\partial\tilde{p}^{wj}(\tau^{*j}, \bar{W}^{*j})/\partial\tau^{*j}$

$= [p^{*j} \cdot W^{*j}_{p*j}]/[W^{*j}_{p*j}$

$+ \tau^{*j}W^{*j}_{pwj}]$ for $j \in \mathcal{N}^*$.

Since the three foreign tariff and welfare levels, $\{\tau^{*j}\}$ and $\{\bar{W}^{*j}\}$, determine a complete set of both world and foreign local prices, they also imply a value for the domestic terms of trade:

$\bar{T}(\{\tau^{*j}\}, \{\bar{W}^{*j}\}) \equiv T(\{p^{*j}(\tau^{*j},$

$\tilde{p}^{wj}(\tau^{*j}, \bar{W}^{*j}))\}, \{\tilde{p}^{wj}(\tau^{*j}, \bar{W}^{*j})\}).$

Finally, by equilibrium condition (11), a value for the domestic local price is implied as well, and we denote it by $\bar{p}(\{\tau^{*j}\}, \{\bar{W}^{*j}\})$. Domestic government welfare can now be written as a function of the three foreign tariffs and foreign welfare levels, or $W(\bar{p}(\{\tau^{*j}\}, \{\bar{W}^{*j}\}), \bar{T}(\{\tau^{*j}\}, \{\bar{W}^{*j}\}))$. Fixing foreign welfare levels and choosing foreign tariffs to maximize the domestic welfare level then defines a point on the efficiency frontier. The first-order conditions are

(A3) $W_p + \bar{\lambda}^{*j}W_T = 0$ for $j \in \mathcal{N}^*$,

where $\bar{\lambda}^{*j} \equiv [\partial\bar{T}/\partial\tau^{*j}]/[\partial\bar{p}/\partial\tau^{*j}]$ and where $\partial\bar{p}/\partial\tau^{*j}$ is nonzero and finite. An implication of (A3) is that Nash tariffs are inefficient. This can be seen by fixing foreign welfare levels at their Nash values and observing that efficient tariffs satisfy (A3), while Nash tariffs satisfy (12a).

Now suppose that a set of tariffs are politically optimal. Then by (A3) and (13a), they will be efficient if and only if $\partial\bar{T}/\partial\tau^{*j} = 0$ for $j \in \mathcal{N}^*$. From the definition of $\bar{T}$, we have

$$(A4) \quad \frac{\partial\bar{T}}{\partial\tau^{*j}} = \frac{1}{M_x} \cdot \left[\left(\frac{\partial E_x^{*j}}{\partial p^{*j}} \frac{dp^{*j}}{d\tau^{*j}} \right. \right.$$

$$+ \left. \frac{\partial E_x^{*j}}{\partial p^{wj}} \frac{\partial\tilde{p}^{wj}(\tau^{*j}, \bar{W}^{*j})}{\partial\tau^{*j}} \right) \cdot (\tilde{p}^{wj}$$

$$\left. - \bar{T}) + E_x^{*j} \cdot \frac{\partial\tilde{p}^{wj}(\tau^{*j}, \bar{W}^{*j})}{\partial\tau^{*j}} \right].$$

But political optimality implies, by (A2) and (13b), that $\partial\tilde{p}^{wj}(\tau^{*j}, \bar{W}^{*j})/\partial\tau^{*j} = 0$, and hence

$$(A5) \quad \frac{\partial\bar{T}}{\partial\tau^{*j}} = \frac{1}{M_x} \cdot \left[\frac{\partial E_x^{*j}}{\partial p^{*j}} \frac{dp^{*j}}{d\tau^{*j}} \right] \cdot (\tilde{p}^{wj} - \bar{T}),$$

which will be zero if and only if tariffs also conform to MFN.

PROPOSITION 7: *An efficient multilateral trade agreement can be implemented under reciprocity if and only if it is characterized by tariffs which conform to the principle of MFN and are set at their politically optimal levels.*

PROOF:

To prove this result we add an additional regularity condition that $\partial E_x^{*j}/\partial p^{*j} > 0$ for

$j \in \mathcal{N}^*$, which will be met as long as substitution effects dominate income effects. We must establish that the only set of world prices for which the outcome of stages 2 and 3 of the Multilateral Negotiation Game rests on the efficiency frontier, when foreign governments make dominant proposals and the proposal of the domestic government is a best response to the foreign proposals, is the politically optimal MFN world price (i.e., the world price associated with politically optimal MFN tariffs). We outline the general argument here; a more detailed argument is found in our discussion paper (Bagwell and Staiger, 1997c).

We begin with the possibility of MFN tariffs. Arguments analogous to the proof of Proposition 5 establish that politically optimal MFN tariffs can be implemented under reciprocity given the politically optimal MFN world price, and by Proposition 6 these tariffs are efficient. Moreover, arguments analogous to those in Proposition 5 establish that efficient tariffs cannot be implemented under reciprocity given any other MFN world price.

We next consider the possibility of discriminatory tariffs. We establish that efficient tariffs cannot be implemented under reciprocity given any set of discriminatory world prices that such tariffs might imply. Again, as each foreign country faces a single world price, arguments analogous to those in the proof of Proposition 5 establish that for any world price $\bar{p}^{wj}$ determined in stage 1 of the Multilateral Negotiation Game, it is a dominant strategy in the subgame corresponding to stages 2 and 3 for foreign government j to propose $\hat{\tau}^{*j} = \tau^{*j0}(\bar{p}^{wj})$ where $\hat{\tau}^{*j} = \tau^{*j0}(\bar{p}^{wj})$ satisfies $W_{p^{*j}}^{*j}(p^{*j}(\tau^{*j}, \bar{p}^{wj}), \bar{p}^{wj}) = 0$. The best response of the domestic government to these foreign proposals is to propose tariffs and bilateral trade shares such that either: (i) its proposal is nonpivotal with each foreign trading partner, in which case it (weakly) desires more multilateral trade volume (at the fixed terms of trade defined by the given set of world prices and the bilateral trade volumes implied by the proposals of its trading partners) than its trading partners are willing at those world prices to accommodate, so that $\{W_p \leq 0, W_{p^{*j}}^{*j} = 0$ for $j \in \mathcal{N}^*\}$, or (ii) its proposal is pivotal with at least one foreign trading partner, in which case the foreign trading partner H with which it shares the least-favorable (highest) world price among all foreign countries with which it trades will obtain (weakly) less trade than it desires at the given bilateral world price, while the domestic government achieves its desired multilateral trade volume (at the fixed terms of trade defined by the given set of world prices and the bilateral trade volumes implied by the pivotal foreign proposals and its proposed bilateral trade volume with H), so that $\{W_p = 0, W_{p*j}^{*j} \geq 0 \text{ for } j \in \mathcal{N}^*\}$. If the conditions in (i) or (ii) hold with strict equality, then the implemented tariffs will be discriminatory politically optimal tariffs, which by Proposition 6 are inefficient. Hence, there are two cases left to consider (we now maintain the assumption that all bilateral trade flows are strictly positive, though this is inessential for the proof):

(i) $\{W_p < 0, W_{p*j}^{*j} = 0 \text{ for } j \in \mathcal{N}^*\}$: In this case, (A2) implies that $\partial \tilde{p}^{wj}(\tau^{*j}, \bar{W}^{*j})/\partial \tau^{*j} = 0$ for $j \in \mathcal{N}^*$, and thus that $\partial \bar{T}/\partial \tau^{*j}$ is given by (A5) for $j \in \mathcal{N}^*$. Then by (A3) and (A5), tariffs must be discriminatory if they are to be efficient, and noting that $\partial \tilde{p}^{wj}(\tau^{*j}, \bar{W}^{*j})/\partial \tau^{*j} = 0$ also implies $\partial \bar{p}/\partial \tau^{*j} > 0$ for $j \in \mathcal{N}^*$, it follows from (A3) that $\partial \bar{T}/\partial \tau^{*j}$ must then be strictly negative for each j if efficiency is to be achieved. But then let k solve $\min_j \{\bar{p}^{wj}\}$ and observe that $\partial \bar{T}/\partial \tau^{*k} > 0$ by (A5).

(ii) $\{W_p = 0, W_{p*j}^{*j} \geq 0 \text{ for } j \in \mathcal{N}^*, \text{ with a strict inequality for at least one } j\}$: In this case, (A3) implies that we have efficiency if and only if $\partial \bar{T}/\partial \tau^{*j} = 0$ for $j \in \mathcal{N}^*$. By (A2), we must have $\partial \tilde{p}^{wj}(\tau^{*j}, \bar{W}^{*j})/\partial \tau^{*j} > 0$ and thus, by (A4), efficiency requires discriminatory tariffs. But noting that $dp^{*j}/d\tau^{*j} < 0$ for $j \in \mathcal{N}^*$, we may then let k solve $\min_j \{\bar{p}^{wj}\}$ and observe that $\partial \bar{T}/\partial \tau^{*k} > 0$, provided that $\partial E_x^{*j}/\partial p^{*j} > 0$ and $\partial E_x^{*j}/\partial p^{wj} < 0$. The latter condition is ensured by our assumption that all goods are normal in consumption, while the former condition is posited above and will be met as long as substitution effects dominate income effects.

REFERENCES

Bagwell, Kyle and Staiger, Robert W. "A Theory of Managed Trade." *American Economic Review*, September 1990, *80*(4), pp. 779–95.

———. "Reciprocal Trade Liberalization." National Bureau of Economic Research (Cambridge, MA) Working Paper No. 5488, March 1996.

———. "Reciprocity, Non-discrimination, and Preferential Agreements in the Multilateral Trading System." National Bureau of Economic Research (Cambridge, MA) Working Paper No. 5932, February 1997a.

———. "Multilateral Tariff Cooperation during the Formation of Customs Unions." *Journal of International Economics*, February 1997b, *42*(1–2), pp. 91–123.

———. "An Economic Theory of GATT." National Bureau of Economic Research (Cambridge, MA) Working Paper No. 6049, May 1997c.

———. "Multilateral Tariff Cooperation during the Formation of Free Trade Areas." *International Economic Review*, May 1997d, *38*(2), pp. 291–319.

———. "Regionalism and Multilateral Tariff Cooperation," in John Piggott and Alan Woodland, eds., *International trade policy and the Pacific Rim*. London: Macmillan, 1999, pp. 157–85.

Baldwin, Richard E. "Politically Realistic Objective Functions and Trade Policy." *Economics Letters*, August 1987, *24*(1), pp. 287–90.

Baldwin, Robert E. *The political economy of U.S. import policy*. Cambridge, MA: MIT Press, 1985.

Berry, Stephen T.; Levinsohn, James A. and Pakes, Ariel. "Voluntary Export Restraints on Automobiles: Evaluating a Strategic Trade Policy." National Bureau of Economic Research (Cambridge, MA) Working Paper No. 5235, August 1995.

Bhagwati, Jagdish. "Aggressive Unilateralism: An Overview," in Jagdish Bhagwati and Hugh T. Patrick, eds., *Aggressive unilateralism: America's 301 trade policy and the world trading system*. Ann Arbor, MI: University of Michigan Press, 1990, pp. 1–45.

———. *The world trading system at risk*. Princeton, NJ: Princeton University Press, 1991.

Bond, Eric W. and Syropoulos, Constantinos. "Trading Blocs and the Sustainability of Interregional Cooperation," in Matthew B. Canzoneri, Wilfred J. Ethier, and Vittorio Grilli, eds., *The new transatlantic economy.* Cambridge: Cambridge University Press, 1996, pp. 118–41.

Bond, Eric W.; Syropoulos, Constantinos and Winters, L. Alan. "Deepening of Regional Integration and External Trade Relations." Center for Economic Policy Research Discussion Paper No. 1317, 1996.

Brock, William A. and Magee, Stephen P. "The Economics of Special Interest Politics." *American Economic Review*, May 1978 *(Papers and Proceedings)*, *68*(2), pp. 246–50.

Caves, Richard E. "Economic Models of Political Choice: Canada's Tariff Structure." *Canadian Journal of Economics*, May 1976, *9*(2), pp. 278–300.

Dam, Kenneth W. *The GATT: Law and international economic organization.* Chicago: University of Chicago Press, 1970.

Dixit, Avinash. "Strategic Aspects of Trade Policy," in Truman F. Bewley, ed., *Advances in economic theory: Fifth World Congress.* Cambridge: Cambridge University Press, 1987, pp. 329–62.

Dixit, Avinash; Grossman, Gene M. and Helpman, Elhanan. "Common Agency and Coordination: General Theory and Application to Government Policy Making." *Journal of Political Economy,* August 1997, *105* (4), pp. 752–69.

Enders, Alice. "Reciprocity in GATT: 1942–1967," in Jagdish Bhagwati, ed., *Going alone: Historical country and sectoral experience.* Cambridge, MA: MIT Press, 1999 (forthcoming).

Feenstra, Robert C. "Estimating the Effects of Trade Policy," in Gene M. Grossman and Kenneth Rogoff, eds., *Handbook of international economics*, Vol. 3. Amsterdam: North-Holland, 1995, pp. 1553–95.

Feenstra, Robert C. and Bhagwati, Jagdish. "Tariff Seeking and the Efficient Tariff," in Jagdish Bhagwati, ed., *Import competition and response.* Chicago: University of Chicago Press, 1982, pp. 245–58.

Fernandez, Raquel and Rodrik, Dani. "Resistance to Reform: Status Quo Bias in the Presence of Individual-Specific Uncertainty." *American Economic Review*, December 1991, *81*(5), pp. 1146–55.

Findlay, Ronald and Wellisz, Stanislaw. "Endogenous Tariffs, the Political Economy of Trade Restrictions and Welfare," in Jagdish Bhagwati, ed., *Import competition and response.* Chicago: University of Chicago Press, 1982, pp. 223–43.

Goldberg, Pinelopi K. "Product Differentiation and Oligopoly in International Markets: The Case of the U.S. Automobile Industry." *Econometrica*, July 1995, *63*(4), pp. 891–951.

Gros, Daniel. "A Note on the Optimal Tariff, Retaliation and the Welfare Loss from Tariff Wars in a Framework with Intra-industry Trade." *Journal of International Economics,* November 1987, *23*(3/4), pp. 357–67.

Grossman, Gene M. and Helpman, Elhanan. "Protection for Sale." *American Economic Review,* September 1994, *84*(4), pp. 833–50.

_____. "Trade Wars and Trade Talks." *Journal of Political Economy,* August 1995, *103*(4), pp. 675–708.

Hillman, Arye, L. "Declining Industries and Political-Support Protectionist Motives." *American Economic Review*, December 1982, *72*(5), pp. 1180–87.

Jackson, John H. *The world trading system.* Cambridge, MA: MIT Press, 1989.

Johnson, Harry G. "Optimum Tariffs and Retaliation." *Review of Economic Studies,* 1953–1954, *21*(2), pp. 142–53.

Kennan, John and Riezman, Raymond G. "Do Big Countries Win Tariff Wars?" *International Economic Review*, February 1988, *29*(1), pp. 81–85.

Kowalczyk, Carsten and Sjostrom, Tomas J. "Bringing GATT into the Core." *Economica*, August 1994, *61*(243), pp. 301–17.

Kreinin, Mordechai E. "Effect of Tariff Changes on the Prices and Volume of Imports." *American Economic Review*, June 1961, *51*(3), pp. 310–24.

Krugman, Paul R. "The Move Toward Free Trade Zones," in *Policy implications of trade and currency zones: A symposium sponsored by the Federal Reserve Bank of Kansas City.* Jackson Hole, WY: Federal Reserve Bank of Kansas, August 22–24, 1991, pp. 7–41.

_____. "What Should Trade Negotiators Negotiate About?" *Journal of Economic Literature*, March 1997, *35*(1), pp. 113–20.

Maggi, Giovanni. "The Role of Multilateral Institutions in International Trade Cooperation." *American Economic Review*, March 1999, *89*(1), pp. 190–214.

Maggi, Giovanni and Rodriguez-Clare, Andres. "The Value of Trade Agreements in the Presence of Political Pressures." *Journal of Political Economy*, June 1998, *106*(3), pp. 574–601.

Mayer, Wolfgang. "Theoretical Considerations on Negotiated Tariff Adjustments." *Oxford Economic Papers*, March 1981, *33*(1), pp. 135–53.

_____. "Endogenous Tariff Formation." *American Economic Review*, December 1984, *74*(5), pp. 970–85.

McLaren, John. "Size, Sunk Costs, and Judge Bowker's Objection to Free Trade." *American Economic Review*, June 1997, *87*(3), pp. 400–20.

McMillan, John. *Game theory in international economics*. New York: Harwood, 1986.

_____. "A Game-Theoretic View of International Trade Negotiations: Implications for the Developing Countries," in John Whalley, ed., *Developing countries and the global trading system: Volume 1*. Ann Arbor, MI: University of Michigan Press, 1989, pp. 26–44.

Olson, Mancur. *The logic of collective action*. Cambridge, MA: Harvard University Press, 1965.

Staiger, Robert W. "International Rules and Institutions for Trade Policy," in Gene M. Grossman and Kenneth Rogoff, eds., *Handbook of international economics*, Vol. 3. Amsterdam: North-Holland, 1995, pp. 1495–551.

Staiger, Robert W. and Guido Tabellini. "Discretionary Trade Policy and Excessive Protection." *American Economic Review*, December 1987, *77*(5), pp. 823–37.

Whalley, John. "Why Do Countries Seek Regional Trade Agreements?" in Jeffrey A. Frankel, ed., *The regionalization of the world economy*. Chicago: University of Chicago Press, 1998, pp. 63–87.

Winters, L. Alan and Chang, Won. "Regional Integration and the Prices of Imports: An Empirical Investigation." *Journal of International Economics*, 1999 (forthcoming).

World Trade Organization. *Analytical index: Guide to GATT law and practice, volume 2*. Geneva: World Trade Organization, 1995.

[13]

The Politics, Power, and Pathologies of International Organizations

Michael N. Barnett and Martha Finnemore

Do international organizations really do what their creators intend them to do? In the past century the number of international organizations (IOs) has increased exponentially, and we have a variety of vigorous theories to explain why they have been created. Most of these theories explain IO creation as a response to problems of incomplete information, transaction costs, and other barriers to Pareto efficiency and welfare improvement for their members. Research flowing from these theories, however, has paid little attention to how IOs actually behave after they are created. Closer scrutiny would reveal that many IOs stray from the efficiency goals these theories impute and that many IOs exercise power autonomously in ways unintended and unanticipated by states at their creation. Understanding how this is so requires a reconsideration of IOs and what they do.

In this article we develop a constructivist approach rooted in sociological institutionalism to explain both the power of IOs and their propensity for dysfunctional, even pathological, behavior. Drawing on long-standing Weberian arguments about bureaucracy and sociological institutionalist approaches to organizational behavior, we argue that the rational-legal authority that IOs embody ~ ~ er independent of the states that created them and channels ~ directions. Bureaucracies, by definition, make rules ~ ~ te social knowledge. They define shared inte~ ~ ate and define new categories of actors (like ~ rs (like "promoting human rights"), and trans ~ ~ d the world (like markets and democracy.) ~ n on impersonal, generalized rules that define ~ l in

We are grateful to John Boli, Raymond Duvall, Ern~ ~ ~t Keohane, Keith Krause, Jeffrey Legro, John Malley, Craig Murphy, M. J. Pete~ ~ ~ck, Andrew Moravcsik, Thomas Risse, Duncan Snidal, Steve Weber, Thomas Weiss, and ~ ~ymous referees for their comments. We are especially grateful for the careful attention of the ed~ors of *International Organization*. Earlier versions of this article were presented at the 1997 APSA meeting, the 1997 ISA meeting, and at various fora. We also acknowledge financial assistance from the Smith Richardson Foundation and the United States Institute of Peace.

International Organization 53, 4, Autumn 1999, pp. 699–732

modern life can also make them unresponsive to their environments, obsessed with their own rules at the expense of primary missions, and ultimately lead to inefficient, self-defeating behavior. We are not the first to suggest that IOs are more than the reflection of state preferences and that they can be autonomous and powerful actors in global politics.[1] Nor are we the first to note that IOs, like all organizations, can be dysfunctional and inefficient.[2] However, our emphasis on the way that characteristics of bureaucracy as a generic cultural form shape IO behavior provides a different and very broad basis for thinking about how IOs influence world politics.[3]

Developing an alternative approach to thinking about IOs is only worthwhile if it produces significant insights and new opportunities for research on major debates in the field. Our approach allows us to weigh in with new perspectives on at least three such debates. First, it offers a different view of the power of IOs and whether or how they matter in world politics. This issue has been at the core of the neoliberal-institutionalists' debate with neorealists for years.[4] We show in this article how neo-liberal-institutionalists actually disadvantage themselves in their argument with real-ists by looking at only one facet of IO power. Global organizations do more than just facilitate cooperation by helping states to overcome market failures, collective action dilemmas, and problems associated with interdependent social choice. They also create actors, specify responsibilities and authority among them, and define the work these actors should do, giving it meaning and normative value. Even when they lack material resources, IOs exercise power as they constitute and construct the social world.[5]

Second and related, our perspective provides a theoretical basis for treating IOs as autonomous actors in world politics and thus presents a challenge to the statist ontology prevailing in international relations theories. Despite all their attention to international institutions, one result of the theoretical orientation of neoliberal institutionalists and regimes theorists is that they treat IOs the way pluralists treat the state. IOs are mechanisms through which others (usually states) act; they are not purposive actors. The regimes literature is particularly clear on this point. Regimes are "principles, norms, rules, and decision-making procedures;" they are not actors.[6] Weber's insights about the normative power of the rational-legal authority that bureaucracies embody and its implications for the ways bureaucracies produce and control social knowledge provide a basis for challenging this view and treating IOs as agents, not just as structure.

---

1. For Gramscian approaches, see Cox 1980, 1992, and 1996; and Murphy 1995. For Society of States approaches, see Hurrell and Woods 1995. For the epistemic communities literature, see Haas 1992. For IO decision-making literature, see Cox et al. 1974; Cox and Jacobson 1977; Cox 1996; and Ness and Brechin 1988. For a rational choice perspective, see Snidal 1996.
2. Haas 1990.
3. Because the neorealist and neoliberal arguments we engage have focused on intergovernmental organizations rather than nongovernmental ones, and because Weberian arguments from which we draw deal primarily with public bureaucracy, we too focus on intergovernmental organizations in this article and use the term *international organizations* in that way.
4. Baldwin 1993.
5. See Finnemore 1993 and 1996b; and McNeely 1995.
6. Krasner 1983b.

Third, our perspective offers a different vantage point from which to assess the desirability of IOs. While realists and some policymakers have taken up this issue, surprisingly few other students of IOs have been critical of their performance or desirability.[7] Part of this optimism stems from central tenets of classical liberalism, which has long viewed IOs as a peaceful way to manage rapid technological change and globalization, far preferable to the obvious alternative—war.[8] Also contributing to this uncritical stance is the normative judgment about IOs that is built into the theoretical assumptions of most neoliberal and regimes scholars and the economic organization theories on which they draw. IOs exist, in this view, only because they are Pareto improving and solve problems for states. Consequently, if an IO exists, it must be because it is more useful than other alternatives since, by theoretical axiom, states will pull the plug on any IO that does not perform. We find this assumption unsatisfying. IOs often produce undesirable and even self-defeating outcomes repeatedly, without punishment much less dismantlement, and we, as theorists, want to understand why. International relations scholars are familiar with principal-agent problems and the ways in which bureaucratic politics can compromise organizational effectiveness, but these approaches have rarely been applied to IOs. Further, these approaches by no means exhaust sources of dysfunction. We examine one such source that flows from the same rational-legal characteristics that make IOs authoritative and powerful. Drawing from research in sociology and anthropology, we show how the very features that make bureaucracies powerful can also be their weakness.

The claims we make in this article flow from an analysis of the "social stuff" of which bureaucracy is made. We are asking a standard constructivist question about what makes the world hang together or, as Alexander Wendt puts it, "how are things in the world put together so that they have the properties they do."[9] In this sense, our explanation of IO behavior is constitutive and differs from most other international relations approaches. This approach does not make our explanation "mere description," since understanding the constitution of things does essential work in explaining how those things behave and what causes outcomes. Just as understanding how the double-helix DNA molecule is constituted materially makes possible causal arguments about genetics, disease, and other biological processes, so understanding how bureaucracies are constituted socially allows us to hypothesize about the behavior of IOs and the effects this social form might have in world politics. This type of constitutive explanation does not allow us to offer law-like statements such as "if X happens, then Y must follow." Rather, by providing a more complete understanding of what bureaucracy is, we can provide explanations of how certain kinds of bureaucratic behavior are possible, or even probable, and why.[10]

We begin by examining the assumptions underlying different branches of organization theory and exploring their implications for the study of IOs. We argue that assumptions drawn from economics that undergird neoliberal and neorealist treat-

---

7. See Mearsheimer 1994; and Helms 1996.
8. See Commission on Global Governance 1995; Jacobson 1979, 1; and Doyle 1997.
9. See Ruggie 1998; and Wendt 1998.
10. Wendt 1998.

ments of IOs do not always reflect the empirical situation of most IOs commonly studied by political scientists. Further, they provide research hypotheses about only some aspects of IOs (like why they are created) and not others (like what they do). We then introduce sociological arguments that help remedy these problems.

In the second section we develop a constructivist approach from these sociological arguments to examine the power wielded by IOs and the sources of their influence. Liberal and realist theories only make predictions about, and consequently only look for, a very limited range of welfare-improving effects caused by IOs. Sociological theories, however, expect and explain a much broader range of impacts organizations can have and specifically highlight their role in constructing actors, interests, and social purpose. We provide illustrations from the UN system to show how IOs do, in fact, have such powerful effects in contemporary world politics. In the third section we explore the dysfunctional behavior of IOs, which we define as behavior that undermines the stated goals of the organization. International relations theorists are familiar with several types of theories that might explain such behavior. Some locate the source of dysfunction in material factors, others focus on cultural factors. Some theories locate the source of dysfunction outside the organization, others locate it inside. We construct a typology, mapping these theories according to the source of dysfunction they emphasize, and show that the same internally generated cultural forces that give IOs their power and autonomy can also be a source of dysfunctional behavior. We use the term *pathologies* to describe such instances when IO dysfunction can be traced to bureaucratic culture. We conclude by discussing how our perspective helps to widen the research agenda for IOs.

Theoretical Approaches to Organizations

Within social science there are two broad strands of theorizing about organizations. One is economistic and rooted in assumptions of instrumental rationality and efficiency concerns; the other is sociological and focused on issues of legitimacy and power.[11] The different assumptions embedded within each type of theory focus attention on different kinds of questions about organizations and provide insights on different kinds of problems.

The economistic approach comes, not surprisingly, out of economics departments and business schools for whom the fundamental theoretical problem, laid out first by Ronald Coase and more recently by Oliver Williamson, is why we have business firms. Within standard microeconomic logic, it should be much more efficient to conduct all transactions through markets rather than "hierarchies" or organizations. Consequently, the fact that economic life is dominated by huge organizations (business firms) is an anomaly. The body of theory developed to explain the existence and power of firms focuses on organizations as efficient solutions to contracting problems, incomplete information, and other market imperfections.[12]

11. See Powell and DiMaggio 1991, chap. 1; and Grandori 1993.
12. See Williamson 1975 and 1985; and Coase 1937.

This body of organization theory informs neoliberal and neorealist debates over international institutions. Following Kenneth Waltz, neoliberals and neorealists understand world politics to be analogous to a market filled with utility-maximizing competitors.[13] Thus, like the economists, they see organizations as welfare-improving solutions to problems of incomplete information and high transaction costs.[14] Neoliberals and realists disagree about the degree to which constraints of anarchy, an interest in relative versus absolute gains, and fears of cheating will scuttle international institutional arrangements or hobble their effectiveness, but both agree, implicitly or explicitly, that IOs help states further their interests where they are allowed to work.[15] State power may be exercised in political battles inside IOs over where, on the Pareto frontier, political bargains fall, but the notion that IOs are instruments created to serve state interests is not much questioned by neorealist or neoliberal scholars.[16] After all, why else would states set up these organizations and continue to support them if they did not serve state interests?

Approaches from sociology provide one set of answers to this question. They provide reasons why, in fact, organizations that are not efficient or effective servants of member interests might exist. In so doing, they lead us to look for kinds of power and sources of autonomy in organizations that economists overlook. Different approaches within sociology treat organizations in different ways, but as a group they stand in sharp contrast to the economists' approaches in at least two important respects: they offer a different conception of the relationship between organizations and their environments, and they provide a basis for understanding organizational autonomy.

IOs and their environment. The environment assumed by economic approaches to organizations is socially very thin and devoid of social rules, cultural content, or even other actors beyond those constructing the organization. Competition, exchange, and consequent pressures for efficiency are the dominant environmental characteristics driving the formation and behavior of organizations. Sociologists, by contrast, study organizations in a wider world of nonmarket situations, and, consequently, they begin with no such assumptions. Organizations are treated as "social facts" to be investigated; whether they do what they claim or do it efficiently is an empirical question, not a theoretical assumption of these approaches. Organizations respond not only to other actors pursuing material interests in the environment but also to normative and cultural forces that shape how organizations see the world and conceptualize their own missions. Environments can "select" or favor organizations for reasons other than efficient or responsive behavior. For example, organizations may be created and supported for reasons of legitimacy and normative fit rather than efficient output; they may be created not for what they do but for what they are—for what they represent symbolically and the values they embody.[17]

13. Waltz 1979.
14. See Vaubel 1991, 27; and Dillon, Ilgen, and Willett 1991.
15. Baldwin 1993.
16. Krasner 1991.
17. See DiMaggio and Powell 1983; Scott 1992; Meyer and Scott 1992, 1–5; Powell and DiMaggio 1991; Weber 1994; and Finnemore 1996a.

Empirically, organizational environments can take many forms. Some organizations exist in competitive environments that create strong pressures for efficient or responsive behavior, but many do not. Some organizations operate with clear criteria for "success" (like firms that have balance sheets), whereas others (like political science departments) operate with much vaguer missions, with few clear criteria for success or failure and no serious threat of elimination. Our point is simply that when we choose a theoretical framework, we should choose one whose assumptions approximate the empirical conditions of the IO we are analyzing, and that we should be aware of the biases created by those assumptions. Economistic approaches make certain assumptions about the environment in which IOs are embedded that drive researchers who use them to look for certain kinds of effects and not others. Specifying different or more varied environments for IOs would lead us to look for different and more varied effects in world politics.[18]

IO autonomy.   Following economistic logic, regime theory and the broad range of scholars working within it generally treat IOs as creations of states designed to further state interests.[19] Analysis of subsequent IO behavior focuses on processes of aggregating member state preferences through strategic interaction within the structure of the IO. IOs, then, are simply epiphenomena of state interaction; they are, to quote Waltz's definition of reductionism, "understood by knowing the attributes and the interactions of [their] parts."[20]

These theories thus treat IOs as empty shells or impersonal policy machinery to be manipulated by other actors. Political bargains shape the machinery at its creation, states may politick hard within the machinery in pursuit of their policy goals, and the machinery's norms and rules may constrain what states can do, but the machinery itself is passive. IOs are not purposive political actors in their own right and have no ontological independence. To the extent that IOs do, in fact, take on a life of their own, they breach the "limits of realism" as well as of neoliberalism by violating the ontological structures of these theories.[21]

The regimes concept spawned a huge literature on interstate cooperation that is remarkably consistent in its treatment of IOs as structure rather than agents. Much of the neoliberal institutionalist literature has been devoted to exploring the ways in which regimes (and IOs) can act as intervening variables, mediating between states' pursuit of self-interest and political outcomes by changing the structure of opportunities and constraints facing states through their control over information, in particular.[22] Although this line of scholarship accords IOs some causal status (since they demonstrably change outcomes), it does not grant them autonomy and purpose inde-

---

18. Researchers applying these economistic approaches have become increasingly aware of the mismatch between the assumptions of their models and the empirics of IOs. See Snidal 1996.
19. Note that empirically this is not the case; most IOs now are created by other IOs. See Shanks, Jacobson, and Kaplan 1996.
20. Waltz 1979, 18.
21. Krasner 1983a, 355–68; but see Finnemore 1996b; and Rittberger 1993.
22. See Keohane 1984; and Baldwin 1993.

pendent of the states that comprise them. Another branch of liberalism has recently divorced itself from the statist ontology and focuses instead on the preferences of social groups as the causal engine of world politics, but, again, this view simply argues for attention to a different group of agents involved in the construction of IOs and competing for access to IO mechanisms. It does not offer a fundamentally different conception of IOs.[23]

The relevant question to ask about this conceptualization is whether it is a reasonable approximation of the empirical condition of most IOs. Our reading of detailed empirical case studies of IO activity suggests not. Yes, IOs are constrained by states, but the notion that they are passive mechanisms with no independent agendas of their own is not borne out by any detailed empirical study of an IO that we have found. Field studies of the European Union provide evidence of independent roles for "eurocrats."[24] Studies of the World Bank consistently identify an independent culture and agendas for action.[25] Studies of recent UN peacekeeping and reconstruction efforts similarly document a UN agenda that frequently leads to conflict with member states.[26] Accounts of the UN High Commission on Refugees (UNHCR) routinely note how its autonomy and authority has grown over the years. Not only are IOs independent actors with their own agendas, but they may embody multiple agendas and contain multiple sources of agency—a problem we take up later.

Principal-agent analysis, which has been increasingly employed by students of international relations to examine organizational dynamics, could potentially provide a sophisticated approach to understanding IO autonomy.[27] Building on theories of rational choice and of representation, these analysts understand IOs as "agents" of states ("principals"). The analysis is concerned with whether agents are responsible delegates of their principals, whether agents smuggle in and pursue their own preferences, and how principals can construct various mechanisms to keep their agents honest.[28] This framework provides a means of treating IOs as actors in their own right with independent interests and capabilities. Autonomous action by IOs is to be expected in this perspective. It would also explain a number of the nonresponsive and pathological behaviors that concern us because we know that monitoring and shirking problems are pervasive in these principal-agent relationships and that these relationships can often get stuck at suboptimal equilibria.

The problem with applying principal-agent analysis to the study of IOs is that it requires a priori theoretical specification of what IOs want. Principal-agent dynamics are fueled by the disjuncture between what agents want and what principals want. To produce any insights, those two sets of interests cannot be identical. In economics this type of analysis is usually applied to preexisting agents and principals (clients

---

23. Moravcsik 1997.
24. See Pollack 1997; Ross 1995; and Zabusky 1995; but see Moravcsik 1999.
25. See Ascher 1983; Ayres 1983; Ferguson 1990; Escobar 1995; Wade 1996; Nelson 1995; and Finnemore 1996a.
26. Joint Evaluation of Emergency Assistance to Rwanda 1996.
27. See Pollack 1997; Lake 1996; Vaubel 1991; and Dillon, Ilgen, and Willett 1991.
28. See Pratt and Zeckhauser 1985; and Kiewit and McCubbins 1991.

hiring lawyers, patients visiting doctors) whose ongoing independent existence makes specification of independent interests relatively straightforward. The lawyer or the doctor would probably be in business even if you and I did not take our problems to them. IOs, on the other hand, are often created by the principals (states) and given mission statements written by the principals. How, then, can we impute independent preferences a priori?

Scholars of American politics have made some progress in producing substantive theoretical propositions about what U.S. bureaucratic agencies want. Beginning with the pioneering work of William Niskanen, scholars theorized that bureaucracies had interests defined by the absolute or relative size of their budget and the expansion or protection of their turf. At first these interests were imputed, and later they became more closely investigated, substantiated, and in some cases modified or rejected altogether.[29]

Realism and liberalism, however, provide no basis for asserting independent utility functions for IOs. Ontologically, these are theories about states. They provide no basis for imputing interests to IOs beyond the goals states (that is, principals) give them. Simply adopting the rather battered Niskanen hypothesis seems less than promising given the glaring anomalies—for example, the opposition of many NATO and OSCE (Organization for Security and Cooperation in Europe) bureaucrats to those organizations' recent expansion and institutionalization. There are good reasons to assume that organizations care about their resource base and turf, but there is no reason to presume that such matters exhaust or even dominate their interests. Indeed, ethnographic studies of IOs describe a world in which organizational goals are strongly shaped by norms of the profession that dominate the bureaucracy and in which interests themselves are varied, often in flux, debated, and worked out through interactions between the staff of the bureaucracy and the world in which they are embedded.[30]

Various strands of sociological theory can help us investigate the goals and behavior of IOs by offering a very different analytical orientation than the one used by economists. Beginning with Weber, sociologists have explored the notion that bureaucracy is a peculiarly modern cultural form that embodies certain values and can have its own distinct agenda and behavioral dispositions. Rather than treating organizations as mere arenas or mechanisms through which other actors pursue interests, many sociological approaches explore the social content of the organization—its culture, its legitimacy concerns, dominant norms that govern behavior and shape interests, and the relationship of these to a larger normative and cultural environment. Rather than assuming behavior that corresponds to efficiency criteria alone, these approaches recognize that organizations also are bound up with power and social control in ways that can eclipse efficiency concerns.

---

29. See Niskanen 1971; Miller and Moe 1983; Weingast and Moran 1983; Moe 1984; and Sigelman 1986.
30. See Ascher 1983; Zabusky 1995; Barnett 1997b; and Wade 1996.

The Power of IOs

IOs can become autonomous sites of authority, independent from the state "principals" who may have created them, because of power flowing from at least two sources: (1) the legitimacy of the rational-legal authority they embody, and (2) control over technical expertise and information. The first of these is almost entirely neglected by the political science literature, and the second, we argue, has been conceived of very narrowly, leading scholars to overlook some of the most basic and consequential forms of IO influence. Taken together, these two features provide a theoretical basis for treating IOs as autonomous actors in contemporary world politics by identifying sources of support for them, independent of states, in the larger social environment. Since rational-legal authority and control over expertise are part of what defines and constitutes any bureaucracy (a bureaucracy would not be a bureaucracy without them), the autonomy that flows from them is best understood as a constitutive effect, an effect of the way bureaucracy is constituted, which, in turn, makes possible (and in that sense causes) other processes and effects in global politics.

Sources of IO Autonomy and Authority

To understand how IOs can become autonomous sites of authority we turn to Weber and his classic study of bureaucratization. Weber was deeply ambivalent about the increasingly bureaucratic world in which he lived and was well-attuned to the vices as well as the virtues of this new social form of authority.[31] Bureaucracies are rightly considered a grand achievement, he thought. They provide a framework for social interaction that can respond to the increasingly technical demands of modern life in a stable, predictable, and nonviolent way; they exemplify rationality and are technically superior to previous forms of rule because they bring precision, knowledge, and continuity to increasingly complex social tasks.[32] But such technical and rational achievements, according to Weber, come at a steep price. Bureaucracies are political creatures that can be autonomous from their creators and can come to dominate the societies they were created to serve, because of both the normative appeal of rational-legal authority in modern life and the bureaucracy's control over technical expertise and information. We consider each in turn.

Bureaucracies embody a form of authority, rational-legal authority, that modernity views as particularly legitimate and good. In contrast to earlier forms of authority that were invested in a leader, legitimate modern authority is invested in legalities, procedures, and rules and thus rendered impersonal. This authority is "rational" in that it deploys socially recognized relevant knowledge to create rules that determine how goals will be pursued. The very fact that they embody rationality is what makes bureaucracies powerful and makes people willing to submit to this kind of authority.

---

31. See Weber 1978, 196–97; Weber 1947; Mouzelis 1967; and Beetham 1985 and 1996.
32. See Schaar 1984, 120; Weber 1978, 973; and Beetham 1985, 69.

According to Weber,

> in legal authority, submission does not rest upon the belief and devotion to charismatically gifted persons. . . or upon piety toward a personal lord and master who is defined by an ordered tradition. . . . Rather submission under legal authority is based upon an *impersonal* bond to the generally defined and functional "duty of office." The official duty—like the corresponding right to exercise authority: the "jurisdictional competency"—is fixed by *rationally established* norms, by enactments, decrees, and regulations in such a manner that the legitimacy of the authority becomes the legality of the general rule, which is purposely thought out, enacted, and announced with formal correctness.[33]

When bureaucrats do something contrary to your interests or that you do not like, they defend themselves by saying "Sorry, those are the rules" or "just doing my job." "The rules" and "the job" are the source of great power in modern society. It is because bureaucrats in IOs are performing "duties of office" and implementing "rationally established norms" that they are powerful.

A second basis of autonomy and authority, intimately connected to the first, is bureaucratic control over information and expertise. A bureaucracy's autonomy derives from specialized technical knowledge, training, and experience that is not immediately available to other actors. While such knowledge might help the bureaucracy carry out the directives of politicians more efficiently, Weber stressed that it also gives bureaucracies power over politicians (and other actors). It invites and at times requires bureaucracies to shape policy, not just implement it.[34]

The irony in both of these features of authority is that they make bureaucracies powerful precisely by creating the appearance of depoliticization. The power of IOs, and bureaucracies generally, is that they present themselves as impersonal, technocratic, and neutral—as not exercising power but instead as serving others; the presentation and acceptance of these claims is critical to their legitimacy and authority.[35] Weber, however, saw through these claims. According to him, the depoliticized character of bureaucracy that legitimates it could be a myth: "Behind the functional purposes [of bureaucracy], of course, 'ideas of culture-values' usually stand."[36] Bureaucracies always serve some social purpose or set of cultural values. That purpose may be normatively "good," as Weber believed the Prussian nationalism around him was, but there was no a priori reason to assume this.

In addition to embodying cultural values from the larger environment that might be desirable or not, bureaucracies also carry with them behavioral dispositions and values flowing from the rationality that legitimates them as a cultural form. Some of these, like the celebration of knowledge and expertise, Weber admired. Others concerned him greatly, and his descriptions of bureaucracy as an "iron cage" and bureaucrats as "specialists without spirit" are hardly an endorsement of the bureaucratic

---

33. Gerth and Mills 1978, 299 (italics in original).
34. See Gerth and Mills 1978, 233; Beetham 1985, 74–75; and Schaar 1984, 120.
35. We thank John Boli for this insight. Also see Fisher 1997; Ferguson 1990; Shore and Wright 1997; and Burley and Mattli 1993.
36. Gerth and Mills 1978, 199.

form.[37] Bureaucracy can undermine personal freedom in important ways. The very impersonal, rule-bound character that empowers bureaucracy also dehumanizes it. Bureaucracies often exercise their power in repressive ways, in the name of general rules because rules are their raison d'être. This tendency is exacerbated by the way bureaucracies select and reward narrowed professionals seeking secure careers internally—people who are "lacking in heroism, human spontaneity, and inventiveness."[38] Following Weber, we investigate rather than assume the "goodness" of bureaucracy.

Weber's insights provide a powerful critique of the ways in which international relations scholars have treated IOs. The legitimacy of rational-legal authority suggests that IOs may have an authority independent of the policies and interests of states that create them, a possibility obscured by the technical and apolitical treatment of IOs by both realists and neoliberals. Nor have realists and neoliberals considered how control over information hands IOs a basis of autonomy. Susan Strange, at the forefront among realists in claiming that information is power, has emphatically stated that IOs are simply the agents of states. Neoliberals have tended to treat information in a highly technocratic and depoliticized way, failing to see how information is power.[39] As IOs create transparencies and level information asymmetries among states (a common policy prescription of neoliberals) they create new information asymmetries between IOs and states. Given the neoliberal assumption that IOs have no goals independent of states, such asymmetries are unimportant; but if IOs have autonomous values and behavioral predispositions, then such asymmetries may be highly consequential.

Examples of the ways in which IOs have become autonomous because of their embodiment of technical rationality and control over information are not hard to find. The UN's peacekeepers derive part of their authority from the claim that they are independent, objective, neutral actors who simply implement Security Council resolutions. UN officials routinely use this language to describe their role and are explicit that they understand this to be the basis of their influence. As a consequence, UN officials spend considerable time and energy attempting to maintain the image that they are not the instrument of any great power and must be seen as representatives of "the international community" as embodied in the rules and resolutions of the UN.[40] The World Bank is widely recognized to have exercised power over development policies far greater than its budget, as a percentage of North/South aid flows, would suggest because of the expertise it houses. While competing sites of expertise in development have proliferated in recent years, for decades after its founding the World Bank was a magnet for the "best and brightest" among "development experts." Its staff had and continues to have impressive credentials from the most pres-

---

37. See Weber [1930] 1978, 181–83; and Clegg 1994a, 152–55.
38. Gerth and Mills 1978, 216, 50, 299. For the extreme manifestation of this bureaucratic characteristic, see Arendt 1977.
39. See Strange 1997; and Keohane 1984.
40. See David Rieff, "The Institution that Saw No Evil," *The New Republic*, 12 February 1996, 19–24; and Barnett 1997b.

tigious universities and the elaborate models, reports, and research groups it has sponsored over the years were widely influential among the "development experts" in the field. This expertise, coupled with its claim to "neutrality" and its "apolitical" technocratic decision-making style, have given the World Bank an authoritative voice with which it has successfully dictated the content, direction, and scope of global development over the past fifty years.[41] Similarly, official standing and long experience with relief efforts have endowed the UNHCR with "expert" status and consequent authority in refugee matters. This expertise, coupled with its role in implementing international refugee conventions and law ("the rules" regarding refugees), has allowed the UNHCR to make life and death decisions about refugees without consulting the refugees, themselves, and to compromise the authority of states in various ways in setting up refugee camps.[42] Note that, as these examples show, technical knowledge and expertise need not be "scientific" in nature to create autonomy and power for IOs.

The Power of IOs

If IOs have autonomy and authority in the world, what do they do with it? A growing body of research in sociology and anthropology has examined ways in which IOs exercise power by virtue of their culturally constructed status as sites of authority; we distill from this research three broad types of IO power. We examine how IOs (1) classify the world, creating categories of actors and action; (2) fix meanings in the social world; and (3) articulate and diffuse new norms, principles, and actors around the globe. All of these sources of power flow from the ability of IOs to structure knowledge.[43]

Classification. An elementary feature of bureaucracies is that they classify and organize information and knowledge. This classification process is bound up with power. "Bureaucracies," writes Don Handelman, "are ways of making, ordering, and knowing social worlds." They do this by "moving persons among social categories or by inventing and applying such categories."[44] The ability to classify objects, to shift their very definition and identity, is one of bureaucracy's greatest sources of power. This power is frequently treated by the objects of that power as accomplished through caprice and without regard to their circumstances but is legitimated and justified by bureaucrats with reference to the rules and regulations of the bureaucracy. Consequences of this bureaucratic exercise of power may be identity defining, or even life threatening.

Consider the evolving definition of "refugee." The category "refugee" is not at all straightforward and must be distinguished from other categories of individuals who

41. See Wade 1996; Ayres 1983; Ascher 1983; Finnemore 1996b; and Nelson 1995.
42. See Malkki 1996; Hartigan 1992; and Harrell-Bond 1989.
43. See Foucault 1977, 27; and Clegg 1994b, 156–59. International relations theory typically disregards the negative side of the knowledge and power equation. For an example, see Haas 1992.
44. Handelman 1995, 280. See also Starr 1992; and Wright 1994, 22.

are "temporarily" and "involuntarily" living outside their country of origin—displaced persons, exiles, economic migrants, guest workers, diaspora communities, and those seeking political asylum. The debate over the meaning of "refugee" has been waged in and around the UNHCR. The UNHCR's legal and operational definition of the category strongly influences decisions about who is a refugee and shapes UNHCR staff decisions in the field—decisions that have a tremendous effect on the life circumstance of thousands of people.[45] These categories are not only political and legal but also discursive, shaping a view among UNHCR officials that refugees must, by definition, be powerless, and that as powerless actors they do not have to be consulted in decisions such as asylum and repatriation that will directly and dramatically affect them.[46] Guy Gran similarly describes how the World Bank sets up criteria to define someone as a peasant in order to distinguish them from a farmer, day laborer, and other categories. The classification matters because only certain classes of people are recognized by the World Bank's development machinery as having knowledge that is relevant in solving development problems.[47] Categorization and classification are a ubiquitous feature of bureaucratization that has potentially important implications for those being classified. To classify is to engage in an act of power.

The fixing of meanings. IOs exercise power by virtue of their ability to fix meanings, which is related to classification.[48] Naming or labeling the social context establishes the parameters, the very boundaries, of acceptable action. Because actors are oriented toward objects and objectives on the basis of the meaning that they have for them, being able to invest situations with a particular meaning constitutes an important source of power.[49] IOs do not act alone in this regard, but their organizational resources contribute mightily to this end.

There is strong evidence of this power from development studies. Arturo Escobar explores how the institutionalization of the concept of "development" after World War II spawned a huge international apparatus and how this apparatus has now spread its tentacles in domestic and international politics through the discourse of development. The discourse of development, created and arbitrated in large part by IOs, determines not only what constitutes the activity (what development is) but also who (or what) is considered powerful and privileged, that is, who gets to do the developing (usually the state or IOs) and who is the object of development (local groups).[50]

Similarly, the end of the Cold War encouraged a reexamination of the definition of security.[51] IOs have been at the forefront of this debate, arguing that security pertains not only to states but also to individuals and that the threats to security may be

45. See Weiss and Pasic 1997; Goodwin-Gill 1996; and Anonymous 1997.
46. See Harrell-Bond 1989; Walkup 1997; and Malkki 1996.
47. Gran 1986.
48. See Williams 1996; Clegg 1994b; Bourdieu 1994; Carr [1939] 1964; and Keeley 1990.
49. Blumer 1969.
50. See Gupta 1998; Escobar 1995; Cooper and Packard 1998; Gran 1986; Ferguson 1990; and Wade 1996.
51. See Matthews 1989; and Krause and Williams 1996.

economic, environmental, and political as well as military.[52] In forwarding these alternative definitions of security, officials from various IOs are empowering a different set of actors and legitimating an alternative set of practices. Specifically, when security meant safety from invading national armies, it privileged state officials and invested power in military establishments. These alternative definitions of security shift attention away from states and toward the individuals who are frequently threatened by their own government, away from military practices and toward other features of social life that might represent a more immediate and daily danger to the lives of individuals.

One consequence of these redefined meanings of development and security is that they legitimate, and even require, increased levels of IO intervention in the domestic affairs of states—particularly Third World states. This is fairly obvious in the realm of development. The World Bank, the International Monetary Fund (IMF), and other development institutions have established a web of interventions that affect nearly every phase of the economy and polity in many Third World states. As "rural development," "basic human needs," and "structural adjustment" became incorporated into the meaning of development, IOs were permitted, even required, to become intimately involved in the domestic workings of developing polities by posting in-house "advisors" to run monetary policy, reorganizing the political economy of entire rural regions, regulating family and reproductive practices, and mediating between governments and their citizens in a variety of ways.[53]

The consequences of redefining security may be similar. Democratization, human rights, and the environment have all now become tied to international peace and security, and IOs justify their interventions in member states on these grounds, particularly in developing states. For example, during the anti-apartheid struggle in South Africa, human rights abuses came to be classified as security threats by the UN Security Council and provided grounds for UN involvement there. Now, that linkage between human rights and security has become a staple of the post–Cold War environment. Widespread human rights abuses anywhere are now cause for UN intervention, and, conversely, the UN cannot carry out peacekeeping missions without promoting human rights.[54] Similarly, environmental disasters in Eastern Europe and the newly independent states of the former Soviet Union and water rights allocations in the Middle East have also come to be discussed under the rubric of "environmental security" and are thus grounds for IO intervention. The United Nations Development Program argues that there is an important link between human security and sustainable development and implicitly argues for greater intervention in the management of environment as a means to promote human security.[55]

Diffusion of norms.   Having established rules and norms, IOs are eager to spread the benefits of their expertise and often act as conveyor belts for the transmission of

52. See UN Development Program 1994; and Boutros-Ghali 1995.
53. See Escobar 1995; Ferguson 1990; and Feldstein 1998.
54. World Conference on Human Rights 1993.
55. UN Development Program 1994.

norms and models of "good" political behavior.[56] There is nothing accidental or unintended about this role. Officials in IOs often insist that part of their mission is to spread, inculcate, and enforce global values and norms. They are the "missionaries" of our time. Armed with a notion of progress, an idea of how to create the better life, and some understanding of the conversion process, many IO elites have as their stated purpose a desire to shape state practices by establishing, articulating, and transmitting norms that define what constitutes acceptable and legitimate state behavior. To be sure, their success depends on more than their persuasive capacities, for their rhetoric must be supported by power, sometimes (but not always) state power. But to overlook how state power and organizational missionaries work in tandem and the ways in which IO officials channel and shape states' exercise of power is to disregard a fundamental feature of value diffusion.[57]

Consider decolonization as an example. The UN Charter announced an intent to universalize sovereignty as a constitutive principle of the society of states at a time when over half the globe was under some kind of colonial rule; it also established an institutional apparatus to achieve that end (most prominently the Trusteeship Council and the Special Committee on Colonialism). These actions had several consequences. One was to eliminate certain categories of acceptable action for powerful states. Those states that attempted to retain their colonial privileges were increasingly viewed as illegitimate by other states. Another consequence was to empower international bureaucrats (at the Trusteeship Council) to set norms and standards for "stateness." Finally, the UN helped to ensure that throughout decolonization the sovereignty of these new states was coupled with territorial inviolability. Colonial boundaries often divided ethnic and tribal groups, and the UN was quite concerned that in the process of "self-determination," these governments containing "multiple" or "partial" selves might attempt to create a whole personality through territorial adjustment—a fear shared by many of these newly decolonized states. The UN encouraged the acceptance of the norm of sovereignty-as-territorial-integrity through resolutions, monitoring devices, commissions, and one famous peacekeeping episode in Congo in the 1960s.[58]

Note that, as with other IO powers, norm diffusion, too, has an expansionary dynamic. Developing states continue to be popular targets for norm diffusion by IOs, even after they are independent. The UN and the European Union are now actively involved in police training in non-Western states because they believe Western policing practices will be more conducive to democratization processes and the establishment of civil society. But having a professional police establishment assumes that there is a professional judiciary and penal system where criminals can be tried and jailed; and a professional judiciary, in turn, presupposes that there are lawyers that can come before the court. Trained lawyers presuppose a code of law. The result is a package of reforms sponsored by IOs aimed at transforming non-Western societies

---

56. See Katzenstein 1996; Finnemore 1996b; and Legro 1997.
57. See Alger 1963, 425; and Claude 1966, 373.
58. See McNeely 1995; and Jackson 1993.

into Western societies.[59] Again, while Western states are involved in these activities and therefore their values and interests are part of the reasons for this process, international bureaucrats involved in these activities may not see themselves as doing the bidding for these states but rather as expressing the interests and values of the bureaucracy.

Other examples of this kind of norm diffusion are not hard to find. The IMF and the World Bank are explicit about their role as transmitters of norms and principles from advanced market economies to less-developed economies.[60] The IMF's Articles of Agreement specifically assign it this task of incorporating less-developed economies into the world economy, which turns out to mean teaching them how to "be" market economies. The World Bank, similarly, has a major role in arbitrating the meaning of development and norms of behavior appropriate to the task of developing oneself, as was discussed earlier. The end of the Cold War has opened up a whole new set of states to this kind of norm diffusion task for IOs. According to former Secretary of Defense William Perry, one of the functions of NATO expansion is to inculcate "modern" values and norms into the Eastern European countries and their militaries.[61] The European Bank for Reconstruction and Development has, as part of its mandate, the job of spreading democracy and private enterprise. The OSCE is striving to create a community based on shared values, among these respect for democracy and human rights. This linkage is also strong at the UN as evident in *The Agenda for Democratization* and *The Agenda for Peace.*[62] Once democratization and human rights are tied to international peace and security, the distinctions between international and domestic governance become effectively erased and IOs have license to intervene almost anywhere in an authoritative and legitimate manner.[63]

Realists and neoliberals may well look at these effects and argue that the classificatory schemes, meanings, and norms associated with IOs are mostly favored by strong states. Consequently, they would argue, the power we attribute to IOs is simply epiphenomenal of state power. This argument is certainly one theoretical possibility, but it is not the only one and must be tested against others. Our concern is that because these theories provide no ontological independence for IOs, they have no way to test for autonomy nor have they any theoretical cause or inclination to test for it since, by theoretical axiom, autonomy cannot exist. The one empirical domain in which the statist view has been explicitly challenged is the European Union, and empirical studies there have hardly produced obvious victory for the "intergovernmentalist" approach.[64] Recent empirical studies in the areas of human rights, weapons taboos, and environmental practices also cast doubt on the statist approach by providing evidence about the ways in which nongovernmental and intergovernmen-

59. Call and Barnett forthcoming.
60. Wade 1996.
61. See Perry 1996; and Ruggie 1996.
62. Boutros-Ghali 1995 and 1996a,b.
63. Keen and Hendrie, however, suggest that nongovernmental organizations and IOs can be the long-term beneficiaries of intervention. See Keen 1994; and Hendrie 1997.
64. See Burley and Mattli 1993; Pollack 1997; and Sandholtz 1993.

tal organizations successfully promote policies that are not (or not initially) supported by strong states.[65] Certainly there are occasions when strong states do drive IO behavior, but there are also times when other forces are at work that eclipse or significantly dampen the effects of states on IOs. Which causal mechanisms produce which effects under which conditions is a set of relationships that can be understood only by intensive empirical study of how these organizations actually do their business— research that would trace the origins and evolution of IO policies, the processes by which they are implemented, discrepancies between implementation and policy, and overall effects of these policies.

The Pathologies of IOs

Bureaucracies are created, propagated, and valued in modern society because of their supposed rationality and effectiveness in carrying out social tasks. These same considerations presumably also apply to IOs. Ironically, though, the folk wisdom about bureaucracies is that they are inefficient and unresponsive. Bureaucracies are infamous for creating and implementing policies that defy rational logic, for acting in ways that are at odds with their stated mission, and for refusing requests of and turning their backs on those to whom they are officially responsible.[66] Scholars of U.S. bureaucracy have recognized this problem and have devoted considerable energy to understanding a wide range of undesirable and inefficient bureaucratic behaviors caused by bureaucratic capture and slack and to exploring the conditions under which "suboptimal equilibria" may arise in organizational structures. Similarly, scholars researching foreign policy decision making and, more recently, those interested in learning in foreign policy have investigated organizational dynamics that produce self-defeating and inefficient behavior in those contexts.[67]

IOs, too, are prone to dysfunctional behaviors, but international relations scholars have rarely investigated this, in part, we suspect, because the theoretical apparatus they use provides few grounds for expecting undesirable IO behavior.[68] The state-centric utility-maximizing frameworks most international relations scholars have borrowed from economics simply assume that IOs are reasonably responsive to state interests (or, at least, more responsive than alternatives), otherwise states would withdraw from them. This assumption, however, is a necessary theoretical axiom of these frameworks; it is rarely treated as a hypothesis subject to empirical investigation.[69] With little theoretical reason to expect suboptimal or self-defeating behavior in IOs, these scholars do not look for it and have had little to say about it. Policymakers, however, have been quicker to perceive and address these problems and are putting

---

65. See Keck and Sikkink 1998; Wapner 1996; Price 1997; and Thomas forthcoming.
66. March and Olsen 1989, chap. 5.
67. See Nye 1987; Haas 1990; Haas and Haas 1995; and Sagan 1993.
68. Two exceptions are Gallaroti 1991; and Snidal 1996.
69. Snidal 1996.

	Internal	External
Material	Bureaucratic politics	Realism/ neoliberal institutionalism
Cultural	Bureaucratic culture	World polity model

FIGURE 1. *Theories of international organization dysfunction*

them on the political agenda. It is time for scholars, too, to begin to explore these issues more fully.

In this section we present several bodies of theorizing that might explain dysfunctional IO behavior, which we define as behavior that undermines the IO's stated objectives. Thus our vantage point for judging dysfunction (and later pathology) is the publicly proclaimed mission of the organization. There may be occasions when overall organizational dysfunction is, in fact, functional for certain members or others involved in the IO's work, but given our analysis of the way claims of efficiency and effectiveness act to legitimate rational-legal authority in our culture, whether organizations actually do what they claim and accomplish their missions is a particularly important issue to examine. Several bodies of theory provide some basis for understanding dysfunctional behavior by IOs, each of which emphasizes a different locus of causality for such behavior. Analyzing these causes, we construct a typology of these explanations that locates them in relation to one another. Then, drawing on the work of James March and Johan Olsen, Paul DiMaggio and Walter Powell, and other sociological institutionalists, we elaborate how the same sources of bureaucratic power, sketched earlier, can cause dysfunctional behavior. We term this particular type of dysfunction *pathology.*[70] We identify five features of bureaucracy that might produce pathology, and using examples from the UN system we illustrate the way these might work in IOs.

Extant theories about dysfunction can be categorized in two dimensions: (1) whether they locate the cause of IO dysfunction inside or outside the organization, and (2) whether they trace the causes to material or cultural forces. Mapping theories on these dimensions creates the typology shown in Figure 1.

Within each cell we have identified a representative body of theory familiar to most international relations scholars. Explanations of IO dysfunction that emphasize the pursuit of material interests within an organization typically examine how competition among subunits over material resources leads the organization to make deci-

---

70. Karl Deutsch used the concept of pathology in a way similar to our usage. We thank Hayward Alker for this point. Deutsch 1963, 170.

sions and engage in behaviors that are inefficient or undesirable as judged against some ideal policy that would better allow the IO to achieve its stated goals. Bureaucratic politics is the best-known theory here, and though current scholars of international politics have not widely adopted this perspective to explain IO behavior, it is relatively well developed in the older IO literature.[71] Graham Allison's central argument is that the "name of the game is politics: bargaining along regularized circuits among players positioned hierarchically within the government. Government behavior can thus be understood as . . . results of these bargaining games."[72] In this view, decisions are not made after a rational decision process but rather through a competitive bargaining process over turf, budgets, and staff that may benefit parts of the organization at the expense of overall goals.

Another body of literature traces IO dysfunctional behavior to the material forces located outside the organization. Realist and neoliberal theories might posit that state preferences and constraints are responsible for understanding IO dysfunctional behavior. In this view IOs are not to blame for bad outcomes, states are. IOs do not have the luxury of choosing the optimal policy but rather are frequently forced to chose between the bad and the awful because more desirable policies are denied to them by states who do not agree among themselves and/or do not wish to see the IO fulfill its mandate in some particular instance. As Robert Keohane observed, IOs often engage in policies not because they are strong and have autonomy but because they are weak and have none.[73] The important point of these theories is that they trace IO dysfunctional behavior back to the environmental conditions established by, or the explicit preferences of, states.

Cultural theories also have internal and external variants. We should note that many advocates of cultural theories would reject the claim that an organization can be understood apart from its environment or that culture is separable from the material world. Instead they would stress how the organization is permeated by that environment, defined in both material and cultural terms, in which it is embedded. Many are also quite sensitive to the ways in which resource constraints and the material power of important actors will shape organizational culture. That said, these arguments clearly differ from the previous two types in their emphasis on ideational and cultural factors and clearly differ among themselves in the motors of behavior emphasized. For analytical clarity we divide cultural theories according to whether they see the primary causes of the IO's dysfunctional behavior as deriving from the culture of the organization (internal) or of the environment (external).

The world polity model exemplifies theories that look to external culture to understand an IO's dysfunctional behavior. There are two reasons to expect dysfunctional behavior here. First, because IO practices reflect a search for symbolic legitimacy rather than efficiency, IO behavior might be only remotely connected to the efficient implementation of its goals and more closely coupled to legitimacy criteria that come

71. See Allison 1971; Haas 1990; Cox et al. 1974; and Cox and Jacobson 1977.
72. See Allison 1971, 144; and Bendor and Hammond 1992.
73. Personal communication to the authors.

from the cultural environment.[74] For instance, many arms-export control regimes now have a multilateral character not because of any evidence that this architecture is the most efficient way to monitor and prevent arms exports but rather because multilateralism has attained a degree of legitimacy that is not empirically connected to any efficiency criteria.[75] Second, the world polity is full of contradictions; for instance, a liberal world polity has several defining principles, including market economics and human equality, that might conflict at any one moment. Thus, environments are often ambiguous about missions and contain varied, often conflicting, functional, normative, and legitimacy imperatives.[76] Because they are embedded in that cultural environment, IOs can mirror and reproduce those contradictions, which, in turn, can lead to contradictory and ultimately dysfunctional behavior.

Finally, organizations frequently develop distinctive internal cultures that can promote dysfunctional behavior, behavior that we call "pathological." The basic logic of this argument flows directly from our previous observations about the nature of bureaucracy as a social form. Bureaucracies are established as rationalized means to accomplish collective goals and to spread particular values. To do this, bureaucracies create social knowledge and develop expertise as they act upon the world (and thus exercise power). But the way bureaucracies are constituted to accomplish these ends can, ironically, create a cultural disposition toward undesirable and ultimately self-defeating behavior.[77] Two features of the modern bureaucratic form are particularly important in this regard. The first is the simple fact that bureaucracies are organized around rules, routines, and standard operating procedures designed to trigger a standard and predictable response to environmental stimuli. These rules can be formal or informal, but in either case they tell actors which action is appropriate in response to a specific stimuli, request, or demand. This kind of routinization is, after all, precisely what bureaucracies are supposed to exhibit—it is what makes them effective and competent in performing complex social tasks. However, the presence of such rules also compromises the extent to which means-ends rationality drives organizational behavior. Rules and routines may come to obscure overall missions and larger social goals. They may create "ritualized behavior" in bureaucrats and construct a very parochial normative environment within the organization whose connection to the larger social environment is tenuous at best.[78]

Second, bureaucracies specialize and compartmentalize. They create a division of labor on the logic that because individuals have only so much time, knowledge, and expertise, specialization will allow the organization to emulate a rational decision-making process.[79] Again, this is one of the virtues of bureaucracy in that it provides a way of overcoming the limitations of individual rationality and knowledge by embedding those individuals in a structure that takes advantage of their competencies with-

---

74. See Meyer and Rowan 1977; Meyer and Zucker 1989; Weber 1994; and Finnemore 1996a.
75. Lipson 1999.
76. McNeely 1995.
77. See Vaughan 1996; and Lipartito 1995.
78. See March and Olsen 1989, 21–27; and Meyer and Rowan 1977.
79. See March and Olsen 1989, 26–27; and March 1997.

out having to rely on their weaknesses. However, it, too, has some negative consequences. Just as rules can eclipse goals, concentrated expertise and specialization can
(and perhaps must) limit bureaucrats' field of vision and create subcultures within
bureaucracy that are distinct from those of the larger environment. Professional training plays a particularly strong role here since this is one widespread way we disseminate specialized knowledge and credential "experts." Such training often gives experts, indeed is designed to give them, a distinctive worldview and normative
commitments, which, when concentrated in a subunit of an organization, can have
pronounced effects on behavior.[80]

Once in place, an organization's culture, understood as the rules, rituals, and beliefs that are embedded in the organization (and its subunits), has important consequences for the way individuals who inhabit that organization make sense of the
world. It provides interpretive frames that individuals use to generate meaning.[81]
This is more than just bounded rationality; in this view, actors' rationality itself, the
very means and ends that they value, are shaped by the organizational culture.[82]
Divisions and subunits within the organization may develop their own cognitive
frameworks that are consistent with but still distinct from the larger organization,
further complicating this process.

All organizations have their own culture (or cultures) that shape their behavior.
The effects of bureaucratic culture, however, need not be dysfunctional. Indeed, specific organizational cultures may be valued and actively promoted as a source of
"good" behavior, as students of business culture know very well. Organizational
culture is tied to "good" and "bad" behavior, alike, and the effects of organizational
culture on behavior are an empirical question to be researched.

To further such research, we draw from studies in sociology and anthropology to
explore five mechanisms by which bureaucratic culture can breed pathologies in IOs:
the irrationality of rationalization, universalism, normalization of deviance, organizational insulation, and cultural contestation. The first three of these mechanisms all
flow from defining features of bureaucracy itself. Consequently, we expect them to
be present in any bureaucracy to a limited degree. Their severity may be increased,
however, by specific empirical conditions of the organization. Vague mission, weak
feedback from the environment, and strong professionalism all have the potential to
exacerbate these mechanisms and to create two others, organizational insulation and
cultural contestation, through processes we describe later. Our claim, therefore, is
that the very nature of bureaucracy—the "social stuff" of which it is made—creates
behavioral predispositions that make bureaucracy prone to these kinds of behaviors.[83] But the connection between these mechanisms and pathological behavior is
probabilistic, not deterministic, and is consistent with our constitutive analysis.
Whether, in fact, mission-defeating behavior occurs depends on empirical condi-

---

80. See DiMaggio and Powell 1983; and Schien 1996.
81. See Starr 1992, 160; Douglas 1986; and Berger and Luckman 1966, chap. 1.
82. See Campbell 1998, 378; Alvesson 1996; Burrell and Morgan 1979; Dobbin 1994; and Immergut
1998, 14–19.
83. Wendt 1998.

tions. We identify three such conditions that are particularly important (mission, feedback, and professionals) and discuss how they intensify these inherent predispositions and activate or create additional ones.

Irrationality of rationalization. Weber recognized that the "rationalization" processes at which bureaucracies excelled could be taken to extremes and ultimately become irrational if the rules and procedures that enabled bureaucracies to do their jobs became ends in themselves. Rather than designing the most appropriate and efficient rules and procedures to accomplish their missions, bureaucracies often tailor their missions to fit the existing, well-known, and comfortable rulebook.[84] Thus, means (rules and procedures) may become so embedded and powerful that they determine ends and the way the organization defines its goals. One observer of the World Bank noted how, at an operational level, the bank did not decide on development goals and collect data necessary to pursue them. Rather, it continued to use existing data-collection procedures and formulated goals and development plans from those data alone.[85] UN-mandated elections may be another instance where means become ends in themselves. The "end" pursued in the many troubled states where the UN has been involved in reconstruction is presumably some kind of peaceful, stable, just government. Toward that end, the UN has developed a repertoire of instruments and responses that are largely intended to promote something akin to a democratic government. Among those various repertoires, elections have become privileged as a measure of "success" and a signal of an operation's successful conclusion. Consequently, UN (and other IO) officials have conducted elections even when evidence suggests that such elections are either premature or perhaps even counterproductive (frequently acknowledged as much by state and UN officials).[86] In places like Bosnia elections have ratified precisely the outcome the UN and outside powers had intervened to prevent—ethnic cleansing—and in places like Africa elections are criticized as exacerbating the very ethnic tensions they were ostensibly designed to quell.

UN peacekeeping might also provide examples. As the UN began to involve itself in various "second-generation operations" that entailed the management and reconciliation of domestic conflicts it turned to the only instrument that was readily available in sufficient numbers—peacekeeping units. Peacekeepers, however, are military troops, trained to handle interstate conflict and to be interposed between two contending national armies, operating with their consent. Some UN staff, state officials, and peacekeeping scholars worried that peacekeepers might be inappropriate for the demands of handling domestic security. They feared that peacekeepers would transfer the skills and attitudes that had been honed for one environment to another without fully considering the adjustments required. According to some observers, peacekeepers did just that: they carried their interstate conflict equipment and mindset into new situations and so created a more aggressive and offensively minded posture than

84. Beetham 1985, 76.
85. See Ferguson 1990; and Nelson 1995.
86. Paris 1997.

would otherwise have been the case. The result was operations that undermined the objectives of the mandate.[87]

Bureaucratic universalism. A second source of pathology in IOs derives from the fact that bureaucracies "orchestrate numerous local contexts at once."[88] Bureaucrats necessarily flatten diversity because they are supposed to generate universal rules and categories that are, by design, inattentive to contextual and particularistic concerns. Part of the justification for this, of course, is the bureaucratic view that technical knowledge is transferable across circumstances. Sometimes this is a good assumption, but not always; when particular circumstances are not appropriate to the generalized knowledge being applied, the results can be disastrous.[89]

Many critics of the IMF's handling of the Asian financial crises have argued that the IMF inappropriately applied a standardized formula of budget cuts plus high interest rates to combat rapid currency depreciation without appreciating the unique and local causes of this depreciation. These governments were not profligate spenders, and austerity policies did little to reassure investors, yet the IMF prescribed roughly the same remedy that it had in Latin America. The result, by the IMF's later admission, was to make matters worse.[90]

Similarly, many of those who worked in peacekeeping operations in Cambodia were transferred to peacekeeping operations in Bosnia or Somalia on the assumption that the knowledge gained in one location would be applicable to others. Although some technical skills can be transferred across contexts, not all knowledge and organizational lessons derived from one context are appropriate elsewhere. The UN has a longstanding commitment to neutrality, which operationally translates into the view that the UN should avoid the use of force and the appearance of partiality. This knowledge was employed with some success by UN envoy Yasushi Akashi in Cambodia. After his stint in Cambodia, he became the UN Special Representative in Yugoslavia. As many critics of Akashi have argued, however, his commitment to these rules, combined with his failure to recognize that Bosnia was substantially different from Cambodia, led him to fail to use force to defend the safe havens when it was appropriate and likely to be effective.[91]

Normalization of deviance. We derive a third type of pathology from Diane Vaughan's study of the space shuttle *Challenger* disaster in which she chronicles the way exceptions to rules (deviance) over time become routinized and normal parts of procedures.[92] Bureaucracies establish rules to provide a predictable response to environmental stimuli in ways that safeguard against decisions that might lead to accidents and faulty decisions. At times, however, bureaucracies make small, calculated

---

87. See Featherston 1995; Chopra, Eknes, and Nordbo 1995; and Hirsch and Oakley 1995, chap. 6.
88. Heyman 1995, 262.
89. Haas 1990, chap. 3.
90. See Feldstein 1998; Radelet and Sachs 1999; and Kapur 1998.
91. Rieff 1996.
92. Vaughan 1996.

deviations from established rules because of new environmental or institutional developments, explicitly calculating that bending the rules in this instance does not create excessive risk of policy failure. Over time, these exceptions can become the rule—they become normal, not exceptions at all: they can become institutionalized to the point where deviance is "normalized." The result of this process is that what at time t_1 might be weighed seriously and debated as a potentially unacceptable risk or dangerous procedure comes to be treated as normal at time t_n. Indeed, because of staff turnover, those making decisions at a later point in time might be unaware that the now-routine behavior was ever viewed as risky or dangerous.

We are unaware of any studies that have examined this normalization of deviance in IO decision making, though one example of deviance normalization comes to mind. Before 1980 the UNHCR viewed repatriation as only one of three durable solutions to refugee crises (the others being third-country asylum and host-country integration). In its view, repatriation had to be both safe and voluntary because forced repatriation violates the international legal principle of nonrefoulement, which is the cornerstone of international refugee law and codified in the UNHCR's convention. Prior to 1980, UNHCR's discussions of repatriation emphasized that the principles of safety and voluntariness must be safeguarded at all costs. According to many commentators, however, the UNHCR has steadily lowered the barriers to repatriation over the years. Evidence for this can be found in international protection manuals, the UNHCR Executive Committee resolutions, and discourse that now weighs repatriation and the principle of nonrefoulement against other goals such a peace building. This was a steady and incremental development as initial deviations from organizational norms accumulated over time and led to a normalization of deviance. The result was a lowering of the barriers to repatriation and an increase in the frequency of involuntary repatriation.[93]

Insulation.   Organizations vary greatly in the degree to which they receive and process feedback from their environment about performance. Those insulated from such feedback often develop internal cultures and worldviews that do not promote the goals and expectations of those outside the organization who created it and whom it serves. These distinctive worldviews can create the conditions for pathological behavior when parochial classification and categorization schemes come to define reality—how bureaucrats understand the world—such that they routinely ignore information that is essential to the accomplishment of their goals.[94]

Two causes of insulation seem particularly applicable to IOs. The first is professionalism. Professional training does more than impart technical knowledge. It actively seeks to shape the normative orientation and worldviews of those who are trained. Doctors are trained to value life above all else, soldiers are trained to sacri-

---

93. See Chimni 1993, 447; Amnesty International 1997a,b; Human Rights Watch 1997; Zieck 1997, 433, 434, 438–39; and Barbara Crossette, "The Shield for Exiles Is Lowered," *The New York Times,* 22 December 1996, 4-1.
94. See Berger and Luckman 1967, chap. 1; Douglas 1986; Bruner 1990; March and Olsen 1989; and Starr 1992.

fice life for certain strategic objectives, and economists are trained to value efficiency. Bureaucracies, by their nature, concentrate professionals inside organizations, and concentrations of people with the same expertise or professional training can create an organizational worldview distinct from the larger environment. Second, organizations for whom "successful performance" is difficult to measure—that is, they are valued for what they represent rather than for what they do and do not "compete" with other organizations on the basis of output—are protected from selection and performance pressures that economistic models simply assume will operate. The absence of a competitive environment that selects out inefficient practices coupled with already existing tendencies toward institutionalizatian of rules and procedures insulates the organization from feedback and increases the likelihood of pathologies.

IOs vary greatly in the degree to which the professionals they recruit have distinctive worldviews and the degree to which they face competitive pressures, but it is clearly the case that these factors insulate some IOs to some degree and in so doing create a tendency toward pathology. The World Bank, for example, has been dominated for much of its history by economists, which, at least in part, has contributed to many critiques of the bank's policies. In one such critique James Ferguson opens his study of the World Bank's activity in Lesotho by comparing the bank's introductory description of Lesotho in its report on that country to facts on the ground; he shows how the bank "creates" a world that has little resemblance to what historians, geographers, or demographers see on the ground in Lesotho but is uniquely suited to the bank's organizational abilities and presents precisely the problems the bank knows how to solve. This is not simply "staggeringly bad scholarship," Ferguson argues, but a way of making the world intelligible and meaningful from a particular perspective—the World Bank's.[95] The problem, however, is that this different worldview translates into a record of development failures, which Ferguson explores in detail.

Insulation contributes to and is caused by another well-known feature of organizations—the absence of effective feedback loops that allow the organization to evaluate its efforts and use new information to correct established routines. This is surely a "rational" procedure in any social task but is one that many organizations, including IOs, fail to perform.[96] Many scholars and journalists, and even the current head of the World Bank, have noticed that the bank has accumulated a rather distinctive record of "failures" but continues to operate with the same criteria and has shown a marked lack of interest in evaluating the effectiveness of its own projects.[97] The same is true of other IOs. Jarat Chopra observes that the lessons-learned conferences that were established after Somalia were structurally arranged so that no information could come out that would blemish the UN's record. Such attempts at face saving, Chopra cautions, make it more likely that these maladies will go uncorrected.[98] Sometimes

95. Ferguson 1990, 25–73.
96. March and Olsen 1989, chap. 5; Haas 1990.
97. See Wade 1996, 14–17; Nelson 1995, chaps. 6, 7; and Richard Stevenson, "The Chief Banker for the Nations at the Bottom of the Heap," *New York Times*, 14 September 1997, sec. 3, 1, 12–14.
98. Chopra 1996.

new evaluative criteria are hoisted in order to demonstrate that the failures were not really failures but successes.

Cultural contestation.   Organizational coherence is an accomplishment rather than a given. Organizational control within a putative hierarchy is always incomplete, creating pockets of autonomy and political battles within the bureaucracy.[99] This is partly a product of the fact that bureaucracies are organized around the principle of division-of-labor, and different divisions tend to be staffed by individuals who are "experts" in their assigned tasks. These different divisions may battle over budgets or material resources and so follow the bureaucratic politics model, but they may also clash because of distinct internal cultures that grow up inside different parts of the organization. Different segments of the organization may develop different ways of making sense of the world, experience different local environments, and receive different stimuli from outside; they may also be populated by different mixes of professions or shaped by different historical experiences. All of these would contribute to the development of different local cultures within the organization and different ways of perceiving the environment and the organization's overall mission. Organizations may try to minimize complications from these divisions by arranging these demands hierarchically, but to the extent that hierarchy resolves conflict by squelching input from some subunits in favor of others, the organization loses the benefits of a division of labor that it was supposed to provide. More commonly, though, attempts to reconcile competing worldviews hierarchically are simply incomplete. Most organizations develop overlapping and contradictory sets of preferences among subgroups.[100] Consequently, different constituencies representing different normative views will suggest different tasks and goals for the organization, resulting in a clash of competing perspectives that generates pathological tendencies.

The existence of cultural contestation might be particularly true of high-profile and expansive IOs like the UN that have vague missions, broad and politicized constituencies, and lots of divisions that are developed over time and in response to new environmental demands. Arguably a number of the more spectacular debacles in recent UN peacekeeping operations might be interpreted as the product of these contradictions.

Consider the conflict between the UN's humanitarian missions and the value it places on impartiality and neutrality. Within the organization there are many who view impartiality as a core constitutive principle of UN action. On the one hand, the UN's moral standing, its authority, and its ability to persuade all rest on this principle. On the other hand, the principles of humanitarianism require the UN to give aid to those in need—values that are particularly strong in a number of UN relief and humanitarian agencies. These two norms of neutrality and humanitarian assistance, and the parts of the bureaucracy most devoted to them, come into direct conflict in those situations where providing humanitarian relief might jeopardize the UN's

---

99. See Clegg 1994a, 30; Vaughan 1996, 64; and Martin 1992.
100. Haas 1990, 188.

vaunted principle of neutrality. Bosnia is the classic case in point. On the one hand, the "all necessary means" provision of Security Council resolutions gave the UN authority to deliver humanitarian aid and protect civilians in the safe havens. On the other hand, the UN abstained from "taking sides" because of the fear that such actions would compromise its neutrality and future effectiveness. The result of these conflicts was a string of contradictory policies that failed to provide adequately for the UN's expanding humanitarian charges.[101] According to Shashi Tharoor, a UN official intimately involved in these decisions, "It is extremely difficult to make war and peace with the same people on the same territory at the same time."[102]

UNHCR provides another possible example of cultural contestation. Historically, the UNHCR's Protection Division has articulated a legalistic approach toward refugee matters and thus tends to view the UNHCR and itself as the refugee's lawyer and as the protector of refugee rights under international law. Those that inhabit the UNHCR's regional bureaus, however, have been characterized as taking a less "narrow" view of the organization's mission, stressing that the UNHCR must take into account the causes of refugee flows and state pressures. These cultural conflicts have been particularly evident, according to many observers, when the UNHCR contemplates a repatriation exercise in areas of political instability and conflict: protection officers demand that the refugees' rights, including the right of nonrefoulement, be safeguarded, whereas the regional bureaus are more willing to undertake a risky repatriation exercise if it might serve broader organizational goals, such as satisfying the interests of member states, and regional goals, such as facilitating a peace agreement.[103]

Although bureaucratic culture is not the only source of IO dysfunction, it is a potentially powerful one that creates broad patterns of behavior that should interest international relations scholars. None of the sources of pathologies sketched here is likely to appear in isolation in any empirical domain. These processes interact and feed on each other in ways that will require further theorizing and research. Moreover, while we have highlighted the organization's internal characteristics, we must always bear in mind that the external environment presses upon and shapes the internal characteristics of the organization in a host of ways. Cultural contestation within an organization frequently originates from and remains linked to normative contradictions in the larger environment. Demands from states can be extremely important determinants of IO behavior and may override internal cultural dynamics, but they can also set them in place if conflicting state demands result in the creation of organizational structures or missions that are prone to pathology. As we begin to explore dysfunctional and pathological behavior, we must bear in mind the complex relationship between different causal pathways, remaining closely attentive to both the internal organizational dynamics and the IO's environment.

101. See Barnett 1997a; David Rieff, "We Hate You," *New Yorker*, 4 September 1995, 41–48; David Rieff, "The Institution That Saw No Evil," *The New Republic*, 12 February 1996, 19–24; and Rieff 1996.
102. Quoted in Weiss 1996, 85; also see Rieff 1996, 166, 170, 193.
103. See Kennedy 1986; and Lawyers Committee for Human Rights 1991.

Conclusion

For all the attention international relations scholars have paid to international institutions over the past several decades, we know very little about the internal workings of IOs or about the effects they have in the world. Our ignorance, we suspect, is in large part a product of the theoretical lens we have applied. From an economistic perspective, the theoretically interesting question to ask about IOs is why they are created in the first place. Economists want to know why we have firms; political scientists want to know why we have IOs. In both cases, the question flows naturally from first theoretical principles. If you think that the world looks like a microeconomic market—anarchy, firms (or states) competing to maximize their utilities—what is anomalous and therefore theoretically interesting is cooperation. Consequently, our research tends to focus on the bargains states strike to make or reshape IOs. Scholars pay very little attention to what goes on subsequently in their day-to-day operations or even the larger effects that they might have on the world.

Viewing IOs through a constructivist or sociological lens, as we suggest here, reveals features of IO behavior that should concern international relations scholars because they bear on debates central to our field—debates about whether and how international institutions matter and debates about the adequacy of a statist ontology in an era of globalization and political change. Three implications of this alternative approach are particularly important. First, this approach provides a basis for treating IOs as purposive actors. Mainstream approaches in political science that are informed by economic theories have tended to locate agency in the states that comprise IO membership and treat IOs as mere arenas in which states pursue their policies. By exploring the normative support for bureaucratic authority in the broader international culture and the way IOs use that authority to construct the social world, we provide reasons why IOs may have autonomy from state members and why it may make sense analytically to treat them as ontologically independent. Second, by providing a basis for that autonomy we also open up the possibility that IOs are powerful actors who can have independent effects on the world. We have suggested various ways to think about how IOs are powerful actors in global politics, all of which encourage greater consideration of how IOs affect not only discrete outcomes but also the constitutive basis of global politics.

Third, this approach also draws attention to normative evaluations of IOs and questions what appears to us to be rather uncritical optimism about IO behavior. Contemporary international relations scholars have been quick to recognize the positive contributions that IOs can make, and we, too, are similarly impressed. But for all their desirable qualities, bureaucracies can also be inefficient, ineffective, repressive, and unaccountable. International relations scholars, however, have shown little interest in investigating these less savory and more distressing effects. The liberal Wilsonian tradition tends to see IOs as promoters of peace, engines of progress, and agents for emancipation. Neoliberals have focused on the impressive way in which IOs help states to overcome collective action problems and achieve durable cooperation. Realists have focused on their role as stabilizing forces in world politics. Constructivists, too, have tended to focus on the more humane and other-regarding features of IOs, but there is nothing about social construction that necessitates "good" outcomes. We do not mean to imply that IOs are "bad"; we mean only to point out theoretical reasons why undesirable behavior may occur and suggest that normative evaluation of IO behavior should be an empirical and ethical matter, not an analytic assumption.

References

Alger, Chadwick. 1963. United Nations Participation as a Learning Process. *Public Opinion Quarterly* 27 (3):411–26.

Allison, Graham. 1971. *Essence of Decision.* Boston: Little, Brown.

Alvesson, Mats. 1996. *Cultural Perspectives on Organizations.* New York: Cambridge University Press.

Amnesty International. 1997a. In Search of Safety: The Forcibly Displaced and Human Rights in Africa. AI Index, 20 June, AFR 01/05/97. Available from <www.amnesty.org/ailib/aipub/1997/10100597.htm>.

———. 1997b. Rwanda: Human Rights Overlooked in Mass Repatriation. Available from <www.amnesty.org/ailib/aipub/1997/AFR/147002797.htm>.

Anonymous. 1997. The UNHCR Note on International Protection You Won't See. *International Journal of Refugee Law* 9 (2):267–73.

Arendt, Hannah. 1977. *Eichmann in Jerusalem: A Report on the Banality of Evil.* New York: Penguin.

Ascher, William. 1983. New Development Approaches and the Adaptability of International Agencies: The Case of the World Bank. *International Organization* 37 (3):415–39.

Ayres, Robert L. 1983. *Banking on the Poor: The World Bank and World Poverty.* Cambridge, Mass.: MIT Press.

Baldwin, David, ed. 1993. *Neorealism and Neoliberalism.* New York: Columbia University Press.

Barnett, Michael. 1997a. The Politics of Indifference at the United Nations and Genocide in Rwanda and Bosnia. In *This Time We Knew: Western Responses to Genocide in Bosnia,* edited by Thomas Cushman and Stjepan Mestrovic, 128–62. New York: New York University Press.

———. 1997b. The UN Security Council, Indifference, and Genocide in Rwanda. *Cultural Anthropology* 12 (4):551–78.

Beetham, David. 1985. *Max Weber and the Theory of Modern Politics.* New York: Polity.

———. 1996. *Bureaucracy.* 2d ed. Minneapolis: University of Minnesota Press.

Bendor, Jonathan, and Thomas Hammond. 1992. Rethinking Allison's Models. *American Political Science Review* 82 (2):301–22.

Berger, Peter, and Thomas Luckmann. 1966. *The Social Construction of Reality.* New York: Doubleday.

Blumer, Herbert. 1969. *Symbolic Interactionism: Perspective and Method.* Englewood Cliffs, N.J.: Prentice-Hall.

Bourdieu, Pierre. 1994. On Symbolic Power. In *Language and Symbolic Power,* edited by Pierre Bourdieu, 163–70. Chicago: University of Chicago Press.

Boutros-Ghali, Boutros. 1995. *Agenda for Peace.* 2d ed. New York: UN Press.

———. 1996a. Global Leadership After the Cold War. *Foreign Affairs* 75:86–98.

———. 1996b. *Agenda for Democratization.* New York: UN Press.

Bruner, Jerome. 1990. *Acts of Meaning.* Cambridge, Mass.: Harvard University Press.

Burley, Anne-Marie, and Walter Mattli. 1993. Europe Before the Court: A Political Theory of Integration. *International Organization* 47 (1):41–76.

Burrell, Gibson, and Gareth Morgan. 1979. *Sociological Paradigms and Organizational Analysis.* London: Heinemman.

Call, Chuck, and Michael Barnett. Forthcoming. Looking for a Few Good Cops: Peacekeeping, Peacebuilding, and U.N. Civilian Police. *International Peacekeeping.*

Campbell, John. 1998. Institutional Analysis and the Role of Ideas in Political Economy. *Theory and Society* 27:377–409.

Carr, Edward H. [1939] 1964. *The Twenty Year's Crisis.* New York: Harper Torchbooks.

Chimni, B. 1993. The Meaning of Words and the Role of UNHCR in Voluntary Repatriation. *International Journal of Refugee Law* 5 (3):442–60.

Chopra, Jarat. 1996. Fighting for Truth at the UN. *Crosslines Global Report,* 26 November, 7–9.

Chopra, Jarat, Age Eknes, and Toralv Nordbo. 1995. *Fighting for Hope in Somalia.* Oslo: NUPI.

Claude, Inis L., Jr. 1966. Collective Legitimization as a Political Function of the United Nations. *International Organization* 20 (3):337–67.

Clegg, Stewart. 1994a. Power and Institutions in the Theory of Organizations. In *Toward a New Theory of Organizations,* edited by John Hassard and Martin Parker, 24–49. New York: Routledge.

———. 1994b. Weber and Foucault: Social Theory for the Study of Organizations. *Organization* 1 (1): 149–78.

Coase, Ronald. 1937. The Nature of the Firm. *Economica* 4 (November):386–405.

Commission on Global Governance. 1995. *Our Global Neighborhood.* New York: Oxford University Press.

Cooper, Frederick, and Randy Packard, eds. 1998. *International Development and the Social Sciences.* Berkeley: University of California Press.

Cox, Robert. 1980. The Crisis of World Order and the Problem of International Organization in the 1980s. *International Journal* 35 (2):370–95.

———. 1992. Multilateralism and World Order. *Review of International Studies* 18 (2):161–80.

———. 1996. The Executive Head: An Essay on Leadership in International Organization. In *Approaches to World Order,* edited by Robert Cox, 317–48. New York: Cambridge University Press.

Cox, Robert, and Harold Jacobson. 1977. Decision Making. *International Social Science Journal* 29 (1):115–33.

Cox, Robert, Harold Jacobson, Gerard Curzon, Victoria Curzon, Joseph Nye, Lawrence Scheinman, James Sewell, and Susan Strange. 1974. *The Anatomy of Influence: Decision Making in International Organization.* New Haven, Conn.: Yale University Press.

Deutsch, Karl. 1963. *The Nerves of Government: Models of Political Communication and Control.* Glencoe, Ill.: Free Press.

Dillon, Patricia, Thomas Ilgen, and Thomas Willett. 1991. Approaches to the Study of International Organizations: Major Paradigms in Economics and Political Science. In *The Political Economy of International Organizations: A Public Choice Approach,* edited by Ronald Vaubel and Thomas Willett, 79–99. Boulder, Colo.: Westview Press.

DiMaggio, Paul J., and Walter W. Powell. 1983. The Iron Cage Revisited: Institutional Isomorphism and Collective Rationality in Organizational Fields. *American Sociological Review* 48:147–60.

Dobbin, Frank. 1994. Cultural Models of Organization: The Social Construction of Rational Organizing Principles. In *The Sociology of Culture,* edited by Diana Crane, 117–42. Boston: Basil Blackwell.

Douglas, Mary. 1986. *How Institutions Think.* Syracuse, N.Y.: Syracuse University Press.

Doyle, Michael. 1997. *Ways of War and Peace.* New York: Norton.

Escobar, Arturo. 1995. *Encountering Development: The Making and Unmaking of the Third World.* Princeton, N.J.: Princeton University Press.

Featherston, A. B. 1995. Habitus in Cooperating for Peace: A Critique of Peacekeeping. In *The New Agenda for Global Security: Cooperating for Peace and Beyond,* edited by Stephanie Lawson, 101–18. St. Leonards, Australia: Unwin and Hyman.

Feld, Werner J., and Robert S. Jordan, with Leon Hurwitz. 1988. *International Organizations: A Comparative Approach.* 2d ed. New York: Praeger.

Feldstein, Martin. 1998. Refocusing the IMF. *Foreign Affairs* 77 (2):20–33.

Ferguson, James. 1990. *The Anti-Politics Machine: "Development," Depoliticization, and Bureaucratic Domination in Lesotho.* New York: Cambridge University Press.

Finnemore, Martha. 1993. International Organizations as Teachers of Norms: The United Nations Educational, Scientific, and Cultural Organization and Science Policy. *International Organization* 47: 565–97.

———. 1996a. Norms, Culture, and World Politics: Insights from Sociology's Institutionalism. *International Organization* 50 (2):325–47.

———. 1996b. *National Interests in International Society.* Ithaca, N.Y.: Cornell University Press.

Fisher, William. 1997. Doing Good? The Politics and Antipolitics of NGO Practices. *Annual Review of Anthropology* 26:439–64.

Foucault, Michel. 1977. *Discipline and Punish.* New York: Vintage Press.

Gallaroti, Guilio. 1991. The Limits of International Organization. *International Organization* 45 (2):183–220.

Gerth, H. H., and C. Wright Mills. 1978. *From Max Weber: Essays in Sociology.* New York: Oxford University Press.

Goodwin-Gill, Guy. 1996. *Refugee in International Law.* New York: Oxford Clarendon.

Gran, Guy. 1986. Beyond African Famines: Whose Knowledge Matters? *Alternatives* 11:275–96.

Grandori, Anna. 1993. Notes on the Use of Power and Efficiency Constructs in the Economics and Sociology of Organizations. In *Interdisciplinary Perspectives on Organizational Studies,* edited by S. Lindenberg and H. Schreuder, 61–78. New York: Pergamon

Gupta, Akhil. 1998. *Postcolonial Developments: Agriculture in the Making of Modern India.* Durham, N.C.: Duke University Press.

Haas, Ernst. 1990. *When Knowledge Is Power.* Berkeley: University of California Press.

Haas, Ernst, and Peter Haas. 1995. Learning to Learn: Improving International Governance. *Global Governance* 1 (3):255–85.

Haas, Peter, ed. 1992. Epistemic Communities. *International Organization* 46 (1). Special issue.

Handelman, Don. 1995. Comment. *Current Anthropology* 36 (2):280–81.

Harrell-Bond, Barbara. 1989. Repatriation: Under What Conditions Is It the Most Desirable Solution for Refugees? *African Studies Review* 32 (1):41–69.

Hartigan, Kevin. 1992. Matching Humanitarian Norms with Cold, Hard Interests: The Making of Refugee Policies in Mexico and Honduras, 1980–89. *International Organization* 46:709–30.

Helms, Jesse. 1996. Saving the UN. *Foreign Affairs* 75 (5):2–7.

Hendrie, Barbara. 1997. Knowledge and Power: A Critique of an International Relief Operation. *Disasters* 21 (1):57–76.

Heyman, Josiah McC. 1995. Putting Power in the Anthropology of Bureaucracy. *Current Anthropology* 36 (2):261–77.

Hirsch, John, and Robert Oakley. 1995. *Somalia and Operation Restore Hope: Reflections on Peacemaking and Peacekeeping.* Washington, D.C.: USIP Press.

Human Rights Watch. 1997. Uncertain Refuge: International Failures to Protect Refugees. Vol. 1, no. 9 (April).

Hurrell, Andrew, and Ngaire Woods. 1995. Globalisation and Inequality. *Millennium* 24 (3):447–70.

Immergut, Ellen. 1998. The Theoretical Core of the New Institutionalism. *Politics and Society* 26 (1): 5–34.

Jackson, Robert. 1993. The Weight of Ideas in Decolonization: Normative Change in International Relations. In *Ideas and Foreign Policy,* edited by Judith Goldstein and Robert O. Keohane, 111–38. Ithaca, N.Y.: Cornell University Press.

Jacobson, Harold. 1979. *Networks of Interdependence.* New York: Alfred A. Knopf.

Joint Evaluation of Emergency Assistance to Rwanda. 1996. *The International Response to Conflict and Genocide: Lessons from the Rwanda Experience.* 5 vols. Copenhagen: Steering Committee of the Joint Evaluation of Emergency Assistance to Rwanda.

Kapur, Devesh. 1998. The IMF: A Cure or a Curse? *Foreign Policy* 111:114–29.

Katzenstein, Peter J., ed. 1996. *The Culture of National Security: Identity and Norms in World Politics.* New York: Columbia University Press.

Keck, Margaret, and Kathryn Sikkink. 1998. *Activists Beyond Borders.* Ithaca, N.Y.: Cornell University Press.

Keeley, James. 1990. Toward a Foucauldian Analysis of International Regimes. *International Organization* 44 (1):83–105.

Keen, David. 1994. *The Benefits of Famine: A Political Economy of Famine and Relief in Southwestern Sudan, 1983–89*. Princeton, N.J.: Princeton University Press

Kennedy, David. 1986. International Refugee Protection. *Human Rights Quarterly* 8:1–9.

Keohane, Robert O. 1984. *After Hegemony*. Princeton, N.J.: Princeton University Press.

Kiewiet, D. Roderick, and Matthew McCubbins. 1991. *The Logic of Delegation*. Chicago: University of Chicago Press.

Krasner, Stephen D. 1991. Global Communications and National Power: Life on the Pareto Frontier. *World Politics* 43 (3):336–66.

———. 1983a. Regimes and the Limits of Realism: Regimes as Autonomous Variables. In *International Regimes*, edited by Stephen Krasner, 355–68. Ithaca, N.Y.: Cornell University Press.

Krasner, Stephen D., ed. 1983b. *International Regimes*. Ithaca, N.Y.: Cornell University Press.

Krause, Keith, and Michael Williams. 1996. Broadening the Agenda of Security Studies: Politics and Methods. *Mershon International Studies Review* 40 (2):229–54.

Lake, David. 1996. Anarchy, Hierarchy, and the Variety of International Relations. *International Organization* 50 (1):1–34.

Lawyers Committee for Human Rights. 1991. *General Principles Relating to the Promotion of Refugee Repatriation*. New York: Lawyers Committee for Human Rights.

Legro, Jeffrey. 1997. Which Norms Matter? Revisiting the "Failure" of Internationalism. *International Organization* 51 (1):31–64.

Lipartito, Kenneth. 1995. Culture and the Practice of Business History. *Business and Economic History* 24 (2):1–41.

Lipson, Michael. 1999. International Cooperation on Export Controls: Nonproliferation, Globalization, and Multilateralism. Ph.D. diss., University of Wisconsin, Madison.

Malkki, Liisa. 1996. Speechless Emissaries: Refugees, Humanitarianism, and Dehistoricization. *Cultural Anthropology* 11 (3):377–404.

March, James. 1988. *Decisions and Organizations*. Boston: Basil Blackwell.

———. 1997. Understanding How Decisions Happen in Organizations. In *Organizational Decision Making*, edited by Z. Shapira, 9–33. New York: Cambridge University Press.

March, James, and Johan P. Olsen. 1989. *Rediscovering Institutions: The Organizational Basis of Politics*. New York: Free Press.

Martin, Joan. 1992. *Cultures in Organizations: Three Perspectives*. New York: Oxford University Press.

Matthews, Jessica Tuchman. 1989. Redefining Security. *Foreign Affairs* 68 (2):162–77.

McNeely, Connie. 1995. *Constructing the Nation-State: International Organization and Prescriptive Action*. Westport, Conn.: Greenwood Press.

Mearsheimer, John. 1994. The False Promise of International Institutions. *International Security* 19 (3): 5–49.

Meyer, John W., and Brian Rowan. 1977. Institutionalized Organizations: Formal Structure as Myth and Ceremony. *American Journal of Sociology* 83:340–63.

Meyer, John W., and W. Richard Scott. 1992. *Organizational Environments: Ritual and Rationality*. Newbury Park, Calif.: Sage.

Meyer, Marshall, and Lynne Zucker. 1989. *Permanently Failing Organizations*. Newbury Park: Sage Press.

Miller, Gary, and Terry M. Moe. 1983. Bureaucrats, Legislators, and the Size of Government. *American Political Science Review* 77 (June):297–322.

Moe, Terry M. 1984. The New Economics of Organization. *American Journal of Political Science* 28: 739–77.

Moravcsik, Andrew. 1997. Taking Preferences Seriously: Liberal Theory and International Politics. *International Organization* 51 (4):513–54.

———. 1999. A New Statecraft? Supranational Entrepreneurs and International Cooperation. *International Organization* 53 (2):267–306.

Mouzelis, Nicos. 1967. *Organization and Bureaucracy*. Chicago: Aldine.

Murphy, Craig. 1994. *International Organizations and Industrial Change*. New York: Oxford University Press.

Nelson, Paul. 1995. *The World Bank and Non-Governmental Organizations.* New York: St. Martin's Press.

Ness, Gayl, and Steven Brechin. 1988. Bridging the Gap: International Organizations as Organizations. *International Organization* 42 (2):245–73.

Niskanen, William A. 1971. *Bureaucracy and Representative Government.* Chicago: Aldine.

Paris, Roland. 1997. Peacebuilding and the Limits of Liberal Internationalism. *International Security* 22 (2):54–89.

Perry, William. 1996. Defense in an Age of Hope. *Foreign Affairs* 75 (6):64–79.

Pollack, Mark. 1997. Delegation, Agency, and Agenda-Setting in the European Community. *International Organization* 51 (1):99–134.

Powell, Walter W., and Paul J. DiMaggio, eds. 1991. *The New Institutionalism in Organizational Analysis.* Chicago: University of Chicago Press.

Pratt, John, and Richard J. Zeckhauser. 1985. *Principals and Agents: The Structure of Business.* Boston: Harvard Business School Press.

Price, Richard. 1997. *The Chemical Weapons Taboo.* Ithaca, N.Y.: Cornell University Press.

Radelet, Steven, and Jeffrey Sach. 1999. What Have We Learned, So Far, From the Asian Financial Crisis? Harvard Institute for International Development, 4 January. Available from <www.hiid.harvard.edu/pub/other/aea122.pdf>.

Rieff, David. 1996. *Slaughterhouse.* New York: Simon and Schuster.

Rittberger, Volker, ed. 1993. *Regime Theory and International Relations.* Oxford: Clarendon Press.

Ross, George. 1995. *Jacques Delors and European Integration.* New York: Oxford University Press.

Ruggie, John. 1996. *Winning the Peace.* New York: Columbia University Press.

———. 1998. What Makes the World Hang Together. *International Organization* 52 (3):855–86.

Sandholtz, Wayne. 1993. Choosing Union: Monetary Politics and Maastricht. *International Organization* 47:1–40.

Sagan, Scott. 1993. *The Limits of Safety: Organizations, Accidents, and Nuclear Weapons.* Princeton, N.J.: Princeton University Press.

Schaar, John. 1984. Legitimacy in the Modern State. In *Legitimacy and the State,* edited by William Connolly, 104–33. Oxford: Basil Blackwell.

Schien, Edgar. 1996. Culture: The Missing Concept in Organization Studies. *Administrative Studies Quarterly* 41:229–40.

Scott, W. Richard. 1992. *Organizations: Rational, Natural, and Open Systems.* 3d ed. Englewood Cliffs, N.J.: Prentice-Hall.

Shanks, Cheryl, Harold K. Jacobson, and Jeffrey H. Kaplan. 1996. Inertia and Change in the Constellation of Intergovernmental Organizations, 1981–1992. *International Organization* 50 (4):593–627.

Shapira, Zur, ed. 1997. *Organizational Decision.* New York: Cambridge University Press.

Shore, Cris, and Susan Wright. 1997. Policy: A New Field of Anthropology. In *Anthropology of Policy: Critical Perspectives on Governance and Power,* edited by Cris Shore and Susan Wright, 3–41. New York: Routledge Press.

Sigelman, Lee. 1986. The Bureaucratic Budget Maximizer: An Assumption Examined. *Public Budgeting and Finance* (spring):50–59.

Snidal, Duncan. 1996. Political Economy and International Institutions. *International Review of Law and Economics* 16:121–37.

Starr, Paul. 1992. Social Categories and Claims in the Liberal State. In *How Classification Works: Nelson Goodman Among the Social Sciences,* edited by Mary Douglas and David Hull, 154–79. Edinburgh: Edinburgh University Press.

Strange, Susan. 1997. *The Retreat of the State.* New York: Cambridge University Press.

Thomas, Daniel C. Forthcoming. *The Helsinki Effect: International Norms, Human Rights, and Demise of Communism.* Princeton, N.J.: Princeton University Press.

UN Development Program. 1994. *Human Development Report 1994.* New York: Oxford University Press.

UN Peacekeeping Missions. 1994. The Lessons from Cambodia. Asia Pacific Issues, Analysis from the East-West Center, No. 11, March.

Vaubel, Roland. 1991. A Public Choice View of International Organization. In *The Political Economy of International Organizations*, edited by Roland Vaubel and Thomas Willett, 27–45. Boulder, Colo.: Westview Press.

Vaughan, Diane. 1996. *The Challenger Launch Decision*. Chicago: University of Chicago Press.

Wade, Robert. 1996. Japan, the World Bank, and the Art of Paradigm Maintenance: The East Asian Miracle in Political Perspective. *New Left Review* 217:3–36.

Walkup, Mark. 1997. Policy Dysfunction in Humanitarian Organizations: The Role of Coping Strategies, Institutions, and Organizational Culture. *Journal of Refugee Studies* 10 (1):37–60.

Waltz, Kenneth. 1979. *Theory of International Politics*. Reading, Mass.: Addison-Wesley.

Wapner, Paul. 1996. *Environmental Activism and World Civic Politics*. Albany: State University of New York Press.

Weber, Max. 1947. *Theory of Social and Economic Organization*. New York: Oxford University Press.

———. [1930] 1968. *The Protestant Ethic and the Spirit of Capitalism*. New York: Routledge.

———. 1978. Bureaucracy. In *From Max Weber: Essays in Sociology*, edited by H. H. Gerth and C. Wright Mills, 196–44. New York: Oxford

Weber, Steven. Origins of the European Bank for Reconstruction and Development. *International Organization* 48(1):1–38.

Weingast, Barry R., and Mark Moran. 1983. Bureaucratic Discretion or Congressional Control: Regulatory Policymaking by the Federal Trade Commission. *Journal of Political Economy* 91 (October):765–800.

Weiss, Thomas. 1996. Collective Spinelessness: U.N. Actions in the Former Yugoslavia. In *The World and Yugoslavia's Wars*, edited by Richard Ullman, 59–96. New York: Council on Foreign Relations Press.

Weiss, Tom, and Amir Pasic. 1997. Reinventing UNHCR: Enterprising Humanitarians in the Former Yugoslavia, 1991–95. *Global Governance* 3 (1):41–58.

Wendt, Alexander. 1995. Constructing International Politics. *International Security* 20 (1):71–81.

———. 1998. Constitution and Causation in International Relations. *Review of International Studies* 24 (4):101–17. Special issue.

Williams, Michael. 1996. Hobbes and International Relations: A Reconsideration. *International Organization* 50 (2):213–37.

Williamson, Oliver. 1975. *Markets and Hierarchies, Analysis and Antitrust Implications: A Study in the Economics of Internal Organization*. New York: Free Press.

———. 1985. *The Economic Institutions of Capitalism: Firms, Markets, Relational Contracting*. New York: Free Press.

World Conference on Human Rights. 1993. Vienna Declaration on Human Rights, adopted 14–25 June. UN Document A/CONF.157/24 (Part I), 20; A/CONF.157/23 DPI/1394/Rev.1 DPI/1676 (95.I.21), 448; DPI/1707 ST/HR/2/Rev.4, 383.

Wright, Susan. 1994. "Culture" in Anthropology and Organizational Studies. In *Anthropology of Organizations*, edited by Susan Wright, 1–31. New York: Routledge.

Zabusky, Stacia. 1995. *Launching Europe*. Princeton, N.J.: Princeton University Press.

Zieck, Marjoleine. 1997. *UNHCR and Voluntary Repatriation of Refugees: A Legal Analysis*. The Hague: Martinus Nijhoff.

[14]

The WTO Dispute Settlement System: A First Assessment from an Economic Perspective

Monika Bütler
DEEP Université de Lausanne, CentER Tilburg University, and CEPR

Heinz Hauser
Universität St. Gallen

We explore the incentives countries face in trade litigation within the new WTO dispute settlement system. Our analysis yields a number of interesting predictions. First, because sanctions are ruled out during the litigation process, the dispute settlement system does not preclude all new trade restrictions. However, the agenda-setting capacity of the com̲ ⸻ ̲luding its right to force a decision, make trade restri̲c̲ti̲ ̲ der the WTO's predecessor, GATT. S̲ ̲ ̲ ̲ provides the losing defendant with sti̲ ̲ ̲ ̲ ̲ ̲ ̲s, and both parties with a possibility ̲ ̲ ̲ ̲ the case. Third, a relatively weak imp̲ ̲ ̲ ̲ ̲rces incentives to violate WTO trade ru̲ ̲ ̲ ̲e likely at an early stage in the process ̲ ̲ ̲ ̲ome of the formal dispute settlement pr̲ ̲ ̲ ̲ a first dataset of cases at an advance̲ ̲ ̲ ̲ ̲cess provides qualitative support for our claims.

1. Introduction

Don't let the European Union make a game of the WTO system[1]

The World Trade Organization (WTO) celebrated its fifth anniversary on January 1, 2000. This was overshadowed by the failure of the Third

---

We are especially indebted to Urs Birchler and Olivier Cadot for their suggestions and advice. Moreover, we would like to thank Andrea Martel, Andreas Ziegler, and a very helpful referee for many valuable insights and comments. The usual disclaimer applies.

Corresponding author: Monika Bütler, DEEP-HEC, Université de Lausanne, BFSH1, CH-1015, Lausanne, Switzerland; email *Monika.Butler@HEC.unil.ch*, tel +41 21 692 3451, fax +41 21 692 3365.

1. *Washington Post*, December 1998. This and other advertisements ("If it's going to have any teeth, the World Trade Organization has to cut them on beef and bananas.") refer to the two prominent agricultural conflicts (DS16/27 and DS26/48, see Table C.1) between the United States and the European Union, and have appeared in major U.S. newspapers in 1998. In both cases, the WTO decided in favor of the United States (the complainant) and requested the European Union (the defendant) to change its practice within a period of 15 months. The European Union failed to implement the recommendations of the dispute settlement system, and the United States subsequently got permission to levy retaliation tariffs on EU products.

504   The Journal of Law, Economics, & Organization, V16 N2

WTO Ministerial Conference in Seattle and two big—though not necessarily representative—agricultural trade disputes between the United States and the European union, which have caught most of the public's attention concerning the WTO in recent months. Unfortunately one of its most important features, the new dispute settlement system, has not attracted the attention it deserves. Although the well-known "banana" and "hormones" cases have indeed uncovered potential weaknesses in the litigation mechanism, a substantial number of disputes have gone through the process successfully, but largely unnoticed by both the public and the economic profession. Our article attempts a first systematic description of the mechanism from an economic perspective. We analyze the WTO dispute settlement system as a game and confront the predictions of the theoretical model with the empirical evidence from its first five years.

The WTO's predecessor, GATT (General Agreement on Tariffs and Trade), was successful in reducing tariffs, but suffered from increasing problems with nontariff restrictions and from a weak and intransparent mechanism to deal with trade disputes. As a consequence, the new WTO established a mandatory and unified dispute settlement system with much broader jurisdiction. During its first five years a large number of cases made this institution by far the most active part of the new international trade organization. WTO and GATT dispute settlement systems have been studied by political scientists and legal experts,[2] but we are not aware of any other economic explanation of the parties' incentives and strategies during the dispute settlement process. Our contribution tries to fill this gap by providing a more formal economic analysis of the mechanism.

The WTO's trade litigation procedures differ not only from dispute handling within the old GATT, but in fact from any previous dispute settlement mechanisms at an international level. Any member country that feels negatively affected by another country's trade measure can bring a case before the dispute settlement system and is granted agenda-setting capacity for a large part of the dispute. Unless a bilateral settlement is reached between the countries involved, the case is decided by a panel established by the Dispute Settlement Body (DSB). The panel's verdict can subsequently be appealed by either country. If the report is in favor of the complainant, the defendant country is given

---

2. See, for example, Croley and Jackson (1996), Vermulst and Driessen (1995), and Palmeter and Mavroidis (1998). A more general perspective on trade legalism is taken by Shell (1995). For a statistical analysis of GATT disputes see Hudec, Kennedy, and Sgarbossa (1993). While focusing on legal aspects, Jackson (1998) provides interesting information on motives and strategies of litigating parties. Petersmann (1997) contains a detailed analysis of the WTO dispute settlement system and its predecessors from a predominantly legal perspective. This book also comprises a large number of illustrating examples, predominantly under GATT.

a limited period to implement the panel's or appellate body's recommendations. In case of the defendant's noncompliance after the granted implementation period, the complainant has a right to ask for compensatory trade concessions. An important difference to dispute settlement under GATT is the elimination of a (factual) unanimity rule. As a consequence, the WTO dispute settlement system prevents single members from blocking the adoption of the final and binding decision.

The new rules seem effective in practice. Already a casual inspection of (nearly) completed cases offers some striking empirical regularities. The first is the large number of cases that have been brought forward for formal dispute settlement: 185 complaints in five years contrasted with fewer than 300 cases in GATT's 47-year history. The large number of cases put forward could be a consequence of the system's inability to prevent trade restrictions or nuisance suits, but could also represent a higher confidence of negatively affected countries in an improved mechanism. The second observation is the apparent popularity of the appellate review. In only four cases was the panel report the last instance of the litigation, whereas 24 panel reports were subsequently appealed.[3] The high proportion of appeals does not seem consistent with the appellate review being an additional legal safeguard only. A third observation, which deserves further analysis, is the mixed success of the system's implementation mechanism. Whether noncompliance is an inherent danger of the system's structure, as the two big agricultural disputes may suggest, is yet an open question. It is clear, however, that a successful implementation stage feeds back into a more powerful procedure. A fourth and last observation is the relatively high ratio of bilateral settlements prior to a panel decision.

Our article attempts to cast some light on these issues. In particular, it aims to answer the following questions:

1. Can the WTO dispute settlement system preclude trade restrictions and nuisance suits?

2. What are the reasons and incentives of the (losing) country to appeal a panel finding? Does the appellate review in practice really play a strictly legal role?

3. How well can WTO rulings and recommendations be enforced given the incentives of the litigants?

4. When are bilateral settlements more likely, and what form might they take? Should they be encouraged by the WTO as they currently are, or rather not?

---

3. These numbers do not include cases for which the granted period to appear had not elapsed by December 31, 1999. Most cases, however, are still at a preliminary stage of the litigation process.

506   The Journal of Law, Economics, & Organization, V16 N2

The importance of strategic interaction between the countries during litigation can be captured by a dynamic game with a succession of sequential moves of the involved players. Time is an important determinant of both parties' payoffs, because rents and costs accrue during the whole litigation process. In the course of the procedure, the appearance of new information and joining third parties, moreover, can change the outcome of the game. Modeling the multistage setting and the rather complicated structure of the system poses a number of difficult questions. The focus of our article clearly lies in finding an appropriate way to map the system into a tractable dynamic game that preserves the most important features, rather than in applying sophisticated game theoretic methods. Although we take an economist's perspective, legal and political aspects are taken into account via their impact on the parties' payoff structure.

Civil suits and international disputes share a number of common features, but differ considerably in other respects.[4] As the most important difference, the payoffs of parties in international litigation accrue predominantly in a nonpecuniary way in the form of political rents and as reputation effects. In most instances, therefore, the issue is not a zero-sum game. Due to the limited number of countries in the organization, moreover, the players' characteristics are supposedly well known. Imperfect information within the dispute settlement system is therefore only of secondary importance.

The article is structured as follows. Section 2 describes the new dispute settlement mechanism in more detail and highlights its most important differences compared to GATT. Section 3 introduces the structure of the game. The core of the article, Section 4, analyses the outcomes of the game. The model's predictions at different stages of the litigation process are compared with a preliminary dataset of completed or nearly completed cases. Section 5 provides a summary of the most important findings and concludes.

2. Dispute Settlement Under GATT and WTO

The WTO dispute settlement mechanism involves a number of stages, the most important of which are illustrated in Figure 1, and by a typical completed case—a complaint by Venezuela against the United States about standards for gasoline—in Appendix B.[5] Obviously the reason for the procedure, and therefore the first stage of the litigation procedure, is a trade-related measure of country D (the future defendant), which

---

4. The existing literature on the economic analysis of legal disputes is predominantly concerned with civil suits. An excellent review of this literature can be found in Cooter and Rubinfeld (1989).

5. A comprehensive description of the dispute settlement system and a wealth of additional information, including panel and appellate review reports, can be found in WTO (1995) and on the WTO's website (www.wto.org/wto/dispute).

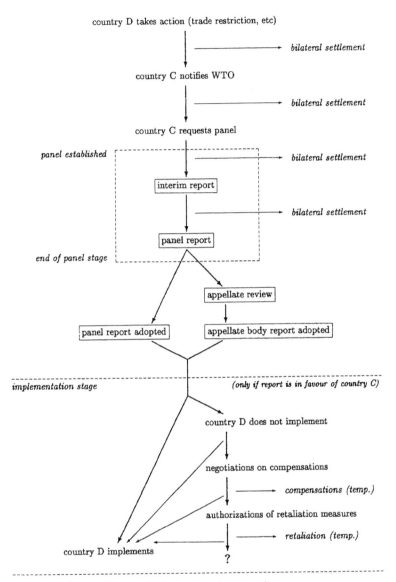

Figure 1. Stages of the new WTO dispute settlement system.

seemingly violates WTO law and nullifies or impairs the benefit of another country C (the future complainant). While most cases within the WTO dispute settlement system have dealt with preexisting measures, this first step must not be neglected, should the role of the dispute settlement be analyzed for future cases. Ideally the WTO

508   The Journal of Law, Economics, & Organization, V16 N2

should prevent countries from taking measures incompatible with WTO law in the first place.

If no bilateral settlement between the two parties can be reached outside WTO procedures, the complainant country C can notify the WTO that it is asking for consultations under the dispute settlement system. This step brings the case to public attention and might attract other countries having similar problems with country D. Countries with a genuine interest in the case can be formally included as third parties in the dispute. Should no agreement be reached after 60 days, the complainant can request the establishment of a panel, which will usually be granted by the WTO's DSB after at most 30 days.

The panel stage, which under normal conditions should not exceed six months, follows a number of intermediate steps and involves both parties. In a careful fact-finding process, the positions of both countries are reviewed. An important step during the panel stage is the interim report, which includes all relevant panel findings and can be viewed as a final draft of the panel's verdict. Revealing the position the panel will take on this particular case, it is thus an important source of information for both parties. The interim report should remain confidential to the parties involved[6] and give them a last opportunity to settle their dispute bilaterally. If no bilateral settlement can be reached, the final panel report, which includes recommendations for implementation, is circulated among all WTO members.

As a novel feature of trade litigation, the WTO dispute settlement system provides an appellate review by a standing appellate body composed of seven independent legal experts. This second—and last—step should provide an additional safeguard against legally wrong panel's decisions. Both involved parties can appeal against legal or procedural aspects of the panel's decision. The introduction of the possibility of an appellate review as a second safeguard is considered to be one of the main new features of the system compared to GATT proceedings. The appellate body has a strictly legal function, such that substantive issues—in principle—cannot be raised during this stage.[7]

Should the binding decision of either the panel or the appellate review be in favor of the complainant, the defendant is given a "reasonable period" (typically not to exceed 15 months) of time to bring the respective trade regulation into conformity with WTO law. In case of

---

6. Often, however, this principle has been violated in the past, notably by the winner in bigger cases, most recently by the European Union in the Foreign Sales Corporations (FSC) dispute with the United States (DS108).

7. However, limiting the permissible subject matter of the appeal is presumably difficult. Petersmann (1997:190) writes: *"Experience with domestic and international appellate review proceedings confirms that distinguishing law from fact, and defining the limits of legal arguments, are notoriously difficult."*

disagreement the period is determined by an independent arbitrator. If the defendant does not conform with the panel's recommendations, compensatory measures can be taken by the complainant. In a first step, the complainant can force the defendant to enter a bargaining process regarding compensatory trade concessions. If the parties do not come to an agreement within 20 days, the complainant is granted the right to take countervailing measures, which have to satisfy certain conditions. Among others, the volume of the retaliation measures must not exceed the complainant's incurred damage. Although both compensation and retaliation measures are supposed to be temporary, it is unclear what happens if the defendant refuses to implement the recommendations of the panel despite countervailing measures.

Between any of these formal stages, bilateral negotiations can take place. Failure to reach a bilateral agreement is a necessary prerequisite for the next step. It usually suffices to notify the WTO about a successful mutual agreement. The outcomes of bilateral settlements are not monitored by the WTO, and their contents are usually not disclosed.

The major differences between the WTO structure and dispute settlement under GATT can be summarized as follows: First, the WTO offers a unified dispute settlement system for trade disputes under all WTO agreements, whereas GATT comprised at least eight different structures for dealing with trade disputes, depending on the nature of the trade restriction. This feature of GATT induced parties to use forum shopping in order to find the most favorable environment. Second, the complainant now has a *right* to have a panel process initiated. Unlike under GATT's factual unanimity rule, there is no way for the defendant to block formal litigation at this stage. In fact, within some limits, the complainant is granted agenda-setting power during the whole litigation process. Third, both parties can appeal against the panel decision. Fourth, the adoption of the final decision (either the panel or the appellate body report) within the WTO dispute settlement system can no longer be vetoed by the losing defendant, as under the old GATT. Finally, the implementation phase has been given more structure. If the losing country does not conform with the panel's recommendations, the complainant has the right to ask for compensation or to take countervailing measures.

3. The Theoretical Model

Our goal is to arrive at a tractable model of the WTO dispute settlement procedure that captures the most important features of the system. The rest of the litigation process is summarized in an appropriate way. We first introduce the participating players and the main stages of the game. The players' payoff structures and the underlying information set are discussed next.

510   The Journal of Law, Economics, & Organization, V16 N2

3.1 Players

The WTO dispute settlement system has two genuine players: The defendant, D, is the country which has taken an action (trade restriction) and which is subsequently accused of violating WTO law by the complainant, C, which files the suit. Both countries are represented by their governments, whose interests are not necessarily identical to those of their population. Throughout the analysis, we assume risk-neutral players and therefore linear utility.[8]

Unlike many private litigation processes, the WTO dispute settlement mechanism allows third parties to participate in the process. Moreover, new information might turn up during the litigation. In our analysis, any new relevant information and the appearance of additional countries are summarized in a change in either the litigation costs or in the probability of a certain outcome of both the panel and the appeal decision.

3.2 Stages of the Game and Timing of Actions

Two kinds of stages are distinguished: First, there are well-defined stages during which one of the two countries or WTO makes a move. Second, there are some intermediate stages in which bargaining between the two countries can take place. The main stages in the former category are illustrated in Figure 2. In a first step (1) the *defendant* introduces a trade-related measure. This can also mean that a preexisting—and previously undisputed—measure can suddenly fall under scrutiny of other countries, notably after a change in WTO law. The next two steps—notification of WTO (2) and panel request (3)—are taken by the complainant and initiate the official WTO procedure. The most important step during the panel phase clearly is the interim report [move (4) by the WTO]. This is the first time during the process when the involved parties know the position of the panel. Both parties can appeal against the panel decision (5). The succession of moves (or simultaneous moves) is not specified here. The appellate review (6) is the final decision by the WTO. The findings of the interim report can be reconfirmed or revised. To simplify matters we summarize the implementation stage as a single step (7). Between any of the above stages, bilateral negotiations can take place. Failure to reach a bilateral agreement is a necessary prerequisite for the next step, and a successful bilateral settlement ends the game at any stage.

We assume that the decisions of the WTO dispute settlement system are unequivocal, either in favor of the defendant or in favor of the

---

8. By postulating linear utility, computations of expected payoffs are kept transparent, even when the dispute stretches over several periods. Moreover, we do not have to specify any distributional assumptions about random components of the payoff structure.

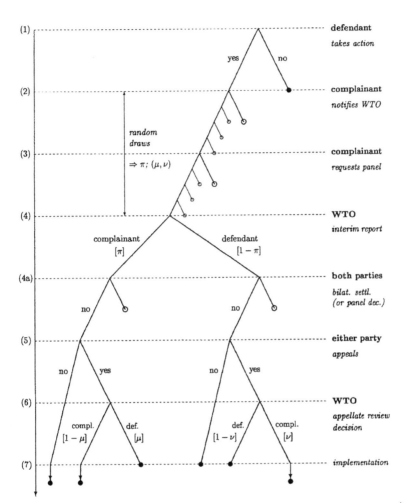

Figure 2. WTO dispute settlement system. Game tree (without implementation stage). Filled dots denote final nodes for which (expected) payoffs are known, circles denote final nodes corresponding to bilateral settlements, for which payoffs are not a priori known. Probabilities are given in square brackets.

complainant. Precluding the possibility of "intermediate" decisions, we thus merely have to state the resulting payoffs in either case.

3.3 Payoff Structure

We distinguish three categories of relevant payoff components (as summarized in Table 1): directly trade-related gains and losses, reputation gains and losses, and litigation costs.

512   The Journal of Law, Economics, & Organization, V16 N2

Table 1. Payoff Elements for Both Players and Probabilities of WTO Decisions

Description	Parameter
Trade related gains/losses	
Loss of complainant (rate, per year)	$l \geq 0$
Continuation loss of complainant	$\tilde{L} \geq 0$
Gain of defendant (rate, per year)	g
Continuation gain of defendant	$\tilde{G}$
Compensation loss, defendant (per year)	p^D
Reputation gains/losses	
Loss of losing panel	R^C_{lose}, R^D_{lose}
Gain from winning panel	R^C_{win}, R^D_{win}
Gain from undergoing appellate review	R^C_{app}, R^D_{app}
Loss of not conforming	$R^D_{impl}[t]$
Litigation costs	
Direct costs (lawyers, etc.)	K^C, K^D
Probabilities	
Panel in favour of complainant	π
Revision by appellate review (panel = complainant)	μ
Revision by appellate review (panel = defendant)	ν

Trade related gains and losses may represent welfare gains and losses to a country, but very often are rents and costs accruing to certain interest groups that translate directly into an implicit political support function. For simplicity, it is assumed that trade-related payoffs are proportional to the time the trade measure is in action. Note that, unlike in most civil suits, gains and losses are not symmetric. The game is therefore not a zero-sum game, even in the absence of reputation costs. If the gains accrue to powerful lobby groups, for example, a trade restriction might well lead to a gain for the defendant in political support which exceeds the complainant's loss.[9] To capture the impact of the duration of the litigation on payoffs, we make a distinction between rents *during* the process and continuation rents *after* the conclusion of the litigation process. During the dispute settlement procedure, the benefit rate for the defendant is denoted by g, and the loss rate for the complainant by l.[10] To simplify the analysis, we refrain from discounting benefits and losses during the length of the dispute. Continuation rents and losses, denoted by $\tilde{G}$ and $\tilde{L}$, respectively, accrue after completion of the litigation process. We assume that they are finite due to discount-

---

9. The U.S. Treasury Department, for example, estimates that the current U.S. FSC regime (DS108, see Table C.1) generates $2–$3 billion in permanent tax savings to U.S. exporters annually. Despite these revenue losses, the U.S. government strongly defends this measure, backed by a powerful lobby of exporters.

10. For a period of time t (given as a fraction of one year), trade-related gains and losses are consequently gt and lt.

ing or due to the fact that new technologies or other changing circumstances might render a previously beneficial or harmful trade restriction irrelevant. A last trade-related payoff is the loss p^D (given as a rate) incurred by a noncomplying defendant via the complainant's retaliation policies during the implementation stage.

Reputation gains and losses are assumed to occur at certain stages of the litigation process. The importance of these payoff elements is emphasized especially by political and legal scientists [see, e.g., Jackson (1998)]. Reputation payoffs depend on the nature and size of the dispute, as well as on a country's size and political structure (i.e., the importance of interest groups, reelection procedures). With one exception they are modeled here as one-time gains and costs: Reputation gains/losses for the complainant (defendant) in case of a positive/negative outcome of the process are denoted by R_{win}^C (R_{win}^D) and R_{lose}^C (R_{lose}^D), respectively.[11] For simplicity, we assume that they only occur during the panel stage and are therefore adjusted for the probability that the subsequent appellate review yields a different outcome. By undergoing the appellate review stage after a negative panel finding, the losing government can signal its determinacy to act in the interest of the involved domestic groups, realizing a reputation gain R_{app}^C (R_{app}^D). Note that for the defendant country, the appellate stage is the first and only stage in which it can actively influence the process.[12] Reputation costs of noncompliance with the DSB's findings are assumed to increase with time and are denoted by $R_{impl}^D[t]$ [i.e., $d(R_{impl}^D[t])/dt \geq 0$]. The fact that the United States, but also other countries, complied even in the absence of explicit implementation procedures under GATT in a number of cases provides some support for the existence of these reputation costs.[13] Their structure will depend on the nature of the conflict.

Litigation costs—that is, the legal and organizational costs of entering the dispute settlement system—are denoted by K^C (K^D). For

---

11. The eagerness of countries to advertise victory or to explain a defeat is obvious from various media reports. In a press statement, the European Union writes: "Until now, there have been only two rulings that have found that certain EU measures are incompatible with WTO provisions. These are the Hormones and Banana cases. It should be remembered that these cases have a long history and involve other considerations than trade, such as public health and development assistance." (EU information on the web (October 98)). Concerning the lost U.S. film case (DS44, see Table C.1), the *New York Law Journal* (February 26, 1998) cites the dean of Brooklyn Law School: "The loss was small in comparison to other victories the U.S. has been setting so far."

12. Especially in the European Union and the United States, the actions of the governments are closely monitored by the involved interest groups. As the headline of its press release, Greenpeace stated: "Greenpeace applauds EU appeal against WTO beef-hormone ruling," Brussels (September 1997).

13. Jackson (1998:170) argues that "even the most powerful trading entities in the world find it difficult diplomatically to ignore the results of the dispute settlement process, although in some sense, they could get away with it."

514   The Journal of Law, Economics, & Organization, V16 N2

simplicity, we assume that litigation costs only matter for the panel stage. They should be interpreted as net additional costs of formal litigation over mutual agreement. The entrance of third parties into the dispute can thus affect the process costs directly (sharing of legal fees) or indirectly (higher coordination costs for cooperating countries in bilateral settlements).

3.4 Information Set and Probability Structure

The analysis assumes a game under uncertainty in which the outcomes of the settlement procedure are not known in advance. The probability of the WTO (panel) deciding in favor of the complainant is denoted by π. The revision probabilities of a potential appellate review are given by μ (the probability of appellate review in favor of the defendant after a panel report in favor of the complainant) and ν (the probability of appellate review in favor of the complainant after a panel report in favor of the defendant). An additional restriction is imposed on the probabilities μ and ν, which allows us to abstract from revision probabilities later in the analysis. We require that the probability π that the panel rules in favor of the complainant equals the overall probability of success for the complainant:[14]

$$\pi = \pi(1 - \mu) + (1 - \pi)\nu. \tag{1}$$

We assume symmetric information about all rents. In the context of the WTO dispute settlement, it can be expected that gains and losses from trade restrictions are public knowledge. The same is true, possibly to a lesser extent, for litigation costs and reputation gains and losses. Under symmetric/complete information, both players have identical beliefs at each stage of the game.

Probabilities and payoff elements are not restricted to remain constant during the game. Apart from WTO's decisions, random draws between notification and the interim report may change the information and cost structure of the game. The probability of a certain outcome is itself random. However, we assume that the best predictor of each payoff component X is always the current value of X,[15] therefore $E(t)X(t + s) = X(t)$, $\forall s \geq 0$. Random changes are assumed to be un-

---

14. As a numerical example, consider a situation in which the complainant has a high probability $\pi = 0.9$ to win. For $\mu = 0.1$, Equation (1) dictates that $\nu = 0.9$, that is, that the probability of a revision in favor of the complainant after a negative panel finding is rather high. For $\pi = 0$, which corresponds to an empty threat of the complainant, $\nu = 0$ and μ can take any value. Similarly for $\pi = 1$, which corresponds to a clear violation of WTO law, $\mu = 0$ and ν is unspecified.

15. Note that probabilities (but not payoffs) are restricted to lie in the interval $[0, 1]$. Consequently there is a probability mass one at both $\pi = 1$ and $\pi = 0$. This means that once a case is clear, it will stay so forever with probability one.

correlated. Consequently we do not have to specify the probability distribution of the payoff components (or of probabilities) in a risk-neutral setting with linear preferences.

The recent Foreign Sales Corporations case (FSC, DS108) between the European Union and the United States provides a nice illustration for time-dependent payoffs. As will be predicted by our theoretical model below, the United States appealed against the negative rulings of the panel. Shortly afterwards it withdrew the appeal, conditional on its right to file a new notice of appeal later. Most probably the United States, hosting the Third WTO Ministerial Conference in Seattle, did not want to be seen as a noncomplying country. After the conference, when public attention was beginning to fade away, the United States did indeed renew its appeal. Apparently the United States experienced a temporary change in its reputation costs.

4. Theoretical Predictions and Empirical Evidence

The game tree is drawn in its extensive form in Figure 2. Taking into account the limited information available on the implementation stage, a simplified treatment will be proposed below. The model is solved backwards to obtain subgame perfect equilibria. Following the solution path, we present the predictions for the implementation stage first, and proceed with an analysis of the appeal stage. The complainant's optimal strategy before the panel and its filing decision are considered next. Finally, we analyze the future defendant's decision to introduce a trade measure. A summary of predicted subgame perfect equilibria and the number of cases corresponding to them can also be found in Table 2.

In the first part of this section, bilateral settlements are ignored, that is, the results are stated as if there was no scope for mutual agreements. A first reason is the very limited information available about the nature of bilateral agreements. It is generally unknown whether a bilateral settlement involves a reduction of the disputed trade measure or compensatory trade restrictions by the complainant. Second, compensation payments—an important ingredient in civil suits—hardly exist between litigating countries. The highly nonpecuniary nature of most payoff components makes it difficult to compare the "cooperative value" of a settlement with the "noncooperative value" of pursuing the dispute. The possibility of bilateral settlements is therefore analyzed separately in the second part of this section.

Each prediction from our model is illustrated with some empirical evidence from WTO dispute settlement complaints filed during the first five years. This analysis rests on a preliminary database prepared by the authors which comprises relevant information on all complaints filed during this five-year period. Unfortunately, only a fraction of all filed suits have been concluded so far, and the vast majority are still at a preliminary stage in the litigation process. Nonetheless, the existing evidence should facilitate an assessment of the predictive power and

516   The Journal of Law, Economics, & Organization, V16 N2

Table 2. Subgame Perfect Equilibria of the WTO Dispute Settlement Game

Stage	1	2	3	4	4a	5		6	Cases
Move by	D	C	C	WTO Intermediate	Panel	D	C	WTO	
I	—	—	—	—		—	—	—	NA
II	Action	—	—	—		—	—	—	NA
III	Action	Notification	Panel	C		Appeal		C	19*
IV	Action	Notification	Panel	C		Appeal		D	2
V	Action	Notification	Panel	D			Appeal	D	1
VI	Action	Notification	Panel	D			Appeal	C	0
Other									6
BS1	Action	BS	—	—		—	—	—	NA
BS2	Action	Notification	BS	—		—	—	—	24
BS3	Action	Notification	Panel	BS		—	—	—	4
BS4	Action	Notification	Panel	?	BS	—	—	—	1

The upper part of the table lists equilibria without an intermediate bilateral settlement and without major random changes to the payoff structure during litigation (* includes two cases in which an appellate review was requested by the winning country). The lower part lists cases, in which a bilateral settlement (BS) can be a possible equilibrium outcome. Only clear empirical cases have been classified. NA = no information available. BS = bilateral settlement; NA = no information available.

potential shortcomings of our theoretical model. For easy reference, all cases mentioned explicitly in this article are numbered by their official WTO label, and are listed in Appendix C (Table C.1).

4.1 The Implementation Stage

After a negative panel or appellate review ruling, the losing defendant is granted a "reasonable implementation period," τ. Although negotiations about compensatory concessions can be requested and retaliation measures can be taken in case of the defendant's noncompliance, the role of the complainant is rather passive. Its only choice variable is thus the time $\tilde{\tau} \geq \tau$ after which it can ask for retaliation.[16]

The optimal strategies of both players during the implementation stage can be summarized in Prediction 1.

Prediction 1 (implementation). The defendant conforms with WTO rulings, if and only if

$$g - p^D I_{[t \geq \tilde{\tau}]} - \frac{d\left(R^D_{impl}[t]\right)}{dt} \leq 0, \tag{2}$$

where $I_{[t \geq \tilde{\tau}]}$ is the indicator function. Consequently,

- The optimal strategy of the complainant is to request compensation or retaliation immediately after the completion of the granted implementation period, thus $\tilde{\tau} = \tau$.
- Given the expected strategy of the complainant, the three possible implementation dates are as follows:
  - At the beginning of the implementation period ($t = 0$), if the reputation costs for nonconforming with WTO law are greater than the trade gains.
  - At the end of the granted implementation period ($t = \tau$), if the impact of compensatory measures is sufficiently large (i.e., if $p^D \geq g - d(R^D_{impl}[t])/dt|_{t=\tau}$).
  - At a time $\tilde{t} \leq \infty$ strictly greater than τ for which $d(R^D_{impl}[t])/dt|_{t=\tilde{t}} = g - p^D$).

Proof. Note that instantaneous trade-related gains g and losses due to retaliation p^D are constant, while reputation costs of noncompliance are assumed to be increasing, that is, $d(R^D_{impl}[t])/dt \geq 0$.[17]

---

16. We view compensatory concessions and retaliations as a combined means to punish a nonconforming defendant.

17. For linear reputation costs, for example, $R^D_{impl}[t] = \rho t$, the three possible implementation equilibria are $t^*_{impl} = 0$, $t^*_{impl} = \tau$, and $t^*_{impl} = \infty$. For exponential reputation costs the defendant always implements after a finite time period: A nonconforming defendant is stigmatized quickly enough to prevent an infinite delay of implementation.

518   The Journal of Law, Economics, & Organization, V16 N2

Even if compensation payments are granted by the defendant or if retaliation measures offset part of the incurred loss of the defendant's trade restriction, the complainant is unanimously better off by a direct implementation of the panel's recommendation. Recall that the trade value of the retaliation measures must not exceed the trade value of incurred losses and the complainant gets no retroactive remedy. Taking into account the fact that the defendant has a strong incentive to delay implementation, the optimal strategy of the complainant country is to request compensation or retaliation as soon as possible.

By the end of 1999, our database contained 11 cases for which information on the implementation status is available. The remaining cases with a final report in favor of the complainant are still within the "reasonable implementation period" granted by the system. While the number of cases is too small to draw reliable conclusions, the clustering of implementation periods, as predicted by our model, is obvious. We can distinguish three different patterns of implementation behavior so far. Two cases ended with an immediate adoption of the panel's or appellate review's recommendations. Both involved relatively minor complaints against the United States in which the direct gains for U.S. interest groups can be presumed to be small relative to reputation losses in delaying implementation (DS24 and DS33).[18]

In seven cases (involving seven different defendants),[19] the losing defendant implemented the panel's finding shortly after the "reasonable implementation period" had elapsed, in most cases after 15 months. Once a reasonable period has been specified (either in the final report or by an arbitrator), none of the countries has an incentive to conform before, and the prospect of retaliation measures may have triggered implementation. The affected trade volumes in the seven disputes seem to be in an intermediate range.

In two major agricultural trade disputes between the United States as a complainant and the European Union as the defendant (DS16/27 and DS26/48), the panel's recommendations were not (fully) implemented even after the period determined by the arbitrator. In both cases the

---

18. In the latter case, the United States conformed with the panel's recommendations even before the final appellate review report was adopted. The appeal was actually asked by the complainant to get clarifications on legal, but not substantive issues. (See also the section below on appellate review.)

19. The cases are DS2/4 (defendant United States), DS8/10/11 (Japan), DS31 (Canada), DS50 (India), DS54/55/59/64 (Indonesia), DS56 (Argentina), and DS69 European Union. Complaint DS2/4 is also illustrated in Appendix C. The implementation of four further rulings (DS18, DS46, DS70, and DS58) is scheduled to be evaluated by the original panel because there is considerable disagreement between the litigants about the implementation status after the implementation period had elapsed.

United States asked for, and was granted, compensatory measures immediately after the given implementation period had elapsed. Available evidence suggests that the political gain for the European Union to retain the disputed trade restrictions is high [for public health concerns ("hormones") and the treatment of former colonies ("bananas")].

For the remainder of the analysis, it is assumed that the defendant implements after a period $t_{impl} = \tau$, *before* compensating measures are taken. Any other equilibrium, in particular if the defendant does not comply with a probability γ, can be modeled in an analogous way.

4.2 The Appeal Stage

An appeal by one of the parties suffices to have the issue in question reviewed by the appellate body. "Appellate review" is the equilibrium of the game as long as the expected payoffs for "appeal" are higher than "nonappeal" for one litigant.[20] The optimal strategies of the players are as follows.

Prediction 2 (appellate review). A losing defendant appeals even if the chance of a reversal of the panel's findings μ is zero. A losing complainant appeals if either reputation gains R^C_{app} or the reversal probability ν are strictly greater than zero.

Proof. The claim is easily verified by inspecting the relevant payoffs of the game (see section A.1 in the appendix).

There is an overwhelming incentive for the losing government to appeal against the panel report. Consider for example the case of the losing defendant. There are three reasons for our prediction: First and most important, the negative panel finding, and consequently implementation, can be delayed at least for a certain period of time, resulting in an additional trade-related rent. Second, the government may secure political support from involved interest groups. Especially for sensitive issues, as for example the EU "hormones" and "banana" cases, domestic political pressure to appeal is substantial. Finally, there is a small probability μ that the panel finding is reversed by an appellate review. Consequently the appellate review procedure is likely to be evoked in a large number of cases.

---

20. The strictly legal function and expertise of the appellate body should ensure unity of interpretation of international law and should rule out that the outcome of an appellate review depends on which country appeals. Once one country appeals, it is virtually costless for the other country to appeal too.

520   The Journal of Law, Economics, & Organization, V16 N2

In fact, 24 of 28 cases which have gone through the panel stage so far have been consequently appealed.[21] In 21 disputes an appellate review was requested by the losing defendant,[22] in one by the losing complainant (DS22), and twice by one or both contestants in disputes with ambiguous panel findings (DS69, DS70). Only four panel reports—one in favor of the defendant (DS44),[23] two in favor of the complainant (DS99, DS126), one ambiguous (DS54/55/59/64)—were directly adopted.

The appellate review fully confirmed the findings of the panel report in 21 disputes. In two cases the appeal led to a reversal of the panel findings (DS60, DS62/67/68), and in one case to a partial reversion (DS103/113). A losing defendant obviously appeals even if hopes to win the case are slim. In the latter three cases, the appellate review seems to have fulfilled its anticipated role.

In contrast to the model's prediction, the winning complainant appealed against the findings of the panel report in two cases, the two minor textile cases of developing countries against the United States already mentioned above (DS24 and DS33). Costa Rica as well as India appealed, although the United States had already announced its intention to conform with the panel's findings. A closer inspection of the two cases reveals that the complainants were not primarily interested in the substantive outcome of the review, but rather in legal interpretations and clarifications of the panel's verdict. The reasoning of the appellate review might have been used as (free) legal expertise for future similar trade conflicts.

There is thus empirical support for our prediction that the losing party has an incentive to appeal, in most cases in order to delay the implementation of a negative ruling. Our analysis implies that the high propensity to appeal will not just be a transitory phenomenon likely to disappear after participants have gained greater clarity about the interpretation of WTO law. The decision to appeal is the result of the incentive structure of the game, and is much less influenced by legal

---

21. The 28 considered cases comprise only completed disputes and exclude cases currently under appellate review or within two months after the panel decision. A very interesting analysis of 15 appellate reviews from a legal perspective is to be found in Vermulst, Mavroidis, and Waer (1999).

22. Disputes DS2/4, DS8/10/11, DS16/27, DS18, DS26/48, DS31, DS46, DS50, DS56, DS58, DS60, DS62/67/68, DS75/84, DS76, DS87/109/110, DS90, DS98, DS103/113, and DS121.

23. DS44 is an interesting case: Although the trade conflict was between the United States and Japan officially, the dispute was in fact between two companies (Kodak and Fuji) with no or only minor government involvement. The U.S. government lost the case because there was not sufficient government involvement to defend a nonviolation complaint. Nevertheless, the United States was granted concessions by the Japanese government in competition policy.

uncertainty. Nevertheless, legal aspects during appellate review do play a role. In at least three cases the appellate review has acted as a safeguard against a legally wrong panel decision. The review's legal expertise can also be valuable for winning complainants because it constitutes important and costless information for future cases.

4.3 Complainant's Strategy (Notification and Panel Request)

After the introduction of a potential trade restriction, the complainant can initiate all moves until a first decision is made by the WTO panel. Its optimal strategy in view of the anticipated reaction of the defendant can be summarized by the following predictions:

Prediction 3a (panel request). The complainant always requests the panel at the earliest possible date.

Prediction 3b (filing decision). The probability π to win the trial has to exceed a threshold value $\bar{\pi}$ before a complaint is filed, where

$$\bar{\pi} = \frac{\left(R^C_{\text{lose}} - R^C_{\text{app}} \right) + K^C}{\tilde{L} + \left(R^C_{\text{lose}} - R^C_{\text{app}} \right) + R^C_{\text{win}}} \tag{3}$$

A nuisance suit ($\bar{\pi} = 0$) is only optimal if the domestic political gain of an appeal after a negative panel decision offsets both the international reputation loss of losing the case and the direct process cost ($R^C_{\text{app}} \geq R^C_{\text{lose}} + K^C$).

Prediction 3c (notification). For $\pi \geq \bar{\pi}$, the complainant notifies WTO at the earliest possible date.

Proof. Predictions 3a and 3c are obvious, because any delay reduces expected payoffs.

Equation (3) in Prediction 3b can be derived from the condition that the complainant's expected payoff in the prepanel stage has to be greater than the reservation payoff without a complaint (i.e, $-lt - \tilde{L}$, see Equation (A2) in Appendix A.2).

Note that Equation (3) hinges crucially on the fact that the complainant can force a decision (and attain R^C_{win}), and that the losing defendant complies after the reasonable period τ. In case the latter requirement is not satisfied $\tilde{L}$ has to be replaced by $(1 - \gamma)\tilde{L}$, where $\gamma \geq 0$ captures the probability of noncompliance or any additional delays in implementation. This allows an interesting comparison between the dispute settlement under GATT and WTO. The required confidence level $\bar{\pi}$ depends negatively on both the strength of the implementation mechanism [as measured by $(1 - \gamma)$], and the possibil-

522   The Journal of Law, Economics, & Organization, V16 N2

Table 3. Distribution of Waiting Times Between Notification and Panel Request

$t_{notif-panel}$	0–59	60–89	90–119	120–149	150–179	180–269	270–360	> 360
Cases	6	25	10	7	7	9	4	7

ity to reach a favorable decision (and therefore get R^C_{win}). Both components were certainly weaker in expected terms under the GATT system
(due to blocking of decisions and the absence of an effective implementation procedure) than under the WTO mechanism. It is therefore not
surprising that the new dispute settlement system has led to a substantial increase in complaints.

The agenda-setting capacity of the complainant, moreover, should
lead to a relatively tight schedule of the dispute settlement system. In
most instances, the complainant will not file a suit until his chances to
win the case are sufficiently high. Nuisance suits cannot be completely
excluded in situations in which domestic pressure to sue has a much
higher impact on political support than an expected loss.

In support of Prediction 3a, Table 3 shows the distribution of waiting
times between notification and panel request (74 cases). The data show
a peak at time periods between 60 (the legal minimum) and 90 days, but
also a considerable dispersion. Note that many cases are delayed due to
bundling of panel requests for related cases or to holidays. Waiting
times of less than 60 days represent disputes in which the complainant
could prove to have notified the defendant in an acceptable way outside
the official procedure. Preliminary evidence suggests that multicom-
plainant settings lead to a longer waiting time between notification and
panel request, presumably due to coordination problems.

Unfortunately empirical support for the complainant's filing decision,
and hence on Prediction 3b, is only indirect. For completed cases there
is no evidence of nuisance suits. Among the 44 panel decisions, only 2
were entirely in favor of the defendant. In both cases (DS22 and DS44)
the complainant "lost" because WTO law was not applicable to the
trade measure in question. Two other cases led to verdicts in favor of
the defendant only after a reversal of the panel's findings by the
appellate review (DS60 and DS62/67/68), which means that the cases
were far from being clear-cut ex ante. The same is true for four cases
with an ambiguous verdict. The remaining 38 cases ended with clear
decisions in favor of the complainant.

In the vast majority of cases, the initiation of the trade restriction is
unknown. Prediction 3c is thus not directly verifiable. Moreover, the
substantial changes in the structure of the dispute settlement mechanism might have led to a backlog and clustering of cases, which
complicates the analysis even if the onset of a trade restriction were
known.

4.4 Introduction of a New Trade Measure

Given the parties strategies during litigation, does the dispute settlement system discourage the introduction of new trade restrictions? Trade-related payoffs for the defending country accrue with certainty during the whole process. Positive expected payoffs are therefore feasible even for a very small probability $1 - \pi$ of being able to maintain the trade measure after the conclusion of the dispute. The defendant's optimal strategy can be stated as follows:

Prediction 4 (new trade restriction). The future defendant introduces a trade measure if

$$(1 - \pi)\tilde{G} + gt + \pi\left(R^D_{app} - R^D_{lose}\right) + (1 - \pi)R^D_{win} - K^D \geq 0.$$

When $\pi = 1$ (i.e., when both parties are certain of panel finding in favor of the complainant), the condition for the introduction of a trade restriction is $gt + R^D_{app} \geq R^D_{lose} + K^D$: The future defendant will introduce the trade restriction, if rents anticipated to accrue during the whole process plus reputation gains from satisfying domestic interest groups exceed the expected reputation loss of a lost trial plus direct process costs.

Proof. Follows directly from the defendant's expected payoff [Equation (A1)] in Appendix A.

If domestic pressure to introduce and maintain a trade restriction is larger than (international) reputation losses plus litigation costs, the dispute settlement system cannot prevent a welfare decreasing policy. If we allow for the possibility that noncompliance is the optimal strategy, incentives for introducing trade restrictive measures are stronger yet, even if the probability of losing is one. The agenda-setting capacity of the complainant, together with the elimination of blocking should limit the potential direct gains of the trade restriction (as measured by gt) during WTO litigation. The possibility of appeal, on the other hand, provides the losing defendant with a potential (domestic) reputation gain. If the former effect dominates, the number of new trade distortions should decrease compared to GATT.

Of course, direct empirical evidence of our prediction is not available, as the motives of trade policy measures are not verifiable. Potential gains from a trade restriction accruing during the litigation process are most likely to be anticipated, however. In the recent Foreign Sales Corporation conflict between the United States and the European Union (DS108) with an affected trade volume of several billion dollars, gains due to the delay in the procedure and the absence of retaliation

524   The Journal of Law, Economics, & Organization, V16 N2

measures before the end of a reasonable implementation period have even been advertised.[24]

4.5 The Scope for Bilateral Settlements

Bilateral settlements between the two parties are feasible if they provide a higher expected payoff for both countries than a continuation of the formal litigation process. The refusal of either party to accept an informal solution suffices to continue the formal dispute settlement procedures. The noncooperative game without intermediate bargaining therefore constitutes a lower bound—and thus the threat point—for both parties' expected payoffs at every stage of the formal dispute settlement system. By a mutual agreement, the parties forego potential future reputation gains and losses, but save litigation costs at early stages. In addition, direct trade gains and losses are reduced in relation to the litigation time saved.

Pecuniary compensation payments between two countries are rather uncommon (but not excluded, e.g., in the form of additional development assistance). Therefore bilateral settlements will very likely result in a compromise on the trade measure in question. This can also entail that the complainant is granted the right to some compensating trade restrictions. In order to avoid arbitrary assumptions about the nature of the bargaining between the two countries and its possible outcomes, we merely consider the polar cases "trade restriction maintained" and "trade restriction suspended" (see Appendix A.3 for the respective payoffs). For each possible settlement period we compute the sum of payoffs for both polar cases as a proxy for the *cooperative value* of the settlement. In an analogous way, the players' payoffs from completing the formal dispute settlement procedure are computed as a proxy for the *noncooperative value* of the game.[25]

Bilateral settlements can be expected to be less clear cut in favor of either party than decisions by the WTO DSB. The retreating party (either the defendant abolishing the trade restriction or the complainant giving up the complaint) has to be compensated for potential reputation payoffs, and for the probability that he might have won the case after all. If the expected panel decision unclear (i.e., $0 < \pi < 1$),

---

24. PricewaterhouseCoopers Tax News Network, for example, states in February 1999: "Because WTO-ordered change in the FSC regime would be prospective in application, and would not likely be effective until 2001, it may still be worthwhile to set up a FSC if the start-up costs can be recouped in about one year or less."

25. If payoffs were pecuniary, a nonstrategic bargaining model would assume that disputes will always be settled informally when the cooperative value is perceived to be greater than the noncooperative value of the game, whereas disputes will finally be decided by the WTO when the former is perceived to be smaller. Although a direct application of this rule is not possible in our much more complex situation, we hopefully still get some information from such an exercise.

the country with the larger absolute gain or loss will have an advantage in bilateral settlements, as it is more difficult for its opponent to offer sufficient compensation in order to retain its previous position. For the two polar cases $\pi = 0$ and $\pi = 1$, only the forgone net (political) reputation gains have to be considered. This is also true after the conclusion of the interim report when the position of the WTO is relatively clear.

Prediction 5a. Bilateral settlements are biased toward the expected outcome of the formal dispute settlement procedure for values of π close to 1 or 0, and especially so after the conclusion of the interim report.

For intermediate values of π, the cooperative value of the game is largely dominated by the relative size of the trade-related continuation gains and losses $\tilde{G}$ and $\tilde{L}$. A mutual agreement is biased toward the country with the higher absolute gain or loss.

Proof. The claim can be derived by comparing cooperative and noncooperative values of the game (as stated in Appendix A.3).

An additional variable of interest is the timing of bilateral settlements. In the absence of shocks to the probability and cost structure, there are three windows for bilateral settlements: Between notification and the establishment of a panel; during the panel stage (when both parties experience direct process costs K^D and K^C), but before the completion of the interim report; and finally between the interim report (when most uncertainty is resolved) and the circulation of the final panel report. Note that although interim and panel reports hardly ever differ, there are notable differences in payoffs between the two stages, because some reputation costs and gains are only relevant when the DSB's findings become public knowledge, that is, after the conclusion of the panel report. The parties can still settle at this point as the content of the interim report is kept confidential. As we have shown above, a potential mutual agreement after the interim report will be biased toward a large reduction in the disputed trade restriction. Moreover, the larger $R^D_{\text{lose}} - R^D_{\text{app}} - R^C_{\text{win}}$, the more probable is a bilateral settlement at this point. A complainant with a minor (reputation) stake in case of victory will agree to terminate the case at this point in time, in exchange for a sufficient reduction or suspension of the trade measure.[26]

---

26. Petersmann (1997) argues that the willingness of developing countries to terminate panel proceedings at this stage might reflect the relatively low gain from winning the case R^C_{win}, such that their gain from a bilateral settlement is much larger. However, under the new WTO dispute settlement system only a single case could be observed so far.

526   The Journal of Law, Economics, & Organization, V16 N2

After the panel report has been circulated among the WTO members, there is little scope for a bilateral settlement. The implementation of the panel's findings is closely monitored by the DSB. Predications 5b and 5c summarize the likelihood of mutual agreements at different stages of the dispute:

Prediction 5b. The larger $R^D_{\text{lose}} - R^D_{\text{app}} - R^C_{\text{win}}$, the more likely a bilateral settlement after the conclusion of an interim report, but before the circulation of the panel report.

Prediction 5c. Mutually agreed solutions are more likely at an early stage of the process, in particular before the complainant is granted a panel.

Proof. For Prediction 5b, note that the noncooperative value of the game is a decreasing function of $R^D_{\text{lose}} - R^D_{\text{app}} - R^C_{\text{win}}$, while the cooperative values are constant. Prediction 5c follows from the fact that before the panel stage, the avoidance of litigation costs K^C and K^D can favor a bilateral settlement.

The appearance of new information and the joining of third parties can change payoff components, above all, direct process costs $K^{C,D}$ and the probability π of success of a complaint. Their impact on the likelihood of bilateral settlements can be summarized as follows:

Prediction 5d. The likelihood of a bilateral settlement

- Increases in π if the defendant's net payoff loss from losing the case $(R^D_{\text{lose}} - R^D_{\text{app}})$ is sufficiently high.
- Decreases in π if the complainant's payoff gain from winning the suit is sufficiently high.
- Increases in direct litigation costs K^C and K^D.

Proof. The claim follows from a comparison of cooperative and noncooperative values of the game. It is also illustrated below.

Let us assume that trade-related payoffs of the disputed restriction are perceived as being symmetric, that is, $\tilde{G} = \tilde{L}$ and $g = l$. Then the noncooperative value of the game is

$$\Phi^C + \Phi^D = \pi\left(R^D_{\text{app}} - R^D_{\text{lose}} + R^C_{\text{win}}\right) + (1 - \pi)\left(R^C_{\text{app}} - R^C_{\text{lose}} - R^D_{\text{win}}\right)$$
$$- K^D - K^C,$$

which can be larger or smaller than zero, depending on the payoff components. A situation in which previously $\Phi^C + \Phi^D \geq 0$ can suddenly open up room for a bilateral settlement in various cases: The costs of undergoing the formal procedure may increase for the defendant if third parties enter in favor of the complainant (K^D increases). An increase (decrease) in π opens up opportunities for mutual agreements, provided the sum $(R_{lose}^D - R_{app}^D) + R_{win}^D + (R_{lose}^C - R_{app}^C) - R_{win}^C$ is positive (negative). Bilateral settlements become more likely if the defendant's payoff loss from losing the case is high, and less likely if the complainant's payoff gain from winning the suit is high.

Although many cases that are settled bilaterally do not enter official records, at least 29 cases (seem to) have been settled without recourse to the formal procedure. In support of our prediction, a majority of 24 cases have been settled after notification but before the establishment of the panel. In five of these cases, the complainant requested a panel before a mutual agreement could be reached. Four settlements could be observed after the establishment of the panel, but before a first decision of the WTO DSB. Only one of the disputes ended in a mutual agreement right after the conclusion of the interim report which prevented circulation of the panel report—and consequently the disclosure of its findings.

5. Summary and Conclusions

Based on the analysis of the different stages of the WTO dispute settlement system, we can now answer the questions formulated in the introduction and try to draw some conclusions for possible improvements of an international dispute settlement system.

First, the preventive power of the WTO dispute settlement system is too limited to discourage new trade restrictions. Even if the probability of winning a case is slim, countries have an incentive to introduce trade restrictions, as rents continue to accrue during the litigation process, and sanctions or compensations for past damages do not exist. On the other hand, the likelihood of a nuisance suit against a well-behaved country is rather small. A complaint is only filed if the probability of winning is sufficiently high.

Second, there is a strong tendency for the losing government to appeal against the panel decision, even if the chances of a revision are slim. An appeal delays the implementation of negative findings and suits the interests of domestic groups. This obviously has consequences for the way the parties perceive the dispute settlement process, as they plan for an appeal right from the start.[27] The appellate review's legal

---

27. As Petersmann (1997) points out, this could—especially in the long run—weaken the authority of first-instance panel reports. According to Petersmann (page 188), the strong tendency to appeal an unfavorable panel decision *"might even lead to the view that governments be granted the right of direct access to the quasi-judicial appellate body rather than be obliged, without exception, to undergo the time and effort of a preliminary panel procedure prior to the final appellate body report."*

528   The Journal of Law, Economics. & Organization, V16 N2

expertise might be used even by winning complainants with a view to accumulate arguments for future disputes on similar issues.

Third, the implementation stage, together with the absence of sanctions for damages during litigation, are the weakest elements of the new dispute settlement system. In case of a panel/appellate review decision in favor of the complainant, the defendant has strong incentives to delay implementation. Unless reputation losses of nonconforming countries are sufficiently high, the limited threats of compensation payments or retaliation measures fail to provide the loser country's with an incentive to implement the panel's recommendations quickly.

Fourth, bilateral settlements are more likely to be observed at an early stage of the litigation process. In clear-cut cases, the results of bilateral settlements should be similar to the expected ruling of the DSB. The losing party can avoid reputation losses (often at the price of giving up its position immediately) by agreeing upon a mutually accepted solution. Changes in the expected outcome of the process and in payoff elements, in particular by joining third parties, have an impact on the scope for bilateral settlement.

Compared to the GATT mechanism, the new dispute settlement system is more effective. WTO decisions cannot be blocked by a single country, which limits the (political) gains from trade distortions. The relatively tight schedule of the new dispute settlement system (the complainant has control over many timing decisions) reduces the gains and losses of inefficient trade measures by limiting the period during which they are effective. This impact is twofold: It leads to a reduction in the threshold level to sue, and consequently triggers a higher number of justified complaints. On the other hand, trade distortions may now prove unprofitable due to the limited time they can be active, which may reduce the number of potential complaints.

Some features of the new dispute settlement mechanism are well designed, while others are not. The complainant's agenda-setting capacity obviously limits the time a trade restriction can remain active. This is, however, partially offset by the weak enforcement mechanism during the implementation stage. Moreover, the lack of effective sanctions for noncompliance with WTO law further weakens the threat of the system, unless nonconforming countries experience sizable reputation losses. Nevertheless, the great number of dispute settlement cases so far should be interpreted as a signal of confidence in the new litigation process rather than as a failure of the WTO's aim to maintain an internationally liberal trade regime.

Appendix A: Payoffs

In this appendix we keep track of all the payoffs of the game. Note that payoffs Φ^C and Φ^D are always understood as (expected) payoffs and are computed from the time the decision is made. Subscripts mark the stage of the dispute settlement process at the relevant decision nodes.

A.1 Appellate Review

Depending on the outcome of the panel report, the expected payoffs for complainant and defendant undergoing appellate review are as follows:

$$\Phi^D_{[app|panel=C]} = \mu\tilde{G} + g(t_{impl} + t_{app}) + R^D_{app} \geq gt_{impl} = \Phi^D_{[no\text{-}app|panel=C]}$$

$$\Phi^D_{[app|panel=D]} = (1-v)\tilde{G} + g(t_{impl} + t_{app}) \leq \tilde{G} + g(t_{impl} + t_{app})$$

$$= \Phi^D_{[no\text{-}app|panel=D]}$$

$$\Phi^C_{[app|panel=D]} = -(1-v)\tilde{L} - l(t_{impl} + t_{app}) + R^C_{app}$$

$$\geq -\tilde{L} - l(t_{impl} + t_{app}) = \Phi^C_{[no\text{-}app|panel=D]}$$

$$\Phi^C_{[app|panel=C]} = -\mu\tilde{L} - l(t_{impl} + t_{app}) \leq -lt_{impl} = \Phi^C_{[no\text{-}app|panel=C]}$$

Note that in computing these payoffs we suppose that the losing defendant complies after t_{impl} $(= \tau)$.

A.2 Prepanel Stages

Note that t denotes the expected time until the end of the litigation process. The defendant's expected payoff is

$$\Phi^D_{prepanel} \equiv \pi\left[\Phi^D_{[app|panel=C]} - R^D_{lose} + (1-\pi)\{\Phi^D_{[app|panel=D]} + R^D_{win}\}\right.$$

$$+ gt - K^D$$

$$= \pi\mu\tilde{G} - \pi R^D_{lose} + \pi R^D_{app} + (1-\pi)(1-v)\tilde{G}$$

$$+(1-\pi)R^D_{win} + gt - K^D$$

$$= (1-\pi)\tilde{G} + gt + \pi\left(R^D_{app} - R^D_{lose}\right) + (1-\pi)R^D_{win} - K^D.$$

$$\tag{A1}$$

The last equality follows from our restricting assumption about revision probabilities in Equation (1). Correspondingly the complainant's expected payoff can be written as

$$\Phi^C_{prepanel} \equiv \pi\{\Phi^C_{[app|panel=c]} + R^C_{win}\} + (1-\pi)\{\Phi^C_{[app|panel=d]} - R^D_{lose}\}$$

$$- lt - K^C$$

530 The Journal of Law, Economics, & Organization, V16 N2

$$= -\pi\mu\tilde{L} + \pi R_{\text{win}}^{C} - (1 - \pi)(1 - \nu)\tilde{L} + (1 - \pi)R_{\text{ann}}^{C}$$
$$- (1 - \pi)R_{\text{lose}}^{C} - lt - K^{C}$$
$$= -(1 - \pi)\tilde{L} - lt + (1 - \pi)\left(R_{\text{app}}^{C} - R_{\text{lose}}^{C}\right) + \pi R_{\text{win}}^{C} - K^{C}.$$

$$(A2)$$

From Equation (A2) the minimum level $\bar{\pi}$ to file can be computed from the condition $\Phi_{\text{prepanel}}^{C} \geq -\tilde{L} - lt$ (the reservation utility without complaint).

A.3 Bilateral Settlements

The threat point and consequently the noncooperative value of the game is the sum of the expected payoffs of the reference scenario without bilateral settlements. We also consider the two polar cases "trade restriction maintained" (denoted by a $+$) and "trade restriction suspended" (denoted by a $-$).

After the interim report, the noncooperative values of the game (conditional on which country has won in the interim report) and the two polar outcomes (as cooperative values) are as follows:

$$(\Phi^{C} + \Phi^{D})|_{\text{interim}=C} = \mu(\tilde{G} - \tilde{L}) + t(g - l) + R_{\text{app}}^{D} - R_{\text{lose}}^{D} + R_{\text{win}}^{C}$$

$$(\Phi^{C} + \Phi^{D})|_{\text{interim}=D} = (1 - \nu)(\tilde{G} - \tilde{L}) + t(g - l) + R_{\text{app}}^{C}$$
$$+ R_{\text{lose}}^{C} + R_{\text{win}}^{D}$$

$$\Phi^{C,-} + \Phi^{D,-} = 0$$

$$\Phi^{C,+} + \Phi^{D,+} = (\tilde{G} - \tilde{L}) + t(g - l).$$

Before the interim report, the threat point and the two polar cooperative outcomes are

$$\Phi^{C} + \Phi^{D} = (1 - \pi)(\tilde{G} - \tilde{L}) + t(g - l) + \pi\left(R_{\text{app}}^{D} - R_{\text{lose}}^{D} + R_{\text{win}}^{C}\right)$$
$$+ (1 - \pi)\left(R_{\text{app}}^{C} - R_{\text{lose}}^{C} + R_{\text{win}}^{D}\right) - K^{D} - K^{C}$$

$$\Phi^{C,-} + \Phi^{D,-} = 0$$

$$\Phi^{C,+} + \Phi^{D,+} = (\tilde{G} - \tilde{L}) + t(g - l).$$

Assume that the disputed trade measure is perceived as a zero game in trade-related rents from both parties views, that is, $\tilde{G} = \tilde{L}$ and $g = l$.

Then the noncooperative value of the game is

$$\Phi^C + \Phi^D = \pi\left(R_{\text{app}}^D - R_{\text{lose}}^D + R_{\text{win}}^C\right) + (1 - \pi)\left(R_{\text{app}}^C - R_{\text{lose}}^C + R_{\text{win}}^D\right)$$
$$- K^D - K^C. \tag{A3}$$

Appendix B: United States—Standards for Reformulated and Conventional Gasoline, Complaint by Venezuela (DS 2)

On January 23, 1995, Venezuela requested consultations with the United States concerning standards for reformulated and conventional gasoline. The dispute related to a U.S. domestic legislation called the "Clean Air Act of 1990," and especially to the "Regulation of Fuels and Fuel Additives—Standards for Reformulated and Conventional Gasoline" enacted by the U.S. Environmental Protection Agency. This regulation was enacted to control toxic and other pollution caused by the combustion of gasoline manufactured in or imported into the United States.

Consultations were held between Venezuela and the United States on February 24, 1995, but the parties failed to reach a mutually satisfactory solution. Consequently Venezuela requested the establishment of a panel on March 25, 1995 (61 days after notification of WTO). On April 10, 1995, the DSB established a panel. At the same time, Brazil requested consultations with the United States concerning the same facts, and—after their failure—required the establishment of a panel (reference DS 4). The DSB decided that the case was to be taken over by the previously established panel for Venezuela.

On January 17, 1996, the panel report was circulated among WTO members. The DSB followed the arguments of the complainants. On February 21, 1996, the United States notified the DSB of its decision to appeal certain issues of law and legal interpretations in the panel report. The report of the appellate review was circulated among WTO members on May 20, 1996. The appellate body upheld the findings of the panel/DSB. The United States was granted a standard implementation period of 15 months. Approximately 17 months later, on October 17, 1997, the United States informed the WTO of its compliance with the requirements of the DSB.

Appendix C: Data

The database has been prepared by and is available from Monika Bütler upon request. Table C.1 contains cases mentioned explicitly in this article. They are numbered by their official WTO label. Additional information, including panel and appellate review reports, can also be found on the WTO's webpage (www.wto.org/wto/dispute).

Table C.1

DS No.	Defendants	Complainants	Disputed Matter
2, 4	US	Venezuela, Brazil	Standards for Reformulated and Conventional Gasoline
8, 10, 11	Japan	EU, Canada, US	Taxes on Alcoholic Beverages
16, 27	EU	Ecuador, Guatemala, Honduras, Mexico, US	Regime for the Importation, Sale and Distribution of Bananas
18	Australia	Canada	Measures Affecting the Importation of Salmon
22	Brazil	Philippines	Measures Affecting Desiccated Coconut
24	US	Costa Rica	Restrictions on Imports of Cotton and Man-Made Fibre Underwear
26, 48	EU	US, Canada	Measures Affecting Meat and Meat Products (Hormones)
31	Canada	US	Certain Measures Concerning Periodicals
33	US	India	Measure Affecting Imports of Woven Wool Shirts and Blouses
44	Japan	US	Measures Affecting Consumer Photographic Film and Paper
46	Brazil	Canada	Export Financing Programme for Aircraft
50	India	US	Patent Protection for Pharmaceutical and Agricultural Chemical Products
54, 55, 59, 64	Indonesia	EU, Japan, US	Certain Measures Affecting the Automobile Industry
56	Argentina	US	Certain Measures Affecting Imports of Footwear, Textiles, Apparel and Other Items
58	US	India	Import Prohibition of Certain Shrimp and Shrimp Products
60	Guatemala	Mexico	Anti-Dumping Investigation Regarding Imports of Portland Cement
62, 67, 68	EU, UK, Ireland	US	Customs Classification of Certain Computer Equipment
69	EU	Brazil	Measures Affecting Importation of Certain Poultry Products
70	Canada	Brazil	Measures Affecting the Export of Civilian Aircraft
75, 84	Korea	EU, US	Taxes on Alcoholic Beverages
76	Japan	US	Measures Affecting Agricultural Products
87, 109, 110	Chile	EU	Taxes on Alcoholic Beverages
90	India	US	Quantitative Restrictions on Imports of Agricultural, Textile and Industrial Products
98	Korea	EU	Definitive Safeguard Measure on Imports of Certain Dairy Products
99	US	Korea	Anti-Dumping Duty on Dynamic Random Access Memory Semiconductors (DRAMS) of One Megabit or Above
103, 113	Canada	US, NZ	Measures Affecting the Importation of Milk and the Exportation of Dairy Products
108	US	EU	Tax Treatment for "Foreign Sales Corporations"
121	Argentina	EU	Safeguard Measures on Imports of Footwear
126	Australia	US	Subsidies Provided to Producers and Exporters of Automotive Leather

References

Cooter, Robert D., and Daniel L. Rubinfeld. 1989. "Economic Analysis of Legal Disputes and Their Resolution," 27 *Journal of Economic Literature*, 1067–1097.

Croley, Steven P., and John H. Jackson. 1996. "The WTO Dispute Procedures, Standard of Review, and Deference to National Governments," 90 *American Journal of International Law* 193–213.

Hudec, R. E., D. L. M. Kennedy, and M. Sgarbossa. 1993. "A Statistical Profile of GATT Dispute Settlement Cases: 1948–89," 2 *Minnesota Journal of Global Trade* 1–113.

Jackson, John H. 1998. "Designing and Implementing Effective Dispute Settlement Procedures: WTO Dispute Settlement, Appraisal and Prospects," in Anne O. Krueger, ed. *The WTO as an International Organization*. Chicago: University of Chicago Press, 193–213.

Palmeter, David, and Petros C. Mavroidis. 1998. "The WTO Legal System: Sources of Law," 92 *American Journal of International Law* 398–413.

Petersmann, Ernst-Ulrich. 1997. *The GATT/WTO Dispute Settlement System: International Law, International Organizations and Dispute Settlement*. London: Kluwer Law International.

Shell, Richard G. 1995. "Trade Legalism and International Relations Theory: An Analysis of the World Trade Organization," 44 *Duke Law Journal* 829–927.

Vermulst, Edwin, and Bart Driessen. 1995. "An Overview of the WTO Dispute Settlement System and its Relationship with the Uruguay Round Agreements: Nice on Paper but Too Much Stress for the System?" 29 *Journal of World Trade* 131–162.

Vermulst, Edwin, Petros C. Mavroidis, and Paul Waer. 1999. "The Functioning of the Appellate Body After Four Years: Towards Rule Integrity," 33 *Journal of World Trade* 1–50.

WTO. 1995. *The WTO Dispute Settlement Procedures*. Geneva: WTO.

[15]

International Studies Quarterly (2001) 45, 1–26.

Institutional Effects on State Behavior: Convergence and Divergence

LILIANA BOTCHEVA AND LISA L. MARTIN

Harvard University

We develop a new typology for examination of the effects of international institutions on member states' behavior. Some institutions lead to convergence of members' practices, whereas others result, often for unintended reasons, in divergence. We hypothesize that the observed effect of institutions depends on the level of externalities to state behavior, the design of the institution, and variation in the organization and access of private interests that share the goals of the institution. We illustrate these propositions with examples drawn from international institutions for development assistance, protection of the ozone layer, and completion of the European Union's internal market. We find that significant externalities and appropriately designed institutions lead to convergence of state behavior, whereas divergence can result from the absence of these conditions and the presence of heterogeneity in domestic politics.

States frequently choose to institutionalize their interactions with one another. This empirical pattern has been reflected in theories of international politics, which have struggled to understand the logic of international institutions. The recent research agenda on institutions has concentrated on establishing that international institutions could have an influence on state behavior. Institutionalist work attempting to show that institutions "matter" gave rise to a strong response from those who discount both the logic and empirical validity of institutionalist claims (Mearsheimer, 1994–95). Our paper addresses one important empirical criticism, arguing that in order to identify institutional effects accurately we need a more finely grained set of expectations about what effects institutions should have and under what conditions they should have these effects. The first generation of rationalist models of institutions aimed primarily at establishing an existence proof: finding situations in which institutions had observable effects on state behavior. Too much of this work relied on single cases and counterfactual arguments, leaving itself open to charges of selection bias and other empirical problems.

We argue that accurate identification of institutional effects requires that we recognize that different types of institutions should have different effects under specified conditions. In other words, researchers require a typology of institutional effects and theoretically grounded hypotheses about the conditions under

---

Authors' note: We thank the following individuals for their comments on previous drafts of this paper: Larry Hamlet; Celeste Wallander; Ron Mitchell; Jeff Frieden; participants in a Program on International Political Economy and Security (PIPES) seminar at the University of Chicago, especially David Edelstein, Duncan Snidal, and Fubing Su; and participants in seminars at the Olin Institute (Harvard University) and the Ohio State University.

which we should observe them. We offer a typology of convergence and divergence effects, hypotheses about when we will find these effects, and evidence from three issue areas to establish the plausibility of both the typology and our hypotheses.[1] Although this evidence cannot be taken as definitive proof of our hypotheses, it does strongly suggest that the typology is a valuable addition to the institutionalist research program. Studies of patterns of convergence and divergence can fruitfully supplement studies of international cooperation.

The first section of this paper develops the argument for considering variation in institutional effects as an important test of the institutionalist research program. The second section argues that simple models of externalities and collective action in complete-information settings lead to predictions of divergence or convergence of member state behavior. The third section specifies our hypotheses more fully, allowing for incomplete information and bringing in considerations of institutional design and domestic politics. We argue that convergence will occur when the cooperation problem states are trying to solve involves substantial externalities to state behavior and when the institutions states craft have adequate mechanisms to overcome these collective dilemmas. Divergence effects, in contrast, are likely to be observed only when externalities are minimal, enforcement mechanisms are weak, and states exhibit significant variation in the organization and power of interest groups attentive to the issues covered by the international institution. A branching model, asking first about externalities, summarizes our expectations about institutional effects.

The fourth section of the paper provides empirical examples of convergence and divergence effects. International attempts to reduce destruction of the ozone layer and the European Union's (EU's) attempt to complete the internal market illustrate convergence effects. In both cases it is easy to identify strong externalities to state behavior, and in both, states have constructed enforcement mechanisms appropriately designed to overcome the collective-action problems created by these externalities. In contrast, the example of development assistance demonstrates that international institutions can contribute to divergence of member state behavior. In this case, states recognize few externalities to their behavior, and the institutions they create have inadequate or nonexistent enforcement mechanisms. We might expect that in such cases institutions would make no difference (i.e., that they would not lead to any observed variation in state behavior). Yet we see that in some states, the creation of formal institutional standards and norms of behavior have served as tools that have increased the influence of domestic interest groups that supported the institution's agenda. In these states, the institution did lead to a change of state behavior, whereas member states that lacked these organized groups were resistant to institutional norms. The result was divergence of behavior, as some members moved closer to the norms established by the institution whereas others showed no response.

Institutional Effects: Cooperation, Compliance, and Effectiveness

Numerous studies over the last two decades have searched for, and sometimes identified, institutions that have had a causal effect on the behavior of their member states. However, such studies have been less persuasive than an institutional theorist might wish. One reason is that researchers have not thought in a sufficiently differentiated way about institutional effects. They have primarily attempted to show that institutions sometimes matter through demonstration of individual examples where outcomes are difficult to understand without taking into account the role of institutions. Although this work has made a major contribution, it suffers from too heavy a reliance on counterfactual argument,

---

[1] For an initial presentation of this typology, see Martin and Simmons, 1998.

selective choice of cases, and an inability to explain why institutions sometimes have intended effects and sometimes do not. Empirical and theoretical progress requires that we develop a more nuanced picture of institutional effects and specify conditions under which we expect to observe alternative effects. This agenda requires that we develop a typology that moves beyond the focus on cooperation, compliance, and effectiveness that characterizes existing work.

Much of the empirical work by institutionalists attempts to show that cases exist in which institutions encourage cooperation, influencing states to cooperate in circumstances in which they would otherwise find cooperation difficult. The dependent variable in this research agenda is international cooperation. Studies of compliance, or whether international institutions are effective, have drawn from the same analytical framework. Empirical research has found instances in which institutions seem to lead states to behave in a more cooperative manner than they otherwise might have. Institutions have enhanced patterns of cooperation in issues including military force levels (Duffield, 1992), oil pollution (Mitchell, 1994), and economic sanctions (Martin, 1992a). Studies of compliance with international agreements on environmental issues (Victor, Raustiala, and Skolnikoff, 1998a) and international regulatory agreements (Chayes and Chayes, 1995) further the agenda of studying the effects of institutions while maintaining a focus on cooperation, compliance, and effectiveness as dependent variables.

These studies suffer from a number of methodological flaws that have led skeptics to challenge their validity. Many rely heavily on counterfactual analysis rather than observable patterns of variation across actual cases. Some do not control adequately for alternative explanations, particularly changes in patterns of interests. Few empirical studies specify the conditions under which institutions should have the predicted effects. The search to find cases that allow researchers to show that "institutions matter" leads to selection bias in favor of cases where institutional effects would be most pronounced. Few of these studies take the problem of institutional endogeneity seriously. These failings, particularly the last, allow skeptics to argue that since institutions are obviously endogenous— they do change in response to changes in structural variables and often serve as agents of state interests—they are epiphenomenal. In other words, the causal significance of institutions remains inadequately demonstrated.[2] This identification of endogeneity with epiphenomenality is a mistake, but overall the criticisms of empirical studies are telling.

These problems of empirical studies have needlessly undermined the promise of institutionalist theory. We propose that one way to begin addressing these problems is to develop a more discriminating dependent variable (i.e., a typology of institutional effects). Effects of institutions typically have been treated as a single, dichotomous variable: cooperation or no, compliance or its lack. This crude dichotomization of the vast variety of state behavior has perhaps obscured as much as it has revealed.

Relying on the standard definition of cooperation—resolution of collective-action dilemmas—also forces us to assume that all institutions are designed to confront similar problems of collective action and market failure. Studies asking whether institutions are effective or whether states comply likewise assume that the goal of institutions is to overcome a specific kind of collective-action problem. Focusing on cooperation thus fits uncomfortably with the notion, highlighted by those who consider variation in institutional design, that different institutions are designed to solve different problems. If institutions confront a variety of problems, forcing all instances of institutionalized interaction into a

---

[2] See Mearsheimer, 1994–95, and, for a response, Keohane and Martin, 1995.

category called "cooperation" is unlikely to highlight most interesting patterns of variation.

A further difficulty with the emphasis on cooperation–no cooperation as the only relevant dependent variable is that it does not provide a language in which to assess possible unintended, even perverse, effects of institutions. Policy analysis is replete with examples of such effects. Peacekeeping operations may induce combatants to put off finding permanent resolution to their disputes. The European Monetary Union (EMU) could allow undisciplined members to forgo fiscal stringency. Such unintended and undesired effects of institutions constitute one of the major normative, as well as theoretical, charges against modern institutionalist theory (Gallorotti, 1991). Yet the language of cooperate–do not cooperate does not provide us with the necessary tools to explore this darker side of possible institutional effects.

The typology of effects we propose does not provide a complete response to all these weaknesses of existing theory and research. But it does identify a start. We shift the focus away from cooperation to an analysis of variation in state behavior. Some institutions lead to convergence of state behavior; others lead to divergence. Some have no effect at all. This typology allows us to specify conditional hypotheses about variation in institutional effects. The concept of convergence, as explained below, is consistent with traditional emphasis on market failure problems and cooperation. Highlighting the possibility of divergence, however, allows us to assess unintended effects more accurately. It also provides a lever for bringing the actions and influence of organized domestic interests into models of institutions, something that institutional theory has been prompted to do for years (Haggard and Simmons, 1987; Moravcsik, 1997).

From a methodological standpoint, the typology developed here provides a guide to more precise measurement of institutional effects. Variation in state behavior is measured prior to institutional creation and after. Change in variation then provides an indicator of institutional effects and a dependent variable that can be used to test alternative theories. Changes in the mean, although not the focus of this paper, remain important as measures of cooperation. Our approach provides a tool for a more rigorous research agenda that responds to criticisms of selection bias and distinguishes between different types of institutional effects. This framework allows us to move away from counterfactual analysis by providing concrete measures of state behavior for comparison at different points in time or across different institutional settings. It directs our attention away from process tracing to consideration of variation in outcomes. It allows us to specify conditional hypotheses rather than the broad and undifferentiated claim that "institutions matter." It also opens an avenue to addressing institutional endogeneity, as the hypotheses specified below take into account variation in institutional design, recognizing that it responds to structural challenges but in an uneven manner.

Externalities and Convergence or Divergence

We propose that studies of institutional effects should concentrate directly on patterns of member state behavior. The particular outcome variable that institutions might influence depends on the specific problem being addressed. Environmental institutions are designed to limit emissions of pollutants. Trade institutions are designed to limit protectionist barriers. Development aid institutions are designed to change flows of development aid. Empirical studies of institutional effects should directly examine these outcome indicators. One particularly fruitful way in which to do this is to ask whether state behavior on these dimensions tends to converge or diverge as the result of institutional action. In this section, we analyze the impact of externalities on the likelihood of convergence or divergence. We do so using simple games that treat states as rational and unitary and that neglect informational problems. In the next section we build on the analysis of externalities by adding the complexities of incomplete information and domestic politics to the model.

Most international institutions are designed to influence issue-specific, observable measures of state behavior. Informal institutions may not clearly specify what measures of state behavior should change. For example, APEC (the Asia-Pacific Economic Cooperation forum) has set no specific targets for member state behavior. Yet even in this case we can specify that member states of APEC generally intend their efforts in this forum to gradually reduce barriers to exchange among them. Thus, protectionist barriers are the target variable for APEC. In more formal settings, specifying the target variable is more straightforward. The World Trade Organization and North American Free Trade Agreement set precise standards of state behavior that can be used as indicators of whether states are living up to their commitments. Development aid institutions, such as the Development Assistance Committee (DAC) of the Organization for Economic Cooperation and Development (OECD), establish targets for the flow of development aid from member states to developing countries. Military alliances agree on standards of military spending. The point is that when we focus on a specific international institution and ask whether it has an effect on state behavior, a promising place to begin will be member state agreements on targets, floors, ceilings, or other standards for their behavior.

Cooperation could perhaps be operationalized by how close states come to these targets and the extent to which the targets require them to change former patterns of behavior. One common descriptive statistic is the average or mean level of state behavior. Measuring cooperation could involve looking at changes in this average. However, asking only about average state behavior obscures some potentially intriguing institutional effects. Another statistic relevant to the overall pattern of state behavior is a measure of variation or diversity in that behavior, such as a standard deviation or variance. Our approach to specifying institutional effects directs attention away from changes in the mean to changes in the standard deviation. We do not intend to imply that changes in the mean are uninteresting. However, because such changes have already received extensive attention in studies of cooperation, we concentrate here on the more novel idea of measuring the standard deviation.

Thinking about changes in the variance or standard deviation of state behavior means asking whether institutions might contribute to convergence or divergence in patterns of behavior. Convergence means a reduction in the standard deviation; divergence means an increase. Average state behavior (the mean) tells us only the central tendency of observed behavior. It thus hides much potentially valuable information about the overall pattern of behavior, information that can be recovered by looking at changes in the standard deviation. In particular, we need to know about more than just the central tendency if we are interested in bringing domestic politics into our analysis, allowing for the possibility that different types of states respond to institutional incentives differently. The mean cannot tell us whether different states are responding differently to institutional incentives. Measuring convergence or divergence tells us whether all or only some member states are responding as expected.

In order to begin thinking about the overall pattern of member state behavior, consider some very simple standard games. In order to clarify the logic of convergence and divergence, we begin by focusing only on the level of externalities that characterize different types of interactions among states. The games illustrated in Figure 1 are differentiated from one another by the level of external-

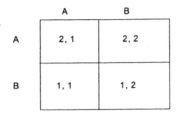

FIG. 1. High- and low-externality games.

ities or interdependence.[3] The top panel of Figure 1 shows two paradigmatic examples of high-externality games, a coordination (battle of the sexes) game and a prisoner's dilemma (PD).[4] These are the situations considered in most studies of international institutions, such as those regulating trade, the environment, or choices of technical standards. The bottom panel shows a low-externality game, one in which the payoffs to each state are not affected by the choices made by the other. An example of a low-externality game could be the choice of labor standards in a situation of low factor mobility among countries. With low mobility, policy choices by one state are likely to have minimal consequences for others.

Consider first the coordination game. A typical coordination problem involves high positive externalities, in that states can benefit from choosing the same course of action. Figure 1 shows a simple coordination problem, where states have only two possible courses of action, A or B. Payoffs are ranked from 4 (the best) to 1 (the worst), with the payoff to State 1 listed first. State 1 (which chooses the row) prefers A, whereas State 2 (which chooses the column) prefers B. However, positive externalities are present in that both states strongly benefit from choosing the same course of action. This full-information game results in two pure-strategy equilibria: one where both states choose A, and one where both choose B. Outcomes where states choose different courses of action are not equilibria, since both states have an incentive to change their choice in order to coordinate with the other state.

---

[3] Thomas Schelling (1980) refers to situations that involve externalities to state behavior as problems of interdependent decision.

[4] Snidal (1985) and Stein (1983) draw on a similar set of games to develop propositions about institutional design.

LILIANA BOTCHEVA AND LISA L. MARTIN   7

This coordination game shows in the most direct way the logic of convergence in the presence of high externalities. It might represent a choice of technical standards, such as standards for high-definition television or railway gauges. Because of the presence of multiple equilibria, the exact outcome cannot be predicted. However, we can make one clear prediction from this exercise: states will converge on one particular outcome. Diversity of state behavior, with each state using a different standard, is not persistent in this setting. Thus, convergence should characterize such positive-externality coordination settings.

Consider next the logic of the PD. Here we also expect a tendency toward convergence, but through a slightly more complex logic than in the coordination case. In a single-shot, simultaneous-move version of the PD, there is only one equilibrium, because both states have dominant strategies to defect. Mutual defection (the BB outcome in Figure 1) represents convergence in its most trivial form.

Allowing for repeat play of the PD opens a wide range of additional equilibria, including mutual cooperation (AA in Figure 1). For our purposes, what is important about equilibria in the iterated PD is the highly interdependent nature of state choices. Choosing to cooperate is always, regardless of the particular punishment strategy that states choose, contingent on the other state's ongoing cooperation. Outcomes where one state defects and the other cooperates (AB or BA) may occur for a round or two, for example, if states are using a forgiving strategy of reciprocity. But defection will eventually lead to punishment in the form of reciprocal defection by the other state. If the punishment strategy is effective it will lead the initial defector to return to a cooperative strategy, as will the punishing state. Thus, effective punishment strategies lead to convergence on the cooperative outcome in this simple iterated PD.

If the payoff from short-term defection is too high or the shadow of the future too short, punishment will not be effective in returning states to a cooperative equilibrium. In this case, states will converge on the noncooperative equilibrium. By examining the logic of punishment through reciprocity, we can see that any outcome will be characterized by converging behavior on the part of rational unitary states. To make this logic a bit more concrete, think of the PD as an exercise in lowering barriers to trade. The A choice represents reduced barriers to trade, whereas choice B means maintaining high barriers. If trade is a PD, states gain from mutual reductions but prefer to cheat and impose high barriers if they can get away with it. If their interaction is repeated over time, they can reap the benefits of low barriers to exchange by threatening to return to the high-barrier outcome in the case of cheating by the other state.[5] The logic of the repeated PD relies on reciprocity as an enforcement mechanism. Reliance on reciprocity should show up behaviorally as convergence of state behavior.

In the simplest PD, behavior should be absolutely uniform: all defect or all cooperate. In practice we do not observe such uniformity, even in situations with some negative externalities. Even before states agree on a particular cooperative equilibrium, they generally show some heterogeneity in their behavior. It seems likely that the level of heterogeneity is related to the level of externalities that characterize the issue: very high externalities, as in our simple PD, should minimize heterogeneity even when states are all defecting. Though we allow for initial heterogeneity in state practices, we claim that high externalities should create a tendency to convergent state behavior in the presence of complete information.

---

[5] Bagwell and Staiger (1999) present a model of international trade as an iterated PD that emphasizes the role of reciprocity.

The bottom panel of Figure 1 shows a game without the high externalities that characterize the games in the top panel. In contrast to the previous analysis, here the payoffs to states are not interdependent. Each has a dominant strategy, with state 1 preferring A and state 2 preferring B. Perhaps state 1 is a rich, industrialized country with stringent protections and benefits for labor (choice A), whereas state 2 is a developing country that cannot afford to provide such protections. If factors are not mobile between these two states, their payoffs should not depend much on the choice that the other makes about its treatment of labor. With high externalities, we do not expect outcomes AB or BA to be stable. In contrast, the only equilibrium in the low-externality game shown here is AB.

Low externalities thus provide the necessary conditions for divergent patterns of state behavior. Of course, if all states happen to prefer the same course of action, behavior will converge even if externalities are low. Thus, low externalities are only a necessary, not a sufficient, condition for divergence. But we expect that low externalities combined with diverse state preferences will lead to divergence. One insight emerges from this analysis: that we will have to pay attention to the sources and nature of state preferences in low-externality environments. In contrast, when externalities are high, states' behavior will be much more responsive to that of other states, drawing our attention away from the domestic to the international level. We summarize this insight in the next section in our branching model of institutional effects.

Now that we have introduced the logic of convergence and divergence, let us make the distinction between them a bit more formal. Our typology concentrates on the level of variation in state behavior with respect to target outcome variables, such as aid expenditures or levels of trade protection. Prior to creation of the institution, states generally exhibit some level of variation with respect to the target variable. They have varying levels of trade protection; some spend more on development aid than do others.[6] One useful way to measure the effect that an institution is having on its members' behavior is to ask whether, after the institution is in place, this variation increases, decreases, or remains the same. If the variation increases, the institution is having a divergence effect, as it has led to increased divergence in state behavior.[7] If variation decreases, the institution could be credited with having a convergence effect.

It is of course possible that an institution would have a constant effect on all member states' behavior, shifting it by an equal amount. The variance would thus remain the same, but the institution would nevertheless have an effect, changing the mean. Looking for changes in the mean will be especially important when states exhibit little initial variation in their behavior. A constant effect is associated with standard ways of thinking about international cooperation.

To highlight the innovative aspects of our approach to institutional effects, we will not concentrate on constant effects here. We wish to draw attention to the fact that state behavior prior to institutional creation is typically heterogeneous. Looking only at the average of state behavior does not allow us to measure heterogeneity and how it changes. It is important to emphasize that we are not suggesting that convergence or divergence are alternative measures of cooperation. They are, instead, additional conceptions of possible effects on state behavior. Convergence does not necessarily equal institutional "success," nor divergence "failure."

Figure 2 illustrates divergence and convergence effects. Assume that the outcome variable of interest for this institution is tariff levels. Prior to creation of

---

[6] As discussed above, in the presence of very high externalities we may not see this initial heterogeneity of state behavior.

[7] Of course, the institution itself can be credited with this effect only after controlling for other potential explanatory variables. This ceteris paribus clause holds throughout the following discussion.

LILIANA BOTCHEVA AND LISA L. MARTIN   9

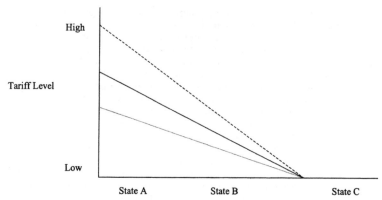

Note: The solid line indicates tariff levels prior to institutional creation. The dotted line indicates a convergence effect, as States A and B's tariff converge to the level of State C's. The dashed line indicates a divergence effect, as institutional creation leads States A and B to increase their tariff levels.

FIG. 2. Divergence and convergence effects.

the institution, State A has high tariffs, State B intermediate tariffs, and State C low tariffs. This situation is represented by the solid line. The relevant question for institutional effects is how variation changes once the institution is created. The dotted line illustrates a convergence effect. Here, States A and B have both lowered their tariffs. The slope of the line is now shallower than it was before, indicating less variation in state behavior. If we were to measure the standard deviation of member state tariffs, we would find that it had decreased since institutional creation. This is an example of a convergence effect.

The dashed line, in contrast, illustrates an instance where States A and B have increased their tariff levels after institutional creation. Perhaps the institution was improperly designed so that it motivated import-competing groups in these countries to organize and thus had the unintended effect of increasing levels of protection in the already more protectionist countries. Here, we see that the slope of the line is steeper, indicating divergence of state behavior. A measure of standard deviation or other measure of variation in tariffs would increase in this example, showing a divergence effect.

For clarity, we draw one further distinction. Figure 2 illustrates a strong divergence effect. The effect of the institution on some states is the opposite of that intended. This could result from mobilization of anti-internationalist forces in reaction to institutional rules or practices with which they disagree. The possibility of strong divergence effects is intriguing and not out of the question empirically. For example, we may see such a reaction in the United States as the inefficiency and practices of some UN bureaucracies lead to mobilization of isolationist forces in Congress and a declining contribution by the United States to the United Nations. However, perhaps a more common pattern would be a weak divergence effect. This could result if an institution had the intended effect on the behavior of some member states, but no effect on that of others. A weak divergence effect is shown in Figure 3. We develop hypotheses about weak and strong divergence effects together, since both are likely to result from differential mobilization of domestic interest groups and both are stable outcomes only when externalities are low.

10 *Institutional Effects on State Behavior*

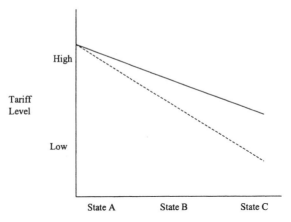

FIG. 3. Weak divergence effect.

In the highly simplified world of 2 × 2 games and complete information, we do not need to consider institutions in order to develop expectations about convergence or divergence of state behavior. These tendencies follow directly from the presence or absence of externalities in states' interactions with one another. However, actual interaction between states is far more complex and involves persistent problems of bargaining and enforcement, bringing in a role for institutions that we consider in the following section. This typology of divergence and convergence effects allows the institutionalist research program to move forward in a progressive manner by allowing for clearer specification and testing of hypotheses about the effects of institutions on state behavior.

Hypotheses: The Role of Institutional Design and Domestic Politics

In the previous section, we argued that issues that involved high externalities to state behavior should produce a tendency toward convergence. Extending our analysis to low-externality situations, we suggested that divergence of state behavior may also sometimes be a stable outcome. Moving toward expectations about the conditions under which international institutions are likely to enhance patterns of convergence or divergence requires that we introduce informational concerns and bring domestic politics into the picture. We do so here. Our overall explanatory framework is a branching model. If externalities to state behavior are high, we expect patterns of behavior to be determined more by the design of international institutions than by domestic factors. If externalities are low, we expect domestic politics to play a more determinative role.

When states are in a PD situation they can realize high benefits from joint movement to a cooperative outcome. However, in spite of these incentives to convergent behavior in a situation of negative externalities, states also face the temptation to renege. Thus convergence to a cooperative equilibrium is far from automatic. Instead, states need to craft mechanisms that will allow them to implement effective strategies of reciprocity. These mechanisms center around the necessity for accurate, prompt information about other states' behavior. Contractual theory has drawn attention to the role of international institutions in providing information and allowing for effective punishment of those who renege. Monitoring of state behavior is an essential component of any attempt to overcome a PD. If states anticipate that they can renege without discovery, they will do so. Without effective monitoring, institutions are unlikely to have any substantial effect on state behavior in a situation of negative externalities.

The functions that institutions perform to assist states in overcoming coordination problems differ from those they perform in a PD but are still concentrated on the provision of information. The type of information that states need to deal effectively with coordination problems is not the monitoring of state behavior that is essential in the PD (Martin, 1992b), since states face no incentives to renege on a cooperative outcome. Instead, they need to resolve bargaining problems to settle on a particular equilibrium. Bargaining problems are also in large part about information, such as the reservation point, costs of holding out, and patience of each player. International institutions, by providing an ongoing forum for overlapping, dense sets of negotiations, enhance the quality of such information about one's bargaining partners. In coordination, information provision is essential to effective solution of collective dilemmas. If international institutions do anything at all, they should provide this information.

Because the type of information necessary to resolve collective-action dilemmas depends on the particular dilemma, the nature of institutions that will most effectively provide information varies from issue to issue. In PD situations, institutions will be most effective if they provide timely and accurate information about member state behavior. An "appropriately designed" institution in a PD situation will have strong monitoring capacities, allowing members to implement enforcement strategies. An appropriately designed institution in a coordination situation, in contrast, will facilitate bargaining by encouraging a dense network of relations among state officials. Hypothesis 1, below, uses the term "appropriately designed." Whether an institution is designed appropriately can be determined ex ante, using the criteria just specified.

The logic of externalities and benefits from convergent state behavior minimizes the explanatory leverage of domestic factors. When externalities to state behavior are high, governments have incentives to coordinate their behavior regardless of precise domestic arrangements. Domestic groups may mobilize and pressure governments to shirk their international commitments. However, such outcomes will be unstable internationally because of the high level of externalities that states will bear as a result of uneven compliance with cooperative agreements. If we observe that member state behavior within an institution is converging, it means that states are adopting similar policies regardless of their particular domestic configurations. Thus, domestic politics has little explanatory power when externalities are high.[8]

Overall, the logic of externalities and information leads us to the following hypothesis, H1, about the conditions under which we should see international institutions leading to convergence of state behavior. (All hypotheses and subhypotheses are stated with the usual "all else equal" clauses and in probabilistic terms.)

H1:   *Convergence Effects.* **International institutions will more likely result in convergence of member state behavior when the following two conditions are met:**

   1a. **States recognize substantial externalities to their behavior. These may take the form of costs for reneging on cooperative agreements or of coordination problems.**

---

[8] If states have similar preferences in a low-externality situation, their behavior is likely to converge. However, convergence in this case cannot properly be called an institutional effect, unless institutions have somehow fundamentally changed preferences. By putting the analysis of externalities first in our branching model, we clarify when convergence might be an institutional effect, rather than a coincidence.

1b. Institutions are designed adequately, having either monitoring mechanisms in place that allow for enforcement of cooperative behavior or procedures that facilitate negotiation, depending on the underlying collective-action problem.

If institutions are created in response to collective-action dilemmas, and these dilemmas induce convergence in the behavior of rational actors, why would institutions ever lead to divergence? When we recognize that some institutions address issues where the externalities to state behavior are small or nonexistent, and that member states can exhibit a great deal of variation in their propensity to comply with these institutions' standards because of variation in their domestic politics, divergence of state behavior emerges as a potentially stable institutional outcome. We argue that we are most likely to observe divergence when the organization and access of domestic interest groups varies across member states.

Studies of international institutions have recently gone beyond the traditional focus on collective-action dilemmas to consider social issues such as human rights, development aid, and labor standards (Moravcsik, 1995; Keck and Sikkink, 1998). Institutions in these new issue areas often have purely aspirational goals. That is, they set standards for their member states and work through a long-term process of persuasion to encourage movement toward these standards. The goals are aspirational in that there are no enforcement mechanisms specified and in that member states do not expect that failure to meet these standards will result in any punishment from other members or the institution itself.

Institutions with such purely aspirational goals are classically "weak" institutions. Two prominent questions emerge about them. First, why do states create and join them? Second, by what causal mechanisms might they influence members' behavior? In response to the first question, a condition for joining a weak institution must be the absence of any significant externalities. In the presence of externalities, states will bear high costs from attempting to cooperate when inadequate monitoring and enforcement mechanisms are in place. However, when externalities are minimal, the potential costs associated with other members' reneging are not high. On many social issues, actors aspire to move to higher standards of behavior, but divergence in the performance of states has few direct cross-border effects. Consider the example of development aid. Some modest benefits may result from coordination of donor policies in this area. However, since the amount of development aid is small in relation to donor budgets and the potential benefits of coordination are far in the future, uncertain, and not of great magnitude, the externalities associated with failure to coordinate aid policies are not high. This situation has resulted in the creation of an institution that sets goals but with little prospect of enforcing penalties for failure to comply with these goals.

In spite of the lack of incentives to coordinate behavior and weak institutions, researchers have argued that aspirational institutions do have effects on the policies of some states. They point to the actions of private groups, particularly nongovernmental organizations (NGOs) or domestic interest groups, in using internationally agreed-upon standards to raise public awareness and pressure governments to move toward compliance. Keck and Sikkink (1998) find that NGOs with principled beliefs have made a difference in the policies of governments on various social issues. NGOs exercise influence by using international agreements, such as human-rights conventions, to generate publicity about government policies and to mobilize grassroots pressure on governments to change. Gurowitz (1999:415) finds a similar dynamic in a study of immigration policy in Japan, where explicit international norms led to the mobilization of domestic actors and changes in Japanese policy.

However, there is a great deal of variation in the capacity of such groups and in their ability to influence state policy. When private organizations are severely repressed by their governments, as for example was the case with Guatemalan human-rights organizations during the 1970s, they have little opportunity to use international norms as a mechanism for generating pressure on the government for policy change (Martin and Sikkink, 1993). In such cases, there is little reason to expect weak institutions to effect any change in government policies. At the same time, governments that are not completely resistant to these international norms and are relatively open to pressure from organized interest groups can be persuaded to move in the direction of international norms. Moravcsik (1995) finds this is the case for European human-rights regimes, as Martin and Sikkink (1993) find in the case of Argentina in the 1970s.

Thus, weak institutions that express aspirational goals in the context of minimal externalities and variation in the organization and access of private groups to member governments can result in a pattern of divergence of state practice. Some members will move toward institutional goals; others will exhibit no effect of these goals on state practice. In the previous section, we argued that the lack of significant externalities created the permissive conditions for divergence of state behavior. By adding the activities of domestic interest groups to the picture, we specify when divergence is most likely to occur.

Above, we introduced a distinction between strong and weak divergence effects. The preceding discussion has focused on weak divergence effects, which result when institutions have the desired effect on only a subset of member states. A strong divergence effect would be more extreme, with an institution having the opposite of the desired effect in some subset of states. In either case, however, the logic of divergent effects on different member states results from differential mobilization and influence of domestic interest groups within member states and requires low externalities. The logic of divergence is summarized in the following hypothesis, H2.

H2: *Divergence Effects.* **International institutions will more likely result in divergence of member state behavior when the following two conditions are met:**
   2a. States do not recognize substantial externalities to their behavior.
   2b. Member states exhibit variation in the organization and access of relevant interest groups to government policymaking.

The purpose and effects of institutions in low-externality situations have received little attention in the literature. One obvious question is why such institutions exist in the first place. Our presumption concentrates on the role of powerful domestic actors. Typically, aspirational institutions reflect the agenda-setting powers of ambitious, well-organized private actors.[9] It therefore seems empirically accurate that aspirational institutions adopt "high" standards of behavior, since these groups hope to use the persuasive power of institutions to "improve" the practices of states. The assumption that aspirational institutions set high standards, rather than just codify the central tendency of current state behavior, is essential to our proposition that they can lead to divergence.

Figure 4 summarizes our explanatory framework. It can be summarized as a branching model. The first variable is the level of externalities to state behavior. If externalities are substantial, we then ask whether international institutions have been adequately designed (as defined above) to address collective-action problems. If the answer is yes, we expect a pattern of convergence. If no, we

---

[9] See Lumsdaine (1993:46) on the role of private interests in putting development aid on the international agenda.

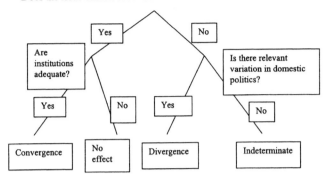

Does the issue exhibit substantial externalities to state behavior?

FIG. 4. A branching model of institutional effects.

expect institutions to have little effect on state behavior. If externalities are not high, we ask about variation in domestic structure. If there is little variation in domestic structure, we have indeterminate predictions; it is not at all obvious what institutions might do in such cases. If we have substantial domestic variation in a situation of minimal externalities, we have the necessary conditions for a pattern of divergence. Developing a rigorous test of these hypotheses would require measures of the level of externalities appropriate to a variety of issue areas as well as measures of the adequacy of institutional mechanisms and the behavior of states. In order to establish the plausibility and value of our typology and these hypotheses, we turn now to examples that are illustrative of convergence and divergence effects.

Empirical Illustrations

The examples discussed below are selected to maximize the variation in the level of international externalities to state behavior. We review three cases: the establishment of the Single European Market (SEM) within the framework of the EU, international cooperation to limit stratospheric ozone depletion, and development aid cooperation among OECD countries. The first two issues exemplify high negative externalities to divergent state behavior. Trade liberalization in Europe can be described in terms of a PD. Although cooperation among states to establish a common market would increase the welfare of each player, there are strong incentives to renege and to maintain barriers. Such opportunistic behavior generates high negative externalities for states that abide by the agreement.

Similarly, the efforts of a subset of countries to eliminate ozone-depleting substances (ODSs) will be dwarfed if other states release such compounds. The continued emission of ODSs can ultimately result in the destruction of the ozone shield. A unilateral reduction of the use and production of ODSs furthermore entails economic externalities. It will impose disproportionate costs on the chemical industry in the state that undertakes such reductions, undermining its economic welfare and international competitiveness.

Contrary to international trade and environmental cooperation, development aid coordination is characterized by low externalities. The increase or reduction of official development assistance (ODA) allocations by any single industrialized country would not affect other OECD members in any significant way. Perhaps improved coordination among donors could increase the volume and efficiency of financial assistance to developing states, contributing to their growth and to closer economic integration with the industrialized world. The collective benefits of such coordination, however, are likely to be small and uncertain.

Thus, we have chosen examples that can be clearly identified as high- or low-externality issues. Our case selection allows us to probe the plausibility of the theory of institutional effects elaborated here. In the instance of international cooperation on development aid, the effect of international institutions on state behavior is likely to be one of divergence. In contrast, the effect of international institutions in the issue areas characterized with a significant level of negative externalities is expected to be one of convergence, provided that the institutions have been designed to supply information and to allow for enforcement.

Institutions for Development Aid

The late 1950s and early 1960s marked the beginning of a coordinated international effort to channel financial assistance to developing countries. At this time, there was increasing concern in industrialized democracies about poverty in third-world states and strong leadership by the United States in support of development aid initiatives. The OECD and its Development Assistance Committee (DAC) emerged as the center of donor cooperation to improve the flow of aid for development.

The DAC defined a set of goals for industrialized countries. These included increasing the volume of aid, equitable contributions by DAC members, softening the financial terms of aid, and redirection of aid to poorer states. To further the goal of equitable and increasing contributions by member countries, the organization adopted specific targets for aid volume. The target was initially defined as 1% of national income for total aid flows, later changed to 0.7% of gross national product (GNP) annually (OECD, 1985).

Despite the fact that the OECD has adopted a specific numeric target, there are no sanctions against members who fail to comply with it. The rules advanced by the organization are viewed as guidelines and aspirations rather than as firm and enforceable standards.[10] Any effect of the institution does not stem from improving the contractual environment to facilitate compliance with a clear set of rules.

The DAC seeks to increase compliance with the 0.7% target by providing information and exerting informal pressure on member states. The organization publishes periodic reviews of the foreign-aid policies of members and annual statistics on aid volume, allocation, and performance. This information serves as a basis for criticism, exchange of experiences, and international pressure for improved performance (OECD, 1985:43). Reference to a specific, mutually agreed-upon target is instrumental in the exercise of "shaming" and peer pressure. As one former DAC chairman points out: "it was clearly necessary to have a uniform statistical procedure year after year to discourage retrogression in the total volume and quality of aid and to encourage increased effort" (OECD, 1985:47).

The OECD also strengthened development aid bureaucracies and their capacity to influence and execute national programs. The adoption of an international target for the volume of aid and the availability of compliance information have been used as ammunition by domestic supporters of development assistance, enhancing their ability to pressure the government. The OECD target

---

[10] Ruggie (1983:435–436, n. 17) qualifies the development aid regime as a "quasi-regime" for the following reasons: "(1) it was fully understood by donor countries that certain norms, particularly those concerning the quantity of aid (0.7% of GNP for ODA, for example), represented aspirations rather than commitments; (2) the various component parts of the would be regime were almost completely unrelated; and (3) the compliance mechanisms were few and weak."

16   *Institutional Effects on State Behavior*

provides a focal point for domestic political bargaining: "Aid authorities in the countries below the one percent level found the simple numbers very helpful in their internal efforts to raise aid budgets" (OECD, 1985:47).

The DAC seeks to advance a set of aspirational goals in the context of minimal externalities to divergent behavior by member states. What has been its effect on state behavior? Studies of the evolution and effectiveness of the regime conclude that its influence on governmental policies can be understood only in conjunction with other factors such as domestic concern, economic prosperity, and foreign-policy interests (OECD, 1985; Lumsdaine, 1993). Total ODA from DAC states has grown continuously, raising the level of total aid from $6.9 billion in 1970 to $28.6 billion in 1984 and $56.8 billion in 1996 (OECD, 1985:175; OECD, 1997:A11). In this generally upward trend, a shrinking U.S. contribution has been compensated for by an increase in aid from "new donors," most significantly the Nordic countries and the Netherlands. Despite the rise in the total flow of aid, however, the level of aid, measured as a percentage of GNP, has not changed dramatically. Nor did the OECD succeed in its goal of promoting "equitable burden sharing" and national convergence with the 0.7% of GNP target.

There are persistent differences in the performance of OECD countries with respect to compliance with the target of 0.7%. The pattern of ODA performance of DAC member countries over time approximates a divergence effect (see Figure 5). Since the 1970s, only four DAC countries—Denmark, the Netherlands, Norway, and Sweden—have consistently complied with and surpassed the 0.7% target. Figure 5 also indicates that the most significant positive change in national ODA allocations, measured as a percentage of GNP, occurred in these four countries. In 1960–61, the Netherlands, Denmark, Sweden, and Norway spent an average of 0.17% of GNP for foreign aid, with the average rising to 0.85% in 1997. At the same time, the performance of the United States has deteriorated

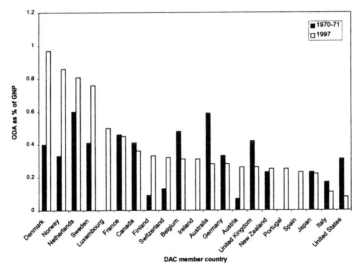

Sources: OECD statistics: ⟨http://www.oecd.org/dac/htm/dacstats.htm⟩; OECD, 1985.

FIG. 5. ODA performance of DAC countries through time (net ODA, measured as percentage of GNP, 1970–71 and 1997).

dramatically, with 0.56% of its GNP allocated to development assistance in 1960–61 and merely 0.08% in 1997. Some former colonial powers exhibit a similar decline in ODA allocations. The volume of development assistance has dropped from 0.56% of GNP in 1960–61 to 0.26% in 1997 for the United Kingdom, and from 0.82% of GNP in 1960–61 to 0.31% in 1997 for Belgium.

As discussed above, a quantitative measure of the degree of divergence in member state behavior is the standard deviation of the target variable. The ODA standard-deviation figures show an interesting trend, lending further support to our divergence hypothesis.[11] The standard deviation of ODA among DAC countries began at a high level, 0.40, in 1959. A process of convergence occurred over the next 15 years, with the standard deviation bottoming out at 0.14 in 1974. After 1974, the standard deviation gradually rose to 0.29 in 1983 and has held fairly stable since. These figures indicate that the 0.7% OECD target, set in 1969 and intended to be implemented by 1975, reflected a preexisting process of convergence. However, once the target was in place, it stimulated divergence.

The international standards established by the development aid regime found fertile ground in some OECD countries but had little impact in others. The overall result was a weak divergence effect. The degree of domestic support for the norms and principles advanced by the institution provide an important clue to understanding these divergent responses. Where strong domestic concern about international poverty and inequality existed, the OECD helped magnify that concern and translate it into specific development aid commitments. In societies with little organized support for redistributive programs at home and abroad, DAC targets had little influence. Case studies of development aid policies in Sweden and the United States reveal contrasting responses to the OECD development aid norms.

The international volume target is described as "a most influential guide" in the evolution of Swedish ODA policies, reinforcing domestic commitment and support (Ohlin, 1973). In the early 1960s, the official development program in Sweden was relatively weak and barely established. By 1975, Sweden was the first country to reach the 0.7% target. The rapid change in Swedish development aid policies was initiated in 1968 by the Social Democratic government. In its activist position, the government relied on strong public support and the involvement of private organizations that already had considerable experience in channeling private assistance to third-world countries. The reference to a specific numerical target for volume of aid helped domestic supporters to advance and sustain the leading position of Sweden. As Steven Hook (1995:98) observes:

> Consistent with the targets articulated by the United Nations and the DAC, the Swedish government pledged to raise ODA appropriations until they reached 1 percent of Swedish national income. This target, officially adopted in 1968 and achieved in 1975–1976, became the focal point of ongoing domestic debate.... Communists and Liberal Party leaders advocated a more aggressive aid program, whereas members of the Moderate and Centrist parties generally argued for more modest appropriations.

Even after the Swedish Parliament decided to abandon temporarily the 1% of GNP commitment in 1995, domestic supporters of development programs have been able to refer to the OECD "level of shame" target to muster a commitment by the government that "the aid budget volume will not be allowed to fall below 0.7 per cent of GNP" (OECD, 1996:33).

In contrast, the United States has been vocal in disagreeing with OECD development aid standards. Despite the United States' leadership role in establishing

---

[11] Data on standard deviations are from Van der Veen, 1998:ch. 7.

the international regime, the specific norms and targets advanced by the DAC have had little influence on U.S. development aid policies. Analysts attribute the limited resonance in the United States to the absence of a tradition of redistributive spending, the dominance of laissez-faire ideology, and the lack of strong organized support for overseas assistance (Lumsdaine, 1993; Hook, 1995). U.S. development assistance policies in the immediate postwar period were often justified as another means of advancing the national interest and the "geopolitical objective of communist containment" (Hook, 1995:121). With change in U.S. foreign-policy strategies, its international aid programs fell considerably below the OECD targets. U.S. policy on ODA reflects that toward other international organizations where the United States has not played a role in setting international targets: it is not strongly influenced by these targets, which are perceived as having been set by "outsiders."

The cases of the United States and Sweden suggest that the effect of development aid institutions on donor states' policies ultimately depends on domestic concern about overseas poverty and the capacity of domestic groups to use international standards to strengthen their country's commitment to international aid programs. Lumsdaine (1993:216) advances this argument in a more comprehensive study of the development aid regime through the 1980s. Lumsdaine's study finds that countries with the "strongest domestic commitment to eradicating poverty, and the strongest public interest in international poverty, were those which had the most vigorous foreign aid programs."

In some cases, international regimes tend to magnify domestic preferences that are in line with the goals promoted by the regime but have a negligible role in states where no such preconditions exist. Divergence driven by domestic concerns can persist because the externalities to state policy are minimal. The aid case also highlights the point that divergence by no means implies the "failure" of institutions but can signal partial "success."

Convergence toward a Single Market in Europe

The Single European Act (SEA), signed by the heads of state of the European Community (EC)[12] in 1986, set the objective of establishing a free economic zone in Europe. This ambitious political project was based on the proposals of the European Commission White Paper, presented to the European Council in 1985. The White Paper outlines specific steps that states should take to create a common market free from barriers to the flow of people, goods, and services (Commission of the European Communities, 1985). The SEA reflected to a large extent the interests of member states, and most importantly, of the three big players (Britain, Germany and France) in further internal trade liberalization. Under the pressures of growing global interdependence, the SEM presented a strategy that would best advance the welfare and competitiveness of the EU (Moravcsik, 1998, 1991).

The goal of completing the SEM has commanded the support and commitment of EU members. Despite this similarity of state preferences, however, national governments are often tempted to avoid or delay the application of internal-market regulations. The risk of opportunism is a problem for completion of the internal market, as for many other instances of international cooperation (Lake, 1999:52). Implementation failures can result from pressure by domestic interests seeking protection from foreign competition or governmental priorities that are not congruent with supranational objectives (Bronckers, 1989). Opportunistic behavior is associated with significant negative externalities. Failure to adopt

---

[12] Since the ratification of the Maastricht Treaty (1992), the European Community has been referred to as the European Union. The paper uses both terms, depending on the period being discussed.

LILIANA BOTCHEVA AND LISA L. MARTIN   19

internal-market regulations will delay and disturb the functioning of the single market, undermining the efforts of the countries that do comply with the regulations. It will impose costs on export-oriented businesses and may give the laggard countries an unfair competitive advantage. The adverse implications of asymmetrical compliance with White Paper directives are summarized by Colchester and Buchan (1990:132):

> Uneven implementation of EC rules could distort competition across the market quite as much as having no rules at all. . . . If some states enforce EC law punctiliously, while others either fail to get EC decisions onto their statute books or pay scant attention to them, there could be a backlash from the virtuous states, leading to bureaucratic tit-for-tat, and a "single market" sliding back into an anarchy of covert protectionism rather as the Common Market did in the 1970s.

Under such conditions, it is not surprising that the states of the EU have delegated significant authority to institutions to ensure adequate monitoring that would facilitate the application of single-market directives. Starting with the adoption of the White Paper in 1985, the European Commission has been instrumental in speeding up the completion of the internal market:

> The white paper greatly facilitated agreement and implementation of the internal market by providing transparency and standardization. Its directives made clear what each government committed itself to do, thus reducing the fear that some states would be doing more than others. The Commission, under the direction from the Council and the EP [European Parliament], contributed to the transparency of the process by agreeing to publish semi-annual reports on the progress of the white-paper directives (Martin, 2000:171–72).

Mounting concern about delays in the implementation of the single-market regulations has motivated even greater activism on the part of European institutions.[13] The Single Market Action Plan, proposed by the commission and adopted in 1997, outlines initiatives for greater transparency and the simplification of single-market rules as well as for strengthening monitoring systems. Member states are required to notify the commission of timetables for implementing all outstanding single-market directives and to designate oversight centers for resolving single-market problems on a bilateral basis. The commission intensified its direct monitoring by the publication of a semi-annual "Scoreboard" that highlights any discrepancies between the political commitments of member states and their actual performance. It identifies members with the worst and best records and monitors the economic impact of single-market regulations (European Commission, DGXV, 1997a, 1997b, 1997d).

The Single Market Action Plan also requires that states set up clearly identified contact points for citizens and interested businesses. Under the plan, the existence of such contact points, details of how to get in touch with them, and information about the main enforcement structures must be widely advertised to citizens' and business groups (European Commission, DGXV, 1997b, 1997c). The commission also advanced a proposal for a regulation to establish a rapid-intervention mechanism. Infringement of this regulation could lead, within a short time, to a referral to the European Court of Justice (European Commission, DGXV, 1997a).

---

[13] Single Market Commissioner Mario Monti provides the following rationale for undertaking quick action for improved compliance with single-market directives: ". . . violations of the free movement of goods can seriously disturb the orderly functioning of the Single Market and cause major damage to economic operators. I am therefore convinced the all measures at the disposal of Member states have to be implemented, as the credibility of the Single Market is at stake" (European Commission, DGXV, 1997a:1).

20   *Institutional Effects on State Behavior*

Through these mechanisms, the institutions of the EU monitor and provide information on the application of internal-market directives. Such information has facilitated the decentralized enforcement of single-market rules through domestic courts and procedures. It has also magnified the direct international pressure for compliance with the provisions of the White Paper. Thus, the institutions of the EU have contributed to a trend of progressive convergence of the behavior of member states toward the adoption of single-market regulations. Data on the rates of transposition of White Paper directives confirm this effect. In 1990, the variation in the level of implementation ranged from a low of 43% in Italy to a high of 88.1% in Denmark, with a rate of 73.4% for the EU as a whole. In 1997, the range of variation had decreased, with a low of 91.4% for Belgium, a high of 97.6% for Denmark, and 93.8% for the EU as a whole (see Figure 6). Furthermore, a press release from February 1998 concludes that the recent move to increase pressure for greater compliance "has proved to be very effective": there has been a 20% improvement since November 1997 in the rate of transposition of single-market directives, narrowing the transposition gap even further, with a low of 92% for Belgium and a high of 97.7% for Finland (European Commission, DGXV, 1998). The standard deviation of the target variable in this case provides a quantitative measure of the trend of policy convergence among EU members. In 1990, the standard deviation in the level of implementation by EU countries was 12.12. The standard deviation dropped considerably to 5.02 in 1994 and 2.14 in 1997 (even with the addition of new member states).

The SEM case supports the hypothesis that in the presence of significant externalities to divergent state behavior and adequate mechanisms for monitoring and enforcement, the institutional effect is likely to be one of convergence. Furthermore, the case demonstrates that if such an effect does not materialize

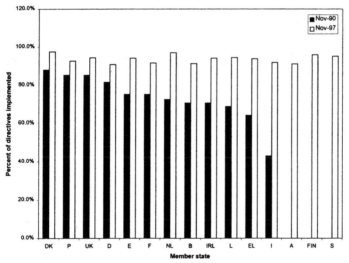

Note: DK = Denmark, P = Portugal, UK = United Kingdom, D = Germany, E = Spain, F = France, NL = Netherlands, B = Belgium, IRL = Ireland, L = Luxembourg, EL = Greece, I = Italy, A = Austria, FIN = Finland, S = Sweden.
Source: European Commission, DGXV, 1998.

FIG. 6. Implementation of EU internal-market directives through time.

initially, there should be strong incentives to strengthen the compliance and monitoring procedures of the institutions so as to stimulate a change in state behavior toward greater convergence over time.

International Institutions to Save the Ozone Layer

An article by Molina and Rowland (1974) first described the likely impact of the environmental externality associated with the use of a particular class of chemical substances. The authors posited that chlorofluorocarbons (CFCs) released into the Earth's atmosphere are decomposed in the stratosphere, releasing significant amounts of chlorine, which could lead to stratospheric ozone depletion. The destruction of the ozone shield would expose the Earth to higher levels of ultraviolet radiation, with a number of harmful effects on ecosystems and human health, including a discernible increase in nonmelanoma skin cancer. Since this seminal work, there has been a growing scientific consensus on the ozone-depleting potential of CFCs and other dangerous chemicals (Benedick, 1998; Parson, 1996). Edward Parson (1993:28) describes two broad stages in the scientific development of the ozone issue: "about ten years of confusion and concern, with newly discovered information frequently revising estimated risks both up and down; then, since 1985, a period of convergence in the basic science coupled with new observations that give steadily increasing grounds for concern."

During the early stage "of confusion and concern," when the threat was perceived as relatively small and uncertain, only the Nordic countries demanded strong controls. These proposals met with little support on the part of other influential actors: the United States, Japan, and the EU. As a result, the Vienna Convention for the Protection of the Ozone Layer (1985) stated a general commitment to cooperation in research and control of ODSs but did not include any specific regulatory mechanisms (Oye and Maxwell, 1995).

A growing scientific consensus against ODSs, the ability to resolve contractual problems, and the lack of strong resistance on the part of big chemical firms all contributed to an agreement on controlling ODSs in Montreal in 1987. The Montreal Protocol committed industrialized countries to 50% cuts in CFC production and use by 1999 and a freeze of halons at 1986 levels by 1993. Following stronger scientific evidence, the London (1992) and Copenhagen (1994) amendments to the Protocol provided for the full phase-out of CFCs by 1996 and of halons (except for essential uses) by 1995 and added new chemicals to the list of regulated substances. The obligations of developing countries that are parties to the Montreal Protocol under Article 5 were delayed by 10 years.[14] The London amendment provides for technology transfer and the establishment of a Multilateral Fund to facilitate the implementation of commitments in Article 5 countries.

The consensus about the harmful effects on human health of ODSs required institutional mechanisms to ensure convergent behavior toward their elimination. The institution created to house these mechanisms also had to deal with possible economic externalities that might result from the content of the international agreement or uneven compliance with its requirements. It was critical to set up the rules of the regime in such a way as not to allow any country's industry to gain a competitive advantage and to ensure against opportunistic behavior (Oye and Maxwell, 1995).

The Montreal Protocol creates transparency of state interaction through the requirement that parties report annual data on production, exports, and imports of controlled substances. It provides for regular reviews of policies and treaty provisions, establishing a mechanism for iterated interaction that would allow

---

[14] Since these countries are covered under Article 5 of the Montreal Protocol, they are often referred to as "Article 5 countries."

states to demonstrate their commitment repeatedly, reducing the uncertainty about one another's action and intentions. The provision of restrictions on trade with nonparties in regulated substances and related products further affect states' interest in participation in the internationally negotiated strategy to save the ozone layer. Finally, the financial transfers channeled through the Multilateral Fund and the Global Environmental Facility provide positive incentives and enhance the capacity of developing countries and East European states to meet their commitments. An interlinked compliance and review system contributes to the protocol's effectiveness and has evolved gradually in response to implementation challenges.[15]

Through a variety of mechanisms, institutions for saving the ozone layer have been instrumental in creating incentives for states to commit to significant reductions in ODSs:

> The control measures enacted in 1987 and 1990 clearly increased everyone's willingness to undertake national controls. Even the activists were willing to go further with confidence that their measures will be reciprocated. Not even the most activist governments made serious, costly reductions until the treaty was signed. . . . For nations that formerly resisted the treaty, the enactment of formal controls also gives incentives to join: the confidence that they will not be placed at a competitive disadvantage by joining, and the desire to avoid trade sanctions and isolation (Parson, 1993:66–67).

During the 13 years since the signing of the Montreal Protocol, there has been significant convergence of state behavior toward achieving the reductions prescribed by the treaty and its amendment (Jacobson and Brown Weiss, 1998; Victor, Raustiala, & Skolnikoff, 1998b; Parson, 1996). Data on the production and use of CFCs and halons for 1995 indicate that all industrialized countries have significantly reduced the consumption and production of these substances (UNEP, 1997). Russia and the other transitional countries, which faced significant political and economic turmoil recently, constitute an important exception to the trend of convergent behavior.[16] In Article 5 countries, levels of both production and consumption have increased since 1986, as the protocol allows, but have remained small relative to the pre-1986 levels of consumption of the industrialized world (UNEP, 1997).

The reduction in the use of ODSs in industrialized states has drastically decreased the diversity in production and consumption patterns between Article 5 and non-Article 5 parties and across regions of the world (see Figures 7 and 8). We can calculate the standard deviation of production and consumption of CFCs and halon for all members, measured in metric tons, on the basis of data from the United Nations Environment Program.[17] All figures show a strong pattern of convergence, comparing 1986 to 1994, even as new member states join the protocol. The standard deviation for production of CFCs decreased from 88,000 to 12,000, and that for halons decreased from 81,000 to 4,000. The standard deviation for consumption of CFCs decreased from 46,000 to 10,000; the figure

---

[15] For instance, the explicit linkage between financial transfers from the Global Enviornmental Fund (GEF) and Multilateral Fund (MLF) and the official Non-Compliance Procedure has been essential for dealing with some implementation problems, such as poor data reporting on the part of developing countries and compliance failures in East European states (Victor, 1998). See Green, 1998, for a detailed description of the system for implementation and review in the ozone regime and an analysis of its effectiveness, and Victor, 1998, for an analysis of the use and effectiveness of the Non-Compliance Procedure.

[16] There has been some decrease in the production and use of ozone-depleting substances in these countries as well, but mainly as a result of a general economic downturn.

[17] Data from http://www.unep.ch/ozone/, accessed August 5, 1999.

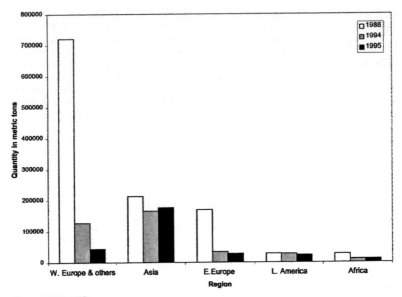

Source: UNEP, 1997.

FIG. 7. Consumption of ozone-depleting substances (CFCs and halons) over time, by region.

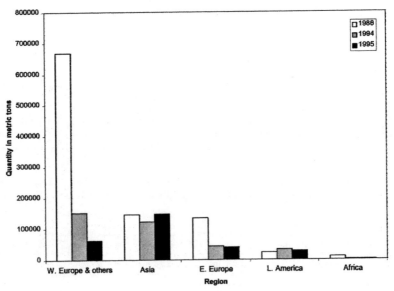

Source: UNEP, 1997.

FIG. 8. Production of ozone-depleting substances (CFCs and halons) over time, by region.

for halons decreased from 33,000 to 2,600. These data illustrate a convergence effect in an exemplary form.

The implementation history of the Montreal Protocol supports the proposition that in the face of significant negative externalities (in this case both environmental and economic) and strong institutions, the effect on state behavior is that of convergence over time. The future realization of the targets of the international treaty will, furthermore, provide an additional and more difficult test of this hypothesis. The capacity-building and redistributive mechanisms embedded in the protocol to ensure the participation of developing countries may need to be significantly strengthened to ultimately achieve the goal of global phase out of ODSs.

Conclusion

Do international institutions have significant effects on the behavior of their member states? If so, under what conditions and through what causal mechanisms? These questions have generated a dynamic research program on international institutions. However, empirical attempts to demonstrate institutional effects and test propositions about when and how they occur have been hampered by the lack of a careful conceptualization of how to identify and measure institutional effects. Institutionalists' understanding of effects has been constrained to a focus on international cooperation that may hide as much as it reveals.

We propose a new typology of institutional effects as an additional mechanism for improving the quality of empirical research on international institutions. We suggest that some institutions lead, as intended, to convergence of state behavior. This pattern is most likely to emerge when states create institutions in response to standard collective-action dilemmas and when states delegate to these institutions adequate monitoring capabilities to allow for effective enforcement. On the other hand, we observe that some institutions have led instead to divergence of members' behavior. We argue that such an effect is most likely to obtain when the issue area is not characterized by significant externalities to state behavior and members demonstrate variation in the organization and access of private interests that favor the goals of the institution.

Our intention in this paper is to outline a new research agenda and to provide some conceptual tools for pursuing this agenda. Studies of convergence and divergence should not be seen as substitutes for studies of cooperation, compliance, and effectiveness but as additional dependent variables of interest. We provide preliminary evidence relevant to our two hypotheses. The example of development assistance illustrates a divergence effect. This issue meets the conditions that we identify for divergence effects, with low externalities and diverse organization of private interests in member states. In contrast, the issues of protection of the ozone layer and completion of the internal market in the EU are classic PD-type situations with high externalities in which fairly strong institutions have been created. Both have resulted in convergence of member state behavior. Our hypotheses can be summarized in a branching model that first asks about the level of externalities to state behavior, then concentrates either on the design of international institutions or on domestic interest groups. Measuring and explaining variation in member state behavior promises to be an important tool for testing alternative theories of international institutions.

References

BAGWELL, K., AND R. W. STAIGER (1999) An Economic Theory of GATT. *American Economic Review* 89:215–248.

BENEDICK, R. E. (1998) *Ozone Diplomacy: New Directions in Safeguarding the Planet.* Cambridge: Harvard University Press.

BRONCKERS, M. C. E. J. (1989) Private Enforcement of 1992: Do Trade and Industry Stand a Chance against Member States? *Common Market Law Review* **26**:513–533.

CHAYES, A., AND A. H. CHAYES (1995) *The New Sovereignty: Compliance with International Regulatory Agreements.* Cambridge: Harvard University Press.

COLCHESTER, N., AND D. BUCHAN (1990) *Europe Relaunched: Truths and Illusions on the Way to 1992.* London: Economist Books.

COMMISSION OF THE EUROPEAN COMMUNITIES (1985) *Completing the Internal Market. White Paper from the Commission to the European Council.* Brussels: Commission of the European Communities.

DUFFIELD, J. S. (1992) International Regimes and Alliance Behavior: Explaining NATO Conventional Force Levels. *International Organization* **46**:819–855.

EUROPEAN COMMISSION, DGXV (1997a) The Commission Proposes an Intervention Mechanism to Safeguard Free Trade in the Single Market. *Europa*, DGXV web page ⟨http://europa.eu.int/comm/dg15/⟩.

EUROPEAN COMMISSION, DGXV (1997b) Single Market Action Plan. *Europa*, DGXV web page ⟨http://europa.eu.int/comm/dg15/⟩.

EUROPEAN COMMISSION, DGXV (1997c) Single Market Action Plan Sets Agenda. *Europa*, DGXV web page ⟨http://europa.eu.int/comm/dg15/⟩.

EUROPEAN COMMISSION, DGXV (1997d) Single Market Scoreboard. *Europa*, DGXV web page ⟨http://europa.eu.int/comm/dg15/⟩.

EUROPEAN COMMISSION, DGXV (1998) Informal Meeting of Internal Market Ministers, Cambridge, 13–14 February, 1998. *Europa*, DGXV web page ⟨http://europa.eu.int/comm/dg15/⟩.

GALLAROTTI, GIULIO M. (1991) The Limits of International Organization: Systematic Failure in the Management of International Relations. *International Organization* **45**(2): 183–220.

GREEN, O. (1998) "The System for Implementation Review in the Ozone Regime." In *The Implementation and Effectiveness of International Environmental Commitments: Theory and Practice*, edited by D. Victor, K. Raustiala, and E. B. Skolnikoff, pp. 89–136. Cambridge: MIT Press.

GUROWITZ, A. (1999) Mobilizing International Norms: Domestic Actors, Immigrants, and the Japanese State. *World Politics* **51**:413–445.

HAGGARD, S., AND B. A. SIMMONS (1987) Theories of International Regimes. *International Organization* **41**:491–518.

HOOK, S. W. (1995) *National Interest and Foreign Aid.* Boulder, Colo.: Lynne Rienner.

JACOBSON, H. K., AND E. BROWN WEISS (1998) "Assessing the Record and Designing Strategies to Engage Countries." In *Engaging Countries: Strengthening Compliance with International Accords*, edited by H. K. Jacobson and E. Brown Weiss, pp. 511–554. Cambridge: MIT Press.

KECK, M. E., AND K. SIKKINK (1998) *Activists beyond Borders: Advocacy Networks in International Politics.* Ithaca, N.Y.: Cornell University Press.

KEOHANE, R. O., AND L. L. MARTIN (1995) The Promise of Institutionalist Theory. *International Security* **20**:39–51.

LAKE, D. A. (1999) *Entangling Relations: American Foreign Policy in Its Century.* Princeton, N.J.: Princeton University Press.

LUMSDAINE, D. H. (1993) *Moral Vision in International Politics: The Foreign Aid Regime, 1949–1989.* Princeton, N.J.: Princeton University Press.

MARTIN, L. L. (1992a) *Coercive Cooperation: Explaining Multilateral Economic Sanctions.* Princeton, N.J.: Princeton University Press.

MARTIN, L. L. (1992b) Interests, Power, and Multilateralism. *International Organization* **46**:765–792.

MARTIN, L. L. (2000) *Democratic Commitments: Legislatures and International Cooperation.* Princeton, N.J.: Princeton University Press.

MARTIN, L. L., AND K. SIKKINK (1993) "U.S. Policy and Human Rights in Argentina and Guatemala, 1973–1980." In *Double-Edged Diplomacy: International Bargaining and Domestic Politics*, edited by P. B. Evans, H. K. Jacobson, and R. D. Putnam, pp. 330–362. Berkeley and Los Angeles: University of California Press.

MARTIN, L. L., AND B. SIMMONS (1998) Theories and Empirical Studies of International Institutions. *International Organization* **52**:729–757.

MEARSHEIMER, J. J. (1994–95) The False Promise of International Institutions. *International Security* **19**:5–49.

MITCHELL, R. B. (1994) Regime Design Matters: Intentional Oil Pollution and Treaty Compliance. *International Organization* **48**:425–458.

MOLINA, M., AND F. S. ROWLAND (1974) Stratospheric Sink for Chlorofluoromethanes: Chlorine Atom Catalyzed Destruction of Ozone. *Nature* **249**:10–12.

MORAVCSIK, A. (1991) Negotiating the Single European Act: National Interests and Conventional Statecraft in the European Community. *International Organization* **45**:19–56.

MORAVCSIK, A. (1995) Explaining International Human Rights Regimes: Liberal Theory and Western Europe. *European Journal of International Relations* **1**:157–189.

MORAVCSIK, A. (1997) Taking Preferences Seriously: A Liberal Theory of International Politics. *International Organization* **51**:513–553.

MORAVCSIK, A. (1998) *The Choice for Europe: Social Purpose and State Power from Messina to Maastricht.* Ithaca, N.Y.: Cornell University Press.

OHLIN, G. (1973) "Swedish Aid Performance and Development Policy." In *European Development Policies: The United Kingdom, Sweden, France, EEC, and Multilateral Organizations*, edited by B. Dinwiddy, pp. 50–62. New York: Praeger.

ORGANIZATION FOR ECONOMIC COOPERATION AND DEVELOPMENT (OECD) (1985) *Twenty-Five Years of Development Co-operation.* Paris: OECD.

ORGANIZATION FOR ECONOMIC COOPERATION AND DEVELOPMENT (OECD) (1996) *Development and Co-operation Review Series: Sweden.* Paris: OECD.

ORGANIZATION FOR ECONOMIC COOPERATION AND DEVELOPMENT (OECD) (1997) *Development Co-operation: Efforts and Policies of the Members of the Development Assistance Committee.* Paris: OECD.

OYE, K. A., AND J. H. MAXWELL (1995) "Self-Interest and Environmental Management." In *Local Commons and Global Interdependence: Heterogeneity and Cooperation in Two Domains*, edited by R. O. Keohane and E. Ostrom, pp. 191–221. London: Sage.

PARSON, E. A. (1993) "Protecting the Ozone Layer." In *Institutions for the Earth: Sources of Effective International Environmental Cooperation*, edited by P. Haas, R. O. Keohane, and M. Levy, pp. 27–73. Cambridge: MIT Press.

PARSON, E. A. (1996) "International Protection of the Ozone Layer." In *Green Globe Yearbook 1996*, pp. 19–28. Oxford: Oxford University Press.

RUGGIE, J. G. (1983) "Political Structure and Change in the International Economic Order: The North-South Dimension." In *The Antinomies of Interdependence: National Welfare and the International Division of Labor*, edited by J. G. Ruggie, pp. 423–487. New York: Columbia University Press.

SCHELLING, T. (1980/1960). *The Strategy of Conflict.* Cambridge: Harvard University Press.

SNIDAL, D. (1985) Coordination versus Prisoners' Dilemma: Implications for International Cooperation and Regimes. *American Political Science Review* **79**:923–942.

STEIN, A. A. (1983) "Coordination and Collaboration: Regimes in an Anarchic World." In *International Regimes*, edited by S. D. Krasner, pp. 115–140. Ithaca, N.Y.: Cornell University Press.

UNITED NATIONS ENVIRONMENT PROGRAM (UNEP) (1997) "Report to the Secretariat on Information provided by the Parties in Accordance with Article 7 and 9 of the Montreal Protocol." Presented to the Ninth Meeting of the Parties to the Montreal Protocol on Substances that Deplete the Ozone Later, Montreal, 15–17 November 1997. UNEP/OzL.Pro.(/3/Add.1).

VAN DER VEEN, M. (1998) "National Identity in Foreign Policy: The Politics of Official Development Assistance." Ph.D. dissertation, Harvard University, Cambridge, Mass.

VICTOR, D. G. (1998) "The Operation and Effectiveness of the Montreal Protocol's Non-Compliance Mechanism." In *Implementation and Effectiveness of International Environmental Commitments: Theory and Practice*, edited by D. G. Victor, K. Raustiala, and E. B. Skolnikoff, pp. 137–176. Cambridge: MIT Press.

VICTOR, D. G., K. RAUSTIALA, AND E. B. SKOLNIKOFF, EDS. (1998a) *Implementation and Effectiveness of International Environmental Commitments: Theory and Practice.* Cambridge: MIT Press.

VICTOR, D. G., K. RAUSTIALA, AND E. B. SKOLNIKOFF (1998b) "Introduction and Overview." In *Implementation and Effectiveness of International Environmental Commitments: Theory and Practice*, edited by D. G. Victor, K. Raustiala, and E. B. Skolnikoff, pp. 1–46. Cambridge: MIT Press.

[16]

Multilateralizing Trade and Payments in Postwar Europe

Thomas H. Oatley

The liberalization of intra-European trade in the years immediately following World War II offered potentially large welfare gains to European societies. In this period European trade flowed through a network of two hundred bilateral agreements. In the two years after the war intra-European trade increased rapidly within this bilateral framework, but by 1947 the growth had halted.[1] Shifting from this bilateral system to a multilateral clearing union could have provided a first step toward trade expansion. In spite of the potential benefits multilateral clearing offered, however, it was not until September 1950 that European governments established an effective multilateral clearing union, the European Payments Union (EPU).

Once established, the EPU had a dramatic impact on intra-European trade. The clearing union freed trade credit and greatly reduced European governments' need to resort to discriminatory quantitative restrictions for balance-of-payments considerations. Trade liberalization within the framework of the Organization for European Economic Cooperation (OEEC) quickly followed. By 1954 80 percent of intra-European trade had been freed from quantitative restrictions, and governments had begun to consider meaningful tariff reductions as well.[2] Thus, inducing European governments to enter a multilateral clearing union in 1950 marked the critical first step toward nondiscriminatory trade in postwar Europe.

I use the Rational Design framework to explore how the institutional structure supporting the multilateral payments arrangements facilitated Europe's shift to

Earlier versions of this article were presented at the Program on International Politics, Economics, and Security at the University of Chicago, February 1998; the Rational Design conference, Chicago, May 1998; and the 1998 Annual Meeting of the American Political Science Association. For helpful comments, I thank Barbara Koremenos, Charles Lipson, Lisa Martin, Walter Mattli, Tim McKeown, Jim Morrow, Robert Pahre, John Richards, Duncan Snidal, Terry Sullivan, the Comparative Politics Discussion Group at the University of North Carolina at Chapel Hill, and the editors and anonymous reviewers of IO.

1. See Eichengreen 1993; and Diebold 1952.
2. Asbeek-Brusse 1997, 83.

International Organization 55, 4, Autumn 2001, pp. 949–969

© 2001 by The IO Foundation and the Massachusetts Institute of Technology

multilateralism. This question has received little explicit attention in the existing literature. Standard accounts of the Marshall Plan, in which the EPU figures prominently, and the one detailed history of the EPU largely ignore the strategic and institutional aspects of Europe's shift to multilateralism.[3] Barry Eichengreen's work on the EPU is more explicitly institutionalist.[4] Eichengreen suggests that European governments chose the EPU over full convertibility because domestic political considerations—in particular, the need for business and labor agreement on wage moderation and investment levels—made them unwilling to accept the real income losses full convertibility would necessarily entail. What Eichengreen neglects, however, is the fact that the very concerns that made European governments reluctant to adopt full convertibility also made them reluctant to adopt more limited multilateral clearing arrangements like the EPU. Thus, existing work provides little insight into how distributive conflict, uncertainty, and enforcement problems blocked Europe's transition to multilateralism or into how specific elements of the EPU's institutional framework facilitated this transition.

In examining Europe's postwar shift to multilateralism I evaluate six conjectures drawn from the Rational Design project. The specific conjectures relate three dimensions of institutional design—flexibility, centralization, and control—to four of the project's independent variables: distributional problems, enforcement problems, uncertainty about the state of the world, and asymmetry of contributions. To evaluate the conjectures linking these variables, I first demonstrate that the independent variable did in fact frustrate European governments' transition to multilateralism. I then examine the degree to which the institutions that governments designed in response to these characteristics of the bargaining environment are consistent with the expectations of the Rational Design framework. The results are quite encouraging. Five of the six conjectures I examine receive very strong support. The sixth conjecture receives only moderate support, but this is more a result of idiosyncratic features of the Marshall Plan than of a weakness in the Rational Design framework.

The article proceeds as follows. I first describe the postwar bilateral trade system in western Europe and explain how multilateral clearing arrangements would work. In the second section I focus on distributional problems and uncertainty about the state of the world. I explain how distributive conflict and uncertainty about the state of the world made European governments reluctant to adopt multilateral arrangements; I then elaborate how the flexibility and centralization imparted to EPU institutions reduced the severity of these problems and thereby facilitated the transition. In the third section I focus on enforcement problems. I explain how the enforcement problem made U.S. officials reluctant to capitalize the payments union and how U.S. policymakers responded by designing centralized institutions that helped limit the kind of behavior they feared. In the final section I summarize the

3. See Hogan 1987; Kaplan and Schleiminger 1989; and Milward 1984.
4. Eichengreen 1993.

degree to which the case supports the Rational Design conjectures and offer some concluding comments.

Bilateralism and Multilateralism in Postwar European Trade

Bilateral agreements in postwar European trade were necessitated by the inconvertibility of European currencies and designed to ensure that imports from particular trading partners were paid for by exports to the same partner.[5] Each bilateral agreement established a list of commodities that the contracting governments agreed to import from each other in specified amounts. Many of these agreements also predetermined prices for these commodities. While bilateral agreements were oriented toward bilateral trade balance, most also contained short-term "swing" credit arrangements that allowed temporary departures from balanced bilateral trade. Bilateral deficits larger than the credit lines offered in the agreement often required settlement in 100 percent hard currency.

While the bilateral system allowed intra-European trade to reemerge in the immediate postwar period, by 1947 bilateralism had reached the limits of its usefulness. The assumption on which bilateral agreements were based, that bilateral trade would be balanced, proved incorrect. Intra-European trade was in disequilibrium. As Table 1 shows, Belgium, Italy, France, Sweden, and Switzerland ran net surpluses on their European trade, while the other countries ran net deficits.[6] These persistent imbalances exhausted available credit, and as a result "downward pressure was placed on the entire network of Europe's trade."[7] When the credit lines available in a bilateral agreement were exhausted, governments either used quotas to restrict their imports from specific countries or in extreme cases stopped trading with some partners altogether. France, for example, ceased importing entirely from Belgium in late 1947, as did Sweden in March 1948. The persistent imbalances and limited credit that characterized postwar bilateralism, therefore, constrained the expansion of trade. Moreover, heavy reliance on quotas to restrict trade when credit limits were reached introduced considerable distortions into European trade, as governments purchased goods from countries with which they had a bilateral surplus or that were willing to grant credit rather than making purchases from producers offering the lowest price.

A multilateral clearing union offered a solution to the problems posed by bilateralism. While the specific elements of clearing mechanisms can be complex,

---

5. For a description of this system see Patterson and Polk 1947; and Diebold 1952.

6. The British trade deficit in 1949 is, to some extent, misleading. This large deficit reflected the overvaluation of sterling. After the 1949 devaluation, the United Kingdom moved into surplus on its European trade. However, because of the problem of sterling balances, the British bargaining position shared more in common with the other European debtor governments than with the other European creditors.

7. Eichengreen 1993, 16–17.

TABLE 1. Net balances on European trade, 1949 (in thousands of $US)

Country	Net trade balance
Austria	−107,756
Belgium-Luxembourg	277,550
Denmark	39,851
France	49,350
Greece	−134,250
Italy	243,214
Netherlands	−120,037
Norway	−108,284
Portugal	−53,783
Sweden	113,783
Switzerland	93,817
Turkey	18,597
United Kingdom	−297,127
West Germany	−14,925

Source: The Operation of the Clearing Union, 20 February 1950, in File: Finance, P.; Finance and Trade Division, 1949–52; RG469.2.2, NACP.

the underlying principle is simple. Under a bilateral system each government has multiple bilateral balances; some of these bilateral balances will be in deficit, and others will be in surplus. Under a multilateral clearing arrangement the credits available in surplus bilateral accounts are used to settle the debts owed in the deficit bilateral accounts. A stylized example can illustrate. Suppose that Britain has a $6 million deficit with Italy, Italy has a $6 million deficit with Belgium, and Belgium has a $5 million surplus with Britain. Under a multilateral clearing system Italy could use its credit with Britain to settle its debt to Belgium.

Multilateral clearing offered two advantages to bilateralism. First, clearing would reduce total outstanding credit obligations. In the stylized example, multilateral clearing would reduce outstanding obligations from $17 million to $11 million.[8] The $6 million of cleared credit could then be used to finance additional trade. In the real world, it was estimated in 1948 that full multilateral clearing could cancel $278.9 million of an existing $762.1 million debt in the European trade system. Second, multilateral clearing would allow governments to focus on their net position against the OEEC as a whole rather than on individual bilateral positions. This in turn would allow governments to remove the discriminatory quantitative restrictions they had

8. Under the bilateral agreements, Britain owes Belgium $5 million, Italy owes Belgium $6 million, and Britain owes Italy $6 million, for a total debt of $17 million. Under multilateral clearing, Italy transfers its $6 million credit with Britain to Belgium, thereby paying its debt. The only remaining debt is Britain's $11 billion debt to Belgium (the $5 million of its own deficit and the $6 million arising from the Italian transfer).

relied on to balance bilateral trade, thereby reducing the distortions that character-ized European trade.

In spite of the apparent benefits to be realized from multilateral clearing, however, European governments were extremely reluctant to relinquish the system of bilateral agreements in favor of multilateral arrangements. The Council for European Economic Cooperation (CEEC) proposed multilateral clearing in 1947–48, but European governments showed little interest in the proposed multilateral scheme. The first clearing under this system, undertaken in 1948, eliminated only $1.7 million of the possible $278.9 million that could have been cleared, and total clearings throughout the agreement's lifetime amounted to only $51.6 million.[9] European governments' resistance to full multilateral clearing persisted throughout 1948 and 1949. U.S. officials consistently pressed Europe to move toward multi-lateral clearing arrangements, but met little success. As a consequence, multilateral clearing had little effect on European trade. Robert Triffin estimated that between 1947 and June 1950, the effective starting point of the EPU, multilateral arrange-ments "cleared only about 4 percent of the positions which would have been cleared under a system of full and automatic multilateral compensation such as was adopted later under the EPU agreements."[10]

Uncertainty, Distributive Conflict, and Europe's Shift to Multilateralism

European governments' reluctance to move toward multilateral clearing arrange-ments during the late 1940s was caused by the interaction between governments' uncertainty about how multilateral clearing would affect their hard-currency receipts and obligations and an underlying distributive conflict. Distributive conflict in an environment of hard-currency scarcity made European governments unwilling to cede even partial control over their external payments obligations to a centralized clearing union. Rational Design conjecture F2, FLEXIBILITY increases with DISTRIBU-TION problems, and conjecture C2, CENTRALIZATION increases with UNCERTAINTY ABOUT THE STATE OF THE WORLD, suggest that in such circumstances governments should seek to create centralized institutions to reduce uncertainty and flexible institutions to reduce the severity of the distributive conflict. The institutions created in 1950 strongly support both conjectures. A U.S. decision to capitalize the payments union relaxed Europe's hard-currency constraint and made possible a centralized clearing union based on a set of clearing rules that imparted considerable flexibility into creditor-debtor relations. This institutional framework enabled European govern-ments to adopt multilateral clearing arrangements.

---

9. Bean 1948, 408.
10. Triffin 1957, 149.

TABLE 2. Gold and dollar reserves, 1951 and 1938 (in millions of $US)

	1951		1938	
	Gold and dollar reserves	Months of imports covered	Gold and dollar reserves	Months of imports covered
Belgium	897	4.3	828	12.7
France	899	2.3	2,944	26.8
Italy	635	3.6	193	3.9
Netherlands	524	2.5	1,100	16.7
Switzerland	1,973	17.4	920	30.1
United Kingdom	2,335	2.6	3,313	8.8

Source: OEEC 1952, 60.

Uncertainty, Distributive Conflict, and Europe's Reluctance to Multilateralize

Uncertainty about the state of the world arose from European governments' inability to predict how multilateral clearing would affect their hard-currency payments and receipts. European governments held little hard currency in the immediate postwar period. The severity of the hard-currency constraint is shown in Table 2, which compares gold reserves in 1951 with prewar holdings. Before the war, European governments (excluding Switzerland) held, on average, reserves sufficient to cover almost fourteen months of imports. In contrast average reserves in 1951 (excluding those in Switzerland) were only about three months of imports.

The shortage of hard currency created problems for European governments. Postwar reconstruction depended on imports from the dollar area that had to be paid for with hard currency, while European exports to the dollar area were quite limited. European countries therefore ran deficits with the dollar area. The scarcity of hard currency coupled with the need to import from the dollar area to achieve reconstruction objectives made European governments extremely concerned about how intra-European trade would affect their hard-currency reserves. Bilateralism was adopted as the safest way to manage European trade in this environment. Bilateral agreements allowed governments to tightly control the amount of hard currency they expended through trade within Europe. By balancing trade on a bilateral basis, imports from a given trading partner could be paid for with exports to the same partner and no hard currency would need to change hands. Bilateral agreements also enabled European governments to shut off imports from a given country if the bilateral balance became unfavorable and threatened to impose hard-currency obligations. In other words, in an environment of hard-currency scarcity bilateral agreements allowed European governments to manage their external balance and conserve hard currency.

The problem with multilateral arrangements, given the scarcity and importance of hard currency, was that governments could not easily predict how multilateral clearing would affect their total hard-currency receipts and obligations. This is clear in creditor and debtor governments' reactions to a multilateral clearing arrangement proposed by the CEEC in 1947–48. The CEEC proposed that each government's bilateral credits and debits be pooled to produce a single net position against the entire CEEC. Debtors' total obligations to the system's creditors would be allocated across all creditor governments in proportion to each creditor's share of the system's total credit. Debtor governments would then settle in hard currency any debts above the credit lines established in the relevant bilateral agreement.

Uncertainty about how the proposed arrangement would affect hard-currency payments caused creditor and debtor governments to object to the proposal. Creditor governments objected to the proposed arrangement because the CEEC plan could reduce the amount of hard currency they earned from European trade. Pooling under the CEEC plan would distribute each creditor government's credits across all of the system's debtor governments. Belgium, for example, which under its bilateral arrangements might have a total hard-currency claim of 100 against Britain, France, and the Netherlands, might find that in the multilateral system it had a total hard-currency claim of 80 distributed across a large number of debtors.[11] By reducing the total claim and by distributing this claim across a larger number of debtor governments, Belgium might find that its intra-European trade surpluses were generating less hard currency under the multilateral arrangement than they would under bilateral agreements. Moreover, some of the governments against which Belgium gained claims as a result of pooling might not have the hard currency required to settle.

Debtor governments objected to the proposed system because it reduced their ability to control their gold obligations.[12] Under the bilateral system, debtor governments could avoid external demands for hard currency by shifting the source of their imports. If they reached the hard-currency payment point in one bilateral agreement, they could stop imports from that country and begin to import from a country with which they had a surplus or that was willing to offer credit. Under a multilateral system these techniques would no longer be effective. Because debts would be distributed across all of the system's creditor countries, shifting imports from one country to another would do little to economize on hard-currency obligations. Thus, debtor governments faced potentially larger gold demands under multilateral clearing than they would face under the bilateral system.

Creditor and debtor governments both preferred the certainty of existing bilateral arrangements to the uncertainty of the CEEC proposal. Instead of adopting the CEEC plan, European governments adopted a multilateral system that provided each government full control over its hard-currency receipts and obligations. The

---

11. This example comes from Bean 1948, 410.
12. See Hogan 1987, 119–21; and Diebold 1952.

First Agreement on Multilateral Monetary Compensation, as this system was called, distinguished between two categories of clearing. First category clearings were those that did not increase any bilateral balances. For example, if France owed Norway $3 million, Norway owed Britain $5 million, and Britain owed France $4 million, multilateral clearing would eliminate the French debt to Norway, reduce Norway's debt to the United Kingdom to $2 million, and Britain's debt to France to $1 million. Because these clearings did not increase any bilateral balances, they were to be conducted automatically among the system's full members. Second category compensations were those that did increase a bilateral balance. Because second category clearings would increase balances in certain bilateral trade accounts, they could occur only if all the parties involved—the primary debtor, the primary creditor, and the government whose currency was being transferred—agreed. In other words, rather than accept full automatic multilateral clearing, European governments created a multilateral clearing system in which they retained a veto over any clearings that would alter their hard-currency receipts or payments. But even with this veto, multilateral clearing proved too large a step. Only five governments joined the system as full members. Eight other governments joined as "occasional members" who reserved the right to veto even first category clearings. As a result, the First Agreement had a negligible effect on European payments arrangements, clearing only $56 million of the total debt in the system.[13]

An injection of hard currency into Europe could reduce European governments' resistance to multilateral clearing arrangements, and as we will see such an injection was an important part of the solution. A permanent shift to multilateralism, however, would require a solution to an underlying distributive conflict. This distributive conflict pitted European debtor governments against European creditor governments and revolved around one basic question: who would bear the costs arising from the existing imbalance in intra-European trade? Would creditor governments with current account surpluses have to reduce the size of their surpluses by importing more, or would debtor governments with current account deficits have to reduce the size of their deficits by importing less? This distributive conflict focused on two distinct, though intrinsically linked, sets of issues: financial arrangements and macroeconomic policy.

Distributive conflict over financial arrangements revolved around the role hard currency and credit facilities would play in any multilateral clearing system. Led by the Belgians, creditor governments saw that their surpluses in European trade could be a potential source of hard currency that could be used to cover their deficits with the dollar area. Creditor governments therefore sought to maximize the amount of hard currency used in settling debts with the clearing union and to minimize the degree to which these imbalances would be settled through credit. Led by the British, debtor governments saw that their deficits in European trade represented a potential claim on their hard-currency reserves, and this potential claim competed

---

13. Bean 1948, 408.

with their need to import goods from the dollar area. The more that debtor governments were required to use hard currency to settle intra-European deficits, the less hard currency they would have available to make necessary purchases from the dollar area. Debtor governments therefore sought to maximize the amount of credit available to finance trade with Europe and to minimize the amount of hard currency used to settle their European accounts. In short, creditor governments wanted to draw more hard currency from any clearing union that was created than debtor governments were willing to pay.

Distributive conflict over macroeconomic issues arose from different macroeconomic priorities. Debtor governments, the Scandinavians and British in particular, were putting the greatest emphasis on achieving full employment, whereas creditor governments, the Belgians and Italians in particular, were putting the greatest emphasis on domestic price stabilization. The combination of domestic demand stimulus in one set of countries and restrictive monetary policies in a second set of countries was one of the primary causes of the imbalance in European trade.[14] Liberal multilateral trade in Europe, therefore, would force either creditor or debtor governments to alter their macroeconomic policies.

The recognition that full multilateral trade would require macroeconomic adjustment predictably generated conflict. Creditor governments argued that the imbalance in European trade was due to the overly expansionary macroeconomic policies being pursued by governments in the deficit countries. Balanced European trade could be attained only if these governments concentrated on domestic stabilization. Governments in the debtor countries argued that their commitment to full employment and expansionary macroeconomic policies was defensible. The imbalance, they argued, was due to the zealous manner in which governments in the creditor countries pursued orthodox policies. For the debtors, the imbalance should be corrected by relaxing macroeconomic policies in creditor countries.

The distributive conflicts over gold and macroeconomic adjustment were intrinsically connected. In a fully automatic multilateral clearing union, hard settlement rules, that is, rules under which hard-currency payments played a large role and credit a small role, would produce creditor-favorable macroeconomic adjustment. As hard currency flowed from deficit countries in payment of their debts, deficit governments would exhaust their hard-currency reserves and be forced to adopt restrictive policies to balance their external account. Thus, under hard settlement rules debtor governments would bear the costs of multilateral arrangements by being forced to reduce their commitment to Keynesian strategies in favor of more orthodox policies. As Sir George Bolton, Governor of the Bank of England, told one

---

14. See Disadvantages of Pro-Debtor Proposals—Clearing Union—Full Employment, 24 January 1950; and Disadvantages of Pro-Creditor Proposals—Clearing Union, PS/AAP(50)14 AAP Policy Series, 24 January 1950; File: European Cooperation; Records of Special Assistant for Staff Planning Henry J. Tasca, 1949–51 (Tasca Papers 1949–52); Records of the Office of the United States Special Representative in Europe, Record Group 469.2.2 (RG469.2.2); National Archives at College Park, Md. (NACP).

U.S. policymaker, hard settlement rules would represent "a return to the old gold standard. [They] would cause extreme difficulties in the UK and the sterling area, a 4 percent decrease in European trade, and millions of unemployed in the UK."[15] A multilateral clearing union based on soft settlement rules, that is, rules in which hard-currency payments were minimized and credit facilities were maximized, would produce debtor-favorable macroeconomic adjustment. As credit expanded in surplus countries, domestic demand would increase, and domestic prices would rise. Expanded demand and rising prices would tend to reduce surpluses in the external account. Thus, under soft settlement rules creditor governments would bear the costs of multilateral arrangements by being forced to reduce their commitment to price stability in favor of more rapid credit creation.

In summary, uncertainty about the state of the world and distributional problems made European governments unwilling to abandon bilateralism in favor of multi-lateral clearing arrangements. Uncertainty about the state of the world, specifically about how multilateral clearing would affect their hard-currency receipts and payments, made governments cling to the certainty that bilateral agreements provided. And even with an increase in hard currency, European governments would need to solve two connected distributive conflicts arising from the existing imbalance in European trade: how much credit should be made available and who, the creditors or the debtors, should bear the costs of adjustment?

Flexibility, Centralization, and Europe's Shift to Multilateralism

The Rational Design project suggests three conjectures relevant to the problems that European governments faced. First, conjecture C2, CENTRALIZATION increases with UNCERTAINTY ABOUT THE STATE OF THE WORLD, suggests that European governments should have sought centralization as a solution to their uncertainty about the state of the world. Second, conjecture F2, FLEXIBILITY increases with DISTRIBUTION problems, suggests that European governments should have sought flexible institutions to solve their distributive conflict. Third, conjecture F1, FLEXIBILITY increases with UNCERTAINTY ABOUT THE STATE OF THE WORLD, suggests that European governments should have sought flexible institutions as a solution to their uncertainty about the state of the world. As these three conjectures suggest, the institutional framework that allowed European governments to make the transition to multilateral trade combined centralization and flexibility.

A U.S. decision to capitalize the clearing union (a decision examined in greater detail in the next section) yielded a highly centralized clearing union that substan-tially reduced creditor and debtor governments' uncertainty about how multilateral clearing would affect their hard-currency holdings. As discussed earlier creditor governments had objected to the multilateral system proposed by the CEEC in

---

15. Memorandum of Conversation, Hebbard and Bolton, 24 January 1950; File: Finebel-Fritalux; Tasca Papers 1949–52; RG469.2.2; NACP.

1947–48 in part because under this plan the credits that they had offered initially on the basis of the credit-worthiness of the individual borrower government would be transformed into claims against all debtor governments with little or no account taken of their individual credit-worthiness. Pooling in the CEEC proposal, therefore, could potentially transform ex ante hard-currency claims into worthless paper claims. Creditor governments were highly uncertain, in other words, about how decentralized pooling would affect the value of their credits.

The U.S. capitalization of the EPU allowed pooling to be highly centralized. Under the EPU, pooling generated claims against the clearing union rather than individual governments. Moreover, U.S. capitalization allowed the clearing union to hold sufficient hard currency to ensure payment of claims against it. Pooling under the EPU, therefore, protected the hard-currency value of credits in a way that the CEEC proposal had not.[16] Centralizing pooling and capitalizing the EPU therefore eliminated creditor governments' uncertainty about the ex post value of their credits. Once they were assured that any credit they advanced through a multilateral clearing union would not be transformed into claims against nonexistent hard-currency reserves of weak-currency governments, creditor governments became willing to extend credit on a multilateral basis.

Centralization also reduced debtor governments' resistance to multilateral clearing. By creating debts to a centralized clearing union rather than to individual governments, and by writing explicit rules (discussed later) about how much hard currency would be required to settle debts to the union, debtor governments became less uncertain about how multilateral clearing would affect the hard-currency obligations generated by a given set of bilateral balances. At the same time, creditor governments' willingness to extend multilateral credit through the EPU allowed debtor governments to balance their trade with OEEC members over a medium term.[17] Normal seasonal fluctuations in exports alongside a constant import stream, for example, could generate a large deficit in one month and a large surplus the next. Without credit mechanisms, governments facing deficits would be forced to choose between making hard-currency payments or tightening quantitative restrictions to limit imports to the level of exports. Given the scarcity of hard currency, European governments were likely to prefer the latter solution to the former. The clearing union's credit mechanisms relaxed this short-term constraint by allowing governments to borrow from the union against future export revenues to pay for current imports. The credit made possible by centralized pooling therefore made deficit governments more willing to expose their economies to the fluctuations inherent in liberal international trade than they would have been otherwise.

Of course, creditor governments were not willing to extend credit without limit, nor were debtor governments willing to enter into a clearing union irrespective of how much credit was made available. Thus, credit mechanisms were themselves the

---

16. Triffin 1957, 172–74.

17. Joel Bernstein to Henry Tasca, The Reconciliation of Intra-European Payments Objectives, 14 March 1950; File: Finance, P; Finance and Trade Division 1949–52; RG469.2.2, NACP.

object of considerable distributive conflict between creditors and debtors. The important point here, however, is that centralization reduced creditor and debtor governments' uncertainty about how multilateral clearing would affect their hard-currency receipts and obligations. The reduction of this uncertainty made governments more willing to enter into multilateral arrangements.

EPU institutions also provided substantial flexibility to creditor-debtor relations. The Rational Design framers conceptualize flexibility in two ways. First, institutions can allow governments to temporarily opt out of existing commitments by invoking escape clauses. Second, flexibility can be provided by substituting a series of short-term agreements for one permanent agreement. To these two types of flexibility, I add a third: flexibility as pliability. Pliable institutions are based on rules that have been designed to impart slack to what otherwise would be tightly binding constraints.

All three types of flexibility were evident in the design of the EPU. First, an escape clause was incorporated into the OEEC's broader trade liberalization program. In this regard it is important to recognize that the over-arching purpose of the multilateral payments system was to facilitate the liberalization of intra-European trade. To achieve this objective the OEEC Code of Liberalization was implemented in conjunction with the EPU.[18] The first step in the liberalization process was to eliminate quotas. While multilateral clearing would eliminate the need for discriminatory quotas—because gold obligations would arise from the deficit with the EPU as a whole rather than through bilateral debts—the possibility remained that a country developing a deficit with the union that it would be unwilling to settle with hard currency might find it necessary to resort to quotas to conserve hard currency. The OEEC trade liberalization program, therefore, allowed governments to suspend temporarily their liberalization programs and reimpose nondiscriminatory quantitative restrictions under a set of broadly defined events. This escape clause was embodied in Article III of the OEEC Code of Liberalization. This article gave governments the right to suspend or only partially implement the required liberalization measures if, "its economic and financial situation justifies such a course"; "any measures of liberalisation of trade ... result in serious economic disturbance"; and "despite any recommendations made [by the OEEC Council] the deficit of a member country with the Union is increasing at a rate which it considers serious in view of the state of its reserves."[19] Thus, governments were allowed to opt out temporarily of the trade liberalization if this process proved too disruptive to a government's general economic objectives or to its narrower balance-of-payments objectives.[20] The flexibility that the escape clause provided

18. On trade liberalization, see Diebold 1952; and Asbeek-Brusse 1997.
19. OEEC Code of Liberalization, 1948.
20. While Article III did lay out the general conditions under which governments could opt out of the trade liberalization program, the article contained no explicit constraint on governments' ability to invoke these clauses. Determining whether opting out was necessary appears to have been left to the discretion of the government. Also not imposed were explicit penalties for invoking Article III or explicit

reduced the degree to which European governments' uncertainty about the state of the world—particularly their concerns that future shocks could create balance-of-payments problems—made them reluctant to embark on trade and payments liberalization.

Flexibility as pliability was imparted through the system's settlement rules. The U.S. decision to capitalize the EPU made it possible to write settlement rules that explicitly allowed creditor governments to withdraw gold from the union at a faster rate than debtor governments were required to pay gold in. The EPU's settlement mechanism worked in the following way. Each government's quota was broken into five tranches of equal size. In the first tranche settlement was entirely in credit and no hard currency changed hands. For all credits above the first tranche the clearing union's obligations to net creditors were settled in 50 percent hard currency and 50 percent credit. Debtors, however, faced a less steep escalation of gold payments. Twenty percent gold payment was required in the second tranche, 40 percent in the third tranche, 60 percent in the fourth tranche, 80 percent in the fifth tranche, and 100 percent once the quota was exhausted.[21] Consequently, in the second and third tranches debtors paid less gold into the clearing union than creditors withdrew. The impact of these settlement rules on intra-European gold flows can be best illustrated by comparing actual gold payments between creditors and debtors in the period October 1948 through March 1950 with the gold payments that would have occurred had the EPU's settlement rules been in operation during this period. According to calculations by the Economic Cooperation Administration, creditor governments would have received $535.5 million under EPU settlement rules compared with the $152 million they did receive. Debtors, in turn, would have paid less: a total of $106 million under EPU rules compared with actual payments of $152 million.[22] The gap between the EPU's hard-currency payments and receipts would be covered by the U.S. funds that capitalized the union.

This settlement mechanism had two effects on the distributive conflict. First, and most obvious, it broke the tight link between creditor hard-currency receipts and debtor hard-currency payments. As a result, the hard-currency consequences of multilateralism were acceptable to both groups. Second, loosening the link between hard-currency payments and receipts weakened the pressure for macroeconomic

requirements that the government doing so engage in some costly signal, as Rosendorff and Milner suggest one should see. Rosendorff and Milner, this volume. Rather than explicit penalties, an informal process does seem to have emerged, driven largely by the handling of the German crisis in 1950–51. See Kaplan and Schleiminger 1989, chap. 6.

21. Diebold 1952, 92–95.

22. See Gold Settlements Under EPU, April 1950; and Gold Payments Under EPU Compared with Actual Intra-European Gold Payments Since October 1948, 20 June 1950; both in File: Finance, P; Finance and Trade Division 1949–52; RG469.2.2; NACP. U.S. policymakers also reduced British concerns about sterling balances being cleared through the EPU by insuring British gold against this risk: "In the event that EPU operations should unexpectedly result in British dollar payment obligations beyond some agreed danger point, ECA would be prepared to consider the allotment of special dollar aid to the United Kingdom." Secretary of State to the British Secretary of State for Foreign Affairs, Aide Memoire, EPU, 11 May 1950. U.S. Department of State 1950, 3:655–56.

policy adjustments that multilateral trade would otherwise produce. Under these settlement rules, a balance-of-payments deficit of a given size would be less costly in terms of hard currency than under rules calling for 100 percent hard-currency payment. Deficit governments would therefore face a less-binding reserve constraint when pursuing expansionary macroeconomic policies.

Finally, the EPU was a short-term agreement that had legal standing for only two years. Of course, the short-term nature of the clearing union was due largely to the system's role as a stepping-stone to full currency convertibility. But it is precisely the longer-term goal of full currency convertibility that makes the EPU's evolutionary approach significant. With European governments unwilling to move directly from bilateralism to full convertibility, the EPU provided an evolutionary path toward this final objective. As originally designed, the system's settlement mechanism was to be gradually hardened over time. If any credit was to survive in the system, this was to take the form of strict swing credits that would be repayable in gold after twelve months.[23] Moreover, European governments were to be pressed during the two-year period of the first agreement's lifetime to move to general convertibility, that is, to 100 percent gold settlements for net deficits. Thus, over a medium-term period the flexibility provided in the short term was to be gradually eliminated from the system, thereby tightening the constraints European governments faced and pushing them gradually toward full convertibility.[24]

In summary, the institutions created to promote multilateral clearing in postwar Europe both centralized and imparted considerable flexibility to creditor-debtor relations. The combination of centralization and flexibility reduced uncertainty over the state of the world and distributional problems, thereby greatly reducing European governments' reluctance to abandon bilateralism in favor of multilateralism. Centralization was achieved by using a U.S. capitalization to create country positions against a gold-backed clearing union. Centralization reduced creditor and debtor uncertainty about how multilateral clearing would affect their hard-currency receipts and obligations. Flexibility was provided through temporary opt outs that allowed governments to conserve hard-currency reserves, by relaxing the constraints that multilateral trade and payments would otherwise impose on creditor-debtor relations, and by an evolutionary hardening of settlement terms. Flexibility reduced the severity of the problems caused by hard-currency scarcity, distributive conflict, and uncertainty about the state of the world, and made European governments willing to enter a multilateral clearing arrangement.

---

23. See Intra-European Credits in EPU, 8 May 1950, RG469.2.2, NACP; and National Advisory Council (NAC) Minutes, meeting no. 158, 29 June 1950; Minutes of Council Meetings 1945–70 (Minutes); Records of the NAC on International Monetary and Financial Problems and the NAC on International Monetary and Financial Policies, Record Group 56.12.1 (RG56.12.1); NACP.

24. In the event, these expectations proved optimistic. The EPU was renewed every two years until finally dismantled in 1959. Settlement mechanisms were not greatly hardened until the 1954 renewal, at which point all debts and all surpluses were settled in 50 percent gold and 50 percent credit. See Kaplan and Schleiminger 1989.

And while it is true that the central aspects of these institutions, the creation of the system's credit mechanism and the asymmetric settlement terms, were made possible by the United States' willingness to capitalize the clearing union, it is important to recognize how this U.S. contribution affected the outcome in Europe. U.S. assistance was not used as a simple side payment, that is, as cash payments to induce cooperation. Instead, the capitalization was used to create a centralized payments union and to write a set of rules that imparted flexibility to this system in a manner that allowed creditor and debtor governments to see clear benefits from participation. In other words, U.S. assistance made a difference through the institutional design that it made possible.

Enforcement Problems and the U.S. Capitalization of the EPU

The creation of the multilateral clearing union in 1950 suggests a puzzle I explore here. The U.S. decision to capitalize the EPU made it possible to create institutions that reduced uncertainty and softened distributive conflict between debtor and creditor governments and thereby allowed Europe to begin the transition to multi-lateralism. Yet not until two years after the Marshall Plan was adopted were U.S. policymakers willing to devote Marshall aid funds to a clearing union. It was not that U.S. officials were unaware of the problems blocking the adoption of multi-lateral clearing arrangements. As early as fall 1947, during the preliminary discus-sions over Marshall aid, European governments had made it clear to U.S. policy-makers that distributive conflict and hard-currency scarcity would block their transition to multilateralism. Moreover, European governments requested at that time that a portion of U.S. aid be used to capitalize a clearing union. Without such a contribution, they told U.S. officials, the transition to multilateral arrangements would be delayed significantly.[25]

Why were U.S. policymakers reluctant to capitalize a clearing union between 1947 and 1950, and how did the institutions created in 1950 alleviate theses concerns? U.S. policymakers were reluctant to capitalize the clearing union because they faced an enforcement problem: they feared that using Marshall aid to finance European trade would lead to a multilateral system that could be sustained only through continued European discrimination against U.S. goods and continued injections of U.S. aid. The Rational Design framers offer two conjectures relevant to the U.S. role in Europe's transition to multilateralism. Conjecture C4, CENTRAL-IZATION increases with ENFORCEMENT problems, and conjecture V2, asymmetry of

---

25. See Memorandum of Conversation, Meeting of the Representatives of the U.S. Advisory Steering Committee with the CEEC Delegation, 3:30–6:00 p.m., 22 October, 1947; File: Memoranda of Conversation and Questions for Discussion; Lot 123; Formulation of the European Recovery Program; General Records of the Department of State, Record Group 59; NACP.

CONTROL increases with asymmetry of contributors (NUMBER), receive some degree of support here, though conjecture V2 receives weaker support than conjecture C4.

The Enforcement Problem: Moral Hazard and the Financing of European Trade

In contemplating the use of Marshall Plan aid to finance intra-European trade U.S. policymakers faced a moral hazard problem. The nature of this problem was straightforward: using dollars to finance intra-European trade could alter European governments' behavior and make it more difficult to achieve the Marshall Plan's broader objective of returning Europe to full convertibility and nondiscriminatory trade.

Moral hazard arose in two distinct ways. First, financing intra-European trade with U.S. funds could give European governments an incentive to expand their consumption by the amount of the U.S. contribution. Thomas Schelling, who worked for the ECA in Paris at the time, noted that "if [recipients] were to believe that their own ... shortfalls would be made up by U.S. expenditure, those deficits would be enlarged by the very evidence of American willingness to fill the gap."[26] This concern was explicitly discussed in the October 1947 Washington conversations between European and U.S. representatives. In these discussions Frank Southard (U.S. Department of the Treasury) asked the European CEEC delegates, "Suppose that one of the CEEC countries were to import from others some relatively less essential items ... through reliance on settlement in dollars. Suppose further that you got a fair degree of freedom of trade. Would it, then, possibly be the case that the country would be piling up, or running the risk of piling up, a debit in the account, while the country which was supplying the relatively less-essential commodities would be, in a sense, earning dollars which have come in through the United States?"[27] Were this to come to pass, any shift to multilateralism could persist only for as long as the United States continued to inject hard currency into European trade. The reasoning behind this concern was straightforward. If U.S. funds allowed consumption to expand, imports would expand. These additional imports could be paid for in hard currency, however, only as long as dollars were injected into the system. Once dollar inflows stopped, imports would drain hard-currency reserves, causing governments to resort once again to trade restrictions to limit their imbalances and conserve hard currency. As one U.S. Treasury official commented, a European payments plan "can't work after U.S. dollars cease to be put in."[28]

---

26. Schelling 1955, 609.
27. See Memorandum of Conversation, Meeting of the Representatives of the U.S. Advisory Steering Committee with the CEEC Delegation, 3:30–6:00 p.m., 22 October 1947; File: Memoranda of Conversation and Questions for Discussion; Lot 123; RG59 Lot 123; NACP.
28. NAC Minutes, 14, 19, and 23 January 1950; File: Minutes, 21 August 1945–25 October 1968; Minutes; RG56.12.1; NACP.

Second, a U.S. hard-currency contribution might reduce European governments' incentives to become competitive in the dollar area.[29] The dollar gap was the primary problem that Marshall aid had been created to solve, and the solution to this problem lay in generating the productivity improvements necessary to allow European governments to export enough goods to the dollar area to earn the hard currency they needed to pay for their imports from the dollar area. If European governments were suddenly allowed to earn dollars by exporting to other European countries, they would have less incentive to make the economic adjustments necessary to become competitive against U.S. goods. At the extreme, allowing European governments to earn dollars by exporting to Europe might, according to one Treasury official, "make it impossible for the European countries to earn dollars from exports to the dollar area. . . . After the initial stages, [a European clearing union] would be used as a device to discriminate against American trade and would defeat the entire objective of the ECA program."[30]

Confronted with this moral hazard problem, U.S. policymakers initially opted to maintain tight control over all Marshall Plan resources used to finance intra-European trade. In the first two years of the Marshall Plan, the United States allocated only a small amount of aid to intra-European trade and maintained tight control of these resources through the offshore procurement program.[31] Under the offshore procurement system, each European dyad forecast its net bilateral trade balance for the forthcoming fiscal year, and the government expected to be in surplus offered a drawing right in local currency to the other government equal to the expected imbalance. The grantee then used these drawing rights to purchase goods from the grantor, who was then compensated with ECA dollar aid. As the State Department noted, financing intra-European trade through offshore procurement rather than through free dollars provided "greater control over any United States contribution to European multilateral clearing than would be the case if dollars were made directly available to settle these accounts."[32]

Limiting Moral Hazard: Centralized Institutions

The Rational Design framers suggest that U.S. policymakers should have responded to the problems they confronted in their decision to capitalize a European clearing union in two ways. First, conjecture C4, CENTRALIZATION increases with ENFORCEMENT problems, suggests that U.S. policymakers should have sought a highly centralized institution to mitigate the enforcement problem they faced. Second, conjecture V2, asymmetry of CONTROL increases with asymmetry of contributors (NUMBER), suggests

---

29. NAC Minutes, 14 January 1950; File: Minutes, 21 August 1945–25 October 1968; Minutes; RG56.12.1; NACP.
30. NAC Minutes, 19 January 1950; File: Minutes, 21 August 1945–25 October 1968; Minutes; RG56.12.1; NACP.
31. For State Department views on free dollars, see The Acting Secretary of State to the Embassy in France, 26 August 1947, in U.S. Department of State 1947, 3:386–87.
32. U.S. Department of State 1948, 50.

that given the asymmetric contribution made by the United States, U.S. policymakers should have sought greater control over EPU decision making.

U.S. policymakers did push for an institutional framework that combined a high degree of centralization with majority rule decision making in order to promote macroeconomic policy coordination among European governments.[33] The payment union's decision-making powers were vested in a managing board rather than in national governments. Thus European governments would not directly participate in the system's operation. The managing board was given the role of encouraging governments to adopt macroeconomic policies that minimized their trade imbalances with the union. Governments with large credits or debits against the EPU were required to justify their macroeconomic policies in front of the EPU's managing board, which could then recommend macroeconomic policy adjustments.[34] Decisions by the board about particular governments' macroeconomic policies were made by majority rule, thus preventing any single actor from blocking action.

The administrative apparatus worked in conjunction with the system's settlement schedule to minimize the moral hazard problem. As shown in the previous section, the EPU's settlement rules were "debtor friendly" in the lower tranches of the quotas because they required zero or small fractional gold payments in the settlement of debts to the union. Thus for relatively small amounts of short-term credit the system provided considerable flexibility. As a debtor government moved into its quota's higher tranches, however, the gold content of payments to the EPU increased. As the gold portion of repayments increased, debtor governments faced increasing pressure from gold outflows to adopt macroeconomic policy adjustments. Thus, while the system easily accommodated short-term deficits, more persistent deficits generated automatic pressure for tighter macroeconomic policies. As Triffin, one of the architects of the system, observed, "the rising schedule of gold payments, on the one hand, would place increasing pressures on persistent debtors to adopt readjustment politics." These pressures would be further reinforced by two factors. First, the administrative authority conferred on the managing board was designed to "foster and support national or mutual policies aiming at the correction of excessive surpluses or deficits."[35] In other words, the managing board would promote a process of macroeconomic policy coordination among European governments oriented toward sustainable trade positions. Second, the evolutionary nature of the EPU was to be used to gradually tighten the settlement terms as the system progressed. Thus, initially soft terms—a lot of credit relative to hard currency— would gradually evolve into sequentially harder terms until the clearing union was functionally equivalent to full convertibility. An explicit process of macroeconomic coordination around relatively conservative policies would place European govern-

---

33. See, for example, Proposal for the Establishment of a European Monetary Authority, PS/ AAP(49)10 (draft), AAP Policy Series, 5 December 1949; File: European Cooperation; Tasca Papers 1949–52; RG469.2.2; NACP.

34. See Hogan 1987, 295–96; and Van der Beugel 1966, 203.

35. Triffin 1957, 170–71.

ments on the path to an early return to full convertibility and nondiscriminatory multilateral trade.[36]

European governments were reluctant to accept the degree of centralization the United States desired, resisting in particular a managing board empowered to make binding decisions through majority rule. Another Rational Design conjecture helps explain this behavior: conjecture V3, CONTROL increases with UNCERTAINTY ABOUT THE STATE OF THE WORLD. As Koremenos, Lipson, and Snidal observe in the volume's introduction, "because states are risk-averse with respect to distributional issues, they design institutions that protect them from unforeseen circumstances."[37] It was precisely this concern that motivated European bargaining positions during negotiations over the EPU's decision-making procedures. Given the underlying distributive conflict over the costs of adjustment and uncertainty about who would control a majority of the EPU's managing board, creditor and debtor governments both preferred the certainty of unanimity rule.[38] The most that debtor governments were willing to grant to the managing board was the authority to demand policy changes in connection with "special assistance" extended above the EPU's regular quotas. Creditor governments did see some advantage to decision-making procedures that would force debtor governments to adopt the policies necessary to service their debt. Yet creditor governments feared that a majority rule managing board could force them to adopt more expansionary policies. Uncertainty about who would control the majority on the managing board in conjunction with the underlying distributive conflict caused European governments to prefer the certainty provided by a veto to the uncertainty implied by majority rule.

While the Europeans were unsuccessful in blocking majority rule in the managing board, they were able to require that all board decisions would be adopted by the OEEC Joint Trade and Payments Committee and Executive Committee, where decisions were taken through unanimity rule. Thus European governments maintained veto power over board decisions through the wider OEEC.[39] In addition, the board was given limited authority. The original agreement did not give the board the right to "initiate proposals about economic and financial policies," nor did it give the board explicit authority to make proposals addressed to governments that generated substantial trade deficits.

U.S. policymakers did not gain greater influence over EPU operations than the European governments, an outcome that is inconsistent with conjecture V2, asymmetry of CONTROL increases with asymmetry of contributors (NUMBER). The lack of support for this conjecture in this case owes more to the idiosyncrasies of the OEEC

36. See, for example, OSR to Secretary of State, Relations EPU with International Monetary Fund, (draft) 23 January 1950; and Answer to Treasury Paper to NAC, 23 January 1950; File: Finance; Finance and Trade Division, 1949–52; RG469.2.2; NACP.

37. Koremenos, Lipson, and Snidal, this volume.

38. For creditor and debtor government positions, see Experts' Report on EPU—Suggested OSR Position; and The Reconciliation of Intra-European Payments Objectives, 14 March 1950; File: Finance; Finance and Trade Division, 1949–52; RG469.2.2; NACP. See also Diebold 1952.

39. See Van der Beugel 1966, 202; and Diebold 1952.

than to a problem with the conjecture's logic. The EPU was a part of the OEEC, and thus formal rights of participation were restricted to those governments that were members of this broader organization. The OEEC was created by European governments for the purpose of coordinating the administration of Marshall Plan assistance, and the United States was not an official member; therefore it could not acquire a larger share of the control over EPU decisions.

In summary, the institutions that facilitated Europe's move to multilateral payment arrangements combined centralization and control to reduce the severity of the underlying enforcement problems. U.S. policymakers were reluctant to use Marshall aid dollars to finance European trade because of an enforcement problem arising from moral hazard. Financing intra-European trade with U.S. dollars could create a European soft-currency area that could be sustained only through additional U.S. aid and continued European discrimination against U.S. goods. As the Rational Design conjectures suggest, U.S. policymakers responded to this enforcement problem by seeking institutions that combined centralized institutions and a relatively autonomous managing board empowered to make decisions with majority rule. Their ability to achieve this objective was limited, however, by European governments' responses to concerns arising from uncertainty about the state of the world. Uncertain who would control a majority of the managing board, creditor and debtor governments both preferred the certainty of unanimity rule.

Conclusion

Interaction between distributional problems, uncertainty about the state of the world, and enforcement problems complicated Europe's movement toward multilateralism in the immediate postwar period. Distributive conflict accentuated by uncertainty about the state of the world generated by hard-currency scarcity made European governments reluctant to adopt multilateral arrangements without substantial financial support from the United States. Concern about moral hazard made U.S. officials reluctant to provide the necessary support. European governments' shift to multilateral arrangements was greatly facilitated by the EPU's institutional framework. This institutional framework allowed U.S. policymakers to reduce the severity of the moral hazard problem, thereby making them willing to capitalize a clearing union. The U.S. capitalization relaxed Europe's liquidity constraint and made it possible to write a set of rules that imparted considerable flexibility to intra-European payments relations, thereby reducing European governments' concerns arising from distributive conflict.

In examining Europe's shift to multilateral payments arrangements, I have focused on six conjectures linking four characteristics of the bargaining environment to three dimensions of EPU institutions. I conclude with a brief discussion of the case's principal findings organized along the three institutional dimensions the case examined: flexibility, centralization, and control. The Rational Design project suggested that the degree of flexibility in the EPU should have been influenced by the severity of the underlying distributional problem (conjecture F2) and by uncertainty about the state of the world (conjecture F1). The case provided strong support for the conjectures as well as for their underlying rationales. Distributional problems and uncertainty about the state of the world did make European governments reluctant to engage in multilateral trade and payments cooperation, in spite of the large benefits such cooperation offered. Flexibility, provided by an escape clause, by the use of credit mechanisms and settlement rules to relax the constraints multilateral clearing would otherwise impose, and by the evolutionary nature of the EPU mitigated both of these obstacles to cooperation. Credit mechanisms, settlement rules, and the evolutionary nature of the agreement softened creditor and debtor distributive conflict and made common participation in multilateral clearing possible. The escape clause mitigated governments' concerns about how possible future shocks would affect balance-of-payments positions. As the conjectures suggest, therefore, flexibility reduced the severity of the distributional problem and uncertainty about the state of the world.

The Rational Design framework suggests that the degree of centralization in European multilateral clearing arrangements should have been shaped by the severity of the enforcement problem (conjecture C4) and by uncertainty about the state of the world (conjecture C2). These two conjectures were also supported. Once U.S. officials decided to capitalize the EPU, they addressed their enforcement problem by creating a highly centralized institutional structure that could constrain European governments' abilities to develop unsustainable trade positions. Centralization in the form of a gold-backed clearing union reduced creditor governments' uncertainty about the post-clearing value of their credits, thereby making them more willing to participate in multilateral arrangements.

Finally, the Rational Design framework suggests that the balance of decision-making power in the EPU, and the EPU's decision rules themselves, institutional components summarized in the variable CONTROL, should be influenced by asymmetry of contributions (conjecture V2), on the one hand, and by uncertainty about the state of the world (conjecture V3), on the other. The EPU provides mixed support for these conjectures. Conjecture V2 receives only weak support in this case, largely because U.S. policymakers could not participate directly in EPU decision making. U.S. policymakers did try to create a decision-making structure that limited European governments' direct control over EPU operations, but European governments' uncertainty about the state of the world had a much more transparent impact on CONTROL. Uncertain about whether a pro-creditor or a pro-debtor majority would dominate the EPU's managing board, creditor and debtor governments both insisted on maintaining the right to veto board decisions.

Overall, therefore, Europe's transition from a network of bilateral trade agreements to multilateral clearing provides strong support for the approach elaborated by the Rational Design framers. Five of the six conjectures investigated here, linking four of the project's independent variables to three of its institutional dimensions, are strongly supported by this case.

References

Asbeek-Brusse, Wendy. 1997. *Tariffs, Trade, and European Integration, 1947–1957: From Study Group to Common Market.* New York: St. Martin's Press.

Bean, Robert W. 1948. European Multilateral Clearing. *Journal of Political Economy* 56 (5):403–15.

Diebold, William. 1952. *Trade and Payments in Western Europe: A Study in Economic Cooperation, 1947–51.* New York: Harper and Brothers.

Eichengreen, Barry J. 1993. *Reconstructing Europe's Trade and Payments: The European Payments Union.* Ann Arbor: University of Michigan Press.

Hogan, Michael J. 1987. *The Marshall Plan: America, Britain, and the Reconstruction of Western Europe, 1947–1952.* Cambridge: Cambridge University Press.

Kaplan, Jacob J., and Gunther Schleiminger. 1989. *The European Payments Union: Financial Diplomacy in the 1950s.* Oxford: Clarendon Press.

Milward, Alan S. 1984. *The Reconstruction of Western Europe, 1945–51.* London: Methuen.

Patterson, Gardner, and Judd Polk. 1947. The Emerging Pattern of Bilateralism. *Quarterly Journal of Economics* 62 (1):118–42.

Schelling, Thomas C. 1955. American Foreign Assistance. *World Politics* 7 (4):606–26.

Triffin, Robert. 1957. *Europe and the Money Muddle: From Bilateralism to Near Convertibility. 1947–1956.* New Haven, Conn.: Yale University Press.

Van der Beugel, Ernst H. 1966. *From Marshall Aid to Atlantic Partnership: European Integration as a Concern of American Foreign Policy.* Amsterdam: Elsevier.

[17]

The Optimal Design of International Trade Institutions: Uncertainty and Escape

B. Peter Rosendorff and Helen V. Milner

International institutions differ g̲ _____ ates included, the decision-making mechanis̲ _____ he degree of centralized control, and the ext̲ _____ substantially from one institution to the next. _____ this article, as part of the larger Rational Design project on the design of international institutions, we claim that such variation can be accounted for as part of the rational, self-interested behavior of states. We show that at least one important aspect of institutional design can be explained as a rational response of states to their environment.

Almost all international trade agreements include some form of "safeguard" clause, which allows countries to escape the obligations agreed to in the negotiations.[1] On the one hand, such escape clauses are likely to erode both the credibility and the trade liberalizing effect of international trade agreements. On the other hand, they increase the flexibility of the agreement by adding some discretion for national policymakers. The first question we address is the institutional design issue that escape clauses raise: when is such increased flexibility rationally optimal for states making international trade agreements? The answer to this question hinges on the costs of using escape clauses and retaining the overall agreement compared with not using them and abrogating the agreement.

Our second question concerns the effects of different institutional designs. If escape clauses allow states more flexibility in meeting their obligations, what impact does this have on their compliance with the agreement? What are the consequences

We thank the editors of the Rational Design project for their efforts: Barbara Koremenos, Charles Lipson, and Duncan Snidal. We are also grateful to two anonymous reviewers, and to James Morrow, Robert Pahre, Lisa Martin, Chris Canavan, and the editors of *IO*, David Lake and Peter Gourevitch, for many helpful comments and suggestions.
    1. Hoekman and Kostecki 1995, 161.

International Organization 55, 4, Autumn 2001, pp. 829–857

of increased flexibility for institutional performance: is cooperation enhanced, and is it more durable?

An escape clause is any provision of an international agreement that allows a country to suspend the concessions it previously negotiated without violating or abrogating the terms of the agreement. Escape clauses are a prominent feature of many international agreements and are included in most trade agreements. Not all international agreements, however, have such clauses; for instance, some international arms control agreements, such as the Strategic Arms Limitations Treaty (SALT) agreements, do not contain such escape mechanisms. Most trade agreements do contain them, but their nature often differs across agreements and they are usually vigorously contested in negotiations. For example, in both the North American Free Trade Agreement (NAFTA) and the General Agreement on Tariffs and Trade (GATT) Uruguay Round negotiations, antidumping and countervailing duty laws were critical issues that impeded agreement among the countries. Since its inception in the 1940s GATT (and the subsequent World Trade Organization, WTO) has slowly built an arsenal of safeguard mechanisms to protect states from import pressures in the wake of extensive trade liberalizing agreements. These include an escape clause, countervailing duty penalties, antidumping statutes, and a national security exception. For each of these, GATT (now the WTO) specifies the conditions under which a government can grant relief to an industry from import competition, and industries then have the option of choosing which mechanism to file their complaints under. In each of the GATT negotiating rounds, the inclusion and/or modification of these different laws have been the subject of intense debate among the signatories.

Many have noted that these different clauses can be substitutes for one another. Bernard Hoekman and Michael Leidy and Wendy Hansen and Thomas Prusa suggest that countervailing duty and antidumping laws are really "a poor man's" escape clause.[2] Antidumping and countervailing duty complaints allege that exporting countries are playing unfairly and thus the harmed country avoids the payment of compensation that GATT requires on use of the escape clause. They are thus means for industries to limit import competition on the cheap: they enable a country to abrogate some portion of its treaty obligations under GATT and to pay a lower penalty than were they to use the escape clause. These and other measures, such as the infant industry and balance-of-payments exemptions in GATT, are all designed by governments to reduce domestic pressures to withdraw from the entire agreement when protectionist pressures grow at home. While these laws are generally seen as substitutes, they do differ substantially in the costs they impose on the countries using them. Usually antidumping and countervailing duty clauses are seen as less costly to use than traditional escape clauses. This type of variation is important, as we will explain later.

---

2. See Hoekman and Leidy 1989; and Hansen and Prusa 1995.

We make three central claims here. First, escape clauses are an efficient equilibrium under conditions of domestic uncertainty. When political leaders cannot foresee the extent of future domestic demands for more protection at home (and/or more open markets abroad), such clauses provide the flexibility that allows them to accept an international agreement liberalizing trade. A more general statement is that the greater the uncertainty that political leaders face about their ability to maintain domestic compliance with international agreements in the future, the more likely agreements are to contain escape clauses. In issue-areas where the impact of high uncertainty about domestic pressures to comply is less, governments are less likely to desire such safeguard measures.

We show that the use of an escape clause, a flexibility-enhancing device, in institutional design increases institutional effectiveness whenever there is domestic political uncertainty. We offer support therefore to Rational Design conjecture F1, FLEXIBILITY increases with UNCERTAINTY, as developed in the framing article by Barbara Koremenos, Charles Lipson, and Duncan Snidal.[3] This conjecture suggests that uncertainty about the state of the world rationally leads to the creation of institutional flexibility. Note that flexibility in this context refers to the ability to adapt and respond to unanticipated events within the context of a well-designed institutional system. The system itself is not subject to renewed bargaining. Alternative flexibility-enhancing devices are, of course, available: sunset provisions or anticipated renegotiations are often used. But we think that these mechanisms are even more costly and hence less used than the ones we examine.

Second, for escape clauses to be useful and efficient they must impose some kind of cost on their use. That is, countries that invoke an escape clause must pay some cost for doing so, or else they will invoke it all the time, thus vitiating the agreement. Paying this cost signals their intention to comply in the future. But the different costs of alternative escape clause measures will affect the frequency of their use. Less costly measures will be used more often. If governments understand this, they should rationally prefer the set of escape clauses that best matches the extent of protectionist pressure they expect to experience from domestic interests. Thus we anticipate that the architects of international agreements will design such agreements so that the costs of the escape clauses they most desire are balanced by the benefits of future cooperation. Variation in the nature of the escape clause mechanism, primarily its cost, is thus an important feature of different agreements. If states rationally design such agreements, we should expect such variation to be an important element of the bargaining process.

The exact size of the cost will depend on the gains from cooperation relative to the benefits of defection; they are a function of what might be called the "preference configuration." The costliness of the escape clause is crucial to the effectiveness of the escape clause regime, and the preferences of the domestic players in the negotiating countries will affect the optimal choice of this cost. We claim, therefore,

---

3. Koremenos, Lipson, and Snidal, this volume.

that domestic preferences and institutions matter in the design of optimal international institutions.

Third, we argue that including escape clauses makes initial agreements easier to reach. Their flexibility allows states to be reassured about the division of the long-term gains from the agreement. Indeed we claim that without escape clauses of some sort many trade agreements would never be politically viable for countries. This fits with Rational Design conjecture F2, FLEXIBILITY increases with DISTRIBUTION problems; that is, increased flexibility (necessary to deal with the uncertainty about future states of the world) lessens the problems of bargaining and distribution that may plague an initial agreement.

We use a formal model to examine why countries might desire escape clauses and how this type of institutional design might affect an institution's performance. We examine a two-stage game: an international bargaining game where an agreement over the design of the institution is adopted and then a repeated trade (sub)game where the countries set their trade policies, given the design of the institution.

Escape Clauses and Political Uncertainty

The key factor that renders escape clauses desirable is the presence of uncertainty. In each period the political pressure for protection at home (and/or for more open markets abroad) is subject to a shock. Some unanticipated change in the economy or political system produces a bigger or smaller value for the impact of domestic firms' demands for protection. We model this shock very generally; it is any exogenous and unanticipated change in the state of the world (such as price or supply changes, technological change, political change) that affects domestic firms' demand for, or ability to lobby for, protection of their markets.

Although we model uncertainty as a political shock, we recognize that the strength of the political support for protection (or for liberalization) is determined by many factors, for instance,

- unexpected price or supply shifts that intensify international competition may induce enhanced lobbying efforts by domestic firms;

- changes in production technology that reduce employment in a sector, and hence its political clout;

- changes in a country's political institutions or preferences: tastes might change in favor of enhanced protection, or campaign finance reforms might alter the political pressure that firms can apply;

- changes in domestic political cleavages or alignments that might make a previously pivotal sector less influential in domestic politics, implying that protection is politically less expedient.[4]

---

4. For analytical tractability, we assume in the model that the shocks in each country are independent. Price shocks—for example, an unexpected rise in the price of an input or the emergence of a

We assume that in the current period leaders in each country know their own domestic political situation but that both sets of leaders are equally uninformed about the degree of political pressure at home and abroad in all future periods. We show that uncertainty about the state of the world creates conditions favorable for the use of escape clauses. That each country has limited knowledge about the domestic politics of the others is central to our argument; furthermore, this uncertainty has a lasting impact because each country faces new shocks in each period that determine the amount of political pressure that domestic groups exert.[5]

The two stages of the model combine the two critical elements of cooperation theory: bargaining and enforcement. The trade game played by the countries is a modified version of a repeated Prisoners' Dilemma. In this second stage enforcement is critical; the temptation to cheat makes cooperation very difficult, especially in international politics where third-party enforcement is absent. Countries must be punished if they protect, but sometimes because of domestic shocks leaders will be forced to protect when they would otherwise want to maintain the agreement—or, forced to undertake "involuntary defection," as Robert Putnam calls it.[6] Such equilibria to the Prisoners' Dilemma are often supported by the requirement that each player automatically punish the other when cheating is observed, and continue to punish forever or for long periods of time. If their discount value is high enough and punishment is sure and strong enough, then they will resist the temptation to cheat. This set of results has often been used to argue that cooperation in international politics is possible, if not frequent.[7] But such punishment often implies abrogation of the entire agreement.

George Downs and David Rocke show that shorter punishment periods can also support cooperation.[8] They identify domestic political uncertainty as an explanation for "imperfect" treaties, where imperfection is measured relative to the "most cooperative" agreement possible. Using a repeated Prisoners' Dilemma game with trigger strategies, where defections are punished by the other player for a limited number of periods, they argue that domestic political uncertainty leads to agreements with shorter punishment periods and therefore less cooperation. But what if

---

third-country competitor—that affect the lobbying strength of firms at home may simultaneously affect the lobbying strength of firms abroad. Allowing for correlated shocks would not alter our central result; agreements with escape clauses allow countries the option to temporarily exit when political pressure is unexpectedly intense, and when this defection is tolerated by the trading partners in the interests of the system's stability.

5. Uncertainty here concerns the "future state of the world": the configuration of political pressure in future periods is not known with certainty. Uncertainty regarding the preferences of key domestic players is another possibility, one we consider elsewhere in an investigation of the effect of elections on the design of international agreements (Milner and Rosendorff 1997). Alternatively, the agreement itself is too complex (or time is too valuable) for the domestic policymakers to fully understand the consequences of its passage, and policymakers therefore rely on the information provided by lobbies and other interested third parties. Milner and Rosendorff 1996.

6. Putnam 1988.

7. See Axelrod 1984; and Oye 1986.

8. Downs and Rocke 1995.

countries every now and then face intense pressure to cheat yet do not want to spark retaliation and a breakdown in cooperation? Can an alternative institutional structure be devised to maintain a cooperative agreement, even in these periods of high political pressure to protect? In the presence of exogenous shocks, international institutions may be much better served by allowing countries to make temporary, ad hoc use of escape clauses that permit them to break the rules for a short period and pay a cost to do so. There is no retaliation. The defection is tolerated, exactly because the other side may wish to use the same instrument in the future.[9] Cooperation, as we demonstrate, is deeper and more likely, and international trade institutions are more durable, with escape clauses than without them. In the choice between rules and discretion, therefore, rules with costly discretion may be better than no discretion when the future holds unexpected, unpleasant surprises. Our first key result is that greater domestic uncertainty makes the inclusion of escape clauses more likely in international agreements.

Many trade agreements include such escape clauses; indeed, all GATT agreements have at least one type, if not several types, of such escape clauses. Moreover, these alternative escape mechanisms have different costs for their use. In general a country appealing to an escape clause is allowed, under the institution's rules, to protect the affected industry for the duration of that period, as long as it (in effect) voluntarily and publicly incurs some penalty. This voluntary penalty is consistent with the reciprocity norm of GATT, which requires a country that applies a temporary trade barrier to reciprocate by lowering some other barrier elsewhere so that its trading partners are unaffected by the action or to face equivalent trade barriers by its partners.

But this penalty may take any number of forms. For example, countries using GATT's escape clause must negotiate compensation with the affected exporter or face equivalent retaliation from the exporter. For other safeguard measures, the cost is often smaller and less explicit. Sometimes there is a presumption that a country invoking the escape clause will be forced to devise and implement a plan of structural adjustment for the affected industry; such plans have costs, both economic and political. Moreover, the costs of filing an escape clause, antidumping, or countervailing duty complaint are also part of the cost that the import-competing firms must face. For many of these the technical and legal requirements for producing evidence of injury are sufficiently high to merit consideration. In any case each safeguard mechanism entails some costs when it is used, although these costs do differ in important ways.

After invoking the safeguard, in the next period the country returns to the cooperative regime, having preserved its reputation as a cooperator. Moreover, no supranational enforcement agency must force the country to pay this penalty; the

---

9. Very little retaliation for treaty violations is actually observed. Under current WTO rules, any punishment can only come after a finding by the dispute settlement procedure at the WTO, and frequently the dispute is "settled" before punishments are applied. The pre-Uruguay Round rules in fact made findings of allowable retaliation quite rare. Rosendorff 1999.

country (and everyone else) realizes that paying the penalty will preserve its credibility in the future. The institution serves as a verification agency, much as the Law Merchants institution does;[10] it monitors whether defection occurs with a penalty.

Low Costs, Frequent Escape

The cost a state must pay for using the escape clause is of great importance. If the penalty is set at an appropriate level, a country may temporarily use the escape clause and then return to the cooperative path. If the cost is too high, countries will abandon the institution and defect when they experience a severe shock. If the cost is too low, there is repeated recourse to the escape clause, and the agreement enforces little actual cooperation over time. Escape clauses will thus be used more often when their costs of use are lower. This implies that policymakers should attempt to design efficient escape clauses; they should act so that the incentive to exercise relief is balanced with the gains from cooperation. Variations in the costs of different escape clause mechanisms will be an important feature of the rational design of international trade agreements.

The first stage in the model focuses on bargaining over the size of the escape clause penalty. When will countries be able to agree to such escape clauses? In particular, when will they be able to agree to impose a cost on themselves for using the escape clause, and when will this be credible? Furthermore, when will they pick a level of costs so that the optimal degree of cooperation is induced? To address this issue, we model a first stage before the trade barrier setting game is played. In this stage the countries bargain with each other over the penalty they are willing to pay for using an escape clause. One can think of this as bargaining over the nature of the trade agreement itself. Thus making an agreement means agreeing on a value for the penalties that all countries will (voluntarily) pay to use an escape clause. We show that the countries negotiate an optimal penalty, one that balances the need for as much cooperation as possible, while allowing some flexibility in times of domestic political pressure. Such a penalty must not be too high or it will eliminate any flexibility and make the system unstable; but it must also not be too low or it will render "cooperation" ineffective. In effect international institutions that are able to adopt an escape clause should do so in ways that generate more durable and stable cooperative regimes.

The escape clause itself is endogenous to the model: choosing a prohibitive cost for invoking the escape clause is equivalent to ruling it out of the institutional structure. Yet in equilibrium we show that the negotiating parties adopt an escape clause with moderate costs. While such bargaining can have distributional consequences, we study only the symmetric case here where the two countries are identical; nevertheless, our model combines both bargaining and enforcement problems.

---

10. Milgrom, North, and Weingast 1990.

Agreements Are Easier to Conclude

Our model also touches on a point made by James Fearon. He uses a model somewhat like ours, which combines a bargaining game in the first stage and a Prisoners' Dilemma game in the second. He points out that "as the shadow of the future lengthens, both states choose tougher and tougher bargaining strategies on average, implying longer and longer delay till cooperation begins."[11] That is, as the possibility of durable cooperation grows in the second-stage Prisoners' Dilemma, the possibility of stalemate in the first-stage bargaining game rises. Hence, making agreements easier to enforce may make them harder to initially conclude, since the distribution of gains set initially will be so important and fixed throughout the future.

Here, the inclusion of escape clauses may reduce this dynamic. That is, if in future periods players can deviate, pay a penalty, and return to cooperation, this escape clause may mean that their initial distributional bargaining is not so important. The pattern of distributive gains agreed upon today may be altered in the future through the use of the escape clause. Therefore, inclusion of an escape clause may have another benefit: it may make agreements easier to conclude initially! We provide some evidence that certain agreements would not have been politically feasible had they not included escape clauses. This is our third result.

The Model

Consider a world with two countries, home and foreign, that trade a single good. The good is produced by a single firm in each country, and hence there is reciprocal dumping or cross hauling. The profits of the home firm depend therefore on the trade barriers at home, t, which raise the domestic price and are good for profits, and the trade barriers abroad, t*, which reduce exports and induce a fall in the home firm's profits; hence, firm profits are a function of both, that is, $\Pi(t, t^*)$.

Government Objectives

A government's utility depends on the sum of consumer surplus, $CS(t)$, which falls with t, producer surplus or profits, $\Pi(t, t^*)$, which rise with t and fall with t*, and tariff revenues, $tM(t)$, which first rise and then fall with the level of the barriers. Let $\gamma > 0$ denote the weight that a government attaches to the firm's profits. The home government's (one period) utility function then is $W(t, t^*) = CS(t) + \gamma\Pi(t, t^*) + tM(t)$. Similarly, for the foreign government, $W^*(t, t^*) = CS^*(t^*) + g\Pi^*(t^*, t) + t^*M^*(t^*)$, where $g > 0$ is the weight of the foreign firm's profits in its government's utility function.

This objective function is "politically realistic" in Richard Baldwin's sense; that is, governments desire to maximize consumer surplus because it helps them recruit

---

11. Fearon 1998, 282.

votes, but they also value firm profits for the contributions and political support that firms can give them.[12] This utility function is also consistent with the objective function used in Gene M. Grossman and Elhanan Helpman's model of lobbying and campaign contributions.[13] Here, governments are concerned with their reelection and hence have political economy motivations.

In the following sections we use these utility functions to define the payoffs for each outcome that the governments can arrive at in a simple noncooperative trade barrier setting game. These payoffs resemble those of a standard Prisoners' Dilemma: mutual cooperation, which we call the Pareto optimal outcome; mutual defection, or the Nash equilibrium; unilateral defection; and the sucker's payoff. This defines what happens in the second-stage trade game.

Political Uncertainty

Policymakers seeking to maximize their political support choose to adopt trade policies that redistribute revenue among politically salient groups. Here policymakers are balancing the interests of consumers with those of the firms. In each period the political pressure exerted by firms is subject to a shock. Some unanticipated change in the economy or political system allows firms to exert a larger or smaller amount of political pressure. We have deliberately chosen to be vague about the specific nature of this shock—for example, whether it is political or economic. This gives our model greater explanatory breadth. Any exogenous and unexpected change that alters the impact of domestic firms on the demand for protection is relevant. In some periods, firms' political influence will take on a "low" value; in others, however, the pressure applied by the domestic industry is "abnormally" high. The same is true in the other country: its leaders have the same objective function and face the same forms of political pressure. Notice that the firms can be either import competitors or exporters. As defined here, a period of unusually "high" political pressure applied by the firms means a heightened demand by the firms for higher trade barriers at home and lower ones abroad.[14]

In any period, γ and g are stochastic and are independently and identically distributed with distribution Φ: this captures the notion that ex ante policymakers are not fully informed about the degree of political pressure to protect local industry that they might experience in any future period. At home, some unanticipated change in the economy or political system creates a larger or smaller value of γ. The same is true in the other country: its leaders have the same objective function and face the same forms of political pressure. For simplicity, we assume that in the

---

12. Baldwin 1987.
13. Grossman and Helpman 1994.
14. The reader may be tempted to draw a contrast with Milner 1988. There export interests organize in favor of lower domestic tariffs. That is an equilibrium outcome, however, not a statement about preferences. In that model, exporters simply prefer lower tariffs abroad, and adopt, for strategic reasons, political action domestically so that tariff concessions at home can be traded for concessions abroad. A similar dynamic is at work here: firms are willing to trade lower tariffs at home for lower tariffs abroad.

current period each country knows its own state of politics but not the other's, and that both are equally uninformed about the values of γ and g (at home and abroad) in all future periods. That each country has limited knowledge about the domestic politics of the other is central to our argument; furthermore, this uncertainty has a lasting impact because each country faces new shocks in each period that determine the amount of political pressure domestic groups exert. Uncertainty about the state of the world in the other country creates conditions favorable for the use of escape clauses.

While we model the political uncertainty as exogenous (and hence as uncertainty about the state of the world), national preferences are actually an aggregation of the preferences of the domestic groups. Individual preferences per se do not change, but national ones might as the intensity of firms' demands change. Each player thus is uncertain about how influential various domestic groups are likely to be in the future when policymakers choose their trade policies. In the future each government may be easily capturable by the protectionist lobby, or it may be able to stand firm in the face of protectionist pressure. Neither player knows beforehand which of these types the other is likely to be.

Without an Escape Clause: Prisoners' Dilemma Game

Under Political Optimum (Cooperation)

First, we find the pair of trade barriers that maximize the sum of the two governments' utility functions. If γ and g are known, we can define the cooperative solution:

$$(t^P(\gamma, g), t^{*P}(\gamma, g)) = \arg \max_{(t, t^*)} (W(t, t^*) + W^*(t, t^*)).$$

Denote the utility of each of the governments under the political optimum as

$$P(\gamma, g) = W(t^P, t^{*P}) \quad \text{and} \quad P^*(\gamma, g) = W^*(t^P, t^{*P}).$$

Under Nash Equilibrium

Under the Nash equilibrium (NE), each player chooses a level of domestic trade barriers as a best response to the behavior of the opponent. In any period in which γ and g are known we can solve for the Nash equilibrium in trade barriers for that period. Let

$$t(t^*) = \arg \max_t W(t, t^*) \quad \text{and} \quad t^*(t) = \arg \max_{t^*} W^*(t, t^*).$$

Solving these simultaneously leads to the Nash pair of trade barriers (t^N, t^{*N}). Denote home government's utility under the Nash equilibrium as

$$N(\gamma, g) = W(t^N(\gamma, g), t^{*N}(\gamma, g)).$$

Defection

Home's optimal defection (when foreign cooperates) is

$$t^D = \arg \max_t W(t, t^{*P}),$$

and its utility under the optimal defection is

$$D(\gamma, g) = W(t^D(\gamma, g), t^{*P}(\gamma, g)).$$

If instead foreign defects and home cooperates, home receives the sucker's payoff:

$$S(\gamma, g) = W(t^P(\gamma, g), t^{*D}(\gamma, g)).$$

Prisoners' Dilemma

So we have $D(\gamma, g) > P(\gamma, g) > N(\gamma, g) > S(\gamma, g)$, a Prisoners' Dilemma game as represented by the standard 2×2 normal form matrix:

	P*	D*	
P	$P(\gamma, g), P^*(\gamma, g)$	$S(\gamma, g), D^*(\gamma, g)$	(1)
D	$D(\gamma, g), S^*(\gamma, g)$	$N(\gamma, g), N^*(\gamma, g)$	

To simplify the notation, $D(\gamma, g) - P(\gamma, g) \equiv B(\gamma, g)$. Each player is susceptible to political pressure both to protect against foreign imports and to open export markets; in the future both are equally unsure how much pressure each will experience. Hence, home must make its best guess about the value of raising domestic trade barriers (defecting) in any period by taking expectations over g; we denote this best guess by

$$B(\gamma) = \int_g B(\gamma, g) d\Phi.$$

Similarly, both players are completely uninformed about the possible draws of γ and g in any future period. Hence, the values of $P(\gamma, g)$ and $N(\gamma, g)$ are unknown for future periods. Expectations can be formed however; denote

$$P = \int_\gamma \int_g P(\gamma, g) d\Phi d\Phi \quad \text{and} \quad N = \int_\gamma \int_g N(\gamma, g) d\Phi d\Phi.$$

The Prisoners' Dilemma in Matrix (1) is played in the presence of uncertainty; as in the standard Prisoners' Dilemma; however, a cooperative equilibrium in trigger strategies can be supported by a large enough discount rate.

LEMMA 1. A pair of grim trigger strategies (cooperate until a defection is observed, then punish forever) is an equilibrium to the game in Matrix (1) for all

$$\delta > \frac{\max_\gamma B(\gamma)}{P - N + \max_\gamma B(\gamma)}.$$

The (expected) incentive to defect in any period with draw γ is $B(\gamma)$. The largest value that $B(\gamma)$ can take is $\max_\gamma B(\gamma)$. If this maximal incentive to defect is less than the present discounted expected value of future punishments $[\delta/(1 - \delta)] \times (P - N)$, cooperation is possible.

Escape Clause Game

In any period of the Escape Clause game, a player can take the Pareto action, that is, play P as in the Prisoners' Dilemma above; or it can exercise an escape clause EC at cost k; or it can defect D as before. The stage game is now 3 by 3:

	P*	EC*	D*
P	P(γ, g), P*(γ, g)	S(γ, g), D*(γ, g) − k	S(γ, g), D*(γ, g)
EC	D(γ, g) − k, S*(γ, g)	N(γ, g) − k, N*(γ, g) − k	N(γ, g) − k, N*(γ, g)
D	D(γ, g), S*(γ, g)	N(γ, g), N*(γ, g) − k	N(γ, g), N*(γ, g)

Define "cooperation" as the play in any period of P or EC. Define defection as the play of D in any period.

DEFINITION 1. An escape clause strategy (for home) is a strategy in which home plays D if D* has been played in any period in the past, otherwise home plays P if $B(\gamma) < k$, plays EC if $k \le B(\gamma) \le K$, and plays D if $B(\gamma), k > K$ for some K to be defined later.

The extent of the exogenous shock determines the gains to be had from defection in this period; these gains rise with the political pressure that the firms can bring to bear; that is, $B'(\gamma) > 0$. If these gains are small ($B(\gamma) < k$), the government sticks to its Pareto optimal strategy, play P. If the penalty is not too onerous ($k < K$), moderate gains from defection ($k \le B(\gamma) \le K$) cause the government to appeal to the escape clause, EC. If the gains from defection are very large and the escape clause penalty is large, that is, $B(\gamma)$, $k > K$, the government ceases to cooperate entirely. A useful way to summarize the government's strategy is to say that the government cooperates (by playing P or EC) when $\min(B(\gamma), k) \leq K$, and defects otherwise.

The critical value of K is determined as the cost that would make any player of this game exactly indifferent between exercising the escape clause and then returning to the cooperative regime, and defecting and exiting the system forever. It is intuitive, therefore, that if the costs of the escape clause and the gains from defection are large, the government will cease to cooperate entirely.

PROPOSITION 1. *A pair of escape clause strategies is a Nash equilibrium.* All the proofs are in the appendix. Notice that in the standard Prisoners' Dilemma game, Matrix (1), cooperation is sustained only for discount factors that are large enough; that is,

$$\delta > \frac{\max_\gamma B(\gamma)}{P - N + \max_\gamma B(\gamma)}.$$

However, in the escape clause equilibrium here cooperation can be sustained for any value of the discount factor as long as $k \leq K$. Recall that at cost K, any player is indifferent between the escape clause and defection; if δ falls, future cooperation is valued less, and the critical K falls. Hence, the cost of exercising the escape clause must fall as well. So a low discount factor can still produce cooperation. Cooperation now is more flexible in that temporary defection is now possible—unlike in the standard Prisoners' Dilemma, where no defection of any kind was permissible.

One particularly appealing aspect of this equilibrium in the context of institutional design is that the penalty associated with the escape clause is self-enforcing. Any country that wishes to exercise the escape clause in an agreement must visibly penalize itself; no external enforcement agency is required. For a defector to avoid being punished, it must pay the penalty k in a visible way. The international institution is an information provider rather than an enforcer here: it is entrusted as an agent of the contracting states to check that each country that adopts an escape clause pays a penalty and to inform the others of this. Only when penalties are not paid do the states need to punish each other.

COROLLARY 1. *There exists an agreement with an escape clause that Pareto dominates one without it in the presence of political uncertainty.*

In any period in which the escape clause is exercised, there is no "true" cooperation: the escaping player is defecting, and the defection is being tolerated. Hence, the value of the game under an escape clause equilibrium will decrease as the use of the escape clause increases. If the escape clause is used infrequently or not at all, there is more "true" cooperation; however, domestic political uncertainty is likely to lead at some point to a complete breakdown of the regime, and then the punishment phase will be applied forever. This corollary establishes that either there is an escape clause with a level of cost that induces enough cooperation and no breakdown such that the value of the game in an escape clause equilibrium is larger than that of the same game without an escape clause, or the cost of escape is too high and the escape clause equilibrium is the same as the grim-trigger equilibrium of the standard Prisoners' Dilemma. Hence, there is an escape clause cost such that the escape clause equilibrium Pareto dominates (perhaps weakly) the grim-trigger equilibrium of the game without an escape clause.

Notice that the more salient the domestic political uncertainty, or the greater its likely impact on electoral returns, the more likely are political leaders to view an escape clause as an essential element of any agreement.

Uncertainty and Escape Clauses: Implications and Some Evidence

As already noted, most international trade agreements include at least one form of escape clause, and many include several. Our claim is that this prevalence of escape clauses is due to the high levels of domestic uncertainty that surround trade politics. We predict that domestic uncertainty affects the use of escape clauses. Greater domestic uncertainty, or situations where political leaders are more sensitive to unanticipated changes in political pressures, should be associated with more reliance on escape mechanisms. An interesting test of our model would be to identify those political institutions that magnify the effect of unanticipated shocks and see whether countries with these types of institutions are more likely to devise and use escape clauses in their trade relations. Another test would be to deduce which issue-areas are more subject to unanticipated domestic shocks and see if they are more likely to have escape clauses associated with them. Such an exercise, unfortunately, is beyond the scope of this article. However, we can suggest two facts about escape clauses that accord with our theory: certain countries that arguably are more sensitive to domestic pressures are the main proponents and users of escape mechanisms, and certain issue-areas seem more likely to have escape clauses than others due to their greater levels of uncertainty.

Escape clauses in trade policy exist both at the national and the international level. Interestingly, international usage has often copied domestic laws. It is notable that several countries dominate the international use of all forms of escape clauses and that all of these countries have tended to use escape clauses domestically first. The main countries using GATT (now WTO) antidumping, countervailing duty, and safeguard clauses are the same ones that earlier developed a battery of domestic laws to use these trade remedies. By and large, the United States, Canada, the European Union, and Australia are the main users of these clauses.[15] These are the same countries that initially built domestic trade laws around such escape mecha-

---

15. Trebilcock and Howse 1995.

nisms. The first instance of an antidumping law was Canada's 1904 dumping regime.[16] In 1947 the United States instituted the world's first safeguard clause.[17] And the United States and Canada were both the early designers of countervailing duty laws. This suggests that the need for escape clauses may be associated with democracies. It may well be that unanticipated shocks are far more damaging for political leaders in democracies than in nondemocracies. These shocks may be more likely to get them ejected from office as the negatively affected groups mobilize against the incumbents in election periods. If so, this would account for why these types of countries are more likely to have such national escape clause provisions and why they are also more likely to be proponents of these provisions at the international level.

In the realm of safeguard clauses, for example, it is the United States that has the oldest domestic laws and has been the most vocal proponent of them in international trade negotiations. U.S. trade law puts the escape clause into practice through Section 201 of the Trade Act of 1974. Following a petition—from the industry or from government (the president, the U.S. Trade Representative, or Congress, among others)—the U.S. International Trade Commission (ITC) conducts an investigation to evaluate whether imports have threatened to injure or been a substantial cause of injury to the domestic industry. After an affirmative finding by the ITC, the president may grant protection for up to five years, with the possibility of extending it for another three.[18] This practice has been followed closely in GATT, largely at the United States' insistence. Article XIX of GATT permits a member to escape from its obligations not to raise trade barriers when one of its industries is suffering an economic downturn and is experiencing "serious injury."

In the realm of antidumping and countervailing duties the same association is apparent. U.S. and Canadian laws have preceded international ones and set the pattern for them. Article VI of GATT, and the Second Antidumping Code of the Tokyo Round, which define practice in antidumping and countervailing duty law, allows member states to apply duties when imports are sold at "less than fair value," following U.S. practice. Ronald A. Cass and his colleagues describe the U.S. antidumping laws (and those of other countries) as "miniature escape clauses," in that the antidumping code extends protection to smaller cases on which agreement would be impossible ex ante.[19] Similarly, the U.S. countervailing duty code (which is consistent with GATT's Art. VI) allows member states to apply a countervailing duty when a subsidy is being provided to the foreign industry.[20] Other forms of the

16. Ibid., 172.

17. Ibid., 227.

18. Between 1975 and 1990, ninety-two cases under sec. 201 were initiated, of which thirteen industries received relief and seven more received trade adjustment assistance. High profile cases included color televisions in 1982, which received protection on $1,543 million of imports that year, and nonrubber footwear, $2,480 million in 1981. Hufbauer and Rosen 1986.

19. Cass et al. 1997, 24.

20. Between 1994 and 1999 alone, 77 antidumping petitions were filed in the United States. Stern 1997. Worldwide, the antidumping clause has been invoked over two thousand times since 1970.

escape clause appear throughout GATT. Balance-of-payments exceptions (Art. XVIII and XII), infant-industry protection (Art. XVIII), and tariff renegotiation (Art. XXVII) allow temporary escape from a member's obligations under the agreement.

Trade is, of course, an area where governments are likely to face strong domestic pressures for import protection from time to time. When imports surge or when economic conditions facing an industry turn downward, pressures for protection may suddenly appear. Unfortunately, governments may not be able to anticipate perfectly the magnitude of such pressures or their origin. Cass and his colleagues claim that these safeguard mechanisms allow "protectionist sentiment to hold sway" when political pressures are large.[21] Democratic leaders may be especially vulnerable to such unexpected changes, and hence may seek escape clause protection more than leaders in other systems. The greater impact of uncertainty in democratic systems may make their leaders particularly desirous of escape clause mechanisms in trade.

The need for escape clauses may also vary by issue-area. It is widely believed that trade is an area where governments face domestic uncertainty that has significant costs; such international economic exchanges are susceptible to swift changes due to price or supply shocks, technological change, and/or foreign government policy changes. The same is true in the macroeconomic area. Fixed exchange-rate systems may be especially vulnerable to unanticipated domestic pressures to devalue. High uncertainty over the timing and magnitude of these domestic pressures seems likely. Thus we see escape clause measures in many fixed exchange-rate agreements. In the Bretton Woods regime, for example, the simple rule was the requirement to maintain fixed exchange rates. But a country could devalue in the event of "fundamental disequilibrium," a vague phrase allowing escape from the simple rule since even economists were unable to agree on what balance-of-payments equilibrium meant. The regime did not dictate in advance the size of the devaluation. Instead, it required a member state to seek approval from the International Monetary Fund (at least for an exchange-rate realignment of more than 10 percent).

The European Payments Union, the postwar multilateral trade-deficit clearing system, gave signatories the right to suspend liberalization measures in the event of serious economic disturbance or if liberalization was too disruptive.[22] Similarly, Europe's Exchange Rate Mechanism required member states to maintain bilateral exchange rates within clearly demarcated target zones, but did allow for realignments of the parity. While the architects of the mechanism recognized the need for occasional parity realignments, they did not specify exactly when such realignments should take place. Instead, realignments were required to be negotiated among all

21. Cass et al. 1997, 24.
22. Oatley, this volume.

members.[23] In all three cases, escape clause mechanisms were included in the design of these institutions to deal with situations where policymakers face high levels of domestic uncertainty over the pressures that will arise for them to abrogate any international agreement they sign.

Notice that under all three regimes (Bretton Woods, European Payments Union, and Exchange Rate Mechanism), devaluation (the use of an escape clause) was not without cost. Devaluation was permitted only in concert with other measures designed to bring core macroeconomic aggregates back to within "acceptable" levels. Devaluation was therefore frequently associated with fiscal and monetary contraction and policy liberalization and reform, all of which come at a domestic political price.

In some noneconomic issues, uncertainty may be consequential enough so that temporary noncooperation may arise as an equilibrium in isolated cases. James D. Morrow, for instance, argues that prisoners of war treaties are often robust in the face of frequent battlefield violations of the rules of war in an environment where monitoring and acquiring accurate information are very costly.[24] Moreover, similar to our model, violations must be policed by the violators themselves, and punishment (in the case of gross violation) must be publicly implemented for cooperation to be sustained. But in other noneconomic areas, it seems that domestic uncertainty is less pervasive and consequential. In an area like arms control, the public and interest groups tend to be less organized and involved. The most important constituent of these agreements is often the military, which may take part in the negotiations and hence shape them directly. The impact of unexpected changes in this area may be less for political leaders than in areas like trade. Notably, arms control agreements have frequently not included escape clauses. The Antiballistic Missile Treaty, most of the SALT agreements, and the Intermediate-range Nuclear Forces treaties do not contain escape mechanisms; some of these allow countries to withdraw with certain notification provisions, and some have definite time limits, but none seem to contain clauses that allow temporary abrogation of the agreements. This suggests, if our claims are correct, that arms control is an area where domestic uncertainty is less important for leaders. Unexpected shocks that greatly increase pressures for leaders to cheat on the agreement (or pay substantial domestic costs), are less common in this area. Hence, one would not expect states to be as concerned about including escape clauses in these agreements as they are in trade and the monetary area. Where domestic uncertainty is less consequential for leaders, escape clauses will be less important and hence less used. We return to this question later.

The Optimal Penalty: Institutional Design

If the cost of exercising the escape clause is too high, the gains from temporary defection and preserving one's cooperative reputation are more than likely out-

23. Canavan and Rosendorff 1997.
24. Morrow, this volume.

weighed by the penalty associated with the use of the escape clause. In such circumstances, the cost of exercising the escape clause is too high, that is, k > K. Then, in any period where a large shock is experienced, the escape clause option is too expensive, and the system breaks down entirely. As a corollary to Proposition 1 above, the same equilibrium strategies in an environment where k > K lead to an equilibrium path in which P is played until $B(\gamma) > k$, in which case home plays D and the system beaks down. Over time, if the escape clause is too costly, the system breaks down with probability 1 (as long as the discount rate is not too high).

But this raises a question of implementation: when will countries be able to agree to escape clauses that do not lead to the breakdown of all cooperation? In particular, when will they be able to agree to impose a cost on themselves for using the escape clause, and when will this be credible? Furthermore, will they pick the optimal level of costs so that the optimal degree of cooperation is induced? To address this issue we model a first stage before the trade barrier setting game is played. In this stage the countries bargain with each other over the penalty they are willing to pay for invoking an escape clause. One can think of this as bargaining over the nature of the trade agreement itself. Much of the bargaining in trade talks concerns escape clauses and exceptions to the agreement rather than the general amount of liberalization. Thus making an agreement means agreeing on a value for the penalties that all countries will (voluntarily) pay to use an escape clause.

Therefore, we add a pregame negotiation phase over the size of k. We consider the symmetric case where both countries are identical. Each wants to choose a penalty that maximizes the value of playing the game. But the value of the game is the same for both players (they are identical), so they agree merely to the level of k that maximizes the value of the game.

PROPOSITION 2. Let V_C and V_C^* be the present discounted expected value of the escape clause equilibrium for home and foreign, respectively. Then both countries agree on $k^* = \arg \max_k (V_C + V_C^*)$ when $k^* \leq K$; they agree on K otherwise.

Larger distributional questions arise when the assumption of symmetry is relaxed. If one country has a greater capacity to absorb exogenous shocks, or alternatively is immune to capture by political interests, this country would prefer a larger value of k; a country that is easily captured by special interests will instead prefer a smaller k. The outcome of this bargaining among asymmetric countries will have important consequences for the international institutions, but it is a subject that we leave for future consideration.

On the Design of Escape Clauses

We have established that escape clause equilibria exist, and that for the escape clause to be exercised in equilibrium, it cannot be too expensive to adopt. This also points to an important trade-off in the design of international institutions between rigidity and stability. As the system becomes too rigid—or as k rises—it becomes

TABLE 1. The trade-off between rigidity and stability

Size of penalty	Regime stability	Regime rigidity
$k \leq K$	High	Low
$k > K$	Low	High

increasingly unstable (Table 1). At low values of k, the system is stable. For any value of the shocks, either pure cooperation or the escape clause is exercised; there is never any exit from the system and hence the regime is very stable. But this comes at a cost: At low values of k, the escape clause is cheap to adopt, leading to many periods in which defection is being tolerated in exchange for the benefits of long-term stability.

Instead, if the cost of exercising the escape clause is too high, it is never used, and as soon as the shocks become severe, the system breaks down and exit occurs. The regime is now too rigid and becomes unstable. It becomes clear then that the traditional Prisoners' Dilemma game without an escape clause is equivalent to this game with a large k: cooperation will break down at some point.

COROLLARY 2. As the costs of using an escape clause rise, it will be used less frequently.

Costs and Use of Escape Clauses: Some Empirical Implications and Evidence

If we are right that governments rationally design escape clause mechanisms, we should see that variations in their cost lead to variations in their usage. Low-cost escape mechanisms should have much appeal; those with high costs should not. A good deal of evidence seems to suggest that this argument is valid. For instance, in U.S. trade law, the escape clause (Sec. 201) has been used far less often than have various other safeguard mechanisms. Wendy Hansen and Thomas Prusa show that the average number of escape clause cases filed has never gone above eleven a year, whereas for antidumping and countervailing duty cases the average reached a peak of ninety-two a year in the early 1980s.[25] Moreover, escape clause complaints have been decreasing steadily, with less than one a year filed in the early 1990s. In contrast, antidumping and countervailing duty cases have been growing over time. What accounts for this difference in usage?

We argue that it is the greater cost of invoking escape clauses that makes firms less likely to do so. Hanson and Prusa claim that the lower probability of success

---

25. Hansen and Prusa 1995, 299, tab. 1.

encourages firms to file antidumping and countervailing duty complaints instead. But our claim is that the lower probability of success results from the fact that escape clause actions when implemented cost the importing country more and thus make policymakers less likely to accept petitions for them. Thus firms see the mechanism as less successful and choose other means. The main reason they cost more is that exporters have a right to demand compensation for escape clause relief and, if it is not forthcoming, to retaliate. Compensation and retaliation create large domestic costs for governments, and thus they try to avoid such measures.

GATT also provides evidence that greater costs mean less use. Under GATT rules, exporters were entitled to compensation or retaliatory action if Article XIX, which involved the escape clause, was invoked. Moreover, the standards of proof for "serious injury" caused by imports needed to invoke the escape clause have been the highest of all. Among all the various safeguard means in GATT, Article XIX was among the least used. It was invoked only 150 times from 1950 to 1994. And its use has declined over time: 3.9 times a year from 1950 to 1984, and 3.2 times a year from 1985 to 1994. In contrast, the antidumping clause is much more frequently invoked: over two thousand times since 1970 alone.[26]

Moreover, scholars have noted that the costliness of escape clause actions has led to the proliferation of so-called voluntary export restraints. As Jeffrey Schott states,

> Most major trading countries, however, have been deterred from invoking Article XIX less by its requirements than by the availability of less onerous and more flexible channels of protection. These have included coercing trading partners to accept VERs [voluntary export restraints] and other so-called gray area measures, as well as frequent recourse to unilateral relief actions under Article VI (i.e., antidumping and countervailing duties).[27]

Voluntary export restraints are less costly to use than escape clauses because they do not assume compensation or allow retaliation from the affected exporter. But an importing country using them may incur costs. Unlike a tariff or quota, which provides rents for the importing country, a voluntary export restraint transfers those rents to the exporter. As Bernard M. Hoekman and Michael Kostecki maintain,

> Affected exporters tended to accept VERs because they were better than the alternative—often an AD [antidumping] duty—as they allowed them to capture part of the rent that was created. Instead of being confronted with a tariff, the revenue of which is captured by the levying government, a VER involves voluntary cut-backs by exporters in their supplies to a market. This reduction in supply will raise prices—assuming that others do not take up the slack. Exporters therefore get more per unit sold than they would under an equivalent tariff. . . . The key point to remember about VERs is that they imply some direct compensation of affected exporters and selectively target exporters. Thus

---

26. Hoekman and Kostecki 1995.
27. Schott 1994, 94.

they practically meet GATT-1947's compensation requirement, while allowing for circumvention of its nondiscrimination requirement.[28]

Hence, voluntary export restraints were preferred to escape clause actions because they were less expensive to employ, but even they imposed costs on the importing country.[29]

Interestingly, GATT recognized that the costliness of using the escape clause was hurting the system and pushing states to develop other means, such as voluntary export restraints, to deal with domestic pressures. Many GATT officials found other safeguard remedies—such as antidumping, voluntary export restraints, and countervailing duties—very undesirable. They preferred that countries use the escape clause mechanism. But they also realized that this process was too costly and thus underused.

In the Uruguay Round, GATT officials made several changes to reduce the costs of the escape clause relative to other safeguards. First, they banned the use of voluntary export restraints in the agreement on safeguards.[30] This in effect raised the costs of such measures. Second, they decided that it was necessary to reduce the costs of the escape clause option. So they proposed, and countries agreed, that one way to do this was to eliminate the right of retaliation. In the WTO, countries that use the escape clause no longer have to pay compensation and the injured exporters can no longer legally retaliate for the first three years of its use.[31] As Hoekman and Kostecki note, "by the time of the Uruguay round the major objective of 'target' countries was to constrain the use of AD and VERs and assert the dominance of Article XIX in safeguard cases . . . Two options were available: either to tighten the discipline on the use of AD, or to reduce the disincentives to use Article XIX. Both approaches were pursued."[32] Lowering the costs of using the escape clause was therefore seen as a key way to shift countries away from using alternative safeguards like antidumping and countervailing duties, and toward using more escape clause actions. This seems to provide some evidence that leaders do indeed rationally design international agreements.

In the international monetary arena, the costs of exercising relief have varied both across institutions and within institutions over time. Again, one could argue that these variations are the rational responses of political leaders to the problems associated in part with domestic uncertainty. The Bretton Woods system's vagueness about the conditions under which a devaluation could occur meant that it was frequently appealed to, and effective cooperation was limited. The European Payments Union and the Exchange Rate Mechanism both were more specific about

28. Hoekman and Kostecki 1995, 168–69.
29. Similarly, Rosendorff establishes that voluntary export restraints are preferred by policymakers to antidumping duties because they generate higher electoral returns at lower costs when policymakers experience political pressures for protection. Rosendorff 1996.
30. Schott 1994, 94.
31. See Preeg 1995, 100–101; and Schott 1994, 94–97.
32. Hoekman and Kostecki 1995, 169.

the terms of realignments; moreover, the Exchange Rate Mechanism became increasingly more restrictive about the conditions under which escape was possible as the system moved toward monetary union, and accordingly less tolerant of realignments. Consequently, the system became somewhat more rigid and less flexible, leading to more periods of instability and exit, as happened in Britain and Italy in 1992.[33]

Fearon's Dynamic

The escape clause adds flexibility to an agreement that might be difficult to sustain in the presence of uncertainty. Hence, bargainers are not stuck in a commitment to a distributional outcome for the infinite horizon, thereby making initial bargains easier to strike. This result lies in contrast to Fearon's concern that infinite horizon models with large discount factors make agreements difficult to strike.

COROLLARY 3. Agreements should be easier to achieve when escape clauses are included than otherwise.

As many analysts have noted about GATT, signing would have been impossible for many countries had it not included various safeguards. John Gerard Ruggie, for example, has argued that all of the international economic agreements, or regimes, negotiated after World War II had to embody the norms of "embedded liberalism," by which he meant that they had to combine multilateralism with the requirements of domestic stability.[34] Domestic safeguards that allowed countries to protect their economies were thus essential parts of this norm in both the trade and monetary areas. Without such safeguards, countries would never have signed the trade and monetary agreements.

Moreover, Hoekman and Kostecki claim that "political realities often dictate that there be a mechanism allowing for the temporary reimposition of protection in instances where competition from imports proves to be too fierce to allow the restructuring process to be socially sustainable. Indeed, a safeguard mechanism is likely to be a pre-condition for far-reaching liberalization to be politically feasible."[35] Or as Alan Sykes has shown, "when self-interested political officials must decide whether to make trade concessions under conditions of uncertainty about their political consequences, the knowledge that those concessions are in fact 'escapable' facilitates initial trade concessions."[36] Following Kenneth Dam,[37] Sykes maintains that

unanticipated changes in economic conditions may create circumstances in which the political rewards to an increase in protection (or the political costs of

33. Canavan and Rosendorff 1997.
34. Ruggie 1982.
35. Hoekman and Kostecki 1995, 191.
36. Sykes 1991, 259.
37. Dam 1970, 99.

an irrevocable commitment to reduce protection) are great. Consequently, in the absence of an escape clause, trade negotiators may decline to make certain reciprocal concessions for fear of adverse political consequences in the future. But, with an escape clause in place the negotiators will agree on a greater number of reciprocal concessions, knowing that those concessions can be avoided later if political conditions so dictate.[38]

Our point is that the inclusion of escape clauses should make reaching an initial agreement easier.

This argument shares much with the theory of efficient breach used in legal theory. This theory advances the idea that "there are circumstances where breach of contract is more efficient than performance and that the law ought to facilitate breach in such circumstances."[39] In order to do so, there must be mechanisms that can determine and compel payment of the appropriate levels of damages for such breach. Jeffrey L. Dunoff and Joel P. Trachtman also note that "entry into contract may be facilitated by the understanding of parties that breach may be permitted under certain circumstances."[40] They point out that the WTO's safeguard system and its notion of compensation or retaliation provides just such a mechanism for efficient breach.

An alternative flexibility-enhancing device is to build into any agreement the opportunity for regular renegotiation, as in GATT, or the International Coffee Agreement.[41] John E. Richards notes that the International Air Transport Association, an airfare-setting cartel, allowed suspension of current agreements for the one-year period in which renegotiation occurred.[42] In the same way that an escape clause adds the necessary flexibility and does not fix the distributional impact immutably, Barbara Koremenos suggests that allowing for renegotiation and finite duration reduces the distributional impact of the agreement, making bargaining over an initial agreement easier, without reducing the effect of the "shadow of the future" in enforcing the agreement.[43] The escape clause, like the opportunity for renegotiation, reduces the effects of Fearon's dynamic. We do think, however, as does Sykes, that renegotiation of an entire agreement is likely to be the most costly means by far and to have a lower probability of success than will the mere inclusion of escape clauses in the original agreement.[44]

There is a second reason escape clauses may diminish Fearon's dynamic. In our model the countries are in a position similar to John Rawl's "initial position," where one is behind the veil of ignorance and cannot tell exactly how one will benefit (or lose) in the future from agreements made now.[45] Because shocks occur in each

38. Sykes 1991, 279.
39. Dunoff and Trachtman 1999, 24.
40. Ibid., 26.
41. Koremenos, Lipson, and Snidal, this volume.
42. Richards, this volume.
43. Koremenos 1998.
44. Sykes 1991, 280.
45. Rawls 1971.

future period that cannot be predicted beforehand, the players do not know the future distribution of gains and losses from the initial agreement with certainty. Hence this is likely to mitigate how hard they bargain in the first place. For these two reasons in our model, Fearon's argument may not hold: the length of the shadow of the future may play no role in affecting the bitterness of bargaining over the initial agreement. Moreover, including escape clauses may make both enforcement and distributive bargaining easier!

Conclusion

International institutions vary substantially. Their design reflects the rational calculations of, as well as the strategic interaction among, countries creating them. These different designs also have implications for the functioning of these institutions. International institutions matter, but so do their forms.

We have shown that international institutions that include an escape clause can generate more durable and stable cooperative regimes. The escape clause itself is endogenous to the model: choosing a prohibitive cost for using the escape clause is equivalent to ruling it out of the institutional structure. Yet we have shown that in equilibrium the negotiating parties will adopt an escape clause with moderate costs when faced with domestic political uncertainty. Indeed, this particular institutional feature—the escape clause—is determined endogenously as an equilibrium outcome to the strategic game between the countries. Thus our model not only derives the rational form of an institution but also shows the impact of that institution once in place. We think future research should explore this result when more than two players are involved and/or when the countries are assumed to be different, such as Giovanni Maggi does.[46]

We make three claims here. One is that escape clauses are an efficient equilibrium under conditions of domestic political uncertainty. When political leaders cannot foresee the extent of future domestic demands for protection, such clauses provide the flexibility that allows them to accept an international agreement liberalizing trade. One testable proposition is that the greater the domestic uncertainty that political leaders face about their ability to maintain domestic compliance with international agreements, the more likely leaders are to negotiate agreements that contain escape clauses. In issue-areas where governments face less uncertainty about future domestic pressures to comply, they are less likely to design such safeguard measures. This may help account for the differences between international trade agreements, where escape clauses are prevalent, and arms control agreements, where they appear to be less salient. Another testable proposition would involve examining whether certain domestic political institutions that reduce domestic uncertainty reduce the incentives for leaders in these countries to pursue escape clauses. Our model's results thus support Rational Design conjecture F1, FLEXIBILITY

---

46. Maggi 1999.

increases with UNCERTAINTY ABOUT THE STATE OF THE WORLD. Future research to examine the empirical hypotheses we have outlined would lend credence to this conjecture.

Our second claim is that escape clauses are useful and efficient only when they impose some kind of cost for their use; that is, importing countries must pay for invoking them or else they will be invoked all the time, thus vitiating the agreement. Paying the cost signals an intention to comply with the agreement in the future. Hence, another testable proposition is that the different costs of different escape clause measures should affect their use. Less costly measures for the importer should be used more often. We assume that governments understand this dynamic. And we anticipate that the architects of international agreements will rationally design such agreements so that the types of escape clauses they most desire will be neither too cheap (encouraging frequent use) nor too expensive (discouraging their use altogether). Furthermore, since paying the penalty is self-enforcing, we expect that the institution's role will be less that of an enforcer making countries pay this penalty and more that of an information provider telling others that the penalty has been paid. Thus we expect that countries will pay penalties, while looking to international institutions for information on whether others have done the same. The role of international institutions here is to provide a particular kind of information about other states' behavior. Again, this is a testable proposition that might warrant future attention.

Our third claim is that escape clauses make initial agreements easier to reach. Fearon's dynamic breaks down; the flexibility provided by escape clauses ensures that the division of the long-term gains from the agreement is not immutable. This result of our model provides theoretical support for Rational Design conjecture F2, FLEXIBILITY increases with DISTRIBUTION problems. Our argument also shares much with the legal theory of efficient breach, where the inclusion of measures allowing parties to later breach a contract may make initial agreement on a contract more likely. Indeed, we claim that without escape clauses of some sort many international agreements would never be politically viable for political leaders to sign in the first place. And this explains why rational political leaders design flexibility into their international commitments when they are uncertain about the future.

Here we have investigated whether the inclusion of escape clauses in international agreements could be a rational response of political leaders to their domestic problems, especially to unanticipated domestic political pressures. These escape mechanisms help political leaders to maintain international cooperation without sacrificing their domestic political positions; they thus reduce the costly, contradictory pressures that can emanate from domestic and international politics, helping to make international cooperation more compatible with domestic political success. As we have argued elsewhere,[47] such solutions to the two-level game faced by political leaders are essential for successful international cooperation. Rationally designing

---

47. See Milner and Rosendorff 1996; and Milner 1997.

flexibility into international agreements thus is important for political leaders when faced with domestic uncertainty and international distributional problems. The likelihood of and the probability of success of international institutions thus depends on their internal design, as well as other factors.

Appendix

DEFINITION 2. Let $N(\gamma, g) - S(\gamma, g) \equiv A(\gamma, g)$.

DEFINITION 3. Denote

$$I(\gamma) = \int_g I(\gamma, g) d\Phi \quad \text{and} \quad I = \int_\gamma \int_g I(\gamma, g) d\Phi d\Phi$$

for any function $I = A, B, P, D, N, S$.

DEFINITION 4. Let $p = \Pr(P \mid \text{cooperation})$.

That is, p is the probability of playing P given that P or EC is to be played. Consider the current period in which nature has drawn (γ, g). Home knows γ but is unsure of g, and hence is unsure of the behavior of the foreign country. Since the countries are symmetric, we know that foreign plays P* with probability p and plays EC* with probability $1 - p$. If home plays P, then home earns in that period $pP(\gamma) + (1 - p)S(\gamma)$; whereas if home plays EC, home earns $p(D(\gamma) - k) + (1 - p)(N(\gamma) - k)$. Then P is played if $pP(\gamma) + (1 - p)S(\gamma) > pD(\gamma) + (1 - p)N(\gamma) - k$, that is, if $k > pB(\gamma) + (1 - p)A(\gamma)$. Hence, $p = \Pr(k > pB(\gamma) + (1 - p)A(\gamma))$.

LEMMA 2. For any k, the function $\Lambda(p; k) = \Pr(k > pB(\gamma) + (1 - p)A(\gamma))$ has a fixed point, $p = \Lambda(p; k)$.

Proof. For any k, Λ is a continuous function of p mapping from $[0, 1]$ into $[0, 1]$. Now $[0, 1]$ is a compact, convex set. Therefore, a fixed point exists by Brouwer's Fixed Point theorem.

Lemma 2 implies that there exists a distribution function Γ such that $p = \Gamma(k)$.

LEMMA 3. $\Gamma(0) = 0$ and $\lim_{k \to \infty} \Gamma(k) = 1$.

Proof. $\Gamma(0) = \Pr(0 > A(\gamma)) = 0$, since $A(\gamma) > 0$ for all γ; $\lim_{k \to \infty} \Gamma(k) = \lim_{k \to \infty} \Pr(k > pB(\gamma) + (1 - p)A(\gamma)) \to 1$, since $B(\gamma)$, $A(\gamma)$ are finite for all γ and $p \in [0, 1] \forall k$, since p is a distribution function.

PROOF OF PROPOSITION 1. A pair of escape clause strategies is a Nash equilibrium.

The expected current period return from defection at home is $D(\gamma)$, and hence the gains from defection are $D(\gamma) - \max(P(\gamma), D(\gamma) - k) = \min(B(\gamma), k)$. Consider the event that a deviation has been observed in some period. From then on, the one-shot Nash strategies are

The Optimal Design of International Trade Institutions   855

played, yielding the Nash payoff (in expectation, since the draws in the future periods are unknown, forever). That is, the aggregate Nash payoff (starting in the next period) is

$$V_D = \frac{\delta}{1 - \delta} N.$$

What is the forgone cooperative aggregate payoff? If cooperation occurred in the last period, in the next each player has the option of cooperating again or defecting. The value of the game in a cooperative phase is the earnings from the play in that period plus the continuation value, $V = p[p(P + \delta V) + (1 - p)(S + \delta V)] + (1 - p)p(D - k + \delta V) + (1 - p) \times (N - k + \delta V)]$.

Solving we have

$$V = \frac{1}{1 - \delta} (p^2 P + p(1 - p)(S + D) + (1 - p)^2 N - k(1 - p))$$

$$= \frac{1}{1 - \delta} (p^2(A - B) + p(-A + D - N) + N - k(1 - p)).$$

Hence,

$$V - V_D = \frac{1}{1 - \delta} (p^2(A - B) + p(D - N - A + k) + N(1 - \delta) - k).$$

Recall that $p = \Gamma(k)$. The no defect condition in any period is therefore

$$\min(B(\gamma), k) < \frac{1}{1 - \delta} ((\Gamma(k))^2(A - B) + \Gamma(k)(D - N - A + k) + N(1 - \delta) - k).$$

Let

$$Z(k) \equiv \frac{1}{1 - \delta} ((\Gamma(k))^2(A - B) + \Gamma(k)(D - N - A + k) + N(1 - \delta) - k),$$

and define K to be a fixed point of $Z(k)$, that is, $Z(K) = K$. Setting $z(k) = Z(k) - k$, we have

$$z(k) \equiv \frac{1}{1 - \delta} ((\Gamma(k))^2(A - B) + \Gamma(k)(D - N - A + k) + N(1 - \delta) - k(2 - \delta)).$$

Now $z(0) = N > 0$ and as $k \to \infty$, $\Gamma(k) \to 1$, and $z(k) \to -\infty < 0$ from Lemma 2. Then we have a nondegenerate fixed point by the intermediate value theorem. Then K is the upper bound on any penalty in order to invoke EC, and home plays P if $B(\gamma) < k < K$; plays EC if $k \leq B(\gamma) \leq K$; and plays D if both $B(\gamma)$, $k > K$. Hence, a pair of escape clause strategies is an equilibrium.

PROOF OF PROPOSITION 2. Let k* satisfy

$$k^* = \frac{1 - \Gamma(k^*)}{\Gamma'(k^*)} - 2\Gamma(k^*)(A - B) - (D - N - A),$$

then both countries agree on k* when k* ≤ K and agree on K otherwise.

The value of the game to either player in which an escape clause equilibrium is played is

$$V(k) = \frac{1}{1 - \delta} ((\Gamma(k))^2(N - S - D + P) + \Gamma(k)(S + D - 2N + k) + N - k)$$

when k < K. What value of k maximizes this value? We solve k* = arg max$_k$ V(k). The first order condition V'(k*) = 0 yields

$$k^* = \frac{1 - \Gamma(k^*)}{\Gamma'(k^*)} - 2\Gamma(k^*)(N - S - D + P) - (S + D - 2N).$$

Checking the second order condition, note that V"(k*) < 0 iff

$$\Gamma''(k^*) < (1 + (A - B)\Gamma'(k^*)) \frac{-2(\Gamma'(k^*))^2}{1 - \Gamma(k^*)}.$$

A sufficient condition for this to hold is that Γ(·) has an increasing hazard rate, and A − B > 0. Moreover, we know that at k = K, each player is indifferent between exercising the escape clause and defecting permanently. If k* > K, then V(k*) < V(K), implying the optimal choice of penalty is K.

PROOF OF COROLLARY 1. An agreement with an escape clause Pareto dominates one without in the presence of political uncertainty.

This follows from the previous proposition. Any escape clause game with k > K is equivalent to a game without an escape clause. This is because if k > K, the escape clause is never exercised, and at some point defection occurs (unless the discount rates are very high). However, countries optimally choose k ≤ K; hence, an agreement with an escape clause dominates one without.

PROOF OF COROLLARY 2. As the costs of using an escape clause rise, it will be used less frequently.

In any escape equilibrium, the probability that the escape clause is used is 1 − p = 1 − Γ(k). As k rises, 1 − Γ(k) falls, reducing the frequency with which the escape clause is exercised.

PROOF OF COROLLARY 3. Agreements should be easier to achieve when escape clauses are included than otherwise.

With escape clauses, true cooperation occurs as long as k ≤ K; there is no restriction on the discount factor δ. That is, given any discount factor δ, there exists a penalty k ≤ K such that an escape clause equilibrium exists. In the standard Prisoners' Dilemma in the face of uncertainty, cooperation occurs whenever

$$\delta > \frac{\max_\gamma B(\gamma)}{P - N + \max_\gamma B(\gamma)}.$$

Hence, the set of discount factors under which the standard Prisoners' Dilemma under uncertainty can support a cooperative equilibrium is

$$\left[\frac{\max_\gamma B(\gamma)}{P - N + \max_\gamma B(\gamma)}, 1 \right] \subset (0, 1],$$

the set of discount factors under which an escape clause equilibrium exists. Hence, if we were to draw a discount factor at random, we are more likely to be able to support an escape clause equilibrium than a cooperative equilibrium in a game without an escape clause.

References

Axelrod, Robert. 1984. *The Evolution of Cooperation*. New York: Basic Books.

Baldwin, Richard. 1987. Politically Realistic Objective Functions and Trade Policy. *Economics Letters* 24 (3):287–90.

Canavan, Christopher, and B. Peter Rosendorff. 1997. How the EMU Killed the ERM: International Regimes with Temporary Relief Clauses. Unpublished manuscript, University of Southern California, Los Angeles.

Cass, Ronald A., Richard D. Boltuck, Seth T. Kaplan, and Michael Knoll. 1997. Antidumping. USC Law School Working Paper Series, 97–15. Los Angeles: USC Law School.

Dam, Kenneth W. 1970. *The GATT: Law and International Economic Organization*. Chicago: University of Chicago Press.

Downs, George W., and David M. Rocke. 1995. *Optimal Imperfection? Domestic Uncertainty and Institutions in International Relations*. Princeton, NJ.: Princeton University Press.

Dunoff, Jeffrey L., and Joel P. Trachtman. 1999. Economic Analysis of International Law. *Yale Journal of International Law* 24 (1):1–59.

Fearon, James D. 1998. Bargaining, Enforcement, and International Cooperation. *International Organization* 52 (2):269–305.

Grossman, Gene M., and Elhanan Helpman. 1994. Protection for Sale. *American Economic Review* 84 (4):833–50.

Hansen, Wendy L., and Thomas J. Prusa. 1995. The Road Most Taken: The Rise of Title VII Protection. *World Economy* 18 (2):295–313.

Hoekman, Bernard M., and Michel M. Kostecki. 1995. *The Political Economy of the World Trading System from GATT to WTO*. Oxford: Oxford University Press.

Hoekman, Bernard M., and Michael P. Leidy. 1989. Dumping, Antidumping, and Emergency Protection. *Journal of World Trade* 23 (5):27–44.

Hufbauer, Gary Clyde, and Howard F. Rosen. 1986. *Trade Policy for Troubled Industries*. Washington, D.C.: Institute for International Economics.

Koremenos, Barbara. 1998. Constructing International Agreements in the Face of Uncertainty. Unpublished manuscript, UCLA, Los Angeles, Calif.

Maggi, Giovanni. 1999. The Role of Multilateral Institutions in International Trade Cooperation. *American Economic Review* 89 (1):190–214.

Milgrom, Paul R., Douglass C. North, and Barry R. Weingast. 1990. The Role of Institutions in the Revival of Trade: The Law Merchant, Private Judges, and the Champagne Fairs. *Economics and Politics* 2 (1):1–23.

Milner, Helen V. 1988. *Resisting Protectionism: Global Industries and the Politics of International Trade*. Princeton, N.J.: Princeton University Press.

———. 1997. *Interests, Institutions, and Information: Domestic Politics and International Relations*. Princeton, N.J.: Princeton University Press.

Milner, Helen V., and B. Peter Rosendorff. 1996. Trade Negotiations, Information, and Domestic Politics: The Role of Domestic Groups. *Economics and Politics* 8 (2):145–89.

———. 1997. Democratic Politics and International Trade Negotiations: Elections and Divided Government as Constraints on Trade Liberalization. *Journal of Conflict Resolution* 41 (1):117–46.

Oye, Kenneth A., ed. 1986. *Cooperation Under Anarchy*. Princeton, N.J.: Princeton University Press.

Preeg, Ernest H. 1995. *Traders in a Brave New World*. Chicago: University of Chicago Press.

Putnam, Robert D. 1988. Diplomacy and Domestic Politics: The Logic of Two-Level Games. *International Organization* 42 (3):427–60.

Rawls, John. 1971. *A Theory of Justice*. Cambridge, Mass.: Harvard University Press.

Rosendorff, B. Peter. 1996. Voluntary Export Restraints, Antidumping Procedure, and Domestic Politics. *American Economic Review* 86 (3):544–61.

———. 1999. Stability and Rigidity: The Dispute Settlement Procedure of the WTO. Unpublished manuscript, University of Southern California, Los Angeles, Calif.

Ruggie, John Gerard. 1982. International Regimes, Transactions, and Change: Embedded Liberalism in the Postwar Economic Order. *International Organization* 36 (2):379–415.

Schott, Jeffrey J. 1994. *The Uruguay Round: An Assessment*. Washington, D.C.: Institute for International Economics.

Sykes, Alan O. 1991. Protectionism as a "Safeguard." *University of Chicago Law Review* 58 (1):255–305.

Trebilcock, Michael J., and Robert Howse. 1995. *The Regulation of International Trade*. London: Routledge.

[18]

International Studies Quarterly (2001) 45, 487–515.

F02

F53

Treating International Institutions as Social Environments

ALASTAIR IAIN JOHNSTON

Harvard University

Socialization theory is a neglected source of explanations for cooperation in international relations. Neorealism treats socialization (or selection, more properly) as a process by which autistic non-balancers are weeded out of the anarchical international system. Contractual institutionalists ignore or downplay the possibilities of socialization in international institutions in part because of the difficulties in observing changes in interests and preferences. For constructivists socialization is a central concept. But to date it has been undertheorized, or more precisely, the microprocesses of socialization have been generally left unexamined. This article focuses on two basic microprocesses in socialization theory—persuasion and social influence—and develops propositions about the social conditions under which one might expect to observe cooperation in institutions. Socialization theories pose questions for both the structural-functional foundations of contractual institutionalist hypotheses about institutional design and cooperation, and notions of optimal group size for collective action.

It is fair to say that for most international relations theorists there are two main ways in which involvement in international institutions changes state behavior in more cooperative directions. The first is through material rewards and punishments: in pursuit of a (mostly) constant set of interests or preferences a state responds to positive and negative sanctions provided exogenously by the institution (rules, membership requirements, etc.) or by certain actors within the institution. The second is through changes in the domestic distributions of power among social groups pursuing (mostly) a constant set of interests or preferences such that different distributions lead to different aggregated state preferences.

Few would deny that these are plausible, observable, and probably quite frequent ways in which policies change direction after a state enters an international institution. But constructivists would expand this list, and ask if and how involvement in international institutions changes state behavior in the absence of these two conditions, and in the presence of conditions that are unique to social groups *qua* social groups, namely, socialization processes. How would one know if socialization processes were critical in producing cooperative behavior? Why it is important for IR theory to figure out an answer to this question?

Author's note: I am grateful for comments and criticisms from Marc Busch, Jeff Checkel, Martha Finnemore, Peter Katzenstein, Jeff Legro, Lisa Martin, Celeste Wallander, participants in Harvard's Ethics and International Relations Seminar, the research seminar at Stanford's Center for International Security and Cooperation, the Security Studies seminar at the Massachusetts Institute of Technology, the International Relations colloquium at the University of Virginia, and several anonymous reviewers.

This article starts from a very simple (and unoriginal) premise: actors who enter into a social interaction rarely emerge the same. For mainstream international relations theories this is both an uncontroversial statement and a rather radical one. It is uncontroversial because mainstream IR accepts that social interaction can change behavior through the imposition of exogenous constraints created by this interaction. Thus, for instance, neorealists claim that the imperatives of maximizing security in an anarchical environment tend to compel most states most of the time to balance against rising power. Contractual institutionalists also accept that social interaction inside institutions can change behavior (strategies) in cooperative directions by altering cost-benefit analyses as different institutional rules act on fixed preferences.

It is a radical statement for IR theory if one claims that the behavior of actors changes because of endogenous change in the normative characteristics and identities of the actors. Put differently, change in the behavior of the participants in a social interaction may have little to do with exogenous constraints on the individual and the group and a lot to do with socialization (Wendt, 1994:384). This is, essentially, the claim made by those involved in the "sociological turn" in IR theory. The implications for IR theory should not be underestimated: the claim focuses attention both on how cooperative norms are created under anarchy (something contractual institutionalism has little to say about) *and*, logically, therefore, why conflictual norms are not epiphenomena of anarchy (something that realist theories cannot fathom). Understanding how socialization works is central to testing the claim, put forward so succinctly by Wendt, that "anarchy is what states make of it." But constructivists, as Checkel (1998) has pointed out, have not been very successful in explaining the microprocesses about how precisely actors are exposed to, receive, process, and then act upon the normative arguments that predominate in particular social environments, such as international institutions.

Given its potential to provide new insights into the production of cooperative and conflictual norms in IR, it is important that those who work with the concept are crystal clear in explicating the microprocesses of socialization and then in systematically testing for their effects. For this reason, this article focuses on three interrelated themes: why socialization approaches may offer different insights into the conditions for cooperation in IR; why, in order to offer such insights, socialization approaches have to be much more precise about at least two different social microprocesses at the heart of conformity to norms; and why, empirically, explaining cooperation inside international institutions is an important test for the validity of socialization approaches. To these ends the article begins with a review of the status of socialization in IR theory, paying particular attention to the differences between contractual institutionalist and sociological approaches to explaining cooperation in institutions. It then defines socialization and disaggregates its microprocesses. Finally it offers some theoretical and methodological reasons why international institutions are useful places to look for evidence of how precisely socialization works.

Socialization in International Relations Theory

Socialization is quite a vibrant area of inquiry in a range of social sciences. It is a core concept in studies in linguistics and the acquisition of language (Schieffelin and Ochs, 1986), sociology and social psychology and theories of in-group identity formation and compliance with group norms (Turner, 1987; Napier and Gershenfeld, 1987; Cialdini, 1987; Nisbett and Cohen, 1996), political science and the acquisition of basic political orientations among young people or explanations of social movements (Beck and Jennings, 1991), international law and the role of shaming and social opprobrium in eliciting treaty compliance (Chayes and Chayes, 1996; Young, 1992; Susskind, 1994; Moravcsik, 1995), and anthropology and the diffusion of cultural practices, among other fields and topics. It ought to be a vibrant area in world politics as well since socialization would seem to be central to some of the major topics in international relations theory today: the formation and change of preferences;[1] national identity formation; the creation, diffusion of, and compliance with international norms; and the effects of international institutions, for example.

It is curious, though, how undertheorized socialization is in much of IR, despite the fact that most noncoercive diplomatic influence attempts by most actors most of the time are aimed at "changing the minds" of others, of persuading, cajoling, or shaming them to accept, and hopefully internalize, new facts, figures, arguments, norms, and causal understandings about particular issues. The goal of diplomacy is often the socialization of others to accept in an axiomatic way novel understandings about world politics.[2]

Yet predominant IR theories either ignore the possibility of socialization or are unprepared or unwilling to theorize about it. Classical realism (and neoclassical realism) seems torn between its impulse to essentialize the drive for power in a self-help world on the one hand and its sensitivity to historical contingency on the other. Morgenthau, for example, left open the possibility that definitions of power and interest are culturally contingent, implying at least that there is variation in how actors are socialized to conceptualize legitimate ways of pursuing legitimate interests (Morgenthau, 1978:9). But by accepting the contingency of power and interests Morgenthau would logically have had to accept that the realpolitik impulses that characterize world politics are in fact not given, but learned, and that there can be, potentially, vast disjuncture between actors' estimates of this world and the "real" world of material power distribution and realpolitik pursuits of interest. If this disjuncture can exist, then, in principle, the "real world" has less independent, predictable effects on actor behavior. As such the "realities" of anarchy, relative material power imbalances, and so forth are no longer so determinative. Yet for classical (and neoclassical) realism there is no obvious theory of socialization to explain variations across time and space in interpreting the meaning of power and interest.

Neorealism uses socialization to describe the homogenization of self-help balancing behavior among security-seeking states interacting under conditions of anarchy (Waltz, 1979:127–128). However, the neorealist process of homogenization is not really socialization in common-sense usage. Rather it is a process of selection and competition: states that do not emulate the self-help balancing behavior of the most successful actors in the system will be selected out of the system such that those remaining (assuming there are no new entrants) will tend to share realpolitik behavioral traits.[3]

Yet it is not obvious that this kind of selection even occurs. The death rates of states have declined dramatically in the twentieth century. Unsuccessful actors—those that eschew self-help and that do not balance internally or externally—simply do not disappear anymore. New states have emerged in the latter half of the twentieth century in an era when failed or unsuccessful states are not routinely eliminated. These new states retain heterogeneous traits and characteristics, supported by institutions and rules (e.g., norms against aggression, arms

---

[1] This is particularly relevant when trying to explain how new states, "novices," decide on the content and institutional structure of their foreign policies, not an unimportant topic when looking at the effects of decolonization or the collapse of the Soviet empire.

[2] As Nadelmann remarks in the context of prohibition regimes, "The compulsion to convert others to one's own beliefs and to remake the world in one's own image has long played an important role in international politics—witness the proselytizing efforts of states on behalf of religious faiths or secular faiths such as communism, fascism, capitalism, and democracy" (1990:481).

[3] For a sophisticated discussion of the neorealist concept of emulation see Resende-Santos, 1996.

control agreements, a concept of sovereignty that "equalizes" unequal actors, among others) somewhat analogous to those that support socially weak and "failed" individuals in many domestic societies.[4] The characteristics of the system structure are thus more varied and complex than the simple tending-toward-balances anarchy of a neorealist world. In such an environment it should not be surprising if "socialization" leads to less homogenization in state characteristics and behavior than neorealism expects.

Contractual institutionalism generally does not focus on socialization processes in international relations per se. The notion that social interaction can change preferences and interests or fundamental security philosophies and ideologies is not a central concern. This is odd. Given the prominence of coordination games and focal points in institutionalist theorizing about social norms, habits, customs, and conventions that constrain rationally optimizing behavior, one might expect more curiosity about the social and historical origins of focal points, for instance.[5] Instead, modeling usually assumes that preferences are fixed for any particular actor. Social interaction inside institutions is assumed to have little or no effect on the "identities" or "interests" of actors, or at least institutionalists are divided as to whether there are any effects.[6] The quality or quantity of prior social interaction among players should be irrelevant to the calculus of whether or not to defect (Frank, 1988:143). For example, being enmeshed in an iterated but potentially finite prisoners' dilemma does not make the D,C payoff less desirable, in principle. All it does is change the costs and benefits of pursuing these preferences.

The undersocialized nature of institutions in contractual institutionalist arguments is highlighted by the factors that contractualists *do* focus on when theorizing how cooperation is elicited inside institutions. The first is issue-linkage where (per)suasion is simply an effort to change the cost/benefit calculations of the defecting player with exogenous positive or negative incentives so as to secure cooperation. It does not change that player's underlying desire to defect.[7] The second is reputation. The desire to establish a trustworthy reputation for future exchanges can be an incentive to engage in norm-conforming, pro-social behavior (Kreps, 1992). Reputation in this sense is an instrument; the rewards come from the private material benefits of future exchange, not the social or social-psychological benefits accrued by cultivating a status and image that is rewarded by the group. The final factor—perhaps the most important one for contractualists—is information. Interaction in institutions can provide new information that can reduce uncertainty about the credibility of others' commitments, and thus help actors' expectations converge around some cooperative outcome (Martin, 1997). Information only affects beliefs about the strategic environment in which the actor is pursuing fixed preferences. If information has an effect on preferences it is mainly through its impact on elite change: information about the failure of some strategy, for instance, could lead to a loss of support

---

[4] History matters here. Many of these norms and practices that protect the survival of "unfit" states evolved in the twentieth century out of movements for self-determination and the diffusion of the principle of sovereign equality into the postcolonial world. My thinking here has been informed by Brenner's helpful discussion of the distinction between evolutionary algorithms and learning processes in explaining social evolution (1998).

[5] Morrow admits that the conspicuousness or prominence of an equilibrium outcome in a coordination game that turns it into a focal point can be a function of socialization in a shared "culture" (Morrow, 1994:96).

[6] I am grateful to Celeste Wallander for pointing out to me some of the divisions over institutions and preferences in the contractualist camp. Wallander allows for variation in interests but argues that institutions do not cause this variation (see Wallander, 1999). Other contractualists claim to the contrary that interests can be changed through involvement in institutions, mainly via complex learning. Explicating this learning process ought to be high on the institutionalist research agenda (see Keohane, 1984:132). But it is not clear what the causal mechanisms would be, nor whether the process would be endogenous to the institution itself or a function of shifting domestic coalitions.

[7] See Martin's discussion of suasion games (1993:104).

for one set of elites pursuing preferences and their replacement by another set with different preferences.

There is sort of an infinite regress problem with much of the work on information, however. What makes the meaning of information conclusive enough to affect behavior unless there is prior agreement on the criteria for the credibility of information? What leads to prior agreement on these criteria? Presumably information about the validity of these criteria that all actors find credible. What leads to this kind of agreement on the credibility of the criteria about credibility? Information about the credibility of the credibility of the credibility of these criteria, and so on. At any stage one could simply state, unproblematically, that actors received credible information about a phenomenon and leave it at that for the purposes of modeling interaction from that point on. But this does not escape the problem that at any given point the criteria for establishing the credibility of new information often *is* problematic.

Instead, contractualists often assume that the credibility of information rests on costliness to the provider of the information. In practice they see costliness mostly in terms of some loss of material welfare or political power. No doubt costs often take this form, but contractualists have no theoretical advantage here, no theory of the conditions under which new information will influence preferences, beliefs, or strategies and by how much.[8] They often leave out the social context of information. The social origins of common definitions of costliness, essential for information to be credible, are unexamined. Yet empirically we know that the same information, even economic information, will be interpreted differently depending on whether it comes from "people like us" (the information is more authoritative and persuasive), or from a devalued "other" (Kuklinski and Hurley, 1996:127; Halpern, 1997; Valley, Moag, and Bazerman, 1998:230). Even in prisoners' dilemma (PD) relationships, information about the other as an opportunist is not static. Hayward Alker (1996) reports on iterated PD games where after a string of mostly cooperative moves the players reinterpret the meaning of identical information. Defections that were interpreted as signals of the other's malevolent or stupid nature before the cooperation streak were interpreted as situational or chalked up to random misperceptions afterward. Thus social context is an important variable in *how well* information reduces uncertainty in a transaction, and in which direction this uncertainty is reduced (e.g., clarifying the other as a friend or adversary).

To be fair, contractualist arguments do not *a priori* reject the possibility that information changes preferences instead of just beliefs about strategic environments. The advice is sometimes to test for both, but in practice the tendency is to discount the possibility of the former. This is primarily because preferences and changes in them are difficult to observe. What often may appear to be a change in preferences may, instead, be a change in strategies. Any likely source to which one might turn to "observe" preferences (e.g., from statements through to actions) could well be itself a product of strategic interaction, hence unrepresentative of true preferences. It is easier, therefore, to assume fixed preferences.[9]

This seems to be a reasonable, cautionary argument for a sound methodological choice. It does reveal, however, an implicit disciplining move that constrains

---

[8] I just want to underscore that what constructivists focus on are changes in fairly fundamental beliefs, not relatively shallow, transient, or low-level attitudes about the efficacy of certain political choices and strategies. The difference is not always obvious, but new information as it pertains to socialization (e.g., persuasion) is interesting precisely because it encourages basic reevaluations of collective "thought styles" (Farkas, 1998:43) that can include preferences or strategies, as long as these strategies pertain to basic methods for achieving basic goals (e.g., multilateralism vs. unilateralism as a "cause" of security). This aligns constructivist work somewhat with more traditional work in political socialization that focuses on fundamental ideological dispositions (e.g., Beck and Jennings, 1991; Kinder and Sears, 1981; and Kinder and Sanders, 1996).

[9] See Frieden, 1999, for a sophisticated statement of this argument.

efforts to think about changing preferences through new information acquired via social interaction inside an institution. Contractualists, I believe, overestimate the ease with which one can deduce preferences from some *a priori* features of an actor. It is often not logically obvious what the preferences of actors ought to be from observing their position in society, or their organizational constitution as actors. This is especially likely when the arena of action is not economics but security, politics, ideology, and culture where utilities and their metrics can vary dramatically. Thus, for instance, the preferences of military organizations (e.g., that they favor offensive doctrines and capabilities) cannot be pristinely deduced from some prior assumptions about the universal characteristics of military organizations (Kier, 1997).

And contractualists overestimate the difficulty of observing preferences and changes in them. To be sure, the validity and reliability of measures for accessing the preferences of actors are problematic since the only way to observe is to look at some phenomenon external to their cognition (e.g., a speech act, a gesture, a decision that might itself be strategic). But given the theoretical importance of the question it seems premature to give up trying to observe change (see Herrmann, 1988:180). Moreover, there are quite well-developed social and psychological survey and content analysis techniques that have been used for years in fields that take socialization seriously, including political socialization studies, and that do wrestle with validity and reliability questions. But most students of IR are not exposed to these technologies during their training.

For social constructivists, socialization is a central concept. As Onuf puts it, "social relations *make* or *construct* people—*ourselves*—into the kinds of beings we are" (1998:59). In their accounts of the creation and diffusion of international norms constructivists mostly focus on the "logics of appropriateness"—pro-norm behavior that is so deeply internalized as to be unquestioned, taken for granted.[10] This naturally raises questions about which norms are internalized by agents, how and to what degree. Kratochwil and Ruggie (1986) imply that by treating institutions as social institutions "around which actor expectations converge" the interesting question becomes the processes by which this intersubjective convergence takes place. So some process of socialization must be going on.

Yet for much of the constructivist literature, socialization processes are unclear. There are a number of reasons for this. First, some constructivism inherits much of the epistemology of sociological institutionalism. A fair amount of empirical work in this regard has tended to focus on macrohistorical diffusion of values and practices (such as rationalism, bureaucracy, and market economics), measured by correlations between the presence of a global norm and the presence of corresponding local practices (Price, 1998; Eyre and Suchman, 1996; Finnemore, 1996b). It tends to assume that agents at the systemic level have relatively unobstructed access to states and substate actors from which to diffuse new normative understandings. Once actors are interacting inside institutions, the diffusion and homogenization of values in the "world polity" seems virtually automatic, even, and predictable. This leaves variation in the degree of socialization across units— the degree of contestation, normative "retardation," the processes by which unit-level actors understand, process, interpret and act upon lessons that are "taught" by international institutions as agents—unexplained.[11] And it leaves the causal

---

[10] I use the term *pro-norm* to indicate action that is consistent with the norm in question, whether done because the norm has been internalized or because some kind of consequentialist calculation makes it useful to follow. I do not mean that an actor is necessarily consciously "for" the norm.

[11] Even Finnemore's detailed causal story of teaching often stops at the point where agents at the international level deliver norm-based lessons to rather passive students (1996b). In their discussion of the cognitive and social processes behind the evolution of security communities Adler and Barnett (1998) do not have much to say about resistance to such processes either. This characteristic of the literature is, perhaps, the natural result of a desire to show first of all that persuasion and socialization "matter."

processes unexplicated.[12] This neglect in the literature is surprising, given constructivists' focus on reflective action by multiple agents: if this kind of agency exists in the diffusion of norms, what happens when it runs into reflective action by multiple agents at the receiving end of these "teaching" efforts?[13]

Second, when constructivists do begin to look at these microprocesses of socialization and the constitutive effects of social interaction, the focus is almost exclusively on persuasion. Here, however, there is a fair amount of variation in how the term is used. For some the term is something akin to the noncoercive communication of new normative understandings that are internalized by actors such that new courses of action are viewed as entirely reasonable and appropriate. Here they often borrow in some form or another from Habermas's theory of communicative action (Risse, 1997; Risse and Sikkink, 1999:13; Black, 1999:102–103). The argument is that social interaction is not all strategic bargaining. Rather prior to strategic bargaining actors have to arrive at "common knowledge"; that is, they must first come to share basic assumptions about the deep structure of their interaction: who are legitimate players and what is a legitimate value to be bargained over? Even more important, this agreement needs to be narrow enough so that a vast range of potential equilibria that could arise in their strategic interaction becomes off-limits, beyond the pale. In other words, for them to even interact strategically they need to establish focal points that are so deeply accepted as to be stable (Johnson, 1993:81). Thus, right from the start, bargaining involves argument and deliberation in an effort to change the minds of others.[14] As Hasenclever et al. put it, "the parties enter a discourse where they try first to bring about agreement concerning the relevant features of a social situation and then advance reasons why a certain behavior has to be avoided. These reasons—as far as they are *convincing*—internally motivate the parties to behave in accordance with the previously elaborated interpretation and the justified expectations of others" (Hasenclever, Mayer, and Rittberger, 1997:176–177, emphasis mine; see also Knoke, 1994:3; James, 1998:7).

For others, persuasion can mean both something akin to communicative action *and* something more normatively coercive, entailing shaming or opprobrium. Here compliance with a norm need not be a function of internalization but is, rather, a function of state elites' aversion to public criticism (Risse and Sikkink, 1999:13–14; Keck and Sikkink, 1998:16).

There are a couple of issues here. First, it is not obvious why, from the perspective of actually doing empirical research on socialization in IR, one should focus on Habermas to the neglect of a very rich research tradition on persuasion in communications theory, social psychology, and political socialization. Habermasian approaches are unclear as to what constitutes a "convincing" argument. This is a huge requirement for argumentation and thus far constructivists have not really shown how debates over common knowledge, for example, "convince"

---

[12] See, e.g., Meyer et al., 1997, and Haas, 1998:26. Haas posits that "interpersonal persuasion, communication, exchange and reflection"—socialization—occurs in thick institutional environments where epistemic communities are active, but there is no discussion of microprocesses of persuasion nor conditions under which variation in the effectiveness of persuasion—hence the completeness of socialization—might be observed. Nadelmann identifies normative persuasion as a central process by which prohibition regimes emerge, for instance, anti-slavery norms in British diplomacy, but it is unclear why political leaders and government officials were persuaded by moral arguments (1990:494). Keck and Sikkink (1998) go a long way in looking at the microprocesses by which transnational activist networks "persuade," but international institutions as social environments per se are not the focus of their research. Adler (1998:133) also notes that the OSCE has an explicit mission to socialize members by trying to persuade them that they are, or ought to be, like "us"—liberal, cooperative, and sharing in a European identity. But it isn't clear why this persuasion ought to work on initial members who are somewhat illiberal and noncooperative. This neglect of microprocesses may change as scholars pick up on Finnemore and Sikkink's insightful summary of some plausible causal processes (1998).

[13] For similar critiques see Checkel, 1998:332, 335; Moravcsik, 1997:539; and Risse, 1997:2.

[14] For an excellent exegesis of Habermas's theory of communicative action see Risse, 2000.

actors to agree to a "mutually arrived at interpretation" of social facts. Under what social or material conditions is "communicative action" more likely to be successful?[15] How would one know? The conditions seem to be quite demanding, involving a high degree of prior trust, empathy, honesty, and power equality. Some constructivists seem to rely on an identity argument here; that is, persuasion is more likely to occur when two actors trust one another such that each accepts the "veracity of an enormous range of evidence, concepts and conclusions drawn by others" (Williams, 1997:291). Put simply, identification leads to positive affect and positive affect leads to a greater probability that the arguments and interpretations of the other will be accepted as valid, and internalized. There is an endogeneity issue here, though nothing that complex adaptive systems epistemology would worry about. And the empirics have yet to be tested in much detail.

There is also a second, more important issue. While it is understandable why constructivists would want to focus on persuasion—this is their trump card in disputes with neorealists and contractualists over whether social interaction can change actor preferences and interests in pro-social ways, and it is the purest type of socialization—often the term is conflated with an entirely separate effect of social interaction that can also lead to pro-norm behavior in the absence of exogenous material threats or promises.[16] This effect has been termed *social influence*. This term encompasses a number of subprocesses—backpatting, opprobrium or shaming, social liking, status maximization, etc.—where pro-norm behavior is rewarded with social and psychological markers from a reference group with which the actor believes it shares some level of identification. A focus on communicative action and/or the conflation of persuasion and social influence means that constructivists have a hard time distinguishing among the range of microprocesses that mediate between "teaching" attempts on the one hand and pro-norm behavior emanating from a foreign policy process on the other. This means they have a hard time explicating systematically the institutional conditions under which one or the other of these microprocesses might be at work. In the next section I focus on how one might distinguish between these microprocesses.

Socialization: Definitions and Microprocesses

There is general agreement across the social sciences that socialization is a process by which social interaction leads novices to endorse "expected ways of thinking, feeling, and acting." In Stryker and Statham's words, "Socialization is the generic term used to refer to the processes by which the newcomer—the infant, rookie, or trainee, for example—becomes incorporated into organized patterns of interaction" (1985:325). Berger and Luckmann define the term as "the comprehensive and consistent induction of an individual into the objective world of a society or sector of it" (1966:130). Thus socialization is aimed at creating membership in a society where the intersubjective understandings of the society become taken for granted.

Political scientists have not wandered far from these basic themes in their definitions of socialization. Ichilov refers to political socialization as "the universal processes of induction into any type of regime." These processes focus on "how citizenship orientations emerge" (1990:1). Siegal refers to political social-

---

[15] See the conditions explicated by James (1998:7–11, 15–17)

[16] Keck and Sikkink, for instance, refer to human rights networks being able to embarrass norm violators such that in order to save face they adjust their behavior (1998:24). But it is not clear why a norm violator would care about pressure that does not come with concrete threats of sanctions that affect wealth and relative military power. In one of their cases, for example, Argentina under military control in the 1970s, the differential effects of image per se and a desire to "restore the flow of military and economic aid" are not obvious (107).

ization as the "process by which people learn to adopt the norms, values, attitudes and behaviors accepted and practiced by the ongoing system" (cited in Freedman and Freedman, 1981:258). IR theorists have generally simplified socialization to processes "resulting in the internalization of norms so that they assume their 'taken for granted' nature" (Risse, 1997:16; see also Ikenberry and Kupchan, 1990:289–290).

There are a couple of common themes in the political science literature on socialization: the first is that socialization is most evidently directed at, or experienced by, novices and newcomers, whether they are children, inductees into a military, immigrants, or new states and their rulers. The second is the internalization of the values, roles, and understandings held by a group that constitutes the society of which the actor becomes a member. Internalization implies, further, that these values, roles, and understandings take on "taken-for-grantedness" such that they are not only hard to change, but that the benefits of behavior are calculated in abstract social terms rather than concrete consequential terms. Why should one do X? "Because . . . ," or "because X is the right thing to do . . . ," or "because X is consistent with my social category or identity."

One should assume, however, that there can be degrees of internalization, given that not all actors are always exposed to exactly the same configuration of social pressures, nor do they enter into a social interaction with exactly the same prior identifications. Thus, while pro-social behavior because of its "appropriateness" may be the ideal, at the opposite end of the spectrum should be pro-social behavior because of its material consequences (positive and negative). At this point, pro-social behavior cannot be attributed to internalization or socialization in pro-social norms of the group.

But if internalization of pro-social values is the hallmark of socialization, and if the other end of the spectrum is behavior motivated by the calculation of material costs and benefits, this leaves a vast amount of pro-social behavior produced by neither process.

This leads to a key point. The focus on internalization tends to lead constructivists to focus on persuasion. This is, as noted, what really distinguishes them from neorealists and contractual institutionalists. But beyond persuasion, the literature on socialization (outside of IR theory) identifies a range of reasons why one might see pro-norm behavior in the absence of exogenous material (dis)incentives. Axelrod, for instance, lists identification (the degree to which an actor identifies with the group), authority (the degree to which "the norm and its sponsor are seen as legitimate"), social proof (essentially mimicking of a valued in-group's behavior), and voluntary membership (where defection from group norms carries costs in self-esteem) as critical mechanisms for reinforcing pro-norm behavior (1997a:58–59). All of these depend on the acquisition of some kind of identification with or affective attachment to a group. Ikenberry and Kupchan list two routes to pro-norm behavior that do not involve persuasion: exogenous shocks that lead to elite transformation in a state; and exogenous material inducements that lead, over time (and somewhat mysteriously) to the internalization of norms that were once adopted for instrumental reasons (1990:290–292). Beck and Jennings refer to three possible, somewhat overlapping, socialization processes whereby adolescents acquire the political orientations of their parents: parents provide social identities that bring with them political interests; power and affect relationships establish certain communication patterns in the family such that parents influence political personalities of younger members; or the political traits of parents are transmitted through a process of inheritance or mimicking (1991:744). Constructivism has tended to neglect many of these microprocesses.

Arguably these multiple processes boil down to two: persuasion and social influence. A critical question, then, is when and to what degree do these separate processes help explain why actors change their behavior in pro-norm or pro-social ways. In practice these processes are likely to be interactive. But separating them out is important because the answer will help point to how durable pro-social conformity is over time and what kinds of institutional designs are most conducive to this durability. Since one should expect variation in the durability of norms depending on the type of socialization microprocess, it does matter, then, whether one can observe internalization or not. Holding preferences constant for the purpose of modeling prevents one from exploring this important issue. Thus, broadly speaking, the speed, uniformity, and effectiveness of norm diffusion in international relations ought to depend a great deal on what kind of institutional social environment leads to what kind of socialization microprocess.

Persuasion

Persuasion has to do with cognition and the active assessment of the content of a particular message. As a microprocess of socialization, it involves changing minds, opinions, and attitudes about causality and affect (identity) in the absence of overtly material or mental coercion. It can lead to common knowledge, or "epistemic conventions" (that may or may not be cooperative), or it can lead to a homogenization of interests. That is, actors can be persuaded that they are indeed in competition with each other, or that they share many cooperative interests. The point is, however, that the gap or distance between actors' basic causal and affective understandings closes as a result of successful persuasion.

Persuasion is a prevalent tool in interpersonal relations. Social psychologists have shown, for instance, that in relationships with another, people tend to rank changing the other's opinions very high in a list of influence strategies, regardless of whether the other is considered a friend or an enemy (Rule and Bisanz, 1987:192). Some political scientists have called persuasion the "core" of politics, the "central aim of political interaction" (Mutz, Sniderman, and Brody, 1996:1). In Gibson's view, politics is all about persuasion: "Real politics involves arguments; it involves people drawing a conclusion, being exposed to countervailing ideas, changing views, drawing new conclusions" (1998:821). Communications theorists have argued that all social interaction involves communications that alter people's "perceptions, attitudes, beliefs and motivations" (Berger, 1995:1).

How persuasion works therefore is a focus of a great deal of research in communications theory, social psychology, and sociology. There is no obvious way of summarizing such a disparate and complex literature,[17] but essentially there are three ways in which an actor is persuaded. First, s/he can engage in a high intensity process of cognition, reflection, and argument about the content of new information. The actor weighs evidence, puzzles through "counterattitudinal" arguments, and comes to conclusions different from those he/she began with; that is, the "merits" of the argument are persuasive, *given* internalized standards for evaluating truth claims. Arguments are more persuasive and more likely to affect behavior when they are considered systematically and, thus, linked to other attitudes and schema in a complex network of causal connections and cognitive cues (Wu and Shaffer, 1987:687; Petty, Wegener, and Fibrigar, 1997:616; Zimbardo and Leippe, 1991:192–197).

This process of cognition, linking one set of attitudes to another, is more likely to occur when the environment cues and allows for the actor to consider these connections. That is, it is less likely to be spontaneous than it is promoted. As Gibson has shown with political intolerance among Russian voters, intolerant

---

[17] See Zimbardo and Leippe, 1991:127–167. Despite the volume of this literature, "To date there is precious little evidence specifying who can be talked out of what beliefs, and under what conditions" (Berger, 1995:8).

attitudes toward political opponents will change in more tolerant directions if counterattitudinal arguments are presented to respondents in ways that compel them to "think harder" about the implications of their initial attitudes. Thinking harder simply means people are cued, and have the time, to connect the implications of their initial attitude to outcomes that might affect their interests based on different sets of attitudes. Thus an initially intolerant view might change to a more tolerant one if the respondent is cued to think about the implications of cycles of intolerance for political stability or for opportunities for themselves to present their own political opinions in the face of opposition (Gibson, 1998:826–831). The probability of some change in attitudes through cognition increases in an iterated, cognition-rich environment where there is lots of new information that cues linkages to other attitudes and interests.

Second, the actor is persuaded because of her/his affect relationship to the persuader: here the persuadee looks for cues about the nature of this relationship to judge the legitimacy of counterattitudinal arguments. Thus information from in-groups is more convincing than that from out-groups. Information from culturally recognized authorities (e.g., scientists, doctors, religious leaders) is more convincing than that from less authoritative sources. This will be especially true for novices who have little information about an issue on which to rely for guidance (Zimbardo and Leippe, 1991:70; Gibson, 1998:821). Information from sources that are "liked" is more convincing than that from sources that are disliked. Liking will increase with more exposure, contact, and familiarity. The desire for social proofing means that information accepted through consensus or supermajority in a valued group will be more convincing than if the group were divided about how to interpret the message (Petty et al., 1997:612, 617, 623, 627, 629; Kuklinski and Hurley, 1996:129–131; Napier and Gershenfeld, 1987:159; Isen, 1987:206–210, 211; Axsom, Yates, and Chaiken, 1987:30–31).[18]

Third, the persuasiveness of a message may be a function of characteristics of the persuadee her/himself. This can refer to a range of variables from the cognitive-processing abilities of individuals in a group, to the strength of existing attitudes (usually these are stronger if developed through personal experience than if based on hearsay or indirect experience, for example), to what appears to be a deeply internalized desire to avoid appearing inconsistent, to the degree of independence an agent might have in relation to a principal. Thus, for example, an attitude associated with an explicit behavioral commitment made earlier will be more resistant to change later because actors experience discomfort at being viewed as hypocritical and inconsistent. Conversely, a new set of attitudes will be more persuasive if associated with a new, high-profile behavioral commitment (Cialdini, 1984; Wu and Shaffer, 1987:677). Thus a focus on the characteristics of the persuadee means looking at the individual features that can either retard or propel persuasion. All this means is that actors entering a social interaction bring with them particular prior traits that, interacting with the features of the social environment and other actors, leads to variation in the degree of attitudinal change.[19]

---

[18] Using different language, Habermasian constructivists make a similar point: "trust in the authenticity of a speaker is a precondition for the persuasiveness of a moral argument" (Risse, 1997:16; see also Williams, 1997:291–292). Game theorists have come to a similar conclusion, only using another language. Lupia notes that persuasiveness rests basically on the persuadee's belief that she or he shares common interests with the persuader and that the information the persuader is offering benefits both (1998). He does not specify what kind of information leads to the first belief. But it could, in principle, be anything from the list in the above paragraph.

[19] Of course, persuasion in practice is likely to be a combination of all these microprocesses. Jorgensen et al. found in a study of televised political debates in Denmark, for example, that the most persuasive debaters were those who used a small number of extended, weighty discussions of specific qualitative examples. The use of these specific, straightforward and logical examples seemed to accentuate the authoritativeness of the debater and were easier for viewers to assess and adjudicate (see Jorgensen, Kock, and Rorbech, 1998).

Lupia and McCubbins argue that all of these conditions and characteristics are simply indicators of more basic conditions for persuasion, namely, that the persuadee believes the persuader to be knowledgeable about an issue and that his or her intentions are trustworthy. The more certain the persuadee is about these beliefs, the more likely the persuader will be persuasive. Both these characteristics can be a function either of familiarity and extensive interaction that, over time, reveals them, *or* "external forces" that make it difficult or costly for the persuader to hide knowledge (or lack thereof) and trustworthiness (e.g., mechanisms for revealing knowledge, penalties for lying, costly actions that reveal the position of the persuader). Any other factors, such as ideology, identity, culture, and so forth, are only predictors of persuasion to the extent that they reveal information to the persuadee about the persuader's knowledge and trustworthiness (1998).

Lupia and McCubbins present a rigorous formal model of persuasion that is probably correct in stripping the process down to these two pieces of perceived information. But this does not avoid the more interesting question about the empirical frequency with which *social* variables such as perceived ideology, identity, and/or cultural values are in fact the primary cues that people use to determine the degree of knowledge and trustworthiness of a persuader, and thus come prior to beliefs about knowledge and trustworthiness. On average is perceived shared identity between persuadee and persuader more likely to be used by the persuadee as an authoritative measure of a persuader's knowledge and trustworthiness than other kinds of cues?

The answer has important implications for how social interactions lead to socialization and how different institutional designs might lead to different socialization paths. Lupia and McCubbins tend to focus, as befits their interest in signaling games, on the role of external forces in clarifying beliefs about the knowledge and trustworthiness of persuaders. They argue that since social and political environments are rarely ones where persuader and persuadee interact face to face over long periods of time, the familiarity/personal interaction route to beliefs about the persuader's knowledge and trustworthiness tends to be less common. This may be true at the national level of persuasion (e.g., political messages from politicians aimed at masses of voters), but it is not necessarily true at the level of social interaction in international institutions among diplomats, specialists, and analysts. Here the first route—familiarity, iterated face-to-face social interaction—may be more common, hence affect based on identity, culture, and ideology may be more critical for persuasion than external forces and costly signals. Institutions, therefore, that are weak in terms of these external forces, nonetheless may create conditions conducive to persuasion—and convergence around group norms—even though there are few material incentives for the persuader to deceive and few material costs for the persuadee to defect from the group. I will come back to this at the end.

Persuasion in the end is a combination of all three processes above and it is hard to run controls that might isolate the effects of any one process. People are more likely to think hard and favorably about a proposition, for instance, when it comes from a high affect source, in part because affect helps kick in resistances to information from other sources (Mohr, 1996:81–82). On the other hand, one can identify ideal combinations that could, in principle, be tested. Given an effort by a persuader to provide information with a view to changing basic principled, causal, or factual understandings, there are certain kinds of social environments that ought to be especially conducive to persuasion. These conditions imply that certain institutional designs will be more effective for persuasion than others. These conditions occur

- when the actor is highly cognitively motivated to analyze counterattitudinal information (e.g., a very novel environment);

- when the persuader is a highly authoritative member of an small, intimate, high-affect in-group to which the persuadee also belongs or wants to belong;
- when the actor has few prior, ingrained attitudes that are inconsistent with the counterattitudinal message, say, when the actor is a novice or an inductee in a new social environment, or when perceived threat from counterattitudinal groups is low;
- when the agent is relatively autonomous from the principal (e.g., when the issue is highly technical requiring a high degree of agent expertise, or when the issue is ignored by the principal); and
- when the actor is exposed to counterattitudinal information repeatedly over time.

In practice, as I will come to in a moment, these conditions are more likely to hold in some kinds of institutions than in other kinds.

Assuming an actor enters the institution and its particular social environment with preferences and beliefs that are at odds with those of the group, if persuasion is at work one should expect to see (after exposure to this environment) the actor's convergence with these preferences and beliefs, and conformist behavior later in the interaction with the group that would not have been expected earlier on. In short, you should get increasing "comfort" levels with group values and normative practices even as the demands placed on the actor by the group for pro-social behavior increasingly violate the initial preferences and beliefs of the actor.

Social Influence

Social influence refers to a class of microprocesses that elicit pro-norm behavior through the distribution of social rewards and punishments. Rewards might include psychological well-being, status, a sense of belonging, and a sense of well-being derived from conformity with role expectations. Punishments might include shaming, shunning, exclusion, and demeaning, or dissonance derived from actions inconsistent with role and identity. The effect of (successful) social influence is an actor's conformity with the position advocated by a group as a result of "real or imagined group pressure" (Nemeth, 1987:237). The difference between social influence processes and persuasion is neatly summarized by the phrase Festinger used to describe compliance due to social pressure: "public conformity without private acceptance" (cited in Booster, 1995:96). Persuasion would entail public conformity with private acceptances. Persuasion, at least of the kind where the authoritativeness of the persuader is what convinces, has been called "mediated informational influence" (e.g., "I thought the answer was X . . . but everybody else said Y, so it really must be Y"). Social influence can, instead, come in the form of "mediated normative influence" (e.g., "I believe the answer is X, but others said Y, and I don't want to rock the boat, so I'll say Y" [cited in Betz, Skowronski, and Ostrom, 1996:116]). The rewards and punishments are social because only groups can provide them, and only groups whose approval an actor values will have this influence. Thus social influence rests on the "influenced" actor having prior identification with a relevant reference group. Social influence involves connecting extant interests, attitudes, and beliefs in one "attitude system" to those in some other attitude system (e.g., attitudes toward cooperation get connected to seemingly separate attitudes toward social standing, status, and self-esteem in ways that had not previously occurred to the actor [Zimbardo and Leippe, 1991:34]).

There is considerable evidence that identification with a group can generate a range of cognitive and social pressures to conform. But, like persuasion, the microprocesses of social influence are multiple, complex, and still the subject of much debate. Generally, however, the literature on social influence has isolated a number of possibilities:

- cognitive discomfort associated with perceived divergence from group norms generates strong internal pressures to conform to the group's practice, that is, the trauma to self-esteem from this divergence can motivate an actor to reduce discrepancies through greater conformity;[20]
- the sense of comfort that comes from interacting with others with whom she/he is perceived to share traits (social liking) leads to an increased willingness to comply with the requests of friends (Cialdini, 1984, 1987); and
- the discomfort with being perceived as inconsistent or hypocritical in relation to past actions and commitments, and conversely the positive moods with being viewed as consistent with one's self-professed identity, leads people whose consistency is challenged to respond by greater conformist behavior (consistency theory). Membership in a group usually entails "on the record" statements or behaviors of commitment (e.g., pledges of loyalty, participation in group activities, commitments to fulfill a membership requirement). These behaviors, even if relatively minor, establish a baseline identity such that behavior that diverges from these identity markers are discomforting inconsistencies. The more the identity-conforming behavior is repeated, the more extreme, and tenaciously held, the actor beliefs and attitudes become, thus reinforcing his/her commitment to the group (Petty et al., 1997:612, 620; see also Cialdini, 1984, 1987).

The most important microprocess of social influence, or at least most relevant to international relations theory given the prevalence of status language in interstate discourse, is the desire to maximize status, honor, prestige—diffuse reputation or image—and the desire to avoid a loss of status, shaming, or humiliation and other social sanctions. Status refers to "an individual's standing in the hierarchy of a group based on criteria such as prestige, honor, and deference." Typically, status is closely related to others' "expectations of ability or competent performance" (Lovaglia, 1995:402). Choi offers a useful definition: "An individual's status is communal certification of his or her relative proficiency in conventions" (1993:113). Thus, competency or proficiency need not mean a mechanical ability to do some task, but can mean a high ability to represent some normative ideal. A competent nonproliferator is, in the eyes of an antiproliferation community, a responsible actor and a consistent, effective proponent of nonproliferation norms. Image is the public manifestation of status. Image refers to the package of perceptions and impressions one believes one creates through status-consistent behavior.

There are numerous motivations behind maximizing status. Often status brings with it power, wealth, and deference, and vice versa. Gilpin, for instance, refers to prestige as "a reputation for power." States are at the top of the status hierarchy because of their economic and military power (1981:30–33). Moreover, in Gilpin's view, status is highly coercive: status markers are forced out of subordinate states through superior power, often through military victory. This is fine as far as it goes, but often status markers and immediate material gains are not correlated. For example, status markers such as citations, medals, or public recognition may have no obvious material reward. Moreover, the desire to maximize status need not entail efforts to defeat others to seize status: it can entail group-conforming behavior designed to "buy" status. The reward is psychological well-being from backpatting; the punishment is psychological anxiety from opprobrium.

---

[20] On SIT and the psychological discomforts of nonconformity see Turner, 1987; Gerard and Orive, 1987; Stryker and Statham, 1985; Barnum, 1997; Axelrod, 1997a.

A second possible motivation is to maximize reputational effects attributed to particular status markers. Here status is an instrument: a good image can encourage actors to deal with you in other arenas, can help build trust leading to reciprocity and decentralized (uninstitutionalized) cooperation (Kreps, 1992). In this sense, image can also be used deceptively—one might want a positive image to convince other states to cooperate, setting them up for the sucker's payoff in some exploitative prisoners' dilemma game. There are two problems with this conceptualization, however. The first is, as Frank points out, if people know about this instrumentality, then an actor's image or reputation as a cooperator has no advantage (1988). So it is in the actor's interest to make cooperation automatic, deeply socialized, in order to make the reputation for cooperation credible. But then no advantages can be accrued, since deception is abandoned. The second problem is that instrumentality assumes the actor is seeking some concrete, calculable benefit from having a good image, an image that can be translated into leverage in some explicit, linked, immediate issue area. Yet often there are no obvious concrete benefits, or they are quite diffuse and vague. Indeed, sometimes there are concrete material costs. In this case, sensitivity to image may be related to identity.

This is the third reason for a concern about status. A particular high status image may be considered a good in and of itself. Frank argues that the desire to maximize prestige and status has physiological and psychological benefits (1985:32). Harre attributes the drive to people's "deep sense of their own dignity, and a craving for recognition as beings of worth in the opinions of other of their kind." To be fulfilled, this desire necessarily depends on *public* affirmation of one's status (1979:3, 22). Hatch notes that "the underlying motivation is to achieve a sense of personal accomplishment or fulfillment, and the individual does so by engaging in activities exhibiting qualities that are defined by the society as meritorious" (1989:349). Franck argues, in reference of the fact that most states abide by most institutional legal commitments most of the time in IR, conformist behavior is due mainly to a desire to be a member of a club and to benefit from the status of membership (1990:38).

An actor will be sensitive to arguments that her/his behavior is consistent or inconsistent with their self-identity as a high-status actor. This sensitivity ought to depend as well on who is making these arguments. The more the audience or reference group is legitimate, that is, the more it consists of actors whose opinions matter, the greater the effect of backpatting and opprobrium (Dittmer and Kim, 1993:9, 14–15). The legitimacy of the audience is a function of self-identification. Actors more easily dismiss the criticisms of enemies and adversaries than they do of friends and allies. If, for example, an actor completely rejected the social norms of a particular group, then no matter what the size of that group it could not generate backpatting or shaming effects. Thus the strength of backpatting and opprobrium depends on two related factors: the nature of the actor's self-categorization, and which other actors, by virtue of this self-identification, become important, legitimate observers of behavior. Changes in identities mean that different audiences matter differently.

All of this hinges, of course, on an intersubjectively agreed upon notion of what socially valuable behavior looks like. I would argue, then, that the production of positive and negative social sanctions sufficient to induce cooperation in the absence of material side-payments or threats rests on two tiers. First, there must be an intersubjective normative consensus about what "good" behavior looks like.[21] Without this shared standard, then the "fact" of some particular action will have no agreed interpretation, and consequently it will have no

---

[21] Franck makes a similar point about symbolic validation of participation in international institutions (1990:117).

meaning, generating no shaming or backpatting effects. Thus, while social influence is not as direct or pristine an example of socialization (persuasion leading to changes in preferences), it could be considered a secondary socialization process because it requires at least some prior change to an actor's understanding of the group's normative preferences.

Second, even if there is a shared interpretation of the meaning of a particular behavior, these actions will not generate social pressures if they are unobserved and private. Thus the second layer is a forum or institution that makes acting a particular way public and observable. The forum could be something as loose as a process where voluntary reporting on some agreed commitment is scrutinized, where defectors would stand out by either not submitting a report or by submitting shoddy and incomplete ones. Or it could be something as strict as a multilateral negotiation process where actors are required to state bargaining positions, justify them, and then "vote" in some form on the proposed solution.

Thus constructivists and institutionalists are both right. Constructivists are right that socially induced cooperation requires shared understandings of what appropriate behavior looks like. But this may not be enough without an institutional structure that provides information about the degree to which actors are behaving in ways consistent with this shared understanding.[22] This information makes the distance between an actor's behavior and the socially approved standard public. It is this distance that generates backpatting and shaming effects. In principle, the larger the relevant audience of cooperators, the more powerful these effects are.

The converse of social backpatting is shaming or opprobrium derived from violating status-related norms and practices. It is widely accepted in a number of subfields that fear of opprobrium is a motivation for group conformity, even if suboptimal from a welfare perspective. As Oran Young remarks *a propos* of international institutions, "Policy makers, like private individuals, are sensitive to the social opprobrium that accompanies violations of widely accepted behavioral prescriptions. They are, in short, motivated by a desire to avoid the sense of shame or social disgrace that commonly befalls those who break widely accepted rules" (1992:176–177; see also DiMaggio and Powell, 1991:4). The specific microprocesses that compel people to avoid opprobrium are similar to those that encourage the accumulation of backpatting.

It is important to note that pro-social behavior motivated by status maximization is not altruistic or pro-group per se. Rather it reflects an actor's egoistic pursuit of social rewards and avoidance of social sanctions (Batson, 1987:65). But these rewards and sanctions cannot exist without the prior existence of a group and without a common understanding of the value or meaning that the group places on putative status markers. This much, at least, must be shared by the actor and the group.

If these are the reasons why actors might be sensitive to backpatting/opprobrium markers, how might this sensitivity affect the decision calculus of an actor who would prefer an outcome where she/he defects while others cooperate? Here we need to look at the effects of these social rewards and punishments on this actor's calculation of the costs and benefits of cooperation.

Assume, for the moment, that the actor in question has internalized a traditionally realpolitik concern about shielding relative power (military and economic) from potentially constraining commitments to international regimes. One can model the actor's diplomacy using a simple N-person's prisoners' dilemma model (Figure 1). The C line represents the payoffs to the actor who cooperates

---

[22] Keohane notes, for instance, that one of the things international institutions do is provide a forum in which an actor's conformity with group standards can be evaluated. He links this to a more instrumental notion of reputation than I do here, however (1984:94)

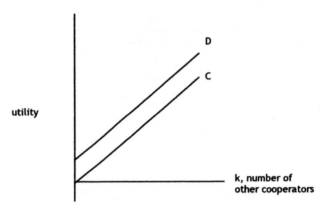

FIG. 1. Free-riding.

when exactly k other players cooperates, in the sense of limiting their military activities. The D line represents the payoffs to the actor from defection when exactly k other players cooperates, in the sense of limiting their military activities. If the realpolitik actor were the only cooperator (e.g., if it were the only one trying to reduce some global security "bad" while others continued to maximize their relative power) it would be constraining its relative power while having little effect on stabilizing the security environment. If it did not cooperate while others also defected, then, although it could not derive any benefits from the cooperation of others, it would be better off than if it unilaterally cooperated. Thus it would pay not to cooperate even if there were no other cooperators. This payoff from defection would hold even as the number of cooperators increased. As these players contributed to a public good the actor would benefit from the provision of this good, but by free-riding it would not incur the cost of providing its share of the good. Thus the payoff line from defection will always be greater than the payoff line from cooperation.

However, if this actor is also sensitive to social rewards and punishments, then social interaction can induce caution in the pursuit of a defection strategy that might have an adverse effect on status. Within international organizations and institutions the participating/cooperating audience can be relatively large. While the opportunities to free-ride are potentially greater—given the number of potential cooperators—the scrutiny of each player is more intense and state behavior is often more transparent than in bilateral relations, due to the rules of these institutions. In this context, a concern about image has two very different effects on a realpolitik actor's payoff structure, corresponding to the effects of backpatting and opprobrium.

Backpatting is a benefit incurred from being seen as a cooperator or an active pro-social member of a group. An actor receives recognition, praise, and normative support for its involvement in the process. Backpatting can reaffirm an actor's self-valuation, its self-categorization as a high-status actor, with concomitant payoffs for self- and public legitimation. *Ceteris paribus*, as the size of the cooperating audience grows, the actor accrues more backpatting benefits. Thus for every additional member of the institution, a potential defector receives a certain added payoff from backpatting as long as it cooperates. The benefits are cumulative. As Figure 2 indicates this increases the slope of the payoffs from cooperation (from C to C').

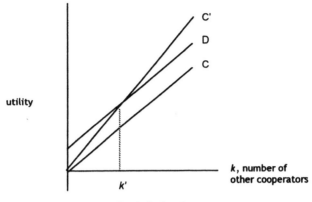

FIG. 2. Backpatting.

Opprobrium, of course, carries social costs—a denial of the prior status and prestige of the actor—as well as psychological ones—a denial of the actor's identity as one deserving of backpatting. Opprobrium can also be modeled as an accumulation of shaming markers that diminishes the value of free-riding as the number of participants/cooperators in a regime increases. A certain social cost is incurred with each additional participant/observer in the reference group. As the group increases the criticisms accumulate, and this increases the costs of defection. The effect, as shown in Figure 3, is to depress the slope of the payoffs from defection (from D to D'). At a certain point, an increase in the slope of the payoffs from cooperation and/or a decrease in the slope of the payoffs from defection may create a crossover point in the two lines. This is the point where the size of the audience (k') is such that the backpatting benefits and opprobrium costs change the cost-benefit analysis. It is at this point that it begins to pay to cooperate as the size of the audience increases.

When backpatting benefits and (implicit or threatened) opprobrium costs are combined this can dramatically reduce the size of the audience needed to make it pay to cooperate (this is shown by k'' in Figure 4).

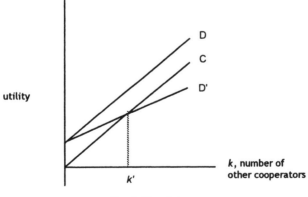

FIG. 3. Opprobrium.

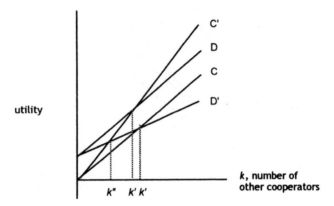

FIG. 4. Backpatting and opprobrium.

Note that the *net* effects of social influence on the cost-benefit calculus of cooperation in an institution appear to be similar to the provision of material side-payments and sanctions. It is important to point out, however, that backpatting and shaming change this cost-benefit calculus in a very different way than side-payment or sanctions. Typically (though not always) side-payments or sanctions, whether provided by the institution or by a key player or players in the institution, have a constant effect on an actor's utility regardless of how many others backpat or shame. Put graphically (Figure 5), the effect of the side-payments and sanctions is to raise the entire C payoff line and/or depress the entire D payoff line, respectively, while not changing their slopes, such that C′ payoff line ends up above the D payoff line, or D′ payoff line ends up below the C payoff line. A sanction for defection (imposed by an enforcer or hegemon, for instance) is equally costly regardless of the size of the group cooperating. Coop-

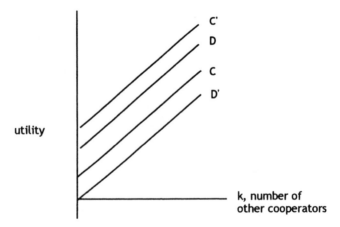

FIG. 5. The effects of material side-payments and sanctions.

eration brings higher utility than defection regardless of what other members of the group do. Thus the audience size and its legitimacy are irrelevant.

Put differently, cooperation as a result of material side-payments or sanctions is not a social effect of the institution. Cooperation due to social influence, however, is a social effect *only*, and would not exist without interaction with a group. Therefore backpatting and opprobrium are uniquely social inducements to cooperation, requiring a forum for social interaction in which the behavior of the potential free-rider is judged. Backpatting and opprobrium lose their impact outside of a social group. The fact that this forum is legitimately designed to promote cooperation accentuates the legitimacy and weight of the social back-patting and opprobrium directed at potential defectors. These forms of social influence would not carry any weight if unilaterally directed by one actor at another in a bilateral, institutionless relationship.

But how would one know if social influence had led to pro-social/pro-normative behavior in international institutions? Controlling for effects on relative power and the presence or absence of material side-payments and punishments, if social influence is at work, one should expect to see the following effects:

- commitments to participate and join power-constraining institutions should take place in the absence of material side-payments or threats of sanctions;
- arguments for joining or participating should stress backpatting and image benefits, diffuse reputation benefits, and opprobrium costs; and
- initial bargaining positions, if stuck to, will put the state in distinct minority, isolating it from the cooperating audience or reference group. Thus, commitments to pro-social behavior will only be made when it is clear that noncommitment will be highly isolating.

Empirical Issues

We need to know at least three things in order to test for the presence and effects of socialization. First, what are the characteristics of the social environment in which agents are interacting at time *t?* If this environment has agentlike "teaching" properties, what are the norms and associated behaviors that actors in the environment are supposed to adopt and, hopefully, internalize? In other words, what is the predominant ideology in the social environment? Second, what are the characteristics of individual agents involved in the social environment at time *t?* How do these characteristics retard or propel the socialization process? Third, how do these agents then interact with this environment at time *t* + 1? What are the policy processes through which newly socialized agents act upon the broader social environment?

The net effect of socialization, therefore, will be a function of the characteristics of the environment interacting with the characteristics of the agent in an ongoing tight, mutually constitutive or feedback relationship and mediated by a policy process. One way of testing for socialization in IR, then, is to use international institutions on the one hand and individuals and small groups involved in state policy processes on the other as, respectively, the social environment and individual agents of interest. My reasoning is as follows:

For the most part, when IR specialists or sociological institutionalists look for the effects of socialization the unit of analysis has tended to be the state (or state elites in a fairly aggregated way) (Eyre and Suchman, 1996; Meyer et al., 1997; Finnemore, 1996a, 1996b; Waltz, 1979). This presents obvious problems when examining particular institutions as social environments since states as unitary actors do not participate in institutions; rather, state agents do (e.g., diplomats, decision-makers, analysts, policy specialists, and nongovernmental agents of state principals). Moreover, treating the unitary state as actor presents problems when applying the socialization literature found in social psychology, sociology, communications theory, and even in political socialization theory. For most of this literature the unit of analysis is the individual or small group.

A constructivist ontology allows (even demands) that the unit of socialization be the individual or small group. As Cederman points out, constructivism's ontology can best be captured by the notion of complex adaptive systems whereby social structures and agent characteristics are mutually constitutive, or locked in tight feedback loops, where small perturbations in the characteristics of agents interacting with each other can have large, nonlinear effects on social structures (1997; see also Axelrod, 1997b, 1997c; Hamman, 1998).[23] Thus it matters how individual agents or small groups are socialized because their impacts on larger emergent properties of the social environment can be quite dramatic.[24] This focus on individuals and small groups also enables constructivists to deal with the legitimate critique from proponents of choice-theoretic approaches that what is observed as the normatively motivated behavior of a group at one level may be the aggregation of the strategic behavior of many subactors at a lower level (Lake and Powell, 1999).

Thus, there are good reasons for studies of socialization to "go micro" and focus on the socialization of individuals, small groups, and, in turn, the effects of these agents on the foreign policy processes of states.[25]

But why choose international institutions as the "agentlike" environments for socialization? After all, state actors experience a myriad of socializing environments from bilateral interactions at the state level, to intra-bureaucratic environments at the policy level, to training and work environments inside bureaucratic organizations themselves.

There are a couple of reasons to focus on institutions. The most obvious is that because sociological approaches offer a clear alternative to contractual approaches to explaining cooperation, it makes sense to focus on the forum or arena on which contractualism itself focuses—institutions under anarchy.

But another powerful, though less obvious, reason is that in the late twentieth and early twenty-first century, international institutions are likely to be the one arena of inter-state activity where the effects of "anarchy" are likely to be checked. Even contractualists make this claim. They argue, of course, that institutions are a rational response to the interest in cooperation when anarchy makes such cooperation difficult to enforce. The argument is that anarchy—institutionless—will make it too dangerous for states to explore cooperation. This claim is rooted in neorealistic logic even though, unlike neorealism, it assumes institutional effects are not necessarily epiphenomena of power distributions.

Constructivists, on the other hand, will have to argue that one of the important checks on anarchy is actor socialization in non-realpolitik directions. To do this, they have to also argue that realpolitik behavior is a product of socialization in realpolitik ideology. Put differently, one of the critical claims constructivists make is that "anarchy is what states make of it." In other words, material power structures do not determine state interests or practices, and thus realpolitik practice by unitary rational actors is not an immutable "fact" of international

---

[23] For research tractability, however, it makes sense to look at separate parts of these feedback loops, as I suggest here, separating out the institutional "teaching" from the "individual socialization" from the impact on state policy from the impact on institutional ideologies, each process endogenized and exogenized at different stages.

[24] This is, after all, the point of much of the work on how transnational networks affect state behavior (Keck and Sikkink, 1998; Evangelista, 1999), "teaching" and the diffusion of norms, and the creation of national interests (Finnemore, 1996b). The roots of this complex adaptive systems approach, as it relates to normative structures in IR, go back to Durkheim's work on the creation and re-creation of "social facts" through the interaction of individual normative agents (see also Ruggie, 1998:29).

[25] Ruggie calls this a focus on "innovative micro-practices," a hallmark of constructivist research (1998:27).

politics. In order to make this case, constructivists and their fellow-travelers have, for the most part, underscored the empirical "deviations" from realist or material power-interests theories: altruistic foreign aid; weapons taboos; "autistic" force postures in developing states; "autistic" military doctrines; and limits on the conduct of war (Lumsdaine, 1993; Price and Tannenwald, 1996; Eyre and Suchman, 1996; Kier, 1997; Legro, 1995; Finnemore, 1996c). These have been important cases that have gone far in undermining the mainstream realist edifice. But at some point the critique needs to go beyond so-called deviant cases to look at cases and phenomena that realist theories claim they can explain; that is, constructivists are going to have to examine the argument that realpolitik practice is a reflection of realpolitik ideology and norms.[26] Critics of constructivism have a simple answer to this issue: realpolitik ideology is simply an epiphenomenon of anarchical material structures, the ideational superstructure that one should expect to find if states are trying to ensure their security in an uncertain world of shifting power distributions.

But the story cannot end there because two radically alternative explanations for the same phenomenon exist. The proper next step is to set up a critical test where one spins out alternative but *competitive* propositions and expectations from the two sets of explanations to see which additional set of empirical observations is confirmed or disconfirmed. One additional empirical implication that could provide an important test of constructivist versus material realist accounts of realpolitik is the phenomenon of counter-realpolitik socialization. If constructivist arguments are right, realpolitik ideology and practice ought to be changeable—independent of material power distributions and "anarchy"—when actors are exposed to or socialized in counter-realpolitik ideologies. If materialist realist theories are right, realpolitik discourse is epiphenomenal to realpolitik practice and neither should change in the presence of counter-realpolitik ideology.[27]

This is where international institutions come in. Constructivists suggest that international institutions in particular are often agents of counter-realpolitik socialization. They posit a link between the presence of particular normative structures embodied in institutions and the incorporation of these norms in behavior by the actor/agent at the unit-level. It is in institutions where the interaction of activists, so-called norm entrepreneurs, is most likely, and where social conformity pressures are most concentrated. Institutions often have corporate identities, traits, missions, normative cores, and official discourses at odds with realpolitik axioms, indeed at odds with the socialization pressures that many realists argue come with being sovereign, insecure actors operating in anarchy.[28] Where else, indeed, would state agents who have internalized real-

---

[26] I define realpolitik ideology, or strategic culture, fairly specifically to mean a worldview where the external environment is considered to be highly conflictual, where conflicts with other actors tend toward zero-sum, and where, given these conditions, the use of military force is likely to be quite efficacious in the resolution of conflicts. Vasquez calls this a power politics paradigm (1993:86–120). I do not define realpolitik simply as the "prudent" pursuit of the power interests of nation-states, as some realists do. This, it seems to me, is too vague and thus its presence or absence is empirically hard to falsify.

[27] Note that I do not accept that an actor's sensitivity to changes in relative power confirms material realism. I've argued elsewhere that one could argue this sensitivity is ideationally rooted. Indeed this is the whole point of testing for socialization. Similarly, when I conclude that cooperation occurs despite relative power concerns, this does not mean that I believe "relative power concerns" is a phenomenon exclusive to, hence confirming of, material realist arguments, or that socialization arguments necessarily expect cooperative behavior and a rejection of realpolitik pathologies. Socialization can go in both directions—actors can be socialized into or out of realpolitik practices. But to deal with the important charge that realpolitik ideology and practice are both epiphenomena of material structures, the critical test necessarily involves looking for evidence of non-realpolitik socialization.

[28] For a discussion of organizations and their "goals" see Ness and Brechin, 1988:247, 263–266. See also Muller's discussion of the ideology of the nonproliferation regime and how the causal and principled ideas of the regime relate to its norms and proscriptive regulations (1993). See also Alter's discussion of the legitimacy of the European Court of Justice's legal culture and doctrine and how this constrains states from challenging the ECJ even when its rulings run against state preferences (1998:134–135).

politik ideologies be exposed to alternative "theories" about the nature of world politics and the routes to security? They are unlikely to be exposed to these sorts of arguments in the domestic policy process or inside their organizations or through contact with the myriad channels through which the state constructs a competitive, often zero-sum picture of the external world (e.g., education systems, propaganda systems). Quite literally, for many of these agents the only sustained exposure to counter-realpolitik arguments and normative structures is often in international security institutions whose own ideology emphasizes cooperation, transparency, confidence-building, and demilitarization.

Thus, for example, some arms control institutions expose actors to an ideology where *inter alia:* multilateral transparency is normatively better than unilateral nontransparency; where disarming is better than arming as a basis of security; where common security is better than unilateral security; and where evidence of the potential for cooperative, joint gains in security in the international system is greater than evidence that the environment is a fixed, conflictual one. All of these axioms and assumptions challenge the core assumptions of realpolitik ideology. So, if there is any counterattitudinal socialization going on, it ought to be happening in particular kinds of security institutions.[29] I do not mean to imply that institutions are the only fora in which socialization in IR occurs. Since the focus is on microprocesses, obviously state agents and principals in the policy process are exposed to a wide variety of socialization experiences and interactions inside their own states. The question is simply how broader non-realpolitik norms in international security might be diffused. Institutions are an obvious first place to look, especially when testing the hypothesis that socialization occurs in the first place.[30]

Note, however, that treating institutions as social environments means positing that different social environments vary in terms of their persuasiveness and social influence. This means asking how institutions as social environments vary in ways conducive to socialization. We need, then, a typology of institutional forms or institutional social environments. Unfortunately, we don't have one. One could imagine, though, at least several dimensions for coding institutions as social environments. Here I am expanding on the typology of domestic institutions developed by Rogowski (1999):

1. membership: for example, small and exclusive or large and inclusive.
2. franchise: for example, where the authoritativeness of members is equally allocated, or unevenly (though legitimately) allocated.
3. decision rules: for example, unanimity, consensus, majority, supermajority.
4. mandate: for example, to provide information, to deliberate and resolve, or to negotiate and legislate.
5. autonomy of agents from principals: low through high.

Recalling my earlier discussion of the conditions under which different kinds of socialization effects will occur, then, different institutional designs (combinations of measures on these five dimensions) should create different kinds of social environments, leading to differences in the likelihood and degree of persuasion and social influence. For instance, to take one extreme ideal persuasion is likely to be the most prevalent and powerful socialization process when membership is small (social liking and in-group identity effects on the persuasiveness of counterattitudinal messages are strongest); when franchise recognizes

---

[29] Risse makes a similar point, suggesting that communicative action should be more frequent inside institutions than outside of them (1997:17).

[30] Or as Shambaugh put it: "The more provocative question is whether an actor's preference, interests and identity can be altered initially as a result of its association with an international institution and vice versa" (1997:8).

the special authoritativeness of a couple of actors (the authoritativeness of the messenger is likely to be high); when decision rules are based on consensus (this requires deliberation where cognition effects will be strongest); when the institution's mandate is deliberative (this, again requires active complex cognition; agents may also be more autonomous since there is no obvious distribution of benefits at stake and thus there is less pressure to represent the principal); and when the autonomy of agents is high (e.g., when the issue is narrowly technical or when the principal just doesn't care much, or when the principal is less attentive or relevant). All these design-dependent effects will be enhanced for novices who are exposed to the environment over long periods of time (Zimbardo and Leippe, 1991: ch. 5).

Conversely, backpatting and opprobrium are more likely to be at work when membership is large (this maximizes the accumulation of backpatting/shaming markers); when the franchise is equally allocated (there are no obvious "authoritative" or "persuasive" sources of new information); when decision rules are majoritarian (behavior is on record and consistency effects may be stronger); when the mandate involves negotiations over the distribution of benefits; and when the autonomy of agents is low (agents have to represent principals thus reducing the effects of persuasion on agents).

But how would one know if persuasion or social influence had led to pro-social/pro-normative behavior in international institutions? First, as I noted above, one would have to show that social environments in institutions are conducive to persuasion or social influence. Second, one would have to show that after exposure to or involvement in a new social environment, attitudes or arguments for participation have indeed changed, converging with the normative/causal arguments that predominate in a particular social environment, or that they reflected social influence pressures emanating from that environment. Third, one would have to show that behavior had changed in ways consistent with these arguments. Finally, one would have to show that material side-payments or threats were not present, or at least were not part of the decision to conform to pro-social norms.

Implications

If my general arguments about socialization are plausible, a focus on institutions as social environments raises at least two implications that challenge predominant arguments in IR theory about the conditions for cooperation inside international institutions.

The first implication has to do with persuasion and institutional design. Typically, contractual institutionalists argue that efficient institutional design depends on the type of cooperation problem (e.g., a PD-type problem requires information (monitoring) and sanctions; an assurance problem primarily requires reassurance information). The flip side is that one can identify inefficient institutional designs for a particular cooperation problem as well (e.g., an institution that is designed only to provide assurance information but has no monitoring or sanctioning capacity would be inefficient for resolving PD-type problems). Additionally, Downs et al. argue that so-called transformational institutions (inclusive institutions that bring genuine cooperators and potential defectors together in an effort to instill norms and obligations in the latter) are less likely to provide efficient solutions than a strategic construction approach. This latter approach to institutional design stresses exclusive memberships of true believers where decisions are made on the basis of super-majority rules. The gradual inclusion of potential defectors under these conditions ensures that the preferences of the true believers predominate as the institution evolves. Their critique of the transformational approach rests explicitly on skepticism that the *preferences* of potential defectors can change through social interaction (Downs, Rocke, and Barsoom, 1998).

It is not clear whether this skepticism rests on empirical evidence or simply on the methodological difficulties of assuming and then trying to observe preference change. In any event, if one relaxes that assumption then one is forced to revisit the contractual institutionalists' notions of efficient institutional design. An institution that appears inefficient to contractual institutionalists (e.g., an assurance institution for a PD problem) may actually be efficient for the cooperation problem at hand. If, say, a player with PD preferences can be socialized (persuaded) to internalize stag hunt preferences through interaction in a social environment with no material sanctioning or side-payments, then "assurance" institutions may work in PD-like cooperation problems. An efficient institution might then be reconceived as the *design* and *process* most likely to produce the most effective environments for socializing actors in alternative definitions of interest. As I have argued, the literature on socialization microprocesses suggests such an institution may have to be informal, weakly institutionalized, consensus-based—the opposite of an institutional design that contractualists believe is effective for dealing with PD problems.

The second implication comes from arguments about social influence and has to do with the problem of collective action inside institutions. Social influence effects may provide insights into how groups resolve the collective action problem that hinders resolving collective action problems. That is, traditionally scholars have argued that a critical solution to free-riding is to offer material side-payments (and sanctions) to make collective action pay for the individual. The conundrum has been, however, that offering side-payments is itself a collective action problem. Who will take up the burden of offering side-payments? Hegemons and activists are usually part of the answer to this puzzle (though why activists should exist in the first place is hard for collective action theorists to specify *a priori*). Social rewards and punishments, however, are a particularly interesting kind of incentive to overcome collective inaction. They are relatively cheap to create, but are infused with a great deal of value. This means that new status markers can be manufactured and distributed without necessarily diminishing their value. In principle any member of a group therefore can provide social side-payments at relatively low cost, indeed at zero cost if the member can also receive these kinds of side-payments for providing them to others. This is, after all, what backpatting entails—a mutual, virtuous circle of bestowing and receiving social rewards. Cheap, but social, talk, then, can indeed be cheap to produce but nonetheless still be considered credible precisely because of its social value.[31] Thus, because status markers are so highly valued, it doesn't take much of a "costly commitment" by providers of these markers to establish the credibility of promises to bestow, or threats to retract, these markers. All this suggests, then, is that one reason why collective action problems are often less frequent and debilitating than theorists expect (Green and Shapiro, 1994:72–97) may have to do with the fact that actors are also motivated by the desire to maximize social rewards and that these are relatively easy for groups to produce and distribute.

Following from this argument about collective action, social influence arguments also challenge the conventional wisdom about the optimal size of institutions and groups. From a contractual institutionalist perspective, *ceteris paribus*, more actors makes cooperation more difficult (collective action problems, problems of monitoring and punishing defection, etc.). Transaction costs increase with more actors. Decentralized institutions are therefore handicapped in dealing with "problems of transaction costs and opportunism" (Abbott and Snidal,

---

[31] This is not dissimilar to Johnson's argument that cheap talk, in the context of persuasion whereby interests and identities converge inside a social relationship, establishes focal points that are necessary to reduce the strategic indeterminacy of bargaining games (see Johnson, 1993).

1998:15). From a social influence perspective, however, more may be better. Status backpatting and opprobrium effects are likely to be stronger when the "audience" or reference group is larger.

References

ABBOTT, K. W., AND D. SNIDAL (1998) Why States Act Through Formal International Organizations. *Journal of Conflict Resolution* **42**:3–32.

ADLER, E. (1998) "Seeds of Peaceful Change: The OSCE's Security Community-Building Model." In *Security Communities*, edited by E. Adler and M. Barnett, pp. 119–160. Cambridge: Cambridge University Press.

ADLER, E., AND M. BARNETT (1998) "A Framework for the Study of Security Communities." In *Security Communities*, edited by E. Adler and M. Barnett, pp. 3–28. Cambridge: Cambridge University Press.

ALKER, H. (1996) "Beneath Tit for Tat." In *Rediscoveries and Reformulations: Humanistic Methodologies for International Studies*, edited by H. Alker, pp. 303–331. Cambridge: Cambridge University Press.

ALTER, K. (1998) Who Are the "Masters of the Treaty"? European Governments and the European Court of Justice. *International Organization* **52**:121–147.

AXELROD, R. (1997a) "Promoting Norms: An Evolutionary Approach to Norms." In *The Complexity of Cooperation*, edited by R. Axelrod, pp. 44–68. Princeton, NJ: Princeton University Press.

AXELROD, R. (1997b) "A Model for the Emergence of New Political Actors." In *The Complexity of Cooperation*, edited by R. Axelrod, pp. 124–144. Princeton, NJ: Princeton University Press.

AXELROD, R. (1997c) "The Dissemination of Culture: A Model with Local Convergence and Global Polarization." In *The Complexity of Cooperation*, edited by R. Axelrod, pp. 148–177. Princeton, NJ: Princeton University Press.

AXSOM, D., S., YATES, AND S. CHAIKEN (1987) Audience Response Cues as a Heuristic Cue in Persuasion. *Journal of Personality and Social Psychology* **53**:30–40.

BARNUM, C. (1997) A Reformulated Social Identity Theory. *Advances in Group Processes* **14**:29–57.

BATSON, C. D. (1987) Prosocial Motivation: Is It Ever Truly Altruistic? *Advances in Experimental Social Psychology* **20**:65–122.

BECK, P. A., AND M. K. JENNINGS (1991) Family Traditions, Political Periods, and the Development of Partisan Orientations. *Journal of Politics* **53**:742–763.

BERGER, C. R. (1995) "Inscrutable Goals, Uncertain Plans and the Production of Communicative Action." In *Communication and Social Influence Processes*, edited by C. R. Berger and M. Burgoon, pp. 1–28. East Lansing: Michigan State University Press.

BERGER, P. L., AND T. LUCKMANN (1966) *The Social Construction of Reality: A Treatise in the Sociology of Knowledge*. New York: Anchor Books.

BETZ, A. L., J. K. SKOWRONSKI, AND T. M. OSTROM (1996) Shared Realities: Social Influence and Stimulus Memory. *Social Cognition* **14**:113–140.

BLACK, D. (1999) "The Long and Winding Road: International Norms and Domestic Political Change in South Africa." In *The Power of Human Rights: International Norms and Domestic Change*, edited by T. Risse and K. Sikkink, pp. 78–108. Cambridge: Cambridge University Press.

BOOSTER, F. J. (1995) "Commentary on Compliance-gaining Message Behavior Research." In *Communication and Social Influence Processes*, edited by C. R. Berger and M. Burgoon, pp. 91–113. East Lansing: Michigan State University Press.

BRENNER, T. (1998) Can Evolutionary Algorithms Describe Learning Processes? *Journal of Evolutionary Economics* **8**:271–283.

CEDERMAN, L.-E. (1997) *Emergent Actors in World Politics: How States and Nations Develop and Dissolve*. Princeton, NJ: Princeton University Press.

CHAYES, A., AND A. H. CHAYES (1996) *The New Sovereignty: Compliance with International Regulatory Agreements*. Cambridge, MA: Harvard University Press.

CHECKEL, J. T. (1998) The Constructivist Turn in International Relations Theory. *World Politics* **50**:324–348.

CHOI, Y. B. (1993) *Paradigms and Conventions: Uncertainty, Decision Making, and Entrepreneurship*. Ann Arbor: University of Michigan Press.

CIALDINI, R. (1984) *Influence: The New Psychology of Modern Persuasion*. New York: Quill Books.

CIALDINI, R. (1987) "Compliance Principles of Compliance Professionals: Psychologists of Necessity." In *Social Influence: The Ontario Symposium*, vol. 5, edited by M. P. Zanna, J. M. Olson, and C. P. Herman, pp. 165–184. Hillsdale, NJ: Lawrence Erlbaum.

DIMAGGIO, P. J., AND W. W. POWELL (1991) Introduction to *The New Institutionalism in Organizational Analysis*, edited by W. W. Powell and P. J. DiMaggio, pp. 1–38. Chicago: University of Chicago Press.

DITTMER, L., AND S. S. KIM, EDS. (1993) *China's Quest for National Identity.* Ithaca, NY: Cornell University Press.

DOWNS, G. W., D. M. ROCKE, AND P. N. BARSOOM (1998) Managing the Evolution of Multilateralism. *International Organization* **52**:397–419.

EVANGELISTA, M. (1999) *Unarmed Forces: The Transnational Movement to End the Cold War.* Ithaca, NY: Cornell University Press.

EYRE, D., AND M. SUCHMAN (1996) "Status, Norms, and the Proliferation of Conventional Weapons." In *The Culture of National Security,* edited by P. J. Katzenstein, pp. 79–113. New York: Columbia University Press.

FARKAS, A. (1998) *State Learning and International Change.* Ann Arbor: University of Michigan Press.

FINNEMORE, M. (1996a) Norms, Culture, and World Politics: Insights from Sociology's Institutionalism. *International Organization* **50**:325–347.

FINNEMORE, M. (1996b) *National Interests in International Society.* Ithaca, NY: Cornell University Press.

FINNEMORE, M. (1996c) "Constructing Norms of Humanitarian Intervention." In *The Culture of National Security: Norms and Identities in World Politics,* edited by P. J. Katzenstein, pp. 153–185. New York: Columbia University Press.

FINNEMORE, M., AND K. SIKKINK (1998) International Norm Dynamics and Political Change. *International Organization* **52**:887–917.

FRANCK, T. M. (1990) *The Power of Legitimacy Among Nations.* New York: Oxford University Press.

FRANK, R. (1985) *Choosing the Right Pond: Human Behavior and the Quest for Status.* New York: Oxford University Press.

FRANK, R. (1988) *Passions Within Reason: The Strategic Role of the Emotions.* New York: W. W. Norton.

FREEDMAN, P. E., AND A. FREEDMAN (1981) "Political Learning." In *The Handbook of Political Behavior,* vol. 1, edited by S. Long, pp. 255–303. New York: Plenum Press.

FRIEDEN, J. (1999) "Actors and Preferences in International Relations." In *Strategic Choice in International Relations,* edited by D. Lake and R. Powell, pp. 39–76. Princeton, NJ: Princeton University Press.

GERARD, H. B., AND R. ORIVE (1987) The Dynamics of Opinion Formation. *Advances in Experimental Social Psychology* **20**:171–202.

GIBSON, J. L. (1998) A Sober Second Thought: An Experiment in Persuading Russians to Tolerate. *American Journal of Political Science* **42**:819–850.

GILPIN, R. (1981) *War and Change in World Politics.* Cambridge: Cambridge University Press.

GREEN, D. P., AND I. SHAPIRO (1994) *Pathologies of Rational Choice Theory: A Critique of Applications in Political Science.* New Haven, CT: Yale University Press.

HAAS, P. (1998) "Constructing Multilateral Environmental Governance: The Evolution of Multilateral Environmental Governance Since 1972." Paper presented at the Center for International Affairs, Harvard University, April 16.

HALPERN, J. J. (1997) Elements of a Script for Friendship in Transactions. *Journal of Conflict Resolution* **41**:835–868.

HAMMAN, H. L. (1998) "Remodeling International Relations: New Tools from New Science?" In *International Relations in a Constructed World,* edited by V. Kubalkova, N. Onuf, and P. Kowert, pp. 173–192. Armonk, NY: M. E. Sharpe.

HARRE, R. (1979) *Social Being: A Theory for Social Psychology.* Oxford: Basil Blackwell.

HASENCLEVER, A., P. MAYER, AND V. RITTBERGER (1997) *Theories of International Regimes.* Cambridge: Cambridge University Press.

HATCH, E. (1989) Theories of Social Honor. *American Anthropologist* **91**:341–353.

HERRMANN, R. (1988) The Empirical Challenge of the Cognitive Revolution: A Strategy for Drawing Inferences About Perceptions. *International Studies Quarterly* **32**:175–203.

ICHILOV, O. (1990) Introduction to *Political Socialization, Citizenship Education and Democracy,* edited by O. Ichilov, pp. 1–8. New York: Teachers College Press.

IKENBERRY, G. J., AND C. KUPCHAN (1990) Socialization and Hegemonic Power. *International Organization* **44**:283–315.

ISEN, A. M. (1987) Positive Affect, Cognition and Social Behavior. *Advances in Experimental Social Psychology* **20**:203–253.

JAMES, M. R. (1998) "Communicative Action and the Logics of Group Conflict." Paper prepared for the American Political Science Association Annual Meeting, Boston, September.

JOHNSON, J. (1993) Is Talk Really Cheap? Prompting Conversation Between Critical Theory and Rational Choice. *American Political Science Review* **87**:74–86.

JORGENSEN, C., C. KOCK, AND L. RORBECH (1998) Rhetoric That Shifts Votes: An Exploratory Study of Persuasion in Issue-oriented Public Debates. *Political Communication* **15**:283–299.

KECK, M. E., AND K. SIKKINK (1998) *Activists Beyond Borders: Advocacy Networks in International Politics.* Ithaca, NY: Cornell University Press.

KEOHANE, R. O. (1984) *After Hegemony.* Princeton, NJ: Princeton University Press.

KIER, E. (1997) *Imagining War: French and British Military Doctrine Between the Wars.* Princeton, NJ: Princeton University Press.

KINDER, D. R., AND L. M. SANDERS (1996) *Divided by Color: Racial Politics and Democratic Ideals.* Chicago: University of Chicago Press.

KINDER, D. R., AND D. O. SEARS (1981) Prejudice and Politics: Symbolic Racism Versus Racial Threats to the Good Life. *Journal of Personality and Social Psychology* **40**:414–431.

KNOKE, D. (1994) *Political Networks: The Structural Perspective.* London: Cambridge University Press.

KRATOCHWIL, F. V., AND J. G. RUGGIE (1986) International Organization: A State of the Art on an Art of the State. *International Organization* **40**:753–775.

KREPS, D. M. (1992) "Corporate Culture and Economic Theory." In *Perspectives on Positive Political Economy,* edited by J. E. Alt and K. A. Shepsle, pp. 90–143. London: Cambridge University Press.

KUKLINSKI, J. H., AND N. L. HURLEY (1996) "It's a Matter of Interpretation." In *Political Persuasion and Attitude Change,* edited by D. C. Mutz, P. M. Sniderman, and R. Brody, pp. 125–144. Ann Arbor: University of Michigan Press.

LAKE, D. A., AND R. POWELL (1999) "International Relations: A Strategic-Choice Approach." In *Strategic Choice and International Relations,* edited by D. A. Lake and R. Powell, pp. 3–38. Princeton, NJ: Princeton University Press.

LEGRO, J. W. (1995) *Cooperation Under Fire: Anglo-German Restraint During World War II.* Ithaca, NY: Cornell University Press.

LOVAGLIA, M. J. (1995) Power and Status: Exchange, Attribution, and Expectation States. *Small Group Research* **26**:400–426.

LUMSDAINE, D. (1993) *Moral Vision in International Politics: The Foreign Aid Regime, 1949–1989.* Princeton, NJ: Princeton University Press.

LUPIA, A. (1998) "Who Can Persuade Whom: How Simple Cues Affect Political Attitudes." (http://weber.ucsd.edu/~alupia/AJPS97.html)

LUPIA, A., AND M. D. McCUBBINS (1998) *The Democratic Dilemma: Can Citizens Learn What They Need to Know?* Cambridge: Cambridge University Press.

MARTIN, L. L. (1993) "The Rational Choice State of Multilateralism." In *Multilateralism Matters: The Theory and Praxis of an Institutional Form,* edited by J. G. Ruggie, pp. 91–121. New York: Columbia University Press.

MARTIN, L. L. (1997) "An Institutionalist View: International Institutions and State Strategies." Paper prepared for the Conference on International Order in the 21st Century, McGill University, May 16–18.

MEYER, J. W., ET AL. (1997) The Structuring of a World Environmental Regime, 1870–1990. *International Organization* **51**: 623–651.

MOHR, L. B. (1996) *The Causes of Human Behavior: Implications for Theory and Methods in the Social Sciences.* Ann Arbor: University of Michigan Press.

MORAVCSIK, A. (1995) Explaining International Human Rights Regimes: Liberal Theory and Western Europe. *European Journal of International Relations* **1**:157–190.

MORAVCSIK, A. (1997) Taking Preferences Seriously: A Liberal Theory of International Politics. *International Organization* **51**:513–553.

MORGENTHAU, H. (1978) *Politics Among Nations: The Struggle for Power and Peace,* 5th ed. New York: Alfred A. Knopf.

MORROW, J. D. (1994) *Game Theory for Political Scientists.* Princeton, NJ: Princeton University Press.

MULLER, H. (1993) "The Internalization of Principles, Norms, and Rules by Governments: The Case of Security Regimes." In *Regime Theory and International Relations,* edited by V. Rittenberger, pp. 361–388. Oxford: Clarendon Press.

MUTZ, D. C., P. M. SNIDERMAN, AND R. A. BRODY (1996) "Political Persuasion: The Birth of a Field of Study." In *Political Persuasion and Attitude Change,* edited by D. C. Mutz, P. M. Sniderman, and R. Brody, pp. 1–14. Ann Arbor: University of Michigan Press.

NADELMANN, E. A. (1990) Global Prohibition Regimes: The Evolution of Norms in International Society. *International Organization* **44**:479–526.

NAPIER, R. W., AND M. K. GERSHENFELD (1987) *Groups: Theory and Experience,* 4th ed. Boston: Houghton Mifflin.

NEMETH, C. J. (1987) "Influence Processes, Problem Solving and Creativity." In *Social Influence: The Ontario Symposium,* vol. 5, edited by M. P. Zanna, J. M. Olson, and C. P. Herman, pp. 237–246. Hillsdale, NJ: Lawrence Erlbaum.

NESS, G. D., AND S. R. BRECHIN (1988) Bridging the Gap: International Organizations as Organizations. *International Organization* 42:245–273.

NISBETT, R. E., AND D. COHEN (1996) *Culture of Honor: The Psychology of Violence in the South.* Boulder, CO: Westview Press.

ONUF, N. (1998) "Constructivism: A User's Manual." In *International Relations in a Constructed World,* edited by V. Kubalkova, N. Onuf, and P. Kowert, pp. 58–78. Armonk, NY: M. E. Sharpe.

PETTY, R. E., D. T. WEGENER, AND L. R. FABRIGAR (1997) Attitudes and Attitude Change. *Annual Review of Psychology* 48:609–647.

PRICE, R. (1998) Reversing the Gunsights: Transnational Civil Society Targets Landmines. *International Organization* 52:613–644.

PRICE, R., AND N. TANNENWALD (1996) "Norms and Deterrence: The Nuclear and Chemical Weapons Taboos." In *The Culture of National Security: Norms and Identity in World Politics,* edited by P. J. Katzenstein, pp. 114–152. New York: Columbia University Press.

RESENDE-SANTOS, J. (1996) Anarchy and the Emulation of Military Systems: Military Organization and Technology in South America, 1870–1930. *Security Studies* 5:193–260.

RISSE, T. (1997) "Let's Talk." Paper presented to the American Political Science Association Annual Conference, Washington, D.C., August.

RISSE, T. (2000) Let's Argue: Communicative Action in World Politics. *International Organization* 54:1–39.

RISSE, T., AND K. SIKKINK (1999) "The Socialization of International Human Rights Norms into Domestic Practices: Introduction." In *The Power of Human Rights: International Norms and Domestic Change,* edited by T. Risse and K. Sikkink, pp. 1–38. Cambridge: Cambridge University Press.

ROGOWSKI, R. (1999) "Institutions as Constraints on Strategic Choice." In *Strategic Choice and International Relations,* edited by D. A. Lake and R. Powell, pp. 115–136. Princeton, NJ: Princeton University Press.

RUGGIE, J. G. (1998) *Constructing the World Polity: Essays on International Institutionalization.* London: Routledge Press.

RULE, B. G., AND G. L. BISANZ (1987) "Goals and Strategies of Persuasion: A Cognitive Schema for Understanding Social Events." In *Social Influence: The Ontario Symposium,* vol. 5, edited by M. P. Zanna, J. M. Olson, and C. P. Herman, pp. 185–206. Hillsdale, NJ: Lawrence Erlbaum.

SCHIEFFELIN, B. B., AND E. OCHS, EDS. (1986) *Language Socialization Across Cultures.* Cambridge: Cambridge University Press.

SHAMBAUGH, G. E. (1997) "Constructivism, Entrepreneurship and the Power to Socialize Rogue States." Paper presented to the American Political Science Association Annual Meeting, Washington, D.C., August.

STRYKER, S., AND A. STATHAM (1985) "Symbolic Interaction and Role Theory." In *The Handbook of Social Psychology.* vol. 1, edited by G. Lindzey and E. Aronson, pp. 311–378. New York: Random House.

SUSSKIND, L. (1994) *Environmental Diplomacy: Negotiating More Effective Global Agreements.* London: Oxford University Press.

TURNER, J. C. (1987) *Rediscovering the Social Group.* Oxford: Basil Blackwell.

VALLEY, K. L., J. MOAG, AND M. H. BAZERMAN (1998) "A Matter of Trust": Effects of Communication on the Efficiency and Distribution of Outcomes. *Journal of Economic Behavior and Organization* 34:211–238.

VASQUEZ, J. A. (1993) *The War Puzzle.* Cambridge: Cambridge University Press.

WALLANDER, C. (1999) *Mortal Friends, Best Enemies: German-Russian Cooperation After the Cold War.* Ithaca, NY: Cornell University Press.

WALTZ, K. (1979) *Theory of International Relations.* Reading, MA: Addison-Wesley.

WENDT, A. (1994) Collective Identity Formation and the International State. *American Political Science Review* 88:384–396.

WILLIAMS, M. C. (1997) "The Institutions of Security." *Conflict and Cooperation* 32:287–307.

WU, C. H., AND D. R. SHAFFER (1987) Susceptibility to Persuasive Appeals as a Function of Source Credibility and Prior Experience with Attitudinal Object. *Journal of Personality and Social Psychology* 52:677–688.

YOUNG, O. (1992) "The Effectiveness of International Institutions: Hard Cases and Critical Variables." In *Governance Without Government: Order and Change in World Politics,* edited by J. N. Rosenau and E.-O. Czempiel, pp.160–194. Cambridge: Cambridge University Press.

ZIMBARDO, P. G., AND M. R LEIPPE (1991) *The Psychology of Attitude Change and Social Influence.* New York: McGraw-Hill.

[19]

Delegation to International Organizations: Agency Theory and World Bank Environmental Reform

Daniel L. Nielson and Michael J. Tierney

In the early 1980s, the World Bank came under fire for having financed multiple projects that led to spectacular environmental disasters in Brazil and Indonesia. As a result, an international coalition of environmentalists organized protests and lobbied the Bank's staff for a change in lending practices. But Bank policy did not waver.

When direct appeals to the Bank failed, these critics turned to the Bank's member governments in the developed world, where environmental issues had become politically salient. They focused most of their attention on the U.S. government, which appropriates the largest share of Bank funds, appoints the Bank president, and controls the largest bloc of votes on the Bank's executive board. During the mid-1980s, the U.S. Congress threatened to withhold future funds from the Bank unless the organization changed its practices. The Bank complied, but only in part. In 1994, Congress followed through on the previous threat, withholding $1 billion from the Bank. Of equal importance, U.S., European, and Japanese representatives on the board sought to ensure that the Bank's promised behavioral changes would actually be implemented. Shortly thereafter, the World Bank adopted sweeping institutional reforms and significantly altered its lending portfolio by increasing environmental lending and decreasing projects that caused environmental harm.

Several people gave us helpful comments on earlier drafts of the manuscript. In particular, we thank Lisa Baldez, Michael Barnett, T.J. Cheng, Scott Cooper, David Dessler, Daniel Drezner, Jay Goodliffe, Darren Hawkins, Wade Jacoby, Robert Keohane, Ralf Leiteritz, Dave Lewis, Mona Lyne, Scott Morgenstern, Sue Peterson, Brian Sala, Steve Swindle, Mike Thies, Robert Wade, Kate Weaver, Sven Wilson, and Bennet Zelner. We owe a special debt of gratitude to Lisa Martin and two anonymous reviewers, as their criticisms were the most painful—and helpful. We also thank the participants in the faculty research seminars at Brigham Young University, the College of William and Mary, and Duke University. The research for this article would not have been possible without support from BYU's David M. Kennedy Center for International Studies and College of Family, Home and Social Sciences, Duke University's Political Science Department, and the Reves Center for International Studies at the College of William and Mary. For research assistance, we are grateful to Nate Bascom, Spencer Bytheway, Adam Ekins, Eric Hatch, Jen Keister, Jennifer Neves, Chris O'Keefe, Joshua Wheatley, and, especially, Kari Sowell.

International Organization 57, Spring 2003, pp. 241–276
© 2003 by The IO Foundation.   DOI: 10.1017/S0020818303572010

This case presents a puzzle for international relations theory. The World Bank exhibited significant independence from its member governments for nearly a decade, then suddenly and repeatedly changed its behavior in response to increasingly coordinated demands by member governments. Neither neorealism nor neoliberalism, as currently conceived, can accommodate such autonomous action by international organizations (IOs) within their state-centric ontologies. This case, like many others in the study of IOs, requires a theory that can explain organizational autonomy as well as responsiveness to the demands of member governments. Extending neoliberal institutionalism, we propose a theoretical alternative that may fill this gap in the literature and have broad application for the study of IOs. We advance a principal-agent (P-A) model of international organization in which groups of member governments sometimes empower their IO agents with real decision-making authority.

However, three understudied factors complicate agency problems in the case of IOs, delimiting the conditions under which the insights of conventional P-A theory hold. First, member countries must solve collective-action problems multilaterally before motivating their agents. Such multilateral decision making highlights the problems faced by any "collective principal." Second, IOs often receive marching orders from organizationally distinct principals—particularly in the case where legislatures and executives in member countries act independently and have separate contracts with the same agent, creating the problem of "multiple principals." Third, IO agents act at the end of a long "chain of delegation," complicating the transmission of demands from the ultimate principals to the IOs.

If problems related to collective action, multiple principals, and agent proximity can be overcome—hardly a foregone conclusion—principals can then employ various tools to rein in errant behavior by IO agents. They can "screen and select" IO personnel more carefully, so that the new staff members more closely reflect their principals' interests. Principals can engage in "oversight" of the IO, not only through direct monitoring of agent behavior (police-patrol oversight), but also by enlisting the aid of third parties (fire-alarm oversight). Principals can generate "procedural checks and balances" within the IO, so that one set of agents has the authority to monitor other agents and report back independently to the principal, or even veto decisions made by other agents. Finally, principals can draft new "contracts" with the IO personnel, requiring modified behavior to achieve anticipated reward, or insuring punishment if behavior is not consistent with the interests of the principal.[1]

To evaluate our model, we examine multiple instances of institutional reform and behavioral change at the World Bank from 1980 to 2000.[2] We trace the pro-

---

1. See Kiewiet and McCubbins 1991; and McCubbins and Schwartz 1987.
2. While we discuss numerous kinds of "Bank behavior" in the case study, we focus our attention on lending behavior—what type of loans does the Bank make, and does this change over time? After all, loans are the primary means by which the Bank shapes economic, political, and environmental outcomes in international relations.

cesses that brought about modest changes after 1986, and then the major institutional reforms of 1993–94. We then highlight the political process linking those institutional reforms to the punctuated and significant changes in the Bank's lending portfolio.

IR Theory and International Organizations

Although neorealism and neoliberalism have dominated international relations (IR) theory debates for twenty years,[3] a number of scholars have convincingly argued that neither paradigm can account for many important features, behaviors, and effects of IOs.[4] These are serious criticisms because most multilateral cooperation now takes place within the context of IOs, the number of IOs is growing rapidly, and IOs seem to be exercising more authority than they ever have in the past.[5]

Realists have largely not perceived IOs as worthy of explanation. On the rare occasions when realists have attempted to explain the behavior, the persistence, or the reform of IOs, they typically fail, sometimes flamboyantly.[6] The thinness of realism's state-centric ontology may explain these failures. Realists leave no place for IOs in their models; hence, international outcomes are determined by state power and interests alone.[7] Substantive IO rules are created and maintained by the most powerful state(s) in the system.[8] As the distribution of power changes, so too will IOs. Hence, IOs are not important arenas within which states interact, and IOs are certainly not autonomous actors in their own right. It follows from realist theory that outcomes in international politics would be the same with or without IOs.[9]

Neoliberals have successfully exploited the empirical and analytical failures of realism, and they have done so with a virtually identical ontology.[10] Unitary states are still the only significant actors in international politics, and states are still fundamentally concerned with survival in an anarchic system. A key difference between the two paradigms follows from an assumption about the role of information in international politics. For realists, information is always scarce and unreliable, thus risk-averse states assume the worst about their neighbors, and security dilem-

3. See, among many others, Waltz 1979; Krasner 1983; Keohane 1984 and 1986; Grieco 1988; Baldwin 1993; and Powell 1994.
4. See Barnett and Finnemore 1999; Moravcsik 1998; Adler 1998; Risse-Kappen 1996; and McCalla 1996.
5. See Ruggie 1993; Shanks, Jacobson, and Kaplan 1996; and Finnemore and Sikkink 2001.
6. See Mearsheimer 1990 on the imminent collapse of NATO and the European Union (EU). See Waltz 1996 on the likelihood of war in the Baltics or a Sino-Russian alliance to counterbalance NATO expansion. Both Gilpin 1972 and 1987 and Krasner 1976 and 1979, deduce the decline of GATT, rather than its institutionalization in the form of the World Trade Organization (WTO).
7. See Strange 1983; and Mearsheimer 1994 and 1995.
8. Gilpin 1981.
9. Mearsheimer 1994 and 1995.
10. See Keohane 1984; Aggarwal 1981; Duffield 1992; and Martin 1992.

mas result. For neoliberals, the quality of information in the international system varies significantly. As the quantity and quality of information increase, so do the prospects for cooperation. Crucially, IOs enable states to gather and share important information.[11] Thus for neoliberals, IOs do matter, but they matter only as structural constraints on state behavior, not as autonomous actors. Therefore, because neoliberals largely share the realist ontology, they have not fully considered how IOs might be treated as agents of state principals and thus actors—albeit subordinate ones—in their own right.

This shortcoming of neoliberalism is both ironic and unfortunate. Pursuing the question of IOs as agents of their member states would have been the logical next step in applying the theory of the firm to international relations. Recall that Keohane began this application in 1984, noting persuasively how IOs might solve Coase's classic problems of information asymmetries, transaction costs, and the absence of property rights.[12] Once economists had developed the functional theory of the firm, they moved on to problems of its organization, including how shareholders attempt to control managers. However, international relations scholars have only recently begun to take the corresponding step for IOs.[13] An explicit application of the theory of the firm to international relations would complement the extant neoliberal theories of IO creation and persistence with a more general theory of IO governance, behavior, and change.[14]

This amendment may prove indispensable because, in its present form, neoliberalism simply has no theoretical apparatus to deal with IO agency. If IOs are important for cooperation in international relations because they reduce transaction costs, mitigate information asymmetries, and provide quasi-legal frameworks, then whether and how well IOs perform these tasks should greatly influence prospects for cooperation. If IOs have autonomy from their creators, they may actually undermine the purposes for which they were created. Given enough autonomy, one can even imagine pathological IOs actively sabotaging the interests of the states that created them.[15] In fact, this vision of IOs running amok is pre-

---

11. Axelrod and Keohane 1985.
12. Keohane 1984.
13. See Pollack forthcoming; Keohane and Martin 1999; Gould forthcoming; and Vaubel 1991.
14. The first generation of neoliberal theorists were constrained from making this seemingly progressive move in their research program because of their need to demonstrate the weakness of neorealist theory while employing a neorealist ontology. Keohane did deduce important systemic outcomes that were distinct from realist predictions by using Coase's model of transaction costs. But the cases he employed reveal an important limitation of neoliberal theory. For example, Keohane finds the International Energy Agency (IEA) staff doing things that influence the amount and type of international cooperation, and notes "a remarkable delegation of authority" to the IEA. We do not doubt these empirical claims, but we also note the inability of Keohane's neoliberal model to accommodate such IO autonomy. See Keohane 1984.
15. For organizational theorists such as Barnett and Finnemore 1999, IOs are like global Frankensteins terrorizing (or more often benefiting) the international countryside. Once IOs have been created, they take on a life of their own and are largely beyond the control of their creators. Barnett and Finnemore advocate an approach that can "explain both the power of IOs and their propensity for

cisely the world that some scholars (and politicians) envision today. Without a theory of IO behavior and reform, neoliberalism has no ability to address such empirical patterns.

Thus neoliberalism finds itself in much the same condition that Coase, Williamson, and other transaction cost economists did during the early 1960s. It is time to apply the insights of the theory of the firm to multilateral cooperation within IOs.[16] Below, we propose a parallel and progressive shift within the neoliberal paradigm that would elaborate the microfoundations of international organization. Our model illuminates the conditions under which IOs will be given autonomy to pursue their preferences, and the conditions under which they will be reined in by member governments.

A Principal-Agent Model of International Organization

We thus develop a model of institutional and behavioral change in IOs, based on logic derived from agency theory in microeconomics.[17] Member governments (making up the principal) hire an IO (agent) to perform some function that will benefit the members. In this framework, member governments establish the goals that IOs will pursue and then allow the IO to pursue those goals with little interference most of the time. Generally, IOs should be observed to act "on their own." As long as agents are producing policies that are broadly consistent with the preferences of principals, P-A theory suggests that member governments will not pay the significant costs associated with micromanaging the organization. But during periods when member governments and IOs differ with regard to preferred outcomes, we can assess the mechanisms that drive IO institutions and behavior. In our P-A framework, we should observe significant institutional reforms and intervention by the member governments if and only if the IO strays from its principals' mandated objectives or the preferences of member governments change in concert.[18]

---

dysfunctional, even pathological, behavior." Barnett and Finnemore 1999, 699. Barnett and Finnemore offer a theoretically coherent explanation for such dysfunctional IO behavior. For discussions about how organizational theory (or constructivism more generally) can be tested empirically and whether it should be conceived as a complement or an alternative to P-A theory, see Nielson and Tierney 2001; and Weaver and Leiteritz 2002.

16. When distinguishing between neorealist and neoliberal predictions regarding the fate of NATO after the Cold War, Keohane 1993, 287, claims, "Institutionalists would expect NATO to use its organizational resources to persist, by changing its tasks." While little within Keohane's original theory can support this assertion, neoliberal institutionalism can be usefully adapted to encompass IO independence. In fact, neoliberals are shifting this way in recent research. See Keohane and Martin 1999; Wallander and Keohane 1997; and Martin 2002.

17. For a more detailed introduction of the P-A approach in IR, see Pollack 1997. For classic works in agency theory, see Coase 1937; Alchian and Demsetz 1972; Williamson 1975; and Fama 1980.

18. If the preferences of only a subset of members change, IO institutional change will depend on the decision rules within the IO and the relative power of various members.

Previous Arguments

For early agency theorists, the creation of a firm provided its founders with a way to internalize transaction costs and delegate decision-making authority to realize efficiency gains that follow from specialization. However, the structure of a firm presents a problem for its founders: How does one delegate authority without losing control? According to Kiewiet and McCubbins, a principal faces three specific difficulties when delegating.[19] First, the agent can "hide information" from the principal whose revelation would hurt the agent and help the principal. Second, the agent can do things behind the principal's back, "concealing actions" that the principal would sanction if known. Third, the principal faces "Madison's dilemma"—in which the need to delegate authority may give powers to the agent that can be used against the principal. Because the interests of principal and agent are never completely coincident, there will always be agency slippage between what the principal wants and what the agent does.

However, the principal is far from powerless. Principals write initial employment contracts, and they can renegotiate—or threaten to renegotiate—those contracts. Although threats and institutional reform may have costs to principals, they can employ these tactics strategically to modify agent behavior. In an efficiently designed P-A relationship, the contract is self-enforcing. That is, institutional constraints induce the self-interested agent to abide by the wishes of the principal.

Principals possess at least four tools to help them design self-enforcing contracts and thus mitigate agency slippage. First, the principal can carefully screen the potential agent when hiring. Such "screening and selection" mechanisms may enable the principal to employ someone whose interests are similar to the principal's, or someone who has demonstrated obedience and diligence in the past. Second, the principal can "monitor" the agent's actions, either directly through "police patrol oversight" mechanisms or indirectly, by inducing third parties to perform the oversight functions and thus mitigate the cost of monitoring through "fire alarm oversight."[20] Third, the principal may employ contracting arrangements that include credible commitments to punish or reward the agent for specified behavior.. Fourth, the principal can construct checks and balances that require coordination or competition between two or more agents.[21] If designed properly, checks and balances can reveal information to the principal about agent behavior and can also inhibit agent behavior that is detrimental to the principal.

P-A models have been fruitfully applied in American and comparative political contexts. The most influential findings from this literature demonstrate that the previously widespread view among scholars—that all-powerful bureaucrats often run amok in the policy process—is dramatically overstated, if not false. Because bureaucrats were observed to have a distinctive culture, to be lobbying politicians,

---

19. Kiewiet and McCubbins 1991.
20. McCubbins and Schwartz 1987.
21. Kiewiet and McCubbins 1991.

to be expanding their range of tasks—in short, to be doing more; and because bureaucracies were growing in size and number, many scholars incorrectly concluded that these organizations were gaining power at the expense of elected officials.[22] This "abdication hypothesis" in American and comparative politics parallels recent claims about IOs in the international relations literature.[23]

P-A Complications and Theoretical Solutions

The perception of "abdication" to agents may persist in the IO literature because IOs introduce a set of complicating factors that the extant P-A literature has not adequately addressed. Initially, models of P-A relationships were kept simple— one principal, one agent—as suggested by our discussion of the literature summarized above. However, this stylized model of delegation imperfectly mirrors the great complexity involved in governing IOs. In particular, such simplifications overlook the problems of common agency and long delegation chains.

Common agency: Collective principal or multiple principals.   A recent literature in political economy addresses the issue of common agency, where principals must solve problems of collective action and incompatible incentives before, and while, they resolve issues of agency slippage.[24] Contributors to this literature continue to conflate two analytically distinct situations that may result in important empirical differences. Specifically, as Lyne and Tierney note, a delegation relationship can have one or more principals, and a principal can either be an individual or a corporate entity.[25] Hence, when an agent has more than one employment contract with organizationally distinct principals, we say this is a delegation relationship with "multiple principals." When an agent has a single contract with a principal, but the principal happens to be composed of more than one actor, we call this a delegation relationship with a "collective principal."

The most familiar delegation relationships in politics and government involve a collective principal. Voters delegate to politicians, legislators delegate to party leaders, and nation-states delegate to IOs. In all these situations, a group of actors reaches agreement among themselves and then negotiates a contract with an agent to do something. If the group cannot come to an agreement a priori (whether because of restrictive decision rules, cycling, or preference heterogeneity), then they cannot change the status quo. This is true for initial hiring decisions, for proposals to renegotiate the agent's employment contract, or for giving the agent novel authoritative instructions. In all these scenarios, there is a single contract between an agent and the collective principal.

---

22. See Niskanen 1971; Lowi 1979; and Dodd and Schott 1979.
23. See Adler 1998; Finnemore 1996; Barnett and Finnemore 1999; and Williams 1994.
24. See Dixit, Grossman, and Helpman 1997; and Kiewiet and McCubbins 1991.
25. See Lyne and Tierney 2002; and Lyne forthcoming.

International Institutions in the New Global Economy

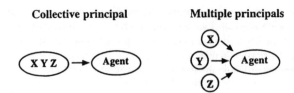

FIGURE 1. *Types of common agency*

Ironically, while delegations from a collective principal are quite common in the world of politics, political scientists have written more extensively on the question of multiple principals.[26] For example, in American politics there is a vigorous debate about the independent influence of Congress and the president on bureaucratic behavior. Neither the Congress nor the president requires the consent of the other to reward, sanction, or monitor the same agent.[27] Hence, the interbranch politics of agency control entails delegation from multiple principals that can unilaterally renegotiate the agent's contract without the consent of other principals.[28]

However, the individual principals in these models of American politics do not seem to suffer from any internal coordination problems, even though both the House of Representatives and the Senate are themselves collective principals. While this assumption may be reasonable in the case of a domestic legislature organized along party lines, it is less plausible for independent governments attempting coordination within an IO. Within a collective principal, if one actor or some combination of actors within the collective principal has a veto, then any decision to remove the agent or reform the agent's incentives must be preferred to the status quo by the veto player. This makes the status quo stickier than many extant common agency models imply. In the strategic situation discussed below, an agent at the status quo may be insulated from meddling principals, especially if coordination within the collective principal is costly or if any member or group of members with the power to veto a change is inclined to do so.

Ceteris paribus, agency slippage has a tendency to increase with the number of actors doing the delegating.[29] As the number of actors grows, coordination within the collective principal gets more complicated. Fortunately, many collective prin-

---

26. A recent review of the delegation literature fails to mention the concept of a collective principal and instead focuses solely on delegation from a single principal and from multiple principals. Bendor, Glazer, and Hammond 2001.

27. See Calvert et al. 1989; and Hammond and Knott 1996.

28. For example, the president can promote, demote, or fire bureaucrats, and Congress can increase organizational budgets, decrease them, or even eliminate them entirely—each without the cooperation of the other. Among IOs, the European Commission is now responsible to both the Council of Ministers and the European Parliament—a clear case of multiple principals.

29. See Olson 1965; and Hardin 1982.

cipals employ decision rules and institutional devices that induce a clear preference aggregation function for the group. Hence, if electoral rules are carefully designed, then millions of voters can coordinate as a collective principal and hold an elected official accountable.

Preference homogeneity within the collective principal may have similar effects.[30] However, if actors within the collective principal do not agree on proposed policy changes or institutional reforms, and the agent is cognizant of this disagreement, then the agent may be able to play members of the collective principal against each other. Such a situation makes it difficult for the collective principal to alter, or credibly threaten to alter, the agent's contract.[31] Hence, agents can more easily ignore threats and refuse to modify their behavior.

Depending on decision rules, the equilibrium outcome will be somewhere within the combined preference sets of the members of the collective principal, but where exactly is indeterminate without prior knowledge of the status quo and the institutional rules that govern the decisions of principals. The good news is that most IOs have formal decision rules. To the extent that these rules are efficacious, one should be able to deduce behavioral outcomes if one can specify the preferences of principals and the power of the principals defined in terms of voting share.

The Delegation Chain: Proximate Principals and Leapfrogging

The nested P-A relationships that are common to IOs further complicate our use of agency theory. This complication has received even less attention in the extant literature.[32] Figure 2 illustrates the numerous P-A relationships that are typical for IOs, with agency slack increasing as the delegation chain grows longer. If there is some slippage at each link in the delegation chain, then the ultimate principals within member countries (citizens) face the possibility that they will pay the costs of membership without receiving the policy payoff promised by the initial delegation.[33]

One solution to the problem of nested P-A relationships emerges through institutional design. Institutions can be designed so that pressure on agents to alter their behavior is only effective if it operates through the "proximate principal"— that is, the principal with the formal authority to hire, fire, or otherwise alter the agent's employment contract. This is so even if portions of the "ultimate principal"—say, voters within member countries—are the ones demanding change. The proximate principal may be designed to receive the petitions of its immediate principals in the chain of delegation, aggregate those demands, sort them, and re-

---

30. See Nielson and Tierney 2002; and Martin 2002.
31. Martin 2000.
32. For an exception, see Bergman, Muller, and Strom 2000. Unfortunately, this work neglects the impact of actions at one link in the chain on outcomes at subsequent links.
33. On problems of IO accountability to the "ultimate principals" within member countries, see Keohane and Nye 2001.

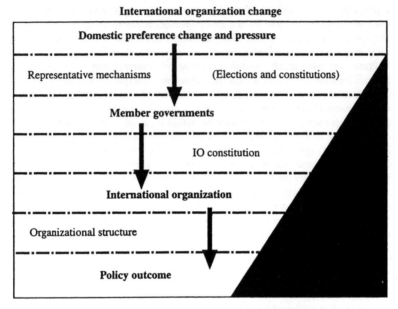

International organization change

Domestic preference change and pressure

Representative mechanisms   (Elections and constitutions)

Member governments

IO constitution

International organization

Organizational structure

Policy outcome

FIGURE 2. *Nested principal-agent relationships*

spond to them. Proximate principals filter messages coming down the chain, so that erroneous or exaggerated information is not conveyed to the agent. Proximate principals have decision rules expressly designed for these purposes, whereas an agent once or twice removed by a link in the chain is suited to receive demands only from its proximate principal and no other. Thus pressure on IO agents is unlikely to succeed until it is filtered through authoritative institutional channels.[34]

Because staff members at IOs are not rewarded, and may even be punished if they respond too vigorously to stimuli other than the demands of their proximate principal, they should tend to ignore or discount demands made by interest groups in given member countries. Hence, as we show in the case study below, attempts to "leapfrog" intermediate links in the chain of delegation will likely fail.[35] Agents

34. Alternatively, principals may design procedures to ensure that agents are receptive to demands from specific constituents. See McCubbins, Noll, and Weingast 1987 and 1989.

35. This remains consistent with principals' use of fire-alarm oversight mechanisms. For example, while nongovernmental organizations (NGOs) and private actors are encouraged to provide the World Bank's executive board with information about the behavior of Bank staff, the authority to sanction IO agents has been—by design—strictly guarded by member governments. Shihata 1994. Recent criticisms of the Bank's inspection panel by NGOs make it clear that the inspection panel has not allowed NGOs to capture or block projects preferred by the board.

(IO management and staff) that are more than one link removed from the ultimate principal (member-country electorates) in the P-A chain will not be equipped with mechanisms to discern whether activists' demands are representative of the distant principal as a whole.[36] Such institutionalized insulation actually ensures that IO agents will not change standard operating procedures without a clear indication from member governments that such changes are desired. The proximate principal will thus prove most important when agents are sifting through conflicting demands for behavioral change.

Thus at both domestic and international levels we adopt a strictly formal notion of power, which flows through authoritative rule structures specified in constitutions, articles of agreement, or charters. This approach may seem blasphemous to those familiar with the literature on IOs, in which readers are constantly reminded that formal rules and codified treaties often obscure the actual distribution of power and rules of the game within a given IO.[37] However, the formal approach adopted here allows us to deduce a clear set of behavioral expectations and aggregate outcomes—something that is missing from much empirical work on IOs. If formal rules are not efficacious within IOs, then our hypotheses are likely to be falsified.

Hypotheses and Methods

A number of hypotheses that relate to collective principals, multiple principals, preference heterogeneity among principals, and the amount and type of agency slippage can be deduced from our P-A argument, but many of these hypotheses are better tested by employing statistical methods on cross-sectional quantitative data from different IOs.[38] In this article we are interested in demonstrating the plausibility of the P-A model by closely tracing the process of reform efforts and illuminating the causal links between our independent and dependent variables. To these ends we deduce the following hypotheses:

H1. When agent behavior diverges from principal preferences, credible threats by the principal to recontract with the agent will reduce the gap between the principal's demands and the agent's subsequent behavior. However, behav-

---

36. As Canadian Prime Minister Jean Chretien explained in response to calls for greater "democratization" by anti-globalization demonstrators in Quebec City, "This meeting is the result of a democratic process. Each of the thirty-four governments represented here is responsible for the well-being of its own people and each government at this meeting has been democratically elected. Who elected these protesters?" MSNBC news broadcast, 21 April 2001.

37. In a typical review of this literature we are told that "informal power" and weakly institutionalized authority structures at the international level "make it difficult for these theories to offer accurate explanations." Middlemas 1995. He may be right. But we note that Middlemas never actually tests hypotheses derived from any theory that assumes the efficacy of formal rules. We believe it is more prudent to empirically test such theories before discarding them out of hand.

38. Nielson and Tierney 2002.

ioral change will be shallow and short-lived unless institutional reforms are enacted to "lock-in" these changes.

H2. When agent behavior diverges from principal preferences, the probability of institutional reform and the amount of institutional reform will rise as the preferences of multiple principals converge or as the preferences of members within a collective principal converge.

H3. Institutional reform will induce change in agent behavior that more closely conforms to principal demands.

H4. Pressure on the agent from any actor other than the proximate principal will not result in significant behavioral change.

To evaluate the strength of these hypotheses we carefully trace the processes and reveal the causal mechanisms of institutional reform and behavioral change at the World Bank. This task requires a method that can reveal multiple steps within a causal chain, from principals' preference changes/convergence to recontracting threats to IO organizational reform to IO behavioral change. Hence, we employ a qualitative case-study research method.

For three reasons, the World Bank presents a difficult case for our P-A model. First, the opportunities for hidden action and hidden information are extensive. The Bank's staff of more than 10,000 full-time employees and its worldwide operations make it difficult for principals to monitor.[39] Second, unlike most IOs, the Bank generates enough revenue to cover its entire operating budget independently. Also, roughly 80 percent of the money it lends is raised in private capital markets where the Bank enjoys a AAA bond rating.[40] Such figures suggest that the Bank, unlike IOs relying on dues, enjoys significant financial autonomy from member countries. Third, for most of the Bank's history, professional economists and engineers on staff have framed reports and proposals in highly technical language, often obscuring the actions taken or the anticipated outcomes.[41] Also, until quite recently it was very difficult for Bank board members (or the government officials who appointed them) to obtain detailed project documents more than a few weeks before the board vote on a loan, making oversight periods very brief. Bank reports were kept secret in the name of preserving the sovereignty of borrowers.[42]

But no matter how carefully "difficult" cases are selected, readers should be skeptical of attempts to generalize from a single case. We attempt to mitigate the small-n problem in several ways. First, while we do not increase the number of observations by looking across space at other multilateral development banks,[43]

---

39. Staff size as of May 2001. If regular consultants are excluded, the permanent Bank staff is more than 8,500 as of November 2001. By comparison, the IMF has fewer than 2,500 employees.
40. World Bank 2000, 7.
41. Ascher 1992.
42. Upton 2000.
43. For a quantitative test that does precisely this, see Nielson and Tierney 2002.

we do expand the *n* by looking across time. By examining institutional and behavioral outcomes at the Bank over a twenty-year period, we increase the number of observable implications for our theory. Of course, we do not claim that each year is independent from all previous years. However, if we encounter variance over time in our core explanatory variables—principals' preference change and convergence, credible threats to recontract, and institutional reform—then each instance of variation expands the *n*.

To increase robustness, we employ multiple measures to gauge variation in our dependent variables. We assess lending behavior by measuring the portions of money lent in various categories from year to year, by measuring the percentage of loans that fall into each category, and by employing three-year moving averages for both measures. We examine each aspect of institutional reform over time. Moreover, our model entails a causal chain. Principals' threats engender institutional reform, which results in behavioral change. Our model is strengthened if we find evidence suggesting that more significant behavioral changes in lending follow from more significant institutional reform.[44]

Case Study: Environmental Reform at the World Bank

Until the early 1980s, the World Bank's task managers and project officers did just about as they pleased.[45] Most politicians and other elites within donor countries believed the Bank was the organization best suited to meet the lending needs of world development, and therefore left it alone. As importantly, the Bank was not engaged in activities that fundamentally conflicted with the interests of the electoral coalitions holding power in the West.

Ironically, during the 1970s the World Bank was often seen as a leader among IOs on questions of environmental protection. It was one of the only IOs to explicitly discuss environmental issues and (at least rhetorically) incorporate them into policy decisions. But with only three environmental specialists on staff until 1983, the Bank's Office of Environmental Affairs typically rubber-stamped projects late in the approval process, only occasionally making recommendations to reduce environmental "externalities."[46] Despite the public perception that the Bank was more sensitive to environmental issues than other IOs, the environmental staff,

---

44. On qualitative methodology, see King, Keohane, and Verba 1994; and George and McKeown 1985.

45. While individual governments opposed various policies and specific loans before 1980, the Bank did not face the concerted and coordinated pressure from the majorities (and sometimes supermajorities) on the executive board that are necessary to redirect the Bank. Hürni 1980.

46. Wade 1997, 620–29.

without budget or authority within the organization, could neither monitor nor enforce compliance with the organization's environmental guidelines.[47]

However, even the previous perception of the Bank as relatively environment-friendly changed dramatically in the early 1980s. Then, as discussed below, a series of World Bank lending blunders helped to mobilize environmental nongovernmental organizations (NGOs), who succeeded in altering Bank behavior only after their demands were channeled through donor governments and the Bank's executive board.

Common Agency Problems at the World Bank

It is important to revisit here the discussion of common agency, involving a collective principal and multiple principals. Both types of agency relationships are exemplified by the case of the World Bank.[48] The Bank's board of governors meets at least once per year and is composed primarily of member-country finance ministers. It has the authority to alter Bank policies, approve the annual budget, and amend the Articles of Agreement. In practice, and for all decisions over operations and policy, the member governments delegate decision-making authority to the Bank's board of executive directors. This executive board is the Bank's collective principal. A simple majority vote by the board is necessary for most Bank actions except amendments to the Articles of Agreement, which currently require an 85 percent supermajority of the board of governors. While all members of the Bank have voting shares, the Group of 7 (G-7) countries currently control nearly 50 percent of all shares.[49] To force alterations in Bank practice, a coalition on the board must be built. (The collective nature of the Bank's principal is represented in Figure 3 below, where the Bank's three largest shareholders are listed). And coalition building on the board proves difficult without participation of the largest shareholder, the United States.

The U.S. president appoints (and the Senate confirms) the U.S. executive director to the Bank, who controlled 16.5 percent of the voting shares in 2000. That same year, Japan had 7.9 percent of the voting share and Germany had 4.5 percent. The large U.S. share provides an effective veto over major institutional changes at the Bank and facilitates blocking or building coalitions on the executive board. The United States is the only country with a unilateral veto over major institu-

---

47. Ibid., 635.
48. While the collective principal case is clearly illustrated by the World Bank, our choice to model the Bank as an agent of multiple principals is not as analytically clear. However, while the authority relationships are complex, we do gain leverage by conceiving of the Bank as an agent of multiple principals.
49. The size of a government's voting share is determined by its financial contribution to the Bank, which is roughly proportional to the size of its economy.

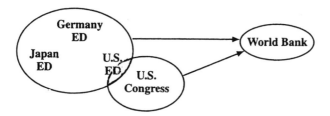

Note: ED = executive director

FIGURE 3. *Principals of the World Bank*

tional changes.[50] The U.S. executive director reports to the U.S. Secretary of the Treasury, and the other G-7 directors report either to finance or foreign affairs ministers of their states. Only eight directors represent single countries.[51] The other seventeen directorships are shared by groups of countries (usually clustered regionally), where individual directors are elected from the group by countries' voting share.

The U.S. president may dismiss the U.S. executive director at any time. As an ultimate tool, the president can end U.S. membership in the Bank unilaterally.[52] However, it is the U.S. Congress that authorizes and appropriates money to the Bank, both through the regular replenishments of the International Development Association (IDA), and when members of the Bank agree to increase their subscriptions. Because subscriptions directly affect voting share, the U.S. Congress can thus unilaterally alter the U.S. contract with the Bank. Thus Congress is an additional proximate principal.[53] Further, the U.S. Senate, through advice and consent, can reject the president's nominee for executive director. Also, Congress can dictate the votes of the director by statute (subject to veto and overrides, of

---

50. The United States has always controlled enough votes to unilaterally veto amendments to the Articles of Agreement. In the 1970s, when the Articles required only an 80 percent supermajority to pass amendments, the United States controlled more than 20 percent of the shares. As the U.S. vote share dropped below 20 percent, the board of governors voted to change the threshold to 85 percent.

51. The United States, Japan, Germany, France, the United Kingdom, the Russian Federation, China, and Saudi Arabia.

52. In fact, we would argue that a U.S. withdrawal from the World Bank—initiated either by the president or Congress—would fundamentally alter the Bank itself. Given the probable shift in priorities, personnel, and headquarters that a withdrawal of the hegemon would entail, the organization that emerged would be a fundamentally different one. The implications of a U.S. withdrawal anchor our claim that both the U.S. president and Congress are independent principals of the Bank.

53. This would hold for any other member country-legislature that exists independently of the executive and can unilaterally recontract with the Bank. This caveat applies to France during periods of cohabitation, and to most Latin American countries. France's voting share is slightly more than 25 percent of the U.S. share. All Latin American countries, even Brazil and Argentina, are much lower. Hence, this multiple principals concept applies most strongly in the case of the United States.

course).[54] Finally, the Congress can end U.S. membership in the Bank by statute (with the same veto caveat applying). Interestingly, the Congress has no direct budgetary authority over the U.S. executive director or the executive director's office, both of which are funded by the Bank. Hence, the U.S. Congress (as represented in Figure 3) has numerous formal sources of authority that allow it to unilaterally recontract with the World Bank, directly through appropriations and membership decisions, and indirectly through its authority over the U.S. executive director.

The Bank thus faces both a collective principal and multiple principals. When preferences diverge on its board, reform of the Bank proves difficult. Also, disagreement between the U.S. Congress and president can give the Bank additional room to maneuver. However, when the preferences of the board members and the two U.S. government branches come together, our model predicts that this convergence will constrain Bank behavior much more tightly.

Rumblings over Rondônia

Beginning in the early 1980s, principals' preferences regarding Bank policy changed and converged markedly in response to Bank actions, both for the U.S. Congress and president and among Bank executive directors. In 1980, the World Bank was invited by the Brazilian government to participate in a transmigration and highway construction project, dubbed *Polonoroeste*, in the heart of the Amazon rainforest. The project was intended to help accommodate the huge resettlement population influx to the state of Rondônia, while also meeting rural infrastructure and agricultural needs. Some members of Bank missions to the Amazon returned dubious about the prospects of the project to meet its stated economic and relocation aims and warned that environmental damage would almost certainly result.[55]

Their warnings went unheeded. Bank staff claimed that the Brazilian government would proceed with or without them. The executive board approved a number of loans for the massive project in the hope that Bank participation could limit some of the project's most destructive consequences. But the Bank failed to prevent the worst of these problems. The road was built; settlers poured into the jungle; indigenous natives died in waves from imported diseases; malaria infected many of the new settlements; and the rainforest burned—impressively and notoriously.[56]

54. The Pelosi Amendment is a case in point. The Pelosi Amendment requires the U.S. executive director to vote against all World Bank projects that are not accompanied by an environmental assessment at least 120 days before a vote is taken on the project by the executive board. Upton 2000.

55. See World Bank 1992; and Wade 1997, 640–42.

56. See Keck 1998; and Rich 1994.

In the rash of finger pointing that followed this debacle, the Bank proved an easy target.[57] Environmental NGOs and a growing number of scientists began to pressure the Bank through direct lobbying of staff and management, by encouraging press coverage, through protests in both Brazil and Washington, D.C., and through testimony in U.S. congressional hearings.[58] Yet, despite a loud and sustained lobbying effort, these groups were unable to stop the project or convince the Bank to halt disbursements on the loans. Similar fiascos following other Bank projects, particularly a comparable Bank-funded transmigration project in Indonesia, amplified the criticisms from the environmental community but did not trigger any change in Bank policies or projects. In fact, Bank officials grew creative in the ways they deflected criticism and ignored critics.[59] After almost three years of well-reasoned critiques, a mountain of scientific evidence and a complete lack of progress, frustrated environmentalists convinced the U.S. Congress to take action.[60]

U.S. Congress Threatens, Treasury Adds Pressure

An odd coalition of environmentalists and fiscal conservatives in Congress joined forces to pressure the Bank. Robert Kasten (R-Wis.), chair of the Subcommittee on Foreign Operations of the Senate Appropriations Committee, fit within both camps. He desired a reduction in Bank-funded projects that caused environmental problems, but he also believed the U.S. Congress should closely scrutinize all money allocated to IOs. Kasten had held multiple hearings on MDB lending and the environment from 1983–85.[61] But more public airing of project foibles had little or no impact on the status of the Rondônia project, others like it, or Bank policy in general. In order to change Bank policy, the management at the Bank needed to believe that those making all the noise could give them something they wanted or take away something that they needed. Senator Kasten understood this; and he was in a position to withhold billions of dollars.

The jugular at the World Bank was the IDA, which makes no-interest loans on a fifty-year repayment schedule to the world's poorest countries. Unlike the larger International Bank for Reconstruction and Development (IBRD), which actually turns a profit, the IDA relies on donor contributions for its allocations. At the behest of environmental groups, Kasten and his congressional allies targeted that Bank vulnerability. The U.S. Congress explicitly threatened to withhold further

---

57. Wade characterizes Polonoroeste as only the most visible of many such projects that allowed environmentalists to go after the Bank. Wade 1997, 658–60.
58. Wade 1997.
59. Ibid., 660–67.
60. See Udall 1998; and LePrestre 1989.
61. Kasten was not alone. Both the House and the Senate held numerous oversight hearings on Bank operations. See LePrestre 1989; and Wade 1997.

IDA replenishments until the Bank addressed environmental problems caused by the projects it financed.[62] In 1985, the Bank responded to Kasten's threat by suspending disbursements to the Polonoroeste project. After a five-month suspension, disbursements resumed, but with minor modifications intended to mollify Congress.[63]

Even when facing threats of funding cuts, Bank responses were sluggish.[64] Subsequently, the U.S. Treasury, the second of the U.S. multiple principals, grew serious about environmental reform at the Bank. The second Reagan administration had become more friendly than the first Reagan administration both to environmental interests and to multilateral development banks. Treasury Secretary James Baker also needed the Bank to manage the Latin American debt crisis. Congressional approval of an IBRD capital increase was vital to the success of the Baker plan for resolving the debt crisis. Now, there were two funding vulnerabilities for the Bank: the IDA replenishment and the IBRD capital increase. Baker thus took Kasten's concerns seriously and added the Treasury's voice to those in Congress calling for environmental reforms at the Bank.[65] The interests of the multiple principals had converged.

The subsequent U.S. pressure was more than rhetorical. On 19 June 1986, the United States became the first country ever to vote against a Bank project on environmental grounds. As Alternate Director Hugh Foster asked the Bank's board before casting his negative vote on the massive Brazil Power Sector loan, "How much confidence can we have that it will be carried out conscientiously when the same [Brazilian government] institutions will be implementing a series of environmental disasters at the very same time?"[66] Despite U.S. opposition, the loan was approved by the board.

Although passage of the loan certainly indicates that the members of the collective principal were divided on the need for serious environmental reform, the loss actually strengthened the resolve of Kasten and his allies in the U.S. Congress to cut IDA financing. Further coordinated efforts of the U.S. legislative and executive branches enhanced the credibility of the threat to IDA funding.[67] Moreover, at this time, interests of other members of the collective principal—notably the Nordic countries, Canada, the Netherlands, and the United Kingdom—were also converging around environmental reforms at the Bank. However, these other directors

---

62. In late 1984, the House Subcommittee on International Development held hearings and made a number of "recommendations" to the Bank. Highlights included the establishment of an Environment Department, hiring more environmental staff, reducing destructiveness of traditional projects, consulting with environmental ministers and NGOs in borrowing countries, and financing more projects that would enhance environmental protection. See U.S. House of Representatives 1984.

63. See LePrestre 1989; Rich 1994.

64. Bank second-in-command Ernest Stern energetically withstood U.S. pressure, particularly demands coming from Congress. Wade 1997, 668.

65. Wade 1997, 667–68.

66. Foster, quoted in Rich 1994, 137.

67. Upton 2000.

applied pressure more subtly, and were more willing to accept Bank explanations for environmental problems at face value.[68]

Waves of Reform at the Bank

With the near certainty of substantial funding reductions, the new president of the Bank, Barber Conable, an environmental sympathizer and former U.S. Congressman, attempted to insure that the IDA would not be gutted.[69] In May 1987, he announced a series of environmental reforms that addressed some of the concerns of the Bank's environmental critics. Most notably, the Bank reorganized its Office of Environmental and Scientific Affairs into a separate Environment Department, boosting staff from a half-dozen people to more than eighty members charged with performing more stringent environmental assessments of projects. In addition, Conable promised to create a new category of free-standing environmental loans. There was no commitment to reducing the dirty "traditional" loans in energy and transportation that were at the heart of the environmental disasters of the 1980s, but Conable did initiate a process that made the Bank's environmental policies more stringent (at least on paper). Over the next several years, the Bank did delay loan disbursements on some of the most controversial projects. However, these actions did little to alter the environmentalists' perceptions of the Bank.[70]

After the 1987 reforms, the Bank increased the number of environmental loans. But many NGOs questioned whether these new loans were in fact "environmental," rather than traditional sector loans with new labels.[71] The incentives of task managers had not been altered by the financial threats of donors, so the Bank continued to favor large (and dirty) traditional loans. For many Bank critics, the behavioral changes that followed 1987 were a step in the right direction, but a very small one.[72]

One reason that the 1987 reforms may have failed to alter core Bank practice was that the threats had been contingent on short-term behavioral changes rather than institutional changes The loan approval process was largely un-

---

68. Wade 1997, 671.

69. Conable was appointed precisely to avert congressional funding cuts and to fix the Bank's environment image. See Wade 1997, 672.

70. See Kraske et al., 1996, 266–68; and Wade 1997, 673–87.

71. In every year from 1987 through 1993, total lending on "brown" projects for water reclamation and pollution abatement was greater than lending for "green" projects aimed at natural resource preservation. The average ratio of brown to green was 3.6:1 for this seven-year period.

72. Our interpretation is at odds with Wade 1997, who emphasized the 1987 reforms as pivotal for environmental improvements at the Bank. However, the facts that NGO criticisms not only persisted but increased, meaningful change occurred sluggishly in traditional sectors, environmental assessment was piecemeal, and Bank approval and board oversight practices remained unaltered, all argue in favor of our interpretation that the 1987 reforms were less important than the 1993–94 reforms. For an interpretation consistent with our position, see Fox and Brown 1998.

changed,[73] with the Bank's board still dependent on project officers for information and the Bank still lacking qualified personnel to conduct all the environmental assessments required by its new policies.[74] While the in-house Environment Department now had a higher profile and more personnel, it was not effectively integrated into the operational side of the Bank and had few levers of power compared to task managers.[75] Hence, over the next few years, environmentalists inside and outside the Bank observed plenty of "bureaucratic drift," but had no institutionalized role in the process through which to restrain such behavior.[76]

Unsurprisingly, the 1987 reforms satisfied neither external critics nor the Bank's executive directors. Evidence of Bank-funded fiascos continued to mount, and a series of documents catalogued Bank shortcomings. Notably, a 1992 report—commissioned by the World Bank but researched and written independently by the Morse Commission—on the Sardar Sarovar dam project in India sharply criticized the Bank for failing to meet its own environmental standards.[77] On the heels of this pointed criticism, an internal Bank document, later known as the *Wappenhans Report*, echoed the Sardar Sarovar criticisms, and noted that 37 percent of Bank projects had proved "unsatisfactory." Wappenhans and his colleagues attributed this massive failure to the "approval culture" inside the Bank, where task managers used project documents—especially the all-important Staff Appraisal Reports (SARs)—as "marketing devices" to ensure loan approval.[78] This criticism stung the Bank's management and further tarnished its public image. Still, Bank officials stonewalled and deflected criticism. It took coordinated actions by both branches of the U.S. government and the Bank's executive board to change this pattern.

Organizational Changes and Reform That Sticks

As the chair of the House Subcommittee on International Development, Trade, Finance and Monetary Policy, Barney Frank (D-Mass.) was acutely aware of the

---

73. While regional vice presidents became more directly involved with loan planning and development, the board still saw project documents for the first time only ten to fourteen days before voting on the loan. See Wade 1997, fn 142; and Upton 2000.

74. Rich 1994.

75. Interviews with World Bank staff member Anjali Acharya, ESSD Network, and John Donaldson, Senior World Bank External Affairs Counselor, Washington, D.C., January 2001. "Task manager" is the title at the Bank for what commercial banks would call a loan officer.

76. McCubbins, Noll, and Weingast 1987 and 1989.

77. By late 1991, a growing number of executive directors simply did not trust the information provided by the Bank's India operations staff. At the behest of the executive board, Bank President Conable appointed an independent review team to investigate the Sardar Sarovar project. The team was chaired by the former director of the UN Development Program, Bradford Morse. See Morse and Berger 1992; Udall 1998.

78. See Wappenhans 1992, 14; and Udall 1998, 401.

Bank's failure to change. With the next round of IDA replenishment looming in 1994, Frank took a page out of Kasten's book and in 1992 threatened to withhold a nearly $4 billion replenishment unless the Bank undertook serious and specific reforms.[79] This time Bank officials fought back with lobbying efforts, venturing repeatedly to the U.S. Treasury Department and to Capitol Hill directly to argue for a reversal of Frank's threat. For the most part they failed. The new Clinton administration was politically committed to environmentalism, and legislators from both parties ignored the issue at their electoral peril. The multiple principals within the U.S. government had converged.[80] Congress did eventually authorize the IDA replenishment, but for two years rather than the customary three. The legislature thus reduced the authorized amount by more than $1 billion. The final increment of $1.25 billion was made contingent on the actual implementation of information disclosure and inspection-panel reforms over the next two years.[81]

Bank officials got the message when U.S. threats were complemented by a resurgent board, which had become more unified on the environment during the early 1990s following the 1992 Earth Summit in Rio de Janeiro.[82] Japan established the Policy and Human Resources Development Fund in 1990, which the Bank would manage. This included grants for technical assistance for a broad range of projects, including issues of health, water and sanitation, but especially environmental and resettlement issues.[83] Additionally, Japan withdrew bilateral aid to India for turbines and generators necessary for the Narmada project.

Meanwhile, the West German Bundestag had been mobilized by the Green Party to support serious environmental reforms at the Bank.[84] European environmental preferences had been converging for another reason as well. As the Single European Act and Maastricht Treaties were signed, Germany, the Netherlands, and Denmark were using their economic strength within the European Union (EU) to both raise, and make uniform, European environmental standards. Even less environmentally sensitive countries, such as Spain and Italy, had implemented more than 80 percent of the EU's environmental rules by 1990. Britain and France had implemented nearly 90 percent.[85] Employing an environmental policy index that we have constructed, this convergence on policy—and, by inference, environmental

79. George Graham, "Developing a More Worldly Bank: Plans at the World Bank for Improving Its Project Management," *Financial Times*, 2–4 July 1993.

80. Wade persuasively argues that the U.S. Treasury Department "above all" pressed the Bank to adopt reforms being championed by environmental NGOs. Wade 2002, 27.

81. But even then, the full amount was to be reduced by $200 million. Several years later the United States did eventually provide the final third of the replenishment. Interview with John Donaldson, Senior World Bank External Affairs Counselor, Washington, D.C., 31 January 2001; and Udall 1998, 403.

82. Nielson and Tierney 2002.

83. See Gyohten 1997; and World Bank 2002.

84. Wade 1997, 662.

85. Steinberg 1997, 255–60.

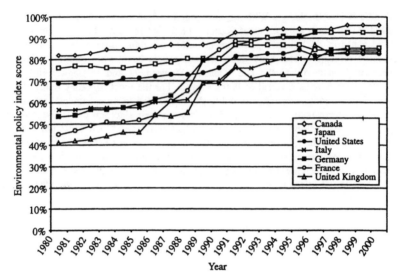

FIGURE 4. *Improvement and convergence of environmental policy in the Group of 7 countries*

preferences—among G-7 countries is shown graphically in Figure 4.[86] The standard deviation on the index among G-7 countries shifts from a standard deviation of 15.6 in 1980 to 6.1 in 1991, and from an average of 60.3 to 84.3.[87]

As the environmental preferences among the Bank's most powerful members increased and converged over time, the board was able to mandate multiple significant reforms. Notably, in 1994 the board empowered an independent inspection panel to hear complaints from groups that Bank projects would directly affect.[88]

---

86. Using the revealed-preferences approach, we have compiled an Environmental Policy Index, patterned on the Environmental Sustainability Index of Esty 2001. In constructing the index we gathered data for 122 countries on twenty-two distinct measures of environmental policy outcomes for the years 1980–2000. The measures ranged from atmospheric sulfur dioxide concentration, to dissolved oxygen levels in freshwater, to number of reporting commitments kept as part of the Convention on International Trade in Endangered Species. We standardized the measures so that each country's index score on any given measure is relative to all other countries on the same measure. Scores were also standardized relative to the base year of 1996, allowing country scores to vary over time as well as cross-sectionally. The overall index score is an average percentile ranking over the twenty-two measures. For details on the construction of the index, see Esty 2001 and Nielson and Tierney 2002.

87. The standard deviation and average for 2000 were 5.4 and 88.1, respectively.

88. This was one of the specific demands of the U.S. Congress. Frank's committee recommended both an independent inspection panel and greater access to project documents for board members, NGOs, and legislators in member governments. On 20 June 1994, the day before Frank's committee was to vote on reauthorization, the Bank released procedural guidelines for the panel that Frank demanded. See Udall 1998, 107–109; and Shihata 1994.

This move conforms closely to the fire-alarm mechanisms noted above.[89] It gave numerous private and public groups an opportunity to bring outside information to the inspection panel and thus the executive board. Now board members found it much easier to get information about the likely impacts of Bank projects before the projects were implemented, as well as information about the conduct of their agents during the implementation phase.[90]

Despite opposition from Bank staff and some borrowing countries, the board enacted sunshine practices and other reporting requirements at the Bank, substantially opening records and documents to the public that had previously been sealed. Since 1994, all project managers have been required to file, and periodically update, a public information document (PID). To ensure that interested societal groups could get relevant information about Bank projects, the board mandated that each PID would contain a section devoted to "environmental aspects" of the project. SARs—now including environmental assessments—were also made public after 1994.[91] These and other sunshine practices were purposely designed as fire-alarm mechanisms that would allow the board to closely monitor its agents: the Bank staff and management.[92]

For good measure, the board increased its police-patrol oversight activities as well. Before 1994, the board received project documents mere weeks before a vote would be taken. This dramatically reduced the probability of any negative decisions by the board, since halting or substantially altering a loan at that late stage of the project cycle would be quite costly and could even shake the credibility of the Bank. After the 1993–94 changes to the loan approval process, board members would be involved early in the planning stages of projects, and they began to exercise their option to question or suggest changes to projects long before they reached the decision phase.[93] As Kapur, Lewis, and Webb, note,

> Issues of accountability and discipline were also complicated by the actions of the Board. Although management held the initiative for bringing projects to the board and the board never turned down any management proposal, it now had influence before projects arrived and in collective discussion of future projects.[94]

89. McCubbins and Schwartz 1987.

90. Of course, not all representatives on the board are enthusiastic about the inspection panel. Board members from borrowing countries see the panel as an intrusion into their domestic affairs. This observation simply highlights the fact that the World Bank responds to a collective principal with a majority-vote decision rule. The coalition led by the G-7 has more than enough votes to sustain the panel even in the face of intense opposition by member states in the minority. Preference convergence within the majority coalition does not imply unanimity on the board. See Umana 1998.

91. This policy only covered SARs written after October 1993.

92. See Shakow 1994; and Shihata 1994.

93. Shakow 1994, 4.

94. Kapur, Lewis, and Webb 1997, 45.

This is precisely what our P-A model suggests we should observe in equilibrium. Bank staff ought to anticipate possible objections by directors and make adjustments so that those projects do not get rejected in later stages of the project cycle.

Finally, in part because of the bureaucratic drift observed after the 1987 reforms, the board now insisted on substantial changes in the type of staff hired by the Bank. The number of environmental economists, biologists, and environmental engineers employed by the Bank dramatically increased between 1993 and 2000.[95] The number of personnel employed as environmental staff had increased from five in 1986 to more than three hundred by March 2000.[96] By hiring agents with training in the environmental sciences, the board could be more certain that Bank staff now had the ability to analyze the environmental impact of projects, but also the interest in seeing that its new goals were realized. This is a classic example of screening and selection to avoid agency slippage.

More important than the fact that the board was hiring scientists, rather than exclusively economists and engineers, was that these scientists were no longer concentrated in the "ghetto" of the World Bank that was the D.C.-based Environment Department or the Regional Environment Divisions. Since 1994, each project with potential environmental impact has been assigned an environmental project manager (typically a non-economist) who is required to assess the environmental impact of each project and include a written evaluation to be sent to the board with other project documents. Having environmental scientists involved in project planning, approval, and implementation is likely to ensure that members of the board get more than mere environmental rhetoric from task managers. Since 1994 board members have received better and more timely information about the environmental impact of Bank projects because the administrative procedures that they passed in 1993 placed numerous checks on the authority of task managers.

Disbursement for any project categorized as environmentally sensitive A or B types now requires two distinct environmental assessments. First, during the project planning phase an environmental impact assessment (EIA) must be submitted and a pilot program must be designed to test for environmental degradation. After data is collected during the pilot phase, a second EIA must be submitted for the project as a whole. This larger EIA reveals practices that negatively affect the environment and recommends alternatives. In the absence of alternatives, the EIA evaluates the cost and feasibility of mitigation options.[97] Loan disbursements cannot commence until these administrative procedures are completed and the documents submitted to the board by authorized environmental staff. This is a direct applica-

95. In 1993, less than 2 percent of Bank staff (roughly 200 people) had advanced degrees in the hard sciences, but by 2000 that percentage had more than doubled to 4 percent (more than 400 professionals). E-mail correspondence with Kristyn Ebro, World Bank External Affairs, June 2001.

96. Nakayama 2000; and e-mail correspondence with Kristyn Ebro, June 2001.

97. See Operational Policy (OP) 4.01, "Environmental Assessments" and OP 4.02, "Environmental Action Plans" in World Bank 1997a and 1997b.

tion of the Madisonian tactic of checks and balances. The principal has hired an additional agent with interests that diverge from those of the original agent, and has also created administrative procedures that check the ability of the original agent to act unilaterally.

These personnel and administrative changes at the Bank were not the direct result of a growing global norm of environmental protection or sustainable development. Such norms preexisted these personnel changes by many years.[98] These administrative and policy changes came as a direct result of a change in the preferences of the Bank's proximate principals and the principals' subsequent employment of mechanisms explicitly designed to reduce agency slippage.

Conspicuous Absences

While reforms at the World Bank are impressive and, as we demonstrate below, have a measurable effect on Bank lending behavior, some notable absences persist. None of the reforms have addressed the basic employment incentives faced by task managers. That is, the collective principal of the Bank has not used the contracting method in an attempt to lock-in preferred agent behavior. Staff incentives to move large amounts of money through big projects persist.[99] Bank critics have repeatedly called for reform of employment incentives,[100] but little in this area has occurred.[101] Bank critics have become intensely frustrated. Because these NGOs have achieved so many of their aims,[102] failure on this front demands some explanation.

First, loans are negotiated settlements. There are at least two parties to all agreements. Despite conventional wisdom that portrays borrowing countries as helpless in the face of a unified "Northern Bloc," developing countries often—if not always—have significant leverage over the architecture of the final loan document.[103] They often find powerful allies within lending institutions that share the developing countries' preferences for traditional, large loans.

Second, our model highlights the fact that NGOs, despite their energy, their activism, and the legitimacy given to their policy positions by a growing number of scientists, are not the ultimate principals of the World Bank. Instead, these groups compete with other social groups to gain the attention of their agents—elected

98. See Keck and Sikkink 1998; and Peritore 1999, 32–36.

99. See Treakle 1998; and Winters 1997. This conclusion was reconfirmed through interviews with members of Bank's upper management on 17 December 2001 and with staff members under the vice president for operations policy and country services on 26 April 2002.

100. See Rich 1985, 1994; Environmental Defense Fund 1998; Nelson 1995; and Cobb 1999.

101. However, the Bank claims that employment incentives are changing. Interview with John Donaldson, Senior World Bank External Affairs Counselor, Washington, D.C., 31 January 2001.

102. In a recent analysis of global social movements O'Brien et al. argue persuasively that environmental NGOs have been more successful than any other issue-oriented NGOs at shaping the policies of multilateral economic institutions. O'Brien et al. 2000.

103. See Fox and Brown 1998, 14–16; and Nielson and Tierney 1999.

TABLE 1. *Summary of institutional reforms*

Category	Pressure	Institutional reform
Screening and selection	Kasten hearings (1985–86) Frank hearings (1991–93) IDA withholding (1994)	• Created Environment Dept. (1987) • New types of professionals hired as environmental staff (1994–) • Mainstreaming personnel (1994–)
Oversight and monitoring	Frank hearings (1991–92) IDA withholding (1994)	• Inspection panel (1994) • Sunshine policies (1994) • Reporting requirements (1993)
Procedural checks	Kasten hearings (1985–86) Frank hearings (1991–92) IDA withholding (1994)	• Environmental assessments (1986, 1991) • Strengthened assessment (1994) • Mainstreaming (1994–)
New contracts	No agreement among proximate principals	• None

officials in developed countries. Because democratically elected governments are agents for a broad range of voters in a winning coalition, we.should not be surprised by policy compromises that dilute the initial demands of particular constituent groups, environmentalists included. In fact, institutional channeling of societal demands may be essential to IO accountability.[104] Further, at each successive level of delegation, we observe some agency slippage. This pattern follows from our model and appears to reinforce the conclusions of leading experts on Bank behavior.[105]

Summary of Qualitative Findings

We have argued that institutional reform resulted from pressure by principals for change, particularly when that pressure was emphasized by threats to recontract with the agent by withdrawing financial support. We argued that this pressure should result in specific outcomes such as new institutions designed for screening and selection, oversight, procedural checks, and new contracts. The findings are summarized in Table 1.

Even the Bank's harshest critics recognize that substantial change has occurred in the organization.[106] And some qualitative analysis has noted that the Bank's

---

104. Keohane and Nye 2001.
105. See Upton 2000, 63; and Wade 1997, 728–34.
106. Interview with Bruce Rich, program manager for the Environmental Defense Fund, August 1995, Washington, D.C.

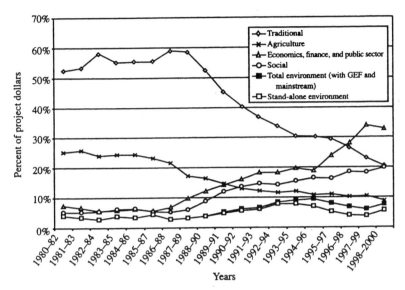

FIGURE 5. *Percent of World Bank project dollars by category (three-year rolling average)*

loan portfolio is altered from the past.[107] However, no researchers have under-taken statistical analysis of Bank lending practices that could offer systematic tests of our P-A model.

Descriptive Statistics

Accordingly, we compiled a large data set that includes every project approved by the Bank's executive board from 1980 to 2000,[108] representing more than 5,300 projects. We aggregated the projects by year and category to reveal overall World Bank lending over time (see Figures 5 and 6).[109] In these figures, we averaged

107. Fox and Brown 1998.
108. At the suggestion of reviewers, we subsequently collected data for 1970 through 1979 (2,120 additional loans). However, in none of the project categories were the trends before 1980 significantly different from the 1980–86 period. To maintain consistency between our case study and our graphical figures below, we exclude the 1970s from the figures. However, the additional data from the 1970s is included in all the regression analysis reported in subsequent footnotes.
109. Because they lack relevance for our particular questions about environmental reform, multi-sector, private-sector and telecommunications/informatics projects are excluded from the presentation of trends in lending categories shown here.

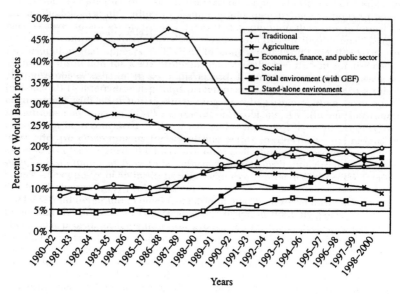

FIGURE 6. *Percent of World Bank projects approved by category (three-year rolling average)*

Bank financing in specific categories for three-year periods, both to accommodate the two- to three-year project cycle and to smooth out year-to-year fluctuations. To ease interpretation of the data (with their large fluctuations in total number of projects and dollars lent from year to year), and to control for the general increase in number and size of World Bank projects over time, the figures represent percentages of projects and project dollars in the three-year periods.

There are two basic approaches to the question: How has the World Bank's portfolio toward the environment changed as a result of principal demands? The first examines projects that actively attempt to preserve and improve the environment. The second considers projects that can harm the environment, particularly "traditional" lending in the areas of energy/electricity, industry, oil/gas exploration, transportation, and urban development. Critics of the Bank have pressed for both increases in environmental lending and decreases in traditional lending.

Alterations in the Bank's environmental portfolio can be seen in Figures 5 and 6 as the lines punctuated by squares. The white squares represent stand-alone environmental projects, or projects aimed primarily at alleviating air and water pollution, protecting parks and wilderness, and improving environmental protection infrastructure in governments.[110] The solid black squares represent total environmental financing, once "mainstreamed" environmental components[111] of traditional loans and Bank-managed Global Environment Facility (GEF) projects are included.[112]

We expected environmental lending behavior to change beginning in 1987 and then again in 1994.[113] Both of these trends occur roughly when predicted and thus support our model. Contradicting our expectations, we found that, beginning in the 1995–97 period (a peak of 9.4 percent of Bank-managed project dollars), environmental projects actually declined as a percentage of project dollars until 1998–2000 (see Figure 5). However, in none of the periods after 1994–96 did stand-alone environmental lending dip below the 1980–86 average level of 3.6 percent.

The fact that the post-1996 decline in stand-alone environmental dollars is flattened when GEF dollars are included suggests that a division of resources has developed at the Bank. Even though the same Bank staffers are initiating, organizing, and managing GEF and IBRD/IDA projects, GEF funds are increasingly being used to finance environmental projects as opposed to IBRD and IDA funds. The member countries that established the GEF in the early 1990s—dominated by the same countries that control the Bank's executive board—likely anticipated this outcome.

Also, the Bank has touted its mainstreaming of environmental dollars into traditional project loans as a way of preventing or solving environmental problems earlier in the project cycle. These mainstreamed environment dollars have diminished in recent years, in part because of the decline in the traditional sectors as a percentage of the Bank's portfolio, also seen in Figures 5 and 6. The post-1993 increase in the environment percentage of total Bank finance is statistically significant.[114]

---

110. Before 1986, the Bank did not label environmental loans as such. But Bank environmental lending, particularly in the area of water reclamation, occurred long before the environmental reforms of the 1980s. Thus, we coded each loan as either primarily environmental or not, independent of the Bank's categorization scheme. Two different researchers coded all of the data from 1970 to 2000. On the few occasions where disagreement arose, the research team coded the loans against the model—ambiguous loans were coded as environmental from 1970–86, and not environmental from 1987–2000. Given controversy over the categorization of forestry projects, we excluded them. See Rich 1994.

111. As we explained in the case study, mainstreamed funds are intended to ameliorate any environmental damage that may result from a given project. These environmental line-items have been included in project appraisal documents and SARs of traditional project loans since 1994.

112. The GEF was created as a small pilot program in 1991 and was funded entirely by contributions from developed-country governments. Replenished in 1995, the GEF provides grants to developing countries for projects that address various environmental problems (biodiversity loss, ozone depletion, climate change, and international waters). The World Bank administers roughly 60 percent of all GEF funds. Only Bank-managed GEF projects are included in the data reported here.

113. These dates are marking from the years that pressure for reform mounted in the U.S. Congress, 1985 and 1992, respectively.

114. Treating each year's total as an independent observation and employing dummy variables for the periods before 1980, after 1986, and after 1993, the 1994–2000 trend is significant at the .01 level. The 1987–93 trend is positive but not statistically significant. The adjusted R^2 is .33 and the F statistic for the regression is 6.07, which is significant at the .01 level. This simple regression is mathematically equivalent to a difference of means test and an analysis of variance (ANOVA) test. The results

When we consider total number of projects as an alternative measure of the dependent variable, rather than dollars lent, the trends toward the environment are more pronounced (see Figure 6). IBRD and IDA environmental projects are smaller on average ($60 million) than projects in traditional sectors ($90 million), and Bank-managed GEF projects are much smaller still ($7.8 million on average). The percentage of stand-alone Bank environmental projects has risen from an average of 4.6 percent of the total number of Bank projects from 1980 to 1986 to 6.0 percent for 1987–93, and to 7.3 percent for 1994–2000.[115] However, when the much smaller Bank-managed GEF projects are included, environment projects as a percent of Bank projects jump from the 1980–86 average of 4.6 to 7.3 for 1987–93 and to 14.9 for 1994–2000.[116] Because managerial effort is much greater per dollar for smaller loans, this shift in overall number of projects represents a large dedication of Bank administrative energy toward the environment. From 1996–2000, more than one sixth of all Bank-managed projects were in the environment category, making it the second largest category (in number of loans) behind the exploding social sector, which includes education, health, and social safety nets.

The sectoral patterns in Bank lending suggest additional support for our argument (see Figures 5 and 6). The sector trends reflect the "do no harm" approach to environmental protection. As we noted in the case study, while unsatisfied principals did pressure the Bank to support environmental protection in borrowing countries, the pressure to halt funding for environmentally damaging projects (such as Polonoroeste and Sardar Sarovar) was arguably even greater. In the 1987–93 period, we witness a sharp decline in Bank lending for traditional categories (energy, industry, transportation, etc.) in both dollars lent and percent of projects. The trend continues in the 1994–2000 period.[117] The same largely holds for the agricultural sector, where most projects also have potential environmental impact.[118] Further, there is little need for environmental amelioration for projects in economics/finance/public sector and the social sectors, where Bank lending is sharply and significantly increasing over time.[119]

---

are qualitatively similar when total dollars lent in the environment category is used as a dependent variable. Of course, such basic analysis does not control for the numerous additional factors that may drive Bank environment finance. We employ such controls in other work, which treats individual loans as independent observations. Nielson and Tierney 2002.

115. The 1987–93 trend is positive, but not statistically significant. The 1994–2000 trend is significant at the .05 level. The adjusted R^2 is .20.

116. The 1994–2000 trend is significant at the .01 level; the 1987–93 trend is significant only at the most modest 0.1 level. The adjusted R^2 is .66.

117. The 1987–93 trend is significant for percent of projects at the .05 level, though it is not significant for project dollars; the 1994–2000 trend is significant at the .01 level for both percent of projects and project dollars. The adjusted R^2 for both regressions is .64.

118. In agriculture, the 1987–93 trend is significant at the .01 level for percent of projects and project dollars. The 1994–2000 trend is significant at the .01 level for percent of projects, though it is not significant for project dollars. The adjusted R^2 for the regressions is .81 and .64, respectively.

119. The trends in finance and social categories are also statistically significant at (at least) the .05 level in regressions for percent of projects and project dollars.

In nearly all cases, the statistical trends are stronger and more significant for the 1994–2000 period than for the 1987–93 period, suggesting that sectoral finance patterns at the Bank changed more profoundly after the 1993 reforms than they did after the much-heralded 1987 reforms. These statistical results reinforce the inferences we make following our case study and offer additional support for our model. Significant behavioral changes that stick follow institutional reforms.

Conclusion

We attempt to accomplish four important tasks in this article. First, we address an interesting empirical puzzle in international relations: How and why did the World Bank initially resist reform, and how did it ultimately come to change its organizational structure and its lending behavior? We offer an agency theory explanation for the observed empirical pattern. Further, we conduct qualitative and statistical analysis of the model.

Second, we provide the first overall (descriptive) statistical analysis of environmental lending at the World Bank and supplement it with an assessment of the entire portfolio.[120] We find it remarkable that no one has done such work during the past ten years, especially considering the mountain of qualitative work done by both academics and activists on these subjects. Not only does this policy debate suffer from a lack of quantitative analysis, but also from an almost complete lack of quantitative data. We help to remedy the latter problem by compiling a large database that bears on various aspects of this debate.[121]

Third, we explain why the next logical step in the neoliberal institutionalist research agenda should parallel a shift that took place in the economic theory of the firm decades ago. Because neoliberal regime theorists based many of their insights on the early work of Coase, it makes sense to pursue a parallel shift toward agency theory in IR in the hope that it will be as productive.

Fourth, in this spirit we outline a P-A model of international organization and discuss some of the special difficulties that we expect agency theory to encounter

---

120. Our findings strongly suggest that Bank critics are wrong when they conclude that the Bank is conducting business as usual when it comes to the environment. Environmental lending has increased significantly since 1987, the Bank has institutionalized checks on the dysfunctional behavior of its staff, the Bank has dramatically decreased lending for traditional "dirty" loans, and member governments have significantly increased their ability to monitor and sanction behavior that is not consistent with official Bank lending practices.

121. Further data collection efforts have produced: A database on voting shares in the eight largest international financial institutions from date of origin through 2000; a database of all MDB loans by type, year and organization over the past twenty years; and an environmental policy index for 122 countries from 1980–2000. We are currently extending our database on "mainstreamed" environmental lending by recoding line items in project documents before 1994. Without such data it is difficult to interpret changes in environmental lending following the 1994 reforms. Finally, we are gathering data on personnel assignments within the Bank and administrative spending by department. These data will help us to conduct much more precise tests of the P-A model at each step in the chain of delegation.

when it is applied to IOs. In fact, our insights about the role of a collective principal, multiple principals, and proximate principals may be germane to researchers in American and comparative politics, whose subjects are either connected by multiple links in a delegation chain or who fit the definition of common agency. Hence, we have not merely employed an existing model to address an empirical puzzle in IR, but have also suggested insights applicable to the broader literature on agency theory.

References

Adler, Emanuel. 1998. Seeds of Peaceful Change: The OSCE's Security Community Building Model. In *Security Communities*, edited by Emanuel Adler and Michael N. Barnett, 119–60. Cambridge: Cambridge University Press.

Aggarwal, Vinod K. 1981. Hanging by a Thread: International Regime Change in the Textile/Apparel System, 1950–1979. Ph.D. diss., Stanford University, Palo Alto, Calif.

Alchian, Armon A., and Harold Demsetz. 1972. Production, Information Costs and Economic Organization. *The American Economic Review* 62 (5):777–95.

Ascher, William. 1992. The World Bank and US Control. In *The United States and Multilateral Institutions: Patterns of Changing Instrumentality and Influence*, edited by Margaret P. Karns and Karen A. Mingst, 115–40. London: Routledge.

Axelrod, Robert M., and Robert O. Keohane. 1985. Achieving Cooperation Under Anarchy: Strategies and Institutions. *World Politics* 38 (1):226–54.

Baldwin, David A., ed. 1993. *Neorealism and Neoliberalism: The Contemporary Debate*. New York: Columbia University Press.

Barnett, Michael N., and Martha Finnemore. 1999. The Politics, Power, and Pathologies of International Organizations. *International Organization* 53 (4):699–732.

Bendor, Jonathan, Ami Glazer, and Thomas H. Hammond. 2001. Theories of Delegation. *Annual Review of Political Science* 4:235–69.

Bergman, Torbjorn, Wolfgang Muller, and Kaare Strom. 2000. Introduction: Parliamentary Democracy and the Chain of Delegation. *European Journal of Political Research*, 37:255–60.

Calvert, Randall, Mathew McCubbins, and Barry Weingast. 1989. A Theory of Political Control and Agency Discretion. *American Journal of Political Science* 33 (3):588–611.

Coase, Ronald H. 1937. The Nature of the Firm. *Economica* 4 (16):386–405.

Cobb, John B., Jr. 1999. *The Earthist Challenge to Economism: A Theological Critique of the World Bank*. New York: St. Martin's Press.

Dixit, Avinash, Gene Grossman, and Ethan Helpman. 1997. Common Agency and Coordination: General Theory and Application to Government Policy Making. *Journal of Political Economy* 105 (4):752–69.

Dodd, Lawrence C., and Richard L. Schott. 1979. *Congress and the Administrative State*. New York: Wiley.

Duffield, John S. 1992. International Regimes and Alliances Behavior: Explaining NATO Conventional Force Levels. *International Organization* 46 (4):819–56.

Esty, Daniel C. 2001. Environmental Sustainability Index. New Haven, Conn.: Yale Center for Environmental Law and Policy. Available online at ⟨http://www.ciesin.columbia.edu/indicators/ESI/⟩.

Environmental Defense Fund (EDF). 1998. Export Credit Agencies: The Need for More Rigorous, Common Policies, Procedures and Guidelines. Washington, D.C.: EDF.

Fama, Eugene F. 1980. Agency Problems and the Theory of the Firm. *Journal of Political Economy* 88 (2):288–307.

Finnemore, Martha. 1996. *National Interests in International Society*. Ithaca, N.Y.: Cornell University Press.

Finnemore, Martha, and Kathryn Sikkink. 2001. Taking Stock: The Constructivist Research Program in International Relations and Comparative Politics. *Annual Review of Political Science* 4:391–416.

Fox, Jonathan A., and David L. Brown. 1998. *The Struggle for Accountability: The World Bank, NGOs, and Grassroots Movements*. Cambridge, Mass.: MIT Press.

George, Alexander L., and Timothy McKeown. 1985. Case Studies and Theories of Organizational Decision Making. *Advances in Information Processing in Organizations*. 2:21–58.

Gilpin, Robert. 1972. The Politics of Transnational Economic Relations. In *Transnational Relations and World Politics*, edited by Robert O. Keohane and Joseph S. Nye Jr., 48–69. Cambridge, Mass.: Harvard University Press.

———. 1981. *War and Change in World Politics*. New York: Cambridge University Press.

———. 1987. *The Political Economy of International Relations*. Princeton, N.J.: Princeton University Press.

Gould, Erica R. Forthcoming. Money Talks: The Role of External Financiers in Influencing International Monetary Fund Conditionality. *International Organization*.

Grieco, Joseph M. 1988. Anarchy and the Limits of Cooperation: A Realist Critique of the Newest Liberal Institutionalism. *International Organization* 42 (3):485–507.

Gyohten, Toyoo. 1997. Japan and the World Bank. In *The World Bank: Its First Half Century*, vol. 2, edited by Devesh Kapur, John P. Lewis, and Richard Webb, 275–316. Washington, D.C.: Brookings Institution Press.

Hammond, Thomas H., and Jack H. Knott. 1996. Who Controls the Bureaucracy? Presidential Power, Congressional Dominance, Legal Constraints, and Bureaucratic Autonomy in a Model of Multi-Institutional Policy-Making. *Journal of Law, Economics and Organization* 12 (1):119–66.

Hardin, Russell. 1982. *Collective Action*. Baltimore, Md.: Johns Hopkins University Press.

Hürni, Bettina S. 1980. *The Lending Policy of the World Bank in the 1970s: Analysis and Evaluation*. Boulder, Colo.: Westview Press.

Kapur, Devesh, John Lewis, and Richard Webb. 1997. *The World Bank: Its First Half-Century*. 2 vols. Washington, D.C.: Brookings Institution Press.

Keck, Margaret E. 1998. Planafloro in Rondônia: The Limits of Leverage. In *The Struggle for Accountability: The World Bank, NGOs, and Grassroots Movements*, edited by Jonathan Fox and David Brown, 181–218. Cambridge, Mass.: MIT Press.

Keck, Margaret E., and Kathryn Sikkink. 1998. *Activists Beyond Borders: Advocacy Networks in International Politics*. Ithaca, N.Y.: Cornell University Press.

Keohane, Robert O. 1984. *After Hegemony: Cooperation and Discord in the World Political Economy*. Princeton, N.J.: Princeton University Press.

———, ed. 1986. *Neorealism and Its Critics*. New York: Columbia University Press.

———. 1993. Institutional Theory and the Realist Challenge After the Cold War. In *Neorealism and Neoliberalism: The Contemporary Debate*, edited by David A. Baldwin, 269–300. New York: Columbia University Press.

Keohane, Robert O., and Lisa L. Martin. 1999. Institutional Theory, Endogeneity, and Delegation. Working Paper Series 99–07. Cambridge, Mass.: Weatherhead Center for International Affairs, Harvard University.

Keohane, Robert O., and Joseph Nye Jr. 2001. Global Governance and Accountability: 'It's Not the Democratic Deficit,' Stupid! Paper presented at IGCC Conference on Globalization and Governance, March, La Jolla, Calif.

Kiewiet, D. Roderick, and Matthew D. McCubbins. 1991. *The Logic of Delegation: Congressional Parties and the Appropriations Process*. Chicago: University of Chicago Press.

King, Gary, Robert O. Keohane, and Sidney Verba. 1994. *Designing Social Inquiry: Scientific Inference in Qualitative Research*. Princeton, N.J.: Princeton University Press.

Kraske, Jochen, William H. Becker, William Diamond, and Louis Galambos. 1996. *Bankers with a Mission: The Presidents of the World Bank, 1946–91*. New York: Oxford University Press.

Krasner, Stephen D. 1976. State Power and the Structure of International Trade. *World Politics* 28 (3):317–47.

———. 1979. The Tokyo Round: Particularistic Interests and Prospects for Stability in the Global Trading System. *International Studies Quarterly* 23 (4):491–531.

———, ed. 1983. *International Regimes*. Ithaca, N.Y.: Cornell University Press.

Le Prestre, Philippe G. 1989. *The World Bank and the Environmental Challenge*. Toronto: Associated University Press.

Lowi, Theodore J. 1979. *The End of Liberalism: The Second Republic of the United States*. 2d ed. New York: Norton.

Lyne, Mona. Forthcoming. The Voter's Dilemma and the Microfoundations of Democracy. In *Citizen-Politician Linkages in Democratic Politics*, edited by H. Kitschelt and S. Wilkinson.

Lyne, Mona, and Michael Tierney. 2002. Variation in the Structure of Principals: Conceptual Clarifications. Paper presented at the Conference on Delegation to International Organizations, May, Park City, Utah.

Martin, Lisa L. 1992. *Coercive Cooperation: Explaining Multilateral Economic Sanctions*. Princeton, N.J.: Princeton University Press.

———. 2000. *Democratic Commitments: Legislatures and International Cooperation*. Princeton, N.J.: Princeton University Press.

———. 2002. Agency and Delegation in IMF Conditionality. Paper presented at the Conference on Delegation to International Organizations, May, Park City, Utah.

McCalla, Robert D. 1996. NATO's Persistence After the Cold War. *International Organization* 50 (3):445–75.

McCubbins, Mathew D., and Thomas Schwartz. 1987. Congressional Oversight Overlooked: Police Patrols vs. Fire Alarms. In *Congress: Structure and Policy*, edited by Mathew D. McCubbins and Thomas Sullivan, 426–40. Cambridge: Cambridge University Press.

McCubbins, Mathew D., Roger G. Noll, and Barry R. Weingast. 1987. Administrative Procedures as Instruments of Political Control. *Journal of Law, Economics, and Organization* 3 (2):243–79.

———. 1989. Structure and Process, Politics and Policy: Administrative Arrangements and the Political Control of Agencies. *Virginia Law Review* 75 (2):431–83.

Mearsheimer, John J. 1990. Back to the Future: Instability in Europe After the Cold War. *International Security* 15 (1):5–56.

———. 1994. The False Promise of International Institutions. *International Security* 19 (3):5–49.

———. 1995. A Realist Reply. *International Security* 20 (1):82–93.

Middlemas, Keith. 1995. *Orchestrating Europe: The Informal Politics of European Union, 1973–95*. London: Fontana.

Moravcsik, Andrew. 1998. *The Choice for Europe: Social Purpose and State Power from Messina to Maastricht*. Ithaca, N.Y.: Cornell University Press.

Morse, Bradford, and Thomas Berger. 1992. *Sardar Sarovar: Report of the Independent Review*. Ottawa, Canada: Resource Futures International.

Nakayama, Mikiyasu. 2000. The World Bank's Environmental Agenda. In *The Global Environment in the Twenty-First Century: Prospects for International Cooperation*, edited by Pamela S. Chasek, 399–410. New York: United Nations University Press.

Nelson, Paul J. 1995. *The World Bank and Non-Governmental Organizations: The Limits of Apolitical Development*. New York: St. Martin's Press.

Nielson, Daniel, and Michael Tierney. 1999. Addressing the Agent: Domestic Institutions and the Demand for MDB Loans. Paper presented at the 96th Annual Meeting of the American Political Science Association, September, Atlanta, Georgia.

———. 2001. Principles or Principals: Constructivism, Rationalism and IO Behavior. Paper presented at 59th Annual Meeting of the Mid-West Political Science Association, April, Chicago.

———. 2002. Principals and Interests: Agency Theory and Multilateral Development Bank Lending. Paper presented at the Conference on Delegation to International Organizations, May, Park City, Utah.

Niskanen, William A. 1971. *Bureaucracy and Representative Government.* Chicago: Aldine.

O'Brien, Robert, Anne Marie Goetz, Jan Aart Scholte, and Marc Williams. 2000. *Contesting Global Governance: Multilateral Economic Institutions and Global Social Movements.* Cambridge: Cambridge University Press.

Olson, Mancur. 1965. *The Logic of Collective Action and the Theory of Groups.* Cambridge, Mass.: Harvard University Press.

Peritore, N. Patrick. 1999. *Third World Environmentalism: Case Studies from the Global South.* Gainesville: University Press of Florida.

Pollack, Mark A. 1997. Delegation, Agency, and Agenda-Setting in the European Community. *International Organization* 51 (1):99–134.

——. Forthcoming. Control Mechanism or Deliberative Democracy? Two Images of Comitology. *Comparative Political Studies.*

Powell, Robert. 1994. Anarchy in International Relations Theory: The Neorealist–Neoliberal Debate. *International Organization* 48 (2):313–44.

Rich, Bruce. 1985. The Multilateral Development Banks, Environmental Policy, and the United States. *Ecology Law Quarterly* 12 (4):681–784.

——. 1994. *Mortgaging the Earth: The World Bank, Environmental Impoverishment, and the Crisis of Development.* Boston: Beacon Press.

Risse-Kappen, Thomas. 1996. Collective Identity in a Democratic Community: The Case of NATO. In *The Culture of National Security: Norms and Identity in World Politics,* edited by Peter J. Katzenstein, 357–99. New York: Columbia University Press.

Ruggie, John Gerad, ed. 1993. *Multilateralism Matters: The Theory and Praxis of an Institutional Form.* New York: Columbia University Press.

Shakow, Alexander. 1994. Press release. *The World Bank's Response to Bruce Rich's Mortgaging the Earth.* Washington, D.C.: World Bank.

Shanks, Cheryl, Harold K. Jacobson, and Jeffrey H. Kaplan. 1996. Inertia and Change in the Constellation of Intergovernmental Organizations, 1981–1992. *International Organization* 50 (4):593–627.

Shihata, Ibrahim F. I. 1994. *The World Bank Inspection Panel.* New York: Oxford University Press.

Steinberg, Richard H. 1997. Trade-Environment Negotiations in the EU, NAFTA, and WTO: Regional Trajectories of Rule Development. *American Journal of International Law* 91 (2):231–67.

Strange, Susan. 1983. Cave! hic Dragones: A Critique of Regime Analysis. In *International Regimes,* edited by Stephen Krasner, 337–54. Ithaca, N.Y.: Cornell University Press.

Treakle, Kay. 1998. Accountability at the World Bank: What Does It Take? Paper presented at the 24th Annual Meeting of the Latin American Studies Association, September, Chicago.

Udall, Lori. 1998. The World Bank and Public Accountability: Has Anything Changed? In *The Struggle for Accountability: The World Bank, NGOs, and Grassroots Movements,* edited by Jonathan Fox and David Brown, 391–436. Cambridge, Mass.: MIT Press.

Umana, Alvaro, ed. 1998. *The World Bank Inspection Panel: The First Four Years (1994–1995).* Washington, D.C.: World Bank.

Upton, Barbara. 2000. *The Multilateral Development Banks: Improving U.S. Leadership.* Westport, Conn.: Praeger.

U.S. House of Representatives. 1984. Committee on Banking, Finance and Urban Affairs, Subcommittee on International Development. *Multilateral Development Bank Activity and the Environment.* 98th Congress, 2d sess.

Vaubel, Roland. 1991. A Public Choice View of International Organization. In *The Political Economy of International Organizations,* edited by Roland Vaubel and Peter Willett, 27–45. Boulder, Colo.: Westview Press.

Wade, Robert Hunter. 1997. Greening the Bank: The Struggle over the Environment, 1970–1995. In *The World Bank: Its First Half Century,* vol. 2, edited by Devesh Kapur, John P. Lewis, and Richard Webb, 611–734. Washington, D.C.: Brookings Institution Press.

——. 2002. U.S. Hegemony and the World Bank: The Fight over People and Ideas. *Review of International Political Economy* 9 (2):215–43.

Wallander, Celeste and Robert O. Keohane. 1997. When Threats Decline, Why Do Alliances Persist? An Institutional Approach. Unpublished manuscript. Harvard University, Cambridge, Mass., and Duke University, Durham, N.C.

Waltz, Kenneth N. 1979. *Theory of International Politics.* Reading, Mass.: Addison-Wesley.

————. 1996. Security Effects of NATO Expansion, Paper presented at Public Lecture at Los Alamos National Laboratory, December, Los Alamos, N. Mex.

Wappenhans, Wili. 1992. *Report of the Portfolio Management Task Force.* Washington, D.C.: World Bank.

Weaver, Catherine, and Ralf Leiteritz. 2002. Organizational Culture and Change at the World Bank. Unpublished manuscript, University of Kansas, Lawrence.

Williams, Marc. 1994. *International Economic Institutions and the Third World.* New York: Harvester Wheatsheaf.

Williamson, Oliver E. 1975. *Markets and Hierarchies, Analysis and Antitrust Implications: A Study in the Economics of Internal Organization.* New York: Free Press.

Winters, Jeffrey. 1997. Down with the World Bank. *Far Eastern Economic Review* 160 (7):29.

World Bank. 1992. *World Bank Approaches to the Environment in Brazil: A Review of Selected Projects, vol. 5: The Polonoreste Program.* Washington, D.C.: World Bank.

————. 1997a. *Environment Matters.* Annual Review. Washington, D.C.: World Bank.

————. 1997b. *Operational Manual: Operational Policies, Bank Procedures. Operations Policy Department.* Washington, D.C.: World Bank.

————. 2000. *The World Bank's Approach to the Environment.* Washington, D.C.: World Bank.

————. 2002. *Japan Policy and Human Resource Development Fund.* Available online at ⟨http://www.worldbank.org/rmc/phrd/phrdbr1.htm⟩.

Name Index